LEGAL NURSE CONSULTING
PRINCIPLES
Third Edition

LEGAL NURSE CONSULTING
PRINCIPLES
Third Edition

Edited by

Ann M. Peterson, EdD, MSN, RN, FNP-BC, LNCC
Lynda Kopishke, MSN, RN, LNCC

Associate Editors

Teddylen A. Guffey, MHSA, BSN, RN, LNCC
Marilyn R. Mason, RN, LNCC
Luanne Trahant, MSN, RN, LNCC
Margaret S. Wacker, RN, PhD

AALNC
AMERICAN ASSOCIATION OF
LEGAL NURSE CONSULTANTS

CRC CRC Press
Taylor & Francis Group
Boca Raton   London   New York

CRC Press is an imprint of the
Taylor & Francis Group, an **informa** business

CRC Press
Taylor & Francis Group
6000 Broken Sound Parkway NW, Suite 300
Boca Raton, FL 33487-2742

Printed in the United States of America on acid-free paper
10 9 8 7 6 5 4 3 2 1

International Standard Book Number: 978-1-4200-8951-6 (Hardback)

Library of Congress Cataloging-in-Publication Data

Legal nurse consulting principles. -- 3rd ed. / editors, Ann Peterson, Lynda Kopishke.
      p. cm.
   Rev. ed. of part of: Legal nurse consulting / American Association of Legal Nurse Consultants. 2nd ed. c2003.
   Includes bibliographical references and index.
   ISBN 978-1-4200-8951-6 (hardcover : alk. paper)
   1. Nursing consultants--Legal status, laws, etc.--United States. 2. Nursing--Law and legislation--United States. I. Peterson, Ann, 1943- II. Kopishke, Lynda. III. Legal nurse consulting.
   [DNLM: 1. Consultants--United States. 2. Nursing--United States. 3. Expert Testimony--United States. 4. Jurisprudence--United States. WY 90 L4956 2010]

KF2915.N8L35 2010
344.73'0414--dc22   2009047506

Visit the Taylor & Francis Web site at
http://www.taylorandfrancis.com

and the CRC Press Web site at
http://www.crcpress.com

Acknowledgment from Ann M. Peterson

This edition reflects the team effort of many contributors working long hours to produce a book that will provide a foundation for LNCs, attorneys, and others involved in the litigation process of health care issues. The authors provided countless hours, sharing their expertise, to the difficult labor-intensive process of revising or writing new chapters.

The reviewers provided excellent feedback to help shape the chapters as being comprehensive, yet practical.

The associate editors were key managers, providing feedback and guidance, while moving the project forward.

The AALNC Board of Directors has provided continued vision, support, and resources over the past three years to ensure this publication would be available for all nurses practicing in the medical-legal arena. It reflects the mission of our association and we are proud to present it to you.

The staff at AALNC provided support and encouragement while assisting in keeping the lines of communication open and keeping the project on course.

I particularly want to thank our families, who have supported the often arduous and time-consuming efforts spent in coordinating the project. Your patience and encouragement throughout this project lightened the task of bringing this book to publication.

Ann M. Peterson, EdD, MSN, RN, FNP-BC, LNCC
Senior Editor

Acknowledgment from Lynda Kopishke

Working on the third edition has been both a labor of love and an opportunity for professional growth. Having the chance to collaborate with Ann Peterson as co-senior editor was a delight. All the authors involved in this process have generously given their time and talents to make this text a success. Your words will shorten the learning curve for many as they journey through their careers as legal nurse consultants. Choosing to expand the previous edition, with specialty practice chapters, begins the process of highlighting emerging areas of legal nurse consulting practice.

No text is ever published but for the assistance and support of the behind-the-scenes professionals: the associate editors who gave selflessly of their time to communicate, edit, and support the authors, and the senior editors. This product would never have come to fruition without your efforts and support. I offer kudos to the associate editors for a job well done!

The reviewers for each chapter added a dimension of content expertise and assisted the authors in honing each topic to make it meaningful to the readers. Many thanks for the great suggestions and support of the reviewers, many of whom burned the midnight oil in order to turn the product around in an expedited manner to meet deadlines.

A huge thanks to the AALNC staff and particularly Emily Palmer for all the support, patience, gentle guidance, and hard work that was required to put this text in the publisher's hands. Emily handled the day-to-day internal operations and logistics of this text, allowing the rest of us to focus on the creative process. Wishing you weekends of peace and fun now Emily! This text would not have evolved to a third edition without the foundation provided by previous editors, authors, and reviewers. The specialty practice of legal nurse consulting owes its history to your persistence in the written word. Many thanks for your guidance and forward thinking.

Lastly, I want to say thank you to my family, who provided unconditional love and support during the many hours of volunteer work required to craft this edition. You deserve recognition, and knowing the time you sacrificed allowing me to finish this project is a precious gift that I will cherish forever.

Lynda Kopishke, MSN, RN, LNCC
Senior Editor

Preface

From the first edition of this book published in 1998, the special practice of legal nurse consulting has grown by leaps and bounds. In the early years, practice primarily focused on the education and support of attorneys practicing in medical litigation areas. The American Association of Legal Nurse Consultants (AALNC) has supported the growth of legal nurse consulting to include a rigorously administered certification process, and a Scope and Standards of Practice published by the American Nurses' Association. Over the past 20 years, the practice of legal nurse consulting has grown to include areas such as life care planning, risk management, administration health law, criminal law, toxic torts, product liability, technical support in the courtroom, and much more. The opportunities for the education of legal nurse consultants have grown as well, with many online and college-based courses utilizing the *Principles and Practices* text as a core for curriculum development.

This third edition seeks to continue the expansion of the specialty practice with focus on emerging areas for legal nurse consultants to explore. This edition was created after a careful analysis of the current practice environment, a focus survey of membership, and a review of the practice analysis undertaken by the American Legal Nurse Consulting Certification Board (ALNCCB). Thoughtful analysis was completed to determine additions and deletions to the text that would best serve readers for several years to come.

The scope of this project was handled in an efficient and thoughtful manner. A talented group of associate editors each volunteered to take on six chapters to mentor, edit, and support. An invitation to previous edition authors was extended to allow past authors to contribute to this edition. A vetting process for new authors yielded many competent chapter authors who were willing to share their expertise in this all-volunteer project. A decision to expand the glossary and acronym sections allows the reader to quickly learn new information. The decision to evolve into a two-volume set took into consideration the needs of both novice legal nurse consultants and advanced practitioners for up-to-date information delivered in a cost-effective manner.

It has been our privilege to incorporate the skills and talents gathered for this project and shepherd them to fruition. It is indeed the opportunity of a lifetime to stand shoulder to shoulder with caring professionals, contributing to the future of nursing. On behalf of the authors, associate editors, reviewers, and staff, we invite you to read with vigor and enjoy!

Lynda Kopishke, MSN, RN, LNCC
Ann M. Peterson, EdD, MSN, RN, FNP-BC, LNCC
Senior Editors

Editors

Senior Editors

Ann M. Peterson, EdD, MSN, RN, FNP-BC, LNCC, president of Ann M. Peterson & Associates, received a diploma in nursing from Boston City Hospital School of Nursing, a Bachelor of Arts in Psychology, a Master of Science in Nursing, and a Doctorate in Higher Education Administration. Dr. Peterson is an experienced legal nurse consultant working with both defense and plaintiff attorneys on medical malpractice, nursing negligence, personal injury, and criminal cases. She has a background in health care administration and advanced clinical practice, has held an academic appointment as an assistant professor at the graduate level, and has multiple publications to her credit. She is a current member of AALNC and the past president of the Rhode Island Chapter of AALNC. She has also served on the Massachusetts Nurses Association (MNA) Congress on Nursing Practice and the Blue Ribbon Commission on Health Policy and Legislation, and is a panel member of the Massachusetts Medical Malpractice Tribunal.

Lynda Kopishke, MSN, RN, LNCC received her diploma in Nursing from St. Francis Hospital School of Nursing in Wilmington, Delaware. After many years of successful practice, Ms. Kopishke returned to Wilmington University, where she obtained a Bachelor of Science and a Master of Science in Nursing. She became certified as a legal nurse consultant in 2000. She served on the Board of Directors of the American Association of Legal Nurse Consulting at both the local and the national level. She is past editor of the *Journal of Legal Nurse Consulting*, a reviewer for the second edition of *Principles and Practices*, and a published author and national speaker on topics associated with nursing and legal nurse consulting. She operates an independent consulting business, Forensic Matters. Ms. Kopishke has been admitted at trial in several states and at the federal level as an expert witness in standards of nursing care as well as in life care planning. She is a nurse educator, researcher, and strong advocate for nursing practice.

Associate Editors

Teddylen A. Guffey, MHSA, BSN, RN, LNCC has worked clinically in both nursing and health care administration for 8 years before entering the field of legal nurse consulting. In the years since, Ms. Guffey has worked as an independent legal nurse consultant (LNC) and as a professional staff member of the law firm team, assisting in the provision of medical malpractice representation and litigation services.

In addition to having her Master's Degree in Health Services Administration, Ms. Guffey has authored numerous articles on various topics ranging from health care rationing to the business realities of the LNC's role within the field of Law. She served 5 years on the board of the Phoenix Chapter of the American Association of Legal Nurse Consultants as president, vice president, past president, and program chair and has given numerous presentations locally and nationally concerning risk and medical malpractice management within the health care field.

Currently, Ms. Guffey is the principal of Guffey & Associates, PC, a law firm specializing in providing business, legal, and risk management services to physicians. She continues to work in the field of legal nurse consulting, risk management, and medical–legal business consulting.

Claire A. Hoffman, MS, RNC, CDDN, CLNC is the president of Hoffman Associates, a health care and medical legal consulting firm, which focuses on all aspects of geriatric care, developmental disabilities, regulatory compliance, and standards of care. She has been in legal nurse consulting for 23 years and has been retained as an expert for both plaintiff and defense law firms throughout the country to conduct record reviews, determine case merit, and consult with attorneys in preparation for depositions/trials, and as an expert witness. Ms. Hoffman has been recognized by the US Congress and professional associations for her advocacy for individuals with developmental disabilities.

Marilyn R. Mason, RN, LNCC has practiced as a legal nurse consultant since 1986. She has worked in both plaintiff and defense litigation, holding positions within law firms as well as practicing in an independent consulting capacity. Her clinical experience includes emergency room, psychiatric, medical–surgical, and administrative nursing. Ms. Mason is currently employed at Winer & McKenna, working in the areas of personal injury, medical malpractice, products liability, and employment law. She received her nursing diploma from Barnes Hospital School of Nursing in St. Louis and her bachelor's degree in health administration from St. Mary's College in Moraga, California. She is a registered nurse through the California Board of Registered Nursing. Ms. Mason has published in national journals and spoken to and consulted with nurses, paralegals, and attorneys, at both the national and the local levels, on medical issues in litigation. She has been a member of the San Francisco State University Faculty, teaching and advising for the legal nurse consulting certificate program. She is a founding member and past president of the American Association of Legal Nurse Consultants (AALNC) and is certified by the AALNC in Legal Nurse Consulting (LNCC).

Tracy Patrick-Panchelli, BSN, RN-BC, CPN has been an AALNC member since 1999 and has had an independent legal nurse consulting practice, focusing on medical malpractice plaintiff and defense work, since 2001. In 2009, she was elected president of the Philadelphia Chapter of AALNC and also became a member of the planning committee for the AALNC National Educational Conference. Tracy earned her Bachelor of Science degree in Nursing from the University of Pennsylvania in 1993 and matriculated in the Master of Science in Nursing—Health Care Administration program at Villanova University in 2009. She is a certified pediatric nurse and is also board certified in nursing professional development. She is employed by Nemours/ Alfred I. duPont Hospital for Children in Wilmington, Delaware, as Coordinator of Nursing Continuing Education and as a staff nurse on the Critical Care Transport Team.

Bonnie Rogers, DrPH, COHN-S, LNCC, FAAN is a professor of Nursing and Public Health and is director of the North Carolina Occupational Safety and Health Education and Research

Center and the Occupational Health Nursing Program at the University of North Carolina, School of Public Health, Chapel Hill. She is an independent legal nurse consultant in occupational safety and health, public health, and malpractice plaintiff and defense work. Dr. Rogers is a nurse ethicist, holds a postgraduate certificate as an adult health clinical nurse specialist, and is certified as a legal nurse consultant, in occupational health nursing and in case management. She is a fellow in the American Academy of Nursing and the American Association of Occupational Health Nurses.

Dr. Rogers has conducted several funded research projects with a major focus on hazards to health care workers. She has worked on several committees with the Institute of Medicine and completed several terms as an appointed member of the National Advisory Committee on Occupational Safety and Health. She is currently on the AALNC Nominating Committee and Editor of the AALNC *Journal of Legal Nurse Consulting.*

Luanne Trahant, MSN, RN, LNCC has been a legal nurse consultant for over 9 years and is the co-owner of Consulting Concepts of Louisiana, Inc. She has been a practicing registered nurse for over 17 years in multiple nursing and administration settings, including medical surgical nursing, orthopedics, rehabilitation, long-term care, home health, hospice, pediatrics, intensive care, cardiology, and psychiatric care. Mrs. Trahant has served her profession as a staff nurse, charge nurse, director of nursing, and administrator in long-term care settings. She received her Bachelor of Science in Nursing from Northwestern State University in 1992, a Master of Science in Nursing from the University of Phoenix in 2005, and is currently completing a postgraduate certificate as a Family Nurse Practitioner. Mrs. Trahant plans to serve the elderly population as an FNP. She is an active member in national, state, and local nursing associations and forums to help advance the nursing profession. Additionally, she is an avid supporter and advocate for the advancement of nursing in long-term care and the elderly population. For the last 9 years, she has provided independent consulting and expert witness services to plaintiff and defense attorneys nationwide in the areas of long-term care, rehabilitation, orthopedics, administration, and general nursing standards.

Margaret S. Wacker, RN, PhD is the director of Nursing at Lake-Sumter Community College, and the president of Wacker and Associates. She is a nationally recognized speaker, writer, and expert witness in pain management. She is an experienced legal nurse consultant working for defense and plaintiff attorneys on issues of nursing negligence and pain management. She is active in professional organizations, received the Florida Nurses Association District 14 Nurse of the Year award in 2006, and has served on the Rhode Island Attorney General's Task Force for End of Life Care since 2001. Dr. Wacker has held academic appointments at the University of Rhode Island and Yale University. She was a graduate of Saint Catherine's School of Nursing, received her Bachelor of Nursing at New York University, a Master of Science degree from Adelphi University, a Master of Arts degree in Anthropology from the State University of New York at Stony Brook, and a PhD in Nursing from New York University.

Cheryl E. White, RN, BS, MSHL, LNCC, LHRM, MSCC, DFSHRMPS has almost 25 years of extensive legal nursing experience. She has an MS in Health Care Law, a BS in Health Care Administration, and over 30 years experience as a registered nurse. Cheryl has been a risk manager for three large health care organizations, works for the Florida Board of Medicine as an inspector of physician offices seeking licensure in levels II and III office surgery, and has worked the last eight years as an in-house legal nurse consultant to a defense firm. Cheryl is also a certified Medicare Set-Aside Consultant.

Contributors

Tonia Dandry Aiken, RN, JD
Nurse Attorney Institute, LLC
New Orleans, Louisiana

Julie Anderson, JD, MSN, RN
Sheehy, Serpe and Ware PC
Houston, Texas

Thomas H. Anderson, RN, BSN, BC
Independent Nurse Consultant
Philadelphia, Pennsylvania

Kathleen Woods Araiza, BA, RN
North Bethesda, Maryland

Gretchen Aumman, PhD, BSN, RN
Houston, Texas

Mary Baldwin
Baldwin Consultants
San Diego, California

Marguerite Barbacci, BSN, RN, MPH,
RNC, LNCC
Manns Choice, Pennsylvania

Sue Barnes, MSN, MSHCA, RN
Catholic Healthcare West
Phoenix, Arizona

Jane Barone, BSN, RN, LNCC
Medi-Law Solutions
Short Hills, New Jersey

Jenny Beerman, MN, RN
Beerman & Associates
Kansas City, Missouri

Julie Bogart
Prairie Village, Kansas

Lorraine E. Buchanan, RN,
MSN, CRRN
Independent Allied Health
    Consultants, Inc.
Blue Bell, Pennsylvania

Michelle Cannon, BSN, RN, CRNI
Green Lane, Pennsylvania

Elena Capella, EdD, MPA, MSN,
RN, CPHQ, LNCC
Central Coast Alliance for Health
Santa Cruz, California

Pat G. Carroll, RN, BSN, LNC,
CAISS
Exponent Failure Analysis Associates
Phoenix, Arizona

Tracey Chovanec, BSN, RN
Dushman, Friedman & Franks, PC
Fort Worth, Texas

Jan Smith Clary, BSN, RN, LNCC
Clary Medical Legal Consulting
Greenwell Springs, Louisiana

April Clemens, MSN, RN
Venice, California

Joyce M. Collins, RN, BSBA, CLNC, LNCC
Collins Medical Legal Consultants, Inc.
Fountain Hills, Arizona

Laura A. Conklin, MSN, MSA, RN, ONC, CWS, LNCC, FCCWS, Dip. AAWM
St. Clair Shores, Michigan

Margo R. Conklin, MSN, RN-BC, LNCC
Conklin Legal Nurse Consulting, LLC
Kingstown, Virginia

Patricia A. Costantini, RN, MEd, LPC, CRC, CCM, CLCP, LNCC, D-ABVE
Costantini Rehab
Pittsburgh, Pennsylvania

Maureen A. Cregan, RN, LNCC
Maron Marvel Bradley & Anderson, P.A.
Wilmington, Delaware

Colleen D'Amico, BS, RN
Preferred LINC LLC
Watertown, Connecticut

Deborah D. D'Andrea, BSN, BA, RN
D'Andrea Consulting, Ltd.
Chicago, Illinois

Cynthia Dangerfield, RN, CPN
Jacksonville, Florida

Doug Davis, BSN, RN, DABFN
Arlington, Texas

Shirley Cantwell Davis, BSN, RN, LNCC
Davis and Associates
Atlanta, Georgia

Nathan Dean
Phoenix, Arizona

Susan Green DeWitt, MSN, RN
Elkton, Maryland

Kara L. DiCecco, MSN, RN, LNCC
MedWise Consulting, Inc.
Bear, Delaware

Kevin Dubose, JD
Hogan Dubose & Townsend
Houston, Texas

Christopher M. Duling, Esq., LL.M.
Maron Marvel Bradley & Anderson, P.A.
Wilmington, Delaware

Jean Dworniczek, BSN, RN-BC
JD Medical Legal Consulting, Inc.
Valparaiso, Indiana

Lucille Evangelista, BS, RN
Succasunna, New Jersey

Diana Faugno, MSN, RN, CPN, SANE-A, SANE-P, FAAFS
Forensic Nurse Consultant
Escondido, California

Karen S. Fox, BSN, RN, LNCC, CPHRM
Th e Medical Resource Network, Inc.
Portland, Oregon

Gail N. Friend, JD, RN
Friend & Associates, LLP
Houston, Texas

Patricia A. Fyler, BS, RN, CEN
Fyler Associates
Brea, California

Margery Garbin, PhD, RN
C-NET
Jersey City, New Jersey

Cheryl Gatti, RN, BSN, LNCC
Lark & Gatti Medical Legal Consultants
Watchung, New Jersey

Adella Toepel Getsch, BSN, RN, LNCC
Robins, Kaplan, Miller & Ciresi
Minneapolis, Minnesota

Madeline C. Good, MSN, RN, LNCC
Fann & Petruccelli, PA
Hollywood, Florida

June Grant-Stafford, MSN, RN
Newark, Delaware

Kathy Gudgell, JD, RN
Healthcare Law Consultants
Lexington, Kentucky

Mary Lou Hazelwood, RN, LNCC
Hazelwood Consultants
Stayton, Oregon

Julianne Hernandez, MPH, BSN, RN
Key Largo, Florida

Sandra Higelin, MSN, RN, CNS, CWCN, CLNC
Palm Springs, California

Karen J. Huff, BSN, RN, LNCC
Steptoe & Johnson PLLC
Charleston, West Virginia

Patricia W. Iyer, MSN, RN, LNCC
Med League Support Services Inc.
Flemington, New Jersey

Rosanna Janes, BSN, RN
Janes and Associates, Inc.
San Diego, California

Betty Joos, MED, BSN, RN
Informed Decisions Inc.
Sautee Nacoochee, Georgia

Patricia Ann Steed King, RN
Duluth, Georgia

Arlene King Klepatsky, JD, BSN, BA, RN
Castro Valley, California

Janet Kremser, BS, RN, C-SN, CDON/LTC
Carriere, Mississippi

Mary Lanz, RN, LNCC
Tolman & Osborne
Tempe, Arizona

Jude Lark, RN, BSN, CCRN
Lark & Gatti Medical Legal Consultants
West Orange, New Jersey

Barbara J. Levin, BSN, RN, ONC, LNCC
Hingham, Massachusetts

Pamela M. Linville, RN, CCRC, CPBT
Lexington, Kentucky

Barbara Loecker, MSEd, BSN, RN
Olathe, Kansas

Mary Lubin, BS, MA, RNC, NHA
San Leandro, California

Linda Luedtke, RN, MSN
MLCS, Inc.
Naperville, Illinois

Joan Magnusson, BSN, RN, LHRM, LNCC
JKM Consulting, LLC
Saint Cloud, Florida

Susan Mahley, BSN, MSN, RNC, C-WHNP
Kansas City, Missouri

Joseph R. McMahon, JD
Metairie, Louisiana

Susan Mellott, PhD, RN, CPHQ, FNAHQ
Mellott & Associates
Houston, Texas

Jane Mihalich, BSN, RN, LNCC
Board of Registration in Medicine
Shrewbury, Massachusetts

Joan E. Miller
Miller Medical Consulting Services, Inc.
Phoenix, Arizona

Phyllis ZaiKaner Miller, RN
Robins Kaplan Miller & Ciresi
Minneapolis, Minnesota

Barbara Noble, RN
Texas Dept of Aging and
    Disability Services
Keller, Texas

Regina Noonan, MSN, RN, LNCC
San Diego, California

Rosie Oldham, BS, RN, LNCC
R & G Medical Consultants, Inc.
Peoria, Arizona

Maureen Orr, BS, RN, CCM, LNCC
Jacksonville, Florida

Marva J. Petty, MSN, RN, LNCC
Vancouver, Washington

Julie Pike, MN, BSN, RN
Kansas City, Kansas

**Patricia L. Pippen, BSN, RN,
LNCC, OCN**
Dallas, Texas

Jennifer L. Rangel, JD
Locke Liddell and Sapp LLP
Austin, Texas

Patricia Raya, RN-C, MBA
PAR Enterprises
Princeton, New Jersey

**Diane L. Reboy, MS, RN, LNCC,
FACFEI DABFN, CFN, CNLCP**
DLR Associates
Kenmore, New York

Sherri Reed, BSN, RN, LNCC
Wilson Kehoe & Winingham
Indianapolis, Indiana

Camille M. Renella, BSN, RN, CME
C.M. Renella & Associates, LLC
Chicago, Illinois

Elisabeth Ridgely, BS, RN, LNCC
Ridgely Associates
Telford, Pennsylvania

Judy Ringholz, BSN, RN
McFall, Sherwood and Sheehy
Houston, Texas

William J. Scott, Esq.
Jacksonville, Florida

Noreen M. Sisko, PhD, MSN, RN
Cape Medical-Legal Consulting
Cape May Court House, New Jersey

Joahnna Evans Songer, RN, CCRN, CLNC
Songer, Valdivia & Associates
    Legal Nurse Consultants
Visalia, California

Therese Steinhardt, MSN, RN
Warren County Department of Health
Belvidere, New Jersey

Barbara Stillwell, MSN, RN
Brown & Kelly
Buffalo, New Jersey

Brett N. Storm, Esq. (deceased)
Houston, Texas

**Anita Symonds, BSN, RN, CFC, CFN,
SANE-A, SANE-P, MS**
Christiana Care Health Systems
Newark, Delaware

**Cassandra Hall Valdivia, RN, BSN,
LNC, CLNCP**
Songer, Valdivia & Associates Legal
    Nurse Consultant
Kerman, California

Edwinna C. Vanderzanden, BSN, JD
Getman, Stacey, Schulthess & Steere
Bedford, New Hampshire

Susan van Ginneken, RN
Eagle Eye Records Review
Lake Stevens, Washington

Diane Trace Warlick, RN, JD
Nurse Attorney Institute, LLC
New Orleans, Louisiana

Eileen Watson, EDD, MSN, RN, ANP, LNCC
Huntington Beach, California

Sheila Webster, BSN, RN, C-HROB, RNC, LNCC
Webster Medical Consulting, Inc.
Glen Ellyn, Illinois

Karen L. Wetther, BSN, RN
Medical Legal Resources
San Diego, California

Renee Wilson, BSN, MS, RN
Houston, Texas

Nancy Wilson-Soga, BS, MS, RN
Warren County Community College
Long Valley, New Jersey

Paula Windler, MS, RN, LNCC
Kent & Wittekind, PC
Tempe, Arizona

Doreen James Wise, EdD, MSN, RN
Medical Research Consultants, Inc.
Houston, Texas

Reviewers

Tracy Albee, BSN, RN, LNCC, CLCP, FIALCP
MediLegal, A Professional Nursing Corp.
Tracy, California

Sue Barnes, MSN, MSHCA, RN
Catholic Healthcare West
Phoenix, Arizona

Jane Barone, BS, RN, LNCC
Medi-Law Solutions, LLC
Short Hills, New Jersey

Catherine Beasley, MS, BSN, LNCC
Chimpoulis & Hunter
Fort Lauderdale, Florida

Jenny Beerman, MN, RN
Beerman & Associates
Kansas City, Missouri

Rachel Boersma, PhD, RN
Fitchburg State College
Fitchburg, Massachusetts

Anthony Bonadies, JD
Bonadies Law Firm
Hamden, Connecticut

Rose Braz, BS, RN, LNCC, CPHRM, FASHRM
Litigation Management
Casper, Wyoming

Bethany Checketts, BSN, RN, LNCC
R&G Medical Consultants
Peoria, Arizona

Mindy Cohen, MSN, RN, LNCC
Mindy Cohen & Associates
Villanova, Pennsylvania

Anna Davies, RN, BSN
Law Offices of Barry G. Doyle, P.C.
Barrington, Illinois

Kara DiCecco, MSN, RN, LNCC
MedWise Consulting, Inc.
Bear, Delaware

Julia Diehl, RN-BC, CDONA/LTC, LHRM
Precision MedLegal Services
Dunnellon, Florida

Angela Duke-Haynes, RN
Legal Nurse Consulting Institute, LLC
Crozier, Virginia

Susan Elkins, RN
Gentiva Health Services
Seneca Falls, New York

Sandra Fandray, RN, BS, LNCC
Dickie, McCamey & Chilcote
Pittsburgh, Pennsylvania

Jessie Hill, JD
Case Western Reserve University School of Law
Cleveland, Ohio

Pam Hollsten, BSN, RN, LNCC
Hollsten & Associates
Yorktown, Virginia

Katy Jones
Chimpoulis and Hunter, PA
Davie, Florida

Suzanne Q. Langroth, BSN, RN, LNCC
Cataula, Georgia

Jane Mihalich, BSN, RN, LNCC
Board of Registration in Medicine
Shrewbury, Massachusetts

Michael G. Monnolly, JD
Alston & Bird, LLP
Atlanta, Georgia

James Thomas O'Donnell, MS, FCP, ABCP, CNS, FACN, R.Ph.
Pharmaconsultant, Inc.
Barrington, Illinois

Noreen M. Sisko, PhD, MSN, RN
Cape Medical-Legal Consulting
Cape May Court House,
    New Jersey

Richard Tucker, JD
Maron Marvel Bradley &
    Anderson, P.A.
Wilmington, Delaware

Susan van Ginneken, RN
Eagle Eye Records Review
Lake Stevens, Washington

Jacqueline VanNorman, RN
Litigation Management Inc.
Seneca Falls, New York

Contents

Chapter 1

The Law, Standards of Care, and Liability Issues

Tonia Dandry Aiken, JD, RN and Diane Trace Warlick, JD, RN

Second Edition
Tonia Dandry Aiken, JD, RN

Contents

Objectives

- Discuss the definition of "law"
- Discuss the types of law
- Define the elements of negligence
- Discuss quasi-intentional and intentional torts
- Define "standard of care"
- Discuss sources of standards of care
- Discuss standards of professional performance
- Define the steps in a trial process
- Define common areas of liability in the health care arena
- Discuss the implications of a malpractice claim on a health care provider's license
- Discuss common documents/materials requested and used to pursue or defend claims

Introduction

In today's legal environment, the legal nurse consultant (LNC) must be knowledgeable in many aspects of law, nursing, and medicine, as well as in the social influences controlling and affecting patient care, legal claims, and litigation. It is extremely important that the LNC be well read on such topics as managed care, case management, health care administrative concerns and issues, advanced practice issues, and health care policy. These are among the legal "hot" buttons that are being "pressed" in today's judicial arena.

Over the centuries, the law has evolved into a quagmire of rules, statutes, regulations, case law, codes, and opinions that, in many instances, will vary from state court to state court, state court to federal court, and jurisdiction to jurisdiction. Laws serve to control and guide people and entities in relationships, unions, and interactions. They are also used to resolve conflicts involving people, corporations, countries, and states. Laws have evolved through the ages and have resulted in major changes in the way people live and work in a modern society.

Sources of Laws

The word *law* originates from the Anglo-Saxon term *lagu*, meaning *that which is fixed*. There are several sources of laws that affect individuals, society, and the medical arena. Sources of laws include constitutional law, statutory law, administrative law, and common law.

Constitutional Law

Constitutional law is a compilation of laws, principles, and amendments derived from the United States and state constitutions that govern and guide federal and state governments, corporations, society, and individuals. The constitutional laws and amendments guarantee individuals certain rights, such as the right to privacy, freedom of speech, and equal protection (see Appendix A). The U.S. Constitution grants certain powers to the federal government and agencies and reserves powers to the states. The Constitution is the supreme law of the land and takes precedence over state and local laws. Constitutional law is the highest form of law in the United States. If not addressed in federal law, then the issue is "given" to the state government. In some instances laws are codified at both the state and federal levels for different circumstances.

An example of a federal act that affects health care providers is the Omnibus Budget Reconciliation Act (OBRA). Enacted in 1987, OBRA regulates the manner in which nursing homes deliver care, monitor quality of care, supply staff, train assistants, and protect the patient's rights. See Chapter 17 for more information about OBRA.

Federal and state governments have the constitutional authority to develop and create laws. In addition to creating laws, they also have the ability to enforce the laws that have been established.

Statutory Law

Statutory laws are laws enacted by federal, state, and local legislative bodies. Many health care providers, special interest groups, legal groups, and attorneys are involved in lobbying for certain bills or amendments to pass, promote, or protect their specific interests. An example of statutory law that every state has addressed is the law outlining the statute of limitations for filing a medical malpractice, wrongful death, or personal injury claim. Other statutory laws related to health care include the reporting of elder and child abuse and communicable diseases.

Administrative Law

Administrative laws originate from administrative agencies that are under the arm of the executive branch of the government. For example, state boards of nursing are state administrative agencies. These agencies promulgate rules and regulations to guide nursing practice in the state and to enforce nurse practice acts. Such nursing board regulations are legally binding. The state boards for health care professionals conduct investigations and hearings to ensure enforcement of the practice acts. Health care professionals can have their licenses limited, revoked, suspended, or probated. They can also receive formal or informal reprimands and fines if it is determined that they have violated the practice act.

The following are examples of violations that can affect a health care provider's license. Check the specific practice act for the acts considered violations in a particular profession or locality.*

- Practicing while using a license or diploma illegally obtained, illegally signed, or unlawfully issued
- Practicing when the license has been revoked or suspended
- Aiding or abetting a felon
- Practicing when the license has lapsed due to failure to renew
- Misappropriating narcotics
- Failing to follow the diversionary or recovering health care provider program
- Failing to exercise appropriate judgment and skills
- Falsifying documents
- Aiding unlicensed practice
- Abusing drugs or alcohol
- Failing to intervene and follow orders
- Delegating care improperly
- Diverting patient medications
- Failing to disclose prior arrests or criminal convictions
- Presenting an illegal prescription

It is important for any LNC working on a matter involving nursing practice, medical practice, or the practice of any health care provider to have access to the statutes that regulate that practice.

Another example of administrative law is an attorney general's opinion. The attorney general may provide an opinion regarding a specific interpretation of a law that cannot be found in a statute or regulation. The opinion is based on statutory and common law principles.

Common Law

Common law was developed in England on a case-by-case basis when the king decided a dispute presented to him in his *divine right*. Common law is used by all states and the federal courts except for Louisiana. Louisiana is the only state that has adopted the Napoleonic Code, developed from a compilation of French, Spanish, and Roman civil law. The Civil Code is a compilation of rules and regulations authorized by the legislature.

Common law comes from the judiciary branch of the government. It is based on court decisions. Court cases that are resolved through the judicial process act as a data bank for those seeking information in various types of cases, whether personal injury, medical malpractice, workers' compensation, admiralty, bankruptcy, or domestic issues. Attorneys search for cases similar to the ones that they are evaluating, mediating, arbitrating, settling, or trying.† The case

---

* For links to individual state nurse practice acts and regulations, see www.nurselaw.com/education and click on state laws.
† Legal research skills are a primary focus of the authors' "Legal Nurse Consulting Course" at Louisiana State University Health Sciences Center School of Nursing. See, www.lsuhsc.edu, click on school of nursing then continuing education.

information provides valuable insight into the value of the case, damages and injuries suffered, experts used, and the "mind-set" of the judge or jury in deciding for or against the plaintiff and awarding damages.

Common law interprets disputed legal issues, statutes, and regulations, and is created by the various courts. Research can be done to determine the value of a case and the decisions made by courts on various legal issues.

Legal doctrines that apply in certain cases include *res judicata*, *stare decisis*, and *res ipsa loquitur*. For example, the doctrine of *res judicata* (a thing or matter settled by judgment) prevents the same parties from trying a case based on the same issues in more than one civil action. The doctrine of *stare decisis* (to stand by things decided) refers to previously tried cases with similar fact patterns that may be governed by the prior court decisions. The doctrine of *res ipsa loquitur* (the thing speaks for itself) is a legal doctrine commonly used in operating room cases where things have been left in the abdomen or other cavities and where the patient's condition is otherwise completely in the control of the person accused of negligence. The doctrine shifts the burden of proving malpractice to the defense, which must disprove the elements of negligence. For example, in *Heastie v. Roberts** the Supreme Court of Illinois decided that *res ipsa loquitor* applied to a case where a patient was alone in a room restrained to a gurney when a fire broke out, and he was severely burned. The court held that expert testimony was not required to prove malpractice, and that the jury was entitled to find the ER staff negligent in the absence of any other rational explanation.

Types of Law

The LNC may encounter practice issues involving civil law, criminal law, contract law, and tort law.

Civil Law

Civil law is law that applies to the rights of individuals or entities, whereas criminal law deals with offenses against the general public. With civil law the remedies for a person or entity involve money or compensation, to make the plaintiff *whole again*. The amount of monetary compensation or *damages* is generally determined by a jury following trial. If a defendant has breached a contract, the court may order the completion of the work known as *specific performance*, or reimbursement of money paid.

Criminal Law

Criminal† law is created to provide guidance and protection to those injured by offenses against society. The criminal justice system has been created to deter, punish, and rehabilitate persons who perform criminal acts. Criminal conduct can include forgery, burglary, murder, assault, battery, theft, rape, and false imprisonment.

A criminal action by an individual is considered a criminal act against society even if it is directed solely at an individual. Nurses have been caught up in the criminal justice system, most

---

* 226 Ill.2d 515, 877 N.E.2d 1064 (Ill.SCt 2007).
† http://www.chicagotribune.com/news/local/ Retrieved on September 12, 2008.

often for drug diversion, nursing home patient abuse, and sexual misconduct. In a case alleging criminal sexual misconduct, the *Chicago Tribune* recently reported the arrest of a school nurse for alleged sexual misconduct with teenage students.

With charges of assault and battery or sexual misconduct, the criminal justice system views the offense as an act against society as a whole. To prove guilt in a criminal action, the level of proof required is *beyond a reasonable doubt*, while in a medical malpractice claim (civil tort law), the proof is met by a *preponderance of the evidence*, or *more likely than not*, which attributes 50.1% or more of fault to the defendants.

Example 1.1

If a person is practicing medicine without a license, is that considered a civil or criminal offense? (This is a criminal offense because it is viewed as an offense against the general public and society.)

Example 1.2

If the state statute requires that child or elder abuse be reported and a nurse or physician refuses to report the abuse, is this considered a civil or criminal action? (Criminal.)

Example 1.3

If a patient receives too much of a medication because the nurse fails to properly administer the correct dose, causing respiratory arrest and brain damage, is this considered a criminal or civil matter? (It is considered a civil matter.)

Contract Law

Contract law involves agreements between parties, individuals, and entities. The three requirements for a contract include offer, acceptance, and consideration. A contract can be in oral or written form, depending on the subject matter and the reason for the contract. However, it is a significant advantage to have a written contract specifically outlining the details of the agreement, along with the payments and other terms agreed upon by parties, in case there is a dispute that arises later. Today, health care providers are faced with many instances that involve contracts, including employee/employer contracts and contracts with health maintenance organizations, suppliers, and facilities. Contract litigation evolves around allegations of failure to perform or a breach of contractual duties.

Tort Law

Basics of Tort Law

Tort law is an area of civil law that encompasses negligence, personal injury, and medical malpractice claims. A tort is a wrongful act that is committed by some individual or entity that causes injury to another person or property. Tort law remedies attempt to make the injured person whole again, usually with compensation in the form of a monetary award. This is in contrast to criminal law, which usually fines and/or imprisons the guilty defendant.

Negligence is a failure to act as an ordinary prudent person or *reasonable man* would do under similar circumstances. Four elements of negligence must be proved for there to be a viable medical malpractice claim:

1. A duty must be owed to the patient. This duty usually occurs when the health care provider accepts responsibility for the care and treatment of that patient.
2. There is a breach of duty or standard of care by the professional. The standard of care for the specialty and treatment must be determined to see if there has been an act of omission or commission that has caused damage to the patient.
3. Proximate cause or causal connection must be evident between the breach of duty and the harm or damages that have occurred to the patient/plaintiff.
4. Damages or injuries must be suffered by the plaintiff. Damages or injuries can take the form of any of the following, including, but not limited to, loss of love and affection; loss of nurturance; pain and suffering; mental anguish; emotional distress; loss of chance of survival; disfigurement; past, present, and future medical expenses; past, present, and future loss of wages; premature death; and loss of enjoyment of life. Some states also recognize damages for the loss of chance for survival due to misdiagnosis, late diagnosis, or failure to diagnose a condition.

Example 1.4

A jury returned a verdict against defendants for $10,232,523. The plaintiffs filed a medical malpractice action against the hospital and physician to recover for damages allegedly suffered by their daughter, who was severely brain-damaged. Allegations of breaches of the standard included failure to adequately treat and discharging a pregnant woman from a hospital when she was leaking amniotic fluid.

The pregnant woman called the physician with complaints of chills, cramping, and diarrhea. She later returned to the hospital in active labor. The infant was born severely distressed, limp, and nonresponsive. The infant was diagnosed with *Staphylococcus aureus* sepsis and severe prenatal asphyxia.

Professional negligence is different from ordinary negligence because professionals are held to certain standards of care dictated by the profession. Ordinary negligence is conduct that involves undue risk of harm to someone caused by the failure to act as an ordinary prudent person would have acted.

Example 1.5

A nursing assistant sees water on the floor in the patient's room but fails to clean the floor. The patient falls and breaks a hip, requiring surgery, along with other medical expenses. This is ordinary negligence, because no professional judgment or standards of care were involved.*

Examples of professional negligence that resulted because health care providers breached acceptable standards of care include failure to

- Detect signs and symptoms of gastrointestinal bleeding, resulting in hemorrhaging and death.

---

* In recent litigation following the death of patients in a hospital flooded and without electricity following Hurricane Katrina, the Louisiana courts wrote lengthy opinions explaining how to distinguish between the medical malpractice versus negligence claims. See *LaCoste v. Pendleton* 966 So.2d 519 (La. 9/5/07).

- Diagnose and treat cancer in time, resulting in loss of chance of survival and untimely death
- Provide a patient with a safe environment, resulting in the patient's molestation
- Properly position the patient in surgery, resulting in a paralyzed limb
- Prescribe the recommended medication, resulting in further patient injury
- Properly monitor restrained patients, resulting in asphyxia, brain damage, or death
- Perform a cesarean section in time, resulting in fetal death or brain injury
- Check properly and administer the correct medication, resulting in death
- Properly evaluate a limb in a cast, resulting in an infection and osteomyelitis
- Perform a procedure properly and in a timely fashion, resulting in a retained foreign body (e.g., lap pad, hemostat, cotton ball, and needle)

Quasi-Intentional Torts

A *quasi-intentional* tort is a tort that involves speech (oral or written). The claim focuses on protection of an individual's interest in privacy, the person's reputation, and freedom from legal action that is unfounded. In contrast to the malpractice cases based on negligence, quasi-intentional and intentional torts are not based on the negligence theory. These torts are intentional, in that the person or entity is reasonably certain that harm will result from his actions.

For example, defamation (libel—written defamation and slander—oral defamation) is a quasi-intentional tort. It is the false communication of information to a third party that in some way causes harm to the person (e.g., economic loss and loss of esteem/reputation in the community). Truth is a defense in such a claim. Breach of confidentiality is another quasi-intentional tort. Health care providers must be especially cautious in *common areas* where such breaches can occur. For example, a health care provider talks about the HIV results of Patient Smith in the elevator. Smith's neighbor hears this information and spreads the news that the patient is HIV positive. Suit may be brought against the facility and health care provider for breach of confidentiality of the patient's protected health information. Health care providers are also entitled to confidentiality. A Texas jury recently held a hospital and physician liable for the publication of actions taken by the hospital to hold his cardiac catheterization privileges in abeyance pending an investigation. The jury held this was defamation as a matter of law because of the harm to his professional reputation.*

Intentional Torts

Intentional torts include assault, battery, invasion of privacy, false imprisonment, trespass to land, and intentional infliction of emotional distress. Assault is an intentional act that causes fear or apprehension that a person will be touched in an injurious or offensive manner. Battery is the actual unpermitted touching. Medical battery is the unpermitted touching of a patient associated with the lack of informed consent to perform the procedure or treatments. Some states no longer recognize *medical battery per se*, but have incorporated the cause into the informed consent law. For example, a surgeon has an informed consent to amputate the right foot because of gangrene but actually amputates the left foot. In such a case, the patient may file a tort claim based on medical negligence along with an intentional tort claim of medical battery for amputation of the wrong foot (Aiken, 2008).

---

* See *Poliner v. Texas Health Systems*, 3:00-CV-1007-P U.S. District Court for the Northern District of Texas, slip opinion dated March 27, 2006. Federal court opinions can be retrieved from the US PACER System by registering at http://pacer.psc.uscourts.gov/ Registration is free. Copies of documents are 0.08 cents per page.

Other intentional torts include the following:

■ Invasion of privacy, which occurs when a person's privacy right has been violated through public disclosure. Disclosure is such that a reasonable person would object to such an intrusion or disclosure. For example, the use of photographs (taken before and after plastic surgery) for an advertisement, without the patient's consent, is an example of an unauthorized disclosure. An important act that focuses on protection of the patient's privacy is the Health Insurance Portability and Accountability Act of 1996 (HIPAA). This act establishes privacy and security standards to protect a patient's health care information. In December 2000, the Department of Health and Human Services issued final regulations governing privacy of this information under HIPAA.*

■ False imprisonment is an intentional tort that is defined as the unlawful intentional confinement of a person through physical, chemical, or emotional restraints so that the person is conscious of being confined and harmed by it. Areas of health care where there are more likely to be claims include emergency rooms and psychiatric facilities. Following hospital restraint policies and documentation is the key to protection of the health care provider from liability.

■ Trespass to land can be both an intentional tort and a negligent act that occurs when a person refuses to leave a place, places something on the property, or causes another person to enter the property of another without permission. For example, a visitor absolutely refuses to leave the hospital after visiting hours and after being asked to leave by facility personnel.

■ Intentional infliction of emotional distress is the intentional invasion of the patient or person's peace of mind by the defendant's outrageous behavior. Some states do not recognize a claim for intentional infliction of emotional distress and others strictly limit its application.

Example 1.6

Wal-Mart and one of its loss-prevention investigations were found liable by a Texas jury for intentional infliction of emotional distress. The jury awarded $13 million for malicious prosecution. A 31-year-old mother was arrested on shoplifting charges. Wal-Mart allegedly gave the police a surveillance tape that the police claimed they did not receive. The defendant's mailman stated that he had seen her on the day of the alleged shoplifting 200 miles from the store where it took place (*Aquilera-Sanchez v. Wal-Mart Stores, Inc.*, 2001).

Standards of Care

The law has numerous rules, regulations, and cases that provide guidance to those persons intended to be protected or regulated, whether it is in the civil or criminal arena. When professionals are the subject of focus of a claim or lawsuit, the LNC must determine the appropriate professional standards of care that apply to the situation.

Standard of care is a term used to designate what is accepted as *reasonable conduct* under the circumstances by a person in the same profession. It is a *measuring scale*. In a malpractice claim, LNCs must determine what the standard of care was at the time of the alleged act or omission that

---

* HIPAA regulations can be found on the U.S. Department of Health website at http://www.hhs.gov/policies/index.html under "Laws and Regulations."

caused damage to the plaintiff. The standard of care is defined as that degree of skill, care, and judgment used by an ordinary prudent health care provider under similar circumstances. The standard of care may recognize more than one reasonable action in a given situation.*

When a plaintiff seeks the advice of an attorney regarding a possible medical or nursing negligence claim, the first documents that must be obtained are the medical records. The attorney or LNC can then review the care and treatment rendered to the patient by examining the records. Routinely, a timeline or chronology of events is done so that it is easier to put things in perspective. Medical records are read *across the board*, meaning that the records are read day by day. In other words, all tests, treatments, medications, and care given are put in chronological sequence for each day. The chronology of events can be based on a minute-by-minute evaluation of the record or a day-by-day evaluation, depending on the allegations of the specific acts of medical negligence. If the LNC is dealing with a product liability case or toxic tort, the standards applicable to the specific set of circumstances must be determined to see if breaches occurred. Product liability claims involve cases where medical products such as defective hip implants, medications, breast implants, and birth-control devices have caused damage or injuries to a patient.

Experts

In most jurisdictions, to prove a malpractice case, an expert witness in the same field of practice as the defendant is required to testify as to what the standard of care is, and whether or not the standard was breached in the particular situation. In addition, an expert witness provides the necessary testimony on proximate cause and damages. If the records must be sent to an expert for review, the records should be organized in a binder with individual sections noted (e.g., Dr. Smith's record). Never send the original records. In the author's opinion, each page should be numbered, if it has not been numbered by the facility. A copy of the complaint or petition for damages should also be included for the expert to evaluate the actual claims being made, if it has been drafted. A table of contents indicating specifically what records, including number of pages of each, are being sent to the expert must be included. An identical duplicate set should be maintained for the attorney so that the expert can talk to the attorney and refer to pertinent pages, information, or entries.

In the letter to the expert, the attorney or LNC should request an objective medical or nursing opinion on whether or not liability exists on the part of the defendant based on the appropriate standards of care. The expert may be asked to provide cites, references, and copies of the appropriate supporting documents for the standards of care. A written report may be required, but the expert should be instructed to call first to discuss his or her findings prior to writing a report. Note that a nursing expert witness should not testify about medical causation.

Example 1.7

In *Flanagan v. Labe*, 446 Pa. Super. 1071 666 A.2d 333, the Superior Court of Pennsylvania held that a nursing expert was not competent to testify on medical causation. Also, the state law forbade nurses from formulating medical diagnoses. The plaintiff presented a nursing expert to prove that the nurse's failure to treat properly led to the development of progressively worsening subcutaneous emphysema. The court would not allow the nurse expert to testify to a *reasonable degree of medical certainty* regarding causation. The Supreme Court of Pennsylvania affirmed this decision stating the nurse's preferred testimony would be a medical diagnosis, therefore it was not allowed

---

* See www.nurselaw.com/ for links to professional organizations and other sources of standards of care.

(Affirmed, 547 Pa. 254, 690 A.2d 183 [pa 1997]). The nursing expert, however, testified as to the breaches of the standard by the nurse, who should have provided reasonable nursing care to a patient who had complaints of pain and breathing problems.

Sources for Standards

If the LNC or expert is requested to obtain the standards of care for a case (e.g., skin care for a diabetic patient), numerous sources can be found. For example, the American Nurses Association has standards of care manuals for nurses in all aspects of nursing (e.g., neurosurgical, perioperative, and school nursing; see Appendix B). National professional organizations also have standards of practice pertinent to their areas of expertise and the U.S. Government has many health care websites that can be resources for standards of care. See Appendix C for a list of many of the national nursing specialty organizations.*

Statutes and regulations also provide minimum standards for how health care providers should practice. For example, in most states, health care providers are required by law to report child and elder abuse. If they are not reported, fines and penalties can be imposed.

Authoritative textbooks are also used as standards. The authors of these textbooks are also often retained as experts by the parties. It is presumed that the textbooks have the most current information on the conditions, treatments, and standards in a particular field of medicine or nursing, although some experts say that by the time a textbook is published, the information is outdated.

The state practice acts are also set standards of care. For example, the act may state that a nurse may not render a diagnosis because this would be considered practicing medicine.

State practice guidelines are also used as standards. Boards determine whether certain treatment, actions, and functions can be performed and/or delegated by licensed health care providers.

Facility and unit policies and procedures may also establish standards of care for the health care provider. Often, health care providers are informed that there are policies and procedures, but fail to take the time to review and understand them. The facility policies and procedures set the standard of practice in the facility and are clearly relevant to negligence claims.

In the following case, the actions of the resident were evaluated in comparison with the standard of care as defined by the hospital and the medical literature:

Example 1.8

A resident in internal medicine became a defendant in a lawsuit after he decided to intubate a 22-year-old woman who was combative and refusing oxygen. After being given several medications, she was intubated and then arrested. Ventricular fibrillation was diagnosed and cardiopulmonary resuscitation begun. Although the resident considered this intubation elective, the anesthesiologist considered it an urgent to impending code or emergency intubation. The plaintiffs alleged that the intubation could and should have been delayed in order to preoxygenate the patient and place monitors for assessment or respiratory and cardiac status. The plaintiffs further alleged that the resident had failed to conduct the cardiac arrest resuscitation of the patient in accordance with hospital protocols and standards set by the American Heart Association. The patient suffered severe hypoxia, permanent brain damage, and neurocortical death, and was left in a persistent vegetative state. The case was settled for $1,750,000. Should the two minor children live their expected life terms, the yield from the settlement structure will be $8,566,343 (Laska, 2002a).

---

* Links to many of the resources can be found at www.nurselaw.com links.

Examples of policies and procedures commonly used to establish the standard of care include the following:

- *Pressure ulcer claims*: Policies and procedures maintaining skin integrity of a diabetic patient.
- *Heating pad burn claims*: Policies and procedures on monitoring and documentation of the skin condition at specific intervals (e.g., to prevent burns) to show that the patient was not monitored properly and in a timely fashion.
- *Fall claims*: Policies and procedures on fall risk assessments and preventative actions.
- *Failure to detect cancer in time claims*: Policies and procedures on diagnostic studies to be done when signs or symptoms of cancer are exhibited.

In the above examples, the policies and procedures are usually requested by the plaintiff's counsel in a Request for Production of Things and Documents. These requests for documents and things by the plaintiff or defendant can cover any and all items in the other party's possession that pertain to the issues of the lawsuit and that may lead to discoverable information. A *subpoena duces tecum* (court order to produce documents) may also be issued by the court to obtain the necessary documents from third parties. It is served on an entity or person who is in control of specific documents and other materials relevant to facts in issue. See Figure 1.1 for a sample subpoena.

Equipment manuals are also used to establish the standard of care in medical device cases. For example, an intravenous (IV) infusion set requires a special filter to be used to prevent an air embolism. If the nurse fails to set up the system properly by omitting the filter, a breach has occurred. It is important that the LNC request personnel files to see whether the staff have received instructions and education on equipment that is the focus of the lawsuit, either before or after the malpractice claim has been made. The attorney and LNC must also decide whether there is the possibility of a medical product liability claim against the manufacturer of the equipment. It may be determined that the medical product is defective in design, use, or material or with inadequate instructions.

Job descriptions can also be used as standards of care. For example, an operating room nurse is required to do three counts in a surgical procedure. If the nurse fails to do the required number of counts for whatever reason, a breach may be alleged because the nurse failed to perform the requirements of her job, resulting in injury to the patient (e.g., lap pad left in the abdomen that caused sepsis). The surgeon may also be liable for a wrong count even though the actual count is delegated to the nursing staff.

Critical pathways or guidelines are not mandatory. If a critical guideline is treated as a standard of care, then it must be followed.

Administrative code regulations, both state and federal, play an important role in certain health care settings (e.g., home health and nursing homes). Such regulations establish minimum standards, which must be met.

Court decisions and administrative rulings are also used as standards. Case law may set out certain guidelines and standards involving malpractice, personal injury, contract, and other areas of laws. A review of case law should be done to determine how the courts have decided on an issue presented by a specific case. This generally is not a duty for the LNC but usually falls to the attorney or paralegal.

The Joint Commission also sets out standards for health care professionals and facilities.

Standards of Professional Performance

Standards of professional performance are described in terms of competency, not reasonable care. Technological advancements provide new and better aids and equipment to treat patients. The criteria to measure compliance with the use of such new technology will also change. Criteria to

CIVIL DISTRICT COURT FOR THE PARISH OF JONES

STATE OF _____

SUBPOENA

No. _____   DIVISION _____   Docket No. _____

BRETT AIKN VS. ALEXES BEAM

TO:

CLERK, CIVIL DISTRICT COURT—Please issue a subpoena to the above party as directed below.

SUBPOENA REQUEST

[ ] YOU ARE COMMANDED to appear in the Civil District Court, Parish of Jones, in Division

"_____," 421 Ratcliff Ave., New Algiers, LA 99999, on the _____ day of _____, 2002, at _____o'clock ___.m., to testify the truth according to your knowledge, in a controversy pending herein between the parties above named; and hereof you are not to fail under the penalty of the law. By order of the Court.

DEPOSITION SUBPOENA REQUEST

[ ] YOU ARE COMMANDED to appear at the place, date and time specified below to testify at the taking of a deposition in the above case.

PLACE OF DEPOSITION   DATE AND TIME

REQUEST FOR WRIT OF SUBPOENA DUCES TECUM

[ ] YOU ARE COMMANDED to produce and permit inspection and copying of the following documents or objects for the _____trial, _____deposition, or _____hearing (state type) _____at the place, date and time specified below (list documents or objects) pursuant to the provisions of article 9999 et seq. of the Code of Civil Procedure.

PLACE   DATE AND TIME

Issued at the request of and fees and costs guaranteed by undersigned.

ATTORNEY _____ Attorney's signature

ATTORNEY'S NAME & BAR NO.

ADDRESS &

TELEPHONE NUMBER

File original and two copies with Clerk, fourth copy for Attorney's File

Figure 1.1   Sample subpoena.

RETURN FOR PERSONAL SERVICE

On the _____ day of _____, 2002, served a copy of the within on _____ in person
_____

_____ ENTERED _____

PAPER   RETURN

SERIAL NO. DEPUTY PARISH   RETURN FOR DOMICILIARY SERVICE

On the _____ day of _____, 2002, served a copy of the within on _____

by leaving same at _____ domiciled or usual place of abode _____ in the hands

of a person of suitable age and discretion, residing therein as a member of _____ domiciliary

establishment, whose name and other facts connected with his service I learned by interrogating the said _____

_____ being absent from _____ domicile at time

of said service.

Return same day

Deputy Sheriff of Jones Parish

Figure 1.1 (continued)

determine the standards of practice are being developed by the specialty areas of medicine and nursing. Standards may be used for different reasons, as evidence for or against a plaintiff or defendant in medical malpractice cases, disciplinary actions, custody matters, workers' compensation claims, commitment proceedings, and personal injury claims.

Liability of Health Care Providers

If the health care professional makes an error in judgment, he is not liable for negligence. Three factors must be present for an action to be called an error in judgment rather than negligence:

1. The health care provider's care must have conformed to the current professional standards of care.
2. The health care provider must possess knowledge and skills similar to those of an average member of the profession.
3. The health care provider must use professional judgment to choose between alternative available treatments or courses of action, both of which would be within the standard of care.

Liability requires that the party or person responsible for injuries or damages be held accountable. Legal accountability requires that the health care provider be held responsible for the actions taken or not taken when providing care and treatment to patients. Vicarious liability occurs when the law, in certain limited instances, imposes liability on a principal for the acts or omissions of an agent. For example, vicarious liability may be placed on an employer for the acts of an employee. Likewise, a hospital is generally vicariously liable for the acts and omissions of hospital employees. *Ostensible authority* is a doctrine of law whereby a hospital may be held liable for the negligence of an independent contractor, if the patient has a rational basis to believe that the independent contractor is a hospital employee. This most frequently applies to emergency department physicians who appear to be hospital employees to patients and their families.

Diagnostic Errors

Allegations of diagnostic errors are common in medical negligence claims. Some of the reasons for errors include a physician's lack of expertise, knowledge base, and experience with the medical problems presented. Errors can also arise from inaccuracies in diagnostic studies or interpretations of the studies, and diseases that have atypical presentations.

LNCs should review the records to determine whether the physicians utilized any of the following strategies in assessing the patient:

- A careful history is important. Is communicating with the patient difficult because of a language barrier? Other factors to be considered are the patient's mental status, or his inability to understand the physician's questions. A red flag should go up as a potential area for liability if this is a factor.
- Careful physical exams can demonstrate evidence of the presence or absence of a disease entity or medical condition.
- Diagnostic tests have limits. The clinical picture may warrant additional testing, even with a previous negative finding. Could the additional testing have discovered that the patient had a subdural hematoma or embolism, for example?
- Did the physician consider all working diagnoses so that all possible tests and evaluations could be done?

Example 1.9

A 37-year-old mother of two minor children was seen by a physician 19 times between January 1995 and April 1998. She reported seeing blood in her stools. The physician diagnosed her as having a small hemorrhoid. Subsequently, the patient reported having rectal pressure, abdominal pain, constipation, and hematochezia (blood in the stool). The physician again diagnosed her as having a hemorrhoid. When seen by a different physician covering the practice, the patient complained again of the same symptoms. She was referred to a gastroenterologist, who performed a colonoscopy, removed polyps, and informed her that they were cancerous. The patient was diagnosed with metastatic colon cancer and died one month after the colonoscopy. The case was settled for $1,800,000 (Laska, 2002b).

Treatment Issues

Treatment issues occur in hospitals, long-term care facilities, and home health settings. Treatment issues involve a wide variety of potential breaches. For example, these may involve failure to

- Treat in a timely fashion
- Provide the correct treatment

- Perform the treatment
- Use equipment properly
- Treat in a timely manner when signs and symptoms of a deteriorating condition are evident

Example 1.10

A 42-year-old diabetic sustained an injury to his right foot. Home care was provided, consisting of wound care, administration of IV antibiotics, and teaching. The plaintiff alleged that the defendant home care agency had failed to treat the foot injury. This resulted in a transmetatarsal amputation of a portion of the plaintiff's right foot. The plaintiff claimed that the nurses should have contacted the physician to relay the information that the patient should have been taking Cipro. The plaintiff's treating podiatrist was seeing him while the defendant home care agency was involved with the plaintiff. The defendant contended that at the time of discharge from the hospital, the amputation was inevitable when the defendant undertook the care of the plaintiff. Prior to trial, the plaintiff settled with the podiatrist for $250,000 policy limits. The jury returned a defense verdict for the home care agency (Laska, 2002c).

Communication Issues

Communication is crucial today because of the many different "players" involved in the care and treatment of the patient. Communication lines must be open between the health care provider and

- The patient
- Other health care providers
- Social services
- The administration
- The risk management
- The case manager
- The insurer

With managed care and case management, communication lines must be open and direct at all times. Otherwise, the patient may suffer injuries, and facilities and insurers may be sued and held liable for damages. Common types of communication failure allegations include failure to

- Communicate at all
- Communicate in a timely fashion
- Document communication with the patient, patient's family, and other health care providers
- Communicate the appropriate information
- Act based on the communication received
- Inform the patient of test results

Example 1.11

In a claim for loss of chance of survival, the plaintiff must establish by a preponderance of the evidence that the patient had a chance for survival (not that he would have survived but for the defendant's negligence) and that the chance was lost due to the defendant's negligence. The court held that the physician and hospital failed to inform the patient that she had an abnormal chest x-ray even though evidence showed that her lung cancer was untreatable when the x-ray was taken. The plaintiff could have had more time to live a normal life before becoming so ill (*Hebert v. Parker*, 2001).

Monitoring

Monitoring a patient involves all levels of health care providers from physicians to nursing assistants. Policies and procedures that set out monitoring responsibilities are important sections in the facility's policy and procedure manuals. Monitoring breaches include failure to

- Properly monitor the care, treatment, and condition of the patient
- Monitor in a timely fashion
- Report deviations (changes in the patient's status when monitoring) to the appropriate person
- Document monitoring
- Use the proper equipment to monitor the patient
- Properly instruct and teach the patient about monitoring her condition (e.g., sugar level to determine the insulin needed)
- Use the equipment properly when monitoring a patient (e.g., silencing the alarm on an infusion pump or telemetry monitor rather than identifying the reason for the alarm)
- Monitor and check equipment and use of equipment

Example 1.12

In a survival action and wrongful death claim, the parents sued for malpractice when their infant was delivered by cesarean section and suffered asphyxia, causing severe brain damage, kidney failure, other complications, and ultimately death. Allegations of breaches of the standard of care included

- Inadequate care
- Administration of Pitocin after a previous test showed fetal distress
- Delay in performing an emergency cesarean section

The negligence was found to be the cause of the baby's injuries. The award was $3,000,000, but was reduced to $500,000 as imposed by the statutory cap. Special damages of $41,833.73 were awarded (*Conerly v. State of Louisiana*, 1997).

Supervision

Supervisory issues have always been an area of great interest, whether they involve the physician in an operating room or a clinical instructor with a student. The common areas of potential liability vary. For instance, with unlicensed assistant personnel, there is great concern over the issue of who is actually supervising the patient.

Supervisory liability focuses on the failure to supervise properly and delegate properly. For example, if a supervisor knows that the staff does not possess the knowledge, experience, and expertise to perform a delegated task, but still delegates it, legal liability may result if the patient is injured.

Additionally, if the supervisor fails to supervise properly or gives incorrect instructions, liability may occur. For example, a nurse asks a supervisor to show her how to z-track because she has forgotten. As she is in a hurry, the supervisor uses her forearm to demonstrate rather than a larger muscle. The nurse enters the patient's room and z-tracks on the forearm, causing severe necrosis and disfigurement. Both the supervisor and nurse may be held liable for their breaches.

Supervisory breaches include failure to

- Supervise properly
- Delegate properly
- Properly evaluate the health care provider rendering treatment
- Educate properly and check that the staff has demonstrated the required skills
- Document that the staff has been oriented, evaluated, and trained
- Use good judgment

Medication

Medication errors are high on the list of potential areas of legal exposure. Errors can be acts of omission or acts of commission. Breaches involving medication may include such things as failure to

- Administer the correct drug
- Administer medication in a timely fashion
- Administer the drug properly using the correct route
- Give the medication to the correct patient
- Assess IV sites for complications (e.g., for signs of infiltration or infection)
- Administer any drug
- Administer the correct dosage
- Confirm or clarify a medication order
- Detect signs and symptoms of drug toxicity
- Order or request an order for drug levels
- Recognize adverse reactions and side effects
- Recognize, and check the chart for, drug allergies that could result in damaging complications
- Document the injection site
- Use the proper-sized needle for the specific drug administered and the required site
- Use aseptic techniques

Example 1.13

A 93-year-old man went to the emergency department for treatment of a bowel blockage. A physician directed one of the nurses to administer 15 mg of Demerol intravenously to the plaintiff. The nurse allegedly programmed the IV pump incorrectly, resulting in a delivery of 70–90 mg of Demerol. After the patient went into respiratory arrest, he was successfully resuscitated, but suffered extensive hypoxic brain damage, resulting in a diminished IQ, and now requires care 24 h a day. The jury returned a verdict of $863,180 (Laska, 2002d).

Falls

Patient falls are extremely common problems and the reason for numerous lawsuits. Geriatric patients, medical-surgical patients, and pediatric patients are all potential fall victims. Patients with the following conditions are more susceptible to falls than others:

- Heavily sedated patients
- Patients with mobility problems

- Patients with cognitive impairments (e.g., Alzheimer's, dementia, and organic brain syndrome)
- Patients who wake up to go to the bathroom or get out of bed for some other reason
- Patients on numerous medications that when combined may cause problems of drowsiness, balance, and coherence
- Patients who have previously fallen
- Patients with predisposing diseases/conditions such as Parkinson's disease, orthostatic hypotension, vertigo, cerebrovascular accident (CVA), seizures, and hypertension
- Patients on multiple medications
- Noncompliant patients

Sometimes it is difficult to predict which patient will fall. Falls can result in injuries that range from minor bruising to subdural hematomas and death. Documentation of all findings discovered at the scene where the fall occurred must be examined by the LNC.

- Was there an order for side rails?
- Did the health care providers follow hospital policies and procedures?
- Was the patient properly managed and treated after the fall? Were there any protocols for monitoring?
- What injuries did the patient suffer?
- Did the fall exacerbate a preexisting condition or cause a new injury?
- Were the policy and procedure with regard to notifying the physician and family followed?
- Were sitters, bed alarms, or more frequent monitoring warranted? If such interventions were ordered, were they in use at the time of the fall?
- If the patient fell, was an incident report written?
- What were the conditions of the surroundings (e.g., the floor where the fall took place)?

All of the above should be considered by LNCs when working on a fall claim, irrespective of whether it is for a plaintiff or a defendant. Also, LNCs should talk to the risk manager and interview those involved in the fall if they are working with the defendant. Obtaining an independent medical examination should be considered if the damages claimed are not consistent with documented damages.

Example 1.14

A wheelchair-bound patient claimed to have fallen from his wheelchair while he was a passenger in the defendant's ambulance and being transported from the dialysis center. He suffered from diabetes, renal failure, peripheral vascular disease, and legal blindness. He contended that the driver made a sharp turn, causing him to fall from his wheelchair and strike his head. He contended that the vehicle was not equipped with a seat belt, the driver claimed that the patient had refused to wear the belt. The plaintiff sustained a hematoma to the scalp, which resulted in gangrene, and removal of half of his scalp to halt the gangrene spread. The action settled for $825,000 (Laska, 2002e).

Restraints

Restraints can cause circulatory damage, nerve damage, brain damage, and death. It is important that the policies and procedures be requested or subpoenaed to determine whether they were followed. For example:

- Was the patient monitored properly and in a timely fashion?
- Was the patient abandoned for a period of time during which he suffered injuries?

- Were all the alternatives to restraints evaluated and employed, if appropriate, prior to the use of restraint?
- Were appropriate and routine body systems performed (e.g., neurological, respiratory, and circulatory)?

Documentation must be evaluated carefully along with an analysis of policies and procedures.

The Lawsuit

Prelitigation Panels for Malpractice Claims

Once a lawsuit is instituted, based on a breach of the standard of care, several steps are involved in the litigation process. In some states, a statutory provision requires the plaintiff to go through a prelitigation or medical review panel process. Panel members may consist of health care providers, lawyers, and judges, depending on the state. Medical records, documents, and materials are submitted to the panel members, who then determine whether malpractice occurred.

Arguments for prelitigation panels include a decreased number of frivolous lawsuits filed. Attorneys can drop cases that the panel has determined have little or no merit. Those opposing the use of prelitigation panels argue that they simply delay the plaintiff from entering the judicial arena and add to the costs of pursuing and defending a case. However, the panel opinion sometimes facilitates settlement.

The Procedural Process

Initiation of a Lawsuit

- The client interview should be detailed, identifying all previous medical providers, past medical history, past surgical history, and social history. All the necessary documents should then be requested and obtained.
- Review and evaluation of pertinent medical/physician records and other documents can be done in the law firm or by an outside expert.
- Determine whether any breaches (acts and omissions) in the standards of care have caused damages to the plaintiff.
- Determine the damages (e.g., lost wages, medical expenses, pain and suffering, loss of chance of survival, disfigurement, loss of society, loss of consortium, loss of love and affection, emotional distress, mental anguish, and diminution of the enjoyment of life). The LNC will focus on special damages such as medical bills while the attorney will address general (non-economic) damages.
- The attorney will file the necessary documents to institute the prelitigation panel process if applicable.
- The attorney will file the Petition for Damages or Complaint in the appropriate court after the panel process is completed; if there is no mandatory prelitigation process, this is the first step in the lawsuit. See Figure 1.2 for a sample complaint.
- There will be an answer by the defendant, who will allege defenses to the allegations or denials. (If not answered in a timely way, entering of a default judgment by the court can occur, which means the plaintiff wins because the defendant did not respond.)

STATE OF _____

IN RE: MEDICAL REVIEW PANEL

NUMBER:

MADELINE OURSO, WIFE OF, INDIVIDUALLY AND

ON BEHALF OF THE ESTATE OF FRANCIS OURSO

VERSUS

CITY MEDICAL CENTER, ABC HOSPITAL,

ANDREA ALI, M.D., and KYLE WAYNE, M.D.

COMPLAINT: REQUEST FOR MEDICAL REVIEW PANEL

The complaint of Madeline Ourso, [is this a fake name] wife of, individually and on behalf of the estate of Francis Ourso, persons of the full age of majority and residents of the Parish of Rabine, State of _____ and proper plaintiff's beneficiary under Louisiana Civil Code Article 2315.1 and 2315.2, with respect represent that:

    I.   Made defendant herein is City Medical Center, which upon information and belief is duly licensed and authorized to do business as a healthcare facility in the Parish of Rabine, State of _____, and at all material times herein rendered care to the deceased, Francis Ourso.

    II.   Made defendant herein is ABC Hospital, which upon information and belief is duly licensed and authorized to do business as a healthcare facility in the Parish of Rabine, State of _____, and at all material times herein rendered care to the deceased, Francis Ourso.

    III.   Made defendant, Andrea Ali, M.D., which upon information and belief is a physician, duly licensed and authorized to and practicing in the State of _____ who rendered care and treatment to Francis Ourso.

    IV.   Made defendant, Kyle Wayne, M.D., which upon information and belief is a physician, duly licensed and authorized to and practicing in the State of _____ who rendered care and treatment to Francis Ourso.

    V.   The above defendants are jointly, severally and in solido liable unto Petitioners for damages sustained by Madeline and Francis Ourso.

    VI.   On or about January 1, 2000, Mr. Ourso sought the services of physicians at the City Medical Center. From January 2000, until his death on December 17, 2001, he was treated by Dr. Ali and Dr. Wayne. Throughout this time period he had complaints consistent with cancer

    VII.   In January of 2001, Mr. Ourso was hospitalized at ABC Hospital for several weeks. Cancer was not diagnosed.

    VIII.   He was also seen at ABC Hospital numerous times for complaints consistent with cancer, e.g., weight loss, rectal bleeding and anemia.

    IX.   On or about December 17, 2001, Mr. Ourso expired. The cause of death according to the Death Certificate was 1. Cardiorespiratory arrest due to or as a consequence of 2. Metastatic adenocarcinoma.

    X.   City Medical Center and ABC Hospital are liable unto petitioners under the doctrine of respondeat superior for the acts and/or omissions of their agents and/or independent contractors, and/or employees, including but not limited to:

        1.   Failure to perform the appropriate and timely diagnostic tests to determine the cause of Mr. Ourso's complaints;

        2.   Failure to properly assess and evaluate patient's serious medical condition;

        3.   Failure to timely diagnose cancer;

        4.   Failure to timely treat cancer;

        5.   Failure to timely refer to an appropriate specialist;

        6.   Failure to recognize signs and symptoms of cancer; and

        7.   Any and all other acts of negligence that may be proven at the trial of this matter.

Figure 1.2 Sample complaint.

XI. Andrea Ali, M.D., and Kyle Wayne, M.D., are liable unto your petitioners for acts and/or omissions including but not limited to:

1. Failure to perform the appropriate and timely diagnostic tests to determine the cause of Mr. Ourso's complaints;
2. Failure to properly assess and evaluate patient's serious medical condition;
3. Failure to timely diagnose cancer;
4. Failure to timely treat cancer;
5. Failure to timely refer to an appropriate specialist;
6. Failure to recognize signs and symptoms of cancer; and
7. Any and all other acts of negligence that may be proven at the trial of this matter.

XII. As a result of defendants' acts and/or omissions, Mr. Ourso has sustained severe pain and suffering, emotional distress, mental anguish, lost wages, diminution of the enjoyment of life, loss of life expectancy, loss of chance of survival, premature death and any other damages to be proven at the trial of this matter.

XIII. As a result of the acts and/or omissions of defendants, Mrs. Ourso has sustained emotional distress, mental anguish, funeral expenses, medical expenses, loss of consortium and any other damages to be proven at the trial of this matter.

XIV. Petitioners demand damages as are reasonable in the premises in accordance with the law; however, they reserve their right to demand a specific dollar amount and prove a specific dollar amount at the trial of this matter.

XV. Petitioners are entitled to and demand that a Medical Review Panel be convened in this matter to determine the negligence of the defendants herein above named. In the event that defendant is not entitled or is not a participant in the state's Patient's Compensation Fund, then Petitioners request to be notified of that fact so that additional filings may be taken.

XVI. Petitioners allege that Rev. Stat. Ann., et seq. is unconstitutional in whole or in part and that by filing this request for a Medical Review Panel as is required, Petitioners do not concede the validity of the statute.

XVII. Wherefore, Petitioners pray that defendants be served with a copy of this complaint and that a Medical Review Panel be convened in this matter to determine the negligence of the defendants and that after due proceedings that there be a decision that defendants violated applicable standards of care and for all general and equitable relief.

Respectfully submitted,

_____

Alexes E. Nekia
123 Sunvalley Road, Suite 200
New Algiers, LA 70355
(903) 999–9999
(903) 999–9998 (fax)

Figure 1.2   (continued)

- There may be filing of a Motion to Dismiss the case based upon a statutory defense. For example, if the complaint is filed in the incorrect jurisdiction or the wrong defendant is named, a Motion to Dismiss the case may be filed.
- There may be possible filing of counterclaims (claims by the defendant against the plaintiff in response to the lawsuit). For example, a defendant hospital may file a counterclaim for unpaid medical bills.
- There may be possible filing of amended and supplemental pleadings by either party (e.g., additional defendant added; Aiken, 1995).

Potential sources of information that will aid the LNC in gathering facts about the case include the following:

- Ambulance run reports
- Emergency department records
- Emergency department logs
- Coroner's report
- Death certificate
- X-ray department
- Code logs
- Switchboard operator's log
- Nursing supervisor shift reports
- Laboratory logs
- Fetal monitor strips
- EKG strips
- Telemetry strips
- Holter monitor strips
- Patient census sheets
- Long-distance phone bills to show calls to physicians or patients
- Employee time cards
- Medication wastage records
- Surveys for long-term care facilities (to determine whether cited for deficiencies)
- Laboratory computer tapes and records
- Employee personnel files
- Police report
- Insurance policies
- Medical records
- Pharmacy bills
- Physical therapy records/bills
- Client's uninsured policy (if applicable)
- Psychiatric records
- Lost wages information
- Other bills (e.g., traction units and cervical collars)
- X-ray diagnostic studies that show injuries [e.g., magnetic resonance imaging (MRI) and computed tomography (CT) scan]
- Toxicology screens (if drugs/alcohol suspected)

Discovery Stage

Discovery Tools

Discovery tools are used to learn about pertinent facts surrounding the circumstances of the claim. Tools include interrogatories, requests for production of things and documents, and admissions of facts and depositions. (These tools are described in detail below.)

Interrogatories

Interrogatories are written questions/requests sent to a party in a suit that are answered under oath and used to "discover" information. For example:

- Please list all places of employment, position, duties, years employed at the facility, and reasons for leaving.
- Please list the names and addresses of any parties listed on your witness list who are or were employees of Aken Hospital.
- Please list any and all exhibits that will be used in the trial of this matter.
- See Figure 1.3 for a sample interrogatory request.

29TH JUDICIAL DISTRICT COURT FOR THE PARISH OF SUN

STATE OF _____

NO: 501–235   DIVISION "O"

ELIZABETH CHAUVIN, WIFE OF, INDIVIDUALLY AND

ON BEHALF OF THE ESTATE OF JOE CHAUVIN

VERSUS

BRETT MACON, M.D.

FILED: _____   _____

                        DEPUTY CLERK

INTERROGATORIES AND

REQUEST FOR PRODUCTION OF DOCUMENTS

TO: BRETT MACON, M.D.

Through his attorney of record,
Alexes E. Nekia
123 Sunvalley Road, Suite 200
New Orleans, LA 70113
(903) 999–9999
(903) 999–9988 (fax)

Petitioner, Elizabeth Chauvin, appearing through her undersigned counsel of record, requests that the defendant answer the following interrogatories, under oath, within fifteen (15) days from the date of service thereof, pursuant to the provisions of Article 1491 of the Louisiana Code of Civil Procedure.

INTERROGATORY NO. 1:
Please list the following information for Dr. Brett Macon:

   1) Have you retained an expert to act on your behalf in any matter pertaining to this action? If so, for each expert state:
      a. Name, office address and telephone number
      b. Occupation and specialty
      c. Brief description of testimony and/or opinion to be given

---

Figure 1.3   Sample interrogatories and request for production.

INTERROGATORY NO. 2:

Please list all fact witnesses that you will call at the trial of this matter:

    a.   Fact witness's name, address, and telephone number
    b.   Scope of facts to which the witness is expected to testify

INTERROGATORY NO. 3:

Is there any person who has knowledge or information concerning the case whose name and address are not listed in the preceding interrogatories? If so, for each such person state:

    a.   His name, address and telephone number
    b.   The address of the place where he is employed, occupation and job title
    c.   What information or knowledge concerning this case does the person possess?

INTERROGATORY NO. 4:

Please list the following information for Dr. Brett Macon:

    1) Were you associated, or in partnership, with any other medical practitioner at the time of the occurrences complained of in this action? If so, state:
        a.   The name, address, specialty and qualifications of each person with whom you were associated or in partnership
        b.   The nature of your business relationship to each such person
        c.   The nature of your professional relationship with Smith Medical Center at the time of the alleged incident
        d.   The number of years of experience you have in your specialty
        e.   A description of the services the defendant has been employed to perform
        f.   Whether defendant has ever been a party in any other lawsuit and, if so, the name of the suit, kind of suit involved, the name of the court and the date of filing, as well as the disposition of the suit

REQUEST FOR PRODUCTION OF DOCUMENTS

REQUEST NO. 1:

Please list the following information regarding Dr. Brett Macon:

    a.   A copy of Dr. Macon's resume/curriculum vitae
    b.   Board certificates, specialties and dates received and rectified
    c.   Educational background
    d.   Employment history
    e.   Publications and/or medical presentations (title, publisher and date published and/or written)
    f.   Any and all agreements, contracts or other documents pertaining to Dr. Macon with Smith Medical Center at the time of the alleged incident

REQUEST NO. 2:

Have you ever written, or contributed to, any medical or nursing textbook or professional journal? If so, for each state:

    a.   Title, publisher and date of publication

Respectfully submitted,

_____

Alexes E. Nekia
123 Sunvalley Road, Suite 200
New Algiers, LA 70355
(903) 999–9999
(903) 999–9988 (fax)

Figure 1.3 (continued)

CERTIFICATE OF SERVICE
I hereby certify that a copy of the foregoing has been forwarded to counsel of record by depositing copy of same in the U.S. mail, postage prepaid and properly addressed, this _____ day of _____, 2002.

Alexes E. Nekia

Figure 1.3 (continued)

Request for Production of Things and Documents

The *Request for Production of Things and Documents* is another discovery tool used to elicit information from the opposing party. This written tool is used to obtain medical records, hospital policies and procedures, personnel records, and other documents or things that may aid in proving that the standard of care was or was not breached. An example of such a request is: Please provide any and all documents, materials, policies, procedures, guidelines, and standards used by the nursing staff at James Hospital from 2000 to 2001 regarding skin care to be administered to diabetic patients.

Admission of Facts

Admission of Facts is a written discovery tool used to streamline information received in a case. For example,

- Do you admit or deny that Patient Alexes Johnanthony was a patient in your practice?
- Do you admit or deny that signs and symptoms of gastrointestinal bleeding can be abdominal guarding, hypotension, and/or tachycardia?
- Do you admit or deny that Ms. Johnanthony had signs and symptoms of a gastrointestinal bleeding?

Depositions

A *deposition* is a structured interview in which the person being interviewed (the deponent) is placed under oath and asked questions about issues of the lawsuit. Depositions are held to

- Discover all available information about the allegations and circumstances surrounding the lawsuit
- Evaluate the demeanor and the credibility of the witness and parties to the lawsuit
- Determine the availability of insurance coverage
- Assist attorneys in assessing the strengths or weaknesses of their cases and their opponents' cases
- Determine the existence of pertinent documents
- Preserve the testimony of a witness who may be unavailable at the time of trial (e.g., the witness may be out of town or a plaintiff who may expire prior to trial as a result of the failure to diagnose cancer in time)
- Refresh the witness's memory or impeach a witness's credibility during the trial

Depositions require preparation and education. Nurses are deposed for many reasons. For example, a nurse may be a defendant (the person sued), a fact or material witness who may have knowledge about facts surrounding allegations and circumstances in the lawsuit, an expert witness (a person who may be able to prove liability or damages), or a holder of important documents (e.g., an emergency room supervisor who has the emergency room log for patients).

The expert witness, fact witness, or defendant who is being deposed should appear professional, confident, organized, knowledgeable, honest, and credible. The witness should

- Review the pertinent documents
- Prepare for the deposition
- Have the medical records available at all times
- Refer to the medical records when needed to answer questions
- Tell the truth
- Dress professionally
- Answer the question asked
- Listen to each specific question and ask for clarification if needed
- Ask for a break if tired, confused, aggravated, or upset
- Wait before answering the question to give the attorney the opportunity to make the proper objection
- Reserve the right to read and sign the deposition. (Rules may vary from state to state as to what changes and additions can be made in a deposition.)
- Ask to see the documents to which the opposing counsel is referring prior to answering the questions
- Speak clearly and slowly and answer verbally
- Listen to the specific objections made by the attorney
- Ask the opposing counsel to break up a compound question
- Ask the opposing counsel for clarification of unclear or complex questions
- Be cautious about hypothetical situations that may not have the exact facts of the case at issue
- Give short and concise answers
- A witness must also avoid displaying hostility, anger, sarcasm; volunteering information; or making assumptions (Aiken, 1995). More information on how to answer questions in a deposition is found in Chapter 14.

Trial Process

Once it has been determined that a breach of the standard that caused damages has occurred, or that the party has a basis to sue, then the lawsuit is filed in the appropriate jurisdiction and venue. Most lawsuits proceed in the following order:

1. Prelitigation conferences may be held
2. Settlements may be proposed
3. Mediation or arbitration may be done to avoid trial
4. Trial of lawsuit
5. Selection of the jury if it is a jury trial: voir dire questioning of potential jurors
6. Opening statements by plaintiff and defendant
7. Plaintiff presents his case

8. Motion for directed verdict against plaintiff
9. Defendant presents his case
10. Rebuttal
11. Closing statements by plaintiff and defendant
12. Jury instructions
13. Jury deliberations
14. Verdict
15. Appeal (optional) 1

See Chapter 14 for more information about preparing for and assisting at trials.

Conclusion

LNCs are in an excellent position to review, evaluate, and analyze potential liability and damage claims. Medical negligence claims, personal injury, workers' compensation, product liability, toxic torts, and automobile cases are all areas of law to which LNCs can apply their skills to assist the attorney in pursuing or defending the claims.

References

Aiken, T. (1995). Depositions: What you need to know. *Journal of Legal Nurse Consulting*, 6(4), 9–10.

Aiken, T. D. (Ed.). (2008). *Legal and ethical issues in health occupations* (2nd ed.). Philadelphia: W.B. Saunders.

Aquilera-Sanchez v. Wal-Mart Stores, Inc., No. 95–61 (Starr Co. Tex. Dist. Ct.). *The National Law Journal*, October 18, 2001; In Touch ... with LTLA, October 26, 2001.

Conerly v. State of Louisiana, 690 So. 2d 980 (La. Ct. App. 1997).

Flanagan v. Labe 666 A.2d 333 (Pa.Super. 1999), aff'd 690 A.2d 183 (Pa. 1997).

Hebert v. Parker, 796 So. 2d 19 (La. Ct. App. 2001).

Laska, L. (Ed.). (2002a). Failure to pre-oxygenate patient. *Medical Malpractice Verdicts, Settlements and Experts*, 3, January.

Laska, L. (Ed.). (2002b). Failure to diagnose bowel cancer leads to death. *Medical Malpractice Verdicts, Settlements and Experts*, January 13.

Laska, L. (Ed.). (2002c). Failure to provide adequate home nursing wound care for diabetic patient leads to partial amputation of foot. *Medical Malpractice Verdicts, Settlements and Experts*, January 20.

Laska, L. (Ed.). (2002d). Nurse administers near-lethal dose of Demerol in emergency room. *Medical Malpractice Verdicts, Settlements and Experts*, January 21.

Laska, L. (Ed.). (2002e). Ambulance driver fails to seat belt wheelchair-bound patient. *Medical Malpractice Verdicts, Settlements and Experts*, January 22.

Additional Resources

www.NurseLaw.com—Current case law and legal updates.

Legal Nurse Consultant link: www.nurselaw.com/education.php—for additional cases and legal updates.

Additional Reading

Aiken, T. D. (Ed.). (2004). *Legal, ethical and political issues in nursing*. Philadelphia: F.A. Davis.

Guido, G. (1997). *Legal issues in nursing* (2nd ed.). Stamford, CT: Appleton Lange.

Iyer, P. (Ed.). (2001). *Nursing malpractice* (2nd ed.).Tucson, AZ: Lawyers and Judges Publishing Company.

O'Keefe, M. (2001). *Nursing practice and the law*. Philadelphia: F.A. Davis.

Test Questions

1. The four elements of negligence include all of the following EXCEPT:
   A. Breach of the standard
   B. Damages
   C. Duty owed
   D. Proximate malpractice

2. Which of the following statements about battery is true?
   A. It is a quasi-irregular tort
   B. It is unpermitted touching
   C. It is based on the stare decisis theory
   D. It is only a criminal offense

3. All of the following are intentional torts, EXCEPT:
   A. Battery
   B. Defamation
   C. Assault
   D. False imprisonment

4. Which of the following statements about the standard of care is true?
   A. It is based on the highest level of care at the time
   B. It is used only in cases involving malpractice
   C. It is based on the current standards for when the suit is filed
   D. It is used to designate what is reasonable under the circumstances

5. Which of the following statements about the standard of care is not true?
   A. It includes the opinion of lay persons
   B. It includes authoritative texts and consensus opinions
   C. It includes statutes and policies
   D. It can be found in the medical records

Answers: 1. D, 2. B, 3. B, 4. D, 5. C

Appendix A: U.S. Constitutional Amendments 1–10 and 14

1. Congress shall make no law respecting an establishment of religion, or prohibiting the free exercise thereof; of abridging the freedom of speech, or of the press; or the right of the people peaceably to assemble, and to petition the Government for a redress of grievances.
2. A well-regulated Militia, being necessary to the security of a free State, the right of the people to keep and bear Arms, shall not be infringed.
3. No soldier shall, in time of peace, be quartered in any house, without the consent of the owner, nor in time of war, but in a manner to be prescribed by law.
4. The right of the people to be secure in their persons, houses, papers, and effects, against unreasonable searches and seizures, shall not be violated, and no Warrants shall issue, but upon proper cause, supported by Oath or affirmation, and particularly describing the place to be searched, and the persons or things to be seized.
5. No persons shall be held to answer for a capital, or otherwise infamous crime, unless a presentment or indictment of a Grand Jury, except in cases arising in the land or naval forces, or in the Militia, when in actual service in time of War or public danger, nor shall any persons be subject for the same offense twice put in jeopardy of life or limb, nor shall be compelled in any criminal case to be a witness against himself, nor be deprived of life, liberty, or property, without due process of law; nor shall private property be taken for public use, without just compensation.
6. In all criminal prosecutions, the accused shall enjoy the right to a speedy and public trial by an impartial jury of the State and district wherein the crime shall have been committed, which district shall have been previously ascertained by law, and to be informed of the nature and cause of the accusations; to be confronted with the witnesses against him; to have compulsory process for obtaining witnesses in his favor, and to have the Assistance of counsel for his defense.
7. In Suits at common law, where the value in controversy shall exceed twenty dollars, the right of trial by jury shall be preserved, and no fact tried by a jury, shall be otherwise reexamined in any Court of the U.S. than according to the rules of the common law.
8. Excessive bail shall not be required, nor excessive fines imposed, nor cruel and unusual punishments inflicted.
9. The enumeration in the Constitution, of certain rights, shall not be constructed to deny or disparage others retained by the people.
10. The powers not delegated to the U.S. by the Constitution, nor prohibited by it to the States, are reserved to the States respectively, or to the people.
14. Section I. All persons born or naturalized in the U.S., and subject to the jurisdiction thereof, are citizens of the U.S. and the State wherein they reside. No State shall make or enforce any law that shall abridge the privileges of immunities of citizens of the U.S.; nor shall any State deprive any person of life, liberty, or property, without due process of law; nor deny to any persons within its jurisdiction the equal protection of the laws.

Appendix B: ANA Nursing Standards

Scope and Standards for Nurse Administrators
Scope and Standards of Advanced Practice Registered Nursing
Scope and Standards of College Health Nursing Practice
Scope and Standards of Diabetes Nursing
Scope and Standards of Forensic Nursing Practice

Scope and Standards of Home Health Nursing Practice
Scope and Standards of Nursing Informatics Practice
Scope and Standards of Nursing Practice in Correctional Facilities
Scope and Standards of Parish Nursing Practice
Scope and Standards of Pediatric Oncology Nursing
Scope and Standards of Practice for Nursing Professional Development
Scope and Standards of Professional School Nursing Practice
Scope and Standards of Psychiatric–Mental Health Nursing Practice
Scope and Standards of Public Health Nursing Practice
Standards and Scope of Gerontological Nursing Practice
Standards of Addiction Nursing Practice with Selected Diagnoses and Criteria
Standards of Clinical Nursing Practice (2nd Edition)
Standards of Clinical Practice and Scope of Practice for the Acute Care Nurse Practitioner
Statement on the Scope and Standards for the Nurse Who Specializes in Development Disabilities and/or Mental Retardation
Statement on the Scope and Standards of Genetics Clinical Nursing Practice
Statement on the Scope and Standards of Oncology Nursing Practice
Statement on the Scope and Standards of Otorhinolaryngology Clinical Nursing
Statement on the Scope and Standards of Pediatric Clinical Nursing Practice
Statement on the Scope and Standards of Psychiatric–Mental Health

Appendix C: National Nursing Specialty Organizations

Academy of Medical-Surgical Nurses (AMSN)
American Academy of Ambulatory Care Nursing (AAACN)
American Association of Critical-Care Nurses (AACN)
American Association of Diabetes Educators (AADE)
American Association of Legal Nurse Consultants (AALNC)
American Association of Neuroscience Nurses (AANN)
American Association of Nurse Anesthetists (AANA)
American Association of Nurse Life Care Planners (AANLCP)
American Association of Occupational Health Nurses (AAOHN)
American Association of Spinal Cord Injury Nurses (AASCIN)
American College of Nurse-Midwives (ACNM)
American Holistic Nurses Association (AHNA)
American Long-Term Sub-Acute Nurses Association
American Nephrology Nurses Association (ANNA)
American Nursing Informatics
American Organization of Nurse Executives
American Psychiatric Nurses' Association (APNA)
American Radiological Nurses Association
American Society for Long-Term Care Nurses
American Society of Ophthalmic Registered Nurses, Inc. (ASORN)
American Society for Pain Management Nurses
American Society for Peri Anesthesia Nurses
American Society of Plastic and Reconstructive Surgical Nurses, Inc. (ASPRSN)
American Society of Post Anesthesia Nurses (ASPAN)

American Urological Association Allied, Inc. (AUAA)
Association of Nurses in AIDS Care
Association of Operating Room Nurses, Inc. (AORN)
Association of Pediatric Oncology Nurses (APON)
Association of Peri Operative Registered Nurses
Association for Practitioners in Infection Control (APIC)
Association for Professionals in Infection Control and Epidemiology, Inc.
Association of Rehabilitation Nurses (ARN)
Association of Women's Health, Obstetric, and Neonatal Nurses (AWHONN)
Case Management Society of America
Dermatology Nurses' Association (DNA)
Emergency Nurses' Association (ENA)
Endocrine Nurses Society
Home Healthcare Nurses Association
Hospice and Palliative Nurses Association
International Nurses Society on Addictions
International Society of Nurses in Genetics, Inc. (ISONG)
International Transplant Nurses Society
Intravenous Nurses Society, Inc. (INS)
League of Intravenous Therapy Education
National Association of Clinical Nurse Specialists
National Association of Hispanic Nurses
National Association of Neonatal Nurses
National Association of Nurse Massage Therapists (NANMT)
National Association of Nurse Practitioners in Reproductive Health (NANPRH)
National Association of Orthopaedic Nurses
National Association of Pediatric Nurse Associations and Practitioners (NAPNAP)
National Association of School Nurses, Inc. (NASN)
National Black Nurses Association, Inc.
National Council of State Boards of Nursing
National Federation of Licensed Practical Nurses
National Federation for Specialty Nursing Organization
National Flight Nurses Association (NFNA)
National Gerontological Nurses Association
National League for Nursing (NLN)
National Nurses Society on Addictions (NNSA)
National Nursing Staff Development Organization
National Organization for Associate Degree Nursing
National Student Nurses Association
Oncology Nursing Society (ONS)
Sigma Theta Tau International Honor Society of Nursing
Society of Gastroenterology Nurses and Associates, Inc. (SGNA)
Society of Otorhinolaryngology and Head-Neck Nurses, Inc. (SOHN)
Society for Urologic Nurses and Associates
Society for Vascular Nursing
Transcultural Nursing Society
Wound, Ostomy, and Continence Nurses Society

Chapter 2

History, Entry into Practice, and Certification

Karen J. Huff, BSN, RN, LNCC; Patricia A. Costantini, RN, MEd, LPC, CRC, CCM, CLCP, LNCC, D-ABVE; and Jane Mihalich, BSN, RN, LNCC

First Edition
Julie Bogart and Rosanna Janes, BSN, RN

Second Edition
Jenny Beerman, MN, RN; Margery Garbin, PhD, RN; Rosanna Janes, BSN, RN; Betty Joos, MED, BSN, RN; Joan Magnusson, BSN, RN, LHRM, LNCC; Regina Noonan, MSN, RN, LNCC; Julie Pike, MN, BSN, RN; Therese Steinhardt, MSN, RN; and Sheila Webster, BSN, RN, C-HROB, RNC, LNCC

Contents

History

Objective

To recognize the role of the American Association of Legal Nurse Consultants (AALNC) in developing, supporting, and promoting the nursing specialty practice of legal nurse consulting.

Introduction

Early Legal Nurse Consultant Practice

It is difficult to determine when nurses gained recognition as legal nurse consultants (LNCs), since attorneys have sought nurses to answer questions for many years regarding medical–legal matters. Nurses have been recognized as consultants to attorneys and have been compensated for their expertise and contribution since the early 1970s. Nurses' earliest and most common experiences in the legal arena have been as expert witnesses in nursing malpractice cases. As the courts began to recognize that nurses, rather than physicians, should define and evaluate the standard of nursing practice, nurses were sought to review cases and offer opinion testimony about nursing care. During the 1980s, nursing malpractice litigation expanded along with medical malpractice. Nurses became more interested and educated about the legal issues impacting health care. The role of the expert nurse witness came to be recognized as an essential professional function. It was clear to both nurses and attorneys that nurses were uniquely qualified to aid attorneys in their medical–legal practices.

During the same period, attorneys were searching for resources to help them understand medical records, medical literature, hospital policies and procedures, and medical testimony. Nurse consultants came to be valued as cost-effective alternatives to physician consultants, who were often unavailable as a result of practice demands. Law firms began to employ nurses for their expertise. Attorneys began to value their input on a broader scope, not just in medical and nursing negligence cases, but in personal injury and criminal cases as well. Since then, the scope of practice of LNCs has considerably broadened from these areas. Many of these areas are discussed in this text.

Formation of the Association

During the 1980s, nurses in California, Arizona, and Georgia, who were practicing as consultants to attorneys, formed local professional groups. Their goals were to educate the legal profession about the effectiveness of the nurse consultant as a liaison between the legal and medical communities, and to provide a network for members to share expertise. Leaders from these three groups became the driving force for founding the national association. On July 29, 1989, a steering committee composed of these leaders met in San Diego and founded the AALNC.

The national steering committee was replaced as the decision-making body of AALNC when the first board of directors was elected in March 1990. AALNC's mission of promoting the professional advancement of registered nurses (RNs) practicing in a consulting capacity in the legal field was inaugurated.

Major Contributions

Chapters

Establishment of Chapters

While AALNC offered national membership benefits to nurses licensed in any state of the United States, it was through the establishment of chartered chapters that AALNC fostered membership growth, networking, and education at the local level. Within 10 years, chapter activity went from the three original local groups to chapters in more than 45 cities in 31 states. The number of chapters continues to increase each year.

Resources for Chapters and Chapter Leaders

AALNC provides local chapters with numerous resources that assist with establishing, running, and maintaining a chapter. The Chapter Leadership Forum is conducted yearly prior to the national conference. This provides information and tools that help local leaders handle chapter governance as well as issues from conducting meetings to managing conflict. AALNC maintains online resources for chapters, including Chapter Leadership Forum presentations and the Chapter Leader Resource Manual. The manual provides resources, information, bylaws, forms, and fact sheets. More information may be obtained by visiting the association's website at http://www.aalnc.org.

Education

National Education Conference

The first annual AALNC educational conference was held in Phoenix, Arizona, in 1990. Since then, this annual conference has been the major networking and educational opportunity for LNCs. The conference offers cutting-edge topics and high-profile speakers as well as sessions for the less experienced LNC. It also includes the AALNC annual business meeting and provides for the transition of the new board members. AALNC chapters also present regional conferences throughout the year.

AALNC offers numerous educational materials in written, audio, and video formats. These are designed to assist nurses at all levels of expertise in legal nurse consulting practice.

Legal Nurse Consulting Online Course

AALNC introduced its Legal Nurse Consulting Online Course in 2007. The course, developed by experienced LNC volunteer content experts, provides RN participants with a convenient and cost-effective method of securing information needed to begin LNC practice. Information regarding all AALNC educational materials is available at the AALNC website.

Certification

Recognizing the importance of nursing certification that incorporates experiential and educational requirements, AALNC established the American Legal Nurse Consultant Certification Board (ALNCCB) in 1997. ALNCCB developed the Legal Nurse Consultant Certified (LNCC®) certification program and credential. The LNCC is the only certification in legal nurse consulting that is endorsed by AALNC. More detailed discussion regarding the LNCC, including its accreditation by the American Board of Nursing Specialties (ABNS), is provided later in this chapter.

Publications

Network News

From its inception AALNC has provided a newsletter to its members called the Network News. This communication tool is used to provide members with professional and organizational information.

Journal of Legal Nurse Consulting

In January 1995, AALNC issued the first edition of the *Journal of Legal Nurse Consulting*, which is the official publication of AALNC. It is a refereed journal providing articles of interest to nurses in the legal nurse consulting specialty and is considered one of the most valued benefits of membership.

Legal Nurse Consulting: Principles and Practice

The first edition of *Legal Nurse Consulting: Principles and Practice* (Bogart, 1998) was published in 1998 as AALNC's effort to provide a core curriculum for LNCs. It became the primary resource text for nurses who wished to learn more about this practice specialty. It also paved the way toward AALNC's goal of developing a certification program for LNCs. The second edition was published in 2003 (Iyer, 2003). This third edition is a continuation of AALNC's ongoing effort to provide nurses with an authoritative reference regarding the practice of legal nurse consulting.

Other Professional Resources

AALNC also publishes a variety of other professional resources available for sale to beginning and advanced LNCs to assist them in establishing and developing their businesses or practices. These materials are designed to give realistic and practical information to enhance the practitioner's knowledge and skills. AALNC online resources offer "eCommunities" for discussions about legal nurse consulting practice as well as an LNC Locator to assist other professionals with finding an LNC or nurse expert witness.

Ethics, Scope, and Standards

Code of Ethics

The Code of Ethics for Legal Nurse Consultants with Interpretive Discussion (AALNC, 1992) was originally adopted in April 1992. It was revised in 2005 and 2009 (see Appendix A). The code provides the guidelines for professional performance and conduct for practice and affirms our responsibility to other professional organizations with which we are aligned, in particular, the American Nurses Association (ANA) (AALNC, 2009).

Scope and Standards of Practice for the LNC

In its initial effort to develop a scope of practice and standards of practice, AALNC conducted a role delineation study in 1992. The survey document contained questions regarding professional activities to identify the essential knowledge and skills for LNC practice. Following the analysis of the data provided by this survey of LNC members, AALNC published the first edition of the *Scope of Practice for the Legal Nurse Consultant* (AALNC, 1994) in January 1994.

In 1995, the AALNC Board of Directors determined that while LNCs need knowledge and skills related to the practice of law, the nursing profession is the basis for the practice of legal nurse consulting. In October 1995, AALNC published *Scope and Standards of Practice for the Legal Nurse Consultant* based on the nursing process model (AALNC, 2002a). In 2005, in collaboration with the ANA, work was begun to update these standards to reflect the evolving practice of legal nurse consulting and to further establish legal nurse consulting as a specialty practice of nursing. A committee of AALNC leaders worked with ANA to develop and define how the practice of legal nurse consulting fits the nursing process model. The ANA's Nursing Scope and Standards of Practice (2004) and Code of Ethics for Nurses with Interpretive Statements (2001) provided a framework for the definition of specialty nursing practice and subsequently, for legal nurse consulting. Although many LNCs have no direct patient contact in their work, the scope and standards clarify precisely how LNC practice fits within the nursing role. LNCs use the information gathered in the research and development of cases to improve care for current as well as future patients, to advocate for patients who have received inadequate care, and to provide education to attorneys, patients, health care providers, and the public. Because LNCs are actively practicing RNs, they must maintain active RN licensure in their locale. The 2005 AALNC position statement entitled *The Specialty Practice of Legal Nurse Consulting* (see Appendix B) further emphasized this mandate (AALNC, 2005).

The first draft of the revised *Scope & Standards of Practice* was distributed to attendees of the 2005 AALNC Annual Meeting. Public comments were solicited there and on the ANA website, which prompted further revisions to the draft. In 2006 *Legal Nurse Consulting: Scope and Standards of Practice* was published (AALNC & ANA, 2006). The *Scope & Standards of Practice*, summarized in Appendix C, and available in complete form through either AALNC or ANA, outlines the expectations of the professional role in which all registered LNCs should practice. Examples of how each standard applies to practice are detailed in the publication.

Position Statements

In 1999, AALNC published its first position statement, *Role of the Legal Nurse Consultant as Distinct from the Role of the Paralegal and Legal Assistant* (AALNC, 1999). The position addressed the distinctions between the nursing specialty practice of legal nurse consulting and the practice of the paralegal and legal assistant as defined by the ABA (see Appendix D). This position was taken in an effort to clarify that nurses do not need to obtain education through programs approved by the ABA in order to be LNCs, since those programs' primary focus is on legal education. Nurses should be reminded that the primary role of an LNC is to evaluate, analyze, and render informed opinions on the delivery of health care and the resulting outcomes rather than focusing on the shared or separate "tasks" of either entity.

AALNC's second position statement, *Education and Certification in Legal Nurse Consulting* (AALNC, 2000), was published in 2000, in an effort to clarify the Association's position on the preferred model for an educational program in preparation for entry into the specialty practice (see Appendix E). The position paper indicates the following: AALNC believes legal nurse consulting education should build on nursing education and clinical experience; AALNC recommends *Legal Nurse Consulting: Principles and Practice* as the core curriculum for legal nurse consulting education; and AALNC recognizes and endorses ALNCCB's LNCC, the LNC certification credential accredited by ABNS. Additional discussion regarding entry into LNC specialty practice and certification is found later in this chapter.

As discussed earlier in this chapter, AALNC published *The Specialty Practice of Legal Nurse Consulting* (Appendix B) in 2005 to define the specialty of legal nurse consulting as an RN practice and to reinforce that the LNC must maintain an active RN license.

Recognizing that the profession of nursing is autonomous from the profession of medicine and other allied health disciplines, and that nursing has the responsibility and knowledge to define its standards of practice, in 2006 AALNC published the position statement, *Providing Expert Nursing Testimony* (AALNC, 2006a). This clearly defines AALNC's position that the only expert who should testify regarding nursing standards and on clinical and administrative nursing issues is a licensed RN (see Appendix F).

Licensure for Expert Witnesses is AALNC's fifth position paper (see Appendix G). This was published in 2006 and provides education and discussion about licensure issues related to LNC expert testimony (AALNC, 2006b).

Professional Relationships

Nursing Organizations Alliance

In January 1994, AALNC was seated as an affiliate member in the National Federation of Specialty Nursing Organizations (NFSNO). In November 1996, AALNC became a regular participant in the Nursing Organization Liaison Forum (NOLF). By 2001, NOLF and NFSNO, noting that both organizations were designed to achieve identical goals, merged to form one organization, the Nursing Organizations Alliance (NOA or The Alliance). AALNC is a member of The Alliance. Delegates from member associations meet regularly to address issues of mutual concern across nursing specialties. Through educational efforts, NOA members work to improve the role of nursing specialties. Through legislative efforts, the Alliance gives input regarding health care legislation.

Legal Organizations/Bar Associations

AALNC has long included as part of its mission the responsibility to increase the awareness of the LNC specialty practice. In addition to ongoing efforts toward building relationships with other nursing organizations, the Association has increased its focus on the legal community. AALNC is committed to enhancing attorney awareness of the value of the LNC. An Awareness Committee has focused specifically on developing resources to assist AALNC chapters with efforts to gain membership status in local or state bar associations, assisting with marketing initiatives regarding the value of LNCs to attorneys, and identifying research of specific interest to LNCs.

Summary of History

This history focuses on the development and continued growth of the specialty practice of legal nurse consulting through efforts of the members and staff of AALNC. AALNC is widely known as the representative voice for LNCs.

Entry into Practice

Objectives

- ■ Define the qualities and traits of an LNC
- ■ Compare entrepreneurial skills with intrapreneurial skills
- ■ Enhance communication skills
- ■ Describe educational options
- ■ Compare certification with certificates

Introduction

The idea of being an LNC is appealing to RNs who are eager to expand their horizons by using their knowledge and experience in a unique way. The possibility of practicing nursing outside the hospital environment and becoming an entrepreneur or working in a law firm or insurance company is intriguing to more and more as the role of the LNC has become more visible.

This chapter is designed to provide an overview of the qualities and traits that set the role of LNC apart from other specialties of nursing. It also discusses the impact of personal and professional changes for a career shift from clinical areas of nursing to legal nurse consulting. Many of the terms and issues discussed represent values familiar to a professional nurse. The technology of nursing science has evolved to a higher level of practice for the professional nurse, and has increased the need for competent practitioners to act as liaisons between the fields of law and health care. The profession of nursing involves a unique body of knowledge and expertise, and nurses are the most appropriate experts to testify to nursing standards of care (*Sullivan v. Edward Hospital*). This chapter will identify types of education that can prepare the LNC and the skills that are essential for successful practice as an LNC.

Qualities and Traits

The three words that make up the acronym "LNC" are self-defining: "legal," referring to the law; "nurse," a professional health care provider; and "consultant," a person who offers advice. What is special about the combination of these words is the union of two independent fields, law and nursing. Each represents years of required formal education from accredited facilities and professional licensure. Each has established standards of practice, a scope of practice defining parameters of professionalism, and a code of ethics. Each in its professional capacity offers advice, guidance, and information to those who seek help. However, law school education does not entitle one to practice nursing and a nursing education docs not allow one to practice law. The intersection of the two professions has been the impetus for the unique services that nurse consultants bring to the legal arena.

Above all, LNCs are licensed RNs. As resolved in 1995 by the board of directors of the AALNC, and reinforced in collaboration with the ANA in 2006 in the *Legal Nurse Consulting Scope and Standards of Practice*, the professional foundation of legal nurse consulting is nursing (AALNC and ANA, 2006). It is this basic foundation of education and experience in a field of nursing that provides the structure for the growth of the specialty of legal nurse consulting. The number-one requirement for an LNC is to be a licensed RN; the service that is provided to those seeking assistance is *nursing knowledge*. The lawyer benefits from the ability of LNCs to integrate their nursing knowledge with the challenges of criminal and civil litigation. It is for this reason that AALNC recommends that in order to be most effective, LNCs should have at least five years of experience as a practicing RN. In 2005, AALNC released a position statement on *The Specialty Practice of Legal Nurse Consulting*, emphasizing that since Legal Nurse Consulting is a specialty practice of nursing, active RN licensure in one's state is required (AALNC, 2005).

An LNC will always be a nurse first. The LNC's area of consultation will depend on experience that has been gained in the field of nursing as well as personal interest and entrepreneurial skills. For nurses, organizational skills and professionalism are integrated within the fundamentals of training and education that prepare graduates for a variety of opportunities upon completion of basic nursing education. The development of nursing expertise that combines on-the-job learning with formal education is essential preparation for those interested in becoming an LNC. Practicing as a nurse is only the beginning of preparing for the role of an LNC.

Specific qualities and traits need to be in place to ensure success as an independent practitioner or an in-house LNC. Attributes such as dependability, efficiency, and a positive attitude are essential, both professionally and personally. So too are good judgment, wisdom, expertise, and intelligence about nursing knowledge, marketing, accounting, and a multitude of other business skills that may need to be used differently as an LNC. To succeed, LNCs must be reliable and competent, as practicing nurses must be, which is demonstrated by effective time management and being prepared to do every job efficiently and accurately.

Successful entry into the specialty practice of legal nurse consulting, whether transitioning to independent practice or to an office setting, will require change. This change will also be impacted by choices made from both a personal and a business perspective, with varying degrees of success, depending on the individual. It is important to keep a positive attitude, be confident in making choices, and believe in a successful outcome. Nursing knowledge, strong work performance, and dependability are attributes basic to quality performance. Other qualities and traits are also needed, and these are described below.

Autonomy

Having the confidence to make lifestyle changes is a stepping-stone quality to beginning the new and exciting role as an LNC. The independence of working for oneself brings with it the need to be self-sufficient, and an ability to set parameters and follow them without the support of a workforce or staff with whom to confer. There is a sense of empowerment that comes from control over the right to choose assignments, hours of work, fees, and expenses. This liberation also comes with the need to initially plan well on how to be emancipated from the traditional role of employee within a structured organization. With determination, a nurse can succeed as an independent LNC, but it takes hard work. Autonomy also provides the opportunity of choosing to work as an in-house consultant in the type of legal setting that has the most appeal and best matches the consultant's experience.

Drive

Drive or determination, as a quality to building a successful practice, requires a significant amount of ambition, energy, and effort in preparing for a specialty practice such as legal nurse consulting. This ambition is grounded in goal-oriented planning, a characteristic that every nurse uses in reaching objectives. One will need to investigate the necessary attributes that are in place and identify the deficits that need to be addressed in order to improve the likelihood of success. Aspiring LNCs should determine whether they are self-disciplined enough to be able to work independently. Some independent consultants are uncomfortable with the lack of structure in working from a home office. It may take a regular routine to provide the daily discipline needed to work without someone looking over your shoulder. This effort is rewarded in the long run by adding proficiency and competence to the list of resources that the legal nurse provides a lawyer-client. The motivation or incentive for joining the specialty of legal nurse consulting is a necessary trait that may spur one to action, but it cannot be fueled impulsively. Enthusiasm, as a quality, can be the driving force behind a great idea, such as being independently employed as an LNC. Assiduousness or hard work is the trait that supports this quality; others are diligence and the thoroughness to see a task to completion with attention to details.

Initiative

Initiative is an intrinsic quality of an experienced nurse; also necessary are the abilities to be clever, inventive, and imaginative. Knowing when to be creative and when to follow a traditional style requires a certain aptitude for insight and forethought. Developing a compelling chart that clearly conveys the primary focus or issues of a case for attorneys can be an invaluable skill. Productivity and creativity as traits of a successful LNC are demonstrated by good organization, competence, and vision. Inspiration and ingenuity support these qualities.

Analytical Skills

To succeed in this profession, an LNC needs to be analytical. Analysis of medical records and other information focuses on critical details related to injuries, timing of events, and completeness of information. The analytical LNC spots the missing record, the sequence of events that seems to be out of order, and the deviations from the standard of care on the part of the health care provider. The role of the LNC often involves the ability to collect and synthesize data in an effort to reconstruct a series of events or determine what should have been done for a patient. Attorneys rely on the knowledge and experience of the LNC, coupled with the ability to place data into a framework that will help the attorney understand the medical information and focus on the critical issues.

Attention to Detail

A keen sense of what is and is not essential is another trait that is important to a conscientious LNC. Being detail-oriented is more than just dotting all the i's and crossing all the t's (although impeccable grammar and spelling are critical). A detail-oriented nurse makes sure that all records are in order, all data are collected, and all filing is completed accurately. Detail-oriented nurses can work through the minutiae of lengthy documents with an eye for the smallest items of importance. The ability to review each element for its potential significance to a case is a valuable service that a detail-oriented nurse can provide a client. Sifting through and clarifying the most significant details or themes of a case are invaluable to the attorney.

Communication Skills

It is important to be an active listener in order to show empathy and be attentive when a client relates the details of a case. Concentrating on facts and at the same time perceiving body language that may or may not be contradictory are basic active listening skills honed by most nurses through years of clinical practice. Being able to systematically and logically list data in a specific manner may not be innate. The ability to accurately yet succinctly document what is heard and observed requires practice and is crucial in discriminating between critical information and pointless items. Decisive writing skills that provide a breadth and depth of information in a succinct manner will be needed to be most effective. Finally, much of what an LNC generates and reviews is in the form of written documentation; the ability to proofread will be needed to correct or amend communications between parties. Fine-tuning a document without modifying the content is another essential skill for LNCs to master. Written and oral communication skills can be improved through several types of educational formats discussed later in this chapter.

Intrapreneurial and Entrepreneurial Skills

Puetz and Shinn (1997) use Pinchot's (1985) definition of intrapreneurship to describe an employee as one "who is innovative, creative, and willing to take risks in the work setting by forging ahead with a new product, idea, or process." Writing for the ANA, Manion (1990) advanced that definition for nurses as "one who creates innovation within the health care organization through the introduction of a new product, a different service, or simply a new way of doing something" (p. 38). In a subsequent article, she identifies many of the same qualities and traits for nurse intrapreneurs that this chapter acknowledges as important attributes of a successful LNC, including being inquisitive, a visionary, and a good salesperson (Manion, 1994).

By comparison, Wilson (1994) identifies an entrepreneur as "a person who organizes and manages an enterprise, especially a business, usually with considerable initiative and risk" (p. 143). The difference between an entrepreneur and an intrapreneur is whether the skills are used independently as a self-employed consultant or as an employee. In either scenario, the successful nurse needs the ability to plan well, problem-solve, and be accountable. The nurse working as an employee can be as creative in developing the legal nurse consulting role for an employer as the independent LNC is in establishing a practice for different clientele, such as attorneys, insurance firms, or pharmaceutical companies. What these authors have confirmed is that nurses must present a professional image of leadership when leading is required or of competent team players when collaboration is necessary.

In an entry-level position as an LNC, it is necessary not only to provide nursing knowledge, but also to have communication, problem-solving, and networking skills as well as political savvy. An intrapreneur may need to fit within an organization, where it can be challenging to get ideas acknowledged. Enthusiasm may need to be channeled in an innovative manner when presenting your perspective and recommendations. As an entrepreneur, the independent LNC is the boss, so the challenge may be to overcome the fear of taking risks in a new market.

An assessment of the work and responsibilities of the LNC, as either the in-house or independent consultant, can be accomplished by researching journals and interviewing others already involved in the practice of legal nurse consulting. Additional insights can be gained by joining AALNC, attending professional conferences sponsored through the association, and attending chapter meetings. Information can be gleaned from accessing AALNC's website, http://www. aalnc.org, which offers a plethora of information about services, products, and other helpful links. Many resources, such as the booklet "Getting Started in Legal Nurse Consulting," and power point presentations for educating attorneys are available through the website. An additional forum is available for AALNC members through web-based discussion groups, or "list serve," enabling interaction with LNC colleagues who have had experience in most issues that arise for those starting out or established.

When considering options, it is helpful to be as objective as possible in listing individual skills and unique qualities. The collection of information and analysis of data may identify issues and outcomes that deal with being a self-starter, organizer, or self-motivated worker, whether self-employed or employed in an office. Other issues may deal with family, personal relationships, and budgeting needed to develop an independent practice. This is the step where the advantages and disadvantages of available options can be identified.

Identifying short-term and long-term goals should be part of planning. Short-term goals can be designed to be achieved within the time frame of a long-term goal. The plan may include learning how to write a business financial and marketing plan for an independent practice. This step may take several weeks to complete. It may require a few days to update a resume or curriculum vitae. The plan may also require attending classes to upgrade communication skills. A written plan provides a ready review of progress, allows for a visual reminder of what comes next, provides organization, and offers a mental boost when items are completed and crossed off the list of "to dos." It is better to list needed items specifically and set a budget and a date for ordering them.

If the plan requires the development of a financial business plan to present to a financial institution for start-up capital as an independent consultant, it is wise to investigate professional resources that offer guidelines for completing this task. The United States Small Business Administration (SBA) can be accessed online at http://www.sba.gov. The SBA offers financing, training, and advocacy for people interested in starting their own enterprises. In addition, SBA works with thousands of lending, educational, and training institutions nationwide that can also provide information and guidance. Another excellent resource is SCORE, a nonprofit organization of experienced volunteers who mentor entrepreneurs through one-to-one business advising sessions on a full range of business topics (www.score.org).

Education

Despite aggressive marketing of various LNC programs to RNs, an entry-level LNC position does not require additional education in a formal program. Many nurses, however, feel more comfortable making the transition following some level of education to familiarize themselves with new challenges. Training in specific areas, such as communication skills, legal terminology, medical research, and writing methods, coupled with a fundamental understanding of the law and the basics of the management of a law or business office, can be reassuring for the novice. There are several ways to increase knowledge of these areas and improve a resume or credentials, which may widen employment opportunities. The choice of formats will depend on the learning style, available time, and financial resources of the nurse. AALNC's website is a comprehensive starting point in the search for continuing education materials that meet the varied needs of aspiring and practicing LNCs. These resources include this current edition of *Legal Nurse Consulting: Principles and*

Practice, the comprehensive core curriculum for legal nurse consulting, which has been used extensively by university-based LNC programs.

AALNC also gathered experienced, successful, actively practicing LNCs to provide their wisdom and expertise in eight interactive modules comprising the Legal Nurse Consulting Online Course. These may be accessed individually to fit one's needs, or in its entirety. Module topics include an Introduction to Legal Nurse Consulting, Practice Roles of the LNC, Legal Fundamentals, the Role of the Expert Witness LNC, Access and Analysis of Medical Records, Research and Report Writing, Effective Case Screening, and Business Principles for the LNC. These resources, and others of benefit to the novice as well as the experienced LNC, are available through the AALNC website.

Formal education is provided by proprietary schools, for-profit businesses and nonprofit businesses, universities, four-year colleges, and community colleges. This education is offered through traditional on-campus programs, telecourses, and distance courses that may be print-based or online. Proprietary schools offer certificates or diplomas, which may include continuing education units. Colleges offer certificates, an associate degree, or a baccalaureate degree, and may also provide continuing education units. In evaluating the merit of any program, the reputation and accreditation of the sponsoring institution should be considered, as well as the cost and length of the program, the convenience of the location or on-line accessibility, and the type of text materials required. Other important aspects of the program to consider are whether it offers a student placement as an externship in a law firm before completion of the program, and what percentage of graduates are being hired by attorneys or businesses in the area. The local chapter is often a good source of information regarding availability of university-based programs and other options in the area.

Although legal education is available to nurses through legal assistant or paralegal education programs, it must be stressed that the education of paralegals and legal assistants is different from the needs of the nurse practicing in the legal arena. "Paralegal" and "legal assistant" are terms that are sometimes used interchangeably in different parts of the country. According to the ABA definition adopted by the ABA House of Delegates in August 1997, a legal assistant or paralegal is "a person qualified by education, training or work experience ... employed by an attorney ... who performs specifically delegated substantive legal work for which a lawyer is responsible" (ABA, 1999). By contrast, the LNC is "distinct from the paralegal or legal assistant" because the LNC "brings specialized education and clinical expertise to the medically related issues of the litigation process." As further clarification, AALNC published a position statement in 1999 delineating the role of the LNC as distinct from that of the paralegal (AALNC, 1999).

The primary focus of legal nurse consulting education must be to build on nursing education, clinical experience, and the function of the nurse in the legal arena. In evaluating a particular program, its mission and purpose should be compared with the standard presented in the position statement on the role of the LNC (AALNC, 2000). AALNC maintains the position that legal nurse consulting education programs must be developed and presented as specialty nursing curricula by nurse educators in partnership with legal educators. The qualifications of the program directors and instructors should be considered when evaluating a program. In general, programs developed and taught by experienced nurse educators who are practicing LNCs are preferred.

As a proprietary provider of education, AALNC offers texts, booklets, home study materials based on actual cases, CDs from conferences, seminars, and the Legal Nurse Consulting Online Course. These methods offer a unique way of increasing both skills and the knowledge base in legal nurse consulting, depending on the novice's needs. AALNC recommends the current edition of *Legal Nurse Consulting: Principles and Practice* as the core curriculum for legal nurse consulting education. Courses based on this curriculum vary in length from 1 day to several semesters. Nurses are encouraged to choose a course that meets their personal requirements and professional goals.

It is important to remember that nursing education is the basic educational requirement for preparation as an LNC, but employment as an in-house LNC may provide experience on the job under the guidance of an attorney or another LNC. Membership and participation in the national organization and local AALNC chapter will afford both the novice and seasoned practitioner the opportunity to remain current with legal nurse consulting practice.

Prospective LNCs frequently inquire about mentoring, or shadowing opportunities, working alongside a more experienced LNC in independent practice, at a law firm, or another setting. AALNC does not have a formal mentoring program, although several chapters have initiated such opportunities. Issues of confidentiality, competition, and effective time management must be addressed prior to implementation. There are also several fee-based mentoring programs available in which sample reports and feedback are provided. An LNC may have success in contacting individual law firms and arranging a limited internship that benefits both parties.

Certification versus Certificates

LNCs beginning in this specialty practice are often confused by the number of different courses that promise "certification" or certificates at the completion of the program, each with its own alphabet soup of credentials (see Table 2.1). While education from any reputable source is helpful and certainly encouraged, it can be difficult for the newcomer to decipher which credentials have

Table 2.1 Certification versus Certificate Programs

Certification	Certificate
Results from an assessment process that recognizes an individual's knowledge, skills, and competency in a particular specialty	Results from an educational process
Typically requires professional experience	For newcomers and experienced professionals
Awarded by a third-party, standard-setting organization, typically not for profit	Awarded by educational programs or institutions often for profit
Indicates mastery/competency as measured against a defensible set of standards, usually by application or exam	Indicates completion of a course or series of courses with a specific focus (different from a degree-granting program)
Standards set through a defensible, industry-wide process (job analysis/role delineation) that results in an outline of required knowledge and skills	Course content determined by the specific provider or institution, not standardized
Typically results in credentials to be listed after one's name (LNCC, ONC, CCRN)	Usually listed on a resume detailing education
Has ongoing requirements in order to maintain; holder must demonstrate he/she continues to meet requirements	Demonstrates knowledge of course content at the end of a set period in time

Source: http://www.aalnc.org/lncc/about/certificate.cfm

meaning to those in the medical legal community. Attorneys usually seek physicians who are Board Certified in their area of specialty when considering them as expert witnesses, the Gold Standard for physician certification (e.g., American Board of Medical Specialties certifications). The legal nurse consulting certification that is most comparable is the LNCC credential, which meets the rigorous standards of the ABNS. The LNCC exam is based not only on expert knowledge of the practice, but also on experience as a practicing LNC; as such it is the Gold Standard of legal nurse consulting certification.

Certification
Objectives

- Identify the purpose of specialty nursing certification
- Describe how the LNCC meets accreditation standards
- Identify key elements in developing the LNCC exam

Introduction

The founding members of AALNC have been credited for their long-range vision for the association and for the specialty of legal nurse consulting. Although their roles may be taken for granted, some very basic decisions had to be made by our founders before the association could move forward. There were several turning points in AALNC's past that left indelible marks on the certification offered by the ALNCCB®. This section will discuss the purpose of nursing certification, the importance of accreditation, and key elements involved in developing the LNCC exam.

Certification in a Nursing Specialty
Definition and Purpose

In 2005, the ABNS published a position statement on the Value of Specialty Nursing Certification. In this paper, ABNS defines certification as "The formal recognition of the specialized knowledge, skills, and experience demonstrated by the achievement of standards identified by a nursing specialty to prompt optimal health outcomes" (ABNS, 2005).

One of the key concepts in this definition is that certification is an indicator of knowledge *and* experience. Unlike state licensure, which is a legal requirement and is achieved at entry into practice, certification is voluntary and reflects expertise in the specialty beyond that of initial licensure (ABNS, 2005).

Professional certification in nursing is widely used to recognize a higher level of nursing skill and expertise within a specialty than is expected from nurses with the minimal qualifications required for entry into the practice setting. Nurses who achieve certification from an accredited certification program in their specialty are considered "board certified." The process is similar to physician board certification, which also requires experience in the specialty prior to sitting for an exam. The public is attuned to the importance of physician board certification, and continued education is needed to heighten public awareness of the significance of nursing certification.

Standards for nursing professional certification programs vary, but three minimum components are generally required:

1. Licensure as an RN
2. Eligibility criteria, which include experience in the specialty, such as clinical experience or a specified number of work hours using skills and knowledge unique to the specialty
3. Identification and testing of a specialized body of knowledge that is distinctly different from the general practice of nursing

In legal nurse consulting, the only certification that currently meets these minimum requirements is the Legal Nurse Consultant Certified, designated as LNCC.

In both medicine and nursing, there is widespread recognition that the professional organization representing practitioners in the specialty is best qualified to set criteria for the certification programs (Ehrlich, 1995). The content of the examination is usually based on a "practice analysis" of critical skills and concepts needed to be proficient in the specialty, as identified by nurses practicing in the specialty.

Nurses in all specialties should discourage the use of unrecognized credentials. If professional certification is to be meaningful to the public and have any value for certified nurses in any specialty practice, nurses must be vigilant about promoting the public's perception that professional certification is granted only to those nurses with demonstrated experience and knowledge in the specialty.

The LNCC is the only certification in the profession endorsed by AALNC and accredited by ABNS. It is comparable to other recognized specialty credentials, such as CCRN, CEN, and RN-BC. Since the LNCC meets the definition of a credential as described above, LNCC becomes part of the professional title, as in Nancy Smith, BSN, RN, LNCC.

Certification in Legal Nurse Consulting

Overview

The LNCC is designed to promote a level of expertise and professionalism by documenting individual performance as measured against a predetermined level of knowledge in legal nurse consulting. It is not intended to determine who is qualified or who shall engage in legal nurse consulting, but allows the public to more readily identify LNCs who have demonstrated a high level of experience, expertise, and commitment to this specialty nursing practice (ALNCCB, 2006).

History of the LNCC

As noted elsewhere in this chapter, the founding members of AALNC have been credited with their visionary leadership and long-range planning for the association. Once important challenges were met and the groundwork was laid, the AALNC Board of Directors was ready to move forward with establishing a certification examination in the specialty. In 1997, a Certification Task Force led by Joan Magnusson was appointed to determine the scope of the program and to seek bids from testing companies. By October 1997, the task force had selected the Center for Nursing Education and Testing (C-NET) as their testing company and was ready to form a Certification

Board. Once the board members were selected, the board began developing policies, establishing eligibility criteria, and creating the examination.

The first Legal Nurse Consultant Certification Examination was offered on October 24, 1998. Of the 156 candidates, 126 (81%) passed and were awarded the LNCC credential (AALNC, 1998). The examination continues to be offered every April and October in various cities around the country as well as at the AALNC annual education conferences.

Setting the LNCC Apart through Accreditation

Early in AALNC's research process, one of the goals for the development of the certification program was to meet the standards necessary for accreditation (Ehrlich, 1995; Janes, 1998). The early certification committees identified ABNS as the accreditation body best qualified to give the certification program the credibility they sought.

The American Board of Nursing Specialties

ABNS was incorporated in 1991 with support from the Macy Foundation. ABNS was formed with the original intention of being "the certifier of certifiers" for nursing specialties. As such, it sought to protect the public and consumers by setting and enforcing standards for certification. The ABNS mission is to provide assurance to the public that the nurse holding the credential from an accredited certification program possesses the knowledge, skills, and competency for quality practice in his or her particular specialty (Bernreuter, 2001).

ABNS has two arms within the organization, which serve distinct functions, membership, and accreditation. Collectively, the member organizations of ABNS represent over half a million certified RNs around the world. An elected Board of Directors governs the membership portion of the association.

An Accreditation Council is responsible for setting accreditation standards and granting accreditation to those programs that meet the rigorous standards. In 2009, the Accreditation Council changed their name to the Accreditation Board for Specialty Nursing Certification (ABSNC). As accredited certification programs transition to the new name, they are encouraged to identify their exam as accredited by ABSNC, formerly known as the ABNS Accreditation Council.

ABNS/ABSNC currently has 18 standards that must be met in order to pass the stringent peer review process by the ABNS Accreditation Council. A shortened version of the standards, with a brief synopsis of what each standard entails, is included in Table 2.2. The longer version of the standards has examples of supporting documentation that must be provided by the applicant organization seeking accreditation. These standards and other information about accreditation, including a list of accredited exams, can be found on the ABNS website at www.nursingcertification.org.

Initial Accreditation of the LNCC Exam

Having built the examination to ABNS standards, ALNCCB determined that the sound psychometric results that had been achieved were the final data needed before making the application for accreditation to the ABNS. With the support of AALNC, ALNCCB was able to submit the extensive application for ABNS accreditation nearly a year earlier than planned. As a result, the ALNCCB program was awarded accreditation at the September 1999 ABNS meeting. The staff

Table 2.2 ABNS Accreditation Standards

#	*ABNS Standard*	*Description*
1	Definition and scope of nursing specialty	The certification examination program is based on a distinct and well-defined field of nursing practice that subscribes to the overall purpose and functions of nursing. The nursing specialty is distinct from other nursing specialties and is national in scope. There is an identified need for the specialty and nurses who devote most of their practice to the specialty
2	Research-based body of knowledge	A body of research-based knowledge related to the nursing specialty exists. Mechanisms are established for the support, review, and dissemination of research and knowledge in the specialty. Activities within the specialty contribute to the advancement of nursing science within the specialty
3	Organizational autonomy	The certifying organization (certifying governing body) is an entity with organizational autonomy governed in part or in whole by nursing members. However, a collaborative relationship exists between the certifying organization and a national or international specialty association that supports the nursing specialty and the standards for specialty practice
4	Nondiscrimination	The certifying organization does not discriminate among candidates as to age, gender, race, religion, ethnic origin, disability, marital status, or sexual orientation
5	Public representation	The certifying organization (certifying governing body) includes at least one public member with voting rights
6	Eligibility criteria for test candidates	The eligibility criteria for basic specialty nursing certification include the following: • RN licensure • Educational and experiential qualifications as determined by the individual specialty certifying organization The eligibility criteria for advanced practice nursing certification include • RN licensure • A minimum of a graduate degree in nursing or the appropriate equivalent, including content in the specified area of specialty practice
7	Validity	The certifying organization has conducted validation studies to assure that inferences made on the basis of test scores are appropriate and justified

continued

Table 2.2 (continued) ABNS Accreditation Standards

#	ABNS Standard	Description
8	Test development	Certification examinations are constructed and evaluated using methods that are psychometrically sound and fair to all candidates
9	Reliability	The certifying organization assures that test scores, including subscores, are sufficiently reliable for their intended uses
10	Test administration	The certification examination is administered in a manner that minimizes construct-irrelevant variance
11	Test security	Procedures are in place to maximize the security of all certification examination materials
12	Passing scores	Passing scores for the certification examination(s) are set in a manner that is fair to all candidates, using criterion referenced methods and equating and scaling procedures that are psychometrically sound
13	Continued competency	The certifying organization has a recertification program in place that requires certificants to maintain current knowledge and to provide documentation showing how competence in the specialty is maintained over time
14	Communications	The certifying organization provides information that clearly describes the certification process to candidates and other stakeholders
15	Confidentiality	The certifying organization assures that confidential information about candidates and certificants is protected
16	Appeals	The certifying organization has an appeal process in place for candidates/certificants who have been denied access to an examination or renewal of certification or who have had certification revoked
17	Misrepresentation and noncompliance	The certifying organization has a mechanism in place to respond to instances of misrepresentation and noncompliance with eligibility criteria or the certifying organization's policies; this mechanism includes reporting cases of misrepresentation and noncompliance to appropriate authorities
18	Quality improvement	The certifying organization shall have an internal audit and management review system in place including provisions for continuous corrective and preventive actions for quality improvement

Source: American Board of Nursing Specialties. (2004). Accreditation standards. Retrieved 2008, from American Board of Nursing Specialties Web Site: http://www.nursingcertification. org/pdf/ac_standards_short.pdf

and volunteer members of AALNC and ALNCCB, as well as the C-NET professionals who were involved in creating a quality certification program, are credited with achieving this goal so early in the program's history.

Reaccreditation

Since the initial accreditation, ALNCCB has continued to ensure that the LNCC program meets or exceeds ABNS standards. To maintain ABNS accreditation, certification programs must apply for reaccreditation every five years. As noted above, the LNCC program was initially accredited in 1999 and reaccredited in 2004. In 2009, the LNCC Program submitted its second reaccreditation application to ABNS. Reaccreditation was granted for another 5 years, or until 2014. Over the life of the exam, the LNCC has been accredited for a total of 15 years. This process is difficult, but necessary in order to uphold the vision and high standards set by our founding members and to preserve our reputation in the industry. Although there are many competitors in the LNC field claiming to award certification, the LNCC is the only certification program in legal nurse consulting that has achieved ABNS accreditation. Accreditation is what sets the LNCC apart from other certificate or certification programs, making the LNCC credential the gold standard in the industry.

The American Legal Nurse Consultant Certification Board

Board Structure and Committees

The ALNCCB was established in September 1997. The board is composed of experienced LNCs with proven leadership who come from a variety of legal nurse consulting work settings with a range of field experience. Geographic diversity is also considered. The ALNCCB bylaws call for terms of three years with a rotation mechanism so that two board members have terms ending each year, with the option to run for re-election for one additional term.

Since the primary goal of nursing certification is to protect the public, ALNCCB also includes a "public member." The role of the public member is to represent the interests of consumers (i.e., the employers of LNCs and the clients they represent). The public member keeps ALNCCB grounded in its duty to the public at large, enhancing the value of the credential outside the nursing community.

Currently, ALNCCB has seven board members, six LNCCs and one public member. One board member is elected to serve as Chair. ALNCCB past chairpersons include Joan Magnusson (1997–2001), Sheila Webster (2001), Peggy Woodward (2002), Patty Costantini (2003–2004), Karen Huff (2005–2006), Marianne Hallas (2007–2008), and Amy Heydlauff (2009).

There are several standing committees appointed by ALNCCB to assist with the mission of the LNCC program, including a separate Item Writing Panel, Audit Committee, and Appeals Committee. Additional committees or task forces are appointed as needed.

Autonomy

ABNS standards call for a "certification board with organizational autonomy," which may continue a collaborative relationship with the nursing specialty organization. In order to meet this standard, ALNCCB has independent responsibility for the certification program. It is the certification board that develops the certification budget, determines the eligibility criteria for the examination, audits applications for compliance with the criteria, sets fees, and sets maintenance criteria for renewal of certification. ALNCCB is charged with the responsibility of maintaining the examination so that it is valid, reliable, and legally defensible. As is common with smaller organizations, AALNC and ALNCCB share some resources while still maintaining separation of power. A Memo of Understanding approved by both boards defines this relationship.

Position Statement on Certification in Legal Nurse Consulting

As mentioned elsewhere in this chapter, confusion exists in the marketplace about certification in legal nurse consulting because of the numerous courses offered by for-profit companies. In an effort to address this issue, ALNCCB published a position statement "Certification in Legal Nurse Consulting" in 2006. See Appendix H for a copy of this position statement, which discusses certification in detail and identifies the LNCC credential as the gold standard in the industry.

LNCC Practice Test

The LNCC Practice Test, published in 2001, was created by ALNCCB in conjunction with the testing company. The test has 100 questions that are mapped to the blueprint, and is designed to help LNCs assess their readiness to sit for the exam. ALNCCB also developed an LNCC Prep Kit, which includes the Practice Test and other certification resources. These products were developed as study aids, and are not intended to guarantee a particular candidate will pass the exam. Both items are available for purchase in the educational products section of the AALNC website.

The LNCC Exam

Necessary Expertise: Working with the Testing Company

ABNS standards have detailed requirements for maintaining statistical validity, reliability, and security of the certification examination. These can rarely be achieved in any nursing organization without help from experts in the testing field. After extensive investigation of companies offering testing services, AALNC signed a contract with C-NET®.

Beginning in October 1997, ALNCCB worked with C-NET to develop the certification program. Standards for developing valid and reliable examinations, including certification and licensure examinations [the Standards for Educational and Psychological Testing (1999)], are published jointly by the American Educational Research Association, the American Psychological Association, and the National Council on Measurement in Education. Standard 14.4 states: "The content domain to be covered by the examination should be defined clearly and justified in terms of the importance of the content for credential-worthy performance in an occupation or profession" (American Education Research Association, 1999).

The same standard also specifies that the knowledge and skills addressed should be those necessary to protect the public. In general, the standard states that the knowledge and skills contained in a core curriculum designed to train people for the profession are relevant. Thus, Legal Nurse Consulting: Principles and Practice, developed by AALNC, is used as a primary resource for test development. In addition, ALNCCB adheres to guidelines of the Equal Employment Opportunity Commission to ensure validity of test content and fairness to all test-takers.

After working with C-NET as their testing company for many years, ALNCCB entered into a partnership with a new testing company in 2008. Schroeder Measurement Technologies (SMT) was chosen as the new testing company after an extensive search process. SMT has experience with computer-based testing, an option under consideration for future test development.

Determining What to Test

A practice analysis provides the primary basis for defining the content domain of a certification examination. The first role delineation survey performed by AALNC took place in 1992; a more extensive and updated practice analysis was needed by 1997. At the first meeting of the ALNCCB and C-NET, a survey was designed to determine the relative frequency and the importance (or criticality) of legal nurse consulting activities and knowledge, taken in part from the 1992 Role Delineation Survey, the AALNC Standards of Legal Nurse Consulting Practice (1995), Legal Nurse Consulting: Principles and Practice (1998), and membership data (Magnusson, 1998). After multiple revisions, the Survey of Legal Nurse Consulting Practice was mailed to 1000 practicing LNCs in February 1998. C-NET analyzed the 221 usable surveys returned, and the final "blueprint" for the certification examination was adopted. The 200 questions found on any edition of the certification examination are matched to the blueprint specifications (AALNC, 2002b).

In 2007, ALNCCB conducted a new practice analysis to ensure that the LNCC examination continues to be a valid assessment of legal nurse consulting practice (Webb & Hallas, 2008). A periodic job analysis is required to meet ABNS standards and maintain accreditation. In addition to its relevance to certification, data gathered through the practice analysis are useful to AALNC in identifying trends in practice.

For the 2007 Practice Analysis, data was collected on 169 LNC tasks and 49 LNC knowledge statements. A URL with a link to the survey was sent to 3487 AALNC members. A total of 369 responses were collected, giving a response rate of 10.6% or 11%. This response rate is comparable to what is currently seen in the certification literature (Webb & Hallas, 2008).

The 2008 LNCC blueprint, as shown in Table 2.3, was developed by using data from the 2007 practice analysis and the blueprint validation committee report. The blueprint is also available on

Table 2.3   2008 LNCC Exam Blueprint: Content Areas of the Examination

Content Area	% of Exam
Medical malpractice	27–31
Personal injury	19–23
Product liability/toxic tort	10–14
Workers' compensation	12–16
Risk management	5–9
Life care planning	4–7
Criminal/forensic	1–4
Administrative health law/regulatory compliance	4–8
Elder law	3–6

Source: Copyright American Legal Nurse Consultant Certification Board (2008). Content areas of the examination. Retrieved 2008, from http://www. aalnc.org/lncc/exam/scope.cfm

the website at http://www.aalnc.org/lncc/exam/scope.cfm. Although the content areas have not changed a great deal since the initial examination in 1998, the test has evolved to show the expansion of practice areas such as Elder Law, Administrative Health Law, and Regulatory Compliance. Table 2.4 shows the evolution of the LNCC certification exam blueprint and compares the data (Hallas, 2008). The practice analysis will be repeated as the specialty evolves, to ensure that the blueprint and the examination are valid measures of current practice in legal nurse consulting.

Developing Test Items

The initial examination questions, or "items," were developed by a group of 12 item writers who were selected from the AALNC membership. The group was selected from experienced LNCs in a wide range of practice settings from all regions of the country. All item writers were required to meet the eligibility requirements for the examination. Under the direction of C-NET, the item writers crafted 250 questions during two intense four-day sessions (Magnusson, 1998).

The original and current examination questions are designed to test the nurse's ability to apply legal nurse consulting knowledge in situations that simulate the actual practice. The majority of questions are in the form of case studies in which a passage describing a legal case is followed by several questions relating to the case (AALNC, 2002b).

Each individual item is coded by the type of case and by one LNC activity. Currently, the categories under "type of case" that are assigned the highest percent of test questions are medical malpractice and personal injury. More than 50% of the questions on any version of the certification examination are likely to concern these two areas (AALNC, 2002b). The percent of questions in these two categories will change if a future practice analysis demonstrates a shift in the percentage of LNCs working in these areas.

Currently the ALNCCB Item Writing Panel is charged with the responsibility of developing new items as needed based on the exam blueprint. The Item Writing Panel continues to add items to the bank via sessions with experts from the testing company to ensure that psychometric testing standards are met.

Validating Test Items

Two pilot tests were developed using the 250 items written. The pilot tests were offered to all LNCs attending the 1998 AALNC National Education Conference in Dallas, Texas. The pilot tests did not exclude LNCs who would not have met eligibility criteria, but a questionnaire included with the pilot tests revealed that most of the 217 LNCs who sat for the pilot tests would have met eligibility requirements. The superior performance by those who met eligibility requirements served as validation that the eligibility criteria did tend to identify those candidates who had reached the level of proficiency measured by the examination (AALNC, 1998).

The pilot tests and each certification examination given since then were subjected to postadministration statistical analysis by the testing company. Each item was reviewed to determine whether it was too easy or too difficult, and whether the item discriminated between high and low scorers. The items that did not meet psychometric standards were eliminated or revised by the ALNCCB members and the testing company before the items were pilot-tested on another certification examination. Any new or revised item is not scored until it can be proven to be a "good" question through statistical analysis (AALNC, 2002b).

ALNCCB continues to regularly evaluate the validity of test items as per ABNS standards with the assistance of the testing company. Postadministration analysis has consistently found the

Table 2.4   Evolution of the LNCC Certification Test Blueprint

1998 Practice Analysis[a]	% of Test	What Our C-NET Application Stated	% of Test	Published in 2008 Practice Analysis Report	% of Test	Final 2008	% of Test
Medical malpractice	30–35	Medical malpractice	28–32	Medical malpractice	28–32	Medical malpractice	27–31
Personal injury	23–28	Personal injury	20–24	Personal injury	20–24	Personal injury	19–23
Product liability/ toxic tort	11–16	Product liability/toxic tort	12–16	Product liability/toxic tort	12–16	Product liability/ toxic tort	10–14
Workers' compensation	10–15	Workers' compensation	12–16	Workers' compensation	12–16	Workers' compensation	12–16
Risk management	5–8	Risk management	4–8	Risk management	4–8	Risk management	5–9
Life care planning	4–7	Life care planning	5–9	Life care planning	5–9	Life care planning	4–7
Criminal/forensic	1–3	Criminal/forensic	1–4	Criminal/forensic	1–4	Criminal/ forensic	1–4
Administrative health law	1–3	Administrative health law	1–4	Administrative health law	1–4	Administrative health law/ regulatory compliance	4–8
Elder law	1–3	Elder law	2–5	Elder law	2–5	Elder law	3–6

Source: Hallas, M. (2008). Evolution of the LNCC Certification Test Blueprint. *AALNC Network News, 10*(4).

[a] Magnusson, J. K., & Garbin, M. (1999). Legal nurse consultant practice analysis summary report. *Journal of Legal Nurse Consulting, 10*(1), 10–18.

examination to be psychometrically sound; it is "valid." In other words, the questions are directly related to the roles of experienced LNCs as identified by the practice analysis, and the majority of LNCs who meet eligibility criteria perform successfully on the examination.

The examination is "reliable" and consistent. Statistical analysis indicates a high consistency of performance of individual candidates throughout the examination. Performance on individual items remains stable from one form of the examination to another, and overall performance on various editions of the examinations is similar. Test forms are statistically equated, so that equally qualified LNCs are neither penalized nor advantaged by sitting for an examination that is more difficult or easier than another edition.

Eligibility Requirements and Recertification

Eligibility requirements to sit for the LNCC exam include (1) current licensure as an RN in the United States or its territories, with a full and unrestricted license; (2) a minimum of five years experience practicing as an RN; and (3) evidence of 2000 hours of legal nurse consulting experience within the past three years.

Certification is valid for five years. LNCCs who wish to renew their certification can do so by submitting 60 nursing contact hours that meet the published criteria for recertification, or by sitting for the exam again. They must meet the same eligibility criteria, except that the experience requirement for renewal is 2000 hours in the past five years. More information about LNCC recertification is available on the ALNCCB website and the LNCC recertification application.

Protecting the Value of LNCC

Nurses who achieve specialty certification want their credential to be meaningful to others. Indeed, the aim of nursing specialty certification and accreditation is to provide assurance to the public that the certification holder is proficient in the specialty practice at a level that exceeds the minimum requirements for entry into practice.

To that end, ALNCCB has taken a number of steps. Both "ALNCCB" and "LNCC" are registered trademarks. No other organization may use "LNCC" to designate certification as an LNC. While it is not necessary to use the registered trademark symbol with the credential, its use may help distinguish the LNCC from the ever-evolving list of entry-level certificates.

ABNS accreditation indicates that the LNCC is comparable to other nursing specialty certifications with high standards and legally defensible programs. The ABNS accreditation process includes a stringent third-party peer-review process of all applications submitted for accreditation.

ALNCCB performs ongoing review of the examination and the individual items, and writes new items as needed. Applications to sit for the examination and for recertification are subject to audit by appointed members of the audit panel. A policy is in place for appeals.

Confidentiality of potential candidates is maintained. Security of the examination is strictly maintained. The testing company is required to safeguard all examination booklets, the item banks, and items still in the development stage in order to prevent the compromise of current and future examinations. Confidentiality regarding test content is a strict requirement for every member of ALNCCB, its staff, and contracted advisers. Test takers are reminded that they should also maintain the confidentiality of the test content. All candidates are required to read and sign a confidentiality statement that appears on the first page of their test booklets.

Ultimately, the public should judge the value of the LNCC credential. As in other nursing specialties, the process of proving the value of certification takes a great deal of time. A specialty as small as legal nurse consulting is at a greater disadvantage in this regard. The LNC's employers and clients usually do not work with enough LNCs to make comparisons between those who have achieved the LNCC credential and those who have not. Consumers, including the LNCC employer's clients, may not even know of the LNCC's involvement in a case, and have no way to judge the LNCC's impact on the case. The complexity of legal processes makes it difficult to measure any one individual's impact on case outcome.

LNCCs and LNCs must be willing to educate their employers and clients about the LNCC credential and about the great lengths to which AALNC and ALNCCB have gone to ensure that the credential is meaningful to them—the consumers of LNC services. Attorneys and other employers need to be made aware that accreditation by ABNS is evidence confirming that the LNCC credential meets the highest standards of nursing certification. The LNCC credential should be promoted as a reliable indicator of an experienced and knowledgeable LNC who ultimately will serve the best interests of the employer's clients.

Education is needed to help consumers differentiate the LNCC from other less meaningful credentials. The AALNC recommends listing certificates and entry-level "certifications" in the education section of a resume or curriculum vitae rather than adding initials that do not represent attainment of specialty nursing certification (AALNC, 2000) to one's title.

Research

Nursing Certification

In describing the purposes of nursing certification in patient care settings, Ann Cary, director of the International Program of Research on the Certified Nurse Workforce, states: "Ostensibly, [nursing certification] protects the public from unsafe and incompetent providers, gives consumers more choices in selecting health care providers, distinguishes among levels of care, and gives better trained providers a competitive advantage" (Cary, 2001). This statement can easily be adapted to the LNC role, even though competent practice by LNCs does not generally involve direct patient care.

In a study of the certified nursing workforce from January 2001, it is reported that nurses hold more than 410,000 certifications in 134 specialties from 67 certifying organizations (Cary, 2001). But the lack of research proving the link between certification and improved outcomes at the bedside or in non-patient-care practice settings has delayed broad-based recognition of the value of many nursing certifications. It is difficult to prove that any individual professional certification fulfills the purposes cited above, even though the achievement of these goals receives at least intuitive support (Cary, 2000).

In recent years, ABNS has begun a focused research agenda in nursing certification, such as the Value of Certification Study described below. Additional research in this area is expected in the future.

ABNS Value of Certification Study

As part of its mission to promote the value of specialty nursing certification, ABNS has developed a focused research agenda to determine the value of certification. The ABNS Value of Certification

Table 2.5   ABNS Value of Certification Survey

Certification	ALNCCB	ABNS
Value Statement	Total respondents (N = 225) percent who strongly agree and agree with the value statement	Total respondents (N = 11,427) percent who strongly agree and agree with the value statement
Validates specialized knowledge	97.7	97.3
Indicates level of clinical competence	85.0	83.5
Indicates attainment of a practice standard	94.9	93.5
Enhances professional credibility	95.3	95.4
Promotes recognition from peers	89.9	88.1
Promotes recognition from other health professionals	80.6	84.0
Promotes recognition from employers	75.5	77.9
Increases consumer confidence	75.3	71.6
Enhances feeling of personal accomplishment	98.6	98.0
Enhances personal confidence in clinical abilities	87.0	88.2
Provides personal satisfaction	99.5	97.3
Provides professional challenge	96.2	95.1
Enhances professional autonomy	83.5	78.3
Indicates professional growth	96.2	95.3
Provides evidence of professional commitment	94.4	94.1
Provides evidence of accountability	89.7	84.4
Increases marketability	78.8	84.8
Increases salary	47.8	41.6

Source: American Board of Nursing Specialties. (2006). ABNS value of certification survey executive summary. Retrieved 2008, from American Board of Nursing Specialties Web Site: http://www.nursingcertification.org/pdf/executive_summary.pdf

Note: Table comparing ALNCCB data with ABNS study findings. The ABNS Value of Certification Survey includes the perspectives of over 11,000 nurse respondents, across 20 specialty nursing certifications organizations, representing 36 different certification credentials. Central to measuring the value of certification, the survey incorporated the Perceived Value of Certification Tool (PVCT[a]), a reliable tool that incorporates 18 certification-related value statements. The PVCT was developed, validated, and copyrighted by the Competency & Credentialing Institute (formally the Certification Board Perioperative Nursing) in 2000–2001. The PVCT consists of 18 items that utilize a five-point Likert-scale response, labeled strongly agree, agree, disagree, strongly disagree, and no opinion.

Study was designed to validate nurses' perceptions, values, and behaviors related to certification. Twenty ABNS member organizations, including AALNC, participated in the study. An equal number of certified and noncertified nurses were invited to participate, with a total sample size of 94,768 nurses. Responses were received from 11,427 nurses for a total response rate of 12.1%. The survey incorporated the Perceived Value of Certification Tool (PVCT®) developed by the Competency and Credentialing Institute (CCI) (ABNS, 2006).

Table 2.5 compares ALNCCB responses (collected from AALNC members) to all ABNS study participants. It is interesting to note the similarities in the perceived value of certification between LNCs and clinical nurses. The top three value statements for LNCs, as shown in this study, indicate that certification provides personal satisfaction (99.5%), enhances a feeling of personal accomplishment (98.6%), and validates specialized knowledge (97.7%).

Future Trends

There are many opportunities for ALNCCB to consider. Computer-based testing (CBT) is one possibility of interest to candidates, especially since members are likely to be computer-savvy, and would appreciate additional testing sites and faster scoring of CBT exams. However, converting from paper and pencil tests to CBT is expensive, so this will need careful consideration. Additional forms of the examination will be required, and the Item Bank will need to be supplemented.

As a member of ABNS, ALNCCB has the unique opportunity of being involved in developing a national research agenda. One of the hot topics in certification currently under discussion is competency and outcomes-based research. Collaborating with other nursing organizations will provide valuable data for AALNC to share with its members and the public, impacting our profession and securing our position as a specialty practice of nursing.

Summary

All LNCs are encouraged to seek certification to validate their knowledge once eligibility criteria are met. As the only certification in the profession endorsed by AALNC and accredited by ABNS, the LNCC is the gold standard sought by experienced practitioners in the industry.

References

American Association of Legal Nurse Consultants. (1992). *Code of ethics for legal nurse consultants with interpretive discussion.* Glenview, IL: AALNC.

American Association of Legal Nurse Consultants. (1994). *Scope of practice for the legal nurse consultant.* Glenview, IL: AALNC.

American Association of Legal Nurse Consultants. (1998). ALNCCB completes certification examination pilot test. *Journal of Legal Nurse Consulting, 9,* 19.

American Association of Legal Nurse Consultants. (1999). Role of the legal nurse consultant as distinct from the role of the paralegal and legal assistant. Retrieved 2008, from American Association of Legal Nurse Consultants Web Site: http://www.aalnc.org/hire/roll.cfm

American Association of Legal Nurse Consultants. (2000). Education and certification in legal nurse consulting. Retrieved 2008, from American Association of Legal Nurse Consultants Web Site: http://www.aalnc.org/edupro/position.cfm

American Association of Legal Nurse Consultants. (2002a). *Scope and standards of practice for the legal nurse consultant.* Glenview, IL: AALNC.

American Association of Legal Nurse Consultants. (2002b). *Handbook for the LNCC practice test.* Glenview, IL: AALNC.

American Association of Legal Nurse Consultants. (2005). The specialty practice of legal nurse consulting. Retrieved 2008, from American Association of Legal Nurse Consultants Web Site: http://www.aalnc. org/images/PositionStatement.pdf

American Association of Legal Nurse Consultants. (2006a). Providing expert nursing testimony. Retrieved 2008, from American Association of Legal Nurse Consultants Web Site: http://www.aalnc.org/images/ ExpWit.pdf

American Association of Legal Nurse Consultants. (2006b). Licensure for expert witnesses. Retrieved 2008, from American Association of Legal Nurse Consultants Web Site: http://www.aalnc.org/images/pdfs/ AALNC_Postion_Statement_on_Licensure_for_Expert_Witnesses_version_2_5.pdf

American Association of Legal Nurse Consultants and American Nurses Association. (2006). *Legal nurse consulting: Scope and standards of practice.* [Brochure]. Silver Spring, MD: NursesBooks.Org

American Association of Legal Nurse Consultants. (2009). *Code of ethics for legal nurse consultants with interpretive discussion.* Chicago, IL: AALNC.

American Bar Association Standing Committee on Legal Assistants. (1999). *More on legal nurse programs. SCOLA update.* Chicago, IL: American Bar Association.

American Board of Nursing Specialties. (2004). Accreditation standards. Retrieved 2008, from American Board of Nursing Specialties Web Site: http://www.nursingcertification.org/pdf/ac_standards_ short.pdf

American Board of Nursing Specialties. (2005). A position statement on the value of specialty nursing certification. Retrieved 2008, from American Board of Nursing Specialties Web Site: http://www. nursingcertification.org/position_statements.htm

American Board of Nursing Specialties. (2006). ABNS value of certification survey executive summary. Retrieved 2008, from American Board of Nursing Specialties Web Site: http://www.nursingcertification. org/pdf/executive_summary.pdf

American Education Research Association, American Psychological Association, and National Council on Measurement in Education. (1999). *Standards for educational and psychological testing.* Washington, DC: American Educational Research Association.

American Legal Nurse Consultant Certification Board. (2006). ALNCCB position statement on certification in legal nurse consulting. Retrieved 2008, from American Legal Nurse Consultant Certification Board Web Site: http://www.aalnc.org/lncc/about/position.cfm

American Legal Nurse Consultant Certification Board. (2008). Content areas of the examination. Retrieved 2008, from http://www.aalnc.org/lncc/exam/scope.cfm

American Nurses Association. (2001). *Code of ethics for nurses with interpretive statements.* Washington, DC: American Nurses Publishing.

American Nurses Association. (2004). *Nursing: Scope and standards of practice.* Washington, DC: NursesBooks. org.

Bernreuter, M. E. (2001). The American Board of Nursing Specialties: Nursing's gold standard. *JONA's Healthcare Law, Ethics, and Regulation, 3,* 5.

Bogart, J. B. (Ed.). (1998). *Legal nurse consulting: Principles and practice.* Boca Raton, FL: CRC Press.

Blueprint validation committee report 7/8/08.

Cary, A. H. (2000). Data driven policy: The case for certification research. *Policy, Politics, & Nursing Practice, 1,* 165.

Cary, A. H. (2001). Certified registered nurses: Results of the study of the certified workforce. *American Journal of Nursing, 101,* 44.

Ehrlich, C. J. (1995). Certification development. *Journal of Legal Nurse Consulting, 6,* 6.

Hallas, M. (2008). Evolution of the LNCC Certification Test Blueprint. *AALNC Network News, 10*(4).

Iyer, P. (Ed.). (2003). *Legal nurse consulting: Principles and practice* (2nd ed.). Boca Raton, FL: CRC Press.

Janes, R., Bogart, J., Magnusson, J., Joos, B., & Beerman, J. (1998). The history and evolution of legal nurse consulting. In J.B. Bogart, (Ed.), *Legal nurse consulting: Principles and practice* (pp. 3–24). Boca Raton, FL: CRC Press.

LNCC Certification Information Handbook and Application.

Magnusson, J. (1998). AALNC's certification exam approaches completion. *Journal of Legal Nurse Consulting, 9,* 26.

Magnusson, J. K., & Garbin, M. (1999). Legal nurse consultant practice analysis summary report. *Journal of Legal Nurse Consulting, 10*(1), 10–18.

Manion, J. (1990). *Change from within: Nurse intrapreneurs as health care innovators.* Kansas City: American Nurses Association.

Manion, J. (1994). How to innovate from within. *American Journal of Nursing, 94,* 38.

Pinchot, G. (1985). *Intrapreneuring.* New York: Harper & Row.

Puetz, B., & Shinn, L. (1997). *The Nurse Consultant's Handbook.* New York: Springer Publishers.

Sullivan v. Edward Hospital, WL 228956 (2004, February 5).

Webb, L. C., & Hallas, M. (2008). 2007 Legal nurse consultant practice analysis. *Journal of Legal Nurse Consulting, 19*(2), 7–13.

Wilson, L. (1994). *Stop selling and start partnering.* Essex Junction, VT: Oliver Wight Publications, Inc.

Additional Reading

For additional reading, see the comprehensive bibliography of nursing certification literature compiled by ABNS. Organized by topic and updated periodically, the list is posted on the ABNS website at http://www.nursingcertification.org/bibliography.htm

Test Questions

1. The primary value of an LNC to an attorney comes from
   A. Legal knowledge gained from educational courses
   B. Medical knowledge and computer skills
   C. Nursing knowledge and experience
   D. Research and organizational skills

2. AALNC recommends that LNCs have
   A. A minimum of five years experience as a practicing RN and active nursing licensure in their state
   B. Paralegal certification from the ABA
   C. Certification as an LNC prior to starting their business
   D. Completed an internship as an LNC prior to starting their business

3. Which of the following are of primary importance for an LNC?
   A. A logo and detailed website
   B. A professional marketing plan
   C. Proficiency in drafting legal documents
   D. Organizational and critical thinking skills, professionalism

4. Three of the following are eligibility requirements to sit for a certification examination in a specialty. Which one is NOT required?
   A. Experience as an RN
   B. Evidence of formal education in the specialty
   C. Current licensure as an RN
   D. Current practice in the specialty

5. Which tool should be used to determine the test specifications (blueprint) of a nursing specialty exam?
   A. A core curriculum
   B. Accreditation standards
   C. A practice analysis
   D. Postexamination statistical analysis

6. The primary goal for nursing certification is to
   A. Protect the consumers of nursing specialty service
   B. Reward skilled nurse specialists
   C. Differentiate placement on an employer's pay scale
   D. Establish who may enter the specialty practice

7. Accreditation of a specialty certification board by the ABNS provides assurance that the
   A. Educational programs in the specialty are of high quality
   B. Bylaws of all specialty certification boards are uniform
   C. Board of the specialty association maintains control of the certification board's decisions
   D. Specialty certification program meets the highest standards

Answers: 1. C, 2. A, 3. D, 4. B, 5. C, 6. A, 7. D

Appendix A: Code of Ethics and Conduct with Interpretive Discussion

Preamble

The Code of Ethics and Conduct of the AALNC is based on beliefs about the nature of individuals and society. The code of professional and ethical conduct provides guidelines to its members for professional performance and behavior. The success of any professional organization results from the competence and integrity of its members. Our goal to those we serve is that they be assured of our accountability.

We recognize a responsibility to other professional organizations with which we are aligned, in particular, the ANA. We accept and abide by the principles of the ANA code of ethics and conduct. By our support of the ANA, we affirm that the right and trust placed in us will not be violated.

1. *The LNC maintains professional nursing competence:* The LNC is a registered nurse and maintains an active nursing license. The LNC is knowledgeable about the current scope and standards of legal nursing practice and advocates for these standards. The LNC does not practice law.
2. *The LNC's primary obligation is to apply their nursing, medical, and healthcare knowledge and expertise to their professional practice:* The analysis of the medical legal implications of legal nursing practice includes applying the nurse's unique insight into the surrounding support systems and clinical circumstances of each case.
3. *The LNC's work is free from bias:* The LNC does not discriminate against any person based on race, creed, color, age, sex, national origin, social status, or disability and does not let personal attitudes interfere with professional performance. Individual differences do not influence professional performance and practice. Financial or other relationships that may give an appearance of or create a conflict of interest will be disclosed. These factors are understood, considered, and respected when performing activities.
4. *The LNC performs as a consultant or an expert with the highest degree of integrity:* Integrity refers to uprightness, honesty, and sincerity. The LNC directs those attributes to the requirements of the profession. Integrity is a personal and sacred trust and the standard against which the LNC must ultimately test all decisions. Honest errors and differences of opinion may occur, but deceit, poor judgment, or lack of principles must not be tolerated.
5. *The LNC uses informed judgment, objectivity, and individual professional competence as criteria when accepting assignments:* The LNC does not purport to be competent in matters in which he or she has limited knowledge or experience. Only services that meet high personal and professional standards are offered or rendered.
6. *The LNC protects client privacy and confidentiality:* The LNC uses confidential materials with discretion. The LNC respects and protects the privacy of the client. The LNC does not use any client information for personal gain.
7. *The LNC maintains standards of personal conduct that reflect honorably upon the profession:* The LNC abides by all local, state, and federal laws and other regulatory requirements. The LNC who knowingly becomes involved in unethical or illegal activities negates professional responsibility for personal interest or personal gain. Such activities jeopardize the public confidence and trust in the nursing profession and is unacceptable to the profession.
8. *The LNC integrates ethical considerations into their professional relationships within the healthcare and legal industries:* The LNC works to achieve their client's goals while at the same time

maintaining their professional responsibility to give accurate, independent nursing/medical/healthcare information, and advice. The LNC contributes to resolving ethical issues in practice, reports illegal, incompetent, or impaired practice, and promotes respect for the judicial system.

9. *The LNC is accountable for responsibilities accepted and actions performed.*

Conclusion

Each individual's personal commitment to the Code of Ethics and Conduct of the AALNC is the ultimate regulator of his or her behavior. By adopting this Code of Ethics and Conduct, we affirm to those with whom we serve that they have the right to expect us to abide by this code.

As members of the AALNC, we pledge to embrace and demonstrate this commitment of integrity and professional excellence.

For more information, contact:

American Association of Legal Nurse Consultants
Toll free: 877/402-2562
Web site: http://www.aalnc.org
Email: info@aalnc.org

Adapted and copyrighted © April 1992
Revised May 2005
Revised August 2009
By the American Association of Legal Nurse Consultants

Appendix B: AALNC Position Statement

The Specialty Practice of Legal Nurse Consulting 2005

Summary

The purpose of this position statement is to define the specialty of Legal Nurse Consulting as an RN Practice and reinforce that LNCs therefore must maintain an active RN license.

Introduction

This position statement is the outcome of extensive discussions and public dialogue about the scope of practice and many roles of LNCs when providing for direct and indirect patient care, as well as consultation and education.

Background

In 2003 the ANA's *Nursing's Social Policy Statement* introduced an updated, contemporary definition of nursing: "Nursing is the protection, promotion, and optimization of health and abilities, prevention of illness and injury, alleviation of suffering through the diagnosis and treatment of human response, and advocacy in the care of individuals, families, communities, and populations."

The *Nursing Scope and Standards of Practice* (2004) and *Code of Ethics for Nurses with Interpretive Statements* (2001) of the ANA provide additional details and further description of nursing and the associated standards of practice. These foundational references provide a framework for the definition of specialty nursing practice, including Legal Nurse Consulting.

Legal Nurse Consulting

The AALNC, the professional nursing specialty organization for LNCs, defines legal nurse consulting as the evaluation and analysis of facts and the rendering of informed opinions related to the delivery of nursing and health care services and outcomes. The LNC is a licensed RN who performs a critical analysis of clinical and administrative nursing practice, health care facts and issues and their outcomes for the legal profession, health care professions, consumers of health care and legal services, and others as appropriate.

As knowledge-based professionals, LNCs use information learned in the research and development of a case to improve future health care for patients, to advocate for remedies for patients who have received inadequate care, and to provide education to clients, patients, health care providers, and the public as appropriate. LNCs seek adequate protection of patients and the public and promote accepted standards of care that will serve to prevent injury and alleviate suffering. Similar to other RNs working in research settings, informatics, administrative positions, and other role settings, LNCs engage in specialty nursing practice that covers many roles, some including direct patient care and others influencing patient care indirectly. For example, the nurse Case Manager or Life Care Planner directly influences patient outcome by assessing patient needs and making appropriate recommendations. The expert witness LNC educates the public when testifying before a jury. As knowledge-based professionals, LNCs use information learned in the research and development of a case to improve future health care for patients. For example, researching and explaining medical issues in malpractice cases may lead to revised nursing policies and procedures; help identify those with legitimate injuries, evaluate the impact of injuries on level of function, and advocate for remedies when these result from receiving inadequate care. LNCs provide education to clients, patients, health care providers, and the public when attending and explaining an independent medical exam or injuries sustained in an accident. By virtue of nursing knowledge, training, and experience (including Legal Nurse Consulting training and experience), all of these roles are implemented by nurses who are considered to be practicing nurses and whose contributions further the nursing profession itself as well as promote effective patient care.

In many jurisdictions, the state nurse practice act and associated regulatory language have conveyed title protection for the term "nurse." When the word "nurse" is used in the professional title, that user must be actively licensed as an RN. Nursing is a knowledge-based profession, and when using that knowledge base the LNC is indeed practicing the profession of nursing.

AALNC

AALNC is the organization that:

- Provides the foundation for best practices within the multitude of LNC roles
- Incorporates cutting-edge clinical and consultative education to promote the practice of legal nurse consulting
- Supports "Legal Nurse Consulting: Scope and Standards of Practice"

Conclusion

Legal Nurse Consulting is an expanding nursing specialty practice. LNCs must maintain an active RN license as an integral requirement of the practice discipline.

Resources

American Nurses Association. (2001). *Code of ethics for nurses with interpretive statements.* Washington, DC.
American Nurses Association. (2003). *Nursing's social policy statement* (2nd ed.). Washington, DC.
American Nurses Association. (2004). *Nursing: Scope and standards of practice.* Washington, DC.
American Association of Legal Nurse Consultants (AALNC). (2003). In P. Iyer (Ed.), *Legal nurse consulting: Principles and practice* (2nd ed.). Boca Raton, FL: CRC Press.

Appendix C: Legal Nurse Consulting Scope and Standards of Practice

Legal Nurse Consulting Standards of Practice and Professional Performance

This is a brief summary of the 15 Standards for LNC practice and professional performance, excerpted from the Legal Nurse Consulting Scope & Standards of Practice created jointly by AALNC and ANA in 2006 and available at http://www.aalnc.org/edupro/profresources/landing. cfm. The complete document expands each Standard and contains additional information regarding the Scope of legal nurse consulting practice, including its evolution, practice characteristics, skills, practice environments and settings, practice roles, specialization, educational preparation, certification, ethics, trends, and issues applicable to legal nurse consulting. All LNCs should familiarize themselves with the expectations for professional practice as an LNC, and with the additional information contained in this document.

Standard 1: Assessment
The LNC collects comprehensive data pertinent to the health case or claim.

Standard 2: Issue or Problem Identification (Diagnosis)
The LNC analyzes the assessment data to determine the issues in the health case or claim.

Standard 3: Outcomes Identification
The LNC identifies expected outcomes for the individualized plan for a given health case or claim.

Standard 4: Planning
The LNC develops a plan that prescribes strategies and alternatives to attain expected outcomes.

Standard 5: Implementation
The LNC implements the identified plan.

Standard 5A: Coordination of Services
The LNC coordinates services related to the health case or claim.

Standard 5B: Health Teaching and Health Promotion
The LNC employs strategies to promote a better understanding of health and safety related to a health case or claim.

Standard 5C: Consultation
The LNC provides consultation regarding a health case or claim to influence the identified plan, enhance and support the contribution of others, and effect change.

Standard 6: Evaluation
The LNC evaluates progress towards attainment of outcomes.

Standard 7: Quality of Practice
The LNC systematically enhances the quality and effectiveness of nursing practice.

Standard 8: Education
The LNC attains knowledge and competency that reflect current nursing practice.

Standard 9: Professional Practice Evaluation
The LNC evaluates one's own nursing practice in relationship to professional practice standards and guidelines, relevant statutes, rules and regulations.

Standard 10: Collegiality
The LNC interacts with and contributes to the professional development of peers and colleagues.

Standard 11: Collaboration
The LNC collaborates with clients and others in the conduct of legal nurse consulting practice.

Standard 12: Ethics
The LNC integrates ethical provisions in all areas of practice.

Standard 13: Research
The LNC integrates research findings into practice.

Standard 14: Resource Utilization
The LNC considers factors related to safety, effectiveness, cost, and impact on practice in the planning and evaluation of the health case or claim.

Standard 15: Leadership
The LNC provides leadership in the professional practice setting and the profession.

Appendix D: AALNC Position Statement

Role of the LNC as Distinct from the Role of the Paralegal and Legal Assistant

The AALNC has defined legal nurse consulting as a specialty practice of the nursing profession. AALNC does not recognize LNCs as a special category of paralegals.

Attorneys and others in the legal arena consult with psychologists and engineers, for example, because of their expertise in their respective professions; similarly, they consult with LNCs because of their expertise in nursing and health care. Many LNCs have bachelor's and advanced degrees in nursing and other health-related fields. Some LNCs practice as independent consultants; others are employed by law firms, insurance companies, and other institutions in a wide variety of roles.

While many LNCs have acquired knowledge of the legal system through such experience as consulting with attorneys and attending seminars, legal education is not prerequisite to the practice of legal nurse consulting. (In contrast, legal education is frequently a requirement for paralegals.) Professional nursing education and health care experience make LNCs unique and valuable partners in legal processes.

The AALNC Code of Ethics and Conduct[1], Scope of Practice for the Legal Nurse Consultant[2], and Standards of Legal Nurse Consulting Practice and Professional Performance[3] describe the specialty of legal nurse consulting. The primary role of the LNC is to evaluate, analyze, and render informed opinions on the delivery of health care and the resulting outcomes.

The following list of activities helps to distinguish the practice of legal nurse consulting:

- Facilitating communications and thus strategizing with the legal professional for successful resolutions between parties involved in health care-related litigation or other medical–legal or health care–legal matters
- Educating attorneys and/or others involved in the legal process regarding the health care facts and issues of a case or a claim
- Researching and integrating health care and nursing literature, guidelines, standards, and regulations as related to the health care facts and issues of a case or claim
- Reviewing, summarizing, and analyzing medical records and other pertinent health care and legal documents and comparing and correlating them to the allegations
- Assessing issues of damages and causation relative to liability with the legal process
- Identifying, locating, evaluating, and conferring with expert witnesses
- Interviewing witnesses and parties pertinent to the health care issues in collaboration with legal professionals
- Drafting legal documents in medically related cases under the supervision of an attorney
- Developing collaborative case strategies with those practicing within the legal system
- Providing support during discovery, depositions, trial, and other legal proceedings
- Testifying at depositions, hearings, arbitrations, or trials as expert health care witnesses
- Supporting the process of adjudication of legal claims
- Contacting and conferring with vendors to develop demonstrative evidence or to collect costs of health care services, supplies, or equipment
- Supervising and educating other nurses in the practice of legal nurse consulting

Confusion about roles arises because in some settings LNCs do some of the same work that legal assistants and paralegals do, particularly in small law offices where they are the only staff available to assist the attorneys.

Legal education programs offered for nurses by legal assistant or paralegal education programs also cause confusion about roles. To the extent that legal education is provided to nurses by legal assistant or paralegal education programs, it should be considered separate from the education of paralegals and legal assistants because of the differences in their practice in the legal arena.

In March 1998, the Standing Committee on Legal Assistants of the ABA decided that "… legal nurses and legal nurse consultants fall squarely within the ABA definition of 'paralegal/ legal assistant' …"[4]. In contrast, AALNC recognizes a clear distinction between the roles of the LNC and the paralegal.

The ABA also determined that "... the educational programs designed to train [legal nurses and legal nurse consultants] are paralegal programs or program options ..." and as such are required to meet ABA guidelines and to be approved by the ABA if offered by an institution with an approved program.[5] AALNC does not support required ABA approval of legal nurse consulting education programs.

AALNC has defined legal nurse consulting as a specialty practice of nursing. AALNC's position, therefore, is that legal nurse consulting education should be developed and presented as specialty nursing curricula by nurse educators in partnership with legal educators.

References

1. American Association of Legal Nurse Consultants. (1992). *Code of ethics and conduct of the American association of legal nurse consultant.* Glenview, IL: Author.
2. American Association of Legal Nurse Consultants. (1995). *AALNC scope of practice for the legal nurse consultant.* Glenview, IL: Author.
3. American Association of Legal Nurse Consultants. (1995). *Standards of legal nurse consulting practice and professional performance.* Glenview, IL: Author.
4. ABA Standing Committee on Legal Assistants. (Winter 1999). *More on legal nurse programs," SCOLA update.* Chicago, IL: Author.
5. Ibid.

Appendix E: AALNC Position Statement on Education and Certification

AALNC has defined legal nurse consulting as the specialty practice of the profession of nursing in which RNs apply their nursing education and clinical expertise to medically related issues of the litigation process. The primary role of the LNC is to evaluate, analyze, and render informed opinions about the delivery of health care and the resulting outcomes.*

The practice of legal nurse consulting predates any specialty organization, training program, or certification. While many LNCs have acquired knowledge of the legal system through such experience as consulting with attorneys and attending seminars, legal or paralegal education is not prerequisite to the practice of legal nurse consulting. In the early days of the specialty, nurses became LNCs without the benefit of formal education, relying on their nursing expertise and informal guidance or "on the job training" from attorneys. Then as now, nurses entered the specialty with a variety of educational backgrounds and practical experiences in nursing. The nurses who founded the AALNC in 1989 were already practicing as LNCs when they came together to share their experience and to promote the specialty by forming a professional association.

Education

Today, numerous educational opportunities are available to nurses who wish to become LNCs. While formal training in legal nurse consulting is not required to practice, some nurses may benefit from a structured introduction to the specialty. AALNC believes that the individual nurse is best able to determine what, if any, program will meet his/her needs and goals.

---

* Refer to the AALNC Position Statement on The Role of the Legal Nurse Consultant as distinct from the role of the paralegal and legal assistant.

While AALNC does not recommend or endorse particular programs, the following criteria should be considered in assessing credible, useful, legal nurse consulting education.

Institution

Legal nurse consulting education is offered by universities, colleges, community colleges, for-profit businesses, and not-for-profit organizations. In assessing the value of these programs, the reputation and accreditation of the sponsoring institution should be considered.

Program

Legal nurse consulting education programs may be found in various colleges or departments, including the School of Nursing, the College of Health Sciences, the Office of Continuing Education, and the Paralegal Department, among others. To the extent that legal education is provided to nurses by legal assistant or paralegal education programs, it should be considered separate from the education of paralegals and legal assistants because of the differences in their practice in the legal arena. The primary focus of legal nurse consulting education should be to build on nursing education and clinical experience and to prepare nurses to function in the legal arena. In evaluating a particular program, its mission and purpose should be compared to this standard.

Program Directors and Instructors

AALNC maintains the position that legal nurse consulting education programs should be developed and presented as specialty nursing curricula by nurse educators in partnership with legal educators. The qualifications of the program directors and instructors should be considered when evaluating a program. In general, programs developed and taught by experienced nurse educators who are practicing LNCs are preferred.

Curriculum

AALNC recommends Legal Nurse Consulting: Principles and Practice as the core curriculum of legal nurse consulting education. Courses of study based on this curriculum vary in length from one day to two years. Nurses are encouraged to choose a course of study that meets personal needs and professional goals.

Certification

Most LNC education programs offer a certificate that testifies to the completion of a course of study and, in some cases, to passing an examination on the course material. Some graduates of LNC certificate programs chose to include letters such as "LNC" after their names, along with their educational degrees and professional credentials. AALNC does not endorse this practice. It is customary to list such certificates in the education section of a resume or curriculum vitae.

These certificate programs should not be confused with the certification programs offered by nursing certification boards, which are commonly affiliated with professional nursing associations. Certification is a process that recognizes an individual's qualifications and demonstrated knowledge in a specialty. In 1997, AALNC established the ALNCCB to administer the LNCC program. The LNCC certification program is accredited by the ABNS.

The purpose of the LNCC program is to promote a level of expertise and professionalism in legal nurse consulting. LNCs must meet the eligibility requirements, which include consulting experience, and achieve a passing score on a multiple-choice examination to earn the LNCC designation. As with many clinical nursing certification programs, the LNCC credential is designed for those who have demonstrated experience and knowledge in the specialty.* Certification is an appropriate goal for those who are committed to a professional legal nurse consulting practice.

AALNC supports the practice initiated by the ANA of listing one's credentials in the following order: highest educational degree, highest nursing degree if different, licensure, and professional certifications. "LNCC" is the only legal nurse consulting credential recognized by AALNC and ABNS.

Appendix F: AALNC Position Statement—Providing Expert Nursing Testimony

Summary

The purpose of this position statement is to establish that RNs are the only health care providers that should provide expert testimony related to nursing standards of care.

Introduction

This position statement is the outcome of extensive review of literature and case law related to physicians testifying on nursing standards. Nurses are uniquely prepared to perform a critical review and analysis of clinical nursing care and administrative nursing practice, which provide the foundation for testifying in nursing negligence issues.

Background and Discussion

Medical malpractice is the failure of a professional health care practitioner to provide reasonable care. The required elements of proof in a medical malpractice case are a duty between the patient and health care practitioner, a breach of duty or departure from accepted practice and the departure being the proximate cause of the alleged injury. Expert opinion is typically required to establish the applicable standard of care and the actual departure from standard practice. The expert witness is required to possess the necessary skill, knowledge, training, and experience to ensure that the opinion rendered is reliable.

It appears elementary that the only expert qualified to render expert opinion testimony would be a member of the same profession who practices in a substantially similar manner to the potential defendant in the case. For many years, physicians have routinely been admitted into evidence to offer testimony to establish the standard of care for the nursing profession. On the other hand, many courts have found that physicians are best qualified to render testimony as to standards of care for physicians and that in many other health care professions, only a member of that health profession is qualified to testify to standards of care for that discipline. Recently, the courts have begun to acknowledge that nurses possess specialized knowledge that physicians do not have unless they have been trained and practice as a nurse.

---

* The LNCC credential can be compared to recognized nursing credentials such as RNC, CCRN, CEN, CPN, and CRRN.

The Supreme Court of Illinois recently held that a board-certified internal medicine physician was not competent to testify as to the standard of care of a nurse. Citing the Amicus Brief submitted by The American Association of Nurse Attorneys, *the court noted:*

A physician who is not a nurse is no more qualified to offer expert opinion testimony as to the standard of care for nurses than a nurse would be to offer an opinion as to the physician standard of care. Certainly, nurses are not permitted to offer expert testimony against a physician based on their observances of physicians or their familiarity with the procedures involved. An operating room nurse, who stands shoulder to shoulder with surgeons every day, would not be permitted to testify as to the standard of care of a surgeon. An endoscopy nurse would not be permitted to testify as to the standard of care of a gastroenterologist performing a colonoscopy. A labor and delivery nurse would not be permitted to offer expert testimony as to the standard of care for an obstetrician or even a midwife. Such testimony would be, essentially, expert testimony as to the standard of medical care (*Sullivan v. Edward Hospital.*, 806 N.E. 2d 645 (Ill. 2004).

Scholars and litigators have long held that

Physicians often have no first-hand knowledge of nursing practice except for observations made in patient care settings. The physician rarely, if ever, teaches in a nursing program nor is a physician responsible for content in nursing texts. In many situations, a physician would not be familiar with the standard of care or with nursing policies and procedures which govern the standard of care. Therefore, a physician's opinions would not be admissible in jurisdictions which hold the expert must be familiar with the standard of care in order to testify as an expert. [Elizabeth W. Beyer & Pamela W. Popp, Nursing Standard of Care in Medical Malpractice Litigation: *The Role of the Nurse Expert Witness*, 23A J.A. HEALTH & HOSP. L. 363–365 (1990)]

Nursing has evolved into a profession with a distinct body of knowledge, university-based education, specialized practice, standards of practice, a societal contract, and an ethical code. The practice of nursing requires decision making and skill based on principles of the biological, physical, behavioral, and social sciences as well as evidence-based research related to functions such as identifying risk factors and providing specific interventions. Each state has a Board of Nursing that is the authorized state entity with the legal authority to regulate nursing practice. State legislature has set forth licensing and regulations for the nursing profession in their respective Nurse Practice Acts and Advanced Practice Nursing Acts. It is evident that under the nursing act, only a nurse would meet the qualifications for sitting for nursing licensure examination, and as such be eligible for licensure as an RN.

AALNC

AALNC is the organization that

- Provides the foundation for best practices within the multitude of LNC roles
- Incorporates cutting-edge clinical and consultative education to promote the practice of legal nurse consulting
- Supports "Legal Nurse Consulting: Scope and Standards of Practice"

Conclusion

The profession of nursing is autonomous from the profession of medicine and other allied health disciplines. The profession of nursing has its own educational and licensing requirements, which serve to identify RNs and, among RNs, further identify those with advanced training and certification in their nursing specialty. Nursing has the responsibility and knowledge to define its standards of practice and indeed has published these standards of care. Therefore, licensed RNs are competent to address these standards of nursing practice in the litigation arena.

It is the position of the AALNC that when applicable nursing standards need to be established through expert testimony, the expert shall be a licensed RN. Further, the only expert competent to testify on clinical and administrative nursing issues is a licensed RN.

Additional References

American Association of Legal Nurse Consultants (AALNC). (2003). In P. Iyer (Ed.), *Legal nurse consulting: Principles and practice* (2nd ed.). Boca Raton, FL: CRC Press.

American Nurses Association. (2001). *Code of ethics for nurses with interpretive statements*. Washington, DC.

American Nurses Association. (2003). *Nursing's social policy statement* (2nd ed.). Washington, DC.

American Nurses Association. (2004). *Nursing: Scope and standards of practice*. Washington, DC.

Kehoe, C. (1987). Contemporary nursing roles and legal accountability: The challenge of nursing malpractice for the law librarian. *Law Library Journal, 79*, 419, 428–429.

Dolan v. Jaeger, 285 A.D. 2d 844, 846, 727 N.Y.S. 2d 784, 786–787 (N.Y. App. Div. 2001).

Cavico, F., & Cavico, N. (1995). *The Nursing Profession in the 1990's: Negligence and Malpractice Liability*, 43 CLEV. ST. L. REV. 557, 558.

Beyer, E., & Popp, P. (1990). Nursing standard of care in medical malpractice litigation: The role of the nurse expert witness. *Journal of Health and Hospital Law, 23*, 363, 365.

National Council of State Boards of Nursing. (1994). *Model nursing practice act*. Chicago: Author

Sweeney, P. (1991). Proving nursing negligence. *Trial, 27*, 34, 36.

State Nurse Practice Acts

State Statutes regulating Expert Witness Testimony

Sullivan v. Edward Hosp., No. 95409, 2004 WL 228956 (Ill. February 5, 2004).

Amicus brief submitted to Illinois Supreme Court—Karen Butler, Esq., American Association of Nurse Attorneys

Vassey v. Burch, 45 N.C. App. 222, 226, 262 S.E. 2d 865, 867.

Appendix G: AALNC Position Statement—Licensure for Expert Witnesses

Summary

The mission of AALNC in this position paper is to protect the public while facilitating the judicial process by recognizing that RN expert witnesses play an integral role in litigation. Confining the availability of an expert witness to those individuals independently licensed within the state where litigation occurs may place an unfair burden on litigants. This position statement has been developed to educate the medical and legal communities, as well as the public at large, on the licensure issue related to LNC expert testimony.

Introduction

This position statement is the natural extension of recently published position papers and professional development of a distinct role for legal nurse consulting within the litigation arena.

The AALNC published a 2005 position statement, *The Specialty Practice of Nursing*, outlining the need for LNCs to maintain an active nursing license. In 2006, the ANA affirmed and recognized Legal Nurse Consulting as a specialty practice of nursing, and published *Legal Nurse Consulting: Scope and Standards of Practice*, setting the benchmark for professional role delineation. In 2006, AALNC adopted a position statement, *Providing Expert Witness Testimony*, further defining and developing the role of RNs who testify as nursing experts.

Given that LNCs will testify to standards of nursing care in multi-jurisdictional settings, AALNC researched and developed this position statement to answer questions regarding nursing licensure and expert testimony across state lines.

Background and Discussion

The issue of licensure for consulting across state lines has been addressed by two other professional associations in the health care field, the American Medical Association (AMA) and the National Council of State Boards of Nursing (NCSBN).

The AMA incorporates language into their expert witness position statements requiring physicians to adhere to a medically acceptable standard of practice while testifying as an expert witness, and goes as far as accepting the role of collaborating with medical boards to discipline physicians who testify falsely under oath (H-265.992 Expert Witness Testimony). The AMA recommends that individual states develop a methodology for granting temporary licensure to physicians who testify as expert witnesses, indicating licensure for exert testimony by physicians has not been addressed by many State Medical Boards (H-265.992 Expert Witness Testimony).

The NCSBN has addressed multi-state licensure through the Nurse Licensure Compact (NLC). In considering actions relevant to the multi-state licensure, the NCSBN determined the most efficient way of enhancing public protection, while retaining state-based authority was to have nurses licensed in their state of residency (http://www.ncsbn.org/ANA7Points120503.pdf). Under the NLC, states maintain the authority for disciplinary actions under the State Nurse Practice Act. The nurse practice acts of most states (including non-compact states) currently authorize Boards of Nursing to take action based on action in another state (http://www.ncsbn.org/NurseLicensureCompactFAQ.pdf).

While recognition of the role of legal nurse consulting as a specialty practice in nursing was affirmed by the ANA in 2006, many State Boards of Nursing have not addressed the nurse expert witness at a local or state level. Wishing to collaborate through guidance and support for LNCs testifying as expert witnesses, judicial systems, and State Boards of Nursing, AALNC holds the following positions:

- Legal nurse consulting be recognized as a specialty practice of nursing within the definition of nursing in each jurisdiction. LNCs acting in the role of RN expert witnesses be held accountable to the scope of nursing practice within each state's definition of nursing practice, without the administrative burden of individual licensure in each state.
- LNCs, testifying as experts, be knowledgeable of the scope of practices within the state where expert testimony is to be delivered, and recognize that testimony as an expert serves a

public interest. The RN expert witness should possess training, education, and experience commensurate with the topic at issue in the expert testimony. The RN expert witness will testify in an impartial clinically competent manner.

- The LNC acting as an RN expert witness be required to hold active license in their residential state, and be held accountable to adhere to standards of care required by the State Board of Nursing in the state in which testimony occurs.
- Any need for disciplinary actions regarding false or misleading testimony be reported to the residential board of nursing for review and disciplinary action as necessary.

Conclusion

While the practice of legal nurse consulting has been recognized by the ANA as a specialty practice of nursing, individual state licensing boards have not addressed the role of the RN expert witness. Until such time as this is addressed by individual Boards of Nursing, the AALNC adopts the above positions as guidance for practice when the LNC functions in the role of RN expert witness.

References

American Association of Legal Nurse Consultants. (2005). *The specialty practice of nursing.* Available at www. aalnc.org

American Association of Legal Nurse Consultants. (2006). *Providing expert witness testimony.* Available at www.aalnc.org

American Nurses Association (ANA). (2006). *Legal nurse consulting: Scope & standards of practice.* Washington, DC. Available at www.aalnc.org

National Council State Boards of Nursing. (2000). *Nurse licensure compact initial adoption by Maryland, Texas, Utah and Wisconsin.* Available at www.ncsbn.org

Appendix H: ALNCCB Position Statement—Certification in Legal Nurse Consulting

Summary

The purpose of this position statement is to define and clarify the role of certification for LNCs and to establish the LNCC program* as the premier certification in this specialty.

Introduction

As a nursing specialty recognized by the ANA, it is vital that LNCs have a pathway to certification that incorporates experiential and educational requirements. The LNCC program is the only certification examination in the field endorsed by the AALNC and accredited by the ABNS.

Background and Discussion

Established in 1997 by AALNC, the ALNCCB is responsible for developing and maintaining a certification program in legal nurse consulting.

---

* The LNCC program is the collective term for all components of the certification process, including policies related to test development, certification, and recertification.

As part of the decision to offer a high-quality certification program, ALNCCB sought accreditation by an outside body and selected ABNS as the most appropriate accreditor. ABNS is an advocate for consumer protection, and is the only accrediting body specifically for nursing certification. ABNS provides a peer-review mechanism that allows nursing certification organizations to obtain accreditation by demonstrating compliance with established ABNS standards.

ALNCCB maintains the only certification in legal nurse consulting accredited by ABNS and endorsed by AALNC. The LNCC program was initially accredited in 1999 and reaccredited in 2004. Accreditation distinguishes the LNCC Program within the field of legal nurse consulting and equates the LNCC credential with credentials from other highly respected programs.

ALNCCB endorses the definition of certification adopted by ABNS: "*Certification* is the formal recognition of the specialized knowledge, skills, and experience demonstrated by the achievement of standards identified by a nursing specialty to promote optimal health outcomes" (ABNS, 2005).

A certification program helps advance the profession, and is one of the required elements for recognition as a nursing specialty. AALNC achieved this milestone in 2006 when the ANA officially recognized legal nurse consulting as a specialty practice of nursing. AALNC, in collaboration with the ANA, published *Legal Nurse Consulting Scope & Standards of Practice*. In this document, the authors note: "Participation in the specialty's certification process demonstrates a level of professionalism and commitment, and allows community recognition of those LNCs who have achieved a higher level of skill and expertise within the specialty" (ANA, 2006).

While RN licensure ensures entry-level competency, certification is the gold standard for demonstrating knowledge and experience in specialty practice. Similar to physician board certification, nursing specialty certification is not achieved at entry into practice. The ABNS Position Statement on the Value of Certification addresses the issue of certification as a standard beyond licensure, noting that: "While state licensure provides the legal authority for an individual to practice professional nursing, private voluntary certification is obtained through individual specialty nursing certifying organizations and reflects achievement of a standard beyond licensure for specialty nursing practice" (ABNS, 2005).

The value of certification also extends to the public. According to ABNS, "The increasingly complex patient/client needs within the current healthcare delivery system are best met when registered nurses, certified in specialty practice, provide nursing care" (ABNS, 2005).

This statement applies to traditional nursing roles as well as legal nurse consulting practice. Similar to certified nurses in other specialties, LNCCs, by virtue of their knowledge and experience in the specialty, can more readily meet the needs of their client than the novice practitioner.

Certification is a commitment that begins at entry into the specialty and continues throughout a nurse's career. Although voluntary, certification allows nursing specialties—including Legal Nurse Consulting—to publicly acknowledge a member's level of experience, judgment, and knowledge. LNCs should commit to building their competency in the field, with a goal of sitting for the LNCC examination.

Conclusion

The LNCC program is designed to promote a level of expertise and professionalism by documenting individual performance as measured against a predetermined level of knowledge in legal nurse consulting; however, it is not intended to determine who is qualified or who shall engage in legal nurse consulting. The LNCC credential allows the public to more readily identify LNCs who have demonstrated a high level of experience, expertise, and commitment to this specialty nursing practice.

LNCs who wish to distinguish themselves in the profession should seek voluntary certification as an LNCC. As the only practice-based certification program that meets national testing standards, the LNCC is comparable to board certification in other nursing specialties. In addition to the personal satisfaction that comes with certification, LNCs who invest their time in achieving and maintaining LNCC certification can be comfortable in the knowledge that they have achieved a credential that has met or exceeded ABNS requirements, and is the gold standard for certification in the specialty.

It is the position of the ALNCCB that

1. Certification is an objective measure of professional knowledge. It demonstrates to the public that an individual has met national testing standards, and has achieved a level of expertise in the specialty.
2. Certification in Legal Nurse Consulting is based on experience and knowledge, and is not achieved at entry into the specialty.
3. The LNCC is the premier certification credential for LNCs, the only certification program accredited by the ABNS.

References

American Board of Nursing Specialties. (2005, March 5). A position statement on the value of specialty nursing certification. Retrieved July 11, 2006, from http://www.nursingcertification.org/position_statements.htm

American Board of Nursing Specialties. (2006). *ABNS value of certification survey executive summary.* Aurora, OH: American Board of Nursing Specialties.

American Nurses Association and American Association of Legal Nurse Consultants. (2006). *Scope and standards of practice for legal nurse consultants.* Silver Spring, MD: Nursesbooks.org.

Iyer, P. W. (Ed.). (2003). *Legal nurse consulting: principles and practice* (2nd ed.). Boca Raton: CRC Press.

Chapter 3

Professionalism, Standards of Practice, and Standards of Professional Performance

Joan Magnusson, BSN, RN, LHRM, LNCC

First Edition
Gretchen Aumman, PhD, BSN, RN and Maureen Orr, BS, RN, CCM, LNCC

Second Edition
Gretchen Aumman, PhD, BSN, RN; Elena Capella, EdD, MPA, MSN, RN, CPHQ, LNCC; Maureen Orr, BS, RN, CCM, LNCC; and Julie Pike, MN, BSN, RN

Contents

Objectives

- Identify the key elements that define a profession relative to nursing practice
- Discuss the relationship between the specialty practice of legal nurse consulting and the profession of nursing
- Define the nursing process as it applies to legal nurse consulting
- Define the Standards of Professional Performance as they apply to legal nurse consulting
- Explain by example how the legal nurse consultant (LNC) can apply the Standards of Practice to a typical case
- Explain by example how the LNC can apply the Standards of Professional Performance to consulting in the legal arena

Introduction

How we define ourselves as a specialized area of nursing practice is the heart of what distinguishes LNCs from other nursing professionals. In order for attorneys, judges and juries, risk managers, insurance adjusters, health care providers, and the public to understand who we are and what we do, we must clearly define our practice and clarify our similarities and differences with other nursing specialties. We are also obligated as professionals to define and ensure our ethics and quality of practice. In practice, our actions must meet criteria that can be measured. Standards provide that basis for practice accountability. The Scope and Standards of Practice were written by the American Association of Legal Nurse Consultants (AALNC) and published by the American Nurses Association (ANA) to meet these professional goals.

    This chapter is designed to provide an overview of how the Standards of Practice and Professional Performance compare the specialty practice of legal nurse consulting with general nursing practice. Because the standards are based on the ANA model of standards and the nursing process, many of the terms in this chapter will be familiar to nurses who have been in active clinical practice. Utilization of the nursing process occurs as second nature to the experienced nurse. With care and thought, that same process is adapted and applied by LNCs to all aspects of their work.

Definition of a Professional

Endeavors have been made to define a profession by identifying various common characteristics. Five attributes generally accepted as essential for an "occupation" to attain recognition as a profession are as follows:

- A high status granted by society because of altruistic motivation and commitment to serve society
- A systematic, unique body of theory, obtained through a university-based education with practical experience to master the knowledge base
- An authority to define the profession and autonomy in its practice
- A code of ethics
- A professional culture that embodies certain values and norms (Chaska, 1990; Moloney, 1998; Oermann, 1991; Quinn & Smith, 1987)

It has been debated for decades whether or not nursing qualifies as a true profession. The discussion itself has promoted recognition of inconsistencies and movement toward solutions, most notably in the areas of educational preparation and control over professional practice. Nursing continues to evolve toward full attainment of these attributes, but it is generally accepted as a professional endeavor.

One of the concepts used to define a profession is that its services are vital to the health and viability of a society. It is generally accepted that nurses provide a valued service based on altruistic motivation. The public assumes that the title of "nurse" carries with it a certain level of expertise and commitment, and accepts nurses as providing essential services desired and needed by society. This assumption, in part, sets the legal precedent of professional *duty*. Many of the changes in health care delivery may further validate nursing as a profession because of its increasing responsibility and authority in public health maintenance as well as illness management.

While the nursing profession may accept various levels of education as entry into practice, a commonality is the knowledge base of health sciences and the nursing process coupled with a minimum level of experience necessary to prepare one for licensure and practice. The continued application of this theory in practice supports the premise of a profession. It is the one common bond that all nurses share.

The concept of autonomy in practice has also been an area of challenge for nursing as well as for many other professions. It is probably true that no single health care professional, with the complexities in providing health care today, can claim absolute autonomy. Changes in the health care system have actually propelled nurses into more autonomous roles (nurse practitioners, clinical specialists, and case managers) as cost-effective providers of health care services.

Professionals have codes of ethics to help regulate their relationships with clients as well as each other. The ANA developed a formal written Code for Nurses in 1985, which was revised to its current version in 2001 (ANA, 2001). Formal codes of ethics are usually based on a set of values and norms that represent the philosophy and practice of the profession.

Professionals have strong values pertaining to their occupational identity. This identity impacts on all aspects of the professional's attitude and behavior toward work and lifestyle. The values established by the profession become the rules of expected behavior among the members of the profession, with expectations of loyalty and adherence.

In examining the role of the nurse as an LNC, one must remember that direct patient care is no longer the defining parameter of what makes a nurse a nurse. How nurses apply health science education and expertise to the ultimate benefactor of the service is the defining parameter. The scope of the practice of nursing may be more aptly defined by using a broad application of the nursing process and applying professional ethics and standards to benefit the health care system and the patients.

Nursing practice in the legal arena seeks to identify and right a wrong, prevent future untoward events, and manage or mitigate injuries resulting from such events. LNCs provide direct and indirect services to that end for patients and the health care system within the legal environment. For example, whether an LNC is working with the plaintiff or defense side of a professional negligence case, the goal is defense of the standard of care. The standard of care directly affects patient care and is defined by the legal as well as the health care practice arena.

Legal Nurse Consulting as a Specialty Practice of Nursing

The AALNC Board of Directors resolved in 1995 that the professional foundation of legal nurse consulting was the practice of nursing, not the practice of law. By applying that foundation in a consulting capacity in the legal arena, AALNC defined a new specialty practice of nursing. The LNC is valued in the legal arena for one's health care education and experience, rather than knowledge of the law. One may apply this special expertise in legal environments that did not previously have the benefit of the nurse's services. In so doing, the quality of the application of the law to health-care-related cases, issues, projects, or practices has been improved. Clients may be attorneys, insurance companies, hospitals, government agencies, or a variety of others. Although knowledge of the law enriches the LNC's contribution, the client depends on the LNC's health care knowledge. The ultimate beneficiary of the LNC's work is the quality of health care.

A duty of any profession is to promulgate standards by which the quality of practice of its members can be assessed. As with other nursing specialty organizations, in 1995 AALNC published the original Scope of Practice and the Standards of Legal Nurse Consulting Practice (AALNC, 1995). In their position statement published in 1996, Role of the Legal Nurse Consultant as Distinct from the Role of the Paralegal and Legal Assistant, AALNC strengthened its affirmation of the development of the specialty practice by calling for nurse educators to develop educational curricula in the specialty in partnership with legal educators (AALNC, 1996).

Standards are authoritative statements by which the profession describes the responsibilities for which its practitioners are accountable. The 1995 Standards of Practice for Legal Nurse Consulting were based on the 1991 ANA model of clinical nursing practice and incorporate the nursing process with adjustments for the context of legal nurse consulting practice. Following ANA's publication of the Nursing's Social Policy Statement in 2003, and the 2004 Nursing: Scope and Standards of Practice, AALNC undertook revising the standards for legal nurse consulting practice. At the time of publishing this book edition, the standards that apply were published in 2006 by AALNC and ANA, entitled *Legal Nurse Consulting: Scope and Standards of Practice*. These standards continue to reinforce the concept that the nursing process provides the LNC with a framework or consistent problem-solving approach to one's specialty practice (see Figure 3.1; American Nurses Association and American Association of Legal Nurse Consultants, 2006).

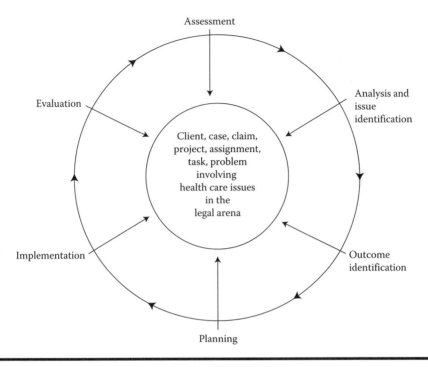

Figure 3.1   Standards of practice for LNCs.

Standards of Practice for LNCs

The Nursing Process as it Applies to Legal Nurse Consulting

The nursing process consists of actions that are logical, interdependent, sequential, but cyclic: assessment, diagnosis, outcomes identification, planning, implementation, evaluation (ANA, 2004). This is a basic problem-solving process or approach to any assignment. Nursing diagnoses are derived from an analysis of the assessment data. All of these actions require critical thinking, the use of clinical experience, and health science education.

In adapting the nursing process to the practice of legal nurse consulting, the following actions are identified: assessment, issue or problem identification, outcomes identification, planning, implementation, and evaluation. The concept of nursing diagnosis is interpreted to mean those opinions formulated by the LNC from analysis of the data to determine health care issues important to resolution of legal claims or cases. Those opinions are called issue or problem identification. The anticipated or hoped-for outcomes of the process are then identified and listed (outcome identification). Planning, implementation, and evaluation of the plan of action follow.

In implementation of the plan, the LNC may assume several roles or functions in coordinating services, health teaching and promotion, or sharing information and decision making that can affect the outcome of the claim (Table 3.1).

The purpose of using the nursing process is to provide the LNC with a framework or consistent problem-solving approach for meeting the needs of the particular case, client, task, or role. This framework also gives the LNC the skills to work with various colleagues in the legal realm so that a successful outcome can be achieved. It also provides the means of measuring how well standards are met by practitioners.

Table 3.1 Comparison of ANA Standards of Nursing Practice and the AALNC Standards of Practice

Clinical Nursing Standards	LNC Practice Standards
Standard 1: Assessment	
The nurse collects data pertinent to the patient's health	The LNC collects data pertinent to the health case or claim
Standard 2: Diagnosis	**Issue or Problem Identification**
The nurse analyzes the assessment data to determine the diagnosis or issues	The LNC analyzes data to determine the issues in the health case or claim
Standard 3: Outcomes Identification	
The nurse identifies expected outcomes for a plan individualized to the patient	The LNC identifies expected outcomes for the individualized plan for a given heath case or claim
Standard 4: Planning	
The nurse develops a plan that prescribes strategies and alternatives to attain expected outcomes	The LNC develops a plan that prescribes strategies and alternatives to attain the expected outcomes
Standard 5: Implementation	
The nurse implements the identified plan	The LNC implements the identified plan
Standard 5A: Coordination of Care/Services	
The nurse coordinates care delivery	The LNC coordinates services related to the health case or claim
Standard 5B: Health Teaching and Health Promotion	
The nurse employs strategies to promote health and a safe environment	The LNC employs strategies to promote a better understanding of health and safety related to a health case or claim
Standard 5C: Consultation	
The nurse provides consultation to influence the plan, enhance the abilities of others, and effect change	The LNC provides consultation regarding a health case or claim to influence the plan, enhance and support the contribution of others, and effect change
Standard 6: Evaluation	
The nurse evaluates progress toward the attainment of outcomes	The LNC evaluates progress toward attainment of outcomes

While the Standards of Practice spell out how LNCs problem-solve and manage tasks, the Standards of Professional Performance constitute the guidelines for the LNC's professional behavior. Adherence to these guidelines will bring a consistency to the practice, so the person engaging in the services of an LNC is assured quality of practice.

Incorporation of the AALNC Standards of Practice and Standards of Professional Performance into one's practice aids in the development of a consistently high standard of practice and job satisfaction, as well as peace of mind that all aspects of an assignment are covered from every possible angle. Meeting the needs of the client generates goodwill and additional work. Having a plan of action to guide the LNC through every assignment results in significant savings of time and energy and ensures a consistent quality product.

The LNC works with a client to obtain the information necessary to make an assessment. After analysis of the case, the issues are discussed jointly. The client often assists with issue/problem identification and outcome identification. Implementation of the plan often occurs in partnership, and evaluation is an ongoing process.

Summary

A plan of action needs thoughtful preparation and a consistent guideline in order to aid professionals in their work. These standards can be adapted and used as such a guide for the LNC. Purposeful thought should be applied to any case or assignment. The steps of assessment, issue and problem identification, outcome identification, planning, implementation, and evaluation will assist LNCs in achieving the best possible outcome of their work.

Application of the Standards of Legal Nurse Consulting Practice and Standards of Professional Performance creates a foundation for the practice. This is illustrated in the examples found in Appendices A and B. LNCs may build on that sound foundation in their own practice based on their individual education, experience, and enthusiasm.

References

American Association of Legal Nurse Consultants (AALNC). (1995). *Scope and standards for the legal nurse consulting practice*. Glenview, IL: American Association of Legal Nurse Consultants.

American Association of Legal Nurse Consultants (AALNC). (1996). *Position statement on the role of the legal nurse consultant as distinct from the role of the paralegal and legal assistant*. Glenview, IL: American Association of Legal Nurse Consultants.

American Association of Legal Nurse Consultants (AALNC). (2005). *Code of ethics and conduct*. Chicago, IL: American Association of Legal Nurse Consultants.

American Nurses Association (ANA). (2001). *Code of ethics for nurses with interpretive statements*. Washington, DC: American Nurses Publishing.

American Nurses Association (ANA). (2004). *Nursing: Scope and standards of practice*. Washington, DC: American Nurses Association.

American Nurses Association and American Association of Legal Nurse Consultants. (2006). *Legal nurse consulting: Scope and standards of practice*. Silver Springs, MD: American Nurses Association.

Chaska, N. L. (1990). *The nursing profession. Turning points*. St. Louis: C.V. Mosby.

Moloney, M. M. (1998). *Professionalization of nursing. Current issues and trends* (3rd ed.). Philadelphia: J.B. Lippincott.

Oermann, M. H. (1991). *Professional nursing practice. A conceptual approach*. Philadelphia: J.B. Lippincott.

Quinn, C. A., & Smith, M. D. (1987). *The professional commitment: Issues and ethics in nursing*. Philadelphia: W.B. Saunders.

Test Questions

1. The key element that *challenges* the premise that nursing is a profession is
   A. The public's perception that nursing services are primarily provided in a hospital setting under the direction of physicians
   B. The lack of a minimum requirement for a university-based education with practical experience to master the knowledge base
   C. The failure of the profession to define nursing and move toward autonomy in practice
   D. The lack of a consistent and uniform Code of Ethics for all nurses

2. To define the nursing process as it applies to legal nurse consulting, the concept of nursing diagnosis equates to
   A. Assessment findings
   B. Outcomes identification
   C. Issue identification
   D. Analysis results

3. To define the Standards of Professional Performance as they apply to legal nurse consulting, which one of the following standards is a function applied primarily in the activities of each of the other standards:
   A. Leadership
   B. Quality of Practice
   C. Research
   D. Ethics

4. After reviewing the testimony of the defendant, the LNC determines that several issues surfaced about the standard of care of another treating physician, which may require other experts be hired in the case. This is known as
   A. Issue identification
   B. Outcomes identification
   C. Planning
   D. Evaluation

5. The best way for the independent LNC to demonstrate one's commitment to the Standard for Professional Practice Evaluation is to
   A. Show one's work product to other LNCs at the local chapter meeting and solicit feedback
   B. Annually track the number of cases each client submits and send Christmas gifts to those who provide the most work opportunities
   C. Compare the amount of income made this year from LNC activities to that made last year
   D. Meet with the client after the submitted work was used in the case to determine whether the materials provided had a positive impact on the resolution

Answers: 1. B, 2. C, 3. A, 4. D, 5. D

Appendix A: Application of the Standards of Practice for the LNC

The following are four examples of activities pertaining to the Standards of Practice. It is important to emphasize that legal nurse consulting is not merely a group of isolated activities, but rather a process. Examples are by no means comprehensive. Not all activities will be undertaken in all assignments. Certain activities may be listed under different headings, depending on assignment or points in time in case progress. Preparation of a chronology, for instance, may be part of assessment in one case, and implementation in another. The examples are meant to give the reader further explanation of how the Standards of Practice can be applied in various situations.

Example 3.1

The LNC working as an investigator for the state licensing board receives a case involving an allegation of sexual misconduct by a psychologist. In this example, emphasis is placed on the LNC's implementation of the identified plan in a reasonable and timely manner, using resources and systems to implement the plan, and the collaboration with colleagues.

Assessment: Data Collection as Basis for Further Activities

The LNC reviews the allegations and pertinent state statutes.

The LNC searches the in-house database and reviews files of two similar previous complaints.

Issue and Problem Identification: Analysis of the Data to Determine the Health Care Issues Related to the Claim

The LNC determines that the case is of a high priority due to seriousness of the charge and previous similar complaints.

The LNC determines that confidentiality is especially critical to all parties due to the nature of the allegations.

Based on the sensitivity of the case, the LNC determines that experts will be needed to testify for the state if probable cause is found.

Outcomes Identification: Results Expected Related to Issue Identification

The LNC determines that the director of investigations should be immediately notified that this is the third complaint regarding this health care provider so that the appropriate board can decide whether immediate temporary action is necessary.

The LNC determines that a completed report should be submitted to the director of investigations within 30 days.

Planning: Plan to Achieve the Expected Outcomes

The LNC asks for case reassignment of two other new cases in order to concentrate on the immediacy of this complaint.

The LNC intimates to the involved parties and witnesses that he or she needs to interview: accused, accuser, and office personnel.

The LNC prepares a list of the accuser's medical records and psychological reports that need to be obtained and reviewed.

The LNC reviews resources to identify which medical experts would be appropriate to conduct a review and give an opinion on the conduct of the accused.

Implementation: Actions Taken to Implement the Plan

The LNC transfers one pending case to another investigator, and places the other on hold as per the supervisor's direction.

The LNC immediately schedules appointments and conducts interviews with the accused, office personnel, and the individual making the accusation.

The LNC reviews and summarizes findings in the accuser's medical records.

The LNC locates and retains an expert psychologist, organizes and submits materials for review, interviews the expert, and summarizes the expert's opinions.

The LNC submits a summary report to the director concluding that the evidence supports the allegations, and makes recommendations for further action.

Evaluation: Determine Progress toward attainment of Outcomes

The LNC notes that the expert psychologist's opinion has confirmed that the behavior of the accused constitutes misconduct.

The LNC follows up with the director to learn whether the recommendations for disposition of the case were followed.

In anticipation of a hearing, the LNC determines whether further information or evidence is needed to support the complaint.

Example 3.2

The LNC working as health care risk manager is notified of the occurrence of a wrong site surgery. In this example, the emphasis is placed on the LNC's coordination of services related to the health case or claim.

Assessment: Data Collection as Basis for Further Activities

The LNC in the role of risk manager obtains a letter of direction from legal counsel to investigate under attorney/client privilege.

The LNC interviews nurses, surgical techs, and physicians involved in the patient's care.

The LNC reviews the medical record documentation and secures the original record for safekeeping.

The LNC reviews the policy on surgical site identification.

The LNC reviews the Joint Commission standards and Sentinel Event Alerts on surgical site identification.

Issue and Problem Identification: Analysis of the Data to Determine the Health Care Issues Related to the Claim

The LNC determines the incident to be a sentinel event in need of a root cause analysis.

The LNC determines the incident to be a potential lawsuit or claim.

The LNC determines that the incident should undergo both physician and nurse peer-review processes.

The LNC determines that appropriate and ongoing communication with patient and family regarding the incident is necessary.

Outcomes Identification: Results Expected Related to Issue Identification

The LNC identifies a need for changes in hospital procedures and practices to prevent a reoccurrence.

The LNC determines, based on current communications with the surgeon, patient, and family, that the claim may be resolved to the satisfaction of the claimant and hospital prior to a lawsuit being filed.

The LNC believes that the process through appropriate peer-review committees will result in improvement in practice of providers.

Planning: Plan to Achieve the Expected Outcomes

The LNC identifies appropriate participants for a working meeting to conduct a root cause analysis.

The LNC arranges for copies of medical records to be sent to counsel and the insurance representative.

The LNC arranges meetings with defense counsel to review the case and schedule interviews with the employees involved.

The LNC discusses patient and family communications with the surgeon and nurse manager to determine the appropriate persons to provide ongoing information.

Implementation: Actions Taken to Implement the Plan

The LNC prepares a packet of information for the root cause analysis team meetings and facilitates the process.

The LNC ensures the implementation of practice and process changes developed in team meetings.

The LNC ensures completion of quality assurance monitoring of practice and process changes.

The LNC reports a summary of the case and root cause analysis to quality committees, hospital board of directors, Joint Commission, and state licensing boards, depending on laws and guidelines.

The LNC works with the attorney and insurance adjuster to arrive at a fair and equitable resolution with the patient and family.

Evaluation: Determine Progress toward attainment of Outcomes

The LNC follows up with the surgeon, surgery department staff, and manager for evaluation of the root cause analysis process.

The LNC evaluates case preparation and the settlement with defense counsel.

The LNC reports the outcome to the hospital board of directors and answers any questions.

The LNC responds to the Joint Commission in the event of an on-site survey.

Example 3.3

The LNC who is skilled in life-care planning is hired by a plaintiff attorney to determine the long-term damages for the adolescent victim of a drunk-driving moving vehicle accident. The teenager suffered a significant closed head injury. This example illustrates the LNC's role in health teaching related to the impact of the illness or injury on a health case or claim.

Assessment: Data Collection as Basis for Further Activities

The LNC reviews the medical records pertaining to treatment of injuries due to the accident.

The LNC requests the adolescent's prior medical records to identify any preexisting physical or mental condition.

The LNC reviews the adolescent's school records and testing for the years preceding and following the accident.

The LNC evaluates the teenager and family in their home.

Issue and Problem Identification: Analysis of the Data to Determine the Health Care Issues Related to the Claim

The LNC determines that the teenager's grades have gone from above average to below average in school.

The LNC determines that the teenager will require long-term cognitive and physical rehabilitation.

Outcomes Identification: Results Expected Related to Issue Identification

The LNC will be able to develop and document a long-term plan of care, detailing costs of care, with the goal of returning the child to the optimum level of function considering the injury.

The plan and costs for care and services will be accepted by the defendants in settlement or by jury at trial.

A video of the child's rehabilitation would favorably impress the defendants at settlement or a jury if the case goes to trial.

Planning: Plan to Achieve the Expected Outcomes

The LNC will set appointments to interview current caregivers, therapists, and neuropsychologist.

The LNC will set appointments to interview the adolescent's teachers.

The LNC recommends to the attorney that a rehabilitation video be produced.

Implementation: Actions Taken to Implement the Plan

The LNC solicits recommendations for future care from current caregivers, therapists, and neuropsychologist.

Based on multiple sources of information, the LNC writes the plan of care and obtains and
calculates costs for all care and services.

With attorney approval, the LNC facilitates the videotape production of the child's daily
rehabilitation program with the videographer and the various rehabilitation caregivers.

Evaluation: Determine Progress toward attainment of Outcomes

The LNC seeks feedback from the attorney regarding the plan data and costs of care report.

The LNC is able to successfully defend the life-care plan in deposition.

The life-care plan is used to support the demand for settlement and facilitates a resolution
prior to trial.

The defense attorney who deposed the LNC calls the LNC three months later requesting
review of a life-care plan submitted to his firm in another case.

Example 3.4

The family of a resident of a long-term care facility who died unexpectedly after undergoing multiple surgeries notified the facility that they are considering filing suit. The LNC has been engaged
by an attorney client to evaluate the claim for merit. This example emphasizes the LNC's role in
consultation regarding a health case or claim to influence the plan, enhance, and support the
contribution of others and effect change.

Assessment: Data Collection as Basis for Further Activities

The LNC reviews medical records from the hospital where the surgeries were performed, the
nursing home facility, and the hospital where the patient was taken prior to her death.

The LNC requests and reviews a copy of the death certificate and autopsy report to determine the cause of death.

The LNC reviews the literature pertaining to the applicable state regulations for medical
care rendered in a long-term care facility.

The LNC obtains and reviews medical literature regarding the indications for, risks of, and
known complications of the surgeries.

The LNC prepares a timeline summary (chronology) of the hospital and nursing home care
from the records obtained.

The LNC attends the attorney's interviews of the decedent's family members to gain more
information regarding the decedent's condition and interaction with the health care
providers prior to death.

Issue and Problem Identification: Analysis of the Data to Determine the Health Care Issues
Related to the Claim

Based on the timeline summary and the state's requirements for documentation, the LNC
determines that a portion of the records pertaining to the care in the nursing home is
missing.

Based on the information from the hospital records, autopsy report, and medical research
information, the LNC determines that the decedent's cause of death was not an expected
or known risk of the surgical procedures.

Based on a comparison of interviews with family members and analysis of the timeline of
events, the LNC identifies long periods of time lacking patient assessment by nursing
personnel and a delay in obtaining appropriate treatment.

The LNC determines that based on current information available, the decedent's death may
have been due to lack of appropriate care in the nursing home.

Outcomes Identification: Results Expected Related to Issue Identification

The LNC determines that the missing records may contain information to support (or refute)
the alleged negligence and should be obtained if they exist.

The LNC determines that an RN (registered nurse) experienced in the care of patients in
long-term care facilities would be an appropriate expert to render an opinion on the
standard of care.

Planning: Plan to Achieve the Expected Outcomes

The LNC recommends that the client request additional records and forward them to the LNC for review.

The LNC recommends that the client retain nursing standard of care experts to review the case and render opinions.

Implementation: Actions Taken to Implement the Plan

The client requests the missing records and informs the LNC that the facility responded that no such records exist.

The LNC interviews three nursing experts in long-term care, verifying qualifications and clinical experience, availability, testimony experience, and fees.

The LNC consults with the client regarding which expert he or she recommends based on the above criteria.

The LNC organizes material to be sent to the expert and sends a memo to the client concerning when to expect a response from the reviewer.

Evaluation: Determine Progress toward attainment of Outcomes

The LNC and the client review the response of the expert to determine whether the issues initially identified were correct.

Based on the expert's opinion, the client determines that the case has merit.

The LNC and the client revise the plan of action to begin pursuit or defense of the claim.

Appendix B: Standards of Professional Performance for the LNC*

The following content includes the complete standards statements from *Legal Nurse Consulting: Scope and Standards of Practice* (pp. 16–35). The application of the professional performance standards in LNC practice involves consideration of the accompanying measurement criteria. The expanded description for each measurement criterion includes specific, but not exhaustive, real life practice exemplars that could be used as performance goals or evaluation metrics.

Standard 7: Quality of Practice (ANA, 2006, p. 25)

The LNC systematically enhances the quality and effectiveness of nursing practice.

The accompanying measurement criteria address the LNC's:

1. Demonstration of quality through documentation of the application of the nursing process. This must be accomplished in a responsible, accountable, and ethical manner.

   Example: The LNC develops a job description for his or her role in a law firm that includes language about using the Standards of Practice being the framework describing and guiding LNC practice.

   Example: The LNC collects and maintains data on the volume, type, and results of the activities performed for each of one's clients

2. Use of results from quality improvement activities to create changes in nursing practice and the health care delivery system.

---

* Standard statements taken from the American Nurses Association, *Legal Nurse Consulting: Scope and Standards of Practice* published by Nursesbooks.org. With permission.

Example: The LNC recommends revision of the firm's current LNC job description based on the findings of a careful analysis comparing the current "as is" business practice model with the desired "to be" future state.

Example: Based on implementation of new policies and procedures for LNCs working in an insurance claim department, the LNC makes recommendations for changes to facilitate processing of claims.

3. Use of innovation and creativity in nursing practice to improve the delivery of legal nurse consulting services.

Example: The LNC evaluates various software programs and purchases a new program that will allow more flexibility in the use of individualized chronologies and reports.

Example: The LNC develops a more convenient and faster mechanism of electronic access to information for clients and experts that ensures compliance with confidentiality mandates.

4. Incorporation of new knowledge to initiate changes in nursing practice. This is especially necessary if desired outcomes are not achieved.

Example: Based on an analysis of client activity, the independent LNC sets meetings with those clients who show a decline in use of their services to identify issues or problems and how services may be improved.

Example: The LNC learns that the jury who heard her expert testimony on nursing standard of care did not find her opinions credible. As a result, the LNC seeks education on improving communication methods and testifying techniques in the future.

5. Participation in activities that improve quality of practice.

Example: The LNC develops policies and procedures for LNCs and others working in an insurance claim department to provide consistency in the method of data collection and report writing.

Example: The LNC drafts a revision of the data collection form pertaining to claimants in a product liability mast tort case to assure all necessary data are collected.

Standard 8: Education (ANA, 2006, p. 27)

The LNC attains knowledge and competency that reflect current nursing practice.

The accompanying measurement criteria address the LNC's:

1. Participation in ongoing educational activities related to appropriate knowledge bases and professional issues.

Example: The LNC reads professional specialty practice, health care and law journals applicable to one's LNC practice.

Example: The LNC attends the annual AALNC educational conference and selects concurrent sessions that are useful to his or her subspecialty.

2. Demonstration of a commitment to lifelong learning through self-reflection and inquiry to identify learning needs.

Example: The LNC seeks information regarding the requirements to maintain licensure in each state in which one is licensed and obtains all necessary knowledge and skills.

Example: The LNC maintains membership in relevant nursing specialty organizations and professional nursing associations to keep current on the issues and developments in the profession and specialty.

3. Efforts to seek experiences that reflect current practice in order to maintain skills and competence in clinical practice or role performance.

Example: The LNC attends continuing education programs pertaining to clinical nursing and medical practice most relevant to his or her LNC practice.

Example: The LNC subscribes to nursing or medical websites that provide regular updated information pertaining to current or new developments in health care.

4. Acquisition of knowledge and skills appropriate to the specialty area, practice setting, role, or situation.

Example: The LNC who works for a plaintiff's medical malpractice firm attends a seminar offered by the American Association for Justice on the latest issues in medical malpractice litigation.

Example: The LNC working in the area of insurance management attends seminars on workers' compensation law and case management.

5. Maintenance of professional records that provide evidence of competency and lifelong learning.

Example: The LNC keeps accurate records for the maintenance and renewal of one's license.

Example: The LNC keeps accurate records for the maintenance and renewal of one's specialty certification.

6. Efforts to seek experiences and formal and independent learning activities to develop and maintain clinical and professional skills and knowledge.

Example: The LNC working primarily with environmental and toxic tort claims attends university courses pertaining to public health.

Example: The LNC earns nursing continuing education credits by completing such offerings in professional nursing journals and other similar publications.

7. Acquisition and maintenance of professional certifications, as available, in the areas of expertise, such as a clinical specialty nursing practice and that of the Legal Nurse Consultant Certified.

Standard 9: Professional Practice Evaluation (ANA, 2006, p. 28)

The LNC evaluates one's own nursing practice in relation to professional practice standards and guidelines, relevant statutes, rules and regulations.

The accompanying measurement criteria address the LNC's:

1. Provision of services in a culturally and ethnically sensitive manner.

Example: The LNC conducts an annual survey of clients to determine how the work product was perceived by the client and the parties in the case.

Example: Based on an analysis of client activity, the LNC meets with those clients who show a decline in use of their services to discuss how services may be improved.

2. Self-evaluation of practice on a regular basis, identifying areas of strength as well as areas in which professional development would be beneficial.

Example: The LNC who has five employees periodically and systematically reviews the business plan, progress of the business, and consults persons or programs with the expertise to recommend improvements.

Example: The LNC employed by a law firm considers one's contribution and role in the firm when determining which educational programs to attend at the national AALNC conference.

3. Efforts to seek feedback regarding ones own practice from peers, professional colleagues, clients, and others.

Example: The LNC asks a coworker LNC to review a life-care plan for accuracy and completeness before it is submitted to the client.

Example: The LNC serving as an expert witness seeks feedback from the client to determine how style of presentation of information to the jury could be improved.

4. Participation in systematic peer review as appropriate.

Example: The LNC employed by a law firm meets on a regular basis with the employer or senior LNC for performance appraisal.

Example: The independent LNC establishes a mentoring relationship with another LNC who works in a similar setting to assist in quality of performance evaluation without breaching client confidentiality.

5. Action taken to achieve goals identified during the evaluation process.

Example: The LNC discontinues recommending medical experts who were not able to meet client deadlines and searches for new qualified experts to replace them.

Example: The LNC providing expert witness testimony plans for more preparation time with the client prior to trial in the future.

6. Provision of rationale for practice beliefs, decisions, and actions as part of the informal and formal evaluation process.

Example: Based on implementation of new policies and procedures, the LNC makes recommendations for changes to facilitate processing of insurance claims.

Example: The LNC elaborates on the potential complications and related expenses in the life-care plan to better provide the information the client is seeking.

Standard 10: Collegiality (ANA, 2006, p. 30)

The LNC interacts with and contributes to the professional development of peers and colleagues. The accompanying measurement criteria address the LNC's:

1. Sharing of knowledge and skills with peers and colleagues as evidenced by such activities as participating in case conferences or presentations at meetings, presenting an educational program at an AALNC meeting, or submitting an article to a professional journal.

Example: The LNC participates in roundtable discussions at the AALNC Networking Luncheon on selected topics pertaining to the organization of work product information.

Example: The LNC who is a certified wound care nurse presents a program to one's local chapter on the standards of practice pertaining to wound care assessment and treatment.

2. Provision of feedback to peers regarding their practice or role performance.

Example: The LNC answers questions posed by a subcontracting LNC regarding the clarity and accuracy of a work product.

Example: The senior LNC in the firm explains to the new LNC the distinction between the roles of the firm's paralegals versus the roles of LNCs.

3. Maintenance of professional, collegial relationships.

Example: The LNC obtains new information regarding the changes in Medicare reimbursement guidelines regarding "never events" and shares it with members at the local chapter meeting.

Example: The LNC participates in online LNC e-communities discussions so as to support and improve the practice of the participants.

4. Contribution to an environment conducive to the education of nurses entering the field of legal nurse consulting.

Example: The LNC welcomes interested nurses who attend the local chapter meetings and encourages them to obtain AALNC written, audio, and video educational resources.

Example: The LNC gives a presentation to the local college LNC program on the LNC's role in preparing a personal injury case for trial.

5. Contribution to an environment conducive to the education of peers, colleagues, attorneys, patients and families, jurors, and others.

Example: The LNC obtains a Groshong catheter and demonstrates its use to the attorney in a case of negligence in which a home health nurse allegedly misused it, causing a severe injury.

Example: The LNC participates in an educational program for an agency of home health nurses on the most common areas of liability in their clinical practice.

6. Action as a mentor to other LNCs and colleagues as appropriate.

Example: The LNC mentors the less experienced LNC just hired by the employer agency by sharing how work product is constructed and offers suggestions on assignments when asked.

Example: The LNC participates in one's chapter mentoring program by offering to be available to answer general practice questions individually or in group settings.

7. Contribution to a supportive and healthy work environment.

Example: The LNC reviews the marketing plan of a colleague and suggests ways to increase visibility among clients.

Example: The LNC evaluates billing procedures for a less experienced colleague and advises changes to improve fee collections.

Standard 11: Collaboration (ANA, 2006, p. 31)

The LNC collaborates with clients and others in the conduct of legal nurse consulting practice.

The accompanying measurement criteria address the LNC's:

1. Communication with members of the legal profession, health care providers, patients and families as appropriate.

Example: The LNC working with the plaintiff's attorney confers with the treating pulmonologist about the medical consequences of inhalation of toxic fumes in a case of inhalation of a combination of burned chemicals.

Example: The LNC working with the defense attorney clarifies with the client what access the LNC will have in gaining information from the defendant or providing information to the defendant.

2. Collaborations with others in creating a documented plan focused on outcomes and decisions related to care and delivery of services.

Example: The LNC with primary expertise in mental health was consulted to review an obstetrical case. Rather than spending days of research and hours of billable time, he refers the case to an LNC who has background in obstetrics and ready access to the research material. Not only is time and money saved for the client, but the credibility of the referring LNC is enhanced.

Example: The LNC meets with the client to discuss whether one medical expert could be used to address the standards of care of the physicians and nurses in a case involving the unexpected death of a patient in an acute care setting.

3. Partnership with others to effect change and generate positive outcomes through knowledge of the patient or situation.

Example: The LNC working as risk manager is presented with a surgical sentinel event in which the patient died in the operating room (OR) in a small rural hospital. A root cause analysis was done and the anesthesiologist and surgeon's management is to be peer reviewed. To obtain an objective review, the risk manager contracts with an appropriate anesthesiologist and surgeon in a nearby community; and presents their reviews to the Department of Surgery for consideration and action as indicated.

Example: The LNC working with a defense firm has accumulated years of data showing how nursing documentation had helped or harmed the attorney in defending that the nursing standard of care was met. The LNC contracts with the client's insurance defense company to present programs to the hospital staff on the appropriateness of nursing documentation.

4. Documentation of communications and referrals as appropriate.

Example: The LNC prepares a memo to the attorney client that summarizes the medical expert's opinions regarding standards of care, injuries, and causal relationships and makes recommendations for other experts that may be needed.

Example: The LNC working for a worker's compensation insurance firm drafts a report to the adjuster after attending a medical evaluation with the patient that details the events that occurred and any recommendations made by the health care provider.

Standard 12: Ethics (ANA, 2006, p. 32)

The LNC integrates ethical provisions in all areas of practice.

The accompanying measurement criteria address the LNC's:

1. Use of the ANA Code for Nurses with Interpretive Statements (ANA, 2001) and the AALNC Code of Ethics and Conduct to guide practice (AALNC, 2005).

Example: The LNC avoids bias in one's opinions on the merits of a case due to the person's social or economic status, personal attributes, or nature of health problems.

Example: The LNC avoids taking assignments or providing information that is beyond the scope of nursing practice or that may be considered as the practice of law or medicine.

2. Advocacy by promoting professional standards of practice.

Example: The LNC bases opinions and recommendations on the published theory and practices of the health sciences, as well as one's knowledge gained through clinical experience.

Example: The LNC acting as nurse expert witness provides an objective opinion regardless of whether engaged by the defense or plaintiff attorney.

3. Maintenance of confidentiality within the legal and regulatory parameters.

Example: The LNC adheres to ethics of confidentiality by refraining from discussing any issues pertaining to the merits of a case with anyone except the client who engaged him or her, the client's employees, or the party whom the client represents.

Example: The LNC providing expert witness testimony clarifies with the client when the LNC's communications and opinions may become discoverable and prepares written reports only on the request of the client.

4. Maintenance of a professional relationship in the health care and legal environment.

Example: The LNC avoids using defamatory language in writing or when talking about the persons involved in any case.

Example: The independent LNC is asked to review a case involving care rendered at a facility that is part of the same hospital chain where the LNC works clinically. The LNC declines the case on the premise that this could be construed as a conflict of interest by the other party or the LNC's employer.

5. Commitment to practicing self-care, managing stress, and connecting with self and others. Example: An attorney who does a high volume of personal injury claims and could be a good source for future work asks the LNC to review several potential claims and prepare a summary of each claim. However, the attorney is not willing to pay for more than 1 hour of review time on each claim. The LNC renegotiates how the assignment will be done on the basis that an adequate and valid review cannot be made with those financial restrictions. Example: At the time of engagement, the LNC establishes with the client an agreed upon deadline for the completion of the scope of work that will meet the client's needs as well as not overburden the LNC's ability to meet other personal and professional commitments.

6. Contribution to resolving ethical issues of patients, colleagues, or systems as evidenced by such activities as participating on ethics committees. Example: The LNC was working for an attorney who is being investigated by the State Bar Grievance Committee. When called to testify, the LNC provides information based on factual knowledge or relevant observations of the attorney's practice. Example: The LNC who is working clinically and witnesses the unethical treatment of a patient cooperates with any committee investigation into identifying the cause and preventing the promotion of such practice.

7. Reporting of illegal, incompetent, or impaired practice. Example: The LNC working as a risk manager provides information to the appropriate regulatory agencies regarding an employee's sexual misconduct with a patient. Example: The LNC working in a large law firm witnesses another LNC misrepresenting herself in a telephone conversation in order to obtain information, and reports the behavior to the supervising attorney.

8. The LNC participates on multidisciplinary and interdisciplinary teams that address ethical risks, benefits, and outcomes. Example:
   A. The LNC on a legal team investigating a personal injury case determines that the medical records indicate the injured child may be suffering physical abuse by the parent and discusses with the attorney client how best to address seeking assistance for protection of the child.
   B. The LNC working as a risk manager participates in hospital and medical staff committees to give input on how committee decisions may impact the risks, benefits, and outcomes of patient safety.

Standard 13: Research (ANA, 2006, p. 33)

The LNC integrates research findings into practice.
   The accompanying measurement criteria address the LNC's:

1. Use of the best available evidence to critically analyze, interpret, and apply research to guide decisions about the health case or claim. Example: The LNC relies on information published by peer-reviewed health care journals, governmental agencies, and evidenced-based medical guidelines and recommendations as resources to determine the facts about standards of care, disease processes, and causative issues. Example: The LNC verifies that the date of publication of the medical literature to be used as a resource or evidence is consistent with the time of the events in the health case or claim.

2. Active participation in research activities such as a formal research committee or program; or by using research findings to evaluate the appropriateness of policies, procedures, and standards of practice as applied to the health case or claim.

Example: The LNC has a strong background in oncology and nursing home administration. She is working in-house for a large firm that is involved in obtaining patents for new pharmaceuticals. The work entails development of spreadsheets that detail the results of the physicians' clinical trials. The LNC's expertise enables him or her to interpret the data and inform the attorneys of the implications of the results.

Example: The LNC completes and returns a practice analysis survey questionnaire developed by one's professional association's certification program.

Standard 14: Resource Utilization (ANA, 2006, p. 34)

The LNC considers factors related to safety, effectiveness, cost, and impact on practice in the planning and evaluation of the health case or claim.

The accompanying measurement criteria address the LNC's 3:

1. Evaluation of factors such as safety, effectiveness, availability, cost and benefits, efficiency, and impact on practice when assessing options that would result in the same expected outcome.

Example: The LNC is asked to review a case in which a patient developed paralysis after an anterior thoracic diskectomy and locate experts to testify on deviation and causation. The surgical reports indicate that the team of physicians included an anesthesiologist, an orthopedic surgeon, and a thoracic surgeon. In searching for expert physicians to assist in the case, the LNC was able to locate an anesthesiologist expert as well as expert neurosurgeon skilled in this surgical procedure who could address the standard of care issues regarding the surgery as well as the causation issues regarding spinal blood supply.

Example: The LNC as risk manager receives a call from a nearby hospital reporting a possible Emergency Medical Treatment and Labor Act (EMTALA) violation by the risk manager's hospital. The risk manager's investigation includes a review of the medical record, and interviews with the emergency room (ER) physician, nursing staff, medical director, and nurse manager. After determining the hospital may not have complied with a key element of the law, the risk manager arranges a phone conference with the hospital's attorney and chief executive officer to present the case, assess liability, and decide whether to self-report to the Center for Medicare and Medicaid Services (CMS).

2. Assignment and delegation of tasks based on the health case or claim as appropriate.

Example: The LNC working in-house for an insurance defense firm supervises their national team of LNCs. A case has arrived on her desk that demands a response in 3 days and involves an incident in a pediatric intensive care unit. The LNC locates a consultant who has recent pediatric intentive care unit experience and who also works well under the pressures of a deadline.

Example: The LNC receives a large stack of medical records, which need to be organized, paginated, and indexed for use as a trial exhibit. The LNC assigns the task to his or her clerk assistant with experience in organizing large volumes of documents for trial.

3. Assistance to the public in becoming informed consumers about the options, costs, risks, and benefits of treatment and care as appropriate.

Example: The LNC prepares a spreadsheet of health care costs and expenses relevant to the treatment of the injuries in the claim for client's use in quantifying this portion of the claim for damages.

Example: The LNC is working on a catastrophic brain injury case with the workers' compensation attorney. The LNC reviews the life-care plan and conducts a survey to locate a suitable rehabilitation facility within the insurance company's providers that will meet the injured person's needs.

Standard 15: Leadership (ANA, 2006, p. 35)

The LNC provides leadership in the professional practice setting and the profession.

The measurement criteria for this standard address the LNC's efforts to provide leadership through diligent practice in this nontraditional nursing role. The LNC's ability to create a successful practice while maintaining healthy professional relationships and ethical practice is a demonstration of leadership. Leadership is also demonstrated by the LNC's commitment to lifelong learning, teaching, and mentoring. The LNC provides leadership by participating in professional associations, committees, councils, and administrative teams whose goals are to improve quality of practice or quality of patient care. Leadership is also exhibited by the LNC who is able to define a clear vision, associated goals, and a plan to implement and measure progress. The LNC leader remains creative and flexible through times of change and demonstrates energy, excitement, and a passion for quality work.

Most of the examples given in each of the previous Standards of Professional Performance illustrate the LNC's leadership activities. The function of leadership may be demonstrated by performing consistent, reliable, and safe practice while promoting others to do the same.

Chapter 4

Elements of Triage
Effective Case Screening of Medical Malpractice Claims

Phyllis ZaiKaner Miller, RN

First Edition
Julie Bogart and Doreen James Wise, EdD, MSN, RN

Second Edition
Marguerite Barbacci, BSN, RN, MPH, RNC, LNCC; Doreen James Wise, EdD, MSN, RN; Susan Mahley, BSN, MSN, RNC, C-WHNP; Julie Pike, MN, BSN, RN; and Renee Wilson, BSN, MS, RN

Contents

Objectives

Upon completion of the chapter, the reader will be able to:

- Define the process of "triaging" medical malpractice cases under investigation
- Discuss how effective triage contributes to building your business
- Name at least five elements to consider when screening every medical malpractice case
- Define the three types of damages and give examples of each
- Explain the difference between negligence and "known complication"
- Name where jury instruction guides can be obtained for each state

Introduction

Legal nurse consultants (LNCs) pride themselves on producing excellent work products. Medical record summaries are created, research on assigned topics is completed, and experts to review and testify on a given topic are identified in the time frame requested. What many LNCs fail to recognize is how their work product fits into the larger picture of the investigation and litigation of a claim. Many LNCs wonder why they do not get repeat business from an attorney who just months before told them their work product was fine. Understanding how the LNC's work fits into the larger picture of claims management will make the LNC work product more valuable to the attorney and provide the attorney with new insights and strategies in the successful pursuit or defense of potential or actual claims. This chapter will make clear the process that LNCs need to implement to provide a product more valuable than completion of singular assignments or tasks. It will explain the critical thinking and analytical concepts necessary to analyze case facts in the context of the legal framework of medical negligence.

Analysis of a medical malpractice claim is as much about medicine as law. Blending the talents of the lawyer who understands the law and the advocacy system with those of an LNC, who is schooled in scientific and medical concepts and has a basic understanding of how the disciplines of law and medicine fit together, makes for a more successful endeavor for the attorney and increased satisfaction for the LNC.

When discussing a new assignment regarding an actual or potential medical malpractice case with an attorney, regardless of whether one is working for the plaintiff or defense, inquire about the elements of triage which are discussed in detail in this chapter. Complete information about the elements of the case will assist the LNC in providing a work product that will be truly helpful to the case. For example, after becoming familiar with the facts and other elements of a case, the LNC may suggest additional or alternative projects from the one assigned that would be more useful and help the attorney to be successful in pursuing or defending a claim.

Not all attorneys handling medical malpractice consider it their area of specialty, and even those who do, do not always understand the subtleties of the science and medicine pertinent to the case. The LNC should discuss the analysis of the elements, and in particular, missing or difficult elements. It might even be the case that analysis of the elements brings up new or different areas of inquiry or research that the attorney had not considered. The LNC who points out issues with the potential to blindside the attorney will be making a valued contribution. No attorney wants to be unprepared.

While the decision to proceed with or defer a potential claim and how to conduct that endeavor ultimately rests with the attorney, giving the attorney warning of potential pitfalls likely to be encountered is a valuable service. Sometimes a lawyer may be eager to pursue a case believing it has the potential for a large settlement or verdict because the client is very injured or because the story has "great jury appeal." After reviewing the case and carefully considering the elements, a knowledgeable LNC may realize that further pursuit of that claim would be difficult at best. The lawyer may not want to hear this at first, but with tact and diplomacy, the LNC's professional analysis and opinion will ultimately be valued. Although the information may not be what the attorney wanted to hear, the attorney will be appreciative as long as the basis for a "less than optimistic" outlook for the potential success of the claim is explained, and is based on sound analysis and judgment. The lawyer will see this contribution as more valuable than summarizing records on a case with little chance of success of pursuit or defense.

Elements of Triage

- Liability/negligence
- Damages
- Causation
- Statute of limitations
- Contributory/comparative negligence
- Economics
- Conflict of interest
- The defendants
- The client
- Other considerations and case types

Each item will be explained with an example given to illustrate the element.

Liability/Negligence

Negligence on the part of a Health Care Provider (HCP) requires four elements to be proved. They are Duty, Breach of Duty, Damages, and Causation. The last two elements will be discussed in detail later in this chapter.

Duty on the part of an HCP is dependent on the existence of a provider–patient relationship (Am Jur, 2002, p. 292). An example of a HCP without such a relationship would be a HCP testifying as an expert regarding the mental health of one of the parties in a divorce claim based on the review of past records.

Breach of Duty is the second component. It is often referred to as liability or negligence. Although states have worded this concept variously, the basic premise is that HCPs have a duty to adhere to the applicable standard of care. They are not required to deliver the highest degree of care possible and they are entitled to exercise individual judgment. They are required to exercise that degree of reasonable skill and care expected of a reasonable competent practitioner in similar circumstances (Am Jur, 2002, pp. 296–297). Breach of duty/liability must be proven through expert testimony that sets forth the applicable standard and the specifics of the deviation from that standard.

The plaintiff's attorney will first hear of the potential case from facts gleaned from the potential client in an interview. The plaintiff should be engaged in a thorough discussion of what the HCP did wrong. The presence of an LNC at this interview can be quite beneficial. Know from the outset that most patients seeking the advice of an attorney regarding a potential claim believe that compensation depends on the degree of injury suffered and the fact that it happened during the course of health care. Many people believe that if they had an infection, allergic reaction, or unexpected unpleasant side effect, they are entitled to compensation. Do not believe that all the elements of a successful claim are present merely because someone is sick or injured. This does not constitute liability (Eisberg, 1990).

Some clients believe that there is compensation due to them if the doctor was rude or late or did not return calls. This likewise does not constitute liability. They also believe that a subsequent treating physician's utterance of "we never do that here" or "this never should have happened" is a defacto statement that there is liability. It is not. The first may only indicate that different HCPs do things differently. The second may only be an expression of empathy, meaning that the new HCP believes things could have gone alright but for this unexpected complication or adverse event. Neither of these statements is an indictment of prior care.

The investigation of liability should not be confined to what the plaintiff thinks went wrong. Listen to the story and always consider that the patient and family are unlikely to be medically sophisticated and often are unable to state what action or omission caused their problem. Many, if not most, patients and their families cannot state the name of their diagnosis or the purpose of the surgery they underwent. Unless the issue is clear, such as operating on the wrong extremity, listen for clues in the story that may reveal the real facts. Do not be afraid to follow a hunch or educated guess in the course of the initial. Many times, through interview of the potential plaintiff and/or review of the records, it will be discovered that what the plaintiff believes to be negligence is actually acceptable care. However, by using critical thinking, the LNC may discover an entirely different act of negligence, never considered by the potential plaintiff, which could be responsible for causing the plaintiff's injuries.

An example of this would be the client recently hospitalized for amputation of her leg after an episode of gangrene. She is angry about a postoperative infection in the stump and the treatments she received for it. Starting a claim based on a theory of infection after a surgery and the difficulties encountered during treatments is not likely to be successful in terms of liability, the most critical element, because infection is a known complication and not generally considered to constitute liability. But, using critical thinking and analysis, the following story emerged. Upon questioning, the caller agreed with the LNC's assumption that she is diabetic and has been for several years. Gangrene in long-standing diabetics is not unusual or thought to be due to malpractice. In asking more questions the LNC learned that a tiny sore had developed on her big toe a year ago. The wound kept getting bigger and deeper, but did not really hurt. Her doctor never gave her any treatment beyond some ointment and never referred her to a wound care expert or surgeon. She did not know what an A1C was, or have regular blood work drawn. She took her insulin or checked her glucose "sometimes when I think I need it." These facts may support a claim of negligence for failure to properly treat diabetes and related complications, ultimately resulting in the amputation. Clearly, to the plaintiff, the amputation is a bigger injury than a stump infection. None of these facts were part of the initial complaint by the patient. The lesson: never assume the client (or the attorney) knows all the facts or understands the medical issues. Just listen, ask, and think critically.

Consider the following as these concepts form the basis for negligence. Has the HCP acted outside the accepted standards of practice? Was something done or not done that any reasonable practitioner would have done or not done under the same circumstances? Known or commonly occurring complications or side effects do not typically constitute liability, while failure to recognize and appropriately treat complications may. However, keep in mind that the occurrence of a highly unusual complication may well suggest a breach of care.

HCPs are allowed wide latitude in their judgment when it comes to choosing treatment in most instances. As long as the treatment chosen was within the bounds of reason, even if the choice does not have a good outcome for the patient, it generally is not negligence. Such an example would be administration of an antibiotic that results in a severe reaction. The patient had no known allergies. Although other antibiotics were available, there was no reason for requiring an alternative. On the other hand, if the prescription was for a medication with known cross reactivity with a known allergy, such a prescription may be considered negligent.

Do not determine liability with the benefit of hindsight. In a case of "failure to diagnose," remember that the potential defendant did not know what the reviewer knows. A defendant's liability must be determined based on the information available to the defendant in that time and place and under the circumstances described. A critically thinking LNC will consider the facts available to the HCP at the time. In considering a potential diagnosis, doctors are trained that "when you hear hoof beats, think horses not zebras." They are also taught that atypical presentations of common diseases are more frequent than typical presentations of rare diseases (Groopman, 2007). These old maxims suggest that HCPs will default to the most likely diagnosis as the first working theory of what might be wrong and begin treatment for it. Even if in hindsight the diagnosis and treatment proved to be wrong, it would be hard to make a successful claim of negligent diagnosis if reasonable HCPs seeing those same signs and symptoms could have reached the same diagnosis.

When doing research to document the standard of care, be sure the research matches the period of time relevant to the care delivered. Standards of care change, new imaging techniques are discovered, and medication regimens change. Do not use literature that is either too old or too new to determine the standard of care.

A time and money saving tip: If for some reason it is difficult to determine if the standard of care has been breached without expending a great deal of time or money, assume that liability exists and proceed with the case review to determine if the other elements of negligence are present. It makes no sense to spend time and money to summarize medical records and retain an expert on standard of care if there are other major problems with the case such as an expired statute of limitations (SOLs). If other elements are present, it may be worthwhile to obtain an expert review on liability.

Damages

Damages are divided into three types: special, general, and punitive. Special damages are those things with a monetary value such as medical bills, wage loss and out-of-pocket expenses incurred by the plaintiff as a result of negligence. General damages are injuries on which the law is unable to place a dollar amount such as "pain and suffering." General damages are sometimes referred to as noneconomic or nonpecuniary damages. Punitive damages, also known as exemplary damages, are monetary compensations exceeding general and special damages intended to punish the defendant, to set an example, and to deter future behavior considered "outrageous." Most jurisdictions determine whether punitive damages can or cannot be awarded, and often set a cap on the amount that can be awarded. Punitive damages are very difficult to prove in medical malpractice cases.

The monetary value of any claim is based on the perceived value of the plaintiff's injuries. Thoroughly discuss with the plaintiff all potential damages from the alleged negligence. Because damage is one of the four required elements of a negligence claim, if there are no damages, there is no case, irrespective of the egregiousness of the conduct (Cardaro, 2000).

Every injury has a theoretical value. The astute LNC will consider the full impact of any claimed injury and over time, will get a feeling for how this translates into the monetary amount the attorney is considering. Ask the attorney what he thinks his case is worth. Imagine sitting on a jury and thinking, "How much this should the plaintiff be awarded?" In assessing damages, determine every way in which the plaintiff's life has been changed as a result of the injury. Permanency of an injury and impairment in ability to work or engage in activities of daily living must all be considered in determining damages (Cartwright, 1987; Egan, 2000). Is the injury permanent and/or serious? In cases of death, consider whether the plaintiff's life expectancy would have been reduced even if there had never been any negligence. An injury resulting in a crooked fifth finger in an arthritic older man is far different from the same injury in a concert pianist.

Some jurisdictions recognize a theory of recovery in medical malpractice cases for a patient's loss of chance of survival or loss of chance of a better recovery. Under this theory, the compensable injury is the lost opportunity to achieve a better result, not the physical harm caused by the plaintiff's initial condition. This theory applies when the patient is suffering from a pre-existing injury or illness that is aggravated by the alleged negligence of the HCP to the extent that (1) the patient dies, when without negligence there might have been a substantial chance of survival, or (2) the patient had a chance of surviving his illness but for the delay in diagnosis. Because of the negligence, that chance has been lost. This is different from the claim that the patient had a more than likely expectation of cure that has now been lost due to negligence (Shandell & Smith, 1999).

Some states, such as Minnesota, do not recognize "loss of a chance." In Minnesota, expert testimony is required to prove that a plaintiff would have had a greater than 50% chance of survival or less damage at the time of the alleged negligence and that the negligence caused the plaintiff's chance of survival or permanent injury to drop to less than 50%. The expert testimony requires the phrase "more likely than not," such as "more likely than not would have avoided the amputation but for the negligence." In cases where the statistics are known and published, such as cancer cases, there would be no claim for negligence that reduced the plaintiff's chance of survival from 49% to 0% or from 95% to 51%, but there would be a claim for negligence that reduced the chance of survival from 51% to 49% (Fennell v. Southern Maryland Hospital, 1990). In this last set, the plaintiff went from "more likely than not to survive (51%)" to "not likely to survive (49%)." Knowing the law in this regard is essential when doing the analysis on cases with a known mortality statistics.

Look carefully at the plaintiff's health history when assessing damages. Pre-existing medical conditions (such as a diagnosis of cancer) or surgeries, medical bills, and disability that would have been encountered even with appropriate care are not elements of damage. Are the plaintiff's injuries severe enough to warrant further investigation? Can the injuries be seen on x-rays, electrocardiograms (EKGs), magnetic resonance imaging, or other medical imaging? If the injury is difficult to understand or empathize with, presenting it to a jury and assigning a monetary value may prove difficult. Cases in which the primary injuries cannot be seen by the jurors, such as soft-tissue injuries, mild head injuries, or mental distress, can pose special problems (Shandell & Smith, 1999). Moreover, many jurors have some ache, pain, or malady they suffer every day. Perhaps they have terrible arthritis or a back full of surgical hardware. If what they deal with every day makes the plaintiff's injuries seem trivial, the jury is not likely to award any sum of money for compensation.

Because the value of a claim in a wrongful death is based in large measure on an estimate of life expectancy, absent the alleged negligence, unexpected findings at autopsy can have a major impact on damages and can totally derail a claim. The discovery of a large bulging aortic aneurysm that could have meant near instant death at any time or severe undiagnosed multi-vessel coronary artery disease can significantly impact the damages argument. It will be difficult at best to argue that this person would have lived 20 years but for the negligence.

Causation

The issue of causation or cause is the main battleground and usually the most difficult element of medical negligence to understand and prove. In a medical malpractice case, causation is not ordinarily a common sense thing. Most of the time causation revolves around medicine, science, physiology, pathology, and natural history of disease and illness (Sloan, Githens, Clayton, Hickson & Partlett, 1993). It is this author's opinion that analysis of causation is the place where the trained and critically thinking LNC can make the most difference.

The precise definition of cause for each state can be found in the jury instruction guides for the jurisdiction in questions. The jury instruction guides state the precise language that a judge will read to the jury when instructing them about the information to consider when rendering a verdict. The questions that the jury will be asked to consider are what the attorney will have to prove in court. Jury instruction guides can be found in a local law library or on the Internet.

An example of a jury instruction on causation in Minnesota, as taken from the Jury Instruction Guides—Civil (1999) is: "A direct cause is a cause that had a substantial part in bringing about the injury/harm." This means the jury will have to decide if the negligence of the defendant played a substantial part in bringing about the harm to the plaintiff. Also understand that the expert opinion on this cause question must be offered by a qualified medical expert and must be given "to a reasonable degree of medical certainty." It is not an opinion that hinges on "might have been" or "could have been" or "maybe." It must be a relatively certain opinion based on the expert's knowledge, education, training, and experience, and grounded in science and clinical medicine.

To understand causation the LNC must think carefully about the following questions: Did the negligence cause the injury or damage? Could it have been caused by something or anything else? Did the negligence cause all or only part of the plaintiff's injury? If only part, which part? Is there any reason why the result would or could have been the same in the absence of the negligence? In death cases, could the plaintiff have died of his disease absent any negligence? If so, what are the statistics on morbidity and mortality for that specific condition?

During the course of a case investigation, as new facts are developed the LNC should rethink causation and how the new information fits the existing causation piece. The relationship between liability and cause can become very fuzzy or extremely complicated over the life of a claim. Fuzzy or complicated scientific issues are difficult to explain to a jury for either side. If the scientific or medical basis of the causation argument is hard for the attorney to grasp even with the assistance of skilled LNC and expert, odds are that an insurance adjuster or a jury will not understand it either (Mooney & Kirshenbaum, 2009).

The application and importance of science, disease theory, and physiology in deciphering cause cannot be understated. Here is a simple example. A plaintiff is claiming that a misfiled or ignored routine mammogram report from 14 months ago resulted in failure to diagnose her breast cancer. At the time of her actual diagnosis she is stage IV with many positive lymph nodes and multiple metastatic lesions in her brain. Common sense implies failure to act on the report was negligent. Common sense and cancer treatment dogma infer that the earlier cancer is diagnosed and treated the better. A common sense cause argument would be: She is now a Stage IV and going to die of her cancer because they missed it. But common sense will not win the day. Science and disease theory infers that breast cancer does not go from curable to Stage IV with multiple positive nodes and visible lesions in the brain over a mere 14 months. Disease theory and statistics hold that she likely already had lesions in her brain and positive lymph nodes and was already at an advanced stage of disease, if not stage IV, 14 months earlier. Therefore, it is likely that even 14 months earlier she would have been in need of much of the same treatment and nearly equally likely to die of her disease regardless of what they did with the mammogram report. Therefore, proving that the ignored report and consequent delay *caused* injury may be next to impossible.

In another example, common sense implies that early and aggressive treatment of septic shock saves lives. Arguments from the defense could be many. They include the fact that according to the American Association of Critical Care Nurses (Balk, 2000), septic shock is lethal to approximately 20–50% of all patients although figures vary by microbe, institution, and underlying comorbidities. The defense might say that the patient was already beyond salvage at the time of presentation. Or that the patient's underlying disease would have prevented his recovery or shortened his lifespan regardless of the care given for his sepsis. Perhaps the type of microbe involved in the patient's sepsis is resistant to many antibiotics and difficult to treat successfully at best. It is the role of the LNC to research, understand, and teach on all of these issues to prepare the attorney to better present arguments and defend his or her position. This means delving into the science and physiology of septic shock and the rationale for the recommendations for diagnosis and treatment. Giving an attorney a common sense answer like "earlier treatment is better" is not dealing with causation.

In the fight for causation, beware the autopsy and death certificate. They are very sharp double-edged swords. Worse, sometimes they are wrong (Smith Sehdev & Hutchins, 2001). Do not assume that all autopsies are conducted with the precision of a television drama. In this author's experience, even experienced medical examiners in large cities admit to rarely glancing at the medical records of a patient who died in the hospital, and often taking the patient history and recitation of events from the HCP who delivered the care. Moreover, the person doing the autopsy may not be a particularly curious person by nature or someone who thinks outside the box. The cause of death listed and filed with the county may be in direct conflict with the history and medical record or what the LNC or attorney think brought about that person's death. The LNC using critical thinking would consider several questions. How do the facts in the medical record or patient history mesh with the findings at autopsy? Was anything missed? What was and was not taken into consideration? Were appropriate samples taken? The LNC may suggest a meeting with the Medical Examiner to fill in any missing information or diplomatically try to discuss any concerns or discrepancies. It has been this author's experience that when presented with an alternative-fact scenario taken directly from the medical records, medical examiners may change or amend the autopsy findings and cause of death. Medical examiners also are familiar with court proceedings and often make excellent witnesses.

At the end of a trial, the jury is sent out to deliberate and when they are ready, fill out a form with their conclusions, called the Verdict form. Although some of these forms are long with multiple defendants and additional questions, the two basic yes/no questions are:

1. Was the defendant negligent?
2. Did the negligence play a direct or substantial part in bringing about the injury to the plaintiff?

In order to reach any kind of monetary compensation for the plaintiff, *the answers to both of those questions have to be yes.* Often the answer to the first question regarding negligence is yes and the second question regarding cause is no. A finding of negligence without cause means the plaintiff has lost. Juries have a much easier time understanding and finding negligence than the much more complex concept of causation (Eisberg, 1990). Remember that all the plaintiffs in a medical malpractice claim had an illness or injury that brought them to health care in the first place. The defense will do everything they can to remind the jury that the underlying illness or injury can and does sometimes have a bad outcome even in the best of hands. Therefore, the LNC must understand the natural history and pathophysiology of the disease or injury at issue as well as the science of what went wrong. Depending on outside medical experts for this preliminary teaching and thoughtful analytical discussion is expensive and time consuming. An LNC with a good understanding of, and ability to teach on, these issues can be particularly valuable to the lawyer.

Statute of Limitations

Every state has a different SOL for medical malpractice claims. The SOL will be different for minors or when a mentally impaired individual is involved. Some states have a different SOL for death claims and/or another tied to the date of the discovery of the injury or negligence. There also may be "notice provisions" that govern what needs to be done. Claims against the Veterans Administration are actually claims against the United States and there is a one-year notice and special paperwork to be filed. The medical records and facts of the case will be the determining factor in setting the SOLs, not what the client believes or remembers.

The LNC needs to carefully identify the act of negligence that actually caused the injury when selecting a tentative SOL. If it was during surgery, count from that date. If it was some several days before or after, identify that date. If there are multiple admissions and providers, or care that crosses state lines, be careful and deliberate and present the relevant facts and dates for the attorney's consideration in setting the SOL.

Although the LNC is not responsible for officially setting this legal deadline, it needs to be factored into the analysis (triage) of all new or potential claims. A statute about to run may not allow enough time for analysis. One that has already expired is barred from the courts. If a statute runs while an attorney or the LNC is investigating it, the attorney stands a good chance of being sued for legal malpractice. Be alert for the applicable dates in the record and raise a flag for the attorney as soon as possible if a potential problem with a close SOL is discovered. Investigation of a case with a close statute must be given a high priority. If the LNC is overcommitted, it may be prudent to decline working on the case rather than risk having the statute run while the file is the LNC's possession.

Contributory/Comparative Negligence

Some states recognize the doctrine of contributory negligence as a complete bar to a plaintiff's recovery. If the plaintiff did anything that could be perceived by a jury as having contributed to his own injury, even if the blame is only 1%, recovery is precluded. In other states where the doctrine of comparative negligence is recognized, the jury can assign a percentage of fault to the plaintiff and deduct that amount from any award. In some jurisdictions, the verdict may be reduced to zero if the percentage of fault attributed to the plaintiff is 51% or more.

For this reason, it is imperative that the actions and inactions of the plaintiff/client be taken into consideration in the analysis of the claim. Because there is a distinct possibility that a plaintiff will walk away from the courthouse with nothing because of these doctrines, attorneys for both sides will consider the plaintiff's actions in determining the value of a case. Did the plaintiff do anything to cause or aggravate his own illness or injury? Was the plaintiff compliant with the prescribed course of care? Did the plaintiff follow the HCP's instructions, keep scheduled appointments, inform his provider of new symptoms or problems, etc.? Was the plaintiff harmed by medication that he continued to take after being instructed to discontinue the medicine (Cartwright, 1987; Eisberg, 1990)?

The following is an example of contributory negligence. A negligent HCP fails to act for over a year on a pap smear report indicating the presence of cervical cancer. This was the 58-year-old patient's first pap smear in 30 years. Who bears the most responsibility for the advanced stage of cancer at the time of diagnosis? A jury could conclude that much of the fault lies with the patient/plaintiff and therefore fail to award damages based on the doctrine of contributory negligence.

Economics

Medical malpractice suits are difficult and costly. Theoretically, any person can attempt to seek compensation for an injury caused by negligence, regardless of its severity, but most plaintiff attorneys will pursue cases only where damages are significant and permanent, which allows for profit after client compensation and payment of costs of the investigation and litigation (Eisberg, 1990; Sloan et al., 1993).

Almost without exception, attorneys representing plaintiffs in malpractice claims work on a contingency basis. This means that the attorney makes no money unless the claim settles or a verdict is reached and damages are awarded. The contingency fee is a percentage of the settlement or verdict. This fee pays the salaries of the attorney and other office staff plus overhead. Costs on the file are an additional burden. These costs include all aspects of the litigation (e.g., record retrieval, consultant and expert services including the LNC, travel, court reporter, etc.). The plaintiff's attorney is only reimbursed for these costs if there is a recovery. Plaintiff's attorneys working on contingency make nothing when a decision is made not to pursue a claim after an investigation has taken place. Defense attorneys will be paid on retainer or hourly by the insurers and the HCPs they represent and will be reimbursed for cost. This makes good triage for both the plaintiff and defense insurers a major economic incentive (Bartimus, 1996).

In recent years many states have enacted caps on noneconomic damages. This means that no matter how severe the injury, things that are not hard provable costs such as pain, suffering, humiliation and misery are compensable only to the limit of the cap. To attain a recovery greater than the cap requires proof of special and future damages such as medical costs, wage loss, special needs such as a modified vehicle, companion services, or housing. A cap on pain and suffering even in the catastrophically injured can significantly limit the recovery. An example of this would be loss of sight in an elderly person. This is a major injury impacting most aspects of quality of life. However, no special medical needs are anticipated to flow from his blindness and his home life will change little as his wife will continue to care for him. He had no income to lose and his pension remains intact. Although totally blind because of negligence, some attorneys in states with a cap on noneconomic damages might find this case potentially too expensive to handle with little in specials and much to spend on records and other costs of litigation. The potential recovery must always be balanced against the costs of investigation and pursuit.

Another cost to the attorney is travel and depositions. In addition to depositions of the parties, some states also require depositions of all experts for both sides. With multiple experts required to prove or defend a case on both sides and no limit on where they come from, criss-crossing the country time and again on a single case would not be unusual. In addition to travel, hotel, and the cost of the court reporter and transcripts, there are the daily or hourly fees charged by the medical experts for their time and participation. All of this can be very costly.

Most malpractice cases take 3–5 years to resolve. The attorney working on contingency may subsidize a case for a long period of time before receiving any reimbursement of expenses if ever. In the meantime, the cost of maintaining the practice continues. To the lawyers on both sides, time is money. If a potential case has low to moderate damages, but the projected number of expensive experts is high and analysis time-consuming, the plaintiff's attorney may well be looking at spending more than can be recovered and a defense attorney spending more than can be saved for the insurer. This is not good business practice. By employing the "elements of triage" LNCs can assist the attorney in making an economically sound decision regarding the investigation and eventual pursuit or defense of the claim (Eisberg, 1990). An understanding of the economics of a legal practice will help LNCs add value to their professional services.

Conflict of Interest

Lawyers need to avoid representing clients when doing so would present a conflict of interest. An example would be representing a physician in his personal and business matters and simultaneously pursuing a negligence claim against him. Most lawyers would also decline to handle a claim against their personal physician, a physician neighbor/acquaintance, or a physician who was about to testify for them on behalf of another plaintiff, even though these situations do not exactly meet the legal definition of conflict. It is important to identify any possible conflicts of interest as early in the investigation as possible. The LNC can assist in this effort by identifying all HCPs that played a role in the care at issue and supplying these names to the attorney for conflict checking.

The Parties

The Defendant

Jurors have a bias toward the HCP. Most lay persons have a great deal of respect for physicians and other HCPs and believe that everyone makes mistakes. If the defendant is well known and regarded in the community, is charming and empathetic, or highly credentialed, this only adds to the jury's bias and the difficulty of identifying medical experts for the plaintiff who would be willing to testify against him or her. If the defendant's area of practice is highly specialized, the pool of potential testifying experts is even smaller and finding an expert might prove next to impossible (Eisberg, 1990; Peters, 2007, 2008; Vidmar, 1998).

The Plaintiff

The LNC should consider the plaintiff's presentation and demeanor. Is the client likable, articulate, and believable? Does the client evoke sympathy? What are the client's motives for bringing a lawsuit? Be alert for issues suggesting credibility problems. If the record says one thing and the plaintiff says another, the argument can rapidly disintegrate to a "he said/she said" contest. Such a contest is almost without exception won by the defendant HCP.

Other Considerations and Case Types

Informed Consent

Claims involving only informed consent issues are generally quite difficult for the plaintiff to win. The burden of proof is high and requires a plaintiff to prove that no reasonable person would have gone along with the treatment, medication, or surgery "if he had only been told" that whatever unfortunate thing has come to pass could possibly have happened. The plaintiff also has to prove, through expert testimony, that the standard of care *required* the particular risk to be disclosed. As a rule, physicians are not required to disclose every possible complication that can occur or every potential or rare side effect of every drug prescribed (see Chapter 7). However, informed consent is sometimes successful when it co-exists with negligence. The LNC's clinical background and experience will be helpful to the attorney in making good decisions about informed consent cases.

An example of a successful informed consent case is presented here. A young man has an obstruction in his subclavian artery near the junction of the carotid. It arises from adhesions in the vessel from a childhood trauma. The obstruction is causing ischemic changes in his arm. A vascular surgeon tells him this can be opened with minimal time away from work and minimal risk, using angioplasty. Consent is given and a few weeks later the procedure is done. During the angioplasty, multiple pieces of clot break off and, unable to flow downstream past the obstruction, the debris floods his brain via the nearby carotid. He suffers multiple strokes and permanent significant brain damage. In this case the main claim was negligence in choosing an inappropriate technique. Open surgery would have allowed clamping of the carotid to avoid stroke and opening of the clogged vessel to clean it out fully. The secondary claim was informed consent; the patient was never afforded the opportunity to discuss the more significant risk of the less invasive procedure.

Wrongful Life and Wrongful Birth

These cases are notoriously difficult to pursue. Many plaintiff attorneys will not even investigate them. The basic injury being claimed is a life that never should have happened. In other words, it puts the parents and their attorney in the position of stating they wish their child had never been born or they wish their child had been aborted. It is a social, moral, and political hot potato that most attorneys would not want to tackle. This author has only worked on one such case. It involved failure to conduct genetic testing after a first child was born with significant mental retardation. The parents stated that if they had only known that the terrible life their first child suffered was due to a genetic defect they carried, a defect that could have and should have been tested for, they surely would have opted to never have another child. They were only told of the genetic issue after the birth of the second child. Abortion was not an issue. The only issue was the tremendous cost of caring for a very disabled child.

Foreign Objects

A surgeon who leaves an unintended object, such as a clamp or sponge in a patient, may be found to be negligent. However, because these objects often do not cause any symptoms or harm, they are often discovered, incidentally, only many years later and often are just left in place. In this instance, there is no damage and therefore no claim. On the other hand, a retained foreign object may cause all manner of pain or illness and require removal. In that instance, the SOL may hinge on when the object was discovered and removed, and if that state has a discovery rule. Some states have adopted special statutes just for discovery of foreign objects versus medical malpractice in general.

Cooperation of a Subsequent Treating Physician

Cooperation or sabotage by a subsequent treating physician can make or break a case, especially where the physician is the only observer of a crucial object or event. For example, in a case involving an allegedly botched surgery, the observations of the subsequent surgeon are of crucial importance. The second surgeon is the only ostensibly "neutral" person who has seen the site of the original surgery. Jurors will therefore often believe the observations of the subsequent treating physician over the opinions of hired experts for either side.

However, subsequent treating physicians or surgeons often have more expertise than the potential defendant. They are often in a position of receiving patients whose care was begun elsewhere and ultimately requires a higher level of expertise or technology or both. Many subsequent treating physicians and surgeons rely on HCPs with lower levels of specialty or experience in surrounding communities for referrals. To testify against these referring physicians or facilities would be the cutting off a crucial source of their own business. A good example is a small rural hospital that waited too long to send a critically ill patient on to a tertiary care center. The receiving doctor is not likely to malign the treatment of the defendant at the rural hospital because it might cause the HCPs at the smaller hospital to feel that their care will be under scrutiny every time they transfer a patient. As a result, the larger hospital and its doctors could see transfers and referrals drop from that facility. Often the only testimony a subsequent treating physician will be willing to give to either side in a malpractice case is a discussion of what they found and what they did, but without offering any opinions regarding prior care. Their input is still often valuable, particularly when gathering information about damages or permanent injury. The LNC can assist the attorney by identifying subsequent treating physicians and gathering information about their specialty or expertise and suggesting those the attorney may want to contact.

Other Worries

Long complicated courses of treatment with multiple providers or multiple facilities all ending with a bad outcome might be impossible to sort out for the plaintiff's attorney considering a potential claim. Figuring out who did what wrong and any causal connection to the injury could be like trying to untangle a spider web. It could also mean several different statutes of limitations and venues.

A case has been rejected by other plaintiff attorneys is also problematic. Has this person been looking for a lawyer for months or even years? If the issues were ever investigated and then turned down by another attorney, it is useful to know the reasons behind the decision, such as inability to find expert support on liability. On the other hand, just because a case has been rejected by one attorney, further investigation should not necessarily be precluded, however, this should be a case of "buyers beware" (Eisberg, 1990).

Cases involving private body parts and functions not typically discussed in public or in front of "polite company" are also cases the plaintiff attorney need to consider carefully prior to beginning an investigation. If the lawyer is embarrassed or uncomfortable discussing the facts, he or she will have a very difficult time at depositions and in front of a jury. Even if the lawyer becomes immune to the topic over time, remember that the jury will not have the same luxury and will hear these things only from the moment the trial begins.

Illustrations and Case Studies of Elements

The following examples set forth the facts as gleaned from the plaintiff and/or medical record, followed by the analysis of the claim.

The Disastrous Hysterectomy

A 47-year-old female had a long history of painful uterine fibroid tumors and very heavy periods. She was prescribed iron supplements, but still had trouble maintaining a normal hemoglobin level. Her condition was unmanageable; she wanted no additional children and opted for a hysterectomy. An abdominal approach for the hysterectomy was planned as her surgeon believed there were too many adhesions from prior cesarean sections and other abdominal surgeries. The surgery was completed "without complication" as stated in the operative report. On postoperative day 3, the patient was distended and complaining of severe abdominal pain. An ileus was suspected. Laxatives were given and ambulation encouraged. On postoperative day 4, the patient was febrile and seemed sicker. An abdominal film was ordered and something beyond an ileus was seen. Additional testing was done and revealed an urinoma. Apparently, during the surgery, the surgeon severed a ureter while trying to free the uterine ligaments from dense adhesions. The patient was returned to surgery for repair of the ureter including stent placement and insertion of a percutaneous nephrostomy tube to drain urine from that kidney while the ureter healed. Days later and still miserable with multiple tubes, the patient was discharged. She was instructed to return 6 weeks later for the removal of the stent and nephrostomy. Subsequent testing showed the ureter to be functioning well with adequate renal function.

Analysis: This case has problems with liability and economics. The injury to the ureter would be considered a complication in the setting of dense adhesions, not an act of negligence. Even the most careful surgeon could have caused this injury under these circumstances. The fact that the injury went unnoticed at the time of surgery is likewise not likely negligent. The delay in diagnosis of the damaged ureter may also be within the standard of care. Judging the care by what was happening at the time without the benefit of hindsight, an ileus is certainly more common and presents just about the same way for many postsurgical patients. In terms of damages, certainly the patient experienced a less than desirable course, but even prompt recognition of the injury in the surgical suite may well have led to the identical course of treatment, albeit a few days sooner. The economics of pursuing a claim based on a few days or even weeks of misery in a patient who was going to be recovering from surgery and out of action for a few weeks anyway does not make sense. The final summary: the patient incurred a known commonly occurring complication not related to an act of negligence and there were no permanent injuries.

The Missed Myocardial Infarction

A 62-year-old man presented to the emergency room of the local hospital with burning chest pain that had developed while he was at work. Upon arrival at the emergency room, the pain had subsided. By history, his cholesterol was "a little high," but he claimed to be "eating better since he found out." He also stated that he "used to take blood pressure pills," but stopped taking them because it was ruining his "married life." An EKG was done and interpreted as showing only nonspecific changes. No other testing was done. He was discharged with a diagnosis of reflux and symptomatic treatment prescribed. A few days later the pain returned, "worse than ever," and continued unabated. He was taken to the emergency room by his wife. An evolving acute myocardial infarction was diagnosed and angioplasty with placement of stents carried out immediately. Three days later, the patient was discharged. Echocardiogram prior to discharge revealed an ejection fraction of 55%. He takes medications for blood pressure, prevention of platelet aggregation, and a statin for elevated cholesterol. A retrospective analysis of the EKG done at the first emergency room visit disclosed that the first EKG had been misread and showed evidence of ischemia.

Analysis: This case has good liability, but has problems with causation, damages, and even possibly contributory negligence, making the potential for success unlikely. The EKG was misread and accepted standards of care for acute coronary syndrome (ACS) including lab work (troponins and enzymes) were not carried out. At the time of the initial emergency room visit, accepted standards of care required admission for evaluation and treatment of the ischemia, evaluation of the extent of disease, likely angiogram and angioplasty and modification of risk factors. These things did not happen at the first visit. That constitutes liability. However, on cause, even if those things had been done, the course of treatment likely would have been exactly the same. Therefore, the negligence did not cause the claimed harm. On damages, there are none caused by the negligence. His ejection fraction is within normal. Moreover, it could be said that he is better off with a stent and proper medications, teaching on his disease and life style modifications of exercise and diet. On contributory negligence, the plaintiff's failure to take his antihypertensive medication as directed may well have contributed to the extent of his cardiac disease.

Delayed Diagnosis of Breast Cancer

A 35-year-old woman was recently diagnosed with breast cancer. She was told by her oncologist that the cancer should have been caught earlier. The patient was shown the missed lesion on a mammogram performed and read as normal 14 months prior to her diagnosis. The patient underwent a lumpectomy and subsequent chemotherapy and radiation. On further questioning, the patient told the attorney that she had a copy of the pathology report and would fax it to the office. The pathology report described the lesion as 2 cm in greatest dimension in the upper outer quadrant of the breast with clear margins. The pathology of the lesion was an infiltrating ductal carcinoma. The sentinel lymph node biopsy was positive with positive estrogen receptors. The patient's cancer was designated a Stage II.

Analysis: At face value, this case represents likely liability on the part of the radiologist for failing to properly interpret the mammogram. The much more difficult elements to prove in a case such as this are causation and damages. Being successful in this claim would require the plaintiff to prove to a reasonable degree of medical certainty that the delay of 14 months led to a progression of her cancer, and that this delay caused her harm. In other words, except for the negligent delay in diagnosis, her outcome (treatment and prognosis) would have been different and better.

In all cancer cases, the first thing the LNC should do is to look up the statistical survivability of the cancer at all stages and how the specific type of cancer diagnosed normally progresses. If the cancer is not likely to be cured and will progress no matter when it is diagnosed, there is little chance of success in proving a significant difference caused by any delay. If there is a reasonable expectation of significantly longer life or significantly easier course of treatment, economics will dictate whether or not the claim is worth pursuing.

Fortunately for the plaintiff, a stage II breast cancer is very curable, and the plaintiff is far more likely to survive than not. In other words, even if it is proven that the plaintiff was a stage I 14 months prior to her diagnosis (no lymph node involvement), progressing from a Stage I to Stage II did not change the likelihood that she would survive the cancer. The delay may have reduced the survival odds a bit, but she is still quite curable. If the attorney wishes to consider the damage to be the change from Stage I to Stage II, beware that not all states recognize "loss of chance" claims. (In this case, loss of chance would be a downward change in the statistical survivability of the cancer.) In terms of treatment change from Stage I to II, even a Stage I cancer would have required surgery and likely radiation. The only change that could be claimed is the need for chemotherapy. And even that could come into play only with testimony that she would not have had positive lymph nodes 14 months prior to her diagnosis.

The Failed Back Surgery

Mr. Jones had a two-level lumbar fusion with placement of hardware, including two pedicle screws and autologous transplant of bone harvested from his iliac crest. After the surgery and weeks of therapy, Mr. Jones was no better. In fact, in some ways his condition was worse. It was determined that the spinal fusion did not take and was not solid. Mr. Jones required additional surgery to have the hardware removed and the fusion redone. He remained in daily pain and was unable to return to work for a period of several additional months. Mr. Jones and his wife were unable to pay the medical bills and went bankrupt. He was certain that his surgery had been done incorrectly or he would not have had the postoperative pain and suffering. Before the surgery, Mr. Jones' doctor assured him that he would be able to return to work six weeks after surgery. Mr. Jones said that his diagnosis now is failed back surgery and believed that if he had been told there was a chance that the surgery would not work, he never would have gone through with the spinal fusion and hardware placement.

Analysis: It would seem that this case is a good example of significant general and special damages in pain and suffering, medical bills, and lost wages. Unfortunately, failed fusions are not uncommon and are considered a risk of the procedure. Unless the plaintiff could prove that the fusion failed not by chance, but due to an act of negligence, there is no liability. On the informed consent issue, it is not likely that the attorney would be able to convince a jury that this man would have opted for the misery he was in before the surgery even if he had been told of a small chance that the surgery would not work. In this author's practice, a recommendation not to pursue the claim would be made.

Failure to Diagnose and Treat Heart Disease

A young mother found herself getting short of breath doing routine things. She was also always tired "to the bone" after an ordinary day. Her doctor told her it was just the burden of working and caring for a young family and suggested more sleep and to have her husband "pitch in more." Things only got worse. A chronic cough complicated the shortness of breath and her physician diagnosed seasonal allergy. Antihistamines were prescribed. When the symptoms persisted into the winter and worsened, a dust allergy was diagnosed and more antihistamines were prescribed. Two years into this episode, when the young woman could hardly walk the stairs in her own home, her doctor sent her to an allergist. He found no allergies and sent her to a pulmonologist who was alarmed at her symptoms and their duration and the huge heart he saw on x-ray. That same day she was diagnosed with end stage idiopathic cardiomyopathy and sent to a major medical center for evaluation for transplant. After six months on an artificial heart, this young mother received a new heart.

Analysis: This is an excellent claim. Symptoms that do not respond as expected or worsen under treatment require further evaluation. Symptoms of unusual fatigue or new onset shortness of breath in a woman should always raise the suspicion of heart disease. On cause: Idiopathic cardiomyopathy reverses with treatment in the majority of cases. In the next percentage class, treatment halts the disease's progress and stabilizes the condition. In a small percentage, the disease progresses despite treatment and transplant is needed. Therefore, medical statistics infer that with treatment, this young woman more likely than not would have avoided transplant and even had her disease reversed with appropriate diagnosis and treatment. The delay in diagnosis caused her to need the transplant.

The damages in this case are also enormous. The cost of her treatment before, during, and after her transplant is over a million dollars. Her life expectancy is reduced to the life of the transplant. Her future medical expenses are also large. Noneconomic damages, her pain and suffering, and the claim of her husband for loss of consortium are likewise huge.

The only worry is the SOLs as it relates to cause. If, for instance, this claim was in a locale with a two-year SOL, then some of the care took place outside of that window. If there are no exceptions for this scenario, then that more distant care cannot be considered. If the last documented negligent care within the SOL was near the time of the actual diagnosis, then causation will be very difficult. It would have to be proved that appropriate treatment on that later date would have given a much better and different outcome. The lesson: Know the SOL and the exceptions in the State the case will be litigated. The first defense a good lawyer will give is that the care complained of is outside the SOL.

Summary

Developing a quality work product often means doing more than was asked. For the LNC, this means expanding from a task-oriented practice to one built on solid analytical and investigative skills. It means going beyond producing a narrative record summary or literature review to applying assessment skills in determining whether the LNC's client, plaintiff or defense, is likely to prevail. Adding value to the LNC's service means that the LNC must consider the case facts fully to know what parts of the medical records are important, what information is necessary and important, and what facts or records can be glossed over. The LNC should think critically. Rather than conducting a random literature search on the illness or injury at hand, research those topics likely to be in contention with or support your position. It means tactfully pointing out to the attorney things in the record that give rise to real concerns about elements of triage beyond liability.

Many attorneys handling malpractice claims are justifiably proud of their advocacy in the courtroom and believe that if they could just "get their case in front of a jury," they would be successful. The attorney is and should be an advocate for their client's position. However, the LNC with unique knowledge and experience can often be most useful by playing the devil's advocate and reminding the attorney of the possible arguments that will surface as the case moves forward. Assuming this role takes assertiveness on the part of the LNC and may take practice to attain a comfort level. But the LNC is uniquely qualified to fill this role and doing so will bring greater satisfaction to the profession of legal nurse consulting.

References

American Jurisprudence. (2002). Physicians, surgeons and other healers. *A modern comprehensive test statement of American law, state and federal* (Vol. 61, 2nd ed., pp. 117–355). Eagan, MN: West Publishing.

Balk, R. (2000). Severe sepsis and septic shock; definitions, epidemiology and clinical manifestations. *Critical Care Clinics, 16*(2): 179–192.

Bartimus, J., & Eaton, C. J. (1996). Should you accept the case? *Trial, 50–52* (May).

Cardaro, T. C. (2000, May). Case Screening and investigation of a potential medical malpractice claim. Presented to the Maryland Trial Lawyers Association, Baltimore, MD, May 2000.

Cartwright, R. E. (1987). Evaluating a case. *Trial, 62–64* (September).

Egan, D. E. (2000). Finding diamonds in the rough, *Trial, 37–45* (December).

Eisberg, J. (1990). *Minnesota medical malpractice*. St. Paul, Minnesota: Merrill/Magnus Publishing.

Fennell v. Southern Maryland Hospital, 580 A.2d 206 (1990).

Groopman, J. (2007). *How doctors think*. New York: Houghton Mifflin Company.

Minnesota District Judges Association (1999). *Jury instruction guides—civil*. St. Paul, MN: Minnesota District Judges Association.

Mooney, C., & Kirshenbaum, S. (2009) *Unscientific America; How scientific illiteracy threatens our future*. Philadelphia, PA: Perseus Books Group.

Peters, P., Jr. (2007). *Doctors and juries*, Article 1453. Michigan Law Review.

Peters, P., Jr. (2008). *Health courts*, Article 227. Boston University Law Review.

Shandell, R. E., & Smith, P. (1999). *The preparation and trial of medical malpractice cases* (rev. ed., chap. 1). New York: Law Journal.

Sloan, F., Githens, P., Clayton, E., Hickson, G. B., & Partlett, D. (1993). *Suing for medical malpractice*. Chicago, IL: University of Chicago Press.

Smith Sehdev, A. E., & Hutchins, M. (2001). Problems with proper completion and accuracy of the cause of death statement. *Archives of Internal Medicine, 161,* 277–284.

Vidmar, N. (1998). *Medical malpractice and the American jury: Confronting myths about jury incompetence, deep pockets, and outrageous damage awards*. Ann Arbor: University of Michigan Press.

Test Questions

1. All of the following are typically considered complications rather than the result of negligence except:
   A. An infection in a surgical wound
   B. A stroke during a carotid endarterectomy
   C. Severe bleeding after lytic therapy for a heart attack
   D. Nerve injury from the stirrups following gynecological surgery

2. In a contingency fee claim, the attorney is paid
   A. A percentage of the settlement or verdict
   B. A percentage of the calculated value of all special damages
   C. Costs plus a percentage of the verdict or settlement
   D. A percentage of the calculated value of the time spent on the claim plus costs

3. Determination of the Standard of Care must be based on
   A. What an expert will testify he or she would do in similar circumstances
   B. Care that is reasonable and acceptable to practitioners of the same community
   C. Medical literature that is current and up to date
   D. Accepted standards of care for practitioners of that specialty with similar resources, as practiced at the time of incidents at issue

4. Contributory negligence might include all except:
   A. Smoking
   B. Obesity
   C. Treated hypertension
   D. Missed clinic appointments

5. Special damages are defined as
   A. Nonpecuniary damages recognized as compensable, but on which the law is unable to place a dollar amount
   B. Out-of-pocket expenses incurred by the plaintiff as a result of negligence
   C. Exemplary damages awarded to punish the defendant and to deter future "outrageous" behavior
   D. Damages awarded when the plaintiff's life has been changed as a result of the injury

Answers: 1. D, 2. C, 3. D, 4. C, 5. B

Chapter 5

Access to Medical Records

June Grant-Stafford, MSN, RN

First Edition and Second Edition
Kathy Gudgell, JD, RN

Contents

Objectives

- Identify the sources of law governing the content and preservation of medical records
- Describe the process for accessing medical and health records, agency records, and other pertinent records
- Explain the reasons for confidentiality of the medical record
- Discuss the appropriate time for disclosure
- Discuss rules of evidence for introducing medical records at trial

Introduction

Legal nurse consultants work with medical records in several different ways. Hours are spent obtaining, reviewing, analyzing, and preparing the medical records for litigation. The LNC must be aware of what is contained in a medical record to know what is missing. The record consists of many parts and the LNC must know how and where to obtain the record and if it is obtainable. The LNC must be familiar with the Rules of Evidence that control the admissibility of a record in a court of law.

Medical Records

The contents of a hospital medical record (see Table 5.1) are regulated by federal, state, and local entities including licensing agencies, accrediting organizations, medical facilities, and professional organizations. The American Health Information Management Association (AHIMA) and the Joint Commission, formerly known as the Commission on Accreditation of Health Care Organizations (JCAHO), also play significant roles.

The Joint Commission (TJC), is one of the largest accrediting bodies for health care in the United States. It grew out of the American College of Surgeons when, in the early 1900s, the College realized that many physicians were performing outside their scope of practice, resulting in

Table 5.1   Contents of Hospital Medical Records

Hospital Administrative Records	1. Administrative data including admission and discharge sheet with basic patient identification data
	2. Primary and secondary diagnoses, final diagnosis, and major procedures performed during the hospital stay
	3. The Conditions of Admission to which the patient consented for basic care. Consent forms specific to the release of information as well as medical and surgical procedures
Hospital Clinical Data Records	1. The history and physical examination that contains a summary of past medical problems, family history, personal and social data, and the complaint or illness that led to the admission. The physical examination portion must be completed in 24 h from the time of admission
	2. A plan of care must be included as well
	3. The physician order sheets must be written, dated, and confirmed by the physician with a signature. Verbal orders given in an emergency situation must be written, signed, and dated at the earliest possible time. Faxed orders are acceptable in some states
	4. Physician progress notes include daily notes or notes documenting any change in the patient's condition. Hospital policy dictates the time line for entries
	5. Special reports or diagnostic studies such as x-rays, magnetic resonance imagings (MRIs), and computed tomography (CT) scans
	6. Medical and surgical procedural reports
	7. Anesthesia records including pre and post assessments
	8. Consultations
	9. Emergency room reports including prehospital information
	10. Laboratory data
	11. Graphs and flow sheets noting intake and output, vital signs
	12. Treatment sheets documenting dates and time of assessments and treatment
	13. Nurses notes
	14. Hospital policy determines a reasonable time period in which the initial assessment must be completed as well as functional status, nutritional status, identification of possible abuse victims, and the frequency of subsequent assessments

continued

Table 5.1   (continued) Contents of Hospital Medical Records

15. Medication administration records should reflect medications ordered, administered, and reasons that a dose was not given

16. Advance directives

17. Transplantation, donations, or implantations with specific documentation of any implanted device and any restrictions that may apply

18. Rehabilitation services

19. Care plans

20. Restraint documentation including a doctor's order for the same

21. An autopsy report may not always be found in the medical record as it depends on the individual patient circumstances

22. Pharmacy records

23. Discharge instructions

24. Billing records including items ordered, specific charges incurred, and any payments received

Source: Joint Commission. (2008). Retrieved February 18, 2009, from http://www.jointcommission.org/SentinelEvents

patient injuries. The College began drafting rules for patient safety due to the improper care by untrained or poorly trained physicians. Nearly half a century later, TJC was created with the coming together of several individual organizations, including the American Medical Association (AMA), that had begun to assert their respective conditions on hospitals.

Today TJC has been granted deemed status by the Health and Human Services (HHS) Department of the Federal government. The HHS inspects TJC on a routine basis to determine whether the deemed status should be revoked or continued. The single condition required by the HHS is that TJC use and confirm that the health care provider is in compliance with the Conditions of Participation (CoP).

CoP are the conditions that all institutions must meet to be accredited for receipt of funding under Medicare and Medicaid. There are varying standards for different health care entities. For hospitals, compliance with standards must be demonstrated in such areas as laws, patient rights, governance, quality assurance, medical staff, nursing services, and medical records, to name only a few.

Manuals published by TJC are consistent with a universal requirement that the medical record contain sufficient information to identify the patient, justify the treatment, document the course of treatment and results, and promote continuity of care by the participating health care providers (Joint Commission, 2008).

TJC guidelines also pertain to long-term care facilities. The medical records should contain similar data including physician orders, physician progress notes, nursing data, assessments, medication documentation, and discharge summaries. Nutritional and activity programs are documented every 90 days. Social services and rehabilitation services are documented with reference to the patient's response to treatment. TJC evaluates long-term care facilities by several methods and from several aspects; the assessment of patients' needs and their response to care, respect for patients' rights, continuity of care and patient education. The Minimum Data Set (MDS) form is a tool used to assess needs and to determine reimbursement, specifically for Medicare and Medicaid (Joint Commission, 2008). Chapter 17 discusses MDS forms in greater detail.

Federal Regulations

Institutions that participate in federal reimbursement programs are subject to federal regulations regarding the content of the medical record. The Center for Medicare and Medicaid Services (CMS) publish the regulations in the Code of Federal Regulations. The regulations are comparable to those of TJC, requiring that the medical record contain data supporting admission and continued hospitalization: support of the diagnosis, data noting the patient's progress, the patient's response to medications, and other patient services. Different types of health care settings have specific regulations. Although states must conform to federal regulations, often state regulations and guidelines are stricter. The LNC must be familiar with the guidelines of the respective state for the individual facilities.

State Regulations

Each state has regulations that define the content of the medical record. The regulations vary from detailed to general requirements, with specific regulations for various health care facilities. The universal requirement, as with federal regulations, is that the medical record contains sufficient information to identify and justify the admission, the diagnosis, treatment, and responses to the treatment and services.

Institutional Regulations

The institutional policies are often related to employee actions. Although physicians are not usually hospital employees, the institution has a duty to monitor a physician's compliance with federal documentation regulations. A physician may have his or her privileges suspended or even revoked for noncompliance. Most institutions follow TJC guidelines. If the policies of the institution are more comprehensive than TJCs, the institution can be held to a higher standard by TJC.

Professional Standards

The AMA has collaborated with the CMS to propose documentation guidelines that would satisfy CMS requirements for justification of approving payments for procedures, care, and medications. In order to avoid charges of fraud or abuse in billing practices, the AMA recommends that the physicians' records be complete, legible, and compliant with general practices of accurate medical record keeping. The AMA further recommends that each encounter with the patient include the reason for the encounter, relevant history and physical examination findings, prior diagnostic tests, assessment and clinical impression or diagnosis, a plan of care, as well as the date and legible identity of the medical provider. Appropriate health risk factors should also be identified. The patient's progress and response to treatment as well as changes in treatment plans or any revision in diagnosis should be included in this documentation (AMA, 2002).

The American Nurses Association (ANA) published the Standards of Clinical Nursing Practice, which require that a nursing assessment be documented in a retrievable form. The diagnosis is required to be documented in a manner that facilitates the determination of expected outcomes, plan of care, interventions, and revision of care (ANA, 1998).

Retention of Records

The holder or custodian of the medical record has the responsibility to safeguard the recorded information once the record is in existence. TJC, federal, state and local regulations, institutional policies, and organizational and professional standards determine the length of time that the medical record should be preserved. Storage space and cost may influence a health care facility's retention of records policy. TJC requirements determine how long medical information is retained based on law, regulations, and the use of patient information as it relates to patient care, legal research, and education. Federal law requires that institutions receiving federal reimbursement, specifically Medicare, retain records for a minimum of five years. Most states require a 5–10-year retention period. Deceased patients may have special rules in some states that permit destruction of records prior to the mandated period. If there are no specific state regulations, the AHIMA recommends health care providers retain records for 10 years from the most recent encounter. Diagnostic images should be retained for five years. Fetal heart monitor records should be retained for 10 years from the date that the infant reaches the age of majority. The age of majority is the age that a person is granted, by law, the rights, and responsibility of an adult. The age is determined by state statute and is usually 18 years of age. Birth, death, and surgical procedure records are retained permanently. Record-keeping policy and institutional policy should be influenced by each state's statute of limitations that control tort and contract actions (AHIMA, 2008). Educational and research facilities may have special needs for retention of medical records that allow for retrospective reviews or long-term monitoring of effects in drug trials. Records may be retained for 75 years.

The retention of school records, Kindergarten through 12th grade is determined by federal and state regulations, as well as local guidelines, much like medical records. Student health records are defined by federal legislation, specifically the Family Educational Rights and Privacy Act (FERPA), to be part of the academic record and thus must be retained in the same way as the academic record. FERPA authorizes school officials to purge immunization and other health records from the student academic file after the student has graduated or left the district, provided that the district has a records retention schedule approved by the respective State Archives.

The Occupational Safety and Health Administration (OSHA) requires certain industries to retain records of employee chemical exposure for 30 years. Medical records must be kept by the business for the duration of employment plus 30 years. In the event that records are converted to microfilm or disc for preservation, the integrity of the record must be maintained. If records are to be destroyed in the normal course of business, AHIMA recommendations dictate that the name of the patient, the date of the destruction, a list of all records to be destroyed, as well as the dates covered in the respective chart be memorialized for future reference. Signatures of those involved in the destruction of the record as well as any witnesses to the record destruction should also be included.

Confidentiality, Privacy, and Privilege

Patients reveal many details of their personal and private lives to their physicians. This is encouraged and expected in order to provide the best medical care to the patient. Therefore, it is the ethical duty of the physician to monitor this information in confidence. This confidence is extended to the information in the written record. The right to confidentiality or protection from the unauthorized release of information is a guarantee by the U.S. Constitution.

Health Insurance Portability and Accountability Act of 1996

Health Insurance Portability and Accountability Act (HIPAA) (Kennedy-Kassenbaum Act 1996) was passed by Congress on August 21, 1996. Among other things, it included rules covering administrative simplification, including making health care delivery more efficient. Portability of medical coverage for preexisting conditions was a key provision of the act as was defining the underwriting process for group medical coverage. Another key element was the provision standardizing the electronic transmission of billing and claims information.

In standardizing the electronic means of paying and collecting claims data, congress recognized the increased potential for abuse of people's medical information. Consequently, a key part of the act also increased and standardized confidentiality and security of health data. HIPAA privacy regulations require that access to patient information be limited to only those authorized, and that only the information necessary for a task be available to them. Last, but certainly not least, personal health information must be protected and kept confidential.

Because Congress did not finalize the actual regulations according to the scheduled time frame, the finalization and implementation passed to the Department of HHS. The final version of the HIPAA privacy regulations was issued in December 2000 and went into effect on April 14, 2001. A two-year grace period was included; enforcement of the HIPAA Privacy Rules began on April 14, 2003. Thus, penalties for noncompliance could be applied from that date.

HIPAA provides for uniformity of rules and regulations from state to state and even from one health care organization to another. Where existing state laws are stricter than the HIPAA guidelines the state law supersedes the federally mandated HIPAA guidelines.

The primary areas covered under HIPAA focus on consumer control over health information, ensuring patients understand their privacy rights, ensuring patient access to their medical records, and providing recourse if privacy regulations are violated. Providers and health plans are required to give patients a clear written explanation of how the covered entity may use and disclose their health information. Patients are generally able to see and obtain copies of their medical records and request amendments in response to information they perceive as inaccurate. Additionally, a history of most nonroutine disclosures must be made available. Individuals now have the right to file a formal complaint with a covered provider or health plan, or with HHS related to violations of HIPAA provisions.

Failure to comply with HIPAA can result in civil and criminal penalties. The latest HIPAA Enforcement Rule was published by HHS in February 2006 (DHHS. Federal Register: Final Enforcement Rule, 2006). This rule applies to all of the major HIPAA rules: the privacy, security, and transaction rules. The previous enforcement regulations applied only to the privacy rule. Under the new rule, HHS can impose fines of up to $100 per violation, to a maximum of $25,000 for violations of an identical requirement during one calendar year, and in some cases, imprisonment. Federal criminal penalties can also be placed upon health plans, providers, and health care clearinghouses that knowingly and improperly disclose information or obtain information under false pretenses. Penalties are higher for actions designed to generate monetary gain. Criminal penalties can be $50,000 and one year in prison for obtaining or disclosing protected health information, $100,000 and up to five years in prison for obtaining protected health information under false pretenses, and as much as $250,000 and 10 years in prison for obtaining or disclosing protected health information with the intent to sell, transfer, or use it for commercial advantage, personal gain, or malicious harm.

Access to Medical Records

Patient Access

Ownership of the physical medical record, including x-rays, and all other reports in the chart belongs to the facility or health care practitioner who created the record, albeit subject to the patient's interest in the information contained therein. HIPAA now provides for universal access by a patient to review and copy his/her medical record. Under HIPAA, the patient can also request that corrections or amendments be made to the record. HIPAA also mandates restrictions on the uses and disclosure to third parties of the information contained in a patient's medical record.

OSHA mandates that an employee have access to their records of exposure to toxic substances and any relevant medical records held by the employer. If no exposure record exists, the employee has the right to review records of other employees with similar job duties. Access to medical records of other employees with similar job duties require specific written consent from the other employee. Please see *Legal Nurse Consulting*, 3rd Edition, Volume 2, Chapter 19, for more information.

The right to request the records of a minor patient resides with the parent or legal guardian. HIPAA uses the term personal guardian. In case of divorced parents, the custodial parent is the one with the right to access for a minor child. For a deceased patient, the administrator of the estate may request the decedent's medical records. Access is defined as reasonable access. The patient or the patient's representative may review the record in the medical record department of a health care facility under supervision at a time that is convenient for the facility, usually during normal business hours. If a notarized request for specific records is received by the facility, the facility has the responsibility to reproduce the record in a timely fashion. The facility cannot refuse to reproduce the record despite nonpayment of other outstanding bills. Most states allow the facility to charge a minimum fee for copying the record. The request for records, by a potential plaintiff, does not have to be a certified copy unless a certified copy is requested. Certification does not guarantee the record is complete; it only guarantees that it is an accurate copy of the record held by the facility (HIPAA, 2002).

Third-Party Access

Information may be released to a third party when the actions of the patient have implied consent or waiver thereof. It is generally assumed when a spouse, family member, or significant other is present during a discussion of the patient's medical condition, the health care practitioner may speak freely concerning private information. The health care practitioner should consult with the patient as to which family members may have access to information at a later date. The health care practitioner must be very careful in the release of information concerning substance abuse. Access to sensitive information such as HIV results or information indicating a diagnosis of AIDS may be denied to nonauthorized individuals. Other sensitive information includes the release of information regarding sexually transmitted diseases, sperm donor, and adoption records. A request for all medical records does not always include the complete record in some states. A specific request may be necessary to identify the exact information that the patient is willing to release. Over the years, accessing records that contain sensitive information has undergone many changes. The seal of secrecy has been changed to allow disclosure of relevant medical information to a child or a child's representative. However, the disclosure is not automatic, but falls under the discretion of the court or governing body upon showing good cause for release of the information.

Disclosure of Medical Records

Mandatory Disclosure

Some types of confidential medical record information must be disclosed. The specific nonvoluntary reporting requirements may vary from state to state, but each state has mandated the reporting of suspected child abuse. Different contagious diseases are also reported in different states. All states require the reporting of AIDS. Some states allow the health care practitioner to disclose a patient's HIV status to the patient's partner, although it may not create a duty to do so. Other mandatory disclosures include deaths, births, specific wounds, accidents, violently incurred injuries, fatalities due to blood transfusions, certain medical devices, workers compensation claims, seizures, particular congenital diseases, and induced termination of pregnancy.

Freedom of Information Act

The Freedom of Information Act (FOIA) was signed into law on July 4, 1996 by President Lyndon B. Johnson, amended in 2002, and went into effect the following year. The act allows for the full or partial disclosure of previously unreleased information and documents controlled by the U.S. Government. The act defines the agency records that are subject to disclosure, outlines mandatory disclosure procedures, and the exceptions to the statute. One exception is disclosure of personal or medical records that would clearly be an unwarranted invasion of personal privacy (FOIA, 2002).

Open Records Act

Most states have Open Records Acts that make medical records at a state hospital available to the general public except for an exemption protecting the confidentiality of the records.

Nondiscoverable Information

Various administrative or monitoring records pertaining to patient care may be sought in a medical malpractice action. These include credentialing surveys, infection control committee reports, departmental logs, risk management data, utilization review reports, peer-review reports, and incident reports. The data are usually discoverable unless protected by a state statue.

Discoverable Information

The information included refers to materials, documents, or witnesses that must be available to the opposing parties in a lawsuit. Discoverable information is not always admissible in court. The judge or other trier of fact makes the final decision about information that is relevant and probable enough to be admitted as evidence. For example, photographs of victims in a fatal motor vehicle accident may be available and discoverable to both sides. The photographs may be extremely graphic and may produce an emotional response in the viewer. Unless the party requesting that the photographs be produced can show that they are needed to prove an issue that is in contention, the judge will probably rule that the photographs are inadmissible because they do not support or defend an issue in the case.

Peer Review

The medical staff of health care facilities is generally charged with the responsibility to ensure the quality of patient care and to oversee the ethical and professional practices of staff members. Part of this responsibility is carried out by peer review, which includes the evaluation of professional performance, ethical behavior, quality of care, utilization patterns, and selected aspects of performance of the staff and health care professionals. Many states have mandated that communications revealed in these conferences are privileged and immune to discovery. The participants cannot be sued for any possible defamatory statements and the records of the meetings cannot be made available to a patient who may be pursuing a legal action against the subject of the peer review. Some states have extended the privilege to all professional committees including Quality Assurance and other states have narrowed the peer-review privilege. The extent of what is discoverable and what is not may be restricted to notes, minutes, and reports. However, continuation or revocation of staff privileges based on the peer review may be discoverable in a subsequent action related to the subject matter reviewed at the meeting.

Incident Reports

The incident report memorializes an event that is not consistent with the routine operation of the hospital or routine care of a particular patient. It may be an accident or situation that could result in an accident. If the incident report is filed as part of the medical record, it may be discoverable and may be admissible in court under the hearsay rule. If the incident report is directed to the legal department of the facility, it may be nondiscoverable and the facility can argue that the report was made in anticipation of litigation. Documents that are prepared in anticipation of litigation are considered to be the attorney's work product and are generally not discoverable.

Computerized Records

The trend toward computerized medical records has continued. Today, most private health care facilities and health care providers have implemented computerized records at some level. Computer technology and HIPAA requirements have revolutionized the management of medical record information. New challenges include mandatory restricted access to confidential records and the risk of loss or destruction of computerized data. In 2006, the United States Supreme Court amended the Federal Register of Civil Procedure (FRCP) and created a category for electronic records naming e-mails and instant message chats as likely to be archived and produced when relevant. The FRCP was completely rewritten and became effective in December 2007. Electronic mail, draft documents, and phone mail are hidden in hard drives, and on servers and backup tapes. If data have been saved it is likely that they can be retrieved, even if they have been deleted. The information is discoverable by attorneys to support their cases. E-mail can provide attorneys with valuable evidence on either side of the case (Rosenberg, 1997).

In a recent national survey of physicians, it was determined that their use of electronic records in the practice environment had been a slow process. Cost, value, and difficulty in finding appropriate hardware and software were cited as reasons. A basic system for laboratory data, clinical notes, and electronic prescribing were sometimes in place, but full electronic systems were in place in the practices of only about 4% of the physicians surveyed. Physicians did state in the survey that some had purchased a system but had not implemented it, or planned to purchase a system in the next several years (DesRoches et al., 2008).

The growing acceptance of computer technology and HIPAA requirements has revolutionized the management of medical information. The health care practitioner or facility has had to adjust to new problems that accompanied the integration of computerized data. New challenges include maintaining restricted access to confidential records along with the risk of loss or destruction of electronic data. Standardized electronic transactions of information approved by HIPAA and unique identifiers for providers, health plans, and employers are now common. Patient identifiers are not far from reality. Transmission of identifiable individual data may be protected by various technical features: passwords; procedural approaches, such as security training and periodic risk assessments; physical safeguards, such as restricting terminal access; and personnel safeguards, such as hiring and educating staff who can abide by confidentiality requirements (Lawrence, 1994).

Legal Access to Medical Records

Statutes of Limitation

The statute of limitations is the time period after which a lawsuit can no longer be pursued. The state legislature determines the time frame, which varies for different causes of action.

If one of the parties involved in litigation refuses to allow the other party access to documents in their possession, the theory of fraudulent concealment may be initiated. This involves hiding essential facts that the opposing party has the right to know. The health care practitioner or facility cannot protect itself from a lawsuit by failing to produce records within the usual statutory time frame as the start of the statute of limitations time period may not be triggered until or when the plaintiff discovers that the defendant is purposefully concealing material information. In some states, the statute of limitations is not triggered until the plaintiff discovers or should have discovered that he suffered an injury due to a tortuous act.

Discovery

When a lawsuit is filed in a state or federal court, the parties begin to investigate the facts or issues of the case through a formal discovery processes. One method of discovery is the request for production of documents. If the document is not produced, the party seeking the document can file a motion with the court to compel production. If the motion is granted, the opposing party must produce the document or face the possibility of sanctions, including a charge for contempt of court (Lobe, 1995).

Record Retrieval by Subpoena

Another method of discovery is the subpoena, which requires the attendance of a party or witness to appear in court or at a deposition. This may be accompanied by a subpoena duces tecum, which is Latin meaning to appear with documents under penalty of law. If the witness, at trial or deposition, is asked to reveal privileged or confidential information, the witness should consult his attorney before responding. The attorney may file a motion for a protective order asking the court to allow the witness to refuse to answer. In the case of substance abuse records, under federal law, a court order must accompany the subpoena stating that disclosure of the confidential information "is more important than what Congress mandated as confidential" (Hirsh, 1995).

Spoliation of Medical Records

Spoliation of evidence refers to any action including destruction, alteration, or concealment of records, which deprives the court or parties to evidence in a dispute (Gilbert, Whitworth, Ollanik, & Hare, 1994). The American legal process relies on the voluntary compliance of the parties to produce documents and other evidence that are in files or in possession of one of the parties. The failure to preserve or produce evidence is one of the worst forms of discovery misconduct and can result in severe consequences, including punitive damages that are not covered by insurance policies.

One of the legal consequences of loss or destruction of a medical record is a jury instruction that can adversely affect the defendant's position at trial, whether the loss was intentional or negligent. The jury may be instructed that they can infer that the evidence that was destroyed was unfavorable to the person who was responsible for its safekeeping. Discovery sanctions, including the entry of a default judgment, can be imposed against the party that destroyed or withheld evidence. Alternatively, the health care facility or practitioner may face professional disciplinary actions or criminal penalties. Spoliation may be an issue when a person claims injury from a defective product. The product thus becomes "lost" and the manufacturer may then attempt to have the case dismissed. Compliance with the discovery process is an ongoing issue in production and preservation of records, especially in medical issues. If the loss or destruction of the evidence is unintentional or not essential to the case, the court is less likely to impose extensive punitive damages.

National Practitioner Data Bank

In 1990, a national data bank called the National Practitioner Data Bank (NPDB) was created as a result of the Health Care Quality Improvement Act. The U.S. Congress became aware of the increasing occurrence of medical malpractice litigation and the need to improve quality of medical care. The intent was to improve quality of care by encouraging state licensing boards, hospitals, other health care facilities, and professional societies to identify and discipline those who engage in unprofessional behavior. It was also developed to restrict the ability of incompetent physicians, dentists, and other health care practitioners to move from state to state without disclosure of a previous medical malpractice payment and adverse action history. Adverse actions include those associated with professional licensure, clinical privileges, exclusions from Medicare and Medicaid, and professional societies. According to TJC, a practitioner must apply for clinical privileges every two years. Each time the application is made, the facility must request information from the NPDB regarding the practitioner. The information is not available to the general public, and facilities must register to access the information.

As part of HIPAA's attempt to combat fraud and abuse, the Secretary of HHS was directed to create the Health Care Integrity and Protection Data Bank (HIPDB), a data bank similar to the NPDB. Health plans and licensing/enforcing federal and state agencies are required to report certain final adverse actions taken against health care practitioners, including nurses, providers, and suppliers. The same entities who must report to the bank are the only agencies that are allowed access to the bank, although legislation is pending to expand HIPDB access (HIPDB, 2008).

Sentinel Events

A sentinel event is an unexpected occurrence that according to TJC "signals the need for immediate investigation and response" (Joint Commission, 2008). If a sentinel event occurs, a facility is expected to perform a root cause analysis and to formulate an action plan that identifies the strategies the organization intends to implement to reduce the risk of similar events occurring in the future. A sentinel event is defined by TJC as any unexpected occurrence involving death or serious physical or psychological injury, or the risk thereof. A recurrence would carry the chance of a serious adverse outcome for the institution. A sentinel event and a medical error are not synonymous. Not all sentinel events occur because of an error and not all errors result in sentinel events. TJC reviews organizations' activities and response to sentinel events during its accreditation process. The goals of the TJC policy include positive impact on improving patient care, treatment, and services; to focus organizational attention to understand the cause and reduce the possibility for recurrence; to increase the general knowledge about sentinel events; and to maintain the confidence of the public and accredited organizations in the accreditation process.

Between January 1995 and June 30, 2008, approximately 5,000 sentinel events were reported to TJC. The majority of the sentinel events were in the general hospital setting (67.5%). The three most commonly reported events were wrong-site surgery (13.3%), suicide (12.3%), and outpatient postoperative complications (11.5%).

A root cause analysis is an internal investigation that should focus on the system, not the individual. Once the facility is notified of an event, a thorough investigation and action plan should be submitted to TJC within 45 days according to TJC guidelines. The self-reporting of the event is not required to be reported to TJC; however, if TJC becomes aware of the event by some other means other than a self-report, the facility will be required to submit the root cause analysis. When facilities report to TJC, they have been advised not to provide patient or caregiver identities. Submitting the report may allow discovery of the report should a medical malpractice claim arise from the underlying event. TJC has agreed to provide the sentinel event documents for review thereof with return of the documents on the same day, or to provide on-site review of the documents (Joint Commission, 2008).

Tell-All Standard

The Institute of Medicine (IOM) is a nongovernmental national organization chartered in 1970. The purpose of the organization is to provide national advice on issues relating to medicine, health, and biomedical science. In November 1999, the IOM reported that between 44,000 and 98,000 people died in hospitals each year as a result of medical errors. The errors included medication errors, diagnostic problems, equipment failure, nosocomial and postsurgical wound infections, blood transfusion errors, and misinterpretations of orders. In response to these reports, TJC proposed new patient safety standards that went into effect on July 1, 2001. Included in the revised standards is a mandate that patients be informed about all outcomes of their care whenever those outcomes differ significantly from the anticipated outcomes.

Rules of Evidence

Just as there are federal and state rules of civil and criminal procedure controlling the process of a legal action, there are federal and state rules controlling what information and witnesses can be used in the courtroom. Since state rules vary, the emphasis in this discussion will be on the Federal Rules of Evidence (FRE). The FRE became federal law on January 2, 1975. The first drafts were begun in 1969 however; Congress made a series of modifications to the rules before they became law (FRE, 2007).

Hearsay Rule

Part of the trier of fact's job in the courtroom, whether the trier of fact is a judge or jury, is to evaluate the witness's perception, memory, and narration of events. The court system attempts to promote these three factors by requiring the witness to take an oath and testify in the personal presence of the judge or jury, but most importantly, by subjecting the witness to cross-examination.

Hearsay is a statement that is made out of court and not under oath and is offered as the truth. Hearsay is not admissible as evidence because cross-examination is not available for accuracy of the statement. In some cases, the court has found the out of court statement to be reliable and trustworthy. These statements have been added to the FRE as exceptions to the Hearsay Rule. Business records fall into the category of reliable and trustworthy evidence that is admissible. Medical records usually fall into the category of business records because they are made by persons who have a duty to record accurate information to assist health care practitioners and health care facilities to care for patients. The document is signed by the responsible individual, the record is made or transmitted close in time to the event, and it is made by persons who had firsthand knowledge of the event. A computerized record may be contested if it does not have a signature. The record must be introduced in a way that fulfills the requirements of the FRE. Another way that the record could be contested is the "double hearsay" problem. The health care practitioner may have documented statements concerning the immediate cause of the injury or assertions about the fault. Unless these statements fall within the exception to the hearsay rule, they cannot be admitted into evidence to prove the cause of injury or fault. The admission of medical records is not usually an issue at trial, because any dispute concerning the records has been resolved in a pretrial conference (FRE, 2007).

Public Records Exception

The public records exception is another exception to the Hearsay Rule that is very similar to the business records exception. Like the business records exception, its reliability for accurateness depends on the recording of data by persons with firsthand knowledge under a duty to make the report. For example, police officers have a duty to record the details of an accident in their report. In a personal injury case, the accident report would be admissible under the public records exception to hearsay. In a medical malpractice suit, the public records exception would generally apply only to records made by public offices or agencies and so would be useful only concerning records of public health care facilities.

Best Evidence Rule

The Best Evidence Rule or the Original Document Rule of FRE requires that the original document, photograph, or recording in evidence be presented if the contents are an issue. If the original document has been destroyed or is lost, a duplicate is admissible unless there is a question of authenticity. Medical records often consist of numerous pages of data. Due to the sheer volume of the record, summaries can be prepared for the court as long as the originals are available. Some states do require exchange of proposed summaries prior to trial.

Exhibits

An exhibit can be anything other than testimony, that can be perceived by the senses and be presented in the courtroom. There are some restrictions as to the information that is acceptable for admission. The exhibit cannot be so prejudicial or inflammatory that it outweighs its probative effect. This determination is made by the judge. The exhibit must be relevant and authenticated and helpful in the witness's explanation of the events to the trier of fact (FRCP, 2007).

Summary

A complete and comprehensive medical record can be a decisive piece of evidence in a case that involves medical issues. The LNC is in a unique position to assist an attorney in gathering, organizing, and reviewing the medical information contained in the record. Familiarity with the standards and rules that pertain to medical records will give the LNC a better understanding of what records should contain, why and when they are confidential, how to obtain them, how long they should be available, and how or why they can be used at trial.

References

American Health Information Management Association (AHIMA). (2008). *Practice guidelines for LTC health information and record systems*. Retrieved, February 18, 2009, from http://www.ahima.org/infocenter/guidelines/ltcs/4.1.asp

American Nurses Association (1998). *Standards of clinical nursing practice (2nd edition)*. Washington, DC: ANA Publishing.

American Medical Association (AMA). (2002). Retrieved February 18, 2009, from http://www.ama-assn.org/ama/pub/category/2386.html

Department of Health and Human Services. Office of the Secretary. (2006, February 16). *Federal Register*. 45 CFR Parts 160 and 164. HIPAA administrative simplification: Enforcement; Final Rule. 71(32). Retrieved February 18, 2009, from http://bulk.resource.org/gpo.gov/register/2006/2006_8390.pdf

DesRoches, C. M., Campbell, E. G., Rao, S. R., Donelan, K., Ferris, T. G., Jha, A., Kaushal, R., Levy, D. E., Rosenbaum, S., Shields, A. E., & Blumenthal, D. (2008). Electronic health records in ambulatory care: A national survey of physicians. *New England Journal of Medicine, 359,* 50–60.

Federal Rules of Civil Procedure (FRCP). (2007). Retrieved February 18, 2009, from http://www.uscourts. gov/rules/civil2007.pdf

Federal Rules of Evidence (FRE). (2007). Retrieved February 18, 2009, from http://www.law.cornell.edu/ rules/fre/rules.htm

Final Enforcement Rule. (2006). Retrieved February 18, 2009, from http://www.hhs.gov/ocr/privacy/hipaa/ administrative/enforcementrule/enforcementfinalrule.html

Freedom of Information Act (FOIA). (2002). Retrieved February 18, 2009, from http://www.gwu.edu/~nsarchiv/ nsa/foia.html

Gilbert, J., Whitworth, R., Ollanik, S., & Hare, F. (1994). Evidence destruction-legal consequences of spoliation of records. *Legal Medicine, 14,* 181–200.

Health Insurance Portability and Accountability Act (HIPAA). (2002). Retrieved February 18, 2009, from http://www.hhs.gov/ocr/hipaa

Healthcare Integrity and Protection Data Bank (HIPDB). (2008). Retrieved February 18, 2009, from http:www.aarc.org/advocacy/state/hip_db.html

HHS Fact Sheet. (2003). *Protecting the privacy of patients' health information.* Retrieved 2008, from http//www.hhs.gov/news/facts/privacy.html

Hirsh, H. (1995). Disclosure about patients. *Legal Medicine,* 312–342.

Joint Commission. (2008). Retrieved February 18, 2009, from http://www.jointcommission.org/ SentinelEvents.

Lawrence, L. (1994). Safeguarding the confidentiality of automated medical information. *Journal of Quality Improvement, 20*(11), 639.

Lobe, T. (1995). *Medical malpractice: A physician's guide.* New York: McGraw-Hill.

Rosenberg, G. (1997). Electronic discovery proves an effective legal weapon. *The New York Times,* D5, March 31.

Test Questions

1. To obtain a client's medical record
   A. A request for certification must accompany the request
   B. A dated and signed request for the record must be made
   C. The client must request the record in person
   D. Payment must accompany the request

2. The statute of limitations is
   A. The time beyond which a lawsuit can no longer be pursued
   B. Consistent for different actions
   C. Suspended when a health care practitioner moves to another state
   D. The limit of damages that can be awarded in a trial

3. A root cause analysis report
   A. Is prepared by JCAHO and must be implemented within 45 days by the health facility
   B. Must include an action plan that focuses on corrective action concerning the individual's behavior
   C. Is automatically discoverable should the incident be the subject of litigation
   D. Stems from an internal investigation regarding the flaws within the system that contributed to a sentinel event

4. Spoliation of the records
   A. Results in a summary judgment for the plaintiff
   B. Includes destruction of records from natural causes
   C. Can result in civil and criminal charges against the health care practitioner
   D. Includes late entries that are inconsistent with earlier entries

Answers: 1. B, 2. A, 3. D, 4. C

Chapter 6

Discovery and Disclosure

Kara L. DiCecco, MSN, RN, LNCC

First Edition and Second Edition
Julianne Hernandez, MPH, BSN, RN; Mary Lanz, RN, LNCC;
Barbara Noble, RN; and Barbara Stillwell, MSN, RN

Contents

Introduction

The purpose of this chapter is not to make the legal nurse consultant (LNC) an expert in the pretrial stages of discovery and disclosure. The legal strategies and nuances of the discovery process far exceed what can be taught in the chapter of a book. While the area of discovery is primarily the domain of the attorney, paralegal, and law clerk, the LNC is a valuable asset in discovery and may play a major role in case development using specialized knowledge.

Objectives

At the completion of the chapter, the LNC will have a basic understanding of the fundamental rules of civil procedure and frequently encountered evidentiary requirements of the federal courts as they relate to discovery in civil actions. The chapter will highlight the stepwise progression of the discovery process in establishing key elements of the case while offering an analysis of the function of each. The final objective is to compare and contrast the roles of the LNC from the plaintiff and defense perspective as well as that of the nurse expert witness.

A Few Words to Clarify

Some clarification is warranted as this chapter begins. First, to lessen confusion and to better delineate the distinct roles of the nurse expert witness and the LNC in the discovery process, we will define these roles to mean "testifying expert" and "behind-the-scenes LNC," respectively. The "behind-the-scenes" LNC may be either in-house or independent. Second, while the terms disclosure and discovery are not mutually exclusive, for our purposes here we will draw the distinction to focus on the subtleties of the definitions. Third, much like physicians, each attorney has distinct styles and preferences. Even though adherence to the jurisdictional rules and guidelines offers a certain measure of flexibility in the pretrial litigation process, the discovery steps outlined here follow the order of the general rule of thumb. It is worth noting, however, similar to health care, that there are always exceptions to the general rule and each step may be influenced by the individual practitioner or judge's preference.

As a technical matter (and paying due respect to gender equality), the pronouns "he" and "she" will be used interchangeably when referring to the professional roles.

Finally, LNCs possess extensive knowledge and may work in a broad spectrum of legal environments, making it a formidable task to present work samples that address the full spectrum of legal settings. For demonstration purposes, the appendices contain samples of work product and provide the rules of procedure and evidence commonly encountered in a medical negligence action. It is important to emphasize that these rules are not necessarily applicable or binding to other areas of law, for example a criminal action or domestic practice, to name just a few. It is essential that the LNC master a basic understanding of the rules of discovery for the specific area in which she practices.

Overview of the Discovery Process

Purpose of Discovery

Discovery is defined as, "The act or process of finding or learning something that was previously unknown. Compulsory disclosure at a party's request of information that relates to the litigation" (Garner, 2001). As this definition implies, discovery is an active process. From the onset, it is important to identify the key elements of the case. A well-conducted discovery will help establish these key elements.

The purpose of discovery is to provide the parties with the opportunity to limit surprises at trial, narrow the issues to be decided, and establish support for their legal positions. The process of discovery is accomplished through the five core instruments: (a) interrogatories, (b) request for production (RFP), (c) depositions, (d) physical and/or medical examination, and (e) requests for admission (RFA) (Fed.R.Civ.P. 30, 33, 34, 35 and 36). Key to the discovery of information sought is that it must be "relevant to the subject matter involved in the pending action" [Fed.R.Civ.P. 26(b)(1)]. This relevancy requirement restrains the tendency to unnecessarily vet the opponent party with requests for material unrelated to the core legal issue, and is the guiding rule for the request of information.

State versus Federal Laws

Because the U.S. Constitution: Bill of Rights provides for the right of states to independently govern their citizens through their legislators, each state is free to choose its own rules of civil procedure and evidence as long as it does not violate the U.S. Constitution (U.S. Const. amend. X). If the individual state so chooses, the state legislature is free to adopt the federal rules in whole, in part, or not at all. Fortunately, many states have chosen to adopt the Federal Rules of Civil Procedure (Fed.R.Civ.P.) and the Federal Rules of Evidence (Fed.R.Evid.). Choosing to follow the Fed.R.Civ.P. and the Fed.R.Evid., provides a measure of continuity and uniformity in our court system. It is incumbent on the LNC however; to be sure she is familiar with the jurisdictional rules and evidentiary guidelines that equate to the federal rules in the state(s) and court(s) in which she practices.

Disclosure

Disclosure assumes a dual role in the law. It is either voluntary or required depending on the information to be disclosed. Disclosure is defined as, "The act or process of making known something that was previously unknown; a revelation of facts" (Garner, 2001). Its dichotomous nature depends on the circumstances of the legal issue itself. For example, voluntary disclosure is expected when a conflict of interest makes itself known to the attorney. It is both anticipated and expected that the attorney will voluntarily divulge such information. This duty also extends to those working as the attorney's agent (paralegal, LNC, law clerk, etc.). If the LNC becomes aware of a potential conflict of interest, she is duty bound to immediately inform the attorney who hired her. This responsibility is imparted to the LNC through the attorney in the American Bar Association's (ABA) Model Rules of Professional Conduct 1.7: Conflict of interest; current clients and 1.16 (a): Declining or terminating representation (2002).

Mandatory disclosure in personal injury litigation is inherent to formal discovery. For example, in a State of Delaware, Superior Court civil action, Form 30 Interrogatories accompany the filing of the complaint and require information from the litigant in the form of seven areas addressing (a) the identification of the names and addresses for any witnesses, (b) names and addresses of any persons with knowledge of facts to the events being litigated, (c) names and addresses of any persons who have been interviewed regarding the events being litigated, (d) identification of persons in possession of documents related to the matter being litigated, (e) name and address of any expert witness presently retained, (f) names and addresses of medical providers, and (g) name/address/policy limit amount of any applicable insurance coverage (Del.Sup.Ct.R.Civ.P., Appendices of Forms, 30).

Claims of Privilege and the Attorney-Work Product Doctrine

Nurses are familiar with the principles of confidentiality as they relate to health care. Our tradition is steeped in the ethics of preserving the confidences of patient communication, diagnosis, and treatment. Similarly the *Attorney–Client Privilege* is primarily addressed in the Model Rule of Professional Conduct 1.6: Confidentiality of information, which directs attorneys regarding their duty to keep client confidences (2002). The hallmark case citing of the intended purpose of this communication privilege is found in *Upjohn Co. v. U.S.* (1981). In part it states that privilege exists to protect "not only the giving of professional advice to those who can act on it but also the giving of information to the lawyer to allow him to give sound and informed advice" (id.389-91). Further rules of communication and privilege are found in Article V of the Fed.R.Evid. The Fed.R.Evid. 501 and 502 and their subsequent rules outline legal protection for communication occurring in defined relationships as they pertain to the attorney's client (see Appendix A, Fed.R.Evid.).

Despite the tendency to use the terms protection and attorney–client privilege interchangeably, there is a clear line of demarcation with regard to their intended purpose. Privilege may extend to documents and the like, but that is not the same as the attorney–client privilege. The attorney–client privilege is intended to address the communication process between the attorney and the client. The *Attorney-Work Product Doctrine* is aimed at protection of the attorney's legal theory, strategically related concepts, legal opinions, and other thoughts and processes as he prepares for trial. The origins of the Attorney-Work Product Doctrine are found in the Supreme Court case *Hickman v. Taylor* (1947), but this protection is extended in the rules to include those materials generated by persons other than the attorney if "prepared in anticipation of litigation" [Fed.R.Civ.P. 26(b)(1–5)].

This protection, however, is not absolute and is subject to production should the opposing party establish an extreme need for such information. Take, for example, a destruction of evidence allegation against a hospital where the only surviving document is the incident report. Normally material prepared in anticipation of litigation compiled by risk management and the hospital's legal counsel is protected. Due to the destruction of crucial evidence, the plaintiff's counsel may be able to show a "substantial need" and "undue hardship" in trying to obtain legal redress for the injured plaintiff without the information contained in the incident report. If the judge determined the incident report was subject to disclosure, the *factual* evidence in the report would be discoverable while the defendant attorney's own spoken and written thoughts [mental impressions] *about* the document would remain shielded by the doctrine [Fed.R.Civ.P. 26(b)(3)].

Discovery and the Behind-the-Scenes Consultant

As a practical matter, work done by a consultant in the employ of the attorney is generally protected under the work product doctrine. An in-house LNC's work product is shielded by this doctrine. However, the LNC in this role should still mark correspondence, e-mails, chronologies/medical summaries, and the like with the disclaimer "attorney-work product, privileged and protected."

Once mistakenly produced or if client confidentiality is breached, even in error, privilege and protection are at debatable risk. For this reason, it is critically important that the consultant keep a strict system of isolating potentially protected documents from those subject to discovery.

The December 2006 amendment to Fed.R.Civ.P. 26(b)(5) does allow one however, in the case of inadvertent production of trial preparation material or privileged information, to assert a protective claim. It provides that once the party seeking protection of materials notifies the receiving parties of the claim and its grounds for asserting protection, the receiving party must return, sequester, or destroy the information. The rule is mute on the waiving of protection and privilege in these circumstances, but bars the receiving party from its use (2006). From a practical standpoint, much like the questionable effectiveness of telling the jury to disregard the shocking statement they just heard, it is better practice to prevent the accidental disclosure in the first place.

Discovery and the Expert Witness

Any individual clearly retained and identified as an expert witness for purposes of testimony will find, at a minimum, their opinions, reports, fee schedule, cancellation schedule, literature, curriculum vitae (CV) or resume, and prior testimony subject to discovery by the other side. Even the expert's draft report of his opinion and personal notations regarding the case are subject to debate about their discoverability. It is safest to assume that all materials generated by the testifying expert witness are potentially discoverable.

The form of interrogatories and deposition questions may seem quite intrusive, even within the guidelines allowed by law. Expert witnesses should anticipate inquiry into whether they personally have ever been the subject of litigation, their class ranking in school, whether they passed licensure boards in their first attempt, the percentage of actual clinical time compared with the time devoted to academic positions or expert testimony, and the total dollar amount they derived from expert testimony in the preceding year, along with numerous other inquiries.

Electronic Discovery

In April of 2006, new amendments to the Fed.R.Civ.P. addressed the need to further clarify the inclusion and scope of requests for information specific to electronic discovery. By December 1, 2006 amendments specific to the discovery of electronic information (Fed.R.Civ.P. 16, 26, 33, 34,

37, 45 and form 35) went into effect and may be viewed at: http://www.supremecourtus.gov/orders/courtorders/frcv06p.pdf.

Known less formally as e-discovery, the scope of electronically stored information (ESI) is both extensive and complex. In the broadest view, it may encompass a vast array of categories, including, but not limited to, active and deleted e-mails and voice mails, archived and back-up systems, cookies, cached pages, audio and graphic files, temporary files, website logs, data, and programs files. In essence, the entire history of electronic information from conception to delivery to demise is subject to potential discovery.

Playing a key role in the evolution of e-discovery is the hidden but traceable text of documents (metadata) that provide a complete historical footprint of changes, deletions, and alterations to a document. While certain areas of litigation are more likely to be the hotbeds of activity (such as toxic tort, class action suits, and patent law), matters of e-discovery are becoming more prevalent in personal injury and health law where issues of federal preemption, corporate compliance, and documents stored on a litigant's *personal* computer take on heightened importance.

A subject as complex as electronic discovery will escape unmitigated definition here. However, there are a few specifics of electronic discovery warranting special attention by the practicing LNC. First, this is an ever-evolving area of litigation, so universally accepted guidelines defining the scope of electronic discovery have yet to be established by the courts. At this writing, as in all areas of the law, the LNC should understand that the parameters governing this area will continue to be shaped and changed as judicial rulings and case law progress.

Second, early timing of the "preservation letter," possibly as early as the pretrial investigative period, is a key component of ESI. In matters where the issue of potential sources of information may be stored electronically, a letter or notice to opposing counsel should be sent via certified mail or served to protect and preserve such information. A well-crafted preservation letter will go a long way toward assisting the attorney in obtaining potentially discoverable information and reserving the information for the discovery process (Ball, 2008). The preservation letter ultimately seeks to prevent the destruction of ESI (2008). The LNC may play a pivotal role in identifying potential electronic information. For example, the LNC may be aware of the existence of videos and monitor tracings that are made as a matter of protocol when performing invasive medical procedures such as cardiac catheterization. The LNC should alert the attorney–client to the possible existence of these electronic formats and should discuss with the attorney the need to send a preservation letter to safeguard against the destruction or deletion of such evidence.

The third multi-faceted concern of ESI is the mechanics of achieving an agreeable exchange of information between parties. A clear definition of terms and expectations, as well as the scope of production by both sides, is paramount to preventing delays or attempts at stalling production. In addition, the bench may be called upon to adjudicate matters such as the reasonableness of the requests, who should bear the cost of producing the requested information (cost-shifting) between the litigants, and who will shoulder the burden of production in fulfilling the request.

Finally, to optimize the production of ESI, the LNC should anticipate the involvement of an information technology (IT) specialist. This role may be filled by in-house IT staff or an independent expert retained by the attorney for litigation support. Similar to the liaison role of the LNC in medical matters, the IT expert will clarify and translate unfamiliar terminology and processes, be familiar with the specifics of maintenance and disclosure of ESI, identify the likely locations and storage protocols of ESI, help establish the trail to the originating system, and alert the attorney to possible manipulation or deletion of materials, whether knowingly or unwittingly, by the adversary. While controversial, the amendments also make allowances forgoing sanctions for ESI lost or destroyed in the process of routine maintenance (Fed.R.Civ.P. 37(f) "safe harbor provision").

Ethical Considerations for Discovery

In the true spirit of discovery, free exchange of information not otherwise privileged or protected should occur. In practice however, attempts to obstruct or evade discovery are not unheard of, and because the court does not directly oversee the process, what gets produced is at the direction and discretion of the attorney. The ABA provides ethical direction for attorneys in their Model Rule of Professional Conduct 3.4: Fairness to opposing party and counsel. In part, the rule states that, "A lawyer shall not unlawfully obstruct another party's access to evidence or unlawfully alter, destroy or conceal a document or other material having potential evidentiary value. A lawyer shall not counsel or assist another person to do such act" (2002). Acting as an agent of the attorney, the LNC consultant is likewise duty-bound by this rule.

Initiating Litigation

Before progressing to the core of the discovery process itself, a brief explanation of the steps leading up to the mandatory exchange of information is needed. Pleading is the umbrella term used for the legal documents that initiate a formal lawsuit. These basic documents frame the issues for trial.

In litigation, the plaintiff filing a *complaint* starts the legal action. The necessary elements of the complaint are (a) a statement regarding the grounds for jurisdiction; (b) short and plain statements of the claims (averments); and (c) demand for judgment (also known as the "prayer for relief" or "Wherefore" clause) [Fed.R.Civ.P. 8(a)]. It is imperative to remember that the *plaintiff* bears the burden of proving what he or she alleges with regard to negligence and damages. In a civil action, this standard is "by the preponderance of the evidence." From a medical causation perspective, this is often defined as "more likely than not" and couched in the phrase "within reasonable, medical (or nursing) probability."

The complaint will specify the factual and legal basis for the lawsuit and must be filed in the court of proper jurisdiction. Also called subject matter jurisdiction, the requirement refers to the court's authority to hear and rule on a specific legal matter. The defendant is the person being sued and is ultimately the recipient of the complaint. Together the plaintiff and defendant are referred to as the parties.

When the complaint is filed, the Court Clerk issues a summons, which along with the copy of the complaint must be served or given to the defendant(s) or their designated agent (in the case of a corporation or business). Together the summons and complaint are known as *the process*. When the summons and complaint have been delivered to the defendant or their registered agent, this is known as service of process.

Service for a complaint must be "perfected" on the defendant within 120 days or risk dismissal unless otherwise extended by the court [Fed.R.Civ.P. 4(m)]. When the process must be served to a nonresident defendant or outside of jurisdictional lines, the process is known as long-arm service. (Attorneys must also be familiar with the unique aspects of service requirements on the Secretary of State, international corporations, governmental agencies, and more.) If additional time is needed to locate or serve the defendant, plaintiff's counsel may file a Motion to Enlarge Time. If granted by the court, this motion will grant a specified extension of time in which to serve the defendant.

Once officially served the complaint and summons, the defendant will need to file a responsive pleading known as the *answer*. The timeframe for filing an answer is subject to the rule outlined in Fed.R.Civ.P. 12. A civil case in federal court would require an answer to be filed within 20 days of service of the complaint and summons unless otherwise ordered by the court. Prior to filing an answer, the defendant's counsel may file a motion to challenge the adequacy of the complaint. For example, the defendant may file a Motion to Dismiss, alleging that the service of process was insufficient, that the court does not have the legal authority to preside over the specific case, or that the complaint fails to state a cause of action.

If the defendant does not file a Motion to Dismiss or the court denies the motion, the defendant must answer the complaint. In the answer the defendant must admit, deny, or plead ignorance to each and every specified fact. The defendant's answer must also contain any defenses and objections (see Appendix B, Fed.R.Civ.P.).

Affirmative defenses are concise statements explaining why the plaintiff's claims are unfounded. The defendant, through their counsel, will assert arguments or new facts that, if valid, would defeat the plaintiff's claim. Affirmative defenses are unique because they shift the burden of proof, which otherwise rests with the plaintiff, to the defendant (i.e., what defense alleges *they* now must prove).

Motion Practice

The filing of one or more motions is often an integral part of the litigation process and the main area of limited judicial intervention in the discovery process. The filing of motions may begin as early as the investigative phase of case development and continue through trial. Motions are simply requests to the court to rule on a matter or take some specific action. Motions in trial may be made orally, for example a Motion to Strike Testimony. Generally, in the discovery period, motions are made in writing and are accompanied by documents supporting the attorney's legal position. As a rule, motions will involve a Notice of Motion specifying the time and date the motion will be heard by the bench, the specific motion itself, exhibits (supporting documents), and a judicial order granting the requested motion in case the judge finds in the moving party's favor. If the judge finds for the party requesting the motion, the order will be signed and filed with the court (see Appendix C, Motion Practice).

Motions can be either dispositive or nondispositive. Granting a dispositive motion, for example a Motion for Summary Judgment, will dismiss or end the case. A nondispositive motion will not have this effect even if granted. An example of a nondispositive motion is a Motion to Compel Discovery. Whenever a motion is filed, the opposing attorney is permitted to file a response. Motions are presented to the presiding judge and may involve brief oral arguments by the attorneys, after which the judge will rule on the request.

Distinct Roles in the Discovery Process

The consulting roles in plaintiff and defense work are at once similar and unique. Both roles require effort toward identifying sources of potential information, which will likely support and give credence to their attorney–client's legal position. Both consultants will identify, strategize, and investigate the necessity of production of documents. Finally, both roles must maintain a fine balance between proving their case and overzealous production of information to the point of proving their adversary's case. The plaintiff and defendant consultants will take these steps specific to establishing the legitimacy of their attorney–client's legal posture, but it is here the commonality ends.

The plaintiff's LNC has the burden of proving and supporting the plaintiff's claim under the attorney's direction. Discovery efforts are aimed at eliciting information that validates the allegations asserted by the plaintiff and revealing potential weaknesses in the adversary's theory of defense. Discovery requests should explore and acquire information on the basis of the defendant's answer to the complaint. Since the burden of proof rests with the plaintiff, the defendant's LNC does not have the same burden. Under the attorney's direction her efforts are geared toward uncovering information that refutes the plaintiff's claim while exposing potential flaws in the adversary's legal strategy. Her focus should explore and acquire information on each allegation asserted in the plaintiff's complaint.

Interrogatories

As a rule, interrogatories are the initial tool of the discovery process. Interrogatories consist of written questions submitted by a party (the proponent) to the opposing party and answered, under oath, by that party (the respondent). In general, the federal rules are more restrictive, allowing only 25 interrogatories (questions), without leave of court (judicial permission) or written stipulation [Fed.R.Civ.P. 33(a)]. Subparts to a question (sometimes known as "branch questions") are counted as separate toward the total. This is an area where states may dramatically diverge on discovery rules from the federal courts. For example, Delaware Superior Court follows the federal rules but does not specify a limit on the number of interrogatories that can be served on the opposing party [Del.Sup.Ct.R.Civ.P. 33(a)]. Again, the consultant should confirm which rules govern the state in which she practices (see Appendix D, Sample Interrogatories).

Interrogatories, prior to the actual questions, will begin with instructions, definitions, clarifications, and clearly worded specifications of the information requested. This is intrinsic to the RFP as well. Providing these clarifications serves to circumvent unfounded objections to the request such as uncertainty about the intended meaning of "communication" or "document" among other terms.

In drafting interrogatories directed at the defendant doctor or nurse, the plaintiff's LNC would inquire regarding the level of skill, board certifications, practical experience, facts at issue, treatment rendered, prior sanctions, and litigation or disciplinary actions. In contrast, the defense's LNC would formulate questions about the plaintiff's medical history, information regarding injuries, accidents, prior litigation, and any background information relevant to the case.

Both plaintiff and defense LNCs will shape questions designed to garner as much information as possible about the medical expert's opinion on the opposing side. Specifically the interrogatories should seek to identify the basis of the expert's opinion. The LNC is most effective in establishing to what literature or treatises the expert will turn, as well as what standards or protocols they are likely to recognize. The LNC should research and obtain any medical literature or authoritative sources identified by their expert. The plaintiff's LNC will need to review the cost of obtaining such information with the attorney–client because the cost is advanced by the plaintiff's attorney, with the cost eventually recoverable from the client *only* if they are successful in litigation. Conversely, the defendant's LNC will need to estimate the cost of obtaining such information with the attorney–client as the cost is passed on to the defendant client (generally the insurance carrier), so the amount of billable hours obtaining the information may be a determining factor.

The interrogatories may also be used to determine the existence of prior testimony by the expert. Obtaining the expert's prior transcripts allows the LNC to review previous statements made under oath for issues of bias or credibility. There are both private and commercial services that provide access to an expert's prior testimony. These "deposition databanks" are usually searchable by the expert's name, and accessible for a fee. Some services may have restricted access for either plaintiff or defense firms.

Once responses to interrogatories are received, the LNC will review the answers, note any objections, and determine with the attorney if supplemental requests should be served.

The federal rules allow the responding party 30 days to assert objections to the request for specific information in the interrogatories and RFP. If the receiving party objects to answering a specific interrogatory (question) or production of a requested item, in addition to the objection, the basis for the objection must also be provided. In the case of a multipart question, the party must still answer those parts of the question to which they have no objection. Appendix E provides several of the common objections encountered in the responses to interrogatories and the RFP. It is important to note, however, that, while commonly encountered, these objections may be considered evasive and nonresponsive since the rule requires the responding party to specify the *exact detail* of the reason for the objection (Fed.R.Civ.P. 26, 33, and 34).

Request for Production

The RFP is submitted to the opposing party to obtain key documents and other tangible items (records, photos, statements of witnesses, etc.) that would assist in proving or refuting the facts asserted in the complaint. The RFP is often filed simultaneously with the interrogatories, although this is not mandatory practice. The RFP again takes the form of a request, although in a statement (see Appendix F, Sample Request for Production).

The law expects that the receiving party will produce all requested information, not otherwise protected, that is within their "possession, custody, and control" pursuant to Fed.R.Civ.P. 34(a). The fact that the information is not immediately contained in the plaintiff's or defendant's file does not necessarily excuse production if the information is within the legal control of the party. For example, a plaintiff's medical records that predate the injuries alleged in the lawsuit are not necessarily in the plaintiff's or their attorney's immediate possession; however, the plaintiff and their counsel are assumed to have control by using an appropriate authorization to obtain them. Likewise, if there is no objection to the production, the responding party must be given at least 30 days to gather and produce the requested documents or items.

From the plaintiff's perspective, the LNC's knowledge of the health care setting is used to make the attorney aware of the existence of videos, monitor tracings, films, internal reports, and written guidelines and policies intrinsic to procedures and treatment. This specialized knowledge also guides the requests to specify the appropriate department if the information is not kept with the primary chart. The plaintiff's LNC will want to conduct investigation into the defendant's history with regard to sanctions, disciplinary actions, and prior litigation. Again, there are commercial services that will provide this information for a fee. In the case of a medical negligence action, the plaintiff's LNC may want to inspect the original medical file on site, looking for inconsistencies in the chart produced earlier. The actual billing statements from the hospital stay or ancillary services should be requested and audited by the LNC. Billing statements will indicate medications dispensed, monitor use, invasive procedures, and equipment usage. In addition, billing statements often contain additional diagnosis and procedural codes for comparison with the chart.

From the defense vantage point, the LNC should closely scrutinize the plaintiff's present and past medical records for clues to alternative causation from pre-existing health problems, prior injuries, medication side effects, and issues of noncompliance. In the case of allegations of cognitive injuries, the LNC should obtain school records to determine a baseline academic performance. In addition, the defense's LNC will want to consider requesting additional medical records of the plaintiff based on results that are copied to the health care providers not otherwise identified and to obtain all pharmacy transmittals. Investigation such as surveillance tapes where permitted, previous insurance claims, and income tax information for wage claims may yield valuable information. Another role of the defendant's LNC may be to determine the location, availability, access, and potential cost of producing broad or potentially immaterial information since sweeping requests by the plaintiff for ESI may not be feasible or warranted.

Both the plaintiff and defense LNCs should review the adversary expert's CV (as well as their own expert's) with an eye for obtaining any publications the expert has authored relevant to their case. Critically analyzing these articles or texts for their strengths and weaknesses can often provide valuable insight into the expert's position. The LNC should also be able to identify any professional resources, associations, licensing boards, and certifications as well as any practice acts because they impact the issues.

The RFP as a discovery tool also permits passage to "inspect the premises or enter the land" [Fed.R.Civ.P. 34(a)]. A site visit may be requested when the location where the injury occurred may afford information important to establish or refute liability: for instance, determining visibility of traffic control devices at an intersection where a motor vehicle accident occurred or inspecting the condition of safety railings at a job site.

Both interrogatories and the RFP are subject to supplementary responses if the original response is incorrect or incomplete, or new and relevant material is made known to the attorney at a later time [Fed.R.Civ.P. 26(e)]. It is also expected that answers to discovery will be generated in a "responsive manner." The responses are to be produced either as kept in the usual course of business or in a labeled and organized fashion that correlates to the numbered sequencing of the original request served [Fed.R.Civ.P. 34(b)]. Determine with the attorney if objections are valid or unfounded. Consider if a Motion to Compel for overdue responses is justified. Likewise, a Motion for Protective Order may be warranted to protect proprietary information or other material.

Organization and Follow-Up

Reviewing answers to interrogatories and taking inventory of opposing counsel's response to the RFP are essential steps throughout discovery. The importance of this step in organization and follow-up cannot be overemphasized in litigation. Responses that contain answers such as "to be provided" or boilerplate objections (which should be challenged) may be overlooked without a tracking system in place. By developing a system of follow-through, the LNC lays the groundwork for support should a motion to compel production be necessary. The LNC will further assist the attorney by alerting her to the possible need for supplemental interrogatories and requests for production, as well as supplemental responses as they relate to medical issues. By paying close attention to and respecting the attorney's and ultimately, the court's deadlines, the LNC best supports and enhances the attorney–client's legal strategy. A systematic approach to protection of privileged information circumvents unnecessary and costly litigation and prevents delays in an otherwise already lengthy process.

Requests for Admission

Fed.R.Civ.P. 36 addresses the RFA as a discovery tool. The intent of the RFA is to limit the issues that will ultimately be presented at trial. These requests take the form of written factual statements that are served upon the other side to which they must admit, deny, or object. If the receiving party does not deny or object to the admission statement(s) within 20 days of receiving the request, the statements are deemed admitted. Likewise the receiving attorney may voluntarily admit to the requests. Regardless of how the statement is admitted, the effect will be the same; that particular fact will not have to be proved at trial. For example, if the defendant admitted all the expenses incurred were valid medical expenses related to the injury the plaintiff sustained, *without conceding liability for the plaintiff's injury*, the total amount of medical bills would not have to be debated in trial (see Appendix G, Sample Requests for Admission).

Deposition

Deposition practice is governed by Fed.R.Civ.P. 30 and 31. More than any other tool in the discovery process, depositions may serve to provide vital information, facilitate negotiations, and reveal the strength or weakness of the opposing counsel's legal position. Till now, questions in the interrogatories may be somewhat reserved and avoid the tendency to reveal too much about the attorney's legal strategy. Questions specifically reflective of the attorney's legal theory or strategy are often withheld *until* the deposition, where answers by the deponent will be more spontaneous and less guarded.

Depositions are fact-finding missions. In addition to finding out what the witness knows, the deposition is designed to size up the witness and determine how he or she would appear to a jury. The witness's demeanor, appearance, and method of delivery can dramatically influence settlement negotiations. Offers of settlement are often increased or withdrawn following the depositions of key witnesses.

Video Depositions

Due to distance, availability, or other constraints, it is sometimes necessary to take depositions by video or from a remote location via satellite. The decision to videotape a deposition is generally made to preserve testimony for trial due to the witness's lack of availability. It is becoming increasingly common, however, to have deponents give even their discovery deposition from a location other than the attorney's office. Many litigation support services will make arrangements for witnesses to be deposed from a specific location, arranging for the court reporter and any equipment needed. Video depositions (even in the best witness) are not the most engaging testimony for the jurors; however, they have the advantage of being reviewed repeatedly to reveal the witness's nervous mannerisms and conflicting body language.

Rule 30(b)(6)

Knowing who is responsible for what information in large organizations can be a daunting task for any attorney. Naming the correct person to depose in an effort to obtain information regarding key documents and policies is the purpose of Rule 30(b)(6). There is a three-fold expectation within the rule: (a) the duty to designate, (b) the duty to substitute, and (c) the duty to prepare. This rule directs corporations, partnerships, associations, or governmental agencies to name the appropriate designee for deposition that is in a position of authority significant enough to provide key answers and information to the deposing attorney [Fed.R.Civ.P. 30(b)(6)]. In part, it provides that in response to a valid 30(b)(6) deposition notice of a party, the deponent organization must either designate one or more of its officers, directors, or managing agents to testify on its behalf, or designate another person who consents to speak for the deponent. If the corporation or organization is not a party to the litigation, a subpoena must be issued to obligate appearance. The rule further specifies that the witness must be prepared to provide binding answers to questions within the scope of the matters specified in the deposition notice. As ESI moves to the forefront of discovery matters, this rule further enhances the effectiveness of a fact-finding deposition as the designated deponent is expected to effectively answer inquiries regarding complex matters of storage and retrieval.

Role of the Behind-the-Scenes Consultant in Deposition

Independent or in-house LNCs are likely to be on the ground floor of identifying witnesses for trial. Both may be recruited to help draft deposition questions based on their review of medical records and the medical research they have conducted.

As the deposition nears, the LNC may become involved in the preparation of the attorney's expert medical witness. Familiarizing the witness with the deposition process will serve to assist with the deposition proceeding smoothly. The LNC may play a role in informing the expert that they will be sworn in and they should remember to answer each question verbally (instead of a nod or "uh-huh"). The LNC should remind the witness, prior to the start of the recorded testimony, that the court reporter will record every spoken word. For example, the expert should avoid talking out loud when looking for something in the record, as this would be recorded and when reviewed may read as though the expert is unprepared or disorganized.

It is helpful, if known, to inform the expert of the deposing attorney's style of questioning (i.e., friendly, aggressive, pressured, etc.). While there is no formula approach to expert testimony, the attorney may wish to discuss how hypothetical questions and matters of the expert's fee should be addressed. Additionally, procedural matters such as waiving the reading of their deposition and the purpose of the *errata sheet* should be reviewed with the expert.

The errata sheet is sent to the deponent's counsel so that the witness will have the opportunity to correct any transcription errors with regard to their testimony. Factual changes should not be made to the testimony, only technical errors. A disclaimer on the errata itself addresses that any changes are also assumed to be under oath. It is important for the LNC to track, through the discovery process, whether or not the expert completed an errata sheet following their deposition.

It is important to review with the expert that objections in deposition are handled differently from those in trial. Objections in discovery depositions are made to preserve the issue for trial and as such are not ruled on until that time. The reasoning is simple; the judge is not there to rule on each and every objection. Stopping the deposition to call the judge for each objection is neither practical nor likely to be appreciated. Once the objection is made, witnesses should pause for instruction from their attorney and should anticipate that the attorney may instruct them to go ahead with their answer. By placing the objection on record, the attorney has reserved the issue for the judge to rule on either prior to or during the trial.

The LNC may be asked to accompany the attorney to the deposition of the opposing side's expert witness. The LNC in this role should be aware of the attorney–client's style and preference in questioning. While most of the LNC's questions will be drafted and reviewed with the attorney prior to the actual deposition, during the deposition the expert may reference something that triggers a follow-up question from the LNC's educated perspective. If the LNC has questions to suggest during the deposition, the attorney and LNC should determine *prior* to the deposition how this should be communicated without obvious interruption.

Additionally, the LNC may formulate a question or point that she feels would be invaluable to the case, only to have the attorney ignore it and conclude questioning. The LNC should not pursue this issue at deposition. It is imperative to understand that attorneys are constantly forming their legal strategy and may reserve this question for trial because of its significance. Conversely, the attorney may choose not to use this question even in trial because by doing so it may open the door to issues she does not want to introduce. The LNC's role, in part, is to appreciate that the lead attorney is the only one who can ultimately decide how to present the case.

Upon entering the deposition room, the LNC will follow her attorney's lead but should anticipate presenting her business card to the court reporter, who will properly record her name and title as among those present for the deposition. The court reporter will also need to note the reason for the LNC's attendance (i.e., whether she was with the plaintiff or defense counsel).

The court reporter is arranged for and paid by the counsel requesting the deposition. The attorney will generally not require the attendance of both the paralegal and the LNC. If the LNC attends, she should confirm with the court reporter when the transcript and errata will be available, and confirm that the court reporter has all the information necessary to send the transcript to the attorney. If the attorney specifically wants an electronic version of the transcript as well, make this known to the court reporter at deposition. When received, the e-transcript should contain a hyperlink to the free software needed to view the transcript. The receiving party will need to click on (open) this link and download the program to their computer to view the transcript.

During the deposition, the LNC will assist the attorney by taking notes, including follow-up questions, noting her observations about eye contact, cues, and body language of the expert witness, potential nonverbal coaching of the deponent by the adversary, recording any inconsistencies in opinion, and noting any areas that need further review. It is helpful to the attorney if the LNC can provide feedback after the deposition regarding the expert's approach to teaching and explanation, as well as her impression of the expert's credibility. It is good practice to have a copy of the outline of the questioning by the attorney. While rare, if any question were missed the LNC would be able to subtly call it to the attorney's attention.

It is helpful for the consultant to track exhibits during deposition by noting which side produces what information. The original exhibits at deposition are returned to the party producing them; however, copies of the exhibits should be included when transcripts of the deposition are received. Be sure to collect any exhibits that belong to the attorney–client after providing a copy for the court reporter. The *original* of the deposition will ultimately be presented at trial and should be kept separate. In the interim, the attorney will work off a duplicate copy of the deposition or a copy saved directly to the attorney's computer as in the case of an e-transcript.

Role of the Expert Witness in Deposition

It is the court's expectation that expert witnesses will offer an honest, well-supported opinion within the scope of their expertise. Based on Fed.R.Evid. 702, the expert brings an opinion to the table that is qualified by specialized education and skill. The opposing medical experts will offer conflicting opinions as to duty, possible breach of duty, proximate cause, and degree of damages. Each attorney is already familiar with his own expert's opinion prior to the deposition, and has received and reviewed the written opinion of his adversary's expert witness.

Therefore, the deposition process is the opportunity for the attorney to find out in detail what the opposing expert is expected to say in trial. In addition, it provides the attorney with the opportunity to size up the expert witnesses and ideally eliminate any surprise testimony. It can safely be assumed that the attorneys will want to depose each other's expert witness and will be sending a notice of their intent to do so. (This is the reverse in trial, where attorneys call their *own* expert(s) and witnesses to testify.)

Depending on attorney and expert experience, the preparation of the expert witness may precede the taking of the deposition by several days or be a brief office consultation (30 min or so) reserved before the actual deposition. Regardless of the time reserved for preparation, the attorney should have provided the expert with all the necessary medical documentation and pertinent information well in advance of their expert's deposition.

In return, it is the experts' professional duty to familiarize themselves with the information provided by the attorney who retained their services in order to deliver an effective deposition. Materials that should be forwarded to the expert should include complete medical records relevant to the matter being litigated, depositions of all health care providers, opinions and the deposition transcript (when available) of the adversary's expert, literature or treatises that the attorney intends to reference, policy and procedures of the institution, facility or office practice, and any other information that has a bearing on the expert's ability to provide an informed opinion. Federal and state rules may differ on the mandatory requirement of current or active clinical practice for qualifying an expert witness; however, this question should be anticipated at deposition and in trial as a strategy to establish or impeach credibility of the witness (see Appendix H, Sample Deposition Questions).

One common pitfall of expert testimony is when the attorney (or his staff) fails to ensure that the expert has received all the updated medical information and dispositive information concerning the plaintiff. More than one expert (and chagrined attorney) has been taken by surprise when the expert's testimony is impeached during deposition because of not having received updated medical records and recent depositions given by parties to the litigation. While the purpose of including the reservation of the right to amend one's opinion in the expert's report (should additional information become available) may help to address such an occurrence, it may cost the expert a measure of credibility in their opinion, as the expert's attorney must now rehabilitate the expert's testimony through follow-up questioning.

From a plaintiff's perspective, when the deposition occurs in the defendant's or expert physician's office, the LNC should note what textbooks, patient educational materials, and references are present on the shelves. It is hard for the expert to deny the reliability of a text or reference he owns. From a defense perspective, the LNC should ensure that the deposition occurs in a conference room or area other than the defendant's or expert physician's private office.

Digesting the Deposition

Digesting a deposition may be done by the attorney's junior associate, paralegal, or law clerk. However, given the nature of complex information in a medical negligence case, the attorney may prefer to have the LNC summarize the deposition. There are a variety of ways to do this, but it largely depends on the attorney's personal preference. One technique involves noting or highlighting every entry of a keyword or statement by page and line number. Another practice is to provide the attorney with a document of the entries. For example, to provide the attorney with a document that shows every time the expert referred to "dehydration" in the deposition, the document would read "dehydration" 3:21, 4:24, 7:18, and so on (i.e., references in the deposition to "dehydration" can be found on page 3, line 21; page 4, line 24; etc.).

Another technique involves contrasting and comparing the written records (expert report or medical record) with the deposition for inconsistencies in opinion or facts. Whether this is done by hand or via a software program depends on the attorney's practice. These key passages or inconsistencies in statements may later be enlarged, highlighted, and used as exhibits in trial. Case management software can save countless hours of manual production by electronically organizing and digesting depositions if the attorney–client's budget allows for this type of technology.

Physical and/or Mental Examinations

As an additional discovery methodology, the defense is permitted to request that the plaintiff attend a medical examination pursuant to Fed.R.Civ.P. 35. In its purest form, the medical examination is meant to provide an objective opinion regarding the nature, extent, and potential recovery/possible permanency of the plaintiff's injuries.

The physician conducting the examination is retained (and their fee paid for) by the side requesting the examination. This invites the debate of whether the exam can be truly objective or unbiased. Given the inherent conflict, this practice is likely responsible for the variety of acronyms associated with the exam: (a) independent medical exam (IME), (b) defense medical exam (DME), or (c) expert medical exam (EME). Regardless of the label, the purpose remains inviolate: to substantiate the extent of injuries as they relate to the plaintiff's allegations.

As Chapter 19 will discuss in depth, the LNC may be asked to attend the exam with the plaintiff. If psychological issues of the plaintiff are at issue, "good cause" must be established by the defense before obtaining a mental examination. As it pertains to the discovery process, whether a physical or psychological evaluation, the plaintiff is entitled to receive a copy of the physician's report detailing his examination findings and ultimate opinion. It is incumbent on the consultant to ensure that a copy of examination is produced in time through discovery, and at the request of the attorney, forwarded to her attorney's expert witness.

Subpoenas

One of the advantages to initiating litigation is the power of a subpoena. Prior to filing a suit, requests for information such as medical records may go unanswered, be subject to significant delays, and result in the receipt of incomplete records. Fed.R.Civ.P. 45 governs the production of documents and things, as well as testimony, of nonparties.

A Notice of Deposition and a Notice of Records Deposition addresses the appearance and production of documents at deposition with regard to deponent *parties* to the litigation. A simple *subpoena* is used to compel the attendance of a *nonparty* deponent or witness. A *subpoena duces tecum* is issued to require a nonparty to produce documents. For example, a medical records custodian may be served with a *subpoena duces tecum* to produce the requested documents in person on or before a specified date and location. If the records custodians produce the requested information on or before the specified date to the requesting party, their physical appearance is not required (see Appendix I, Sample Subpoena Duces Tecum).

A word of caution is warranted here concerning the practice of subpoenas crossing jurisdictional lines. Whether or not a nonresident, nonparty is subject to the legal enforcement of a subpoena will be determined by the controlling jurisdiction. For example, in a Delaware civil action involving a nonparty witness who is a resident of Pennsylvania, the legal procedure requires an Out-of-State Commission to be filed to *request* the cooperation and assistance of the court with jurisdictional authority in Pennsylvania.

Scheduling, Status, and Final Pretrial Conferencing

In general, the scheduling conference falls after discovery is well underway [Fed.R.Civ.P. 16(b)]. This initial meeting provides a framework for important dates related to the litigation process, and is scheduled and conducted by the judge assigned to the case. It requires the attendance of the attorneys representing the parties involved, although the parties themselves do not attend.

From the scheduling conference, a proposed scheduling order of key dates is generated which the judge must approve. The scheduling order specifies when the exchange of discovery documents will stop, when the plaintiff's expert report will be due, when the defendant's expert report will be due, and the date by which all pretrial motions should be filed. The order also provides basic instructions of procedure. During this conference, issues of undisputed facts are determined, matters of law are discussed, and the potential for settlement is reviewed. If settlement is unlikely, a trial date will also be set.

Status conferences (interim meetings) between the judge and counsel occur between the scheduling conference and before the pretrial conference. As the trial date nears, the final pretrial conference is scheduled pursuant to Fed.R.Civ.P. 16(d). The purpose of the pretrial conference is to dispose of duplicative matters, finalize legal positions, address any preliminary objections, and exchange pretrial briefs outlining the key elements of trial including potential exhibits.

Seasoned LNCs often find that familiarity with the judge's particular style and "standing orders" further assists them in maximizing efficiency in the discovery period: for example, knowing the judge's personal bias toward granting or denying pretrial motions filed to extend time in the discovery process. Some judges are more likely to deny an extension of time past the original scheduling date in order to keep their docket of cases moving. Other judges will entertain such requests as long as both attorneys stipulate (voluntarily agree) to the extension, and the request for additional time is reasonable.

Spoliation and Fraudulent Concealment

The intentional destruction, mutilation, alteration, or concealment of evidence is termed spoliation (Garner, 2001). In response to proof of spoliation, the trial judge may allow an instruction to the jury that the missing evidence may be assumed unfavorable to the party responsible. The difficulty in establishing spoliation of evidence lies in the remedy itself. It may be impossible to counterbalance the damage done by the destruction if there is no evidence to view and quantify the degree of prejudice the affected party has sustained.

Fraudulent concealment refers to the intentional suppression of a material fact or circumstance with the intent to deceive or defraud despite a legal or moral duty to disclose (Garner, 2001). For example, a physician fails to disclose that a partner in his practice committed malpractice on a patient now under the second physician's care. As it applies to health care provider negligence, fraudulent concealment may toll the statute of limitations until the plaintiff discovers or should have discovered the negligence.

Both the chain of custody form and evidence log may be helpful in tracking and locating discoverable evidence and are also instrumental in establishing or defeating the charge of willful obstruction in the discovery process.

Summary

The in-house LNC, the independent LNC, and the expert witness who master a basic understanding of the ethical guidelines and rules that govern the process of discovery stand ready to assist the attorney in the presentation of a formidable case. By staying informed of evolving case law and advancing technology, the LNC promotes the true intent of the law in the exchange of information. By displaying integrity and professionalism in the discovery process, the legal nurse demonstrates the essence of the LNC profession. These attributes combined make the LNC an invaluable and irreplaceable member of the attorney–client's litigation team.

References

Amendments to the Federal Rules of Civil Procedure. (2006). Retrieved September 30, 2008, from http://www.supremecourtus.gov/orders/courtorders/frcv06p.pdf

Ball, C. (2008). Piecing together the e-discovery plan. *Trial*, June, 20–29.

Del.R.Ann. Vol. I. Del.Super.Ct.R.Civ.P., 33(a) (2007).

Del.R.Ann. Vol. I. Del.Super.Ct.R.Civ.P., Appendix of Forms 30 (2007).

Fed.R.Civ.P. 4(m)

Fed.R.Civ.P. 8(a)

Fed.R.Civ.P. 8(c)

Fed.R.Civ.P. 12

Fed.R.Civ.P. 12(b)(1–7)

Fed.R.Civ.P. 16

Fed.R.Civ.P. 16(b)

Fed.R.Civ.P. 16(d)

Fed.R.Civ.P. 26

Fed.R.Civ.P. 26(b)(1)

Fed.R.Civ.P. 26(b)(2)

Fed.R.Civ.P. 26(b)(3)

Fed.R.Civ.P. 26(b)(4)

Fed.R.Civ.P. 26(b)(4)(A)(i)

Fed.R.Civ.P. 26(b)(5)

Fed.R.Civ.P. 26(b)(5)(C)

Fed.R.Civ.P. 26(b)(5)(E)

Fed.R.Civ.P. 26(e)

Fed.R.Civ.P. 30

Fed.R.Civ.P. 30(b)(6)

Fed.R.Civ.P. 31

Fed.R.Civ.P. 33

Fed.R.Civ.P. 33(a)

Fed.R.Civ.P. 34

Fed.R.Civ.P. 34(a)

Fed.R.Civ.P. 34(b)

Fed.R.Civ.P. 35

Fed.R.Civ.P. 36

Fed.R.Civ.P. 37

Fed.R.Civ.P. 37(f) (amended 2006)

Fed.R.Civ.P. 45

Fed.R.Civ.P. 56

Fed.R.Evid. art. V

Fed.R.Evid. 501

Fed.R.Evid. 502

Fed.R.Evid. 702

Federal Rules of Civil Procedure with forms. (2007). Committee Print No. 2, 110th Congress, 1st Session (Publication No. 052-070007509-1). Retrieved September 30, 2008, from http://www.uscourts.gov/rules/civil2007.pdf

Garner, B. A. (Ed.). (2001). *Black's Law Dictionary* (3rd. ed.). Minnesota: Thomson West.

Hickman v. Taylor, 329 U.S., 495 (1947).

Model Rules of Prof'l Conduct 1.6. (1983). Retrieved September 30, 2008, from http://www.abanet.org/cpr/mrpc/rule_1_6.html

Model Rules of Prof'l Conduct 1.7. (1983). Retrieved September 30, 2008, from http://www.abanet.org/cpr/mrpc/rule_1_7.html

Model Rules of Prof'l Conduct 1.16(a). (1983). Retrieved September 30, 2008, from http://www.abanet.org/cpr/mrpc/rule_1_16.html

Model Rules of Prof'l Conduct 3.4 (1983). Retrieved September 30, 2008, from http://www.abanet.org/cpr/mrpc/rule_3_4.html

Upjohn Co. v. U.S., 449 U.S., 389 (1981).

U.S. Const. amend X.

Test Questions

1. In response to a valid deposition notice, Fed.R.Civ.P. 30(b)(6) imposes all of the following duties on the named corporation *except*
   A. The duty to designate
   B. The duty to negotiate
   C. The duty to prepare
   D. The duty to substitute

2. The purpose of an errata sheet following deposition is to
   A. Make factual changes to the testimony
   B. Waive the reading of the deposition
   C. Provide the deponent with the opportunity to change their opinion
   D. Correct mistakes in the deponent testimony due to transcription error

3. The attorney work-product doctrine functions to
   A. Protect the attorney/client communications with regard to legal representation
   B. Protect the testifying expert's opinion from discovery
   C. Protect materials prepared by the attorney in anticipation of litigation
   D. Protect confidential information even if inadvertently disclosed

4. All of the following is true about subpoenas *except*
   A. They are subject to the rules of the court of proper jurisdiction
   B. They are served on nonparties to the litigation
   C. They may be the subject of a Motion to Compel Discovery
   D. The receiving party must pay the cost of serving the subpoena

5. All of the following is true about objections to Interrogatories *except*
   A. The objection(s) must be timely filed
   B. The objection(s) must specify the exact reason for the objection
   C. In a multipart question, the respondent does not need to answer the question at all if he objects to any part of the question
   D. May be avoided if definitions and clarifications of terms are provided at the beginning of the document

Answers: 1. B, 2. D, 3. C, 4. D, 5. C

Appendix A: Summary of Select Federal Rules of Evidence

Summary of select Fed.R.Evid as they commonly impact the discovery process. The following is not meant to be an exhaustive list or exact citation of the rules. The specific examples given are for illustrative purposes only. To view the complete Fed.R.Evid. online, go to http://www.law.cornell.edu/rules/fre

Article IV	*Relevancy and its Limits*
Fed.R.Evid. 401: Defines "relevant evidence"	Evidence that supports or refutes the material facts at issue
Fed.R.Evid. 403: Exclusion of relevant evidence on grounds of prejudice, confusion, or waste of time	"The Balancing Test." Gives judge authority to rule whether the evidence's probative (tendency to prove) value outweighs its prejudicial effect. For example, an enlarged photo exhibit of a ventilator-dependent infant. The judge must decide if the picture is too inflammatory so that it plays on the emotions of the jury or is it necessary to show what the parent's are dealing with each day to determine damages
Fed.R.Evid. 409: Payment of medical and similar expenses	Offers or promises to pay medical expenses related to the injury in question, cannot be admitted as proof of liability
Article V	*Privileges*
Fed.R.Evid. 502: Lawyer–client	The client has the privilege to refuse to disclose and to prevent any other person from disclosing confidential communications made for the purpose of facilitating the rendition of professional legal services to the client. This duty to preserve confidences extends to those acting as the attorney's agent as well
Fed.R.Evid. 503: Mental health providers, physicians, psychotherapist–patient	For example, a physician (nor those in his employee) is not permitted to disclose the patient's terminal condition to the family in the absence of the patient's express permission
Fed.R.Civ.P. 503(2) and (3) Exceptions to privilege	For example, court ordered medical examination; because the plaintiff's injury or condition is an element of the claim
Fed.R.Evid. 507: Trade secrets	For example, if the trade secret becomes public knowledge the party will suffer financial harm due to marketplace competition
Fed.R.Evid. 510: Waiver of privilege by voluntary disclosure.	For example, the plaintiff is interviewed by his attorney regarding the events. The plaintiff insists his cousin can stay and gives permission for the cousin to be present for the conversation. The plaintiff has waived privilege should the opposing counsel call the cousin to testify
Article VI	*Witnesses*
Fed.R.Evid. 612: Writings used to refresh memory	For example, at deposition the witness may be asked if he or she can recall who was on duty in the emergency room the night of the alleged negligence. The witness is permitted to view the emergency room record to refresh his or her memory if needed

continued

Fed.R.Evid. 613: Prior statements of witnesses	For example, prior deposition testimony or written opinion of contradictory opinion to the position expert now asserts in this litigation
Article VII	*Opinions and Expert Testimony*
Fed.R.Evid. 702: Testimony by experts	In matters too complex or technical for the average juror to understand, an expert witness of specialized knowledge and education may testify to aid their understanding. For example, how to interpret arterial blood gases and how recognizing the patient's respiratory deterioration may have prevented the anoxic event the plaintiff suffered
Fed.R.Evid. 703: Basis of opinion testimony by experts	Materials and information relied upon by the expert in forming their opinion, not necessarily admitted as evidence. For example, the expert witness testifies the patient's symptoms were consistent with the presentation found in the *Principles of Neurology*, 8th edition. While the expert relies on this information, it would be too cumbersome for the jury to review the text in their deliberations so it will not be admitted as evidence
Fed.R.Evid. 705: Disclosure of facts or data underlying expert opinion	Materials and information relied upon by the expert in forming their opinion not necessarily to be produced for the court; however, the court reserves the right to require production
Fed.R.Evid. 706: Court appointed experts	The parties may agree upon an independent witness or the court on its own volition can appoint an independent expert witness. For example, in *Daubert v. Merrell Dow Pharmaceuticals* due to conflicting opinions, the court appointed three impartial witnesses
Article VIII	*Hearsay*
Fed.R.Evid. 803: Hearsay exceptions; availability of declarant immaterial	As a general rule, hearsay is inadmissible. Below are a few exceptions to hearsay, thereby admissible
Fed.R.Evid. 803(4): Statements for purposes of medical diagnosis or treatment.	For instance, nurse practitioner tells jury that the physician told her the child had a urinary tract infection
Fed.R.Evid. 803(6): Records of regular conducted activity.	For example, medical records, billing statements, on-call schedules for staff physicians, etc.
Fed.R.Evid. 803(8): Public records and reports.	For example, public health statistics or information found at under the Freedom of Information Act http://www.foia.gov
Fed.R.Evid. 803(18): Learned treatises.	For example, a core textbook used for medical students might be considered a learned treatise. Because it would be unrealistic for the author to appear to testify to its authenticity, as long as the expert witness recognizes the text as reliable, she can testify to the information within

continued

Article IX	Authentication and Identification
Fed.R.Evid. 901(a): Requirement of authentication or identification	For example, the need to identify and authenticate voice recognition or handwriting
Fed.R.Evid. 901(b): Illustrations	For example, a trial exhibit may be introduced to show a fractured tibia. The expert will be able to authenticate (through testimony) the illustration is an accurate representation of the plaintiff's injury
Article X	Contents of writings, recordings, and photographs
Fed.R.Evid. 1002: Requirement of original	For example, a Polaroid photo of a ventilator-dependant plaintiff is enlarged to be used as a trial exhibit. The original Polaroid photo should be available for examination by the Court
Fed.R.Evid. 1003: Admissibility of duplicates	For example, a certified copy of the plaintiff's medical record will be accepted in lieu of the original record
Fed.R.Evid. 1006: Summaries	For example, the contents of the plaintiff's medical records are too voluminous to be examined in court, then a summary or chart of the medical records may be presented. The original or copy of the medical records summarized should be available for the court

Appendix B: Summary of Select Federal Rules of Civil Procedure in the Pretrial Period

Summary of select Federal Rules of Civil Procedure in the Pretrial Period. The following is not meant to be an exhaustive list. Due to the complexity of the Fed.R.Civ.P., only *excerpts* of the more commonly encountered rules of discovery by the LNC are listed. The specific examples given are for illustrative purposes only. The Fed.R.Civ.P. may be found online at http://www.law.cornell.edu/rules/frcp/

Fed.R.Civ.P. 3 Commencement of an Action	Filing the complaint
Fed.R.Civ.P. 4 Summons	A court's written order (writ) requiring the defendant to appear in Court. The sheriff is directed to summon the defendant via the writ
Fed.R.Civ.P. 5 Service of process	When the complaint and summons have been served to the defendant
Fed.R.Civ.P. 7 Pleadings and motions	Speaks to the form each document must take

continued

Fed.R.Civ.P. 8 General rules of pleadings 8(a) Claims for relief 8(b) Defenses 8(c) Affirmative defenses	The necessary legal elements and inclusions to properly form a complaint and answer according to court rules
Fed.R.Civ.P. 12 Answer	The defendant must respond to the plaintiff's complaint or file a motion to dismiss based on the adequacy of the complaint
Fed.R.Civ.P. 13 Counterclaims and cross-claims	A counterclaim is a claim asserted by the defendant against the plaintiff. For example, the plaintiff filed suit against the defendant for his responsibility in a motor vehicle accident. The defendant counter sues alleging the plaintiff was at fault A cross-claim occurs when two or more parties being sued believe one or the other should bear the liability. For example, a plaintiff slips and falls on ice in a parking lot. The property owner and the snow removal company are sued. The property owner files a cross-claim against the snow removal company for liability (i.e., they did not remove the snow as contracted and the fault is theirs)
Fed.R.Civ.P. 16 Pretrial conference	Close to the trial date, the Pretrial Conference is conducted to resolve pending matters, the simplification of the issues, counsel may view and address objections to the intended exhibits and other legal matters. The judge has been provided with a pretrial brief from each individual counsel
Fed.R.Civ.P. 26(a)(1–5) 26(b)(1–5) 26(c–g)	Rules regarding discovery including duty to supplement responses, objections, privilege of materials, disclosure, relevancy
26(b)(1) Expert Witness Written Report	Addresses the disclosure of the identity of the expert witness, the written opinion of the expert, the reasons for the expert's opinion, the expert's qualifications and list of publications for the past 10 years, the expert's compensation, and the identifications of cases in which the expert has been deposed or testified in the last four years
26(b)(3) Trial preparation: Materials	Provides limited protection to otherwise discoverable trial preparation and work-product materials. The work-product protection applies only to documents prepared in anticipation of litigation

continued

26(b)(4) Trial preparation: Experts	Parties may depose expert witnesses who may testify at trial
26(b)(5) Claims of privilege or protection of trial preparation materials	The party withholding the information as privilege must provide the opposing side with the nature of documents or information to enable the opposing to assess the claim of privilege
26(b)(5)(c) Covers the right to file a Motion for a Protective Order	For example: A trademark secret (such as a secret recipe) might otherwise harm a company's competitive standing in business if the information was made public by revealing the ingredients to its competitors or a motion may be filed by defense counsel in insurance litigation to protect the claims-handling policies and procedures of a company
26(b)(5)(e) Addresses the duty to supplement responses to discovery	For example, answers must be supplemented when information that was initially correct but now no longer true or new relevant information has been made known to the party
Fed.R.Civ.P. 27 Depositions before an action or pending appeal	For example, the plaintiff is terminal and may not live to testify at trial. The video deposition make be taken in advance of filing the complaint. This deposition is known as *de bene esse* (Latin for "of well-being") and taken in anticipation of a future need
Fed.R.Civ.P. 30 Deposition upon oral exam	Governs the guidelines for taking of depositions
Fed.R.Civ.P. 30(b)(5) Provides that a *party* to the litigation can be compelled to bring documents or tangible things to a deposition for examination, copying, and inquiry	For example, the designated representative of a 30(b)(6) notice is instructed to bring a written list of storage protocols for the defendant's IT department
Fed.R.Civ.P. 30(b)(6) Permits a party to notice the deposition of an organization's key representative and specify "the matters on which examination is requested"	For example, in response to the notice, the organization must designate one or more individuals to testify on its behalf, who must have knowledge of the subjects described in the deposition notice
Fed.R.Civ.P. 31 Depositions upon written questions	For example, counsel may request a written deposition because the deponent is incarcerated and unable to be released from custody to attend
Fed.R.Civ.P. 33 Interrogatories to parties	Written questions served to the opposing party that requires their responses and are asserted under oath by the means of a signed affidavit testifying to the truthfulness of the answers

continued

Fed.R.Civ.P. 34 Request for production	Requests generated for tangible items, such as documents, tapes, photos, equipment, reports, etc.
Fed.R.Civ.P. 34(a) Documents and things	Also, allows for site inspections
Fed.R.Civ.P. 35 Request for physical and/or mental exam	Physical exam: The defendant counsel has the right to have the plaintiff examined by a physician of the defense's choosing to evaluate the alleged injuries asserted in the complaint
	Mental exam: For example, the plaintiff alleges depression as a result of the injuries sustained in a motor vehicle accident. Conversely, a showing of "good cause" to obtain a mental examination will be required of the moving party if the plaintiff has not put their mental condition at issue
Fed.R.Civ.P. 36 Request for admissions: To limit the issues that will need to be presented at trial	For example: Both parties of the litigation agree in writing that the total amount of the medical bills in question is related to the injury. This is not an admission of liability; the trier(s) of fact will still need to determine if the defendant is liable for the injury
Fed.R.Civ.P. 37 Motion to compel and sanctions for failure to make discovery	Example: Defendant fails to produce the requested information despite the timeframe allowed and repeated requests by plaintiff's counsel. A Motion to Compel will be filed with the court, all attempts requesting the documents should be attached as exhibits to show the court the effort made to obtain. In reality, actually imposing sanctions (monetary or otherwise) for failure to comply with discovery requests is largely determined by the individual practice of the judge
Fed.R.Civ.P. 45 Subpoena	Compels a *nonparty* to appear for deposition or testimony. For example, the attorney for the plaintiff may want to take the deposition of a security guard that saw the plaintiff fall in the parking lot
Fed.R.Civ.P. 45 Subpoena *duces tecum*	For example, the attorney may issue a subpoena *duces tecum* to the *nonparty* custodian of medical records to bring the requested documents to a specified time and place. If the records are produced on or before the specified date, the custodian need not appear

Appendix C: Samples of Motion Practice

Samples of Motion Practice as they pertain to the Fed.R.Civ.P. in the pretrial period: The following list is not meant to be exhaustive regarding the Fed.R.Civ.P. in filing motions. Due to the complexity of the Fed.R.Civ.P., only *excerpts* of the more commonly encountered motions in the pretrial period by the LNC are listed.

The specific examples given are for illustrative purposes only.

Motion to Enlarge Time: Fed.R.Civ.P. 6(b)	For example, the Sheriff was not able to serve the defendant at their last known address. As the 120 days to perfect service nears, the attorney may wish to file a motion to permit an extension of time in which to serve the defendant or would risk dismissal of the complaint
Motion to Amend: Fed.R.Civ.P. 7(b)	For example, as the plaintiff's attorney is made aware of additional defendants in a medical malpractice action it may be necessary to amend the complaint to add parties
Motion to Dismiss: (may also be asserted as defenses to the complaint): Fed.R.Civ.P. 12(b)(1–7)	• Lack of jurisdiction over the subject matter • Lack of jurisdiction over person • Improper venue • Insufficiency of process • Insufficiency of service of process • Failure to state a claim upon which relief can be granted • Failure to join a party (under Fed.R.Civ.P. 19)
Motion for Protective Order: Fed.R.Civ.P. 26(c)	For example, the plaintiff's attorney is requesting to schedule a third deposition of the company's maintenance supervisor. Without a showing of "good cause" the court will likely grant the defendant's motion based on a finding of annoyance and undue burden
Motion to Compel Discovery: Fed.R.Civ.P. 37(a)	For example, the plaintiff's attorney has repeatedly requested fetal monitor tracings from the hospital's labor and delivery unit for several months. The attorney has provided a Health Insurance Portability and Accountability Act compliant authorization each time and spoke with defense counsel several times regarding this request with no response. The subpoena *duces tecum* was served and has gone unanswered. The plaintiff's attorney will likely assemble documentation of the attempts to secure the information, as well as applicable case law, and attach them as exhibits in support of her motion to compel
Motion for Summary Judgment (as a Matter of Law): Fed.R.Civ.P. 56	May be filed after an adequate period of discovery. The purpose of the motion is to request the court to enter judgment without a trial. For example, the defendant counsel files the motion on the grounds there is insufficient evidence to support a verdict in the plaintiff's favor (i.e., there is no genuine issue of material fact to be decided by the jury)

Appendix D: Sample Interrogatories

[Court of Jurisdiction]

	:	
John Q. Smith,	:	**C.A. No.: 04-772-BBB**
	:	
Plaintiffs,	:	
	:	**Non-Arbitration Case**
v.	:	
	:	
Healthcare Hospital, a hospital	:	**Jury Trial by Twelve**
corporation, and Max I. Millan, M.D.	:	**Persons Demanded**
	:	
Defendants.	:	
	:	
	:	
	:	

Plaintiffs' Second Set of Interrogatories Directed to Defendant Hospital

These interrogatories are of a continuing nature; therefore, the answers should be kept current.

Throughout these interrogatories, whenever you are requested to "identify" a communication of any type, and such communication was oral, the following information should be furnished:

(a) By whom it was made and to whom it was directed
(b) Its specific subject
(c) The date upon which it was made
(d) Who else was present when it was made?
(e) Whether it was recorded, described, or summarized in any writing of any type; and if so, identify each such writing in the manner indicated below

If you are requested to "identify" a communication, memorandum, or record of any type, and such communication was written, the following information should be furnished (in place of identification, production is acceptable):

(a) Its nature, for example, letter, memorandum, telegram, note, drawing, and so on
(b) Its specific subject
(c) By whom and to whom it was directed

(d) The date upon which it was made
(e) Who has possession of the original and copies

"Written" communications also encompasses e-mail and computer communications. Whenever a person is to be "identified," you should furnish, except as otherwise noted:

(a) Name and present or last known address
(b) If a corporation, the state of incorporation

Interrogatories
1. Did any person, agency, group, committee, board, or faculty in or outside the defendant/institution review the medical records of (plaintiff name) at any time from February 7, 2004 to the present? If your answer is yes, please state:
   (a) The name, address, title, and position of said persons, agencies, groups, committees, boards, or faculty conducting such review
   (b) The reason such review is made
   (c) The date of each such review
   (d) The results of each review of (plaintiff's name) charts and records
   (e) Whether or not any minutes were kept at such review meetings and if so, where the minutes are located and who has custody of them.

Answer

2. Did the defendant hospital have in effect on February 7, 2004 any by-laws, rules, policies, regulations, or procedures which required:
   (a) That the medical staff strives to maintain the optimal level of professional performance of its members
   (b) That the medical staff provide periodic in-depth reappraisal of each staff member?
      If so, please attach a copy of all such instruments which set out the hospital's requirements in regard to those items listed above and written protocol for the achievement of such requirements

Answer

3. Identify by name, address, title, position, and responsibility of all the following persons:
   (a) The nursing administrator responsible for the nursing department on February 7, 2004
   (b) The nursing supervisors responsible for and in charge of the nurses rendering care to patient, (plaintiff name) on February 7, 2004
   (c) The head nurse responsible for and in charge of the nurses rendering care to patient, (plaintiff name) on February 7, 2004
   (d) The charge nurse responsible for and in charge of the nurses rendering care to patient, (plaintiff name) on February 7, 2004
   (e) Each RN, LPN, and nursing assistant who attended and rendered nursing care to patient, (plaintiff name) on February 7, 2004
   (f) Each technician and/or other individual at health care hospital who rendered care to patient, (plaintiff name) at any time on February 7, 2004

Answer

4. Please identify by name, address, title, position, and responsibility of the medical staff and/ or emergency room physician who rendered care to (plaintiff name) at any time on February 7, 2004.

Answer

5. Please identify by name, address, title, position, and responsibility of the nurse practitioner that rendered care to (plaintiff name) at any time on February 7, 2004.

Answer:

LAW OFFICES OF PLAINTIFF

By: _____

Plaintiff Attorney (ID No. 0000)

Address

City, State, Zip Code

Phone Number

Attorney for Plaintiff

DATED:

Appendix E: Anticipated Objections to Interrogatories and Request for Production

Anticipated objections to interrogatories and request for production grounds for objections to material requested in interrogatories and request for production are addressed in Fed.R.Civ.P. 26(b)(1).

"Overly broad, vague"

"Unduly burdensome or unreasonably expensive"

"Not relevant"

"Privileged and Protected"

"Not reasonably calculated to lead to the discovery of admissible evidence"

Appendix F: Sample Request for Production

[Court of Jurisdiction]

	:	
John Q. Smith,	:	**C.A. No.: 04-772-BBB**
	:	
Plaintiffs,	:	
	:	**Non-Arbitration Case**
v.	:	
	:	
Healthcare Hospital, a hospital	:	**Jury Trial by Twelve**
corporation, and Max I. Millan, M.D.	:	**Persons Demanded**
	:	
Defendants.	:	
	:	

Plaintiffs' Second Request for Production Directed to Defendant Hospital

The plaintiff requests defendant to produce for examination and copying at the office of the attorney for the plaintiff on or before thirty (30) days of receipt of this request:

1. A copy of all policies and procedures that were in effect on February 7, 2004, which set out or specified the scope of conduct of patient care to be rendered by the medical staff of the health care hospital emergency department.

Response

2. A copy of all The Joint Commission [formerly Joint Commission of Accreditation of Hospital Organizations (JCAHO)] reports and recommendations regarding the emergency department staff for the years 1997 through the present.

Response

3. A copy of the hospital wide policy on patient's rights and responsibilities.

Response

4. A copy of all policies and procedures that were in effect February 7, 2004 and February 8, 2004, which set out or specified the scope of conduct of patient care to be rendered by the medical staff/emergency room nurses.

Response

5. A copy of the table of contents for every policy and procedure manual located in the emergency department.

Response

6. A list of references and text books in the emergency department.

Response

7. A copy of all written materials regarding the definition of the scope of practice in the emergency department.

Response

8. A copy of all evaluation tools and performance appraisal tools for medical staff and nursing staff in the emergency department.

Response

9. A copy of all policies and procedures regarding staffing and staffing requirements for emergency department nursing service.

Response

10. A copy of all policies and procedures regarding patient assignments.

Response

11. A copy of the log record for all patients admitted to the emergency department at health care hospital for the 24 h period on February 7, 2004.

Response

12. A copy of any incident report, variance report, accident report, unusual occurrence report, exception report, generic screens, quality indicators, or any other report that was completed with respect to (plaintiff name).

Response

LAW OFFICES OF PLAINTIFF

By: _____

Plaintiff Attorney (ID No. 0000)

Address

City, State, Zip Code

Phone Number

Attorney for Plaintiff

DATED:

Appendix G: Sample Request for Admissions

[Court of Jurisdiction]

	:	
	:	
John Q. Smith,	:	**C.A. No.: 04-772-BBB**
	:	
Plaintiffs,	:	
	:	
v.	:	**Non-Arbitration Case**
Healthcare Hospital, a hospital	:	
corporation, and Max I. Millan, M.D.	:	
	:	**Jury Trial by Twelve**
Defendants.	:	**Persons Demanded**

Plaintiff's Requests for Admissions Concerning Medical Bills Directed to Defendants

Pursuant to Rule 36 of the Federal Rules of Civil Procedure, Plaintiff, John Q. Smith, requests that Defendants admit that the following statements are true for the purposes of this action, and with respect to any statements to which your response is not an unqualified admission, plaintiff requests, pursuant to Rule 36 of the Federal Rules of Civil Procedure, that defendants respond to the Accompanying Interrogatories.

Each Request for Admission and Interrogatory incorporates the following instructions.

Instruction

1. If you object to any admission requested, fully state the basis of your objection
2. If you believe you must qualify or deny part of the requested admission, specify so much of the requested admission as you believe true and qualify or deny the remainder
3. If you are unable to admit or deny any of the admissions requested, state your reasons

Request for Admission #1

That each of the following documents, exhibited with this Request, is genuine and authentic.

A-1	Bills from health care hospital, February 7, 2004 to March 11, 2004, in the amount of $22,044.08, page 3
A-2	Bills from Heart Ambulance, February 7, 2004, in the amount of $440.45, pages 4–5
A-3	Bills from Memorial General Hospital, September 20, 2004, in the amount of $5979.00, page 6
A-4	Bills from Max. I. Millan, M.D., February 7, 2004, through November 11, 2004, in the amount of $11,803.00, pages 7–9
A-5	Bills from Expert Rehabilitation Services, June 29, 2004, in the amount of $1137.00, pages 10–11

Answer

Supplemental Interrogatory #1

If the answer to Request for Admission #1 is anything but an unqualified admission, state all facts upon which the denial or partial denial is based.

Answer

Request for Admission #2

That the amount of each bill set forth in request number 1 is reasonable.

Answer

Supplemental Interrogatory #2

If the answer to Request for Admission #2 is anything but an unqualified admission, state all facts upon which the denial or partial denial is based.

Answer

Request for Admission #3

That the treatment for which each bill pertains is related to the incident of February 7, 2004.

Answer

Supplemental Interrogatory #3

If the answer to Request for Admission #3 is anything but an unqualified admission, state all facts upon which the denial or partial denial is based.

Answer:

LAW OFFICES OF PLAINTIFF

By: _____

Plaintiff Attorney (ID No. 0000)

Address

City, State, Zip Code

Phone Number

Attorney for Plaintiff

DATED:

Appendix H: Example of Information Asked of Deponent Expert Witness

While not all-inclusive the following request for information may be anticipated in deposition of the expert medical witness.

1. Name, address, credentials, education
2. Current and past licensure(s)
3. Any past sanctions or disciplinary actions
4. Any licensure revocations
5. Class ranking and/or success with passing boards
6. The extent of prior testimony
7. If the expert's CV produced is current and accurate
8. Whether deposed as an expect witness or subject of litigation
9. Board certifications and specialties
10. Fee for deposition, report, and trial testimony
11. Amount of time in active clinical practice
12. Division of testimony for plaintiff versus defense
13. Listing of previous cases in which expert testified
14. Association with attorney that retained them
15. Basis for their opinion and what they specifically relied on in forming that opinion (i.e., medical literature and/or research, textbooks, etc.)
16. What records they reviewed in forming their opinion
17. Whether or not the expert ever examined the plaintiff
18. If they have reviewed the report (opinion) or deposition of the plaintiff/defendant expert witness and on what points do they agree/differ

Appendix I: Sample Subpoena Duces Tecum

[Court of Jurisdiction]

John Q. Smith	Subpoena in a Civil Case
v.	
Max I. Millan, M.D.	Civil Action No.: 04-772-BBB

To:

Name, Records Custodian

Address of Facility

City, State Zip Code

☐ **You Are Commanded** to appear in the United States District Court for the District of Delaware at the place, date, and time specified below to testify in the above case.

Place of Testimony	Courtroom
	Date and Time

☐ **You Are Commanded** to appear at the place, date, and time specified below to testify at the taking of a deposition in the above case.

Place of Deposition	Date and Time

☐ X **You Are Commanded** to produce and permit inspection and copying of the following documents or objects at the place, date, and time specified below (list documents or objects):

A dispatch log and any audiotape and/or transcript of the 911 call placed by (witness name) regarding an ambulance accident that occurred near the intersection of Driveway Road and Exit Road in Sanderson, Delaware on February 7, 2004 at approximately 1:00 p.m.

Place	Date and Time
Law Office, City, State and Zip Code	April 30, 2006 at 3:00 p.m.

☐ **You Are Commanded** to permit inspection of the following premises at the date and time specified below.

Premises	Date and Time

Any organization not a party to this suit that is subpoenaed for the taking of a deposition shall designate one or more officers, directors, or managing agents, or other persons who consent to testify on its behalf, and may set forth, for each person designated, the matters on which the person will testify. Federal Rules of Civil Procedure, 30(b)(6).

Requesting Party's Name, Address and Phone Number	
Attorney for Plaintiff Name, Address, City, State and Zip Code, Phone Number	
Issuing Party's Signature and Title (Indicate If Attorney for Plaintiff or Defendant)	Date
Attorney for Plaintiff, Plaintiff Name	March 11, 2006

Proof of Service		
Served	Date	Place
Served on (Print Name)		Name of Service
Served by (Print Name)		Title
Declaration of Server		

I declare under perjury under the laws of the United States of America that the foregoing information contained in the Proof of Service is true and correct.

Executed on

_____   _____

Date   Signature of Server

_____

Address of Server

Rule 45, Federal Rules of Civil Procedure, Parts C & D

(c) Protection of Persons Subject to Subpoenas.

(1) A party or an attorney responsible for the issuance and service of a subpoena shall take reasonable steps to avoid imposing undue burden or expense on a person subject to that subpoena. The court on behalf of which the subpoena was issued shall enforce this duty and impose upon the party or attorney in breach of this duty an appropriate sanction which may include, but is not limited to, lost earnings and reasonable attorney's fee.

(2) (A) A person commanded to produce and permit inspection and copying of designated books, papers, documents or tangible things, or inspection of premises need not appear in person at the place of production or inspection unless commanded to appear for deposition, hearing or trial.

(B) Subject to paragraph (d) (2) of this rule, a person commanded to produce and permit inspection and copying may, within 14 days after service of subpoena or before the time specified for compliance if such time is less than 14 days after service, serve upon the party or attorney designated in the subpoena written objection to inspection or copying of any or all of the designated materials or of the premises. If objection is made, the party serving the subpoena shall not be entitled to inspect and copy materials or inspect the premises except pursuant to an order of the court by which the subpoena was issued. If objection has been made, the party serving the subpoena may, upon notice to the person commanded to produce, move at any time for an order to compel the production. Such an order to comply production shall protect any person who is not a party or an officer of a party from significant expense resulting from the inspection and copying commanded.

(3) (A) On timely motion, the court by which a subpoena was issued shall quash or modify the subpoena if it

(i) fails to allow reasonable time for compliance,

(ii) requires a person who is not a party or an officer of a party to travel to a place more than 100 miles from the place where that person resides, is employed or regularly transacts business in person, except that, subject to the provisions of clause (c) (3) (B) (iii) of this rule, such a person may in order to attend trial be commanded to travel from any such place within the state in which the trial is held, or

(iii) requires disclosure of privileged or other protected matter and no exception or waiver applies, or

(iv) subjects a person to undue burden.

(B) If a subpoena

(i) requires disclosure of a trade secret or other confidential research, development, or commercial information, or

(ii) requires disclosure of an unretained expert's opinion or information not describing specific events or occurrences in dispute and resulting from the expert's study made not at the request of any party, or

(iii) requires a person who is not a party or an officer of a party to incur substantial expense to travel more than 100 miles to attend trial, the court may, to protect a person subject to or affected by the subpoena, quash or modify the subpoena, or, if the party in whose behalf the subpoena is issued shows a substantial need for the testimony or material that cannot be otherwise met without undue hardship and assures that the person to whom the subpoena is addressed will be reasonably compensated, the court may order appearance or production only upon specified conditions.

(d) Duties in Responding to Subpoena.

(1) A person responding to a subpoena to produce documents shall produce them as they are kept in the usual course of business or shall organize and label them to correspond with the categories in the demand.

(2) When information subject to a subpoena is withheld on a claim that it is privileged or subject to protection as trial preparation materials, the claim shall be made expressly and shall be supported by a description of the nature of the documents, communications, or things not produced that is sufficient to enable the demanding party to contest the claim.

Chapter 7

Informed Consent

Susan Mellott, PhD, RN, CPHQ, FNAHQ

First Edition and Second Edition
Julie Anderson, JD, MSN, RN

Contents

Objectives

After reading this chapter, the reader will be able to

- Describe informed consent and the process of obtaining informed consent
- Identify major issues related to informed consent
- Describe the aspects of liability involved with informed consent

Introduction

Elements of informed consent are part of the nurses' role regardless of the setting in which the nurse practices. The rights of the patient to be well informed of the risks, benefits, and alternatives to the prescribed elements of their care have become more important than ever as technology evolves and patients are living longer with more complicated diseases and comorbidities.

The American Nurses Association (ANA) revised the Code of Ethics for Nurses to reflect the changes in the healthcare system and expanding roles of nursing practice. The first provision of the 2008 version of the American Nurses Association Code of Ethics for Nurses includes a discussion on self-determination as the foundation of informed consent (ANA Code of Ethics for Nurses, 2008). The nurse's role is to assure that the patient understands the information being presented. If the nurse feels that the patient does not comprehend the information, the nurse must solicit the help of others to assure that there is a complete understanding before the informed consent is obtained. The third provision of the Code discusses the patient's rights regarding being informed about participation in research studies and addresses the new technologies that store personal information concerning the patient. The nurse must also assure that the confidentiality of this protected personal information is maintained according to the Health Insurance Portability and Accountability Act (HIPAA). This chapter will discuss the concept and process of informed consent, as well as limitations of the process. There will also be a discussion concerning informed consent as a theory of liability that can be used in any health care practice regardless of the role or practice setting where the informed consent process is a vital part of communicating with patients.

Informed Consent

Informed consent is grounded in principles of respect for individuals and individual autonomy. Each state has its own laws and requirements for what must be included in the informed consent process. There are federal rules and regulations that apply to certain types of institutions or procedures. Many professional organizations have established ethic white papers that address the informed consent rights of an individual. There are many examples of case law that are also applicable.

Consent to research is grounded in ethical codes, statutes, and administrative regulations also. The informed consent for research has developed from history and the need to protect the subjects of the research. However, patients often do not understand what they are signing and often do not read the information before they sign. If they were to read the document before signing it, research has shown that they frequently do not remember the information that they read (Turner & Williams, 2002). Informed consent leads to better patient safety and more patient autonomy.

When is Informed Consent Required?

There is no inclusive source that lists all procedures and treatments that require informed consent. The most common ideation is that any invasive test or procedure should require informed consent to be obtained prior to the procedure or treatment. If there are side effects of the treatment or procedure that could result in a temporary or permanent loss of limb, function or life, informed consent must be obtained after completely informing the patient of these potential side effects. To begin to determine the procedures and treatments which require an informed consent prior to the start of the procedure or treatment, the Emergency Care Research Institute (ECRI), a nonprofit organization that uses applied science research to develop and identify safe and efficient processes, suggests that organizations refer to state law and regulations, case law, high-risk procedures or low-risk procedures such as are listed in Table 7.1 (ECRI, 2008).

The health code of a jurisdiction should be consulted for the applicable law in that state. In some jurisdictions, specific language is required by statute for certain forms. In Texas, for example,

Table 7.1   Some High-Risk, Low Volume Procedures and Treatments that should have Consents

• Tubal ligation	• Administration of radiation
• Vasectomy	• Insertion of devices or medication
• Administration of psychotropic drugs	• ECT
• Administration of anesthesia	• Genetic testing
• Chemotherapy	• Newborn screening
• Blood administration	• Insertion of central lines
• Surgery	

Source: Adapted from ECRI Institute. (2008, January). *Informed Consent. Healthcare Risk Control Risk Analysis, Vol. 2, Laws, Regulations and Standards.*

the legislature has determined what constitutes the inherent and material risks for a large number of procedures, and these risks, specified in a list titled List A, must be disclosed by the health care professional (Texas Medical Liability Trust, 2006). List A procedures require full disclosure of risks by the physician or health care provider to the patient or person authorized to consent for the patient. If this form is used for disclosure of risks, it is admissible in court and creates a rebuttable presumption that the health care provider has complied with the statutory standard and is not negligent. They have also specified a list called List B which lists procedures that require no disclosure. Examples include local anesthesia, hemorrhoidectomy, myringotomy, needle biopsy or aspiration, lumbar puncture, many invasive radiological procedures, and others. When a procedure is performed that does not fall in either List A or List B, the extent of disclosure for that procedure is governed by the common law.

Federal law requires that patients who are to be transferred (or who have refused recommended transfer) to another facility for health treatment under emergency circumstances must be informed of the risks and benefits of transfer (42 U.S.C. §1395dd, 1996). This federal law also mandates that the hospital, and not the physician, take responsible steps to obtain a patient's informed consent both for transfer under emergency conditions and for refusal of transfer, if transfer is deemed medically necessary.

Courts have generally been reluctant to impose upon a referring physician a duty to obtain informed consent for a procedure that is to be performed by a specialist who presumably is most familiar with the procedure and its risks and alternatives. However, several jurisdictions have held that a physician who actually prescribes the specific diagnostic procedures to be performed by another physician could be held liable for failure to obtain the patient's informed consent (*Bowers v. Talmage*, 1963). These courts reason that the patient's personal physician bears primary responsibility for all phases of treatment, including procedures performed by specialists to assist in the patient's diagnosis. This is not, however, the general rule.

When a physician determines that a patient is not in need of medical treatment, the physician is not required to inform the patient of possible risks and benefits of no treatment. Courts have held that the informed consent doctrine cannot be extended to require disclosure of the risks of a recommendation of no treatment, when the physician, in the exercise of his best judgment, believes no treatment is necessary. This has been litigated in the context of alleged failure to diagnose certain conditions, where the patient/plaintiff alleges that the physician should have performed further testing (42 U.S.C. § 11101 et seq., 2001).

Medical Informed Consent Process

Informed consent, as a process resulting from dialogue between the patient and the physician or health care provider, does not refer simply to a signature at the bottom of a form. The items listed in Table 7.2 are the elements that must be included in the medical informed consent process (American Medical Association, 2008).

Guiding Principles of Informed Consent

The practitioner performing the procedure should be the one to obtain the consent. The practitioner should have a complete understanding of the patient's medical condition and history. The practitioner must assure that the patient is legally and mentally competent to give consent for the procedure. The patient must give consent for a specific procedure, and the practitioner may not

Table 7.2 Informed Consent for Procedures and Treatments

- Nature and purpose of the procedure
- Risks, benefits, and alternatives
- Availability of alternative treatments (including no treatment) and the risks, benefits of the alternative treatment
- Risks and benefits of not having the procedure
- Other items that are required based on the procedures and treatments to be performed
- Other items that are defined by each state
- An assessment of patient understanding
- The acceptance of the intervention by the patient

Source: Adapted from American Medical Association, *Office of the General Council, Division of Health Law, Informed Consent Legal Issues.*

perform any other procedure outside the scope of the consented procedure. The practitioner must give the patient sufficient information at a level that the patient can easily understand regarding the procedure, risks, benefits, and alternatives concerning the procedure. The patient must be given an opportunity to ask questions concerning the procedure and its risks, benefits, and alternatives. The patient must not be coerced into signing the consent form. The patient has the right to refuse treatment or a procedure after the patient has been fully informed of the risks, benefits, and alternatives to the treatment or procedure.

Documentation of Informed Consent

A consent form is the document reflecting the consent process, but it does not replace the dialogue between the patient and the health care provider. In all cases where informed consent is required, it should be documented that such consent was in fact obtained by the person who had the duty to obtain it. Sometimes oral disclosure will be sufficient, but the proof becomes problematic if the only witnesses to the conversation were the doctor and the patient. If a form is not signed by the patient, then the health care practitioner must document what was included in the discussion regarding the informed consent process. Executed consent forms should be a part of the patient's permanent medical record.

Consent forms can be general, such as consent to medical care and the release of certain information on admission to a hospital, or specific to treatment or a procedure, such as the consent form for the administration of blood or blood products. The forms must be signed by the patient or authorized agent and witnessed, usually by a nurse or other person who must ascertain that the patient has, in fact, had a discussion with the physician and has given informed consent based on that discussion. If a patient does not speak English, a translator must be involved in the process, and should also sign the consent form. If no form is required or used in a particular facility, narrative chart notes by the health care provider suffice.

There should be a witness to the signature of the individual giving consent for the procedure and treatments. The witness is not responsible for giving the individual the information required to have informed consent, but rather should ascertain that the individual has received this information from the physician and has no further questions prior to the signature indicating consent. The person witnessing the individual's signature should not be taking part in the treatment or procedure. For example, the same day surgery nurse can witness the consent signature as long as that nurse is not involved with the case in the operating room (McCorkle & Pietro, 2007). The witness should sign and date the informed consent form while in the presence of the patient.

Exceptions to Informed Consent

Emergency Situations

Consent is implied when a patient, who is unconscious or otherwise unable to give express consent, needs immediate treatment necessary to save his life, and the harm from failure to treat is imminent and outweighs the harm threatened by the proposed treatment. In such cases, the physician is not held liable for failing to obtain informed consent, even if complications occur that would be considered both inherent and material. In this context, the rule requiring parental consent for a minor is suspended, if the minor needs emergency treatment and the parents are not available to give consent.

Therapeutic Privilege

In rare cases, that is, where it is "not medically feasible," a physician may withhold information that he reasonably believes could hinder treatment or prove harmful to the patient. This concept is employed by the defendant physician to justify nondisclosure on the basis that it is in the best interests of the patient not to do so. For example, in a case involving the psychotherapeutic drug that resulted in the side effect of tardive dyskinesia, the doctor argued that the patient's schizophrenia rendered him unable to have the reactions of a reasonable person, justifying nondisclosure of the risk. The court disagreed, holding that the patient's right to disclosure was not negated just because his doctor did not believe that his patient was reasonable (*Barclay v Campbell*, 1986).

Compulsory Tests or Treatments

Many states have laws regarding the blood tests that brides and grooms must obtain in order to get a marriage license. Since the couple desire to obtain the marriage license, they must have the blood tests and no informed consent is required.

Who May Sign the Consent Form?

Depending on each situation, the person giving consent is usually the patient unless the patient is unable to do so for some reason. Each situation must be evaluated, and the facility's policy must be followed. Most facilities establish their consent policies based on the laws and regulations of the state in which they are located.

Competent Patient 18 Years of Age or Older

There is a legal presumption that any person who has reached the age of majority (usually 18 years) is competent and may make decisions about medical care. For informed consent, competence refers to decision-making capacity, or the patient's ability to engage in rational decision-making, rather than the patient's clinical condition.

Parent of a Child under 18 Years of Age

In the case of minors, parents must give consent by proxy (Whitstone, 2004). If the parents are divorced, or in a custody battle, the parent with custody of the child at that time should be the one to consent for the child. If parents are unavailable in a given situation, certain others, usually next of kin in a hierarchical fashion, may be authorized under the jurisdiction's family code. The parent must consent for neonatal treatment before a baby is delivered. Many times the nurse in the labor and delivery area obtains the consent for the newborn's treatment at the time when the consent for the mother's treatment is obtained.

Emancipated Minors

The state determines when a minor can consent for themselves. For example, some family codes provide that a minor need not have parental consent in order to obtain treatment for venereal disease, drug addiction, or pregnancy. In addition, emancipated minors (e.g., minors who are married or have been legally adjudicated as emancipated) can consent to treatment without parental participation. What constitutes an emancipated minor differs from state to state, and each state's family code should be consulted for those laws. In 1979, the Supreme Court ruled in *Parham v. J.R.* and established a definite standard for juvenile admissions for states and facilities to use. The parent may authorize the admission of the juvenile, but that a neutral individual would need to determine if statutory requirements for admission have been satisfied (Mohr, 2007).

Mentally Incompetent Persons

The family codes or the mental health codes of a particular state may contain provisions allowing procedures to be performed without the usual consent, when the patient is mentally incompetent or committed to a mental institution and cannot give informed consent because of that mental condition. In Texas, this exception allows for the performance of surgery or other treatment in these circumstances under the advice and consent of three licensed physicians, without consent of the patient's guardian (Texas Health & Safety Code § 551.041, 2001).

Legal Guardian

A legal guardian may be appointed by the legal system to handle the affairs of another individual. This most often occurs when there is a physical or mental issue that prevents the individual from making decisions and caring for themselves, when an individual is in danger of substantial harm to themselves or from others, or when an individual has no person already legally authorized to take responsibility of them, such as when a child's parents are killed in a car accident, and there are no other family members available.

The legal guardianship may be for a limited period of time or for an undetermined period of time. The legal guardian then becomes responsible for the individual's residence, health care, food, and social activity. The guardian should consider the wishes of the individual in any decisions that are made regarding these items. The courts will monitor the decisions made by the legal guardian to ensure that the individual is benefiting from the services of the legal guardian. The courts may terminate a legal guardianship at any time (Larson, n.d.).

Medical Power of Attorney

If a person lacks the decision-making capacity, the physician(s) must determine if there is another individual who can provide the consent or whom the patient had previously identified to do so through a medical power of attorney. A medical power of attorney, or sometimes called the Power of Attorney for Healthcare, is established by a competent individual who identifies another person, known as the "agent," to make decisions regarding the individual's health care, should the individual become unable to do so for whatever reason. The medical power of attorney becomes effective immediately, and remains in effect until it is revoked, replaced by a more recent version, or until the individual becomes competent to make clinical decisions. The agent may begin to make health care decisions for the individual after a physician has certified in writing that the individual is incompetent or unable to make such decisions. A copy of the medical power of attorney must be maintained in the individual's permanent medical record (Texas Medical Association, 1999).

The medical power of attorney may allow for the agent to make all health care decisions, or it may limit the agent's decision-making authority. Regardless of what is stated in the medical power of attorney, states may have specific laws regarding to what the agent may consent. For example, in the State of Texas, an agent named in a medical power of attorney cannot consent for commitment to a mental institution, convulsive treatment, psychosurgery, abortion, or the discontinuance of comfort care (Texas Medical Association, 1999).

The medical power of attorney must be signed in the presence of two witnesses in order for it to be valid. Each state defines who may or may not witness the signature. In most states the following individuals are not allowed to witness the signatures: the agent, a member of the individual's family, a person entitled to part of the individual's estate, an individual's physician, or an employee of the physician or health care facility in which the individual is a patient (Texas Medical Association, 1999).

Specific Populations—Informed Consent

There are federal, state, and facility regulations and policies regarding the extent of informed consent required in different health care settings. Table 7.3 lists the Centers for Medicare and Medicaid Services (CMS) Conditions of Participation regulations where specific information regarding each setting may be obtained.

Hospital Setting

In April 2007, CMS updated the 2004 version of the interpretive guidelines for informed consent. The updates describe in detail what must be included in the informed consent and the information given to the patient concerning the informed consent (CMS, Interpretive guidelines, n.d.).

The 2004 version of the interpretative guidelines requires a completed informed consent form be in the patient's medical record prior to the surgery or procedure, unless it is an emergency. It also required that there be included in the consent a list of the names of all practitioners who will conduct specific and significant tasks during the procedure. This requirement was changed to a recommendation in the 2007 version.

Table 7.3   CMS Conditions of Participation Regulations

Type of Facility	CMS Regulation Number for Conditions of Participation
Ambulatory surgery	42 CFR 416.2, 416.40–49
Community mental health center	42 CFR 410.172
Comprehensive outpatient rehabilitation	42 CFR 485.50–74
Critical access hospital	42 CFR 485.501–645
End stage renal facility	42 CFR 405.2100–2184
Home health	42 CFR 484.1–.55
Hospice	42 CFR 418.3, 418.50–116, 418.58
Hospital	42 CFR 482, 489.20–24
Inpatient rehabilitation	42 CFR 412.20–30, 412.600–632, 482.1–66
Intermediate care facility for mental retardation	42 CFR 435.1009, 440.150–220, 442.118–119, 483.400–480
Long-term care	42 CFR 483
Outpatient rehabilitation	42 CFR 485.701–729
Psychiatric hospital	42 CFR 482.60–62
Psychiatric residential treatment facility	42 CFR 483.350–376
Religious nonmedical health care facility	42 CFR 403.730–746
Rural health clinic	42 CFR 405, 491, 485.601
Transplantation	42 CFR 482.68–104

The 2007 version also detailed that the following information must be included on the informed consent form (CMS, Conditions of participation, 2007)

■ Name of the hospital
■ Name of the procedure or other medical treatment
■ Name of the practitioner performing the procedure or administering the medical treatment
■ Signature of the patient or legal guardian
■ Date and time the consent is obtained
■ Statement that the procedure and anticipated benefits, material risks, and available alternative therapies were explained to the patient or guardian

The CMS goes on to recommend that organizations consider the following elements to be included in their informed consent forms (CMS, 2007):

■ Statement that, if applicable, physicians other than the primary surgeon/practitioner (e.g., residents) will conduct specific significant surgical tasks. Significant surgical tasks include opening and closing harvesting grafts, dissecting tissue, removing tissue, implementing devices, and altering tissues.

■ Statement, if applicable, that qualified medical practitioners who are not physicians will perform important parts of the surgery or administration of anesthesia.

■ Name of the practitioner who conducted the informed consent discussion with the patient or guardian.

■ The date and time and the signature of the professional person witnessing the consent.

■ A list of risks discussed with the patient or the patient's representative.

Behavioral Health Setting

There are several caveats to informed consent with individuals who are receiving behavioral health services. When an individual seeks psychotherapy, it is unknown to the therapist what the individual may reveal and what direction would be the best therapy to pursue. In many cases, the individual receiving these services may not be able to consent to the services, or the therapy may be court ordered. Also, many of these individuals will undergo electroconvulsive therapy (ECT), which in and of itself requires an informed consent every time the treatment is undertaken.

When an individual is legally incapable of giving consent, the therapist must still explain the process and obtain the individual's agreement to the therapy sessions. The therapist must also become a patient advocate keeping the individual's preferences and best interests in mind. Whenever possible, the therapist must obtain the permission for the therapy from a legally authorized person, if one is available. When individuals are receiving therapy due to a court order, the therapist must still explain the nature and process to the individual, and inform the individual about their extent to which they may refuse service (Zur, n.d.).

ECT has evolved into an acceptable therapy for certain behavioral health patients; however, there is still a division of opinions concerning its usefulness. The patient must be well aware of the risks, benefits, and alternatives of receiving this therapy. The requirements for informed consent for ECT vary from state to state. In Texas, an informed consent form and a supplemental statement (§ 405.117) are required prior to each individual ECT treatment. The requirements of the consent include the following: (Texas Administrative Code, n.d.)

■ Indications for therapy for the patient
■ Description of the process
■ Anesthesia risks and side effects
■ Medical evaluation results
■ Results of psychiatric and other medical consultation(s) relevant to ECT
■ For patients 65 years of age or older, known medical conditions that may increase the possibility of injury or death as a result of ECT and a statement signed by two (2) physicians that the treatment is medically necessary
■ Contraindications to therapy
■ Risks of the therapy
■ Benefits of the therapy
■ Alternative therapies that are available

Long-Term Care Setting

In Long-Term Care, CMS addresses informed consent with information on advance directives. In 42 CFR 483.10 Resident Rights, CMS states that "These requirements include provisions to inform and provide written information to all adult residents concerning the right to accept or refuse medical or surgical treatment, and, at the individual's option, formulate an advance directive" (CMS, Conditions of participation—long-term care, n.d.).

Home Health Setting

In the Home Health Setting, it is the nurse who usually must obtain the informed consent from the patient. The Home Health nurse will be performing procedures ordered by the physician, but the physician will not necessarily have seen the patient to explain the risks, benefits, alternatives, and right to refuse the procedure or treatment to the patient. The nurse must document the discussion with the patient and the patient's consent or refusal.

Hospice Setting

CMS does specifically address what must be in a general consent for treatment for hospice patients. In 42 CFR 418.62, CMS states that the hospice must include in the informed consent the specifics of the type of care and services that may be provided as hospice care (CMS, Conditions of participation—hospice, n.d.).

Department of Veteran Affairs Settings

The Department of Veterans Affairs (VA) has its own federal regulations (38 CFR Part 17). Prior to March 8, 2007, only practitioners who were clinically privileged to do so, and who where performing the procedure, could obtain informed consent from the patient. This also included medical and dental residents who, while not privileged, were allowed to obtain informed consent. In the VA, this was limiting since a number of advance practitioners performed procedures or treatment, but were not credentialed to do this. These advance practitioners function under a "scope of practice" agreements or formal delineations of their job which specified what these practitioners were allowed to perform (Federal Register Rules and Regulations, 2007).

On March 8, 2007 the regulation was changed to extend privileges to medical or dental resident, any health care professional, such as dentists, physician assistants, and advance practice nurses and others who are appropriately trained who has primary responsibility for the patient or who performs the procedure or treatment, *must* obtain the informed consent for the procedure/treatment. However, the practitioner must be qualified and per this Federal Regulation, the VA had to establish national requirements in policy and hold the local VA facilities accountable for the implementation of these policies (Federal Register Rules and Regulations, 2007).

Organ Recovery and Transplantation Settings

In 42 CFR 482.45(a)(3), CMS discusses how to obtain consent from the family of a potential donor. Basically, CMS requires that, in collaboration with an Organ Procurement Organization (OPO), the hospital must identify an individual staff member who will/has completed a course offered or approved by the OPO regarding how to approach potential donor families and request the organ or tissue transplant. The OPO will determine if the patient is a potential donor and then the specially trained hospital staff member will approach the family for permission to donate. A member of the OPO frequently joins the designated/trained staff member when the family is approached. The staff member must inform the family member(s) of its options to donate organs, tissues, or eyes, and their right to decline the donation (CMS, Conditions of participation—hospital, 2007).

While the CMS regulations comment on informed consent for the donor, there is currently no legislation or law that requires full consent for the recipient of the transplant organ or tissue. In 2008, the United Network for Organ Sharing (UNOS), the national clearing house for organ allocation, and the Organ Procurement and Transplantation Network (OPTN) were in the process of developing a policy to address disclosure of the donator risk factors. The proposed policy would inform transplant recipients of the known high-risk behaviors of the donor at the time organs become available. Utilizing Centers for Disease Control and Prevention (CDC) guidelines, the high-risk criteria would include behavior and history criteria, pediatric donor criteria, and laboratory and other medical criteria. The recipient could at that time decide to accept or decline those particular organs or tissue. Currently only the recipients of kidney donor organs are permitted to accept or decline organs if they are obtained from an older donor or from a donor who had hypertension or other such disorder (Organ Procurement Transplantation Network and the UNOS, n.d.).

A group of physicians from the University of Pennsylvania School of Medicine are calling for the policy to be modified to require all transplant recipients to be made aware of "all foreseeable risks" when the patient is placed on a waiting list for an organ or tissue. The physicians identify the risks as those which could occur when the transplanted organ or tissue comes from donors who are older, who have any infectious diseases (or risks there of), or donors who suffered a cardiac arrest prior to their death. The physicians further state that the recipient of the organ should not be allowed to accept or decline transplantation at the time the transplant is to take place, but must determine when they are placed on the waiting list that they are aware of the risks but still wish to receive a donor organ. These physicians feel that if the recipient is allowed to reject a particular donor's organ or tissue that the process could lead to "discrimination, inefficiency, and inequity in how organs are allocated" (University of Pennsylvania, 2008).

The UNOS and the OPTN have also developed a resource document regarding informed consent regarding the donation of organs by living donors. The document was developed as a resource to transplant professionals to follow when obtaining informed consent from living donors. The document discusses the risks, benefits, and alternatives that the living donor has as well as the fact that the transplant centers are required to report living donor follow-up information for at least two years after the donation takes place, as this is the only method they have for collection of information regarding the long-term effects of donation on living donors (Organ Procurement and Transplantation Network, n.d.).

Research Informed Consent Process and Research

Informed consent for research studies and medical experimentation on humans first gathered attention after a World War II military tribunal was held in 1947 in the case of the *USA vs. Karl Brandt*, et al. As a result of the testimony and discussion during the trail, the tribunal submitted a memorandum to the United States Council for War Crimes which outlined six points, eventually becoming 10 points, defining legitimate research. The document became known as the Nuremberg Code, but it never became law in the United States nor Germany (U.S. Holocaust Memorial Museum, 1953).

In 1981, the U.S. Food and Drug Administration enacted their regulations regarding the Protection of Human Subjects. This regulation states "No investigator may involve a human being as a subject in research covered by these regulations unless the investigator has obtained the legally effective informed consent of the subject or the subject's legally authorized representative" (Food and Drug Administration, 2008). The regulations state that the consent must be in a language understandable to the subject or representative and that the subject may not waive their legal rights or relieve anyone involved from liability for negligence. There are exceptions to this rule as stated in Sections 50.23 and 50.24 of the regulation.

There are individual state laws that govern the conduct of research and informed consent process and that additional protections for vulnerable populations, such as pregnant women, children, and prisoners, are required by institutional review boards or human research review committees. Special rules for children participating in research apply. The consent process is outlined in the Code of Federal Regulations at 45 CFR Part 46. The Office of Human Research is the federal agency charged with the consent process during research.

The regulations state that the content in Table 7.4 must be included as elements of the informed consent. The regulation further states that the documentation of the consent must be in a written format, approved by the Institution Review Board (IRB) and signed and dated by the subject at the time consent is given. If the information is given orally to the subject, there must be a short form written consent document that states that the information was presented orally, which is signed by the subject. There must be a witness to the oral presentation who will sign both the short form and the copy of the summary that was presented to the subject. The IRB must approve the written summary of what is to be said to the subject. The person obtaining the consent must also sign the summary document. The patient must then receive a copy of the signed short form and the summary form (Food and Drug Administration, 2008).

Academy of Pediatrics on Bioethics has developed a policy regarding consent for Pediatric research that states that parental permission may be given only for medical necessitated treatments. If the treatment is nonessential, then the procedure should wait until the child is at an age where they can consent for themselves (Van Howe et al., 1999). The parent is in essence giving "consent by proxy" since the consent is for someone else. The practitioners must be assured that the parent or guardian is acting in the best interest of the child and not in the parent's own interest. If the practitioner feels that the parent is not capable of decision making, then the practitioner is obligated to act to have another person, such as a "guardian ad litem" appointed by the courts to make medical decisions for the child (Whitstone, 2004).

In *Wisconsin v Yoder*, the U.S. Supreme Court deemed that parental decisions may be limited if the decisions will jeopardize the health and safety of the child. In the *Little v Little* case, the courts maintained that the parents may consent only to the medically necessary treatments. In this case, the guardian ad litem of a 14-year-old mentally incompetent girl applied to the courts for the child's mother to have the girl's healthy kidney removed in order to have it transplanted into the mother's son's body since he was suffering from end-stage renal disease. The courts refused to allow this procedure to be done since it could harm the 14-year-old girl and put her at unnecessary risk for potential harm (Van Howe et al., 1999). According to Van Howe, a review of the literature on pediatric consent supports the test for parental consent for a surgical intervention must have three parts: (1) the intervention must be medically necessary; (2) the intervention must be in the best interests of the child; and (3) it must not place the child at risk for unnecessary suffering or injury.

Whenever possible, the older child or adolescent should be involved in the decision-making process to the extent possible based on their developmental level. It is important that the child or adolescent gives 'assent' to the procedure or treatment if they are developmentally able to do so.

Table 7.4   Elements of Informed Consent

Basic Elements of Research Informed Consent

1. Explanation of the research and the expected duration of the subject's participation, a description of the procedures to be followed, and identification of any procedures that are experimental

2. Description of any reasonably foreseeable risks or discomforts to the subject

3. Description of any benefits to the subject or to others which may reasonably be expected from the research

4. Disclosure of appropriate alternative procedures or courses of treatment that might be advantageous to the subject

5. Statement describing the extent to which confidentiality of records identifying the subject will be maintained and that notes the possibility that the Food and Drug Administration may inspect the records

6. For research involving more than minimal risk, an explanation as to whether any compensation and an explanation as to whether any medical treatments are available if injury occurs and, if so, what they consist of, or where further information can be obtained

7. Explanation of whom to contact for answers to pertinent questions about the research and research subject's rights, and whom to contact in the event of a research-related injury to the subject

8. Statement that participation is voluntary, that refusal to participate will involve no penalty or loss of benefits to which the subject is otherwise entitled, and that the subject may discontinue participation at any time without penalty or loss of benefits to which the subject is otherwise entitled

Additional Elements of Research Informed Consent

1. Statement that the particular treatment or procedure may involve risks to the subject (or to the embryo or fetus, if the subject is or may become pregnant) which are currently unforeseeable

2. Anticipated circumstances under which the subject's participation may be terminated by the investigator without regard to the subject's consent

3. Any additional costs to the subject that may result from participation in the research

4. The consequences of a subject's decision to withdraw from the research and procedures for orderly termination of participation by the subject

5. Statement that significant new findings developed during the course of research may relate to the subject's willingness to continue participation will be provided to the subject

6. Approximate number of subjects involved in the study

Source: Adapted from Food and Drug Administration. Subpart B. *Informed Consent of Human Subjects.* Title 21 Food and Drugs. Federal Register 46 FR 8951, January 27, 1981, as amended at 64 FR10942, March 8, 1999, revised as of April 1, 2007 (21CR50).

Issues with Informed Consent

Many articles have been written and research studies completed that identify issues and limits with the informed consent process. According to Burns et al. (2005), more than 50% of the study patients could not list any treatment-related risks at the time of surgery, even though 90% of the patients were satisfied with the informed consent process and considered themselves well informed (Murphy, 2008). The main issues identified in the literature revolve around the concepts of incomplete disclosure, inadequate consent forms, comprehension, and mental competency.

Incomplete Disclosure

Incomplete disclosure is one of the most debated components of informed consent. Clinicians and researchers have published many articles regarding what should be disclosed to the patient regarding medical care and research informed consents, and what may not need to be disclosed. The keystone case regarding informed consent is the 1914 case of *Schloendorff v. New York Hospital*. The judge in this case concluded "Every human being of adult years and sound mind has a right to determine what should be done with his own body" (Walker, 2006).

In the clinical arena, there is less discrepancy between what to disclose or not to disclose. The main issue of disclosure is regarding what was known and when it was known (Walker, 2006). The effects of asbestos fibers were not known for many years, and as a result there has been a plethora of litigation against the manufacturers of this product, even though the manufacturers were not aware of these effects when the product was introduced.

In the research arena, there is a large amount of controversy between the views of researchers regarding informed consent. One of the main discussion points is that if research participants are given complete information about the study that either the patients would refuse participation or that the results could be biased. In some research, the complete set of risks may not be known until after the research has been completed.

Informed Consent Procedure Forms

Melissa Bottrell et al. (2000) conducted a study to determine if informed consent forms met acceptable standards. These researchers gathered informed consent forms from a random selection of hospitals from the 1994 American Hospital Association (AHA) directory. A total of 540 informed consent forms were obtained from 157 hospitals nationwide. All of the forms were scored based on the six components listed in Table 7.5.

The conclusion of this study was that the content of the forms did not meet acceptable standards of informed consent or patient–physician interaction (Bottrell et al., 2000). Of the 540 consent forms, 96% indicated the procedure, but only 26% of them indicated the risks, benefits, and alternatives in addition to the procedure(s) name. Figures 7.1 and 7.2 indicate the results of this study. The researchers also found that in states where the basic elements of procedure, risks, benefits, and alternatives are required by law, the informed consent forms did no better than those without the state laws requiring such.

Competency

There are many other reasons why a patient may not be competent to give informed consent. Patients who may not give consent are those who are under the age of 18, or who are mentally

Table 7.5   Items Scored from Informed Consent Forms

• Nature of the procedure

• Risks

• Benefits

• Alternatives

• Items that might enhance patient–physician interactions

• Items that might encourage shared decision making

Source: Adapted from Bottrell, M. et al. (2000). *Archives of Surgery, 135,* 26–33.

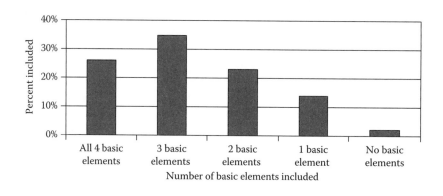

Figure 7.1   Informed consent forms inclusion of basic elements of consent. (Adapted from Bottrell, M. et al. (2000). *Archives of Surgery, 135,* 26–33.)

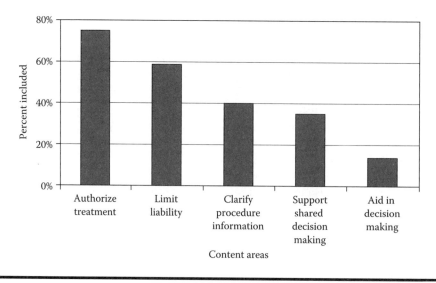

Figure 7.2   Informed consent forms consent. (Adapted from Bottrell, M. et al. (2000). *Archives of Surgery, 135,* 26–33.)

impaired, demented, confused, unconscious, drug dependent, and multiple other categories of patients. In the case of emergencies, it may be difficult for any individual to process the information being given to them regarding informed consent. In emergencies and at other stressful times, individuals are less able to process information, and may in fact be more susceptible to the persuasion of others (O'Neill, 2003).

Alzheimer's and other forms of dementia affect patients in varying degrees. It is often difficult to determine if a patient with these diagnoses is competent. Alzheimer's is a disease that takes many years to manifest itself to the furthest degree. There are many individuals with mild Alzheimer's who remain competent, while others with the same degree of illness who can function socially and express their abilities are not competent to give consent (Kim et al., 2001). A study developed to accurately measure the decision-making capacity of patients with Alzheimer's found it would be difficult to indicate whether a patient was capable or incapable of giving informed consent (Kim et al., 2001).

A practitioner may have questions about a patient's decision-making capabilities when the patient refuses a course of treatment that goes against what the physician is recommending. In such a case, the practitioner must document the decision-making capacity of the patient. Simply because the patient has the ability to consent to a procedure or treatment does not mean that the patient has the capacity to make a decision to refuse treatment. According to Derse (2005), "the concern for the patient's well being must be balanced against the respect for the patient's self-determination" (Derse, 2005). Derse maintains that if the consequences of the decision to refuse treatment may result in a disability or death, the patient must have a higher level of decision-making capability than if the treatment would just be beneficial to the patient. This is one of the ethical dilemmas that physicians must face in determining a course of action on behalf of the patient.

Comprehension and Understanding of Material

According to information published in 2004 from a survey conducted by a Commonwealth Fund, 33% of sick patients who leave the physician's office after an appointment do so without getting all their important questions answered (Woolf et al., 2005). A research study by Engel et al. (2008) indicated 78% of discharged patients had difficulty recalling their diagnosis and its cause, the care received in the ED, the post ED care instructions, and the instructions regarding returning to the ED if needed.

Cassileth et al. (1980) identified three factors that were related to the lack of recall of the information discussed during the informed consent process: education, medical status, and the care with which patients felt that they had read the consent forms. Education and cognitive function are a few reasons for poor comprehension and retention of information provided during the informed consent process. The elderly, those with a below average IQ and those who had impaired cognitive functions, had the most difficulty recalling the information that was provided (Lavelle-Jones et al., 1993). According to the National Institute on Deafness and Other Communication Disorders (NIDCD), the average reading level throughout the United States is between the eighth and ninth grades. However, the average reading age of individuals from low economic classes is at the fifth grade level. The NIDCD also states that two thirds of individuals over the age of 65 and 25% of immigrants have poor literacy skills. Language barriers also pose a significant barrier to informed consent. Many facilities only have informed consent forms in the English, while many of their patients lack English proficiency. The use of translators is haphazard at best, many times utilizing family, other patients, and staff to provide the translation. The quality of their translation is unknown and suspect to being incomplete or incorrect (Betancourt & Jacobs, 2000).

The physician may be held liable if a competent medical interpreter is not utilized to obtain informed consent if the patient speaks a language other than the language spoken by the physician. In the case of *Quintero v. Encarnacion* (2000) the physician obtained consent from a patient who was able to communicate minimally utilizing a few Spanish words (All Language Alliance, 2007). The court ruled that:

> Informed consent cannot be obtained if the explanations were conducted in a language the patient did not understand. If the patient's capacity to understand is limited by a language barrier, and the physician proceeds without addressing this barrier ... the physician may be liable for failing to obtain informed consent from the patient. (All Language Alliance, 2007)

Proof in Court

Informed consent as a theory of liability on which the plaintiff tries to obtain a monetary judgment is most frequently combined with a medical negligence theory rather than being the sole theory in a claim. The elements of the plaintiff's case in an informed consent action are the same as in general medical negligence: duty, breach of duty, and proximate cause of the injury. In other cases, the plaintiff may base the case on battery or fraud, neglect, deceit, misrepresentation, and breach of contract. Medical negligence is the most commonly utilized approach.

Medical Negligence

Medical negligence model is based on four criteria: duty, breach of duty, causation, and damages. The plaintiff must show harm occurred as a result of the procedure at issue, or that the possible harm was not disclosed to the patient at the time of giving the informed consent. Most of these cases include expert testimony that the injury was caused by the performance of the procedure at issue (ECRI, 2008). Plaintiffs asserting informed consent claims must prove that (1) the complication or condition in question was a risk inherent in the procedure performed, (2) a reasonable person fully informed of all inherent risks would not have consented to the treatment in question (decisional causation), and (3) the patient/plaintiff was in fact injured by the occurrence of this complication or condition about which he was not informed (physical causation). The relationship between the failure to disclose a particular risk and the later occurrence of that complication must be shown in order for the patient/plaintiff to prevail in the lawsuit. Generally, expert medical testimony is necessary to prove the plaintiff's case in a negligence action based on informed consent (and to defend a physician's actions in this regard). The expert must testify regarding the inherency of the risk complained of and all other facts concerning the risk that show that knowledge of the risk could influence a reasonable person in making a decision to consent to the procedure (ECRI, 2008).

Decisional causation must demonstrate that if the physician had disclosed the potential risk from the procedure, that the patient would have never consented to having the procedure done, and that other people would have made the same determination.

There are two aspects of decisional causation that may be utilized. The objective finding, that a reasonable person would also have refused the procedure if the information had been disclosed, is the method most typically utilized in court. The reasonable person standard described here requires that one person's behavior is compared to what a hypothetical person who is just like the patient would do given the information about the procedure, its risks and alternatives. The plaintiff must prove that he would not have consented to the procedure if told about the risks or alternatives. It is by utilizing this objective standard that subjectivity is removed from the decision regarding the case (Mehlman, 2008).

The reasonable physician standard is a variation of the reasonable person standard. By utilizing the reasonable physician standard, the defense must demonstrate that the physician presented to the patient the information that any reasonable physician would have presented to another similar patient. This is where the physician experts are utilized to support what the physician told the patient (Mehlman, 2008).

The second aspect, the subjective approach, the jury, or the judge if there is no jury, must decide that the patient would not have had the procedure if additional information regarding the risks and alternatives had been disclosed. In this situation, the jury decides what they would have done in a similar situation. The subjective approach has been adopted by only a small number of states as the way the jury must determine if there was decisional causation (Mehlman, 2008).

Medical negligence informed consent law was established as an intentional tort of battery of the patient. The law protects the patient from unwanted physical touching of a patient's body by someone without permission. For battery to be alleged, one of the following actions had to occur:

- Physician performs a procedure without the consent of the patient
- Physician performs a procedure that is substantially different from the procedure that was consented to
- Physician exceeds the scope of the consent by expanding on the procedures performed
- A different physician performs the procedure other than the physician listed on the consent form

The plaintiff may be compensated with a monetary award even if there is no injury as a result of the failure to obtain the consent (ECRI, 2008).

Fraud, Deceit, Neglect, Misrepresentation, and Breach of Contract

In breach of contract cases, the plaintiff may be able to recover as damages the cost of the procedure, nursing care, medications, and other monetary expenses that result from the breach of contract (ECRI, 2008). A properly executed informed consent may be found to be invalid if obtained by fraudulent misrepresentation, nondisclosure of important information or concealment.

There are some current trends that will address these issues. In some cases, the physician and/or the organization are video taping the consent process, and/or utilizing recorded educational programs to explain the surgery/procedure. Interactive media and websites are other approaches increasingly being utilized to educate the patient about what they are consenting for. There is a growing trend towards transparency where the practitioners are being asked by the patient and other consumers what their complication rate for a procedure is, how many has the practitioner performed, and so forth. Research is currently being conducted to determine the severity of undisclosed risks of a procedure or surgery to assist in the determination of what should or does not have to be disclosed to the patient.

Viability of the Cause of Action

Practically speaking, it is often difficult to persuade a jury in informed consent claims, especially if the procedure or treatment in question is lifesaving, curative, or necessary for a serious medical condition. When lack of informed consent is raised as an issue in a medical malpractice case, it is often difficult to prove what occurred during the informed consent discussion. There are frequently discrepancies between the physician's and patient's version of the information exchanged during this conversation. At times, a dispute between the patient and physician takes place regarding whether a discussion of the risk was actually held, even if there was documentation. Some physicians specifically document the conversation in physician progress notes as well as on an informed consent form. This may occur more often when the physician is getting consent for high-risk surgical procedures.

In cases where the defendant physician or health care provider has proven compliance with a statutory or common law duty, and a properly executed consent form is part of the record, the patient/plaintiff must resort to claiming that the scope of the disclosure was inadequate, or that the validity of the consent is in question. In that regard, the patient may claim that he did not have the capacity to give consent, or that he did not sign the form. Contract defenses such as fraud, mutual mistake, accident, and undue influence are typically employed in such situations.

On the other hand, the reasonable person standard increases the difficulty of a physician obtaining summary judgment, because the defendant must counter the argument that knowledge of a particular risk of injury could influence a reasonable person in making a treatment decision. This is typically a question of fact for the jury rather than a question of law for the court.

Summary

The importance of the informed consent process is not fully understood by many health care professionals. Too often the nurse or other designee has the patient sign the informed consent form without really knowing what the physician has discussed with the patient regarding the treatment or procedure.

Failure to carry out the informed consent prior to any treatment or procedure requiring informed consent could result in litigation. There should be documentation in the medical record that the informed consent was obtained appropriately, that the patient was presented with the appropriate information and understood what was presented. There should be documentation of the methods utilized to overcome any limitations of the consent process that practitioners and staff discover, such as language barriers and readability of the consent documents. It is only through this documentation of what information was discussed with the patient/subject and how the information was presented that the medical record can substantiate the informed consent process utilized if a law suit should result.

References

42 U.S.C. § 1395dd (1996). Retrieved October 10, 2008, from http://assembler.law.cornell.edu/uscode/html/uscode42/usc_sec_42_00001395– dd000-.html

42. U.S.C. § 11101 et seq. (2001). Retrieved October 10, 2008, from www.npdb-hipdb.hrsa.gov/legislation/title4.html

All Language Alliance, Inc. (2007). *Medical interpreters, foreign language barriers and informed consent. Translation for Lawyers September 2007*. Retrieved on July 7, 2008, from http://www.translationforlawyers.com/2008/06/medical_interpreters_foreign_l.html#more

American Medical Association. (2008). *Office of the General Council, Division of Health Law, Informed consent legal issues. March 20, 2008*. Retrieved on August 28, 2008, from http://www.ama-assn.org/ama/pub/category/print/4608.html

ANA Code of Ethics for Nurses. (2008). Retrieved June 27, 2008, from http://nursingworld.org/ethics/code/protected_nwcoe813.htm

Barclay v. Campbell., 704 S.W.2d 8 (Tex. 1986). Retrieved October 10, 2008, from http://bulk.resource.org/courts.gov/c/F2/884/884.F2d.196.88-5615.html

Betancourt, J., & Jacobs, E. (2000). Language Barriers to informed consent and confidentiality: The impact on women's health. *Journal of American Medical Women's Association, 55*(5), 294–295.

Bottrell, M., Alpert, H., Fischbach, R. L., & Emanuel, L. L. (2000). Hospital informed consent for procedure forms. *Archives of Surgery, 135*, 26–33.

Bowers v. Talmage, 159 So. 2d 888 (Fla. Dist. Ct. App.) (1963).

Burns, P., Keogh, I., & Timon, C. (2005). Informed consent: A patient's perspective. *Journal of Laryngology & Otology, 119*, 19–22.

Cassileth, B. R., Zupkis, R.V., Sutton-Smith, K., & March, V. (1980). Informed consent—Why are its goals imperfectly realized? *New England Journal of Medicine, 302*(16), 896–900.

Centers for Medicare & Medicaid Services (CMS). (n.d). *Conditions of participation–Hospice.* Retrieved on July 27, 2008, from http://www.access.gpo.gov/nara/cfr/waisidx_04/42cfr418_04.html

Centers for Medicare & Medicaid Services (CMS). (2007). *Conditions of participation—Hospital.* Retrieved on July 28, 2008, from http://www.access.gpo.gov/nara/cfr/waisidx_04/42cfr482_04.html

Centers for Medicare & Medicaid Services (CMS). (2007, April 13). *Revisions to the hospital interpretive guidelines for informed consent {memorandum online}.* Retrieved on July 26, 2008, from www.cms.hhs.gov/SurveyCertificationGenInfo/downloads/SCLetter07–17.pdf

Centers for Medicare & Medicaid Services (CMS). (n.d.). *Conditions of participation—Long term care.* Retrieved on July 27, 2008, from http://www.access.gpo.gov/nara/cfr/waisidx_01/42cfr483_01.html

Derse, A. R. (2005). What part of 'no' don't you understand?. *Mount Sinai Journal of Medicine, 72*(4), 221–227.

ECRI Institute. (2008, January). Informed consent. *Healthcare risk control risk analysis, Vol. 2, Laws, Regulations, and Standards 4.* https://members2.ecri.org/Components/HRC/Pages/LawReg4.aspx?pfm=true

Engel, K., Heisler, M., Smith, D. M., Robinson, C. H., Forman, J. H., & Ubel, P. A. (2009). Patient comprehension of emergency department care and instructions: Are patients aware of when they do not understand? *Annals of Emergency Medicine, 53*(4), 454–461.

Federal Register Rules and Regulations. (2007). Department of Veterans Affairs 38 CFR Part 17. *Federal Register, 72*(45), 10365–10367.

Food & Drug Administration. (2008). Subpart B. Informed Consent of Human Subjects. Title 21 Food and Drugs. Federal Register 46 FR 8951, January 27, 1981, as amended at 64 FR 10942, March 8, 1999, revised as of April 1, 2007 (21CR50). Downloaded on August 13, 2008, from http://www.accessdata.fda.gov/scripts/cdrh/cfdocs/cfcfr/CFRSearch.cfm?CFRPart=50&showFR=1&subpartNode=21:1.0.1.1.19.2

Kim, S. Y. H., Caine, E. D., Currier, G. W., Leibovici, A., & Ryan, J. M. (2001). Assessing competence of persons with Alzheimer's disease in providing informed consent for participation in research. *American Journal of Psychiatry, 158*(5), 712–717.

Larson, A. (n.d). *The legal guardianship Expert Law.* Retrieved on August 29, 2008, from www.expertlaw.com/library/estate_planning/guardianship.html

Lavelle-Jones, C., Byrne, D. J., Rice, P., & Cuschieri, A. (1993). Factors affecting quality of informed consent. *British Medical Journal, 306*, 885–890.

McCorkle, D., & Pietro, J. (2007). Perioperative nursing malpractice issues. In: P. Iyer & B. Levin (Eds.) *Nursing malpractice* (3rd ed., p. 372). Tucson: Lawyers & Judges.

Mehlman, M. J. (2008). *Informed consent. The doctor will see you now.* Retrieved on February 19, 2009, from http://www.thedoctorwillseeyounow.com/articles/bioethics/consent_3/

Mohr, W. (2007). Psychiatric nursing liability. In P. Iyer & B. Levin (Eds.) *Nursing malpractice* (3rd ed., p. 420). Tucson: Lawyers & Judges.

Murphy, J. (2008). Editorial, Mayo Clinic Proceedings. *Benefits and Challenges of Informed Consent, 83*(3), 272–273.

O'Neill, O. (2003). Some limits of informed consent. *Journal of Medical Ethics, 29*, 4–7.

Organ Procurement and Transplantation Network. (n.d). *Resource document for informed consent of living donors.* Retrieved July 27, 2008, from www.unos.org/SharedContentDocuments/Informed_Consent_Living_Donors.pdf

Organ Procurement and Transplantation Network & United Network for Organ Sharing (UNOS). (2008). *Proposal to require transplant centers to inform potential recipients about known high risk donor behavior.* Retrieved on July 27, 2008, from http://www.unos.org/news/newsDetail.asp?id=948

Texas Administrative Code. (n.d). *Electroconvulsive therapy (ECT)* (Title 25, Part 1, chap. 405, Subchapter E, Rule § 405.108).

Texas Health & Safety Code § 551.041, 2001. Downloaded on October 10, 2008, from http://tlo2.tlc.state. tx.us/cgi- bin/cqcgi?CQ_SESSION_KEY=WQFLKGMLUMDR&CQ_QUERY_HANDLE=126986 &CQ_CUR_DOCUMENT=9&CQ_TLO_DOC_TEXT=YES

Texas Medical Association. (1999). *Medical power of attorney: Patient and health care provider information.* Retrieved on August 15, 2008, from www.texmed.org/Template.aspx?id=65

Texas Medical Liability Trust. (2006). *Informed consent, the third generation.* Retrieved on October 10, 2008, from www.tmlt.org/publications/riskpubs/informedconsentbook.pdf

Turner, P., & Williams, C. (2002). Informed consent: Patients listen and read, but what information do they retain? *Journal of New Zealand Medical Association, 115*(1164), U218.

U.S. Holocaust Memorial Museum. (1953). *Trials of War Criminals Before the Nuremberg Military Tribunals under Control Council Law No. 10.* Nuremberg, October 1946 to April 1949. Washington, DC, U.S. F.P.O. 1949–1953.

University of Pennsylvania. Press Release (2008, June 26). *Disclosure of organ transplant risks: A question of when, not if June 26, 2008.* Retrieved July 27, 2008, from www.uphs.upenn.edu/news/News_Releases/ 2008/06/organ-transplant-risk- disclosure.html

Van Howe, R. S., Svoboda, J. S., Dwyer, J. G., & Price, C. P. (1999). Involuntary circumcision: The legal issues, *BJU International, 83*(Suppl 1), 63–73.

Walker, J. M. (2006, Summer). Beyond informed consent. *Journal of Legal Nurse Consulting, 17*(3), 8.

Whitstone, B. N. (2004). *Medical decision making: Informed consent in pediatrics and pediatric research.* Retrieved on July 16, 2008, from http://tchin.org/resource_room/c_art_18.htm

Woolf, S. H., Chan, E., Harris, R., Sheridan, S. L., Braddock, III, C. H., Kaplan, R. M., Krist, A., O'Connor, A. M., & Tunis, S. (2005). Promoting informed choice: Transforming health care to dispense knowledge in decision making. *Annals of Internal Medicine, 143*(4), 293–301.

Zur, O. (n.d.). *Ethics codes on record keeping and informed consent in psychotherapy and counseling. Zur Institute.* Retrieved on July 24, 2008, from www.zurinstitute.com/ethicsofrecordkeeping.html

Chapter 8

Medical Treatment Decisions
The Patient's Choice

Camille M. Renella, BSN, RN, CME and
Susan Green DeWitt, MSN, RN

First Edition and Second Edition
Gail N. Friend, JD, RN; Jennifer L. Rangel, JD; and
Brett N. Storm, Esq. (deceased)

Contents

Prelude

In the increasingly complex world of health care service and delivery, there are numerous participants involved in the medical decision-making process at the point at which the patient enters the system. To name just a few would include: the federal government, state and local government, public and private health care insurers, hospitals, health care facilities, social service agencies, doctors, nurses, therapists, patients, and, of course, the American taxpayer via the court of public opinion and political debate. The nurse consultant involved in the forensic review of a medical case must be aware of these multiple participants and their various agendas in order to fully understand, and explain if necessary, the rationale behind the decisions reflected in the medical record. A full discussion of all the interests involved in the decision-making process is beyond the scope and purpose of this book.

The authors acknowledge there may, at times, be other decision makers in the medical treatment decisions affecting one individual; however, the decisions made should always respect the patient's expressed wishes; or if the patient's wishes are not known, his or her personal values or best interests should determine the course of medical treatment. Therefore, this chapter will deal with the medical treatment decisions that are chosen by the patient.

Objectives

At the end of this chapter, the legal nurse consultant (LNC) will be able to

- Describe the concept of autonomy as it applies to a patient's informed consent
- Describe the medical professional's responsibilities to a patient when a plan for health care treatment is made
- Understand the parts of an advance directive (AD)
- Articulate when an AD becomes effective and what circumstances negate its instructions
- Describe minor's rights in heath care decisions
- Appreciate standards for substituted decision making when patients do not have the capacity to make decisions for themselves
- Know where to get updated information on the Emergency Medical Treatment and Active Labor Act (EMTALA)

Introduction

"The treatment of the disease may be entirely impersonal; the care of a patient must be completely personal."

Francis W. Peabody—"The Care of the Patient" (1927)

In order to analyze a case for merit, it is our responsibility as LNCs to view the case on multiple levels, including those of which legal clients may not be aware. These perspectives are what distinguish LNCs, as health care professionals, from legal experts. Determining the state of medical compliance in every case will strongly help to affirm or challenge the allegations.

Theory for Making Informed Medical Treatment Decisions

It is the health care professional's obligation to respect the patient's autonomy to make medical decisions that are right for them during the course of medical care. It is then and only then that health care providers fulfill their professional obligation to help the patient and do no harm. In order to accomplish this goal, it is essential to educate the patient and make sure the patient understands the recommended treatments, patient risks, burdens and benefits of those treatments, as well as alternative treatment options and each of their risks, burdens, and benefits (see Chapter 7, "Informed Consent").

Once patients have this information, they have the right to make medical decisions that conform to their life goals, personal values, and individual preferences. Although it is sometimes difficult for health care professionals to care for patients whose values are different from those the provider holds, nonetheless, their decisions are to be respected. Federal laws, such as the Patient Self Determination Act (PSDA), require hospitals to inform patients of their rights to make their own decisions, even if those decisions are medically contraindicated.

Health care is only one part of a person's life. Patients make treatment decisions for reasons that are not medically based and many times health care providers are not privy to their reasoning.

The physician's expertise is knowledge of the disease, diagnosis, and treatment, and it is the physician's obligation to translate medical information into language the patient understands so the patient is able to hear, absorb, and apply it to himself. This professional obligation includes determining the patient's decision-making capacity (DMC) to make the necessary decisions, disclosing information, and truth telling.

Understanding the impact that specific medical treatments play within the context of a patient's life is a part of case analysis that is sometimes overlooked or minimized when determining whether or not "harm" has been done. It should be obvious that "harm" is not always physical. Therefore, harm to a patient's integrity, personhood, values, personal preferences, and goals should be taken into consideration. Documentation should show that respect for holistic, patient-centered care has been provided, including providing the patient every option to make informed decisions.

When analyzing a case with complex medical implications, in-depth analysis is essential in order to understand reasons and ways patients make the medical treatment decisions. It also helps to analyze whether or not health care providers have practiced ethical behavior and patient-centered care. Was patient autonomy respected in obtaining an uncoerced informed consent? Did the health care provider behave paternalistically by withholding information or overriding the wishes of a competent adult patient? Did the provider obtain, and then implement the patient's expressed preferences for the quality of life they want to experience? Was the patient's right to privacy and confidentiality respected?

Patient Autonomy/Self-Determination

The concept of patient autonomy, which governs the act of making informed decisions, has further evolved through laws such as the PSDA and the adoption of professional codes, such as The American Nurses Association Code of Ethics. These documents emphasize the importance of autonomy in proving patient care. "Autonomy refers to a person's ability to be in charge of his or her own life without interference or coercion" (DeWolf & Sue, 2007). In respect to patient autonomy, a patient has the right to be informed of, and a provider has the duty to disclose, the medical treatment that will be given and the reason for it. Respect for patient autonomy and information disclosure are part of the informed consent process (see Chapter 7, "Informed Consent") mandated by the PSDA.

Health Care Provider's Duties

Requirements are provided in the PSDA that health care entities participating in the Medicare program, including HMOs, must meet. Among these requirements is the stipulation that competent adult patients be provided with written notice of state law regarding their rights to consent to or refuse care. Written policies and procedures must be in place addressing the required elements of PSDA (Obade, 2008).

Liability issues may arise when allegations are made that the patient was not fully informed or was given wrong information. Families and surrogate decision makers can complicate the situation if they disagree with a patient's medical decisions to refuse care. Failure to respect a patient's right to refuse medical treatment may give rise to a civil suit by the patient for damages. In addition, withholding or withdrawing treatment pursuant to a patient's alleged wishes can also lead to liability if the family disagrees or claims that the patient did not want treatment to be withdrawn. If a health care provider is in doubt as to the proper course of action, involving the court is a prudent step.

Patient Rights

In 1973, The American Hospital Association issued a Patient's Bill of Rights to be implemented throughout the United States for all hospitals and professionals to follow, to help ensure they were providing holistic patient-centered care. The Patient's Bill of Rights was replaced in 2003 with *The Patient Care Partnership: Understanding Expectations and Responsibilities* (American Hospital Association, 1998). These rights include the following concepts:

- Providing Considerate and Respectful Care: The patient's individual culture, religious beliefs, values, personal preferences, and economic situation should be considered among other aspects of their identified, individual needs.
- Providing Information Regarding Care in Understandable Terms: In addition to verbal communication, health care providers may also include visual, audio, sign language, and other educational options in order to assure their patient's understanding. Sometimes asking patients how they learn best helps the educator apply this concept.
- Providing Informed Consent: A patient's consent to medical treatment is considered to be informed only when they demonstrate an understanding of the risks, benefits, and burdens of the recommended treatment, as well as an understanding of the alternative treatment options and each of their risks, benefits, and burdens. (See Chapter 7, "Informed Consent.")

■ Allowing Treatment Refusal and Knowledge of the Consequences: Treatment refusal includes the choice to withhold, withdraw treatment and make medical choices which are not medically optimal. Patients also have the right to make what health care professionals would identify as bad decisions or less than medically optimal decisions, as long as those decisions are informed—that is, the patient expresses an understanding of the consequences of their decision. Once this determination is made, the patient's decision should be respected without judgment on the part of the health care professional.

■ Providing Privacy, Confidentiality of Medical Records and Communication: This concept applies not only to medical records, but also to talking about patients by name in the elevators, to other health care team members who are not involved in the patient's care, giving information regarding the patient's condition over the phone not knowing the caller's relationship to the patient or without the patient's specific expressed permission, or through discussion outside the health care facility without the patient's knowledge or consent to do so.

■ Providing Access to a Full Range of Patient Services: Providing holistic patient care via a team approach includes social service, nursing, physical therapy, occupational therapy, speech therapy, and community resources, among others.

■ Allowing Refusal to Participate in Research: Care needs to be taken to assure the patient is aware a proposed treatment is experimental and that the patient is fully aware of all the risks and benefits, from participating in the research study. The consent form should include who will be notified if the patient experiences adverse effects by participating in the study. Patients also need to be made aware that if they choose not to participate in the research, standard care will still be provided. They should also be told what care will be provided, who will provide it, where it will be provided, and what that standard care will include.

■ Providing Continuity of Care: Typically when there are multiple disciplines and services caring for one patient, but there is no patient care coordinator, the chance for information being omitted is increased. This type of disconnected care is more vulnerable to miscommunication and poor patient outcomes.

■ Providing Pain Relief: Pain is subjective and should be treated individually and not according to a particular recommended dosage. Sometimes this aspect of analysis is underestimated or misunderstood in determining a patient's ability to comprehend and make rational choices regarding their medical decisions.

■ Providing an Explanation of the Bill: This right is not applicable to medical decisions but should be considered when appropriate.

■ Providing an Explanation of Hospital Rules: The health care institution has an obligation to make sure the patient is informed of any conflict between the patient's values or wishes and the hospital's policies. The patient should know this up front so that he can make choices in line with his values and preferences.

Patients exercise the rights listed above within the framework of their identity. Individual culture and ethnicity influence the decision-making process. It is imperative to understand that the medical profession is a culture within itself. That is, medical professionals have their own belief systems of what is right, wrong, valuable, indifferent, and/or optimal in regard to medical treatment. In contrast, patients have their own deep-stated values from which they launch all their life-long decisions. Their individual medical treatment decisions are based on that same decision-making process and from that same personal value system.

Patient values versus those of the medical profession are another important aspect of case analysis that is buried deep within the context of any case, especially when analyzing the patient's medical decision-making process. It is critical to note that typically when a patient goes along with the medical treatment recommendations, it is accepted without the treating physician's scrutiny. But when a patient hesitates to agree, or outright refuses a medical recommendation, then the reasons for their decisions are more likely to be scrutinized.

In order to ensure a patient's autonomous informed decisions are respected, it is important to consider the impact of the patient's personal values and culture on their care and to carefully review the medical records for evidence of how medical treatment decisions were recommended and made. Such analysis has the realistic potential to reveal hidden aspects of the case that may be crucial to or even change the outcome.

Evidence of the language used to discuss the patient's illness and disease, including the degree of openness in discussing the diagnosis, prognosis, and death, should be in the medical record. Documentation should reflect health care providers' discussions with the patient including education regarding the disease process, treatment recommendations, alternative treatments, risks, benefits, and burdens as well as expectations and outcomes and the patient's response to these discussions. Sometimes within the medical culture, it is uncomfortable to raise the issue of impending death or even the possibility of death. Although the culture is changing, it is something to make note of during case analysis.

Determine whether decisions are made by the patient or a larger social unit such as the family, especially when respecting patient confidentiality. Look for documentation regarding who was present during provider-to-patient discussions and whether or not the patient appeared to voice a choice as to the presence of family members. Was there any evidence the patient felt he had no choice as to how, when, where, and with whom he was comfortable having the discussion?

Consider the relevance of religious beliefs, particularly about the meaning of death, the existence of an afterlife, and belief in miracles. This may help to explain why a patient is making decisions contrary to medical recommendations. A patient, for example, may be choosing to suffer pain in this life so as not to have to endure eternal suffering in the next. Without careful exploration of this type of case, the overt appearance of refusing pain medication can be falsely interpreted as noncompliance.

Another obvious and well-known religious belief is one held by Jehovah's Witnesses in their refusal of blood and blood products. Social workers' and/or chaplains' documentation in the patient's medical records should reflect a health care team's respect for the social and religious dimensions of holistic patient care. Lack of such involvement from either of these two disciplines should raise concern for the LNC reviewing the case.

It is crucial to understand how a patient's personal values, religion, and culture affect his medical treatment decisions. Evidence of how the health care provider assessed and respected the patient's autonomy is relevant in every case analysis. Some things that may be helpful to consider in case analysis are:

- Evidence of how hope for recovery is negotiated within the family and with health care professionals. For example, look for documentation of discussions regarding the family beliefs of a patient who is in a persistent vegetative state. Does the family hope the patient will awake and be cured or is their hope for comfort care or a peaceful death? Are these emotional issues reflected in the orders and code status written for by the treating physicians? Is there documentation that indicates negotiation between family and providers? What is the evidence of the patient's degree of fatalism versus an active desire for the control of events into the future. Does the patient have an AD? Are there documented discussions between patient and physician regarding a medical plan of care? Are there documented information-sharing discussions among family members, health care providers, and treating physician(s) at crucial crossroads during the course of the patient's care?

■ Consider issues of age/generation, gender and power both within the patient's family and with the health care team. For example, in some cultures the wife does not make any decisions for herself. In others, the children depend on their parents to make decisions for them. In still other cultures, the doctor makes all the medical decisions for the patient and the patient would not think of asking questions or challenging the treating physician's medical treatment decisions. Also, some nurses believe they are servants to the physician and do not share their assessments or insights into their patient's values, wishes, preferences, and beliefs. Therefore, the nurse–physician relationship should always be considered.

■ Take into account the political and historical context, refugee status, past discrimination, poverty, and lack of access to care. If the patient has never experienced optimal care due to lack of community, religious, familial, financial or insurance resources, they may have few expectations and may not feel empowered or knowledgeable as to how or what to ask for on their own behalf.

To aid the complex effort of interpreting the relevance of cultural and religious dimensions of a particular case, LNCs should make use of available resources and experts, including community or religious leaders, family members, and language translators. LNCs need to look for evidence that these issues have been considered, because what appears to be patient compliance may not be if this information has been overlooked or not addressed in the patient record.

The merit of the case may change if the patient does not have a clear understanding of the facts due to cultural or language barriers, or has religious objections that were not considered.

The patient's motivation for making treatment choices is important and should always be validated. The case reviewer needs to understand how generalized information translates into the patient's personal decisions, choices, preferences, and wishes. Looking for evidence as to the steps the health care team took in order to determine whether and how the personal religious and cultural beliefs affected the patient's medical treatment choices is yet another key in determining whether or not the patient's autonomous, informed medical treatment decision was respected.

Evidence of the health care team's efforts to understand the context within which the patient made his treatment decisions should also be reflected in meticulous documentation in the patient's medical record. How did the patient describe his reasons for seeking medical treatment? Where did discussions like this take place? Who was present during the discussions? Who provided patient education regarding diagnosis and treatment recommendations? Was the education provided in a language and format the patient understood and was there documentation of the patient's understanding? Were resources consulted in order to understand the patient's religion and culture? Was any effort made related to understanding the community and its values in which the patient lives that might or might not have influenced their behavior?

If these aspects were adequately considered, then evidence of these kinds of discussions should begin the minute the patient seeks medical attention, throughout treatment, until, and beyond discharge from care. LNCs should look for a team approach to the holistic care patients receive, no matter how extensive that team may be. Health care teams may include a doctor and nurse or a full team of social workers, therapists, chaplains, nurses, doctors, and specialists. Look for documentation of multidisciplinary team meetings. What is the routine or policy for addressing these issues within the institution? And most importantly, how was the patient included in these discussions?

This is important since medical treatment decisions made by the patient should reflect the patient's values, wishes, and desires. If the medical decisions are made by a surrogate, the decisions should reflect the patient's values or should be made as the patient would have made. Evidence of whether or not these issues have been addressed appropriately may change the outcome or merit of the case.

Advance Directives

Making medical treatment decisions known ahead of time provides patients with the assurance that their wishes will be honored and offers their providers a clear guide to follow; failure to do so is paramount to choosing to have others make the decisions for them. As patients live their lives they make choices. The same is true for making medical treatment choices. Unless patients share their end-of-life care preferences, their family and health care providers will be forced to substitute their judgment for that of the patient. Not surprisingly, it is possible that the patient will receive medical care they would not necessarily want for themselves.

Patients have the right to make decisions about receiving health care that reflects their values, preferences, and wishes. In order to support this right, federal law requires patients be told of their right to complete an advance directive (AD). An "AD" is a written statement the patient prepares that defines how they want their medical decisions to be if they are incompetent to make them for themselves. If they choose not to complete an AD, it is important they understand they will still receive care.

ADs are written instructions about the patient's future medical care, and go into effect when the patient is no longer able to make his own decisions. ADs allow patients to decide ahead of time what medical procedures they do or do not want to receive. This usually involves decisions about breathing machines, cardiopulmonary resuscitation (CPR), receiving food and water if they cannot take them by mouth, and whether or not to use certain medicines such as antibiotics. They also help the family make decisions based on the patient's wishes and ensure that they are followed if different from their family's wishes. There are two types of ADs: a Living Will (LW) and a Durable Power of Attorney for Health Care (DPAHC).

Living Will

An LW is a legal document, also known as a health care treatment directive, which states the patient's desires about withholding and/or withdrawing treatment in the event he has a condition that cannot be cured and is not expected to live for more than a few months. LWs direct caregivers when the patient is not able to make health care decisions known. It is called a "living will" because it must be signed formally like a regular will but its terms take effect before death.

An LW may:

- Spell out the measures the patient does and does not wish to have taken to extend their life when death is imminent
- State whether or not they want breathing machines, feeding tubes, oxygen, IV fluids, or other medicines to be used
- Lists specific conditions (coma, fatal illness with no hope of recovery or cure, end-stage dementia) under which the terms of the LW are to go into effect

For an LW to be legal, the patient must be competent, and the document signing must be witnessed. All adults are presumed competent unless a judge has declared them incompetent.

Requirements vary from state to state, but usually the witnesses must not be the patient's relative, creditor, heir, doctor, or other professional medical health care provider.

A person should prepare an LW when healthy and not wait until very ill or hospitalized. It is important to note that LWs only cover decisions about a patient's health care in cases of terminal illness and when death is expected in a relatively short time. Some illnesses, such as stroke, may not be covered by an LW. While most states have laws that recognize ADs, some do not recognize ADs as binding and some do not recognize LWs that have been drafted in other states. Consequently, it is necessary to check the laws in the state where the AD was completed and executed. Given the limitations inherent in an LW, patients should have other AD in place so that their wishes will be respected.

Durable Power of Attorney for Health Care

A DPAHC appoints a family member or friend to follow the patient's wishes only in the event the patient is unable to make his own medical treatment decisions. The DPAHC is called the agent or surrogate decision maker and will make medical decisions for the patient unable to make them. The decisions should reflect the patient's own values, preferences, and wishes and not those treatments the agent wants for the patient.

DPAHC is different from an LW in that an LW only goes into effect if the patient is dying. A DPAHC goes into effect any time the patient cannot make medical treatment decisions for himself. That condition can be temporary or permanent. If the patient suffers from a condition that is temporary, such as a coma from a head injury, the patient will resume making his own decisions once awake from the coma and if/when it is determined he has the capacity to make this own decisions.

Some people prefer the DPAHC to an LW because it is more adaptable. The patient must be competent at the time the DPAHC is signed in order for it to be legally valid. Sometimes, due to a medical or mental condition, a person can be confused about time and place but still able to understand choices if they are carefully explained. Health care providers and mental health specialists can assess the patient's ability to make decisions. If the patient is able to demonstrate an ability to understand the questions asked, the medical decision to be made, the risks, benefits, and burdens of that decision, the available alternatives and their respective risks, burdens, and benefits, then the person is said to have DMC and those autonomous, informed decisions should be respected. DMC is different from legal competency, which needs to be established in a court of law.

A court must decide if the person is legally competent. Legal competence is based on whether the person has a condition such as a mental illness or dementia, is able to make or communicate decisions, and is able to manage money or make health care decisions. The patient is said to be "legally competent" if the patient is making an informed decision and understands the consequences of that decision. In addition to DMC and competency, it is required the patient be at least 18 years old (minors are discussed later in this chapter).

If a person is found to be legally incompetent, the court may appoint a legal guardian. Guardianship may cover all areas of someone's life, or it may cover only certain areas. For example, an older person may be able to make decisions about his health but not about money.

Consider the case, for example, where a patient has a progressive medical condition (such as Parkinson's disease). The patient may wish to draw up the DPAHC papers early in the illness. The agent's duty is to follow the patient's wishes, so it is most helpful if the patient takes the opportunity to discuss his wishes regarding treatment while still able to do so. In states that recognize such documents, families and health care providers cannot override a patient's LW or the agent's decision. If it is unclear as to the patient's DMC at the time they completed the LW and/or DPAHC, the court should determine competency. If the patient is not competent to express his wishes or make medical treatment decisions, the court should appoint a legal guardian with the authority to make medical decisions in the patient's best interest.

Once a patient has signed an LW and/or a DPAHC, they should be kept in a safe place that is accessible. It is a good idea for patients to discuss their wishes with their friends, family members, and especially their doctors and provide them with copies of their LW or DPAHC.

Sample forms for writing ADs of an LW and/or a DPAHC are available on-line and conform to the laws of each state. The National Hospice and Palliative Care Organization will also provide a copy of state-specific ADs free of charge. Patients can call 800-658-8898 or visit their web site at http://www.nhpco.org. A patient's state health department, local hospitals, or state bar association may also be able to provide state-specific ADs. Completing an AD does not require an attorney; however, a patient may wish to ask a lawyer for assistance in drawing up an AD.

Do Not Resuscitate

If a patient is in a clinic, hospital, or nursing home, he may be asked to sign a code status sheet. This tells the staff what measures the patient wants to be taken if the patient's heart stops and he is not breathing. The patient may change the code status at any time.

A full code means that the patient wants every effort for revival attempted, including CPR, electrical shock, intracardiac injection to start the heart, and placement on a ventilator. A limited code may exclude being put on a ventilator, dialysis, or other kinds of support. A no code or Do Not Resuscitate (DNR) order may be written.

A DNR order excludes only CPR, an emergency procedure that may save the life of someone whose heart has stopped beating and who is not breathing and does not limit other types of treatment. Patients should receive other necessary medical and nursing care, even if CPR would not benefit them. Laws are different in different states, however. If it is determined in advance that the person has a terminal illness or multi-system failure and death is imminent, and if that condition is established and documented by two or more physicians, then CPR is no longer an option and is not required or offered as a treatment option if the patient's heart stops.

Failing to respect the patient's AD or taking action prohibited by the AD can result in a civil suit being brought against the professional health care provider. Therefore, when reviewing a case involving end-of-life decisions, the LNC should search the record for documentation of discussions about the patient's wishes at the end of life and in the absence of an AD.

Standards for Substituted Decision Making: Health Care Surrogate Act

While it is clear that a competent person makes his own informed medical treatment decisions, most state statutes provide that a person who is incompetent or lacks DMC cannot consent to medical treatment. A person may be incompetent due to a variety of reasons and circumstances. For example, the person may be under the state's legal age of consent, unable to understand the treatment decision they are being asked to make, or they may be unable to communicate their treatment decision. For whatever reason, if the patient is unable to make informed decisions for himself he cannot consent to medical treatment.

As of 2009, all 50 states enacted statutes that create a DPAHC or a health care proxy. In some cases, the only way for the patient to consent to medical treatment is through a surrogate. A surrogate is a person who speaks for the incompetent patient and could be a family member, friend, spouse, or health care provider. Surrogate decision makers look to the law for guidance regarding their authority, the standard that they base their decisions on, and the limits to their authority. Surrogate health care decision makers may derive their authority from statutes that create a health care proxy or from other sources when a proxy is not available.

Ideally, the surrogate decision maker is appointed by the patient with DMC. The patient's wishes, shared with the surrogate, are based on his values, preferences, and whatever other elements important to the informed decision-making process. According to the Massachusetts Health Care Surrogate Act (The Illinois Health Care Surrogate Act in the Appendix is similar to that of Massachusetts), without the expressed wishes of the patient:

> … the surrogate must rely on other factors to consider when making health care decisions as he/she believes the patient would have made for himself/herself. Some of the factors that a surrogate could consider include the patient's present level of physical, sensory, emotional and cognitive functioning, the quality of life, life expectancy and the prognosis for recovery with and without treatment, the various treatment options, the degree of humiliation, dependence and loss of dignity resulting from the condition and treatment, the opinions of family members, the reasons behind those opinions and the motivations of the family in advocating a particular course of treatment (Massachusetts Health Care Surrogate Act).

During case analysis, if a patient's capacity to make health care decisions is in question, care should be taken to review the patient's DMC. If DMC is lacking, then the question must be raised regarding who the patient surrogate is according to the patient's AD. If the patient did not have an AD, the next question is who is the legal surrogate decision maker according to the state's Health Care Surrogate Act? Finally, if the patient has a health care surrogate, is there evidence that the surrogate made health care decisions as the patient would have made?

If, for example, a surrogate makes the decision to continue life support for a patient, is it because he cannot let go of the patient, or is the surrogate buying more time in anticipation of a miracle? In the second instance, the decision not to discontinue life support is based on the surrogate's beliefs, wishes, preferences, desires, and personal grief. Is there evidence the patient would make this same decision, knowing the inevitable outcome of death, based on the patient's own values, wishes, and beliefs? In some cases, the patient would make the same decision. In other cases, the patient may want to die peacefully without the intrusion of a machine. Documentation of discussions with the surrogate, asking them whose wishes they are considering, should be evident in the patient's medical records in order to determine if the surrogate is making medical treatment decisions as the patient would have made for himself/herself.

Standards for Minor Patients

As we have come to have a better understanding concerning how physicians should collaborate with minor patients and parents in making treatment decisions, the concept has been formalized by the American Academy of Pediatrics (AAP). In 1976, the AAP recognized that children should participate in decision-making commensurate with their age and development. According to the AAP, children should provide assent to care whenever reasonable.

Recognizing that the "informed consent" process has limited direct application in pediatrics, that is, it is limited to parents who have the legal right and appropriate DMC for decision making on behalf of their child, the AAP provided an updated analysis of the concepts for:

1. Informed consent
2. The ethics of informed consent
3. The right to refuse treatment
4. "Proxy consent"
5. Parental permission and child assent
6. Informed consent of adolescents

Parents' Rights

The AAP holds that treatment decisions involving the care of all minor children are the shared responsibility of the pediatrician and parents and includes all the elements of the Informed Consent process (as outlined in Chapter 7, "Informed Consent"). Although the law generally provides parents with the authority to make informed decisions for their children, laws also exist which protect children from abuse and neglect, making it clear that sometimes parents can breach their obligations toward their children. Therefore, professionals who provide care to minors have the professional obligation to carefully assess parental decision making as it relates to the best interests of the child. If, in the case of recommended life-saving treatment, the parents' motives and/or capability are questioned and all reasonable attempts have been made to educate them to the importance of the treatment, the health care provider has a professional obligation to protect the child and should consider legal steps to override parental wishes or decisions.

Care Choices in the NICU

The medical treatment of infants should be based on what is in their best interest. However, because the infant's "best interest" is not always clear, parents and health care givers are often faced with difficult treatment decisions when confronted with the situation of a severely ill, extremely premature, or terminally ill infant (American Academy of Pediatrics, 2006).

The rapid advances in medical technology from the late 1960s to the Baby Doe case of 1982 established neonatal care as a legitimate specialty of medical care, separate from the rest of pediatrics and medicine (Lantos & Meadow, 2006).

Consequently parent autonomy, clinical prognosis, and children's rights, in addition to the meaning of futility and inhumane treatment, often stimulate legal battles around treating infants with debilitating birth defects and treating infants for whom the physicians deem efforts to prolong life to be futile. Complex conversations between physicians and parents are often overshadowed by parental emotion and medical uncertainty. Often within minutes or seconds a parent's dreams of a beautifully healthy, bouncy baby girl or boy is suddenly replaced with the harsh possibility of having to care for that same child but who is now disabled or terminally ill. Treatment decisions under these conditions are overwhelming and devastating. When reviewing cases involving any aspect of neonatology, LNCs need to access all related resources in order to fully appreciate the complex medical implications, establish the choices the parents faced, the timing of their education regarding these implications, and the method of teaching to match their learning style. Documentation in these types of circumstances should be detailed, and appear as an on-going multidisciplinary health care team member to parent discussions. (The reader is referred to Volume 2, Chapter 15, "Obstetrical and Neonatal Case Evaluations" for further information.)

Pediatric Assent for Medical Care

Treatment decisions that involve the health care of older children and adolescents should include, to the greatest extent feasible, the assent of the patient as well as the participation of the parents and the physician. According to the AAP, assent should include at least the following:

1. Helping the patient achieve a developmentally appropriate awareness of the nature of his or condition
2. Telling the patient what he can expect with tests and treatments
3. Making a clinical assessment of the patient's understanding of the situation and the factors influencing how he is reasoning (including whether there is inappropriate pressure to accept testing or therapy)
4. Soliciting an expression of the patient's willingness to accept the proposed care. Regarding this final point, the AAP notes that no one should solicit a patient's views without intending to weigh them seriously. In situations in which the patient will have to receive medical care despite his objection, the patient should be told that fact and should not be deceived.

As in the case of informed consent, the emphasis on obtaining assent should be on the interactive process in which information regarding the values of the child and the parents are shared and joint decisions are made. The Academy does not in any way recommend the development of a new bureaucratic mechanism, such as "assent forms," which could never substitute for the rational aspects of consent or assent (American Academy of Pediatrics Task Force on Pediatric Research, 1976).

Examples in which informed permission may be sought from parents/guardians for infants and young children include: Providing immunizations, performing invasive diagnostic testing for a congenital cardiac defect, beginning long-term anticonvulsant therapy to control a seizure disorder, initiating serial casting to correct congenital club foot, or undertaking surgical removal of a suspicious abdominal mass. If parents deny permission, the physician should seek to obtain permission from the courts to initiate treatment based on reasonable clinical judgment before delaying care or risking liability for performing the treatment without appropriate authorization.

Examples of situations where the Academy encourages physicians to seek the assent of the parent as well as the consent of the older school-age child include: venipuncture for a diagnostic study in a nine-year old, diagnostic testing for abdominal pain in a 10-year old, or application of an orthopedic device to manage scoliosis in an 11-year old. While in some cases treatment may proceed over the objection of the patient, physicians and parents should be informed in order to appreciate that overriding the child may undermine their relationship with the child.

Pediatrics and Treatment Decisions

In the situation in which the minor patient refuses to assent (or actively refuses), there should be adequate evidence that the health care professionals made every effort to respect the wishes of the patient in order to understand their situation or come to terms with fears or other concerns regarding proposed care. Evidence of this effort should be found in the medical records. Family meetings should be recorded in detail. In addition, evidence of social service and chaplain involvement are avenues the health care team may explore in their effort to understand and address these concerns. Coercion in diagnosis or treatment should be considered a last resort.

While medical treatment decisions of the minor patient should be meticulously explored during case review, other aspects of the care of the minor should also be considered, including confidentiality and disclosure. The AAP affirms that with the exception of life-threatening situations, confidential care of adolescents is essential to overall health, and parental consent or notification should not be a barrier to receiving medical care. The receipt of medical treatment without parental consent also extends to the disclosure of minors' access to treatment.

Adolescents' Rights

Three specific situations where minors' access to treatment may be disclosed without parental authorization include the following ("HIPAA and Teen Privacy" 2006). Mature Minors: Minors who have been deemed "mature" may have decision making and control over the disclosure of medical information.

1. Emancipated Minors: Emancipation is a legal procedure that frees children from the custody and control of their parents or guardians before they reach the age of majority. (In California this is age 18.) If a minor becomes emancipated, he will be able to do certain things without parental consent, including consent to medical treatment. There are three ways a minor can become emancipated:

   ■ He can get married. (This requires parental consent and permission from the court.)
   ■ He can join the armed forces. (This requires parental consent and acceptance by the service.)
   ■ He can obtain a declaration of emancipation from a judge. This information tells minors only about how to be declared emancipated by a judge. If he/she wants to be declared emancipated by a judge, they must convince the judge that he/she meets ALL of the following requirements:

      (i) At least 14 years old
      (ii) Willingly wants to live separate and apart from his/her parents with the consent or acquiescence of the parents (Parents do not object to the minor living apart from them.)
      (iii) Can manage his finances
      (iv) Has a source of income that does not come from any illegal activity.

2. Sensitive Situations and Issues: These situations and issues include birth control, sexually transmitted diseases, and pregnancy in which minors may not seek medical attention because of reluctance to inform parents or guardians.

   It should also be noted that minors' access to abortion and contraception as well as substance abuse and mental health treatment without parental involvement is often regulated separately by state laws, which vary widely from state to state.

3. Finally, the AAP believes that in most cases, physicians have an ethical and legal obligation to obtain parental permission for recommended medical interventions. In many circumstances, physicians should also solicit patient assent when developmentally appropriate. In cases involving emancipated or mature minors with adequate DMC, or when otherwise permitted by law, physicians should seek informed consent directly from adolescent patients (Committee On Bioethics, American Academy of Pediatrics, 1995).

Health Care Provider Liability Issues Resulting from the Right to Refuse

Patients have the right to refuse recommended medical treatment. In 1973 the American Hospital Association adopted A Patient's Bill of Rights which went through several revisions till 2003 (American Hospital Association, 2003), when the American Hospital Association replaced it with its publication entitled, *The Patient Care Partnership: Understanding Expectations, Rights and Responsibilities.*

The evolution of these documents reflects a major shift in the concept of who the health care plan decision maker is. Where the physician was once the decision maker, with little question regarding his authority, it is now the patient who is the primary decision maker for his health care decisions. In making one's own health care decisions, there are certain rights and responsibilities that pertain to the patient, health care provider, and/or institution. The patient has the right, and is encouraged, to obtain current and understandable information concerning diagnosis, treatment, and prognosis from the physicians and other direct caregivers. Except in emergencies when the patient lacks DMC and the need for treatment is urgent, the patient is entitled the opportunity to discuss and request information related to the recommended specific procedures and/or treatments, the risks involved, the possible length of recuperation, and the alternative medical options along with the accompanying risks and benefits of each (American Hospital Association, 1998).

Emergency Medical Treatment and Active Labor Act

The Emergency Medical Treatment and Active Labor Act (EMTALA) is a Federal law signed into law by President Regan in 1986 as part of a larger body of legislation, the Consolidated Omnibus Budget Reconciliation Act (COBRA). EMTALA incorporates regulations adopted by the Centers for Medicare and Medicaid Services (CMS), a division of the Department of Health and Human Services, to regulate the delivery of necessary emergency services.

The essential provisions of the law is as follows: Any patient who "comes to the emergency department" requesting "examination or treatment for a medical condition" must be provided with "an appropriate medical screening examination" to determine if he or she is suffering from an "emergency medical condition." Once the patient presents to the emergency department, the hospital is then obligated to either provide him with treatment until he is stable or to transfer him to another hospital in conformance with the statute's directives (Strickler, 2006).

EMTALA applies only to hospitals that satisfy two criteria: (1) it receives Medicare funds, and (2) it provides emergency treatment services. It does not matter whether a hospital operates a formal emergency department or not. As long as the hospital provides services to treat emergency conditions, it will be subject to EMTALA and must comply with certain statutory and regulatory requirements. Furthermore, physicians who practice within that hospital are also subject to specific obligations.

Since being signed into law, there have been many updates to clarify portions of the original law. For example, CMS (memo dated July 13, 2006) clarified the concept of "parking" to be, "When Emergency Medical Services (EMS) personnel bring a patient to the emergency department (ED) and the EMS personnel are left in attendance of the patient rather than the ED personnel assuming care" (Assid, 2007). Parking is considered a violation under EMTALA. Other issues such as emergency preparedness will compel EMTALA to evolve.

EMTALA continues to be a law that is in constant flux, requiring clarifications of ambiguities and interpretation by the CMS. For health care institutions that meet the definition of having an emergency department, education on these changes must be ongoing. What the facility does to comply and stay current with the evolution of EMTALA are areas to scrutinize during an investigation. A facility must show that it provides updates on EMTALA and makes compliance efforts on a proactive and continuing basis.

The LNC should stay current on the law, but more importantly, know where to look for the policies and procedures required for a facility to meet EMTALA's guidelines. Moreover, a risk manager (in many cases an LNC) must update and revise policies and procedures and review compliance in her own institution to stay current with EMTALA. The reader is encouraged to visit the following web site for details regarding the law: http://www.emtala.com/faq.htm (*Frequently asked questions about the Emergency Medical Treatment and Active Labor Act*, n.d.).

Conclusion

It is a patient's right to make choices about accepting or refusing medical care. There are, however, life circumstances that could rob the patient of that right unless the patient makes plans in advance about medical treatment. If someone is involved in a motor vehicle accident or has a heart attack with loss of consciousness, but does not have an AD, the physicians and family would have to guess what kind of medical care the patient would have wanted. Patients can maintain their right to accept or refuse treatment if they have provided a written statement of their wishes called an AD.

When the LNC reviews a case, looking for evidence of when and how medical treatment decisions were made, the patient's role in the discussions and understanding of the treatment recommendations may assist in determining the case's merit. Tucked between the lines in every case are clues regarding the ethical behavior of the medical professionals involved. These behaviors help determine if the patient had the opportunity to make informed, individualized, and personal medical treatment decisions that were right for him. LNCs are in a unique position to recognize these clues because of their professional experience. Understanding and looking for evidence of the ethical practices that should define the patient's medical decision-making process will give the reviewing LNC added insight into the validity of the case as well as the edge that may support or challenge the outcome.

References

American Academy of Pediatrics Task Force on Pediatric Research, Informed Consent, and Medical Ethics. (1976). Consent. *Pediatrics, 57*, 414–416.

American Hospital Association. (1998). *A patient's bill of rights.* Chicago, IL, catalog no. 157759.

American Hospital Association. (2003). *The patient care partnership: Understanding expectations and responsibilities.* Retrieved March 8, 2009, from http://www.aha.org/aha/issues/Communicating-With-Patients/pt-care-partnership.html

Assid, P. A. (2007). Emergency medical treatment and active labor act: What you need to know. *Journal of Emergency Nursing, 33*(4), 324–326.

Committee on Bioethics, American Academy of Pediatrics. (1995). Informed consent, parental permission, and assent in pediatric practice. *Pediatrics, 95*(2), 314–317. Retrieved March 8, 2009, from http://www.nocirc.org/consent/bioethics.php

DeWolf, B., & Sue, M. (2007). When respecting patient autonomy may not be in the patient's interest. *JONA's healthcare law, ethics, and regulation, 9*(2), 46–49. Philadelphia: Lippincott Williams & Wilkins, Inc.

Fosmire, M. Sean. (2009). *Frequently asked questions about the Emergency Medical Treatment and Active Labor Act.* (n.d.). Retrieved December 9, 2009, from http://www.emtala.com/faq.htm

HIPAA and Teen Privacy. (2006). *HIPAA Compliance Journal.* Retrieved February 18, 2009, from http://www.hipaacompliancejournal.com/2006/07/

Lantos, J., & Meadow, B. (2006). *Neonatal bioethics: The moral challenges of medical innovation.* Baltimore: The John Hopkins University Press.

Obade, C. C. (2008). Right to refuse treatment. In *Patient care decision-making: A legal guide for providers, Part II. West Law.*

Peabody, F. W. (1927). The care of the patient. *JAMA, 88,* 877–882.

Strickler, J. (2006). EMTALA: The basics. *JONA's Healthcare Law, Ethics, and Regulation, 8*(3), 77–81. Lippincott Williams & Wilkins, Inc.

Additional Resources

Buchanan, A. E., & Brock, D. W. (1989). *Deciding for others: The ethics of surrogate decision making.* Cambridge: Cambridge University Press.

Illinois Health Care Surrogate Act.

Jonsen, A. R., Siegler, M., & Winslade, W. J. (1992). *Clinical ethics: A practical guide to ethical decisions in clinical medicine* (3rd ed.). New York: McGraw-Hill.

Kaye, C. (2006). Introduction to the newborn screening fact sheets. *Pediatrics, 118*(3), 1304–1312. Retrieved March 8, 2009, from http://pediatrics.aappublications.org/cgi/content/full/118/3/1304

Lantos, J. D. (1989). Treatment refusal, noncompliance, and the pediatrician's responsibilities. *Pediatric Annals, 18,* 255–260. National Hospice and Palliative Care Organization. http://www.nhpco.org

The Hastings Center Guidelines on the Termination of Life-Sustaining Treatment and the Care of the Dying (1988). Bloomington, IN: Indiana University Press: Author.

Veatch, R. M., & Fry, S. T. (1987). *Case studies in nursing ethics.* Philadelphia: J.B. Lippincott.

Test Questions

1. What constitutes Informed Consent to a recommended treatment?
   A. The patient allows the surgery
   B. The patient allows the surgery after being informed of its risks, burdens, and benefits as well as the alternative treatments and each of their risks, burdens, and benefits
   C. The patient nods yes when asked if he consents to the medical treatment
   D. The patient has a life-threatening emergency and immediate care must be given

2. If a patient chooses to make "bad" medical decisions, should those decisions be respected?
   A. Yes, it is the patient's choice
   B. No, the health care team of doctors and nurses are in a better position to make the medical choices
   C. Only if this is an informed decision with an understanding of the consequences of his decisions and it is confirmed that the patient has DMC
   D. Only if he or she has a psychological diagnosis

3. What is the difference between an LW and a DPAHC?
   A. A Durable Power of Attorney draws up an LW
   B. They are the same thing
   C. A DPAHC and an LW are both ADs
   D. One must be dying for an LW to go into effect

4. Name one situation where the health care provider should seek assent from an adolescent patient?
   A. Organ donation
   B. Vaccination
   C. Blood transfusion
   D. All of the above

5. What is a hospital's obligation to patients when it is operating under the provisions of EMTALA?
   A. To immediately transfer a patient to a facility with the best medical care specific to treating his particular condition
   B. To stabilize a patient before considering patient transfer
   C. To treat all patients despite their ability to pay medical bills
   D. To give each patient a medical screening exam if the facility provides emergency care and stabilize the patient if necessary before transferring

Answers: 1. B, 2. C, 3. D, 4. D, 5. D

Appendix: Illinois Health Care Surrogate Act
Objective

To comply with the State of Illinois legislation authorizing certain family members and other individuals to make decisions relating to medical treatment on behalf of patients who (1) are no longer capable of making such decisions, and (2) have no applicable AD. For those patients who meet the above criteria and have a "qualifying condition," a decision maker is permitted to make a decision to forgo life-sustaining treatment on behalf of the patient.

Definitions

An AD is an LW or Power of Attorney for Health Care.

The attending physician is the physician selected by or assigned to the patient who has principal responsibility for treatment and care of the patient and who is a licensed physician in Illinois. Neither a resident nor a fellow is the attending physician.

Decisional capacity is the ability to understand and appreciate the nature and consequences of a decision regarding medical treatment or forgoing life-sustaining treatment and the ability to reach and communicate an informed decision as determined by the attending physician.

A qualifying condition is the existence of one or more of the following conditions in a patient: a terminal condition, permanent unconsciousness, or an incurable or irreversible condition. The condition must be certified in writing in the patient's medical record by the attending physician and at least one other qualified physician.

A qualified physician is a physician licensed to practice medicine in all of its branches in Illinois who has personally examined the patient.

Terminal condition is an illness or injury for which there is no reasonable prospect of cure or recovery, death is imminent, and the application of life-sustaining treatment can only prolong the dying process.

Permanent unconsciousness is a condition that to a high degree of medical certainty:

i. Will last permanently without improvement
ii. In which thought, sensation, purposeful actions, social interaction, and awareness of self and environment are absent
iii. For which initiating or continuing life-sustaining treatment in light of the patient's medical condition provides only minimal medical benefit

Incurable or irreversible condition is an illness or injury:

i. For which there is no reasonable prospect of cure or recovery
ii. That ultimately will cause the patient's death even if life-sustaining treatment is initiated or continued
iii. That imposes severe pain or otherwise imposes an inhumane burden on the patient
iv. For which initiating or continuing life-sustaining treatment in light of the patient's medical condition provides only minimal medical benefit

Imminent (as in "death is imminent") is a determination made by the attending physician according to accepted medical standards that death will occur in a relatively short period of time, even if life-sustaining treatment is initiated or continued.

Life-sustaining treatment is any medical treatment, procedure, or intervention that, in the judgment of the attending physician, when applied to a patient with a qualifying condition would not be effective to remove the qualifying condition or would serve only to prolong the dying process. Such procedures can include but are not limited to assisted ventilation, renal dialysis, surgical procedures, blood transfusions, and the administration of drugs, antibiotics, and artificial nutrition/hydration.

A parent is a person who is the natural or adoptive mother or father of the child and whose parental rights have not been terminated by a court of law.

A surrogate decision maker is an adult individual(s) who:

  i. Has decisional capacity
 ii. Is available upon reasonable inquiry
iii. Is willing to make medical treatment decisions including decisions regarding the forgoing of life-sustaining treatment on behalf of a patient who lacks decisional capacity
 iv. Is identified by the attending physician in accordance with the provisions set forth below, as the person or persons who are to make those decisions

Surrogate decision makers are to be identified in accordance with the following order of priority:

1. The guardian of the patient
2. The patient's spouse
3. Any adult son or daughter of the patient
4. Either parent of the patient
5. Any adult brother or sister of the patient
6. Any adult grandchild of the patient
7. A close friend of the patient
8. The patient's guardian of the estate

A close friend is any person 18 years of age or older who has exhibited special care and concern for the patient and who can demonstrate to the attending physician by presenting an affidavit or notarized letter setting forth facts that establish that he or she:

  i. Is a close friend of the patient
 ii. Is willing and able to become involved in the patient's health care
iii. Has maintained such regular contact with the patient as to be familiar with the patient's activities, health, and religious and moral beliefs

The Illinois Medical Surrogate Act sets forth the order of priority among persons who can be appointed as a surrogate. When there are two or more representatives from the same category, a reasonable effort should be made to reach a consensus regarding the treatment decision. If agreement cannot be reached, or if the authority of the surrogate is challenged, it is recommended that advice be obtained from the Ethics Consultation Service.

For those patients who lack decisional capacity and for whom a surrogate decision maker or guardian is not available, decisions concerning medical treatment of those patients may be made by a court-appointed guardian.

Chapter 9

Communication with Clients in the Medical Malpractice Arena

Margo R. Conklin, MSN, RN-BC, LNCC and
Karen S. Fox, BSN, RN, LNCC, CPHRM

First Edition and Second Edition
Sherri Reed, BSN, RN, LNCC

Contents

Objectives

Upon reading this chapter, the legal nurse consultant (LNC) will be able to

- Describe three components of interviewing skills that nurses acquire through their practice and education
- List three skills that LNCs possess as interviewers that give them an advantage over in-house office staff specializing in plaintiff litigation
- Explain two purposes for plaintiff client interviews in a legal setting
- State three roles in which the LNC may interface with health care provider defendants (HCPDs)
- Discuss the role of the LNC during interviews with HCPDs
- State three duties and responsibilities of the LNC when working with defense clients
- State the importance of understanding the philosophy of the company insuring the health care provider or health care system
- Describe the variety of defense clients that the LNC may encounter
- List three potential barriers to communication with clients

Introduction

This chapter addresses the role of the in-house and/or independent LNC during communication with either the plaintiff team or the defense team, taking it from the initial client interview and continuing with ongoing communication with the client team in a civil tort litigation. The chapter provides information about the advantages of utilizing an LNC as a responsible and proficient communicator, with broad health care education and experience, to help the attorney litigate the claim effectively and successfully.

The nursing process, as described below, provides a systematic means for the nurse to demonstrate accountability and responsibility to the law firm's clients during the litigation process. Responsible communication conveys to clients that their feelings are respected, which leads to the clients' commitment to a team approach. Commitment and a team approach lead to successful implementation of strategies in a legal case.

"Communication" Defined

The American Heritage Dictionary defines "communication" as an interpersonal relationship between two or more individuals, involving the "exchange of thoughts, messages, or information"

Table 9.1 Purposes of Client Communication

- Establish and maintain rapport
- Collect data
- Educate client
- Support client

(Miffin, 2003). The primary purpose of communication (Table 9.1) involves the exchange of information or ideas. Meeting a person face to face is just one mode of communication, and often used for "formal discussion or to meet with someone to examine his qualifications or to get information from him" (Miffin, 2003). Communication through interviewing is a fundamental component of the LNC and client relationship. Interviews may be formal or informal, in person or over the phone, but are always goal-directed (Balzer-Riley, 1996). In order for the litigation team to represent the plaintiff or defendant effectively, there must be full, open, and honest communication. Common purposes of client communications are explained in detail in Table 9.1.

Barriers to Communication

It is important to recognize the numerous potential barriers to effective communication between client and attorney or LNC. Such barriers are unique to each situation (see Table 9.2).

In addition, the client's prior legal experience, as well as the attorney's and LNC's previous experience with similar clients and cases, may also present barriers.

Some examples of barriers that an LNC might encounter include a plaintiff who has suffered a stroke and can no longer speak, a plaintiff who does not speak English, or someone who practices a religion that does not allow blood transfusions and cannot understand how that issue might interfere with the prosecution of the case.

With the growth of the electronic age, location and mode(s) of communication might become a barrier. Some examples of these types of barriers that an LNC might encounter include misinterpretation of the written word, that is, e-mail correspondence, misinterpretation of the spoken word, that is, telephonic interference or miscommunication due to dropped or inaudible calls, or misinterpretation of gestures across cultural lines. The natural tendencies to judge, evaluate, approve, or disapprove of a client's statement based on one's own value system or preconceived ideas can be a major barrier to interpersonal communication. Once perceived by the client, this potential

Table 9.2 Potential Barriers to Communication with the Client

- Language
- Age
- Socioeconomic status
- Ethnic background
- Religion
- Client's previous experience with the legal system
- Legal team's previous experience with similar cases or plaintiffs

barrier may inhibit the client's freedom to provide information, place the client on the defensive, or force the client to make choices inappropriate to his or her situation and value system. It may also become a source of dissatisfaction with legal representation if the outcome of the case is unsuccessful or not what the client expected. An accepting, nonjudgmental attitude on the part of the attorney and LNC is essential for an effective relationship with the client.

Communication in the Plaintiff Arena

The objective of the attorney/plaintiff relationship is a mutually satisfactory resolution of the business that the plaintiff brings to the attorney. The objective is a comfortable working relationship between the attorney and the plaintiff. The legal problem is evaluated in terms of whether or not the plaintiff will follow the course of action agreed upon in collaboration with the attorney and other members of the legal team. The plaintiff's actions and attitude depend in part on how the plaintiff feels about the attorney and support staff. The LNC plays a key role in the communication process as the one person on the legal team with both health care and legal experience. For this reason, a special bond is often forged between the LNC and the plaintiff. The LNC becomes a resource for the plaintiff and a liaison with other members of the litigation team. How is this accomplished with the independent LNC?

The independent LNC brings medical/nursing knowledge and information and advanced communication skills, and often has increased flexibility when working with the plaintiff attorney and the plaintiff. It is not uncommon for the LNC to have communication with the plaintiff attorney and/or the plaintiff during the evening or weekend hours. Due to hectic work schedules and travel or location issues, the independent LNC can be invaluable for client meetings. Appropriate communication of information by the LNC helps the plaintiff to understand the risks and benefits of all options presented. Ultimately, the attorney needs to ensure that the plaintiff makes decisions only after the plaintiff has been informed of relevant considerations. The plaintiff's desires in the matter have to be carefully elicited and choices must be made with adequate legal information.

Often, the plaintiff's decisions in litigation proceed more from emotional factors (love, hate, fear, and anger) than the attorney's decisions do. Plaintiffs who have been injured or who have lost a loved one often seek financial retribution, and may also seek a public admission of fault from the defendant. Plaintiffs may be unable to see the facts of the case beyond the injuries sustained. It may be inconceivable to them that the defendant may not have been negligent or that the negligence may not have caused the injuries. Furthermore, they may be shocked to discover that even if the defendant is found negligent, his or her license to practice may not be at risk. The plaintiff's goals must be accurately identified. Education and emotional support can then be appropriately directed at those goals. It is crucial for the LNC to obtain the facts from an objective perspective in order to help the plaintiff and to assist the plaintiff in helping himself or herself.

Purpose of Plaintiff Interview in a Legal Setting

Establishing and Maintaining Rapport through Effective Communication

The rapport established between the plaintiff and the attorney or the LNC at the initial interview may have far-reaching consequences in terms of the accuracy and completeness of information obtained. It might also affect the attorney's ability to counsel the plaintiff effectively when alternative courses of action arise (Nelken & Schoenfield, 1986). Inquiry call forms or intake forms (often individualized by the plaintiff attorney or one of his office staff) can be used to collect information when screening initial calls from potential plaintiff clients. One of the primary roles of the in-house LNC is often to screen phone calls and collect information from potential plaintiffs. For plaintiff attorneys without an in-house LNC, often nonmedical office support staff obtain the initial intake or screen the initial call. In these cases, the independent LNC can support the plaintiff team with follow-up interviews. It is important for the independent LNC and plaintiff's attorney team to have excellent communication skills which will then establish good rapport. The independent LNC might be given the intake interview to review for merit or to follow up for additional information.

The Initial Interview of Plaintiff

The initial interview usually creates lasting impressions for both the plaintiff and the litigation team and the LNC can contribute to this process through follow-up interview and communication by explaining how the plaintiff's medical situation is meshed with the process of the litigation. Throughout a lengthy litigation process, the plaintiff will frequently communicate with the legal support staff, such as the LNC, paralegal, and secretary, more often than with the attorney. The fact-gathering process can be easily sidetracked or blocked if the plaintiff is suspicious of the attorney, resents the attorney as an authority figure, or for any other reason does not have a good rapport with the attorney or other members of the litigation team.

Nurses learn communication and interviewing strategies as part of their basic interpersonal and assessment skills. The skill of active listening means that the interviewer becomes engaged in the plaintiff's thought processes. It requires considerable energy on the part of the nurse interviewer. Nurses are trained to attend carefully to a patient's conversational flow and analyze it as the patient is speaking. The nurse then directs the patient into appropriate problem-solving modes based on the assessment. The same process is used during the initial interview between the potential plaintiff and the LNC.

Successful interviewing skills include a balance of verbal and nonverbal behavior, empathy, assertive responses, and client-centered techniques, each chosen specifically to promote trust (Lindberg et al., 1994). In turn, these skills assist in preparing the plaintiff for deposition testimony or the negotiation process. A trusting plaintiff will be open and receptive to ideas and take the LNC and attorney seriously when discussing these areas. Successful interviewing solicits and provides pertinent information, influences the plaintiff to effect some change or to respond appropriately to a request for medical care compliance, and encourages attitudes that allow the plaintiff to consider settlement alternatives.

Many plaintiff interactions take place over the course of several years of litigation. The LNC is the appropriate contact person for the plaintiff, since these contacts often include obtaining updated medical information, answering medically related questions, or discussing the medical aspects of the case. Plaintiffs will remain more cooperative and receptive to advice or counsel if they feel that they have been listened to attentively. Plaintiffs need to believe that the attorney and the support staff are advocates, working on their behalf, in order to maintain a trusting and amenable relationship throughout the litigation process.

The LNC can assist in initiating a working relationship with the plaintiff in an open, reflective, and supportive atmosphere in the law office, on the telephone, via electronic mail, or in the plaintiff's home. Electronic mailing should never be a substitute for periodic verbal communication on the part of the attorney or LNC. Communication by electronic mailing can be a useful and time-saving way for the plaintiff to update the LNC or attorney on his or her medical care; however, the LNC should always be cognizant of the fact that people can sometimes misinterpret the "tone" of an electronic communication. The LNC realizes that strategies such as active listening, empathic regard for the plaintiff's feelings, and acceptance are sometimes not interpretable via electronic mailing.

The initial plaintiff interview may take place over the telephone, in the attorney's office, at the plaintiff's home, or in a health care facility. The purpose of the initial interview is to introduce the plaintiff to the LNC as a member of the litigation team, obtain background and factual information relating to the events and damages, and ascertain whether a working relationship is possible between the plaintiff and the members of the litigation team. The process of the initial interview might be compared to the initial health history and physical performed by the nurses when the patient is first admitted to the hospital or health care facility. See Table 9.3 for elements of initial interviews with plaintiff clients.

The LNC should begin the plaintiff interview with introductions and an explanation of the LNC's role on the litigation team. The plaintiff is asked to explain briefly what happened or why the plaintiff is calling the law firm and what he or she thinks the health care provider did wrong. It may be clear early on that the plaintiff does not have a valid case. He may be angry because his call light continually went unanswered, but he has no injury. The LNC may provide a brief explanation to the plaintiff, but should avoid telling the plaintiff that the case does not have merit. If the LNC comments on the case's merit, the LNC might be providing information outside his or her professional realm. Instead, the LNC should tell the plaintiff that the information obtained will be provided to the attorney, who will ultimately make the decision about the merits of the case.

Table 9.3   Key Elements of Initial Interviews with Plaintiffs

- Listen carefully to the plaintiff
- Allow the plaintiff to tell the story in his or her own words
- Be empathetic
- Identify date of injury
- Obtain names, addresses, and phone numbers of the plaintiff and close relatives
- Determine conflicts of interest
- Identify the plaintiff's goals and objectives
- Obtain accurate and complete medical information using an assessment tool
- Obtain names, addresses, and phone numbers of current and past treating health care providers
- Describe current compared with previous health and lifestyle
- Solicit occupational history and effects of injury
- Estimate past medical expenses
- Estimate past lost wages
- Introduce key office staff
- Provide the plaintiff with office phone numbers
- Identify potential future health care providers

During the interview, the LNC should obtain the plaintiff's full name, addresses, and phone numbers, and those of the plaintiff's close relatives. The LNC should ask what prompted the plaintiff to contact the attorney and what the plaintiff wishes to accomplish by filing a lawsuit. The LNC may discover that the plaintiff does not necessarily want to file a lawsuit, but only wants to know what happened to cause an injury. The plaintiff may want financial compensation or to "prevent this from happening to someone else."

Early in the interview, it is important for the LNC to identify any conflicts of interest that would prohibit involvement in the case. Names of all potential health care defendants should be solicited. The LNC should also inquire about any previous involvement with the legal system and obtain the names of the attorneys and defendants involved. If it is determined that a conflict exists, the interview may need to be terminated until the conflict is resolved, if possible.

If no conflict is evident, the interview should proceed to solicit more detailed information by asking the open-ended question "What happened to you?" Most plaintiffs are eager to tell their story to a nurse who understands the medical issues of their claim. The LNC must direct the interview efficiently to sort relevant information from irrelevant information by guiding the story with specific questions or requests for additional details. The LNC should allow the plaintiff to tell the story in his or her own words, listen carefully to the plaintiff, and not allow previous experience with similar cases to color the plaintiff's story. If preliminary review of the case indicates that there may be merit, the LNC should refer the case to the attorney for determination of the statute of limitations. The interview should conclude with a brief explanation of the next step of the litigation process and a reminder to the plaintiff to notify the LNC or attorney of any change in his or her medical condition. The plaintiff should also be cautioned not to discuss the lawsuit with anyone outside his or her family. Key office staff may be introduced to the plaintiff and contact phone numbers provided.

Data Collection

With every plaintiff, the attorney must gather sufficient facts to conduct the appropriate research and factual investigation, and enough information about the plaintiff's attitude toward those facts to guide the plaintiff in choosing an appropriate course of action. The initial stage of the interviewing and counseling process should conclude with a clear understanding between attorney and plaintiff of the future course of action, including what steps will be taken, when, and by whom. The attorney should be comfortable with the facts presented as accurate and complete, including pre-existing medical conditions, in order to determine what, if any, role those conditions may play in the liability or causation issues.

The nursing process guides the LNC by providing a systematic means of collecting and assessing health care data accurately and thoroughly. LNCs apply their knowledge and expertise during the assessment to elicit a detailed, accurate clinical health history from the plaintiff. They identify potential damages resulting from the alleged negligence of the defendant and identify information concerning influences of past medical history and care (pre-existing conditions). The LNC might be able to identify other medical conditions the plaintiff may have, based on medications the plaintiff is taking. A plaintiff may not recognize the importance of this information. LNCs also identify factors that will influence compliance with future medical therapy. They anticipate the need for future medical care or evaluations related causally to the incident, such as coagulation studies for monitoring anticoagulation or periodic abdominal series for gastrointestinal conditions. This information can then be added to the damage profile. When collecting data in obstetrical and neonatal cases, it is imperative for the LNC to include the infant's medical history, the family history, and any genetic history.

The assessment process enables the nurse to determine factors in the client's life that promote healthy behaviors and wellness. By eliciting information from the plaintiff regarding social and cultural background, support systems, value systems, or health perceptions, the LNC demonstrates the importance of focusing on the whole person rather than just the signs and symptoms of the medical problem at issue. These additional elements contribute significantly to the pursuit of a successful lawsuit. Such assessments might include understanding why the potential plaintiffs desirous of pursuing a medical negligence claim regarding the care for their fourth child's delivery did not seek medical care for the pregnancy until the time of delivery. Or it could clarify how the choice not to give an infant a recommended or ordered blood transfusion because of religious beliefs might affect the outcome of the claim.

The LNC is aware that a loss can include loss of body parts, functions, independence, or any other type of physical, emotional, or intellectual loss, whether real or perceived. Assessment of the plaintiff's reaction to loss can help the LNC evaluate the plaintiff's psychological status. Identification of the plaintiff's coping skills contributes to an understanding of how the plaintiff will deal with the stress of a lengthy lawsuit. The plaintiff may need to be referred to a psychologist or other mental health professional for help in dealing with unresolved issues related to loss. These needs are a significant part of the damages in a plaintiff's claim. They also may affect the plaintiff's ability to withstand the rigors of a stressful legal process. The LNC uses assessment skills to collect data about a case and formulates diagnoses of the major issues. The attorney and LNC can then prepare a strategic plan of action. The plan directs the work performed by the LNC, whereas the creation of work product can be compared to the implementation of the nursing process. The LNC (and others) evaluates the effectiveness of the plan of action and quality of the work product developed. The plan is altered accordingly as new information about the case is obtained. The new information begins the cycle again.

Legal Issues

In addition to establishing rapport and collecting data, a third purpose of communication with plaintiffs is education. Often, the plaintiff's perception of the legal problem differs from that of the attorney, particularly in a medical malpractice action. For example, the plaintiff should understand that the defendant health care provider's license may not be suspended or revoked in the event of a successful outcome. Loss of monetary compensation may be the only effect suffered by the defendant health care provider. The attorney and LNC may use the initial and ongoing interviews with the plaintiff to educate him or her about the legal process. The LNC may prepare educational materials such as a booklet that can be provided to all plaintiffs. Plaintiffs should be instructed that their role in the litigation process is an active one and that they must respond to requests for subsequent information promptly and fully. Plaintiffs need to understand the possible length of the proceeding and the importance of avoiding discouragement by seemingly endless postponements and continuances (see Table 9.4).

Medical Issues

Plaintiffs often view the LNC as a resource person who can answer questions about their injuries, ongoing medical problems, and care. They want to know what caused their injuries and why. The LNC plays a vital role in educating the plaintiff about the reasons for continuing therapies and the importance of compliance with the medical plan of care.

Table 9.4 Educate the Plaintiff Regarding Legal Issues

- Elements of proof required for successful case outcome
  - Liability
  - Proximate cause
  - Damages
- Process of litigation
  - Interaction with defendant and insurance carrier
  - Medical releases
  - Expert case review
  - Petition/complaint
  - Discovery
    - Interrogatories
    - Requests for production
    - Depositions
  - Arbitration, mediation, medical review panel process, settlement
  - Trial
- Potential length of process
- Importance of compliance with current medical treatment
- Future course of action related to litigation
- Potential outcomes
  - Monetary damages
  - No loss of license or public admission of wrongdoing
  - Confidentiality clauses in settlement agreement

After the plaintiff has explained their concerns, the LNC and the plaintiff should discuss the impact of the injury on health, lifestyle, or job—that is, identify the damages. The complete health history covering all body systems is elicited and reviewed to determine pre-existing conditions. Specific questions about current medical problems caused by the injury and the effect of the injury on the pre-existing medical problems are included. The LNC also gathers available data relative to medical expenses and wage loss. It is important to obtain names, addresses, and phone numbers of all past and current treating physicians or other health care providers and caregivers who may provide information about future medical problems and care related to the injury. It is vital to obtain prescription information and the names and addresses of all pharmacies that the plaintiff might have used. Depending on the age of the plaintiff, it may be essential to obtain work or school records. The LNC should determine whether a third-party provider paid the medical bills. If a third-party provider is involved, the name and address of the company should be obtained. The LNC should also determine whether the initial injury was work related and whether a workers' compensation case has been initiated.

In ongoing contacts with the plaintiff, the LNC must obtain updated medical information and records in order to evaluate and maintain an updated profile of damages. Once a lawsuit has been filed, the updated profile will supplement information to defense counsel. These contacts also serve to evaluate the plaintiff's compliance with subsequent medical treatment recommendations and provide ongoing support to the plaintiff. The LNC, as an educator, understands that assessment through interviewing and questioning is an ongoing process lasting as long as the claim lasts, and that this process should clearly identify strengths and weaknesses in the plaintiff's case. The LNC working for the plaintiff in civil tort litigation is uniquely qualified to interview plaintiffs initially and perform any subsequent interviews.

Communication in the Defense Arena

The Health Care Provider as the Defense Client

LNCs play a vital role in the defense of professional negligence cases and other litigation involving health care issues. Today, many professional liability insurance carriers have integrated LNCs into their companies in roles such as claim specialists, adjusters, health care consultants, or loss-prevention and risk-management consultants. Insurance carriers or self-insured companies retain defense law firms to represent health care providers and health care systems, such as large health maintenance organizations (HMOs). These defense law firms also utilize LNCs, either as in-house employees or independent LNCs on a contract basis. Self-insured hospitals and health care systems may utilize independent LNC firms as an adjunct to their own internal self-administered program.

In the defense arena, the HCPD is often referred to as the client, particularly in the context of a law firm setting. However, independent LNCs currently find themselves in more expansive roles. Their defense clients may include attorneys, insurance companies, third-party administrators (persons or companies hired to oversee and resolve claims), and self-insured hospitals and health care systems. Although many of the principles are similar, there are some additional considerations for the LNC working within the context of a larger defense system, rather than with an individual HCPD. This chapter will look at defense clients in several contexts and at some of the roles that the LNC may fill in working with these clients. Communication will necessarily be defined by the different roles and concerns of the various types of clients.

The LNC as a Liaison

In the defense arena, one of the LNC's most important roles is that of liaison between the HCPDs and their attorneys and liability insurance carriers. Many HCPDs find the prospect of litigation very daunting; the concepts of law and the process of discovery and trial are as foreign to them as the practice of health care is to most attorneys. Fortunately, the LNC provides the bridge between these two disciplines by offering health care and health-science education to attorneys and insurance professionals, and legal-process education to health care providers. On a daily basis, the LNC assists with many aspects of the litigation process, including processing or composing complaints, responding to allegations, preparing answers, composing or responding to discovery requests, preparing or responding to interrogatories, scheduling and preparing for depositions, seeking and retaining medical experts, and performing other aspects of discovery. Most of these terms and processes are unfamiliar and anxiety producing to HCPDs who may be exposed to them for the first time (Carroll, 2006). Explaining legal jargon is a crucial part of assisting the HCPD through the legal process. Describing the expected time frames for the process also helps to prepare the HCPD who is used to a faster course of events. Explaining from the outset that the wheels of justice grind slowly, with the average medical malpractice case taking several years to resolve, may help change unrealistic expectations and decrease the HCPD's apprehension.

The LNC as a Facilitator

LNCs are knowledgeable about health care issues and are most often perceived as nonthreatening by HCPDs. Thus, another role that the LNC performs is that of facilitator for the HCPD in the legal process. Lawyers, even those on the defense team, are often viewed as threatening simply because of the adversarial nature of our justice system (Louisell & Williams, 2007). The pairing of an LNC with a lawyer for initial client interviews provides countless rewards for the defense team. During the initial interview, the LNC has the opportunity to facilitate for HCPDs at times when they may not be able to express an opinion or ask a question adequately. An LNC is usually intuitively aware of difficult issues for the HCPD, and may be able to intervene with therapeutic communication techniques. The LNC can also be useful in identifying areas that need further clarification for either the HCPD or the attorney. Thus, the LNC serves as a translator between the two, asking questions for clarification to be certain that the meanings of words are clearly understood and comprehended by all.

The LNC as a Support Person for the HCPD

HCPD anxiety can be dramatically reduced by the presence of another health care provider, someone who speaks the HCPD's language. Sharing commonalities is a highly effective stress-reducing, team-building technique. The LNC's involvement in the initial interview can build trust between the defense team and the HCPD. The LNC can initiate this connection by sharing stories about previous successful outcomes. The LNC can explain the defense team's role, including a general timeline of case development and a description of what will be expected of the HCPD. When the HCPD views the LNC as an advocate, initial apprehension is eased. Most health care providers who are calm, appropriately assertive, and equipped with knowledge of the legal process can participate fully and effectively in their own defense. Those who are paralyzed with fear or who are suffering damaged self-esteem because of the allegations against them create an extra burden for the defense. Just as providing explanations and information to patients helps decrease anxiety and improves self-care, providing information and guidance to HCPDs can be equally effective. Helping HCPDs see their role in the context of the litigation process, while helping them persevere despite the inherent stress of that process, will improve their ability to be highly functioning defense team members.

The LNC as an Educator and Researcher

The LNC is also an educator and researcher. Videotapes describing the litigation process are frequently available from the HCPD's insurance carrier or from the medical–legal or risk management department of the health care organization. State and local medical and nursing associations are also good resources for state-specific legal information for health care providers. Discovery rules vary considerably from state to state. The LNC must be familiar with the rules in the state where the litigation is filed in order to accurately explain the rules to the HCPD. A simple chart of the legal process, as it relates to a medical malpractice lawsuit, can also be a helpful teaching tool. The LNC may recommend role-playing or suggest videotaping a mock interview or deposition of the HCPD. By employing these tools, the HCPD can watch the testimony in a relaxed atmosphere, critique the performance, and ultimately develop confidence when testifying. Providing a list of available resources early in the litigation process helps HCPDs recognize and anticipate their own needs, thereby making it easier for them to request assistance.

HCPDs are often valuable resources for pertinent medical information related to the medical or nursing care issues in the case. They may have extensive literature collections, including bibliographies, articles, or monographs, on subjects pertinent to the litigation. They may have diagrams or anatomic models that can serve as cost-effective trial exhibits. They are often knowledgeable about the local and national experts who will be needed for evaluation of the standard of care and, potentially, for testimony. They may also direct the LNC to pertinent standards published by professional associations. Such information is readily accessible and serves as an avenue for the HCPD to participate in his or her own defense.

The Initial Interview with the HCPD

To evaluate the HCPD's background and effectiveness as a witness, the LNC should begin the interview process by focusing on questions about education, work experience, certifications, and publications. Most people feel comfortable talking about themselves, and in this way, the interview process starts out in a nonthreatening manner. The LNC and attorney (if present) can use this opportunity to observe and evaluate the HCPD's demeanor, communication style, credibility, and jury appeal (Harney, 1993).

Depending on the practice setting, an LNC may perform the initial interview alone or may work, through a team approach, with the defense attorney, insurance professional, or a claim manager from a self-insured hospital or health care system. If conducting the interview alone, an LNC must take detailed notes in order to prepare a memorandum to the defense attorney, or other client, summarizing findings and recommendations. Providing such documentation is important to keep all the defense team members apprised of the status of the work in progress and to avoid duplication of effort and increased defense costs. To ensure a productive interview, it is important for the LNC to ask that all the plaintiff's medical records in the possession of the client be brought to the interview. Physician HCPDs may have office records, billing records, and radiology films regarding the care of the plaintiff. Imaging films are particularly important if the allegations are radiological in nature.

In preparation for the initial interview with an HCPD, the LNC should prepare a list of questions covering such areas as:

- Clarification of the HCPD's charting
- Independent recollection of the issues
- Chronology of events
- Meetings and discussions with others
- Names of other witnesses
- Additional documents needed
- Theories and ideas for the defense
- Suggestions for experts
- Billing practices and procedures

Having the health care provider go over each chart note helps interpret handwriting and idiosyncratic abbreviations. This review helps refresh the HCPD's memory about the case. It is also an opportune time to seek information about routine care that may have been provided, but not charted. Specific independent recollections about care can also be elicited. If the medical record is too extensive for interpretation during the initial interview, it is often useful to have the HCPD type or dictate the office notes (or other notes) verbatim. This can also be helpful when opposing counsel asks for clarification of the medical record and can save time later during the deposition of the HCPD. The LNC should arrive at the interview with a prepared chronological summary of the chart with annotated page numbers. This material will assist in expediting the interview and targeting information needed to complete any unreadable portions of the chart. A list of page number citations specific to the individual HCPD's chart entries will also help guide and speed the interview process. During the initial interview, the LNC assists the HCPD in identifying pertinent documents not in the chart or office record, which will be important to the case. Considerations may include:

- Any additional medical records in the defendant's possession
- Case-specific hospital or office policies and procedures
- Hospital credentialing materials
- Handwritten personal notes made at the time of incident, but not included in the medical record
- Curriculum vitae of all health care defendants
- Diaries, calendars, logs, or appointment books
- Telephone logs and message books
- Prescription records separate from the office chart
- Transcripts of previous deposition or trial testimony given in other cases

During this initial interview with the HCPD, it is important to obtain information about the HCPD's professional background and history. Has the HCPD been involved in litigation prior to this matter? Has the HCPD had any problems with licensure, suspension, or certifications? Is the HCPD board-certified in his or her specialty? If so, how many times did the HCPD take the certification board before passing? If the HCPD is not board-certified, elicit the reason why. It is important to ascertain this information before opposing counsel does so. Nothing is more embarrassing than having opposing counsel advise defense counsel that the HCPD's history includes a medical license suspension for a period prior to the allegations in the case at hand.

Throughout the case, the LNC serves as the HCPD's medical–legal case manager of sorts, the conveyer of case status reports, and a reservoir of resources and legal-process information. The LNC's practice setting and working relationship with the other members of the defense team are important factors to consider when planning the participation of various team members. As an example, an LNC employed in a law firm may be expected to call the HCPD as soon as he or she receives a verbal report from an expert witness. The LNC may find it necessary to consult with the involved attorney and convey the meaning of the expert review to the HCPD in the context of the case development. Independent LNCs usually provide a summary of expert witness conclusions to their attorney or other type of defense clients, but may not have the opportunity to interact personally with the HCPD. The principles discussed here are useful for all subsequent interactions with HCPDs, such as preparation of interrogatories, deposition preparation, trial preparation, assistance at trial, and coping with the outcome of the case.

The Attorney, Insurance Company, Third-Party Administrator, and Self-Insured Company as Defense Clients

Depending on the practice setting of the LNC, the term defense client, rather than referring to the HCPD, may refer to the defense attorney, an insurance company, a third-party administrator, or a self-insured hospital or health care system. When employed as an independent LNC, defense clients are more often the end payer for the LNC service. The client is considered to be the entity that retains the LNC, rather than the HCPD. It is crucial that the LNC understands the various relationships and coverage issues, as well as the timing and context of his or her role, when working with such defense clients (see Figure 9.1). Clearly defining performance expectations and identifying the parameters of desired involvement are key elements in creating a successful working relationship (Katzenbach & Smith, 1993).

Understanding the Defense Philosophy of the Client

Experienced LNCs frequently develop their own defense philosophies that they may erroneously believe are representative of those of all defense clients. Numerous considerations contribute to the defense philosophy of the party (e.g., the insurance company, the third-party administrator, or the claims-resolution committee of a physician-owned company) who controls the funds spent on the defense of a case or any settlement or award. Past loss experience, economic influences, ethical considerations, religious affiliations, and health care provider ownership are just a few of the variables influencing the overall defense philosophy of a health care organization or an insurance carrier. An LNC must have respect for these factors in order to understand the client and offer services appropriately within the greater defense context.

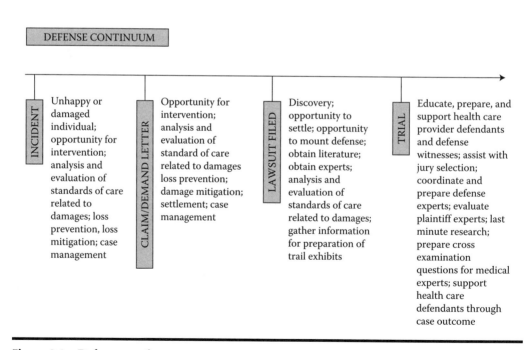

Figure 9.1 Defense continuum.

A self-insured HMO may choose to spend limited funds on early intervention and loss prevention, while applying the greater share of its defense budget to claims containing dollar demands and filed litigation. Another health care organization may have a mission to undertake early analysis and intervention in any untoward patient outcome, instituting loss prevention measures and case management for damage mitigation, even in the absence of medical negligence. It is paramount that the LNC understands and accepts the differences in these defense approaches. Tailoring one's work product to the client's philosophies and goals is probably the most important and challenging task that an LNC must undertake.

Defense philosophies may be elicited during a tactful interview with the client before work is ever undertaken. The LNC's personal philosophies must be identified, isolated, and separated from those of the client for successful meshing of work styles and goals. Attending to the client's needs, rather than personal preferences or beliefs, is client-centered service at its best (Spector & McCarthy, 2005).

Economic considerations are always important to defense clients. Identifying priorities with the client will help with cost containment. Spending hours on projects that the client does not perceive as important or valuable is pointless, even though the projects may be relevant to the case as a whole. Preparation of a detailed timeline chart may be appropriate prior to trial for use as an exhibit, but an insurance carrier may not consider it valuable or cost-effective during the preliminary stages of claim evaluation.

Another consideration to discuss with the defense client is the degree of detail or depth that is expected on a project. Some clients may want every medical word in a report defined parenthetically. Others may be medically sophisticated and request only an explanation of new procedures or treatments. Some clients want extensive medical research with copies of all pertinent articles reviewed and highlighted. Others want the results of medical research simply summarized in memorandum format until trial preparation begins. It is imperative for the LNC who is in doubt about the parameters of a project to clarify the client's expectations prior to undertaking the work. With some clients it may be necessary to do this in writing; other clients may prefer a spoken agreement. Learning to ask the right questions of the client before undertaking the work is a very important part of successful LNC practice.

Defense Perspectives

Chapter 4, "Elements of Triage: Effective Case Screening of Medical Malpractice Claims," presents a detailed discussion of the evaluation of medical negligence cases. The following discussion assumes familiarity with the elements of negligence and evaluating professional negligence cases and focuses on the perspectives that LNCs encounter when working with defense clients.

When beginning the evaluation of a case for a defense client, it is critical to clearly identify the insured or self-insured party for whom the LNC is working. Many incidents, claims, and lawsuits involve a myriad of health care providers, and the professional liability coverage for the providers may stem from a variety of sources. In a staff-model HMO, physicians, nurses, and all other HMO employees are most often covered by the same insurance carrier or self-insured program. The defense of such a case may take on a more unified approach because defense costs and any potential settlement or trial award will come from one source regardless of the specific health care provider found liable for any deviation in the standard of care resulting in damages. For more information, refer to the discussion of HMO liability in Chapter 22, "ERISA and HMO Litigation."

In many health care systems, the nurses and other hospital employees are covered by the hospital's professional liability insurance or self-insurance plan, but each physician has his or her own professional liability coverage. A variety of liability insurance carriers may provide professional liability insurance to different physicians working in the same hospital. Even when several physicians are involved in one case and have the same insurance carrier, each physician will usually be assigned a separate claim representative and separate attorney to work on his or her behalf.

Though evaluation of any case should be thorough and complete, encompassing all involved providers, it is important to understand the economic interests of the LNC's specific client. If the LNC discovers that the party for whom he or she is working has little involvement in the case, the LNC should call this to the attention of the client before undertaking extensive workup of the case. Additionally, if another health care provider is responsible or partially responsible for an injury, and that health care provider has not been named in the lawsuit, the defense client will want to be made aware of that fact. All involved health care providers should be identified for the defense client. Another party may be responsible for sharing settlement costs, if appropriate. Careful attention to providing appropriately targeted, valuable, and fiscally important information throughout the case will strengthen the LNC's relationship with the defense client.

Some states have contributory negligence or comparative negligence laws that mandate evaluation of any act or omission by the plaintiff. In states where the doctrine of contributory negligence is recognized, any blame assigned to the plaintiff will preclude recovery of damages. Even if the plaintiff is found liable for only 1% of the injury and subsequent damages, the plaintiff is barred from any recovery.

When the doctrine of comparative negligence is recognized, the plaintiff's contribution to injury will be compared to any act or omission by any named defendant. Any jury award will be decreased by the percentage of the plaintiff's comparative fault. In some states, recovery is barred if the plaintiff's contribution to injury is deemed greater than 50%. The LNC should be aware of the specific laws governing the state(s) in which he or she practices.

Case Example 9.1

A jury award of $100,000 made to a plaintiff who was found to have a comparative fault of 40% for the injury would result in an actual award of $60,000 to the plaintiff.

LNCs may become involved in the defense of cases at a variety of points on the defense continuum. At each stage, defense clients are interested in determining whether they have responsibility or liability for any injury that has occurred. This determination will help the client decide whether the case should be settled expediently or vigorously defended through trial if necessary. An early evaluation of the standard of care provided by the insured or self-insured health care provider and determination of the cause of any injury will assist in that determination. Upon careful evaluation, some injuries will be determined to be inherent to the claimant or plaintiff's disease process or to be a result of an expected medical complication, rather than due to an act of professional negligence. If injuries are documented and causally linked to deviations in the standard of care, liability is established. LNCs often provide data from the medical record that help to determine whether the standard of care was met. These data include evidence of the health care provider's thought process, monitoring, and response to changes in patient condition. Researching published standards of care, as well as identifying and retaining appropriate clinical experts for standard-of-care reviews, are additional services that LNCs often provide to defense clients.

Early evaluation of an incident may allow for intervention to minimize claimant or plaintiff damages. The provision of an expedient settlement may decrease the overall cost of the case to the defendants, minimize harm to their reputation in the community from adverse publicity, and improve the claimant or plaintiff's overall outcome.

Case Example 9.2

One health care system used a nurse case manager and prepayment for a rehabilitation facility for a patient who broke a hip in a fall from a cardiac catheterization table. Clear liability was identified soon after the incident occurred. Early intervention resulted in an improved patient outcome and made litigation unnecessary. Many cases in which standard-of-care deviations are causal to patient injury are settled at an early point in the defense continuum before a lawsuit is filed, and defense attorneys' fees and trial costs are completely avoided.

When liability has been firmly established, defense clients will be interested in all potential ways of mitigating and minimizing damages. LNCs may find important data during their review of the medical records that will help with this endeavor. Pre-existing illnesses or injuries are important pieces of information to glean from the record. A claimant or plaintiff with a pre-existing chronic illness that will shorten his or her life span will likely also have a decreased number of working years. Thus, economic damages in this case may be lower than for a patient with a normal life expectancy.

Attention to the size and potential value of any case is important when working with a defense client. Regardless of the merits of the case, a case involving an infant with a poor outcome will almost always require a more extensive workup than a case involving a 70-year old with a heel ulcer. Seeking specific preauthorization for any work performed is appropriate for all cases. An LNC must be sensitive to the potential monetary value that each case may represent to the client.

Social issues identified in the medical records are often important in the defense of cases.

Case Example 9.3

The total settlement value of a case involving the death of a 29-year-old mother of four was decreased by an LNC's important discovery in the medical records. The records showed that prior to her death, the mother lost custody of all four children and was not providing any financial support for them. This information made the settlement value of this particular case less than one in which a mother of four was caring for her children in the home and working to support them.

Identifying factors that may make a claimant or plaintiff more or less appealing to a jury is also an important LNC function that is valuable to defense clients. Medical record documentation that describes the claimant or plaintiff's appearance, employment, family structure, and involvement in civic activities is important to point out to the defense client. It is also important to note whether or not the plaintiff missed or canceled appointments or was noncompliant with the prescribed course of care. This information will be utilized as part of the overall assessment of the case. Similar information about the health care defendants that appears in the medical record or is otherwise known to the LNC is also important to share with the defense client. It is extremely important for the defense attorney to be aware of any undesirable attributes of the HCPDs, such as a history of alcohol or drug abuse or a license suspension.

Conclusion

LNCs, as educators and skillful communicators, are critical to the litigation process. Their assessment skills assist them in obtaining useful data for both the plaintiff and defense teams. The LNC assisting the defense team will have a varied application of this chapter according to the practice setting, the timing of the work related to the defense continuum, the relationship with the other defense team members, and the defense philosophy of the health care organization or insurance carrier. Whether working with individual health care providers, defense law firms, insurance companies, third-party administrators, or self-insured health care systems, the LNC will find that his or her health science education and clinical experience serves as a firm foundation for broadened roles as liaison, facilitator, support person, educator, researcher, and legal case manager.

The LNC working for the plaintiff's team is uniquely qualified by virtue of specialized communication and interviewing skills, data-collection and organizational skills, and knowledge of the nursing process to assist the attorney in the initial interview and subsequent plaintiff communication. Effective communication is important during advocacy for plaintiffs and one of the LNC's most effective tools for assisting persons to adapt to life changes and the ongoing stress of litigation. Beyond the nurse/patient relationship, learned and familiar communication skills can be used to successfully assist the litigation team.

References

Balzer-Riley, J. W. (1996). *Communications in nursing* (3rd ed.). St. Louis: C.V. Mosby-Year Book.

Carroll, R. (Ed.) (2006). *Risk management handbook for health care organizations* (3rd ed.). San Francisco: Josey-Bass.

Harney, D. M. (1993). *Medical malpractice* (4th ed.). Charlottesville, VA: Michie LawPublishers (Cumulative Suppl. 1999).

Katzenbach, J. R., & Smith, D. K. (1993). *The wisdom of teams.* New York: Harper Collins.

Lindberg, J. B., Hunter, M.L., & Kruszewski, A. Z. (1994). *Introduction to nursing concepts, issues, and opportunities* (2nd ed.). Philadelphia: Lippincott.

Louisell, D. W., & Williams, H. (2007). *Medical malpractice* (Vol. 6). New York: Matthew Bender.

Miffin. (2003). *The American heritage dictionary of the English language* (4th ed.). Houghton Boston: Miffin Company.

Nelken, M. L., & Schoenfield, M. K. (1986). *Problems and cases in interviewing, counseling and negotiation.* St. Paul, MN: National Institute for Trial Advocacy.

Spector, R., & McCarthy, P. (2005). *The nordstrom way* (3rd ed.). New York: John Wiley & Sons.

Additional Reading

Browne, M. K., & Keeley, S. (2007). *Asking the right questions: A guide to critical thinking* (8th ed.). Englewood Cliffs, NJ: Prentice Hall.

Chay, A., & Smith, J. (1996). *Legal interviewing in practice.* Sydney, Australia: Law Book Company.

Iyer, P., Taptich, B., & Bernocchi-Losey, D. (1995). *Nursing process and nursing diagnosis* (3rd ed.). Philadelphia: W.B. Saunders.

Smith, L. (1998). *Medical paradigms for counseling: Giving clients bad news. Clinical Law Review, 4,* 391.

Test Questions

1. Which of the following statements is NOT true?
    A. An LNC plays a key role in the communication process as the one person on the legal team with health care and legal experience
    B. A plaintiff's attitude and actions depend in part on how the plaintiff feels about the attorney and support staff
    C. The plaintiff can often see the facts of the case beyond the injuries sustained
    D. The plaintiff's goals must be accurately identified

2. Identify the most essential component of data collection in a client interview.
    A. A clear understanding between attorney and client of the future course of action
    B. Identification of factors that influence compliance with future medical therapy
    C. Obtaining updated medical information
    D. Talking to family members every few weeks for additional information

3. An LNC working for the defense of a medical malpractice case may work for all of the following EXCEPT:
    A. A self-insured hospital
    B. A third-party administrator
    C. A defense law firm
    D. An injured patient

4. Which of the following findings from the medical records would be helpful in mitigating damages in a case of clear liability?
    A. The plaintiff was a college graduate
    B. The plaintiff was the sole support for a family of four
    C. The plaintiff was a third-grade graduate
    D. The plaintiff had sole custody of his children

5. After a patient fall resulting in a broken hip, an example of an early intervention that may help avoid a claim or lawsuit is
    A. Completing an incident report to document the details of the fall
    B. Providing nurse case management to improve communication and patient outcome
    C. Notifying the insurance carrier to set adequate reserves for settlement
    D. Conducting a conversation with the facility risk manager

Answers: 1. C, 2. A, 3. D, 4. C, 5. B

Appendix: Personal Injury Inquiry Telephone Screening Form

PERSONAL INJURY INQUIRY CALLS

_____

Name of Caller: _____

Address: _____

Telephone: _____ (home)

_____ (work)

Was call for a specific attorney? _____

   If so, name the attorney. _____

Was the caller referred by another person? _____

   If so, name and address of person. _____

Is caller currently represented by an attorney? _____

   If so, name and address of attorney. _____

Date of incident giving rise to injury. _____

Place of incident. _____

Brief summary description of incident. _____

_____

Brief description of injury. _____

_____

Approximate amount of medical, hospital, and related expenses incurred. _____

Medical and hospital bills _____

COMMUNICATION WITH CLIENTS IN THE MEDICAL

Insurance Carrier _____

Wage loss _____

Date: _____ Person receiving call: _____

Chapter 10

Legal Writing

Edwinna C. Vanderzanden, BSN, JD

First Edition and Second Edition
Kevin Dubose, JD

Contents

Objectives

Upon completion of this chapter, the legal nurse consultant (LNC) will be able to:

■ Understand the philosophical reasons for clear, written communication
■ Identify four principles of clear, concise, readable writing
■ Write more clearly and concisely
■ Provide clients with a more valuable work product

Why "Legal Writing" is a Misnomer

A reference to *legal writing* suggests that written communication by and for lawyers is different from other writing, and that it comes with its own set of rules, stylistic conventions, and expectations. Approaching a legal writing assignment with the mind-set to create a legal writing style merely contributes to the stilted, convoluted, jargon-laden prose that we have come to recognize as legalese or legal speak. Legalese, is known to be exhaustive and convoluted while simultaneously considered the standard of quality for exactness and accuracy in legal legislation, legal documents, or policy statements, it should be avoided by the LNC.

Supreme Court Associate Justice Antonin Scalia received the American Society of Legal Writers' lifetime achievement award, acknowledging his co-authorship of *Making Your Case: The Art of Persuading Judges* (Scalia & Garner, 2008). In his acceptance speech, Justice Scalia reported that he does not "believe that legal writing exists as a separate genre of writing. Rather, I think legal writing belongs to that large, undifferentiated, unglamorous category of writing known as nonfiction prose" (Lawprofessors.typepad.com, 2008).

Legal writing should rarely be different from any other writing. It is the subject matter that distinguishes legal writing from other writing, not the style. Writers who assume a different and unnatural voice in an attempt to "sound like a lawyer" rarely write with clarity and grace, often defeating their own purpose. "Good legal writing is simple, brief, and clear. Unnecessarily abstract or complex words and phrases, flowery language, or literary devices may interfere with the reader's ability to understand the point" (Sobel, 2007). The writer should strive to communicate clearly and concisely, incorporating their own style, for only then will the end product resonate with style ... their own.

Resources for legal writing can be found on the Internet at sites such as Good Business Style Writing (n.d.) and Barger on Legal Writing (2002), which provide links to many useful references.

The Purpose of Legal Writing

The sole goal of writing is communication. Communication is not a self-indulgent process in which writers merely disgorge information. Rather, good communication must include the giving of information and the understanding of that same information. For understanding to occur, writing must be directed to a targeted audience. Good communicators focus on their goal for communicating and tailor their information to a specific audience.

The subject matter of legal writing is unique; however, there are a few other differences between legal and other prose. These differences relate to the sophistication of the intended audience. For instance, a letter drafted by an attorney to a client discussing the merits of their case will read quite differently from a letter to the expert witness in that same case. In the first example, the focus will be on an explanation in simple terms with regard to the legal process in the case, the role of the attorney, and the role of the client. In the latter example, the attorney may focus on more complex legal theory, incorporating medical or mechanical jargon; two different goals for each communication, directed to two diverse audiences.

Good legal writing must anticipate and address the opposing view. The LNC has an ethical duty to inform the reader that there may be a difference in applicable standards of care, or differing opinions among experts as to proper management of particular conditions. The LNC's intent should be to present a balanced case analysis, that is, clear, concise communication in a manner designed to completely inform the intended reader.

A significant difference between legal writing and other technical or professional prose is in the nature and extent of citation. Statements and assertions must be backed up with authority, professional literature, and standards of care, applicable at the time of the injury or negligence. When preparing record summaries or analysis for specially retained experts or counsel, present all reasonable points of view in an objective manner and clearly cite supporting references for every fact in issue. Be sure to address contrary opinions and/or the opposition's expert reports where they have been produced.

The Audience

The knowledge and expertise of the targeted audience will influence the style of writing. It is important for LNCs to pay particular attention to the sophistication of their audience in two areas: law and medicine. Some audiences have expertise in both law and medicine. This category includes attorneys who handle health law claims, expert witnesses with experience in the legal system, those with a doctorate in juris prudence (JD) and a doctorate in medicine (MD), registered nurses who also have a JD, and other LNCs. Other audiences are familiar with the legal system but unfamiliar with medical matters. That group includes judges, attorneys, and legal assistants without experience in health law claims. Other audiences are well versed in medical matters, but inexperienced in legal proceedings. That group includes doctors and nurses without experience in the legal system. Finally, some audiences lack knowledge and sophistication in both law and medicine. This category includes nonmedical clients (usually plaintiffs), family members, and other nonmedical fact witnesses. Table 10.1 summarizes the potential audiences for LNCs' legal writing.

LNCs write for readers with highly variable levels of medical and legal sophistication. Where the intended reader has limited knowledge of the scientific or technical facts of the case, for example, an attorney who has limited medical background, it will be important to establish an initial base of essential facts and terminology for that reader. The LNC preparing a medical factual summary to be presented to opposing counsel in a settlement brochure or the court in a pleading, will want to define the medical terms at issue, citing an authoritative medical dictionary when necessary. If particular professional texts or journal articles are applicable, they also should be accurately cited, and copies of important text provided as exhibits to the writing.

The writing style appropriate for these audiences varies considerably. The writer must assess the audience, and write on a level that is understandable to the audience, without talking down to it.

Table 10.1   LNC Writing Audiences

Area of Expertise	Audience
Law and medicine	Attorneys experienced in health-related claims
	Expert witnesses with legal experience
	JD-MDs
	RN-JDs
Law, not medicine	Judges
	Attorneys without experience in health-related claims
	Legal assistants without experience in health related claims
Medicine, not law	Doctors, nurses without legal experience
Expertise in neither law or medicine	Family members
	Nonmedical fact witnesses

Potential Purposes for Writings by LNCs

Writers must also consider the purpose of the writing. Writing about legal matters serves one of the four purposes:

1. *Informative writing transmits information to the reader.* For LNCs, informative writing includes reports, memoranda, chart analyses, literature summaries, reports evaluating the standard of care, and medical summaries. Informative writing should be an objective, fair presentation of both sides.
2. *Commemorative writing records events.* Medical chart notations and memoranda to document conversations are commemorative writings, as are summaries of client intake interviews and conferences with potential experts. Identify and organize important issues in a logical order.
3. *Inquisitive writing poses questions.* Inquisitive writings include interrogatories and requests for production. Inquisitive writing should be thorough and precise so that unasked questions do not result in withholding critical information.
4. *Persuasive writing tries to persuade.* In litigation, persuasive writings include briefs, motions, and correspondence intended to induce settlement. Persuasive legal writings should be brief, measured, and precise and are slanted in favor of the writer's position (Table 10.2).

Writing style and substance can vary tremendously depending on the purpose. Thus it is essential to keep the purpose of the writing clearly in mind.

No single method of writing is universally preferable. Rather, writers should be mindful of both audience and purpose, and choose a writing style that is appropriate for the circumstances.

Table 10.2   Purposes of LNC Legal Writing

Purpose	Type of Document
Informative	Chart analysis
	Literature summary
	Identification of injuries caused by a defective product
	Complaints
	Mediation and trial briefs
Commemorative	Client intake interview
	Conference with expert
Inquisitive	Interrogatories
	Requests for documents
Persuasive	Settlement brochures
	Mediation and trial briefs

Strive for Reader-Friendly Writing

Regardless of the purpose of the writing, the purpose cannot be achieved unless writers communicate to their readers. Communication is a difficult and uncertain art. However, writers greatly enhance the chance of communication when they make the reader's job easier.

Reasons for Reader-Friendly Writing

All readers engage in two activities: deciphering and comprehending. The deciphering function consists of determining what is being said and how it can be structured in a logical, absorbable framework. The comprehension function consists of digesting what has been deciphered and responding to it. Readers have a fixed amount of time and energy. More time and energy spent on one activity reduces the time and energy available for other activities. Writers should want readers to spend their time and energy on comprehension. Accordingly, the goal of writers should be to minimize the time and energy required for deciphering, so that more time and energy can be devoted to the comprehension function.

Practically speaking, writers want to make a good impression on their readers, whether they are employers, expert witnesses, judges, or opposing counsel. Positive impressions are more likely if the reader does not have to spend time trying to glean the meaning of the writing. Readers who have to work hard are not favorably disposed to writers who place that burden on them. Accordingly, the goal of writers should be to make the reader's job easier.

Attributes of Reader-Friendly Writing

Brevity

Strive to use the shortest, common English words, as well as the shortest possible sentences and paragraphs and omit unnecessary words. Most readers would rather do something other than read legal writing. Judges, lawyers, doctors, and LNCs are all human beings with busy schedules, short attention spans, and limited tolerance for boredom. Readers appreciate writers who reduce the time required for reading. Necessary information should not be sacrificed for brevity. But unnecessary and redundant information should be ruthlessly trimmed so that the product is as short as possible.

Short Words

Long words are common in both law and medicine; choose words appropriate to the knowledge level of the intended reader, always trying to use the shortest word that will clearly convey your point. Writing as if you have a thesaurus in one hand and a dictionary in the other is counter-productive. If writers use words that are unfamiliar to their readers, the readers must look them up in the dictionary (creating more work for readers), guess about their meaning (perhaps incorrectly), or just skip them without understanding them. Each of those consequences is unfavorable. Although the medical and legal professions are full of long, unfamiliar words that have no short, familiar substitute, writers should use shorter words when possible.

Short Sentences

Although it is possible to write clear sentences that happen to be lengthy, the possibilities for confusion and awkwardness increase as sentences get longer. Reading a sentence creates dynamic tension between writer and reader; if the tension is sustained for too long, the reader becomes uncomfortable and the ending is often disappointing. Sentences that exceed three or four lines should be carefully examined.

Short Paragraphs

Dynamic tension also applies to reading paragraphs. People like to receive information with an end in sight. When we read a book, we check to see how many pages it has. When we watch a television show, we check to see how long it lasts. When we read a paragraph, our eyes scan the left margin for the next indentation. Readers are disheartened when they see an entire page without paragraph breaks. Long paragraphs abuse the reader's patience and dissipate dynamic tension. Generally, shorter paragraphs are preferable.

Omit Unnecessary Words

Wordiness and the use of clichés, redundant pairs, qualifiers, and overuse of prepositional phrases (e.g., in, at, for) can distract the reader. Avoid expressions such as "ordered, adjudged, and decreed"; "if and when"; "null and void"; "save and except"; "each and every"; "aid and abet"; and "part and parcel." Do not use several words when one will do. Replace "in the event that" with "if"; replace "on or about" with "on"; replace "prior to" with "before"; replace "subsequent to" with "after"; and replace "for the reason that" with "because." Avoid two-word expressions when one word necessarily implies the other—for example, "past history," "reason why," "mutual agreement," and "sum total."

Avoid meaningless modifiers, including adverbs and adjectives used for effect that add nothing to the sentence's meaning. Adverbs modify verbs and answer how, when, how often, to what degree. Adverbs usually end in "ly," such as "quickly," "extremely," and "generally." All adverbs do not end in "ly," such as, always, never, and soon. Adjectives modify nouns and pronouns and answer what kind, which one, how many. Examples of adjectives are large, negligent, and liable.

Adjectives end in "ly" when modifying a noun, for example likely can be an adjective when it modifies the noun "defendant."

Avoid Statements of Personal Belief

Be wary of beginning sentences with phrases such as "I believe . . . ," "it is my feeling that . . . ," and "it is our position that . . . ." These phrases should always be avoided in persuasive writing. First, it goes without saying that these statements are the writer's belief, feeling, or position. Second, the prefatory phrases weaken the statements that follow, making them sound tentative and uncertain. If writers are sure about their statements, they should make them directly, not qualify them or water them down by statements of personal belief. On the other hand, in informative and commemorative writing, LNCs sometimes are asked to provide personal impressions. In those situations, using a qualification of personal belief is appropriate. Nevertheless, statements of personal belief are over-used and should be scrutinized to determine whether they are necessary and appropriate.

Clarity

Written communication is amazing, even in the best of circumstances. Writers formulate initial ideas and then attempt to give form and expression to these amorphous concepts. Words are assembled and arranged on paper. Readers read those words and form their own ideas. The writer's goal should be for his or her original idea to be as close as possible to the idea ultimately formed in the mind of the reader. Most words in the English language have more than one meaning; when words are used in combination, the possible meanings increase geometrically. The fact that writers' ideas and readers' perceptions ever coincide is phenomenal.

Similarity between beginning and ending ideas is most likely to occur when writers communicate ideas as clearly as possible. Writers should strive to eliminate the potential for multiple meanings, misleading impressions, and confusion. Style and elegance should be sacrificed in favor of clarity. *Drafting Legal Documents, Principles of Clear Writing* (n.d.) offers some tips in improving clarity that the LNC will find applicable when writing a medical analysis.

Most writers are poor judges of the clarity of their own writing. They cannot fairly judge the mental impressions that their words generate in others because they are unavoidably reminded of their original ideas. The best way to evaluate the clarity of a piece of writing is to ask someone else to read it. Putting the work aside for a few days helps somewhat, but there is no substitute for a fresh pair of eyes brought to a writing effort.

Simplicity

Although simplicity is often related to clarity, the two are not synonymous. Complex ideas may be communicated clearly, and simple thoughts may be communicated in a manner that is unclear. As a general proposition, however, simple is more likely to be clear, and vice versa.

Complex and sophisticated concepts have no value if they cannot be communicated clearly to the most simpleminded member of the potential audience. (A list of simpler, readable terms is available at http://www.law.ucla.edu/volokh/legalese.htm.) At best, they are a waste of time. At worst, unfathomable concepts may frustrate and alienate the audience and be counterproductive. Complex writing makes the reader's job more difficult by making the reader spend more time and energy on deciphering, leaving less time and energy for comprehension. Writing should be so simple that the reader can read it once, put it down, and be able to explain what the writing was about.

Table 10.3   Attributes of Reader-Friendly Writing

Attributes	Action
Brevity	Use short words, sentences, and paragraphs
	Omit unnecessary words
Clarity	Communicate the information clearly and concisely
Structure	Prepare detailed outline
	Use headings, subheadings of outline in text

Provide Structure

A report should have an appropriate introduction and conclusion, with topics arranged in a logical sequence and paragraph transitions clear. The human mind is incapable of processing and retaining unstructured information. If writers do not provide a structure that makes the information accessible, readers must do the work required to structure the information. Readers who do that extra work are resentful of the writer, and the opportunity to make a good impression has been squandered. Readers who are unwilling to do the work necessary to process the information allow it to pass quickly through their minds without perceiving or retaining it.

Effective structure requires two steps. First, writers should prepare a detailed outline before beginning to write. An outline forces writers to organize thoughts; it is probably a more important step in the creative process than translating those thoughts into prose. Although modifications may be necessary during the writing process, some form of structure must be maintained rigorously.

The second step to effectively structured writing is communicating the outline to the reader. It should be communicated to the reader with headings, subheadings, boldfaced type, underscoring, enumeration, and any other type-style conventions to enhance the visual accessibility of the outline (Table 10.3).

Reader-Friendly Writing Requires Rigorous Editing

Most writers do not write with brevity, clarity, simplicity, and structure in a first draft. These qualities are developed through rigorous editing, by primary writers and by others. Every paragraph, sentence, phrase, and word should be scrutinized to determine whether it is necessary, whether it is clear, and whether it could be stated more concisely. The timing of drafts and deadlines should allow ample time for editing, with as much time devoted to editing as the writer spent on the first draft. Good editing is hard work that takes a long time. It can make the difference between tolerable writing and great writing.

Reader-Friendly Writing has been Endorsed by the Bar

Organized bar associations have endorsed the concepts of user-friendly legal writing. For example, the board of directors of the State Bar of Texas unanimously passed a resolution urging the members of that state to follow a "Charter for Plain Legal Writing," which contained the following suggestions:

- Write simply. Never use a long word when a short one will do. Never use a Latin or French word when an English one will do. Avoid legal jargon and technical terms unless they are necessary
- Omit needless words
- Provide clear transitions from one idea to another
- Generally, write sentences with an average of fewer than 20 words. Include only one main idea in a sentence
- Prefer the active voice; that is, make sure that the subject of the sentence performs the action of the verb
- Use concrete, specific words instead of abstract, general words
- Make sure that each paragraph has a clear purpose, progresses logically, and contains one main thought
- Use headings, lists, bullets, and ample spacing for appeal and clarity
- Make sure that your documents are well organized, logical, accurate, and immediately comprehensible to the intended reader
- Break a rule rather than say something silly

Similarly, the Canadian Bar Association and the Canadian Banker's Association have drafted "The Ten Commandments for Plain Language Drafting":

1. Consider your reader and write with that reader's viewpoint in mind
2. Write short sentences
3. Say what you have to say, and no more
4. Use the active voice
5. Use simple, "everyday" words
6. Use words consistently
7. Avoid strings of synonyms
8. Avoid unnecessary formality
9. Organize your text in a logical sequence, with informative headings, and with a table of contents for long documents
10. Make the document attractive and designed for easy reading

These rules provide specific suggestions for achieving the qualities of reader-friendly writing articulated in this chapter: simplicity, clarity, brevity, and structure. Writing with those qualities in mind, and with an awareness of the audience and purpose, will make the product more reader-friendly and increase the likelihood of communication.

References

Barger, C. (2002). Barger on Legal Writing. Retrieved on March 11, 2009 from http://ualr.edu/cmbarger/RESOURCES.HTM#cite

Drafting legal documents, principles of clear writing (n.d.). Retrieved on March 11, 2009 from http://www.archives.gov/federal-register/write/legal-docs/clear-writing.html

Good business style writing (n.d.). Retrieved on March 12, 2009 from http://www.techcommunicators.com/pdfs/sharp-01-good-biz-style.pdf

Scalia, A. & Garner, B. (2008). *Making your case: The art of persuading judges*. Washington, DC: West Thompson

Sobel, S. (2007). *Law clerk handbook: A handbook for law clerks to federal judges* (2nd ed.). Washington, DC: Federal Judicial Center.

Volokh, E. (n.d.). *Eschew, evade and/or eradicate legalese*. Retrieved on March 11, 2009 from http://www.law.ucla.edu/volokh/legalese.htm

Additional Reading

Bouchoux, D. E. (2008). *Legal research and writing for paralegals* (5th ed.). Gaithersburg, MD: Aspen Publishers.

Garner, B. A. (1995). *A dictionary of modern legal usage* (2nd ed.). New York: Oxford University Press.

http://lawprofessors.typepad.com/law_librarian_blog/2008/08/former-legal-wr.html

Johns, M. Z. (1998). *Professional writing for lawyers*. Durham, NC: Carolina Academic Press.

LeClercq, T. (2007). *Guide to legal writing style* (4th ed.), Gaithersburg, MD: Aspen Publishers.

National Labor Relations Board. (n.d.). *NLRB style manual: A guide for legal writing in plain English*. Washington, DC: U.S. Government Printing Office. Retrieved on March 11, 2009 from http://www.nlrb.gov/nlrb/legal/manuals/stylemanual.pdf

Stark, S. D. (1999). *Writing to win: The legal writer*. New York: Doubleday.

Strunk, W., Jr., White, E. B., Osgood, C., & Angell, R. (2000). The *elements of style* (4th ed.). New York: Macmillan.

Wydick, R. C. (2005). *Plain English for lawyers* (5th ed.). Durham, NC: Carolina Academic Press.

Test Questions

1. The most important goal of legal writing is
    A. To provide as much information as possible to the reader
    B. To entertain the reader with colorful language and imaginative prose
    C. To make the product easy for the reader to read and understand
    D. To provide tangible evidence of the work you've done

2. Which of the following phrases does not contain needless repetition?
    A. Each and every
    B. Incision and drainage
    C. Aid and abet
    D. Past history

3. Which of the following statements accurately describes the relationship between the purpose of a piece of writing and the appropriate writing style?
    A. Informative writing should provide an objective, fair presentation of both sides
    B. Commemorative writing should be as brief as possible
    C. Inquisitive writing should be careful not to offend by asking for too much
    D. Persuasive writing should be lengthy and thorough to cover every possible angle

4. Effective legal writing always requires
    A. A complex structure subtly embedded in the prose
    B. A liberal sprinkling of legal jargon so that it sounds like a lawyer
    C. Long words, long sentences, and long paragraphs
    D. Rigorous editing

5. Effective communication
    A. Depends on a reader's willingness to work hard to catch up with the writer's level of knowledge and experience
    B. Is impossible when the legal and medical fields intersect
    C. Depends on the writer's ability to express ideas in a manner appropriate and understandable to the audience
    D. Is highly overrated

Answers: 1. C, 2. B, 3. A, 4. D, 5. C

Chapter 11

Researching Medical Information and Literature

Maureen A. Cregan, RN, LNCC and
Christopher M. Duling, Esq., LL.M.

First Edition and Second Edition
Karen L. Wetther, BSN, RN

Contents

Objectives

- Identify the steps in a database search
- List two ways to access information from the National Library of Medicine
- Perform a PubMed search utilizing the "Limits" selections
- State three sources of obtaining hard copies of medical literature
- Identify a source of information to identify a current clinical trial
- List five National Library of Medicine databases other than MEDLINE® that can be helpful in accessing information on specific topics
- List two sources that can be used to research a physician's credentials
- State two ways to determine the validity of published information
- List two sources for locating standards of care or clinical practice guidelines

Introduction

The American Association of Legal Nurse Consultants (AALNC) Standards of Professional Performance professes, "The legal nurse consultant recognizes research as a methodology to further the legal nurse consultant's practice" (American Association of Legal Nurse Consultants, 1995).

As our specialty becomes more familiar to the legal profession, the roles of legal nurse consultants (LNCs) are ever expanding. Attorneys are realizing and appreciating that LNCs have a vast knowledge base and many skills to offer beyond the review and interpretation of medical records. Some attorneys are beginning to think outside the box, realizing that LNCs can be helpful in multiple areas (e.g., domestic, criminal, environmental cases, etc.) including cases where negligence involves critical medical issues. Case in point, a labor law attorney represents a client who was diagnosed with bipolar disorder. The plaintiff was fired from his job and now alleges the behavior which led to the dismissal, was due to his bipolar disease. He is now pursuing a legal claim of discrimination under the American with Disabilities Act. An LNC should be a welcome member of the legal team and be able to research medical and pharmaceutical information as well as interpret psychiatric and pharmacy records in this case.

Depending on the type and stage of the case where the LNC's involvement begins, an LNC may be asked to provide such valuable service as performing all or a portion of the medical research, providing confirmation or rebuttal to the case allegations, determining standards of care and standards of practice, identifying medical literature relevant to the case or authored by an expert or fact witness, identifying potential experts, providing background information for treatment, locating expert witnesses, and determining the necessity of future medical damages and treatment.

Over the past few years, access to computers and the World Wide Web have become commonplace both at home and in the workplace. Information is just a click away on the Web and has become a significant resource relied upon by many on a daily basis.

One of the many valuable services that an LNC offers clients is the ability to identify and locate biomedical information specific to issues in a particular case. Most nurses are relatively comfortable doing research in health sciences libraries and often have had considerable experience in retrieving information from medical and scientific textbooks and journals. However, some may be somewhat less confident performing in-depth medical research using the Web depending on their educational preparation.

The Internet provides access to the most current information via online sources and has revolutionized the way in which LNCs perform their research projects. This information explosion is invaluable and can be expeditiously akin to finding the needle in the proverbial haystack. Information in traditional textbooks relating to medical conditions, medications, procedures, standards, and practice guidelines that was relevant at the time of the subject incident or accident is often key in establishing the necessary elements of the case.

The goals of this chapter are to help the LNC develop the skills of identifying and locating medical information, increasing the LNCs awareness of the many resources available, increasing the LNCs personal knowledge base, and, perhaps more importantly, helping the LNC analyze the medical and scientific information relied upon for its validity and credibility. For ease of reading, at the conclusion of this chapter, Appendix A will provide a complete listing of all referenced websites in addition to multiple other websites.

We live in a high-speed information society. Due to the mechanics of the publication process, much of the state-of-the-art knowledge may not be found in the traditional textbook. Considerable time (possibly years) may pass between the manuscript's acceptance and the textbook's availability. Owing to this, textbooks often do not reflect the most up-to-date information. They do, however, contain a wealth of in-depth material that is invaluable for many research projects pertinent to the timeframe in question.

The Nursing Process in Online Searches

The nursing process serves the LNC well when conducting research. Each element of the process is critical to the development of a research strategy that delivers the best results.

Analysis and Issue Identification

It is essential to know the type of case in order to properly direct the research. After determining the case issue(s), find out from the attorney what questions are in play and what information is needed. Then, analyze what information needs to be accessed in order to meet the attorney's need.

Failure to collect the important data at the outset of the research may result in delays and may produce incomplete or irrelevant results. In addition to knowing the topic to be researched, the LNC should also understand the issues involved in the case, the date of loss (i.e., the date when the incident or injury occurred), the plaintiff's demographics (i.e., age, gender, ethnicity, etc.), any past or concurrent medical conditions of the plaintiff, medications taken, whether the attorney has a preference for textbook information or medical/nursing journals, and any date restrictions to be applied to the information retrieved in the search due to the date of the subject incident.

The LNC must use analytical and critical thinking skills to sort out the primary issues to be addressed. The attorney may have identified one issue she personally considers to be the key issue, whereas the LNC may have a different opinion once the initial data is retrieved and the situation is analyzed. Discussing this difference of perspective with the attorney will usually put the LNC's valuable teaching skills once again into practice.

Example 11.1

An attorney reports to the LNC that his client is a woman who has asked him to file a wrongful death suit against a hospital, arising from the death of her husband. Subsequent to undergoing coronary bypass surgery, the husband became increasingly depressed and agitated. He presented to the emergency department (ED), accompanied by his wife, who informed the triage nurse that her husband was in need of medication to treat worsening depression and agitation as he no longer had any interest in normal activities and refused to eat. His primary physician was paged, but was on vacation. The house physician was paged, but said he could not authorize treatment because he was not one of the patient's Health Maintenance Organization (HMO) providers. A third physician who was an HMO provider was paged, but he failed to respond. The patient waited in the ED for 4 hours, then left, and that afternoon violently committed suicide.

The attorney tells the LNC that he needs to know what the standard of care is for a triage nurse in the ED when a patient offers complaints of depression and agitation. The LNC agrees, but adds that since the nurse attempted to reach three physicians but was unable to obtain authorization for treatment, perhaps the larger issue was the lack of protocol between the hospital and HMO to obtain authorization for treatment.

Outcome Identification

After collecting the initial data from the client, analyzing it, and identifying the primary issues, the LNC must then identify the desired outcome of the research effort. Towards that goal the LNC should consider these questions:

1. What does the attorney need to establish?
2. Is the subject matter controversial?
3. Does the attorney want to view the full articles or are article abstracts or synopses sufficient for the *preliminary* research?
4. Are medical teaching materials needed to educate others on the legal team?
5. What is the time frame for obtaining the materials?
6. Are there considerable budget constraints?

Planning

For the purposes of this chapter, planning involves determining which databases and core textbooks to research (if textbook research is required), researching the applicable standards of practice, and, in the case of a computerized search for journal articles, selecting the most relevant search term for the MEDLINE database, along with choosing appropriate limits in order to retrieve the most relevant articles. This step of the process may also extend to investigation of the defendant physician or expert's credentials. Planning expedites and focuses computerized literature searches.

Example 11.2

The LNC is asked by an attorney to research *abdominal rhabdomyosarcoma* because she has a potential client who claims that a delay in the diagnosis of her 14-year-old daughter's condition resulted in her death in September, 2006. The LNC may decide to look for pertinent information in pediatric oncology textbooks and perform a computerized literature search for medical journal articles relating to this issue via subscription databases as well as online Internet searches.

A search for relevant and authoritative literature may start at the National Library of Medicine's (NLM) website. The NLM is the library of the National Institutes of Health (NIH). The NLM's main search engine for MEDLINE is PubMed®. Using PubMed for retrieval and the single Medical Subject Heading (MeSH®) term *rhabdomyosarcoma* in the query box results in a search that yields 9648 citations. In order to narrow the search further and retrieve only those articles most relevant to the specific case, the LNC may chose to limit the search further by clicking on the *Limits* tab below the query box. The new window will then allow the LNC researcher to reduce the search parameters to adolescents (13–18 years), English language, human studies, and publication years between 2003 and 2008 by using both free-text and checking boxes. In this way, the LNC can reduce the number of citations from 9648 citations to 309.

Noting that many of the articles (citations) retrieved pertain to *rhabdomyosarcoma* at various sites of the body, the LNC may further limit the results by adding *retroperitoneal* to the word *rhabdomyosarcoma* (PubMed will automatically add the Boolean operator AND between *rhabdomyosarcoma* and *retroperitoneal* unless directed otherwise.) This addition again decreases the number of result citations to only one, but it is more pertinent to the primary issue than the 309 citations previously retrieved. The LNC may now decide to expand the date restriction to 10 years rather than just five, by changing the date limitations with publication dates ranging from 1998 to 2008, and now this revised search retrieves eight total citations.

It is also possible to limit the search to *abstracts only*, by selecting the abstract box, although this narrows the results to only those articles containing abstracts. By choosing this option, this may result in some relevant citations being lost or overlooked. However, the LNC may always obtain the articles that do not have abstracts, especially if the titles indicate the articles may be relevant to the topic being searched.

Implementation

Implementation is the act of following through with the established plan. In Example 11.2, the LNC chose the appropriate search term (MeSH terminology is discussed later in this chapter) and chose limiters to restrict the search parameters to match the specifics of the potential case. This decreased the number of citations retrieved from 9648 to eight, a reasonable number to review.

Each case is different, and the LNC must use critical thinking skills to determine whether the resulting number of citations, once limits have been selected, is too small. Limits may be deselected, which results in a larger number of citations, but many of the articles may not be pertinent to the primary issue(s). Also, if the search is limited to *review articles* (by checking the review box), it is likely fewer citations will be retrieved, but review articles will provide an overview of the medical literature on a specific issue or topic. It is worth noting, the LNC researcher should not rely *solely* on either abstracts (due to brevity) or review articles (due to interpretation by someone other than the original author) when formulating final medical trial strategy with the attorney.

To implement the plan, the LNC reviews the eight citations and their abstracts and selects four of those that appear to relate to the client's case. The next implementation step is to print out the selected citations and abstracts. The LNC researcher may then retrieve the four journal articles from the library shelves or an online database or through a document delivery service. The specifics of article retrieval will be discussed later in this chapter.

Evaluation

Prior to obtaining textbook information and articles for the attorney, the LNC should review them to evaluate whether or not the information is relevant to the attorney's case and needs. The attorney may initially need only broad information on a medical topic in an effort to become familiar with a condition or disease before deciding whether or not to accept a case. In contrast, the attorney may need the information before deposing a medical professional or need reliable and authoritative information to support the case strategy. The attorney's specific needs, as mentioned before, should have been determined early in the research process. Once the information is retrieved, the LNC should then reevaluate the literature in the context of its intended purpose and to ensure it will meet the needs of the attorney–client.

The LNC must be able to answer the questions: "Will this information meet my attorney–client's needs for this particular case?" and "Will this information meet the appropriate court's rules and prior precedents concerning what will be allowed into evidence?" If not, "Plan B" must be formulated, followed by implementation of the plan and subsequent evaluation.

If the first three steps of the process (analysis/issue identification, outcome identification, and planning) are completed thoughtfully, implementation and evaluation should successfully follow.

Research Sources

The LNC should consult a variety of sources to identify the best available evidence-based medical information or to research information related to professional medical credentials. Both primary and secondary sources are available for analysis.

In the context of medical research, primary sources comprise experiments and observations conducted for research or scientific purposes and dissertations on behalf of funding agencies (Weishapple, 2001). Two resources for primary research are the NLM's Health Services Research Projects in Progress (HSRP) and the database found at ClincialTrials.gov, which allows access to current research and information pertaining to ongoing, suspended, or terminated clinical trials. Both websites will be discussed later in the chapter.

In the broadest sense, secondary sources may be thought of as a category of resources not originating with the primary author or original research. Secondary sources of information may be obtained via the following:

1. Consultation with a professional in the appropriate specialty or field
2. Textbook research either accessed online or in the library
3. Nonprofit organizations (e.g., American Cancer Society and National Kidney Foundation)

4. The World Wide Web
5. Literature reviews using a bibliographic database such as MEDLINE
6. Directories (e.g., the Official ABMS Directory of Board Certified Medical Specialists, The Health Care Standards Directory, the International Medical Education Directory (IMED))
7. Professional specialty organizations (e.g., American Association of Critical Care Nurses (AACN) and American College of Obstetrics and Gynecology (ACOG))
8. Governmental agencies (e.g., the Food and Drug Administration (FDA), the Centers for Diseases and Control (CDC), and the National Institutes of Health (NIH)) are also invaluable resources

Leading Directories of Organizations and Agencies

The Medical and Health Information Directory (MHID) is a multivolume resource of comprehensive information related to both medical and health care delivery. Volume I is devoted to over 26,500 alphabetical listings, including contact information for organizations, agencies, and institutions pertaining to clinical medicine, basic biomedical sciences, technology, and socioeconomic aspects of health care. Volume II is devoted to alphabetical listings for over 12,000 various publications, libraries, and other resources. Volume III is devoted to more than 35,000 health services, including clinics, treatment centers, care programs, counseling, and diagnostic services.

For instance, the directory listing for In Vitro Fertilization Clinics documents the number of facilities that specialize in In Vitro Reproduction, along with name, address, phone number, and contact person. The clinics are organized both geographically by state and alphabetically by name of the facility. Each of the three volumes may be searched by using the descriptive listings or alphabetical name or keyword search. This resource mainly references sources located in the United States.

The Encyclopedia of Medical Organizations & Agencies provides a subject guide to more than 18,000 associations, foundations, federal and state government agencies, research centers, and medical and allied health schools. The table of contents lists medical organizations and agencies by subject (e.g., birth defects, child abuse and family violence, emergency medicine, chiropractic, nursing, etc.). The reader is then directed to the pages that include listings and a brief description of the organizations that relate to the topic being researched.

For example, the section on obstetrics and gynecology lists 65 national and international associations, including the American College of Obstetricians and Gynecologists (ACOG), the American College of Nurse-Midwives (ACNM), and the American Society for Colposcopy and Cervical Pathology (ASCCP), the International Association for Maternal and Neonatal Health (IAMENEH), the National Perinatal Association (NPA), and the Society for Menstrual Cycle Research. Many of the organizations listed in the encyclopedia are excellent sources of information.

To further illustrate, the LNC who has difficulty reading and understanding chiropractic records or who needs to locate recognized standards for chiropractors might benefit from consulting the section on chiropractics in the Encyclopedia of Medical Organizations & Agencies. The listing for the Commission on Accreditation of the Council of Chiropractic Education includes addresses and phone numbers as well as the chiropractic schools, listed by state, that are approved by the Commission, in addition to professional organizations.

Further sources of valuable information for the LNC are nonprofit organizations such as the American Cancer Society, the Arthritis Foundation, and the National Kidney Foundation, to name just a few. They often provide statistics, resources relating to the condition being researched, prospective medical experts, and other valuable information. Many of their brochures are published in lay language and include simple drawings or diagrams that may help to educate the attorney, the attorney's client, or the jury.

The Health Care Standards Directory is available in hard copy and online. The print version of the directory may be cost prohibitive for the individual practitioner (or facility), which can also make it difficult to locate. The online version of the directory provides easier access but does require a subscription fee. This directory can help the LNC to locate health care standards, guidelines, and recommended practices which often elude the researcher. It includes listings for standards issued by medical societies, professional associations, government agencies, and other health-related organizations. The directory includes:

1. Complete citations to standards, legislation, and referenced articles
2. An alphabetical listing of organizations that have issued standards related to health care (listings include the full name, address, and telephone number of each organization as well as the title of each standard issued by the organization and information relating to price or how to order the standards)
3. An alphabetical listing of federal and state agencies that have issued health-related regulations or guidelines; includes the name, address, and phone number of each agency
4. A quality-of-care bibliography that lists significant articles relating to assessing and providing quality health care

Online Searches

In this information society, numerous sources of information are available on the Web. Awareness of that information and quick access to it can significantly enhance the LNC's value to the attorney. According to Sherman and Price, the Internet is the world's largest computer network, made up of millions of computers allowing information of various kinds to flow from computer to computer around the world (2001).

The Web is one of many interfaces of the Internet, making it easy to retrieve text, pictures, and multimedia files from computers without having to know complicated commands. Online information retrieval is the process of identifying desired information by direct, interactive communication with a computer.

A search engine is an enormous database of websites navigated by a software robot that seeks out and indexes websites, and sometimes other Internet resources as well. A search engine "looks" for databases of documents and information to access based on the researcher's search terms.

There are thousands of search engines (e.g., Google, Yahoo, Alta Vista, etc.) and they vary in speed, skill, depth of indexing, size of database, advanced search features, and presentation of results. Each search engine's method of searching is proprietary, the depth and breadth of its database is unique, and each possesses its particular strengths and idiosyncrasies.

A database is a program that organizes specific information and "virtual" documents enabling a researcher to rapidly access subsets of information from the entire body of information for retrieval (analogous to finding the desired document in a filing cabinet). Medscape, PubMed, TOXLINE are examples of document and image databases.

The Invisible Web (a.k.a. the "deep" or "hidden" web) "consists of material that general-purpose search engines either cannot or perhaps more importantly, *will not* include in their collections of Web pages (called indexes or indices). The Invisible Web contains vast amounts of authoritative and current information" (Sherman & Price, 2001).

Conducting a MEDLINE Search

A MEDLINE search can be performed by accessing the NLM website directly and clicking on PubMed or by accessing MEDLINE from a number of different medical websites. Either way, the following steps should expedite and focus the search to achieve the best results.

1. Collect adequate information from the client to formulate a focused search strategy
2. Formulate the overall search strategy
3. Input common search terms or the MeSH term(s), author, or journal that addresses the focus of the search in the *Query Box* (see the sections on Author Searches and Journal Searches)
4. Chose *limits* for searching, if desired
5. Click *GO* (or *Search*) to retrieve the results of the search
6. View the citations and click on relevant citations to view the abstracts (if available)
7. Print out search results (specifically the list of citations and relevant abstracts)
8. Locate or order articles

MeSH Term Searches

A MeSH term search is the most common type of search used in the MEDLINE database and entails entering one or more MeSH terms in the query (search) box. Either a single term or multiple terms can be entered. Multiple terms can ensure a more focused search. If additional terms are entered, or to further focus the search, Boolean operators (OR, NOT) should be inserted in capital letters between the terms. PubMed now automatically adds the Boolean operator AND for the researcher between multiple terms when retrieving citations.

Example 11.3

The LNC is asked to research *malignant melanoma* for a case in which the primary issue involves the failure of the defendant physician to diagnose melanoma, treat the condition, or refer the patient to a dermatologist in a timely manner. If the LNC performed a search using the single term *melanoma* in the query box, thousands of citations would be retrieved and many would probably be irrelevant to this case. In order to focus the search, keeping the primary issue in mind, the LNC searches using *melanoma AND diagnosis* because the most important articles are those that relate to early diagnosis of melanoma.

Limiting the Search

MEDLINE allows the researcher to limit searches in order to decrease the number of citations retrieved and, more importantly, to retrieve only the most relevant articles. In PubMed, after entering the search terms in the query box, click on the word *limits*. A new window will appear from which the user selects the limits determined to be appropriate for the search. The search can be limited to a specific age group, gender, human or animal studies, the desired language, a range of years, type of article, or a specific journal. The user then clicks on *GO* (or *Search*), and the search results appear in seconds.

Author Searches

Author searches are often used when an attorney wants to review published works of opposing experts or their own experts. The search is usually simple and straightforward, and no search strategy or analysis is required. The researcher enters the author's last name and one or two initials (first and middle names and *no punctuation*) and then click *GO* (or *Search*). If the author's middle initial is not known, it is sufficient to enter the last name and first initial. This calls up all authors with the same name and initial. Entering the middle initial helps to narrow the search, especially if the last name is common. If the physician's last name might be mistaken for a MeSH term (e.g., hand), the searcher can clarify an author search by entering the physician's last name and two initials followed by the field tag for author in brackets: [au]. The author search would then read: hand js [au]. The total number of citations retrieved will appear at the top of the first page (in this case 35). It is important to print out the entire list of citations. The default parameter is indicated next to *show* and is usually 20 citations per page. This parameter may be changed to as little as 5 or up to 500. When a common name is being searched, narrowing the search by date parameters may once again reduce the amount of irrelevant citations the LNC will need to review.

The LNC may be asked to analyze and prepare a synopsis of the author's articles once retrieved. This may be followed by a request to review the expert's publications and deposition transcript (if it has been taken) for any discrepancies that might provide a basis for impeachment.

Journal Searches

Limiting a search to one particular journal is time-efficient in certain situations. For instance, an attorney may learn in an opposing expert's deposition that an article relating to a particular issue in the case was recently published in *JAMA*. However, he or she is unsure of the issue's publication date or the article's title. The attorney may relay this to the LNC so that the article can be retrieved.

To perform this type of search, the LNC should enter the name of the desired journal or the abbreviated title in the query box (search box) instead of, or in combination with, a MeSH term or author's name. A health sciences reference librarian can provide a list of accepted journal abbreviations if needed, and is also accessible in the overview link (left hand menu) provided in PubMed.

Government Resources

Overview of the National Network of Libraries of Medicine

The NLM, which is part of the NIH, is the largest and most prestigious medical library in the world and is based in Bethesda, Maryland. Its progeny, the National Network of Libraries of Medicine (NN/LM), is a nationwide network of regional health sciences and biomedical libraries. The NLM serves as the overall coordinator and as a backup resource for all other regional libraries in the network. The NN/LM provides the nation with access to the most comprehensive collection of biomedical information in the world. Beneath the umbrella of the NLM are the subdivisions of the specific retrieval systems.

PubMed is a Web-based retrieval system developed by the National Center for Biotechnology Information (NCBI) at the NLM. It is the NLM's premiere search system for health information available online without charge. Assistance for searching PubMed is easily accessible and offered with links to an online tutorial, overview of PubMed, help and frequently asked questions (FAQs).

PubMed offers links to full-text articles, some without charge, at participating publishers' websites. Additionally, PubMed offers links to similar articles as well as free access to other third-party sites such as libraries and sequencing centers.

MEDLARS/MEDLINE

The *Medical Literature Analysis and Retrieval System (MEDLARS)* is the computerized system of databases and databanks offered by the NLM. The NLM enters into agreements with public institutions in foreign countries to serve as International MEDLARS Centers. These centers assist health professionals in accessing MEDLARS databases, offer training in searching, provide document delivery and perform other functions as biomedical information resource centers (International MEDLARS, 2008).

MEDLINE (abbreviated from MEDlars onLINE) is the NLM's electronic directory to bibliographic references for over 5200 biomedical journals selected for indexing with MeSH terms. The MEDLINE database contains more than 18 million references and abstracts of articles (2008). Each entry is assigned a PubMed ID (e.g., PMID) number. "The subject scope of MEDLINE is biomedicine and health and is broadly defined to encompass those areas of the life sciences, behavioral sciences, chemical sciences, and bioengineering needed by health professionals and those others engaged in basic research, clinical care, public health, health policy development, and/or related educational activities." (Fact Sheet MEDLINE, 2008).

The MEDLINE database includes the following three traditionally *printed indices*:

1. *The Index Medicus* is a monthly and annual cumulative index of articles references from a global bibliographic listing from over 3000 biomedical journals. (The publisher of Index Medicus actually ceased hardcopy publication with the December, 2004 issue, but it continues to be an online subset for MEDLINE in PubMed.)
2. *The International Nursing Index* contains more than 270 worldwide, indexed nursing journals, in addition to all nursing articles in the 2700 allied health and biomedical journals indexed for Index Medicus. Appendices include nursing books published and a list of publications of organizations and agencies. The Index has been published quarterly in cooperation with the NLM and cumulated annually.
3. *The Index to Dental Literature* includes an alphabetical listing of dental literature from 1839 to 1999, when publication was terminated. Presently, the index is generally employed to locate pre-1966 articles. MEDLINE, the online index, begins with literature published in 1966 (Dental Library, 2008). Free of charge, MEDLINE covers the period from 1949 to the present time. This database includes American and International journals from over 80 countries. Most of the literature is published in English or has abstracts that are written in English. It is accessible either directly through the Internet or via the NLM Gateway.

MEDLINE is revised annually and the *NLM Technical Bulletin* routinely includes information concerning adjustments made during the year-end processing of MEDLINE. Be mindful that MEDLINE does not index all medical articles and errors are occasionally made in MeSH term classifications (Greenhalgh, 1997).

OLDMEDLINE is comprised of citations from international biomedical journals covering areas of medicine, preclinical sciences, and allied health sciences. In 1996, the electronic conversion of the printed indexes *Cumulated Index Medicus (CIM)* and the *Current List of Medical Literature (CLML)* now covering the years 1949–1965 was begun. OLDMEDLINE contains approximately 1,816,000 citations predating 1966 that have been integrated into MEDLINE articles. As part of the conversion, it was necessary to update the older citations utilizing current MeSH vocabulary. To do so, the index terms or keywords used to index in these older citations were digitalized and mapped to current MeSH terms. Once this work is completed, the citations are identified as (PubMed indexed for MEDLINE). Prior to complete indexing and mapping, these citations are tagged (PubMed—OLDMEDLINE) after the PMID number. Most are now included in the MEDLINE database and can be searched in either PubMed or NLM Gateway. Updates to the database with older citations will continue as resources and time permit.

PubMed will search the MEDLINE database for new, current, or older citations. "In process" citations will provide basic citation information prior to indexing with MeSH terms in the MEDLINE database. Some in-process citations may include publisher-supplied citations that may not receive full indexing for MEDLINE because they are not biomedical in nature [e.g., (PubMed—as supplied by publisher)], and will be displayed after the PMID number. Other in-process items may be citations for the Entrez molecular biology databases and citations to author manuscripts of articles published by NIH-funded researchers [e.g., (PubMed—in process)].

NLM Gateway

The *NLM Gateway* is a Web-based system that allows users of the NLM services to initiate searches in multiple retrieval systems from one interface, providing "one-stop searching" for many of NLM's information resources. Initiated in 2000, NML Gateway covers a wider range of information than PubMed. In addition to journal citations, the NLM Gateway collection contains multiple databases, some of which include audiovisual materials, serials, and monographs available for searching and retrieval. NLM's network allows for concurrent searches of multiple databases.

LocatorPlus is one of the NLM free online catalogs. It is a guide to finding records for journals, books, reports, and audiovisuals in the NLM collection; records for serials and books not in the NLM collection, but owned by regional libraries; records for journals, books, reports, and audiovisuals on order, on loan, or in process at the NLM. Updates to LocatorPlus are provided continuously, making new or updated records immediately available to users.

MEDLINE Plus is a consumer-based website offered by the NLM. Easily searchable, the database contains reader-friendly information on drugs, diseases, and treatments. A medical encyclopedia and medical dictionary, directories of health care providers, and other databases are included in this site. A link to PubMed is also available making it more convenient to retrieve medical literature.

Clinical trials are research studies of specific health questions in human volunteers performed in a controlled environment to conduct research for determining new ways to utilize known treatments or to determine efficacy of experimental treatments or therapies inclusive of a broad database of medical diseases. *Clinicaltrials.gov* contains current information on more than 59,000 trials being conducted in all 50 states and over 150 countries both federally and privately funded.

DIRLINE is the NLM's online directory containing over 8000 organizations and records documenting resource data principally focused on health and biomedical topics. This database contains descriptive information relating to projects, research resources, organizations, and other databases. DIRLINE presents resources offered by local, state, and federal government agencies, academic and programs offered at research institutions, professional societies, referral centers, voluntary and self-help groups, and referral centers. Rare and genetic diseases as well as most common diseases are included in this database.

Development and Reproductive Toxicology/Environmental Teratology Information Center (DART/ETIC) is a bibliographic database covering literature on reproductive and developmental toxicology. DART is managed by the NLM and funded by the EPA, the National Institute of Environmental Health Sciences (NIEHS) and NLM. DART/ETIC contains references to reproductive and developmental toxicology literature published since 1965. It also provides meeting abstracts and abstracts of meetings on selected subjects for a limited number of organizations.

Health Services Research Projects in Progress (HSRProj) permits researchers to access information pertaining to ongoing health service research subsidized by public and private grants and contracts awarded to both public and private contractors, federal agencies, foundations, medical schools, hospitals, managed care organizations, pharmaceutical companies, and various state agencies. Access is available for the progression of information about health services before results are available in a published form.

The *Hazardous Substances Data Bank (HSDB)* is a comprehensive, peer-reviewed toxicology database for about 5000 chemicals. It focuses on the toxicology of potentially hazardous chemicals. It is enhanced with information on human exposure, industrial hygiene, emergency handling procedures, environmental fate, regulatory requirements, and related areas. All data are referenced and derived from a core set of books, government documents, technical reports, and select primary journal literature. HSDB is peer-reviewed by the Scientific Review Panel (SRP), a committee of experts in the major subject areas within the databank's scope. HSDB is organized into individual chemical records, and contains over 5000 such records (HSDB Fact Sheet, 2008).

TOXLINE is the NLM's databases pertaining to toxicology, hazardous chemicals, environmental health, and toxic releases from 1965 to the present. TOXLINE contains over 3 million citations, almost all with abstracts and/or index terms and Chemical Abstracts Service (CAS) Registry Numbers. TOXLINE covers much of the standard journal literature in toxicology, complemented with references from an assortment of specialized journals and other sources listed below as well as a direct link to PubMed.

ChemIDplus is a database providing access to structure and nomenclature authority databases used for the identification of chemical substances cited in the NLM databases. ChemIDplus contains over 380,000 chemical records, of which over 289,000 include chemical structures. ChemIDplus is searchable by name, synonym, CAS Registry Number, molecular formula, classification code, locator code, structure, or physical properties. Enhanced structure display is available in ChemIDplus Advanced.

Toxics Release Inventory (TRI) is a series of databases that describe the releases of toxic chemicals into the environment annually for the 1987–2006 reporting years through the EPA.

Genetics Home Reference is the NLM's website for consumer information about genetic conditions and the genes or chromosomes responsible for those conditions. This site references genetic condition summaries; gene summaries; chromosome summaries; glossary; and "Help Me Understand Genetics" (an illustrated, basic explanation of how genes work and how mutations cause disorders). It also includes current information about genetic testing, gene therapy, and the Human Genome Project.

Online Mendelian Inheritance in Man (OMIM) contains information on all known Mendelian disorders and over 12,000 genes. OMIM is intended for use primarily by genetic researchers, physicians, and other professionals concerned with genetic disorders and by advanced students in science and medicine. It is updated daily, and the entries contain copious links to other genetics resources.

Nongovernment Resources

Care Pages are often offered by individual hospitals and medical centers for patients and families to communicate with concerned friends and family. The LNC, researching medical malpractice or any issues relating to a personal injury case, may find it helpful to locate the plaintiff's online Care Page. Most times, these pages will contain a description of the events surrounding the accident (situation) and will have multiple entries documenting progress or delay, health care providers names as well as pictures taken of the injury, surgical site, etc. As with any information relayed during times of duress, some of the entries may contain conflicting information. Generally, however, these entries have an indicia of reliability because they are made prior to any consideration of litigation.

Care Pages will also contain basic information (e.g., dates, names) as well as sources of additional medical records (e.g., ambulance or helicopter transfer records, physical therapy, rehab facility, homecare, etc.). However, it may be more efficient to obtain this information from more direct sources rather than waiting for the LNC to search through several hundreds or thousands of pages in order to locate the same information.

The *Cumulative Index of Nursing and Allied Health Literature (CINAHL)* is an important database containing literature related to nursing, allied health, alternative therapies, biomedical, case management, consumer health, critical care, evidence-based practice, health administration and management, health informatics, library resources, medical equipment and supplies, mental health, and pharmacology. As of early 2007, CINHAL discontinued individual subscriptions. Access to CINAHL is now generally available through academic institutions or medical libraries.

The *Cochrane Collaboration* is an autonomous, international not-for profit organization founded in 1993. A portion of the Collaboration is *The Cochrane Library*, which consists of a regularly updated collection of evidence-based medicine databases, including *The Cochrane Database of Systematic Reviews*. The Cochrane Library (subscription required) contains full-text Cochrane reviews, as well as other databases of reviews and controlled trials. It also provides quality-assessed review evidence on diagnostic tests, health technology assessments, economic evaluations, and methods studies from the world's medical literature. This database includes systematic reviews of health care interventions that are produced and disseminated by The Cochrane Collaboration.

The abstracts of Cochrane reviews (published quarterly) can be obtained free of charge on the website and furnish a useful source of health care knowledge. The reviews are typically prepared by health care professionals who volunteer to work in one of the many Cochrane Review Groups with editorial teams overseeing the preparation and maintenance of the reviews, within the rigorous quality standards for which Cochrane Reviews have become known (Practitioner's Portal, 2008).

EMBASE is a pharmacological and biomedical database with access to over 11 million documents from 1974 to the present, including over 5000 biomedical journals from 70 countries. EMBASE can be accessed through major database vendors (e.g., OVID Online, LexisNexis, and DIALOG). They may be contacted within the United States at (888) 615-4500 or via e-mail at usembaseinfo@elsevier.com.

EMedicine offers free information on 850 common diseases, conditions, tests, and procedures as well as first aid. EMedicine features health-related slideshows, medication information including generic, brand names, dosing, interactions, drug classifications, prescription, or over-the-counter availability. This site contains a multitude of calculators for body mass index (BMI), temperature conversions, weight conversions, blood alcohol concentration estimation, diagrams of dermatomes and burn surface area (BSA).

Google Scholar searches "peer-reviewed papers, theses, books, abstracts and articles, from academic publishers, professional societies, preprint repositories, universities and other scholarly organizations" (Google, 2008).

MD Consult is a reliable online service to enable health care providers to perform expedient research regarding clinical and treatment-based information. The site's content includes over 50 well-respected medical textbooks, as well as more than 80 journals and Clinics of North America, over 1000 peer-reviewed practice guidelines, thousands of patient education aids, online continuing medical education opportunities, medication information, and the ability to search full text journals and links to millions of PubMed abstracts. Over 90% of North American medical schools subscribe to MD Consult (a subscription fee is required, which can be paid either annually or monthly).

Many medical and nursing journals are available online. Several well-known, peer-reviewed journals allow access to their full articles, without a fee. Even those journals that charge a fee for current issues often have archives of the journals available at no cost, although the individual publisher's policies on this may vary.

Medscape offers medical journal articles, access to MEDLINE, free CMEs credits, important conference releases, medical news, and medication information. A free registration is required to access this database.

OVID "offers a premier selection of the world's most respected databases across a wide range of disciplines" (OVID, 2008). OVID is used across the world by librarians, researchers, clinicians, and students from foremost colleges and universities; medical schools; academic research libraries and library consortia; hospitals and health care systems; pharmaceutical, engineering, and biotechnology companies; and HMOs and clinical practices. In North America alone, OVID is used by 93% of medical libraries, 97% of teaching hospitals, and 87% of U.S. hospitals with more than 200 beds, as well as the top 30 pharmaceutical companies (2008). OVID is not accessible to an individual without password granted access through one of the above means.

The Virtual Library (through the University of Sheffield in the United Kingdom) offers links to complete text documents for evidence-based practice.

Accessing Standards and Guidelines

LNCs who are new to the field often expect to find lists of standards of care in books that they can easily refer to when they need to compare a health care professional's conduct to the standard of care that should be followed. Unfortunately, it is usually not that simple. The following resources can be consulted, many of which are available online, when standards of care or clinical practice guidelines are needed:

1. MD Consult: a subscription fee is required, which can be paid annually or monthly
2. The Cochrane Library abstracts of evidence-based guidelines based on extensive literature reviews may be viewed without a fee; however, access to full-text reviews requires a subscription fee
3. Professional Organizations (e.g., the American Heart Association)
4. Medical journals (e.g., *CHEST Journal* from the American College of Chest Physicians)
5. Core curriculum medical and nursing textbooks
6. National Guideline Clearinghouse™ Evidenced-Based Guidelines are produced and updated weekly by the Agency for Healthcare Research and Quality [AHRQ, formerly the Agency

for Health Care Policy and Research (AHCPR)], in partnership with the American Medical Association (AMA) and the American Association of Health Plans (AAHP) Foundation

7. Agency for Healthcare Research and Quality offers an archive of older standards of care and guidelines of practice
8. Health Care Standards Directory (available in medical library's reference section)
9. Nursing care plans and critical or clinical pathways
10. Facility policies and protocols
11. Joint Commission Standards are published in accreditation manuals, which are available for purchase

Retrieving Copies of Medical Literature

For LNCs who are employed by a hospital or medical center, the medical librarian often retrieves and copies articles free of charge. An independent literature retrieval service or LNCs with easy access to a large medical library offer document-retrieval services to other LNCs and will retrieve and scan and e-mail, fax or send full-text articles for a fee with an appropriate copyright and a facility permission. For a proper search, a minimum of three reliable sources are recommended.

Using a Retrieval Service

Loansome Doc is the document retrieval system offered by the NLM. It allows users to order full-text copies of articles located on MEDLINE from a medical library. The user must register with the NLM to use the service. The NLM website walks the user through the registration and ordering processes. An agreement must first be established with a local library that uses DOCLINE. If unsure about which library to contact, the user can call (800) 338-7657 on weekdays between 8:30 a.m. and 5:00 p.m. (all time zones) to connect with the appropriate NLM Regional Medical Library. Loansome Doc service charges a retrieval fee for the article(s).

Independent Retrieval Services

It is also possible to avail the services of an independent medical literature retrieval service. When e-mailing requests, include as much information as possible, to accelerate access of the materials. Complete citations, including authors, title, journal, volume, pages, and date of publication, will insure a timely and accurate delivery of the requested documents.

Libraries

If access to a local medical library is available, obtain the articles and copy them (again with appropriate copyright permission) at the library for a nominal fee. If the LNC is employed at a medical center or large law firm, it may be possible to order the articles from the medical-legal librarians or set up an account with the publishers directly.

Online Sources without the Use of a Retrieval Service

Medical journal articles are occasionally free of charge through PubMed. Links directly to the article archived in PubMed Central (PMC) or in the actual journal are clearly displayed when an article is available for free. Searching the individual journal's website archives may also allow access without charge. Individual journals determine the amount of time before articles may be accessed without a subscription fee. MD Consult, a subscription database, has access to full text articles in over 80 journals, available without an additional charge to the basic subscription fee.

Library Searches
Textbook Research

Well-recognized, core textbooks offer prevailing standards of care, wide-ranging protocols and procedures, and case descriptions. The LNC should not find textbook research particularly challenging as long as access to a health science library is available. Many recognized medical textbooks are available online, although some publishers' Web-based databases require an annual subscription fee. The following pointers will help to safeguard the LNC who relies on printed information to support a position relating to a medical issue or topic:

1. Use grandfather texts, that is, core-curriculum textbooks that are widely accepted in the general medical and scientific community. Grandfather texts are generally those used as textbooks in medical and nursing schools. (E.g.: Kliegman, *Nelson Textbook of Pediatrics*, 18th ed. 2007©, Saunders; Kumar, Robbins and Cotran, 7th ed., 2005©, Saunders; Hoffman, *Hematology*, 4th ed., 2005©, Churchill Livingstone & Ferri, *Ferri's Clinical Advisor 2008*, 1st ed., 2008©, Mosby.)
2. The LNC must be certain that the book is time-appropriate to the case, especially when attempting to locate standards of care or clinical practice guidelines. If the LNC is researching an issue related to an incident in 2001 that is the subject of a medical malpractice lawsuit, the books consulted should have been published in, or prior to, 2001. Any information relating to standards or guidelines would have to have been available to the treating health care practitioners at the time of the subject incident.
3. Refer to a minimum of three authoritative sources to confirm that there is general agreement or controversy among the experts regarding the issues in question. Prior to submitting printed materials (from textbooks and journals) to the attorney, highlight the pertinent information to expedite review of the materials. In some cases, the attorney may want the LNC to prepare a synopsis of each article submitted.

References and bibliographies at the end of textbook chapters may direct the reader to additional information on the subject. Also, editors and authors of authoritative texts may be potential expert witnesses as they are considered experts in their specialties or subspecialties.

Reference Materials

A reliable source of generally accepted textbooks and published journals covering the time frame of 1965–2003 is the Brandon/Hill list. The list was published annually in the *Bulletin of the Medical Library Association* (it included medical, nursing, and allied health literature listed in alternate years). The list can be obtained at medical libraries by asking the reference librarian. It is helpful to make a personal file copy. Unfortunately, publication of this important tool ceased as of 2004. *Doody's Core Titles (DCT)* is working to fill the void and has worked with "an online community of experts to identify and score a core list of titles in 121 health science specialties and disciplines" (Shedlock & Walton, 2006). DCT will be updated on an annual basis and is solely available online.

American Board of Medical Specialties (ABMS) is considered the "gold standard" of physician certification. ABMS has 24 medical specialty member boards supervising the criteria for physician certification. Verification of certification is available online, by phone (866) ASK-ABMS (275-2267), and in hard copy in either a medical or public library. The hard copy includes dates of certification and recertification as well as profile information for each board certified physician.

Advantages to Researching on the Internet or in the Library

The vast amount of information available within seconds with the click of your mouse is equally the major benefit as well as the major drawback. The primary benefits of using the Internet to access information of any type are speed and volume available 24/7. Current technology enables rapid transmission of large files, including those with color images, sound, and motion pictures. With regard to volume, vast numbers of computer users can simultaneously send mail and take part in electronic bulletin board discussions.

A primary advantage of making a trip to a comprehensive medical library is the advantage of having more than the current edition of multiple textbooks and PDRs on the shelves, as is often the case when researching online. Copies of older medical and nursing journals will also be available for reviewing and copying significant articles.

Disadvantages to Researching on the Internet or in the Library

The major drawback of accessing information online is the volume of information one must sort through. Because so much information is available, evaluating the results of a search can be time consuming. As most of the information is relatively current, if information is needed for cases that involve incidents that occurred several years earlier, the information may not be available online.

Careful scrutiny is needed when researching on the Internet. It is critical for the LNC to carefully evaluate and appraise any information to make certain it is accurate, reliable and authentic to the time under research.

The *Health on the Net Foundation (HONcode)* was established in 1995 during an international conference in Switzerland, entitled *The Use of the Internet and World-Wide Web for Telematics in Healthcare*. The purpose is to "promote the effective and reliable use of the new technologies for telemedicine in health care around the world."

In March 1996, their website was one of the first URLs on the Internet to voluntarily acknowledge reliable medical information for both the health care professional and the layman.

Verifying an Author's Credibility

The importance of verifying the author's or potential expert's qualifications to address the particular subject matter at issue cannot be overemphasized. This critical step may be achieved one of several ways:

1. A PubMed search will verify if the physician has published articles on a particular topic in their field of medicine.

2. Curriculum vitae (CV)—May or may not be available for review and verification of credentials/employment/responsibilities.

3. Hospital/medical school faculty biographies may be available on the facilities website.

4. Verify educational credentials—Phone calls to the individual schools and medical facilities cited will usually furnish the needed information.

5. State Licensing Board—Most states have a website with a link to verifying a license. Depending on the individual website, it may be possible to locate comprehensive information related to education, training, board certification(s), dates, and current location.

6. The ABMS may be searched online or contacted to verify board certification status.

7. AMA data of members are available as to office location, board certification(s), medical school, residencies and fellowships, locations of hospital admitting privileges, major professional activity, and group practice participation.

8. Castle Connolly's *America's Top Doctors.* Annual surveys are conducted to gather peer nominations to determine the top 1% of physicians in more than 60 medical specialties and subspecialties. This publication contains in-depth data concerning each physician's education, training, and special expertise.

9. Traditional Internet searches via various search engines, such as Google, may help to locate a physician, their practice, publications, and presentations given to medical groups.

10. Westlaw & LEXIS-NEXIS databases contain very comprehensive information on many physicians, including deposition and trial testimony, *Daubert* challenges and media coverage. However, these databases are generally very costly and usually not needed, unless the author is serving as an expert or possibly a treating physician in a case involving a substantial financial sum.

Assessing the Validity of Medical Literature

It has been said, "you can prove anything you really want to prove." All published information is not valid: the LNC should be mindful of this fact when selecting journal article or using information to support a position while filling the role of a nurse expert.

LNCs learn to develop critical-thinking skills to analyze the facts of their cases. This skill should extend into the area of analyzing medical literature, whether it is obtained from an online source or in the library.

Textbook research should be confined primarily to core curriculum texts. A major portion of these texts have been used for health care education for many years, having been reproduced in several editions since the original publication, and published by reputable publishing houses (including but not limited to Mosby, W.B. Saunders, Lippincott, Williams & Wilkens, and Appleton & Lange). Additionally, the authors or contributors are medical professionals with extensive experience and expertise in the subject area. It is always a good practice to use at least three reputable texts to be sure that there is general agreement or controversy regarding the issues being researched.

Beyond textbooks, there are a host of other sources for medical information, among them scientific journals and continuing education resources available for analysis.

Peer-reviewed journals are generally viewed as more credible than non-peer-reviewed publications. Peer review prior to publication attempts to ensure that the methodology, results, and conclusions of the experiment, observation, study or research are unbiased and meet the criteria for scientific research. Depending on the journal's readership and interest, the topic inclusions may provide input and observations from highly regarded scientists researchers that have passed peer review.

Professional association journals cover emerging trends, standards of care, legal issues, ethical issues, and reports on disciplinary actions, association news, and practice and business articles. Medical periodicals contain information related to emerging trends and techniques, prevailing philosophies on medical issues, practice and business articles and profiles of practitioners. Continuing education information contains emerging practices and protocols, updates on medical issues, state of the science at the time of the conference, seminar, or workshop.

Scientific research may be conducted and medical literature published in any of the following formats. Customary notation for the relative weight carried by the different types of primary study when making decisions about clinical interventions ("the hierarchy of evidence") puts them in the following order (Greenhalgh, 1997):

1. Systematic reviews and meta-analysis are quantitative studies of published results relating to a particular problem (OECD, 2008).
2. Randomized controlled trials with definitive results (confidence intervals that do not overlap the threshold clinically significant effect) (Greenhalgh, 1997).
3. Randomized controlled trials with nondefinitive results (a point estimate that suggests a clinically significant effect but with confidence intervals overlapping the threshold for this effect) (Greenhalgh, 1997).
4. Cohort study is a research study that compares a particular outcome (such as lung cancer) in groups of individuals who are alike in many ways but differ by a certain characteristic (e.g., female nurses who smoke compared with those who do not smoke) (NCI, 2008).
5. Case–control study is a study that compares two groups of people: those with the disease or condition under study (cases) and a very similar group of people who do not have the disease or condition (controls). Researchers study the medical and lifestyle histories of the people in each group to learn what factors may be associated with the disease or condition. For example, one group may have been exposed to a particular substance that the other was not. This is also called a retrospective study (NCI, 2008).
6. Cross-sectional surveys measure the prevalence of health outcomes or determinants of health, or both in a population at a point in time or over a short period (Coggon, Rose, & Barker, 1997).
7. Case report is a detailed report of the diagnosis, treatment, and follow-up of an individual patient. Case reports also contain some demographic information about the patient (e.g., age, gender, ethnic origin) (NCI, 2008).

Junk Science—How it Applies to Medical Literature

It is important to keep in mind that any literature referenced may be subject to *Frye* or *Daubert* standards for admissibility in litigation. Junk science is "evidence that has been offered in evidence that purports to be scientific, but is not accepted in the medical or scientific community" (Weishapple, 2001).

The landmark case of *Daubert v. Merrell Dow Pharmaceutical, Inc.* (1996) defined the elements needed to authenticate scientific testimony and admissibility in trial. Under *Daubert* all expert opinions, theories, and the literature* on which they rely must meet the following criteria: (a) scientific

---

* In a Daubert Motion, medical literature must be cited using Blue Book format not APA format.

methodology, (b) subject to peer review or publication, (c) a known rate of error, and (d) generally accepted within the medical/scientific community. While some states chose to follow the *Frye* rule (general acceptance by the scientific community), the federal courts apply the *Daubert* standard.

Literature Citation Tips

The *American Psychological Association (APA)* style is the accepted format to use when referencing sources of information from the health care professions. Due to the nuances of the APA format for different sources of information, the LNC should make an effort to become acquainted with this resource. The APA website offers citation examples and there are online tutorials available through many educational institutions websites.

Ethics

The procedural guidelines of information retrieval are universal for effective, competent, and ethical research. Below are several guidelines that are applicable to any researcher who acts as an intermediary between an attorney–client and the information, whether the information is obtained from textbooks or by computer. The following guidelines directly apply to LNCs.

1. Use interview techniques to clarify the attorney–client's needs before doing research on any case and consider any budgetary restrictions or time constraints
2. Maintain awareness of the range of information resources to advise the client fairly and impartially
3. Maintain a reasonable and current skill level in the database systems available for performing online searches
4. Avoid bias in the selection of appropriate databases and systems when performing online searches and confirm the reliability, authority, and credibility of the retrieved literature
5. Maintain alertness with regard to information that might be detrimental to the attorney–client's case and keep the attorney–client informed
6. Maintain and respect the attorney–client's schedule and deadline for the production of literature
7. Maintain strict adherence to copyright and reprint permission
8. Maintain confidentiality of all case-specific data

Conclusion

Accessing varied aspects of medical information is challenging, demanding, labor intensive, and trying at times. It is also personally gratifying to enhance your knowledge base as well as discern the information retrieved has been a major factor in the outcome of the client's case.

References

About Google Scholar. Retrieved from http://scholar.google.com/intl/en/scholar/about.html
About Health on the Net Foundation. Retrieved August 20, 2008, from http://www.hon.ch/Global/

American Association of Legal Nurse Consultants. (1995). *Standards of legal nurse consulting practice and professional performance.* Glenview, IL: Author.

Case-control study. (n.d.). In *National Cancer Institute online glossary.* Retrieved August 20, 2008, from http://www.cancer.gov/Templates/db_alpha.aspx?CdrID=348989

Case report. (n.d.). In *National Cancer Institute online glossary.* Retrieved August 20, 2008, from http://www.cancer.gov/Templates/db_alpha.aspx?CdrID=44007

Coggon, D., Rose. G., & Barker, D. J. P. (1997). *Epidemiology for the uninitiated* (5th ed.). *Case-control and cross-sectional studies* (pp. 46–50). Chennai, India: BMJ Publishing Group. Cohort study. (n.d.). In *National Cancer Institute online glossary.* Retrieved August 20, 2008, from http://www.cancer.gov/Templates/db_alpha.aspx?CdrID=285673

Daubert v. Merrell Dow Pharmaceuticals, 509 U.S. 579 (1993).

Frye v. United States, 293 F. 1013 (1923).

Greenhalgh, T. (1997). How to read a paper: Getting your bearings (deciding what the paper is about). *British Medical Journal, 315*(7102), 243–246. Retrieved August 17, 2008, from http://www.bmj.com/archive/7102/7102ed.htm

Meta-analysis. (n.d.) In *Organization for Economic Co-operation and Development online glossary.* Retrieved August 17, 2008, from http://stats.oecd.org/glossary/detail.asp?ID=3718

National Library of Medicine. (2008). *Hazardous substance data bank* [Fact sheet]. Retrieved from http://www.nlm.nih.gov/pubs/factsheets/hsdbfs.html

National Library of Medicine. (2008). *International MEDLARS Centers* [Fact sheet]. Retrieved from http://www.nlm.nih.gov/pubs/factsheets/intlmedlars.html

National Library of Medicine. (2008). *MEDLINE* [Fact sheet]. Retrieved from http://www.nlm.nih.gov/pubs/factsheets/medline.html

National Library of Medicine. (2008). National Institutes of Health, *NCBI bookshelf.* Retrieved on August 20, 2008 from http://www.ncbi.nlm.nih.gov/bookshelf/br.fcgi?book=helppubmed&part=pubmedhelp

Shedlock, J., & Walton, L. (2006). Developing a virtual community for health sciences library: Doody's Core Titles. *Journal of Medical Library Associations, 94*(1), 61–66. Retrieved August 17, 2008, from http://www.pubmedcentral.nih.gov/articlerender.fcgi?artid=1324773

Sherman, C., & Price, G. (2001). *The invisible web: Uncovering information sources search engines can't see.* Medford, NJ: Information Today, Inc.

The Cochrane Collaboration. (2008). *Practitioner's portal.* Retrieved August 20, 2008, from http://www.cochrane.org/index_practicioners.htm

The OVID Experience. (n.d.). Retrieved August 17, 2008, from http://www.ovid.com/site/index.jsp?top=1

University of Toronto, Faculty of Dentistry. (2008). *The index to dental literature.* Retrieved August 20, 2008, from http://www.utoronto.ca/dentistry/newsresources/library/FindArticles.html

Weishapple, C. L. (2001). *Introduction to legal nurse consulting.* Albany, NY: Delmar.

Test Questions

1. Which sources may be utilized to locate Standards of Care?
   A. Well-respected medical and nursing textbooks
   B. The Cochrane Library
   C. The Agency for Healthcare Research and Quality
   D. Professional Organizations
   E. All of the above

2. Which is a primary source of medical information?
   A. Health Care Standards Directory
   B. Food and Drug Administration
   C. Observations conducted for research or scientific purposes
   D. Textbook research
   E. Consultation with a professional in the appropriate specialty

3. Which database will access information pertaining to health organizations?
   A. MEDLINE
   B. MD Consult
   C. The Cochrane Library
   D. DIRLINE
   E. Index Medicus

4. Medical Literature may be retrieved by which of the following?
   A. PubMed
   B. The Internet
   C. Loansome Doc
   D. Retrieval Service
   E. All of the above
   F. None of the above

5. What site may be useful in retrieving archived U.S. Government documents?
   A. The Invisible Web
   B. OLDMEDLINE
   C. CyberCemetery
   D. NIOSH

Answers: 1. E, 2. C, 3. D, 4. E, 5. C

Appendix A: Websites

Function or Specialty	List or Site	Description	URL/Address
	Parent Agency	**Department of Health and Human Services (DHHS)**	**http://www.hhs.gov (formerly http://www.dhhs. gov)**
Primary site of funding and research for disease	National Institute of Health (NIH)	The NIH (part of DHHS) is the primary Federal agency for conducting and supporting medical research	http://www.nih.gov
Molecular biology	National Center for Biotechnology Information (NCBI) at the NIH	National resource for molecular biology information, creates and provides public databases, conducts research in computational biology, instrumental in software tool development for analyzing genome data, and disseminates biomedical information	http://www.ncbi.nlm.nih.gov
Medical library	The National Library of Medicine® (NLM)	Collects materials and provides information and research services in all areas of biomedicine and health care, largest biomedical library in the world, located on the campus of the NIH	http://www.nlm.nih.gov
Retrieval system for NCBI at the NLM	Entrez	Integrated, text-based search system for PubMed; and major molecular biology databases such as Nucleotide and Protein Sequences; Protein Structures; Complete Genomes; Chemical databases, and more	http://www.ncbi.nlm.nih.gov
Part of the Entrez retrieval system but can be accessed directly	PubMed®	Provides free access to MEDLINE, link out to participating publishers, some free text articles are accessible here. Noteworthy are the interactive tutorials that provide instruction on all aspects of searching via PubMed	http://pubmed.gov
Portal to retrieval systems of the NLM	NLM Gateway	A single entry point to access multiple NLM resources	http://gateway.nlm.nih.gov

Citation database	MEDLINE®	Provides citations, abstracts, and some free full-text articles indexed by the MeSH system. Free full-text articles are designated by PubMed Central® icon or similar prompt. May also be searched with natural language	http://www.nlm.nih.gov/pubs/factsheets/medline.html
Part of the MEDLINE database	OLDMEDLINE	Citations that need converting to indexing with MeSH terminology but have not yet been updated	http://www.nlm.nih.gov/databases/databases_oldmedline.html
Part of the MEDLINE database	PREMEDLINE	In-process citations that have not yet been indexed (or may not be depending on content submission) but still accessible	http://www.ncbi.nlm.nih.gov/sites/entrez To access type premedline in the search box
Medical subject headings	MeSH®	MeSH is a medical thesaurus that uses specified terms to locate articles in MEDLINE. MeSH terms are in a hierarchical structure that has broad categories at the top, more specific terms at the bottom. Links to MeSH factsheets and tutorials	http://www.nlm.nih.gov/mesh/
Consumer health information	MEDLINEplus®	Reader-friendly information on a wide range of diseases and conditions, as well as surgery and instructional animated videos	http://medlineplus.gov
Online catalog of the NLM	LocatorPlus®	Provides information about the NLM holdings of monographs, journals, and audiovisuals	http://locatorplus.gov
Document retrieval and delivery system of the NLM	LoansomeDoc® DOCLINE®	The NLM's document retrieval and delivery system. Requires free registration and participating recipient library	http://docline.gov/lonesome/login.cfm
Directory of the SIS at the NLM	DIRLINE®	Directory of organizations and other resources in health and biomedicine	http://dirline.nlm.nih.gov

continued

Function or Specialty	List or Site	Description	URL/Address
Data network for toxicology	TOXNET®	Collection of toxicology and environmental health databases. Including but not limited to ChemIDplus, HSDB, TOXLINE, DART, TRI	http://toxnet.nlm.nih.gov
Toxicology database	Hazardous Substances Data Bank (HSDB®)	Provides information on the toxicology of potentially hazardous substances	http://toxnet.nlm.nih.gov/ cgi-bin/sis/htmlgen?HSDB
Toxicology database	Toxics Release Inventory (TRI)	The NLM provides access to this resource of the EPA which provides publicly accessible information on the release and waste management of toxic substances	http://toxnet.nlm.nih.gov/ cgi-bin/sis/htmlgen?TRI or http://epa.gov/tri
Toxicology database	Tox Town	Information with links for chemical disasters, toxic chemical in areas of living, working, and entertainment	http://toxtown.nlm.nih.gov/
Chemical database	ChemIDplus	Chemical dictionary and structure database. Under the NLM's division of Specialized Information Services (SIS). Also accessible through TOXNET	http://sis.nlm.nih.gov/ chemical.html
Specialized database	AIDSinfo	Provides treatment guidelines, clinical trials, and drug and vaccine information	http://aidsinfo.nih.gov
Clinical trials database	*ClinicalTrials.gov*	Information on clinical research studies on a wide range of diseases and conditions and current ongoing studies	http://clinicaltrials.gov
Reproduction	DART®/ETIC	Covers teratology and other aspects of developmental and reproductive toxicology	http://toxnet.nlm.nih.gov/ cgi-bin/sis/htmlgen?DARTETIC
Consumer database of genetic information	Genetics Home Reference™	Consumer-friendly information about the effects of genetic variations on human health	http://ghr.nlm.nih.gov

Genetics	Online Mendelian Inheritance Online	Compendium of human genes and genetic phenotypes	http://www.ncbi.nlm.nih.gov/**omim**/

Archives of Information

Archived government websites and information	CyberCemetery	A joint venture of the University of North Texas Libraries and the U.S. Government Printing Offices provides information regarding past government agencies and commissions and their final reports	http://govinfo.library.unt.edu
Archive of web pages	The Wayback machine	Searches now defunct web pages by URL and date. Also contains images and audio	http://www.waybackmaching.org

Medical Specialty Sites

Accreditation	Joint Commission on Accreditation of Healthcare Organizations	Information for the general public, health care organizations, professionals, purchasers, employers, and unions	http://jointcommission.org (formerly http://www.jcaho.org)
AIDS	University of California, San Francisco	A project of the University of California, San Francisco (UCSF), AIDS Research Institute; UCSF AIDS Program at S.F. General Hospital; Center for AIDS Prevention Studies; and the Henry J. Kaiser Family Foundation	http://hivinsite.ucsf.edu/
AIDS and Cancer Statistics	National Cancer Institute/Surveillance Epidemiology and End Results (SEER)	AIDS-related guidelines, clinical trials, vaccines, and drugs as well as cancer-related statistics	http://seer.cancer.gov/statistics/
Allergy	Allergy solution	Multiple links to allergy bedding and additional products	www.allergysolution.com
Alternative medicine	Alternative Medicine Homepage	Annotated links to sites related to this topic. Provides access to textbooks from within the site	http://www.pitt.edu/~cbw/altm.html

continued

Function or Specialty	List or Site	Description	URL/Address
Anatomy	Human Anatomy Online	Fun, interactive, and educational views of the human body	http://www.innerbody.com/
Anesthesiology	Martindale's Virtual Center/Anesthesiology and Surgery	Links to guidelines; simulations and videos; textbooks; intubations; equipment; algorithms; dermatomes; and anatomical drawings	http://www.martindalecenter.com/MedicalSurgery.html
Anesthesiology	American Association of Nurse Anesthetists	Patient, professional, and member resources. Including links to Professional Practice Documents; State Legislative and Regulatory Requirements (50-state summaries); to multiple articles related to legal issues and topics	http://www.aana.com
Arthritis	Arthritis Foundation	Offers education and support to patients and families affected by arthritis	http://www.arthritis.org
Cancer	American Cancer Society	Offers education, support and services to patients and families affected by cancer	http://www.acs.org
Cancer	National Cancer Institute	Information regarding clinical trials, research, funding, and statistics	http://www.cancer.gov
Cardiac	American Heart Association (AHA)	Information directed to medical professionals, patients, and caregivers; includes medical guidelines, statistics, signs and symptoms of stroke, and extensive grocery list with heart smart foods listed with brand names	http://www.americanheart.org
		Link to AHA guidelines	http://www.americanheart.org/presenter.jhtml?q=guidelines&identifier=10000015&submit.x=36&submit.y=10
Cardiac surgery	Cardiothoracic Surgery Network	Information or links to clinical trials; International CT Surgical organizations; journals; current outcomes for the State of NJ	www.ctsnet.org

Cardiac monitoring	EKG File Room	Interesting virtual EKGs with analysis and explanation	www.lf2.cuni.cz/Projekty/interna/heart_sounds/ekg4/fileroom.html
Certifications and credentials	American Nurses Credentialing Center	Verify credentials for Nursing specialties, Clinical Nurse Specialists and Nurse Practitioners. Identifies Magnet Organizations	http://www.nursecredentialing.org/
Certification and credentials for advance practice nursing	Nursing Credentialing Acronyms	May 2008 updated credential acronyms for nurse practitioners, clinical nurse specialists, and other advanced specialties	www.medscape.com/viewarticle/575791
Certification and credentials for physicians	Physician Board Certification	Online verification of granted by the American Board of Medical Specialties and contact information for the individual specialty boards and criteria for board certifications	http://www.abms.org
Child abuse	National Data Archive on Child Abuse and Neglect	Disseminates information on child abuse and neglect; provides training and technical support for analysis of the data	http://www.ndacan.cornell.edu/
Chiropractic	Commission on Accreditation of the Council of Chiropractic Education (CCE)	The CCE is the agency recognized by the U.S. Secretary of Education for accreditation of programs and institutions offering the doctor of chiropractic degree	http://www.cce-usa.org/coa.php
Critical care	American Association of Critical Care Nurses	Information on certification, education, and clinical practice	http://www.aacn.org
Critical care	learnICU.com	Links to multiple pediatric and adult critical care guidelines	http://www.learnicu.org/Quick_Links/Pages/default.aspx

continued

Function or Specialty	List or Site	Description	URL/Address
Diet and Nutrition	American dietetic association	Metasite with links to consumer education and public-policy sites; dietetic associations; dietetic practice groups; food, foodservice, and culinary organizations; medical and health professionals; and journals	http://www.eatright.org
Dentistry	University of Toronto Dental Library	Uses both PubMed and OVID for searching. Provides Index to dental literature	http://www.utoronto.ca/dentistry
Drug and pharmaceutical information	Drug Infonet	Sections include Drug Information, Ask the Experts, Pharmaceutical Manufacturer Information, and Hospitals	www.druginfonet.com
Drug and pharmaceutical information	RxList	Drugs currently on the U.S. market or close to approval, keyword search, RXList, top 200 prescriptions	http://www.rxlist.com
Drug and pharmaceutical information	Drugs.com	A to Z drug list; drugs by condition; pill identifier; interactions checker; drug image search; news and articles; new drug approvals; new drug applications; drug side effects; drug imprint codes; FDA alerts; Medical encyclopedia; medical dictionary; clinical trial results	http://www.drugs.com
Endocrinology and diabetes	American Diabetes Association	Comprehensive information on diabetes	http://www.diabetes.org
Environmental science	The National Institute of Environmental Science	Part of the NIH, studying environmental medicine and its impact on human disease	http://www.niehs.nih.gov

Topic	Name	Description	URL
Diabetes and kidney disease	National Institute of Diabetes and Digestive and Kidney Disease	NIH's website dedicated to diabetes information and resources	http://www2.niddk.nih.gov
Evaluation	Health on Net Foundation (HON Code)	Code of conduct for medical and health sites with a query box to locate certified medical sites honoring the code	http://www.hon.ch
Experts	Expert Witness Notebook	Attempts to link attorneys and expert witnesses	http://www.witness.net
Expert witness and deposition databanks	IDEX	Defense-oriented services; national network consisting of more than 4600 defense-oriented law firms, government entities, and corporations. Close to 150,000 experts; fee-based	http://www.idex.com
Expert witnesses	Expert.com	Extensive areas of expert witness's services	http://www.experts.com
Expert witnesses	Expert Pages	Medical and nonmedical experts; directory by state	http://expertpages.com/
Expert witness and deposition databanks	Trialsmith	Plaintiff-oriented online deposition bank for expert investigation; fee-based	http://www.trialsmith.com
Experts and case law	Daubert Tracker	Provides subscription or per session fee to access case law centered on issues of *Daubert v. Merrell Dow Pharmaceutical* and its implications	http://www.dauberttracker.com/
Evidence-based medicine	The Virtual Library	Through access to the University of Sheffield (United Kingdom) a core collection of evidence-based medicine is available	http://www.shef.ac.uk/scharr/ir/core.html

continued

Function or Specialty	List or Site	Description	URL/Address
Family medicine	Family Practice Notebook.com	Over 4316 topics within 616 chapters and 31 subspecialty books	http://www.fpnotebook.com/about.htm
Fitness and exercise	Shape Up America!	Information concerning health and fitness, Cyberkitchen, Body Mass Index Calculation	http://www.shapeup.org
Forensic nursing	International Association of Forensic Nurses	Abstracts from *Journal of Forensic Nursing*, links to chapters and websites, educational programs, and certification information	http://www.forensicnurse.org/
Gastroenterology	Gastroenterology Web	Links to other sites that relate to this specialty: extensive information on liver disease	http://www.cumc.columbia.edu/dept/gi/
General medicine	American Academy of Family Physicians	Information for both the professional and the consumer. Offers links to public health; patient information; quality improvement and multiple other sites; for the consumer links for over the counter medications; women's health; men's health; and senior's health	http://www.aafp.org
General medical resource	MDConsult	Subscription database that provides virtual access to core medical textbooks, journals, patient education materials, and more from within the medical profession. Offers annual or monthly subscriptions	http://www.mdconsult.com
General medical resource	Martindale's Virtual Medical Center	Currently the Medical Center contains over 140,850 medical cases and grand rounds; 1560 courses and textbooks; 67,800 teaching modules and files 550 journals; 4800 databases; atlases and image databases; and over a 1000 videos/movies	http://www.martindalecenter.com/Medical.html

Geriatrics	Alzheimer's Web	Links for both the layperson and the professional for resource organizations and clinical trials	http://www.alz.org
Glossary	Cochrane Collaboration	Glossary of Cochrane Collaboration and research terms	http://www.cochrane.org/resources/glossary.htm
Government	CDC/NCHS	Data and statistics regarding various diseases; HIV /AIDS Surveillance Report; Morbidity and Mortality Weekly Report (MMWR); traveler's health; injury; violence and safety; links to contact information by states to obtain birth, death, marriage, or divorce certificates	http://.cdc.gov
Government licensing, regulation, and recalls	Food and Drug Administration	Links to MedWatch; pharmaceutical warning letters; pediatric therapeutics; medical device registration and listings; E-Code of Federal Regulations; Federal Register; Laws enforced by FDA and Statues; and CFR Title 21 database	http://www.fda.gov http://www.fda.gov/cder/
Governmental Agency	DHHS/Center for Medicare and Medicaid Services	Centers for Medicare and Medicaid Services with links for multiple resources; DHHS also provides various links, among them extensive information regarding HIPAA regulations	http://www.cms.hhs.gov/
Government Statistics	National Center for Health Statistics	FASTATS (fast statistics); National Death Index (epidemiology): Data Warehouse of published and unpublished tables; and FEDSTATS (statistics compiled by more than 70 federal agencies)	http://www.cdc.gov/nchs
Guidelines	National Guideline Clearinghouse	Evidence-based clinical guidelines with links to Guideline Index; Guidelines In Progress; Guideline Archive; What's New This Week; and FDA Advisories	http://www.guideline.gov

continued

Function or Specialty	List or Site	Description	URL/Address
Guidelines	Agency for Healthcare Research and Quality (AHRQ)	Provides access to older guidelines and standards	http://www.ahrq.gov/clinic/cpgarchv.htm (formerly http://www.ahcpr.gov)
Guidelines and standards	The Healthcare Standards Directory	Citations of standards, legislation, and referenced articles. Directory of organizations and government agencies issuing guidelines and standards	http://www.ecri.org
Guidelines in journals	American College of Chest Physicians	Links to health and science policy and evidence-based medicine in the *CHEST Journal*	http://www.chestnet.org/education/hsp/guidelinesProducts.php
Guidelines for endocrinology	American Association of Clinical Endocrinologist	Guidelines with updates available from 2001 to 2008	http://www.aace.com/pub/guidelines/
Infectious disease	MMWR	Published by the CDC; full text of the reports with searchable index; charts and tables available in PDF	http://www.cdc.gov/mmwr
Internal medicine	American Medical Association	Links to peer-reviewed archived full text from several journals from 1998 to present (subscriptions required); medical ethics; legal issues; and physician finder	http://ama-assn.org
Health insurance plans	Americas Health Insurance Plans (AHIP)	Information about health care plans and consumer resources	http://www.ahip.org (formerly http//www.aahp.org)
Home health	PA Association of Medical Suppliers Home Health Resources	JCAHO accredited source for multiple home care supplies	http://www.homehealthresource.com/
Kidney disease	The Kidney Foundation	Offers information and support to those affected by kidney disease	http://www.kidney.org

Category	Name	Description	URL
Managed care	Health Administration Responsibility Project	Links to pertinent sections of the federal and California codes; relevant cases; information on ERISA; mandatory arbitration; torts; contracts; and fiduciary breach	http://www.harp.org
Managed care accreditation	National Quality Assurance Association	Accreditation body for HMO's; and NCQA Accreditation Programs; Health Plan Accreditation (HPA); Managed Care Organizations (MCO); Preferred Provider Organizations (PPO); Managed Behavioral Healthcare Organizations (MBHO); New Health Plans (NHP); Disease Management (DM). Report cards available for various entities	http://www.ncqa.org
Maternal health	International Association for Maternal and Neonatal Health (IAMANEH)	International effort to improve maternal and neonatal health	http://www.gfmer.ch/000_IAMANEH.htm
Medical database	OVID	Subscription service provider for accessing medical information. Used by the majority of medical research librarians and facilities	http://www.ovid.com
Medical education	International Medical Education Directory (IMED)	A joint effort of the Educational Commission of Foreign Medical Graduates (ECFMG) and the Foundation for Advancement of International Medical Education and Research (FAIMER). Provides information about foreign medical schools	https://www.imed.famier.org
Medical journal	Journal of the American Medical Association (JAMA)	Web edition of JAMA back issues with full text from January 1995 to present; Tables of Contents, Abstracts, selected PDFs: May 1992 to November 1997; Tables of Contents and Abstracts only: January 1975 to May 1992; Tables of Contents only: January 1966 to December 1974	http://pubs.ama-assn.org Click on JAMA and Archives Journal in the lower right-hand menu
Medical journal	New England Journal of Medicine (NEJM)	Web edition of NEJM; current week's journal, archives with Full Text and Abstracts: 1993–2008; Abstracts only: 1975–1992 (subscription required)	http://www.nejm.org

continued

Function or Specialty	List or Site	Description	URL/Address
Medical Journal	*British Medical Journal*	Excellent source of articles on medical research and development. Many free full text	http://www.bmj.com/
Medical Library	The Medical Library Association	Connecting information on more than 4000 health sciences, this nonprofit organization exists to provide education, information on research, and continuity of global care	http://www.mlanet.org
Medical Library	National Network of Medical Libraries (NN/LM)	Collaborative effort of medical libraries nationwide to combine knowledge-based sources and much more.	http://nnlm.gov
Medical reference	Doody's Core Titles	Fee-based, provides information regarding core textbooks in medicine. Small subscription fee for list	http://www.doody.com/dct/
Medical reference/ review	Cochrane Collaboration	Provides up-to-date database of evidence-based medicine and literature reviews	http://www.cochrane.org/
Medical directory	Medical and Health Information Directory	Annual directory comprises three volumes. May be cost prohibitive for the individual practitioner but volumes can be purchased separately	http://www.pohly.com In the left-hand menu, choose search this site, and enter the title of the book Volume I: Organizations, Institutions & Agencies Volume II: Public Libraries & Other Information Volume III: Health Services (Clinics, Treatment Centers, Care Programs, Counseling & Diagnostic Services)

Category	Resource	Description	URL
Medical directory	Encyclopedia of Medical Organizations and Agencies	Information about more than 18,000 public and private agencies concerned with medical information, funding, research, education, planning, advocacy, advice, and service	*Author's note:* This resource is also published through Gale Thomson (as above). For purposes of this research, this text was accessed at the Helen F. Graham Cancer Center Library in Newark, Delaware
Medical records	Medical Records Privacy	Factsheets and articles pertaining to medical record privacy	http://www.privacyrights.org/medical.htm
Medical records	American Health Information Management Association	Links to information on coding, emerging issues; article; ICD-10; definitions; guidelines; and health care organizations	http://www.ahima.org/infocenter
Medical records	The Health Policy Institute of Georgetown University-Center on Medical Record Rights and Privacy	Consumer-oriented links to each of the 50 states with information pertaining to the laws governing obtaining and retention of an individual's medical records	http://hpi.georgetown.edu/privacy/records.html
Medical resource	Hardin—MD University of Iowa	Links to multiple medical diseases and conditions by systems with some images available	http://www.lib.uiowa.edu/hardin/MD/
Neurology/neurosurgery	DrDillin.com	Educational tools and information including multiple detailed animations of various spinal procedures	http://www.drdillin.com/
Neurology	Neuroland	Excellent site for any neurological information	http://www.neuroland.com

continued

Function or Specialty	List or Site	Description	URL/Address
Nursing journals	AJN	Articles from 1900 to present (subscription needed to access)	http://www.ajn.org
Nursing research	CINHAL	Hosted by EBSCO, this pay database of premier nursing information and research does provide a free trial	http://www.ebscohost.com/cinahl/
Nurse midwives	ACNM	Education and health care information	http://www.acnm.org/
Nursing resources	Chronic Wound Healing	Extensive graphics; instruction in proper wound care. Good teaching tool for students and attorneys	http://www.nursing.uiowa.edu/sites/chronicwound/
Nursing resources	Medscape for Nurses	Provides up-to-date information and articles directed toward nurses	http://www.medscape.com/nurses
Nursing Journals	Nursing Index	Links to issues of *The Journal for Nurse Practitioners; The Nurse Practitioner; The American Journal of Primary Care; The Journal of the American Academy of Nurse Practitioner; and Journal of Pediatric Primary Care*	http://www.medscape.com/index/section_398_1
Nursing boards	State Boards of Nursing	Contact information for all 50 states and Washington, DC	http://www.ntnnursenet.org/setup_frames/frames_nurse.php
Nutrition and wellness	The North Dakota State University (NDSU) Library	Multiple links to a broad range of nutritional information and statistics	http://www.lib.ndsu.nodak.edu/research/subjects/ag/agfoodnut.php#inter
Obstetrics	American College of Obstetricians and Gynecology (ACOG)	Promoting advocacy, education, research, and practice management	http://www.acog.org

Obstetrics/gynecology	Infertility	Multiple links to topic-based resources	http://www.nlm.nih.gov/medlineplus/infertility.html
Oncology	CancerNet	National Cancer Institute; multiple links to NIH sites relating to cancer	http://cancernet.nci.nih.gov
Oncology	National Cancer Institute	Cancer Stat Factsheets for 27 types of cancer statistics	http://seer.cancer.gov/
Orthopedics	Southern California Orthopedic Institute	Good site for reviewing information on anatomy; basic orthopedics; arthroscopies; and more	http://www.scoi.com
Patient information	Care Pages.com	Offers online support and information regarding hospitalized family members. At admission, enrolled and assigned accessed by major hospitals	http://www.carepages.com http://www.mayoclinic.org/feature-articles/carepages.html (to learn more)
Pathology	Your Pathology Report	Explanation of terminology in breast cancer pathology reports	www.breastcancer.org/symptoms/path_report/
Pathology	The Pathology Guy	Site maintained by a board-certified anatomic and clinical pathologist with links to many educational resources	www.pathguy.com/
Patient safety	AHRQ	Multiple links to a variety of information related to medical errors and patient safety	http://www.ahrq.gov/qual/errorsix.htm
Patient safety	The Kentucky Society of Radiologic Technologists, Inc.	Impressive collection of links to safety issues across a broad spectrum of safety concerns. Everything from A to W	http://www.ksrtinc.org/SafetyResource.html

continued

Function or Specialty	List or Site	Description	URL/Address
Pediatric maxillofacial	Cleft Palate/Craniofacial Differences	Links to information and resources for parents and children.	http://www.childrensmercy.org/Content/uploadedFiles/cleftresources.pdf
Pediatrics and neurology	Pediatric Neurosurgery	Information on a number of pediatric conditions requiring neurosurgical intervention or expertise	http://cpmcnet.columbia.edu/dept/nsg/PNS
Pediatric resources	Children's Hospital of Philadelphia	Links to information for the following: index of children's medical conditions; parenting; safety; vaccines; and common emergencies	http://www.chop.edu/consumer/your_child/index.jsp
Perinatal health	NPA	Provides Family Advocacy Network (FAN), advocacy, transcultural considerations, and position statements	http://www.nationalperinatal.org/
Pharmacology	PharmWeb	Annotated listing of publications; electronic products; and journals related to pharmacology; links to pharmacy-related sites, including pharmaceutical companies	http://www.pharmweb.net
Pharmacology	Drugs.com	Links to pill identifier, drug information; side effects; and drug interactions	http://www.drugs.com/
Pharmacology		Links to identify pharmacies with addresses and phone numbers for all 50 states and Washington, DC	http://www.healthcarehiring.com/pharmacy_delaware.php
Pharmacology	PharmWeb	Annotated listing of publications; electronic products; and journals related to pharmacology; links to pharmacy-related sites, including pharmaceutical companies	http://www.pharmweb.net

Pharmacology	EMBASE	Subscription database for biomedical and pharmacological literature	http://www.embase.com
Physician assistants	American Academy of Physicians Assistants	Links to resources for clinical information; search tools; publications; medical-related associations; U.S. government offices; and insurance information	http://www.aapa.org/resourc.html#clinical
Physician information	American Board of Medical Specialties	Physician board certification verification (free registration required)	http://www.abms.org
Physician professional organization	American Medical Association	Reviewed medical sites; medical society director; database of over 800,000 physicians; and guidelines	http://www.ama-assn.org
Physician licensing	State Licensing Boards	Links to individual states and Washington, DC	http://www.ama-assn.org/ama/pub/category/2645.html
Physician locator	Physician Locator	The NPI database contains over 2.5 million records, with detailed information including medical specialty and multispecialties; business mailing and practice location addresses; contact phone and fax numbers; UPIN; state medical licenses; and insurance company identification. It may be searched by most specialties, although identification numbers (taxonomy codes) have not yet been assigned to all specialties. The database is updated regularly. This is public information, and use of this website is completely free of charge	http://www.e-physician.info

continued

Function or Specialty	List or Site	Description	URL/Address
Psychiatry	The Lundbeck Institute	Located in Denmark, the institute promotes education, partnership, and quality of care for neurological and psychiatric disorders	http://www.brainexplorer.org
		PDF of multiple ratings scales to measure the severity of psychiatric disorders	http://www.brainexplorer.org/factsheets/Psychiatry%20Rating%20Scales.pdf
		For depression: Hamilton depression rating; Montgomery–Åsberg depression rating scale; Geriatric depression scale; Zung self-rating depression scale	
		For mania: Young mania rating scale	
		For anxiety: Hamilton anxiety rating	
		For obsessive–compulsive disorder (OCD): Yale–Brown obsessive–compulsive scale	
		For schizophrenia: Positive and negative syndrome scale; brief psychiatric rating scale; Calgary depression scale for schizophrenia	
		For general psychiatry scales: global assessment of functioning (GAF); clinical global impression (CGI)	
Public health	Health Services and Public Health	Links to federal agencies, associations, data sets and data sources, epidemiology and health statistics, evidence-based medicine and health technology assessment, funding, health policy and health economics, informatics, public health rural health, state resources, and disparities in health care	http://www.atsdr.cdc.gov/HEC/HSPH/hsphhome.html

Topic	Description	URL
Public health statistics	A to Z stats including: aging, births, deaths, disease classification, growth charts, health care, health insurance, injuries, and physical activity	http://www.cdc.gov/nchs/
References	Searchable site includes symptoms, common clinical procedures, laboratory tests, and anatomical drawings for consumers	http://www.merck.com/pubs/mmanual
References	Links to more than 1100 dictionaries, including 19 medical dictionaries and glossaries	http://www.onelook.com
Scholarly literature	Broad search across disciplines and sources for scholarly literature	http://scholar.google.com
Sleep disorders	"Everything you wanted to know about sleep disorders but were too tired to ask."	http://www.sleepnet.com
Surgery	Links to multiple resources and information and organizations	http://www.nlm.nih.gov/medlineplus/surgery.html
Surgery (plastic)	Explanations and photos of various procedures, physician locator, and videos	http://www.surgery.org/
Vaccines	Vaccine Education Center provides information for adults and children	http://www.chop.edu/consumer/jsp/microsite/microsite.jsp?id=75918

National Center for Health Statistics

Merck Manual of Diagnosis and Therapy

OneLook Dictionaries

Google Scholar

SleepNet

MedlinePlus

The American Society for Aesthetic Plastic Surgery

Vaccine Education Center at Children's Hospital of Philadelphia

continued

Function or Specialty	List or Site	Description	URL/Address
Women's health	Mayo Clinic on Menopause	Offers comprehensive overview of menopause covering symptoms, treatment options, and self-care measures	www.mayoclinic.com/health/menopause/DS00119
Women's health	Society for Menstrual Cycle Research	Nonprofit, interdisciplinary research organization. Membership required	http://menstruationresearch.org/
Women's health	ASCCP	Promotes committed to improving the study, prevention, diagnosis, and management of lower genital tract disease	http://www.asccp.org/
Worker's compensation[a]	ExpertLaw	Links to worker's compensation benefits—A State-By-State Guide	http://www.expertlaw.com/library/comp_by_state/
Writing skills	American Psychological Association (APA)	Provides an online resource for APA format	http://www.apastyle.org/elecref.html

® Indicates a Registered Trademark.

[a] See *Journal of Legal Nurse Consulting: Summer 2007* (Vol. 18(3), p. 25) for a comprehensive list of websites pertaining to worker's compensation.

Note: All websites were current at the time of submission. However, it is possible some sites may be inactive at the time of publication.

Appendix B

Checklist for Medical Research on the Internet

- Gather and analyze relevant facts and define the medical issue.
- Determine whether field searches can be used (author, journal).
- Identify and enter MeSH® terms if field searches are not appropriate.
- Utilize BOOLEAN connectors (AND, OR, and NOT) to expand or limit the results.
- Open Limits tab, if needed, to define very specific criteria to be included in the scope of the search.
- Review citations and abstracts.
- Mark the relevant citations.
- Verify the research is time specific to the needs
- Print the search results
- Retrieve the article(s)

Checklist for Library Research

- Gather and analyze relevant facts and define the medical issue.
- Determine the area of medicine to be researched.
- Use the online card catalog to locate learned treatises or books published on this issue and area of medicine.
- Educate yourself on the area of medicine by using textbooks and medical dictionaries.
- Locate scientific and medical journals and peer-reviewed publications that deal with this area of medicine by referencing medical indexes.
- Verify that research is date specific.
- Summarize or photocopy relevant research.
- Create a paper trail of research findings using appropriate citation techniques.

Chapter 12

Medical Record Analysis

Deborah D. D'Andrea, BSN, BA, RN and
Jean Dworniczek, BSN, RN-BC

First Edition
Shirley Cantwell Davis, BSN, RN, LNCC

Second Edition
Shirley Cantwell Davis, BSN, RN, LNCC and
Colleen D'Amico, BS, RN

Contents

Objectives

Upon reading this chapter, the legal nurse consultant (LNC) will be able to

- List three types of medical records that may not be produced in response to a request for complete medical records, and discuss why this may occur
- Outline the key points to be assessed in a complete review of an operative record
- Identify two types of altered records and five ways whereby the LNC can detect alterations
- Discuss the various kinds of medical record summaries that a legal nurse consultant can perform and the advantages of each type of summary
- Describe two examples of common pitfalls in medical record analysis

Introduction

The American Association of Legal Nurse Consultants (AALNC) has defined the primary role of the LNC to be the evaluation, analysis, and rendering of informed opinions on the delivery of health care and the resulting outcomes. This is accomplished in part by reviewing, summarizing, and analyzing medical records along with other pertinent health care and legal documents. These findings are then compared and correlated to plaintiff statements of allegations contained in the complaint (AALNC, 2006a, 2006b).

LNCs are not attorneys and do not practice law. However, they review the legal documents because they address the negligence allegations and reveal the initial legal strategy being used by opposing counsel. This information is invaluable in order to understand and assist the attorney in developing his/her case response. Medical record analysis with the provision of counsel to the attorney has been the foundation of legal nurse consulting practice since the profession first emerged.

Attorneys have no formal training regarding medical record analysis. As a result, they should rely heavily on the LNC to review and interpret the medical records on their behalf as well as that of their clients'. Due to the complexity of medical litigation in today's world, it is essential that all LNCs be able to perform medical record review and analysis in a timely and accurate manner. Small but highly significant details can be overlooked, with potentially disastrous results during discovery and at trial.

Obtaining Medical Records

The AALNC Standards of Legal Nurse Consulting Practice state that assessment of the issues is the first step in approaching any medical–legal case. In order to accomplish this, the LNC needs to collect data from all relevant sources, which then can be used to conduct a systematic assessment of the health care issues involved (AALNC, 2006a, 2006b). For the plaintiff, it is essential that the LNC understands the plaintiff's complaints regarding the injuries and how they occurred. Once the case is filed and in litigation, it is equally critical for the defense to know everything about the incident(s) as well as the plaintiff's complete medical history and comorbidities, in order to evaluate what possible cause–effect relationship exists regarding the incident(s) in question.

Compile Complete Medical Records

In most instances, the medical record must be complete, accurate, and authenticated before it can be introduced into evidence. All states have statutes regarding medical record maintenance. Failure to comply can be grounds for loss of hospital accreditation. Civil liability may also be found against a hospital for breach of duty to maintain accurate records (Pozgar, 2007). The Joint Commission (TJC) (formally entitled JCAHO—The Joint Commission on Accreditation of Healthcare Organization) survey standards require prompt completion of medical records not to exceed 30 days after the discharge of the patient. This time period is spelled out in most medical staff rules and regulations (The Joint Commission, 2007). Persistent failure to complete records by hospital staff members may be used as a basis for suspension of those staff members (Pozgar, 2007).

When requesting medical records, it is always wise to ask for a certified copy of each medical record. Hospitals and other health care organizations ideally should have a health information management administrator who is licensed by the American Health Information Management Association as a registered record administrator (RRA) in charge of the medical records (Pozgar, 2007). The RRA will certify the accuracy and completeness of the copies of the original records. Often, the LNC will have to supply a physician or other health care provider with a fill-in-the-blank certification form when requesting medical records, since many health care providers do not have an official records administrator and are not familiar with certification of copies of their medical records (see Appendix A).

Although the health care organization has certified that the record is a true and complete copy of the original document, the LNC should never assume this to be true. Two-sided forms may not have been completely copied. Portions of the record may have been removed or not included at the time of the copy request. On the plaintiff side, an index of suspicion should be maintained, particularly in the LNC's analysis of medical malpractice claims. For the defense LNC, all records should be subpoenaed as most of the time plaintiff records are incomplete. In addition, under the rule of law, subpoenas mandate the complete record to be supplied, and most importantly, in a timely manner. Whether working with the plaintiff or the defense, the LNC should maintain a listing of records or forms that are felt to be missing from the complete record. This list should then be given to the attorney so that the records can be specifically requested. This list should be updated on a regular basis throughout the discovery process.

Records that may not be Produced as Part of the Medical Records

Frequently, inpatient facilities will have patient-related records they do not consider, or disclose as part of the official chart. The LNC needs to be aware that these records exist and should be obtained for review.

Fetal Heart Monitor Strips

Fetal heart monitor strips are electronic transcriptions of medical information and are considered to be part of the medical record of the mother of the fetus. Failure of a health care provider to keep and produce fetal heart monitor strips can be considered spoliation of evidence.

The LNC should specifically request fetal heart monitor strips for all admissions. Due to their bulky configuration and odd size, it may necessitate that they be stored separately from the medical records. This is particularly true of antepartum testing strips, which usually remain in the labor and delivery suite for comparison, when the patient returns for delivery at a later date. The same is true for monitoring strips in the intensive care unit (ICU).

Some ICUs are going to adopt electronic charting. However, most still keep paper flowsheets, as the large amount of data is cumbersome to view, in the whole, on the computer screen. Also, the nurse is required to record a strip of the heart rhythm (usually in two leads), as well as the waveform analysis of any invasive monitoring such as a right atrial pressure, pulmonary capillary wedge pressure, and pulmonary artery pressure. Waveforms are kept separately for patients on an intra-aortic balloon pump and all of these rhythm strips need to be specifically requested when the patient record is requested.

Radiographic Films

When evaluating any case involving critical radiographic films, the LNC should always obtain copies of the films. For the plaintiff, this may be done prior to filing the claim; for the defense, it should be done as early as possible for evaluation. Loss of original films by the provider does not always imply there was harmful intent to cover up or obscure evidence. Many types of radiographic films, such as CT, MRI, and PET scans, are stored on computer disks. Real-time echocardiograms, angiograms, and ultrasounds are also kept on tape or digital imaging. As most hospitals have now gone digital, these may be provided in DICOM (Digital Imaging and Communication in Medicine) format while the originals are saved on hospital servers. Therefore the request may need to go to the specific department, such as Cardiology, to get a CD for an angioplasty rather than through medical records.

The LNC will often find that radiograph copies are of insufficient quality to provide an accurate interpretation by an outside radiologist. Health care facilities may provide original x-rays to patients if certain conditions are met, but infrequently to LNCs and attorneys. Patients, however, have the right to request their films so they make take them to another doctor for review. If a case is in litigation, original films may be produced by agreement of counsel or by subpoena. The LNC should keep a log to track the receipt, storage, and transmittal of original films and other evidence. Loss of a film, or any type of evidence, once it has been in the possession of an attorney involved in the litigation, has profoundly affected the outcome of more than one medical malpractice case. All x-rays, specimens, or other case evidence received by the LNC should be inventoried and noted in an evidence log for ease of referencing throughout the case.

Radiographic file folders that are normally used to store films by a provider may be another frequently overlooked source of important information. In addition to demographic information, such as the patient's name and address, these file jackets may also contain the patient's complaints, the date and time that the films were taken, and the radiology technician's name.

Special Procedures Reports, Films, and Logs

Special procedure departments such as cardiology, radiology, endoscopy, hemodialysis, and so on have separate reporting and storage systems for reports and films as well as separate systems for obtaining and administering medications during a procedure. Dictated reports as well as films are frequently stored on digital imaging. These reports and imaging are maintained within the specific department and not within medical records, thus requests for such documents or films must be made directly to the appropriate department.

Videotapes or Photographic Documentation of Surgical Procedures or Deliveries

It is important to look for evidence in the medical record documentation that suggest photographs, videotaping, or digital recordings taken during a procedure were obtained. Videotapes and/or CDs of surgical procedures are considered part of the patient's medical record. The health care organization is obligated to retain these tapes. However, the LNC should be alert to the fact that the surgeon may ask the operating room staff to turn off the video camera when difficulties are encountered.

If the case is in litigation, specific questions will be asked in the interrogatories about these recordings. Sometimes the family may record birthing deliveries. Frequently the surgeon may have copies of special procedures made for educational purposes, and often the hospital will have and keep copies. Whoever has evidence of this nature will be expected to produce such evidence in its original condition.

The plaintiff may possess such documentation—for example, a videotape or CD of an exploratory laparoscopy—even though there is no written evidence that videotapes or photographs exist. Cardiopulmonary bypass monitoring records and flowsheets may not automatically become part of the medical record. If a cardiopulmonary bypass procedure was performed, these records may require a special request to the cardiac surgery, radiology, anesthesia, or perfusion departments.

Emergency Medical Services Transport Records

In many states the law requires that a health care facility release only records generated as a result of the care and treatment rendered at that particular facility. Thus, records from a previous treating facility and emergency-transport/ambulance records may need to be requested separately. The LNC should identify whether both a first aid or basic life support (BLS) squad and a mobile intensive care unit (MICU) treated the patient. Each record should be obtained.

Emergency Medical Services (EMS) reports are very useful in personal injury cases. Transport times are important, reflecting the time the call was received, time of dispatch, arrival at the scene, departure from the scene, arrival at the hospital, and so on. Additional information in these records may include a description of the person at the time of the arrival, the types of treatments and interventions utilized. They will identify if a helicopter was contacted or other ambulances were necessary for further transportation. These reports will describe how the injured appeared during the primary or initial assessment, and if there were significant clinical changes that occurred during transportation such as extrication from the injury site with help from the Jaws of Life. The report will reflect the amount of time it took for extrication along with the names of witnesses and others who attended the scene.

Emergency Room Logs/Operating Room Logs/Radiology Logs/Pharmacy Logs

Frequently, intra-departmental logs are created and maintained for a variety of reasons within a health care facility. Depending on the issues under litigation, such logs can be critical sources for information not contained in the "official medical record." The LNC needs to consider obtaining these as additional sources of corroborative information concerning the delivery of patient care.

Autopsy Records

If a patient has died during a hospitalization, the hospital record may not be considered complete without the autopsy results. This is especially true if the autopsy was performed outside the hospital at the medical examiner's or coroner's office. If the death is unexplained or occurs within 24 hr of admission, it may automatically become a "coroner's case." The LNC should ascertain whether (1) the autopsy report is a complete protocol or reflects only the preliminary results, (2) all the microscopic examinations have been performed, and (3) the results of any toxicology tests or special consultations to outside agencies have been received.

Autopsy evidence can be critical not only in confirming a diagnosis causing death, but in disproving certain facts. The LNC should request re-cuts of the original microscopic slides or tissue specimens for independent expert pathological review when the cause of death is in question or the patient had recent surgery. It can take several weeks to complete an autopsy report and several months to obtain it, particularly when specimens are sent to outside specialty laboratories for analysis or toxicology results.

Billing Records

Billing records are helpful in determining what services were provided, the type of equipment used, what medications were given, and many other details of the care and treatment. Billing records can be of extreme importance, especially when the LNC suspects that a diagnostic test result has been removed from the medical record. The LNC should check the billing records to determine whether the diagnostic charge was ever billed to the patient's insurer. The LNC should check all billing records as some facilities will send special lab requests to outside laboratories for processing. The LNC would then need to request those records separately.

Police or Sheriff Reports

In a motor vehicle accident, or other instances in which the police are involved, the police report should always be obtained because it may contain valuable information about the litigant as well as other potential "nonparties at fault." These reports contain a wealth of information that the LNC will want to review and mine. This information may contain the time of the arrival of the first responder–the time the first police officer arrived, the speed of the vehicle(s), witness information, type of damage to the vehicle which will help determine impact and angle of impact which the LNC can correlate to the corresponding injuries. The report will reflect the time the police were notified, who contacted the EMS and at what time. This information is important when tracking long response times that may occur in rural areas or delays due to weather or road conditions. This report will identify any incapacitated persons which will be important during discovery; also it may identify the names of witnesses from the scene that could be helpful to the case. Any photographs of the crash site as well as any computerized drawings detailing the accident can be requested from the police or sheriff departments. These reports assist in evaluating the impact of the collision, rollover details, speed, and distance for stopping in addition to other information that will enhance the details of the accident.

Accident or Work Site Reports

In cases that are related to work site injuries, the LNC will want to review the facility's injury or incident report. These reports are written after the accident/incident and the time frame for completion will depend on the facility's policies—they may be written immediately after the accident, the next day, or even longer after the event. They are usually written by the foreman or immediate supervisor of the area or division where the accident occurred. These reports will include the time of the incident, names of witnesses, and interventions that were undertaken or utilized. While these reports are not always as accurate as police and EMS reports, they may contain some very helpful information such as circumstances prior to the accident and immediately after the accident. Because work-site-related accidents must be reported to the Occupational Safety and Health Administration (OSHA), the LNC will want to compare the facility's injury report with the report submitted to OSHA. Medical care provided by the facility's Occupational Health Department immediately after the accident may be helpful when comparing the initial injury with the subsequent care.

Reference Laboratories

Occasionally, a biological specimen is sent to an outside laboratory for testing with the result sent back to the hospital after the patient is discharged. As a consequence, the results may not be contained in the chart. Therefore, it is important to obtain copies of reference lab results and check for any follow-up visits to the primary care physician as many Health Maintenance Organizations (HMOs) and other insurances require a visit to the primary care provider after any hospitalization. Late lab results and final lab and radiology reports may also be found in the physician records.

Pharmaceutical Records

All pharmacies have computerized drug utilization records for every individual to whom they sell pharmaceuticals. These records, which can be generated in chronological order, are invaluable when a drug utilization history is an essential part of a case, such as in a pharmaceutical product liability case or when there are allegations that the plaintiff had drug-seeking behavior. These records can also be used to demonstrate patient noncompliance when prescriptions are either not filled or sporadically filled. Mail order pharmacies are also able to provide this type of patient information. Even if there are no pharmaceutical issues in the case, pharmacy records can be used to identify treating physicians.

Many hospitals have outpatient pharmacies for their clinic patients or patients being discharged. Their records are not usually considered a part of the hospital medical record and therefore must be requested separately, just as though they were an outside drugstore. Their records should be requested for a specific individual, to avoid the concern of patient confidentiality being breached, for information on other patients that might be included in such a document. If the records cannot be produced in that format, understandably the hospital or institution may insist that the names of other patients be redacted. Unfortunately, the LNC may end up being the most likely person to redact that record. Therefore, to avoid this problem the LNC should always request patient-specific data instead of a database that spans a period of time for all patients served by a pharmacy.

Facility Pharmaceutical Records

Facility pharmacies are required by law to keep records of controlled substances. In cases where there is a dispute over the amounts of narcotics administered, copies of the records reflecting distribution of a controlled substance should be kept by hospital pharmacies. The pharmacy retains a listing, or log, of all medications that are sent to a specific unit, floor, or speciality area such as radiology, cardiology, or gastrointestinal (GI) laboratories in their "floor stock." The pharmacy will keep logs of all drugs stored and used on a crash cart. Some hospitals keep these narcotics in a locked cart.

Other hospitals have a computerized dispensing system for ordered medications. In such a system, each registered nurse (RN) has a code to enter when removing narcotics. With this system, a computer log can be generated with the time and person who removed the drug and often with the provision for a witness RN to verify the "wasting" of a drug when that occurs. In addition to the computerized logs, the hospital can produce a billing list specific for the dispensing system. This system not only lists the medication but also the dose, name of nurse removing the drug, the date and time of dispensing, and the cost of each dispensed medication.

Records of HIV Testing

The physician's order for an HIV test and the result of the testing itself are confidential and cannot be obtained without a standard medical release (see Chapter 7).

Neonatal Transfer Reports

When testing procedures are performed on a critical newborn, the test results are frequently not available at the time of the transfer to a tertiary-care center. A second request for production of medical records may be necessary in order to obtain a complete record from the originating hospital/health care facility.

Specialty Testing

Specialty testing that may not be contained within the normal medical records includes psychiatric and neuropsychology testing, audiology testing, and speech and language testing. The reports and testing results should be requested from the individual departments. When requesting psychiatric and neuropsychiatric evaluations, the LNC will want to obtain not only the summary report, but will also want the actual test booklets for review and comparison.

Operating Room Logs and Medical Equipment or Devices

Operating room logs will contain vital information such as the type of operations that were occurring simultaneously or availability of staff such as the number of anesthesiologists overseeing the procedures. These logs may also contain information critical to product liability cases regarding the presence of a sales representative from a medical supplier or pharmaceutical company who was present at the time of the procedure.

Biomedical Equipment Identification and Maintenance Records

In cases that involve medical equipment, hospital records often identify the equipment involved. Hospitals maintain equipment information, such as the model number, serial number, and the manufacturer's name, address, and phone number. Equipment-repair log sheets or maintenance records may reflect that a specific piece of equipment had a history of problems. These records are usually maintained by the biomedical or engineering department. When cases involve a potentially defective equipment, this information should be obtained without fail.

Medical Records Dictation Logs

Most hospital medical records departments have a telephone dictation system or outside dictation service. In these systems, the time and date of the dictation are automatically recorded. If the dictation is not recorded on a telephone system but instead is recorded with tapes that are dropped off in the transcription department, these tapes are usually logged in with the date and time they were received. If the facility uses an outside agency for their transcription service, usually there will also be a log indicating the date and time the tapes were picked up and returned by the agency(ies). This information along with who transcribed the tapes may end up being invaluable in a medical negligence case. If there is a discrepancy between the injuries documented on an autopsy report and the type and extent of injuries documented on the emergency room physician's report and/or discharge summary, the log in the medical record department can confirm when and by whom the dictation took place.

Other Types of Medical Records

Visiting Nurse or Home Care

Home health care has expanded rapidly in the wake of managed care as has the sophistication of their medical records. Home-care records encompass treatment plans, patient assessments, care, and care outcomes. As such, these records should not be overlooked.

When requesting these records, it is important to obtain not only the daily nursing records but to also obtain all telephone and facsimile physician orders as well as any other message or communication logs that reveal communication between the various caregivers. The home-care records will have laboratory or radiology reports that were ordered by the physician although the tests and results may have been conducted at a local hospital or other outpatient facility. The LNC can identify the providers so these records and bills can be obtained. The home-care agency may provide durable medical equipment, oxygen services, and IV services as well as contracts with other providers. The use of any of these other outside providers should be noted in the home health care records.

Mental Health or Substance Abuse

Because of the confidential nature of records pertaining to mental health or substance abuse, these records usually require specialized consent forms. In most cases, legal counsel will have to prove that the records are essential to the case before a judge will order release of such records.

Nursing Home Records

As part of the Omnibus Budget Reconciliation Act (OBRA) of 1987 (Health Care Financing Department of Health and Human Services 1987), Congress passed the Nursing Home Quality Reform Act requiring substantial changes in nursing-home care with more vigorous and more punitive regulatory enforcement (Sartwelle, 1994). As a result of OBRA, awareness of negligence in nursing homes is increasing. Nursing home records should be obtained and inspected carefully for noncompliance with OBRA and for other general negligence issues. More information on this subject is found in Chapter 17.

Outpatient Therapy or Rehabilitation Records

The LNC should not overlook physical, occupational, and speech therapy records in either the plaintiff or defense of medical malpractice, personal injury, or workers' compensation cases. They may include statements by the plaintiff or observations by the therapists that would not appear in the physician's records and could be damaging to or supportive of the plaintiff's case. The therapist's observations are usually detailed, precise, and legible. The therapists themselves can be excellent witnesses when deposed and at trial.

In medical negligence cases involving inpatient admissions, the therapist's assessments of a patient's behavior and clinical well-being can be compared and contrasted effectively with the nurse's and physician's observations of the patient during the same period. Comparing records from different disciplines often provides clues about what may have gone wrong.

Computerized Medical Records

Increasingly, health care facilities are moving toward greater use of computerized medical records. Most hospitals have computerized laboratory, pharmacy, radiology, electrocardiogram (EKG), and electroencephalogram (EEG) reporting as well as computerized invasive monitoring in the ICU and electronic fetal monitoring in the obstetrical unit. Computerized medication records are being used more frequently because they diminish the possibility of medication transcription and administration error. In many areas of the country, operating rooms are experimenting with computerized anesthetic records.

Computerized nurses' notes and physician order transcriptions are often voluminous when they are printed. The LNC may find computerized information difficult to access and occasionally, understand. However, with a computerized record the LNC is much more likely to be able to determine exactly when a physician ordered medications or tests and when the orders were transcribed compared with many standard physician's order sheets.

The Law and Computerized Medical Record Systems

Laws that are relevant to electronic communication include the Electronic Communications Privacy Act (ECPA) of 1986 (ECPA 1986). This act established the provisions for the access, use, disclosure, interception, and privacy protections of wire and electronic communications. The U.S. Code defines "electronic communications" as "any transfer of signs, signals, writing, images, sounds, data, or intelligence of any nature transmitted in whole or in part by a wire, radio, electromagnetic, photo electronic or photo optical system that affects interstate or foreign commerce." ECPA prohibits unlawful access and certain disclosures of communication contents. The law also prevents government entities from requiring disclosure of electronic communications from a provider without proper procedure.

The proposed Medical Privacy Regulations drafted by the Department of Health and Human Services (HHS) may also have an impact on medical record privacy. These regulations, which are the first federal protections for medical information, apply to both paper and electronic health records. Congress recognized the need for national patient record privacy standards in 1996 when it enacted the Health Insurance Portability and Accountability Act (HIPAA) of 1996 (HIPAA, 1996). HIPAA included provisions designed to save money for health care businesses by encouraging electronic transactions, and it also required new safeguards to protect the security and confidentiality of that information. The law gave Congress until August 21, 1999, to pass comprehensive health privacy legislation. When Congress did not enact such legislation after three years, the law required HHS to craft such protections by regulation.

Under the final rule, patients have significant rights to understand and control how their health information is used:

- Providers and health plans will be required to give patients a clear written explanation of how the covered entity may use and disclose their health information.
- Patients are able to see and get copies of their records and request amendments. A history of nonroutine disclosures must be made accessible to patients.
- Health care providers who see patients are required to obtain patient consent before sharing their information for treatment, payment, and health care operations. In addition, separate patient authorization must be obtained for nonroutine disclosures and most nonhealth care purposes. Patients have the right to request restrictions on the uses and disclosures of their information.
- People have the right to file a formal complaint with a covered provider or health plan, or with HHS, about violations of the provisions of this rule or the policies and procedures of the covered entity.

With few exceptions, such as certain appropriate law enforcement needs, an individual's health information may be used only for health purposes. Health information covered by the rule generally may not be used for purposes not related to health care—such as disclosures to employers or financial institutions—without explicit authorization from the individual.

In general, information disclosures are limited to the minimum amount necessary to meet the purpose of the disclosure. However, this provision does not apply to the disclosure of medical records for treatment purposes because physicians, specialists, and other providers need access to the full record to provide quality care.

Incomplete Medical Records

The usual reason for receiving what appears to be an incomplete medical record from a hospital or other health care facility is that the page or pages in question are not in the expected chronological or sequential order in the chart. Therefore, it is important to organize the medical records properly before further action is taken. It is usually safe to assume that the medical record department is not deliberately trying to thwart the LNC's efforts to get a complete record.

Often an LNC finds the critical "missing" consultation in the middle of the physician's progress notes or some other unlikely place. Sometimes the records are released from the health care facility prior to completion by the attending physicians or before final laboratory compilations have been forwarded to the medical records department. This may happen when records are requested soon after the discharge or death of a patient.

Sometimes, records are missing as the result of an error by the copy technician. Often a letter to the medical records administrator outlining the exact missing records will be all that it takes to procure them. If the hospital denies the existence of portions of the record that, in the LNC's opinion, should exist, the medical record administrator should be asked to document, in writing, that those portions of the record are absent and do not exist.

In some circumstances, the LNC may be permitted to view the original record to look for missing pages and forms. This action requires approval of the attorney who retained the LNC, and a written request to the hospital that permits the LNC, on behalf of the attorney, to review the record. It is not unusual for the LNC to be observed by the risk manager or medical records department personnel to ensure that no documents are removed from the file.

When dealing with a health care practitioner's office, the LNC may find that the custodian of the medical records is often not a trained medical records administrator. Accordingly, records may be missing because the person responding to the medical record request did not understand the specifics of the request. When dealing with a healthcare practitioner's office, the prudent LNC will specifically delineate all portions of the medical record encompassed by the request.

A typical physician's office record consists of handwritten or dictated notes of each visit; correspondence; diagnostic test results; copies of hospital records; copies of consultations or referrals by other physicians; billing records; records of phone calls; insurance forms; copies of prescriptions for drugs, therapy, appliances, or equipment; and return-to-work or work-restriction forms. The LNC should specifically request all handwritten and typewritten notes, memos, billing records, and telephone conference notes. Most health care providers will not send copies of records received from other treating physicians unless specifically asked; some states have laws that prevent this under all circumstances. Once the records are received, the LNC should make certain that the handwritten database or medical history form that the patient filled out on the first visit has been included.

The LNC should be aware whether the law of the state in which the case is being litigated permits an adverse inference to be drawn against a person or facility that is unable to produce a document or study, whether it has been innocuously lost or not, since this may have great impact on the status of a case with incomplete records of any kind (Janulis, 2007).

In all cases of missing records, the LNC should advise the attorney of the specific records that are missing as soon as possible and the reason why collection of those records is essential for thorough case review. Many LNCs working for attorneys in law firms have ongoing authority to request whatever records are necessary. LNCs working independently either advise the attorney concerning which records to obtain or obtain them directly, with a consent form that identifies the LNC as working on behalf of the attorney.

Obviously, it is impossible for the LNC to analyze the medical records thoroughly and accurately if complete medical records are not available. In many cases where there has been a long illness, or in pregnancy/birth trauma cases, it is critical to obtain the medical records from the primary care provider or OB/GYN both before and after the inpatient stay. This may show whether or not there were early signs of the problem that were missed or if the patient was noncompliant with the treatment plan.

Organization of the Medical Records

In order to review medical records in the most complete manner possible, it is essential to organize the records into an easily comprehensible format. LNCs are more qualified to understand the medical records than any other litigation professional. Therefore, it is critical that the LNC supervises the organization of the medical records. Most often this consists of organizing all records into a logical order for ease of review. This organization may differ from case to case and in regard to the use of the record, that is, whether it is going to be used.

Several logical sequences of various types of hospital records are suggested in Appendix B. HMO and physicians' records encompass different types of information from hospital records and require a different organization. A logical sequence for these types of records is also suggested in Appendix B. When organizing physician office records, oftentimes it is important to know what records a particular physician had received from other doctors. Based on this, the LNC may wish to place these records in their own tabbed section that may be labeled "records from outside providers," or "consultations."

Often the records are received in an order that facilitates patient care, but not medical–legal review. A common presentation is to make the physician's orders section one of the first parts of the chart. Although critical in a few cases, the physician's orders are generally not of importance for the majority of medical–legal cases and may be placed farther back in the indexed chart.

There is no one "right" way to organize and sequence medical records. The type of case may suggest the most logical sequence for ease of review or the LNC/attorney may have a specific practice pattern that suits his/her practice style. It is imperative, however, that all persons on the same side of the litigation team have medical records that are indexed in the same manner.

When the LNC has an abundance of medical records that are not critical to the investigation or litigation of a case, for example, long-term nursing care due to brain damage resulting from an anesthesia accident, he/she may want to divide the "excess" records into file folders or notebooks and label them so that the information can be easily retrieved and accessed whenever necessary.

Frequently you may find duplicate forms or pages within the hospital or long-term care facility records. It is suggested that the LNC review each page carefully to make sure that these are actually duplicate pages and do not contain differing information. If the page is indeed a duplicate, then duplicate pages can be collected and retained within their own notebook or divider.

When medical records come double-sided, it is recommended that the records be recopied to single-sided paper and then placed into the proper sequence before they are placed into various notebooks.

Copies of fetal heart-monitoring strips can be difficult to interpret on multiple sheets of paper. The LNC may want to take the extra time to meticulously line up and tape together all the pieces of the fetal heart monitor strips so that the panel numbers correlate chronologically. The same principle applies to ICU flow records when the original encompasses several folding sheets, so that the times for all the data match and can be easily read and interpreted. One technique that works particularly well is to use a colored sheet to divide and label each 24-hour flow sheet. Once the pattern of how the pages are organized is discernible, the LNC can quickly identify which pages are missing. The LNC should spend time doing this only in a case in which the ICU flow sheets are of central importance to the alleged negligence.

Indexing and Paginating Medical Records

Once complete, all medical records should be placed in a loose-leaf binder for ease of review, with subsections of each record tabbed and labeled "Progress Notes," "Medications," and so on. Formulation of an index, such as the one in Appendix C, can be a valuable and time-saving aid. An index identifies the exact nature of the medical record contents, including the dates of treatment and the types of physicians who have treated the patient. Not only is the index helpful to the LNC in his or her continuous dealings with the medical records; it also helps the attorney to obtain a comprehensive assessment of the records at any time during discovery. When medical records are sent to expert witnesses, an index gives a concise record of exactly what information the expert has received and reviewed in order to arrive at his or her opinion. The LNC updates the index as further medical records are collected during the course of case evaluation or litigation. Use of preprinted tabs, purchased from a medical supply company, facilitates the organization of records.

If the medical records are complete and organized, bates stamping will be tremendously helpful in later discovery and trial. Copies of the entire paginated record can be used as invaluable "working copies" during discovery with the advantage of knowing that all the attorneys, experts, and LNCs are referring to exactly the same information. Complete and Bates® Stamped (paginated) records ensure expeditious review of medical records by expert witnesses, which in turn keeps client costs to a minimum. The LNC should not paginate records that are not complete since the numbering system will only cause increased confusion once the remainder of the records are obtained and incorporated.

Alternatively, if paginated medical records arrive from another law firm or a copy service, the records may be stamped a second time with a different type of pagination system that perhaps incorporates letters with the numbers, for example, A001, A002, and so on. Some litigation software products automatically paginate the medical records as the pages are being scanned into the system. When and how to Bates® stamp a medical record continues to be an ongoing challenge in any litigation unless all parties agree to use one, complete Bates® stamped copy of the record.

Paperless Medical Records

As technology continues to advance, the LNC will begin to receive medical records that have been scanned onto a disc instead of receiving boxes and boxes of "hard copy" medical records. As with the paper medical record, organization is of utmost importance prior to having the records scanned into PDF documents. Once the records are organized, there are programs that will paginate or Bates stamp each page of the medical record as it is being scanned in. There are computer programs that are virtual case management systems. These programs provide the ability to upload, store, manage, display, and link scanned medical records. Many record copy businesses are scanning the medical records in color. Color copies will allow the LNC to see different colored ink or read sections that are highlighted and often "greyed or blacked-out" with conventional copying.

Less paper means less storage, and is more friendly to the environment. The LNC no longer needs to lug around those huge notebooks or boxes of medical records. It is easier to read various sections if the writing is very tiny or illegible as the page can be enlarged to over 500 per cent. If it is still difficult to read, the LNC can print that specific enlarged section. PDF files can be tabbed and highlighted and then these pages can be saved as a separate file, thus keeping the "originals" clean and clear. There is a cost benefit to both the plaintiff and defense as the copy and shipping/delivery costs are markedly decreased and, at the end of a case, it is easier and less costly to destroy a computer disk versus shredding multiple boxes of medical records.

Medical records that have been scanned using as a PDF file have the flexibility of performing a word search using PDF editing software. For example, the entire medical record can be searched for the client's weight and every section where the weight is documented will be illustrated. Using the computer to do the word search literally takes seconds to search through pages and pages of progress notes for that one single entry that is significant.

When working with medical records on disc, the LNC may have an initial expense of purchasing a second monitor. These monitors can be set up side by side; one monitor will be used for reading the medical records while the other monitor will be used for the LNC work product. These screens can be "linked" so that when preparing a chronology the LNC can copy from the scanned pages and paste this into the work product, thus decreasing the amount of actual typing. Another way of viewing the PDF records is to use a large-screen monitor and split the screen, thus having the medical records on one side and the work product on the other side of the screen.

Computerized medical record systems can provide record-formatting consistency and the ability to record and store medical information. These systems have audit trails that identify who entered or altered data, and in which field the information was located. The system puts a date and time stamp on each entry, making it easy to identify who entered, altered, removed, or deleted any data within a record. The attorney may wish to order this computer medical record audit log if there are questions pertaining to the documented entries.

A major disadvantage of electronic records relates to the effort it takes to get used to working with records on disk and the differences between a PDF file and a Word file. PDF files condense information, so that when you revert and save it to a Word page the page numbers no longer match up. Therefore, when you reference a page number to someone not using a PDF file, everyone will be confused. The same is true vice-versa from Word to PDF.

There are a wide variety of software systems that will scan and maintain large files for multiple users without having to send individual PDF files to each person. This is especially beneficial when the files contain literally thousands of pages. Services like X-Drive can be used to ensure that all documents are scanned and everyone on the team gets a pass code to log in and view the exact same records.

The point is that the LNC must keep up with the growing trend of electronic records not only from hospital records, but in viewing the records, even handwritten records, electronically. Using the organizational techniques above is an excellent way to focus and keep track of what is essential in a case as well as using the tools built into these systems to find key words, phrases, or even sections of a chart such as pharmacy orders or billing records.

Medical Record Analysis

The AALNC Standards of Legal Nurse Consulting Practice states that once the appropriate data (medical records) has been collected, the LNC must analyze the data and identify the health care issues related to the case or claim (AALNC, 2006a, 2006b). A quick assessment of the medical records should be done during the initial record organization. This assessment can provide an overview of the issues of the case and a mental note of who treated the plaintiff when and where. More important, the overview helps the LNC to determine whether any records are missing.

The LNC may find it helpful in complicated cases to make an outline or chronology of all important events during the review of the medical records. The outline can be used as a guide for a more in-depth and systematic review of the medical records.

Systematic Review of Hospital Medical Records

Face Sheet, DRGs, and ICD-9 codes

The medical record's face sheet provides valuable information about the time that the patient was admitted to the hospital. This can be important in a case involving an alleged delay in an admission. The face sheet may list the date of a previous admission, which alerts the LNC to a potentially missing record. Diagnosis-related groups (DRGs) are the basis for HHS's prospective payment system (contained in the 1983 Social Security Amendments) for reimbursing inpatient hospital costs for Medicare beneficiaries. The key source of information for determining the course of treatment of each patient and the proper DRG assignment is the medical record (Pozgar, 2007). ICD-9 codes are the reimbursement codes for any procedures performed on a patient. Because more and more procedures are added every year, the best source for these codes is an on-line listing of DRG and ICD-9 codes.

The most comprehensive overview of DRGs is St. Anthony's DRG Guidebook (2000) which provides an easy way to reference DRG groupings, relative weights, and mean length of stay statistics. The book can be found in most medical libraries and bookstores. Additional DRG and ICD-9 sources are listed in the references and additional reading sections at the end of this chapter.

Consent Forms

The LNC should be familiar with state statutes regarding the specific informed consent laws for the state in which the case rests. Federal law mandates that the consent be properly witnessed, dated, signed, and timed by the patient and the physician. In addition, the physician is required to have an attestation statement on the consent form. It should also delineate the expected usual, unusual, and rare adverse consequences of the operation or procedure and the risks of nonperformance of the procedure, including the need for, risk of, and alternatives to blood products (TJC, 2007). The alternative treatment options that are available to the patient in the event of nonperformance of the procedure should be listed (TJC, 2007).

The consent form must be completed before the patient is given preoperative medication, which could impair his or her ability to give competent consent (Janulis, 2007). The LNC should check the medication record as to the time sedation or any narcotics were given and the time the consent was signed. The LNC should determine whether the patient or his or her representative agreed to the particular operation or procedure performed and whether any exceptions to that consent were noted.

Discharge Summary and Nursing Instructions

The discharge summary and instructions can be reviewed as an overview of the hospitalization: the dates of the hospitalization, reason for admission, complaints upon admission, course of treatment and significant findings, response to procedures and treatment, any complications that occurred, the status of the patient at discharge, and the instructions, if any, provided to the patient and family (TJC, 2007). The discharge summary can also be used as a barometer against which the effects of any treatments that occurred during the admission can be measured. This is important in terms of damages, because it can indicate whether the patient suffered harm or injuries, to what extent he or she was injured, and how permanent the injuries are.

The LNC should look carefully for details such as when the discharge summary was dictated, since it can have bearing on the subjectivity of the summaries content. The LNC should determine whether there are handwritten additions, deletions, or changes to the original document; when those changes were made; and their relevance to the subject of the lawsuit.

Nursing discharge summaries may provide comprehensive documentation reviewing the entire hospital stay. They may also contain information about patient and family education as well as specific discharge instructions pertaining to activity levels, drain or tube care, dressing changes, medications, and follow-up appointments with physicians or other health care providers. The medications at discharge should include the drug name, dose, route, last dose taken prior to discharge, and the time for the next dose.

Discharge summary and instructions are critical for evaluating these types of cases. The LNC may need to request records from several different departments as they are seldom part of the "hospital" record. The patient usually is admitted to a preop holding area where a nursing assessment and preop checklist is done, consent is obtained, and history and physical by the surgeon, and/or the anesthesiologist is done. Discharge planning is usually initiated, whether the patient is expected to be discharged or admitted. If discharge is expected, any home-care needs are assessed and arrangements started. The patients go to the OR and then to a recovery setting which could be PACU or an outpatient recovery room. The LNC can see that a variety of records need to be obtained and reviewed with attention to all aspects, but especially discharge instructions and the documentation of the patient's score to determine if they were alert enough to understand and ask questions, and what instruction sheets were given.

Emergency Medical Services

The LNC should compare the patient's admission status with the emergency transport records. This may be important in cases in which the patient's condition prior to arrival or resuscitation efforts and response prior to admission are critical elements of the case (Janulis, 2007). The LNC should note how the rescue squad documented the patient's condition at the scene of the accident, whether the patient was dazed or lost consciousness, and look for descriptions of injuries to the vehicle in order to correlate them with the patient's injuries. For example, a squad member may have seen a "star" pattern of broken glass on a windshield resulting from impact with the patient's skull or made comments about the vehicle being "T-boned" (hit broadside) with intrusion of the side of the car into the passenger compartment. This may correlate with injuries to the side of the patient's body. The LNC should look for evidence of dashboard damage if the patient complained of a knee injury from hitting the dashboard and note any documentation of broken seat belts or seats, indicating that great force was exerted against the car. The LNC should note whether the "Jaws of Life" were needed to extract the patient from a crushed car.

Emergency Department

Common problems resulting in litigation in the ER include (1) not treating the patient in a timely manner, (2) failing to accurately diagnose the problem, and (3) prematurely discharging the patient needing further observation and treatment. Knowing this, the LNC should review the time that the patient was triaged, the time seen by the physician, the presenting complaints, and vital signs. Review the assessment and determine whether the appropriate triage classification was made. Determine when the physician initially saw the patient and compare the nurse's assessment of the patient with that of the emergency physician to determine whether the physician ordered the appropriate diagnostic studies and whether the diagnostic studies were performed in a timely manner. Also, note whether there was any evidence that the patient was under the influence of any alcohol or drugs and whether the emergency department health care providers recorded information about alcohol consumption (alcohol on breath [AOB] or ETOH). Look for entries that refer to the use or the nonuse of a seat belt in a motor vehicle accident.

Ascertain whether the patient responded to the treatment rendered. If a patient receives emergency, urgent, or immediate care, and leaves against medical advice, the health care providers are required to make a note of this (TJC, 2007). The LNC should determine whether the patient signed a form to that effect. Some health care facilities consider the records generated in the emergency department as outpatient records, so they may need to be specifically requested.

If a case involves failure to diagnose or premature discharge from the emergency department, the LNC should search for discharge instructions. If a misdiagnosis has been made, the advice and instructions provided on the discharge instruction forms could be critical to evaluating this type of case.

In personal injury, workers' compensation, and criminal cases, the LNC should look for documentation that contains information or declarations by the patient about how the accident or injuries occurred. Note whether the patient described having a loss of consciousness, and correlate this information with the rescue squad record and the history recorded by subsequent treating physician office records. Look for discrepancies between the initial symptoms of the patient as recorded in the emergency room records and subsequent records.

History and Physical Examination

Joint Commission requires through its survey process that a patient's History & Physical (H&P) examination, nursing assessment, and other screening assessments be completed within 24 hr of admission (TJC, 2007). A physician may elect to document his or her H&P examination findings in writing or by dictation. The LNC should determine the date that the typed history was dictated. The information in a history dictated several days after an admission with complications may be suspect. The name of the person dictating the H&P examination may also have significance. If the H&P examination is performed by a nurse practitioner (NP) or a physician's assistant (PA), the LNC should be aware of the state laws and hospital policy pertaining to their documentation.

Unlike an experienced physician, an NP, PA, or resident may not have the knowledge base or the clinical expertise to detect or follow up on subtle test findings. Likewise, a physician covering for a patient's regular physician may not know the patient well enough to be able to evaluate the patient's current situation in the light of a complex medical history.

History

The LNC should look at the patient's chief complaint and history, searching for clues to the present illness. The LNC should evaluate the patient's complaints for validity, for the patient's perception of his or her own illness, and for the prior treatment the patient has received (Janulis, 2007). Sometimes patients give histories that are slightly or radically different during separate admissions. The LNC should compare the histories from all hospitalizations and those from physicians' records, checking for consistency. Often an error in a history becomes a self-perpetuating "fact" as each subsequent consulting physician obtains the history information from the chart instead of the patient. The LNC should be aware of this and look carefully for the origin of all information. He or she should look for historical information regarding medications, drug allergies, and illicit drug and/or alcohol use. The history of prior surgeries, prior medical conditions, illnesses, and injuries can be of extreme importance to the presenting problem. Failure of a physician to ask questions necessary to elicit an adequate history may constitute negligence (Janulis, 2007).

Physical Examination

The physical examination should be thorough and appropriate to the patient's presenting chief complaint. It should include a review of every bodily system and is important as much for what it contains as for what is omitted. Examinations that are fragmented or incomplete should be carefully noted by the LNC and reflect upon an inadequate review of the whole person. System reviews that are overlooked can have critical importance to the accurate determination of the patient's underlying condition, and the correctness of medical decisions based on such incomplete information is then suspect.

Provisional/Differential Diagnosis

Since the provisional diagnosis reflects the physician's preliminary opinions, the LNC should look closely at the physician's conclusions to determine if they are appropriate, whether the treatment plan encompasses an appropriate diagnostic workup, and whether the workup is specific to the diagnoses made.

Operative Records

Operative records consist of numerous types of documentation, including consent forms; preoperative and intra-operative nursing records; preoperative, intraoperative, and postoperative anesthesia records; surgical notes; pathology reports; and post anesthesia care unit records.

Preoperative Nursing Records

Preoperative nursing records are important in determining whether the appropriate preoperative preparation of the patient took place. Documentation of the patient's vital signs, preoperative testing, last food or drink, and signing of the consent form may have important implications for a case.

Perioperative Nursing Records

Nursing notes can be invaluable in documenting exactly who participated in a surgical procedure and the times that those persons were in the operating room, as well as when the procedure began and ended. The LNC should look for information regarding the skin preparation, the type of pre-operative or intraoperative positioning of the patient, and the location of the electrosurgical ground pad. The nurse's operative record will contain specifics regarding any devices implanted during the procedure and, often, specialized types of equipment used by the surgeon. The notes will also include information not found elsewhere regarding drains, sponges, surgical packing, and catheters. Often the nursing portion of the operative record will include clues to what happened during the operative procedure that will not be contained in the anesthesia charting or the surgeon's operative note. The presence of any sales representative should be noted on the perioperative nursing records.

Anesthesia Preoperative Assessment

The anesthesia preoperative workup should be complete and include a history of the patient's response to previous anesthetics, potential problems involving the airway, and current medical illnesses and medications. An assessment of the degree of the patient's illness and his or her risk for anesthetic complications is determined by utilizing the Physical Status Classification System of the American Society of Anesthesiologists (ASA) (ASA, 2001). This assessment process assigns a category based on the ASA scale of P1 (Class 1), which indicates "a normally healthy patient," through P6 (Class 6), the category used to define "a declared brain-dead patient whose organs are being removed for donor purposes." The ASA classification can be used as a barometer to judge whether the appropriate intensity of intraoperative monitoring of the patient occurred. For example, a Class III patient with diabetic neuropathy and cardiovascular disease should have more intense monitoring than a Class I patient with no systemic disease.

At the conclusion of the preoperative workup, the anesthesiologist should draft an operative plan for the patient that reflects the preoperative medication, the type of induction, and the type of anesthesia to be administered. When complications occur intraoperatively, the LNC may want to review the preoperative assessment forms to determine if the preoperative workup was planned by the same person who administered the anesthesia during the operative procedure.

Anesthesia Records

The LNC should ascertain whether an anesthesiologist, a nurse anesthetist, or a PA (often titled anesthesiologist assistant) trained in anesthesia delivered the anesthetic agents as well as find out who monitored the patient. Often the induction is performed by an anesthetist with an anesthesiologist present, but the anesthesiologist subsequently leaves the OR suite to oversee another anesthetist. It is important to ascertain who actually administered the anesthesia.

Depending on the degree of legibility, the actual anesthesia graphic charting and narrative records may be difficult to comprehend. In cases involving intraoperative events, the LNC should look at the types of inhalation agents (gases) and drugs used for induction, the time of intubation, whether there was any difficulty with the intubation, the number of times it took to intubate the patient, and the patient's vital signs in response to these events. Patient positioning can also have significance in cases involving intraoperative complications or postoperative findings such as neuropathies. Events will often be numbered on the graphic record and correspond to the narrative record. The LNC should determine the type of intraoperative monitoring used. An end tidal CO_2 monitor and an oxygen saturation monitor are essential, as recommended by the ASA (ASA, 2001). The LNC should look closely at the patient's vital signs and the anesthetist's response to changes in them. It is important to determine whether the patient's condition is due to the effect of the anesthesia or the surgery being performed. The LNC should note the length of time that the patient was under anesthetic care and the time it took to perform the operation. These times should be compared with those on the intraoperative nurse's notes.

When a case involves respiratory complications that occur at the end of the surgical procedure, the LNC may look to the anesthesia record for information pertaining to which anesthetic agents were administered. Some anesthetic agents are fast acting and dissipate quickly and some anesthetic agents require the administration of reversal medications. The LNC should be aware of the fact that some gases are retained in fatty tissue and therefore obese patients may have respiratory problems and difficulty in waking up. This in turn should lead the LNC to review what anesthesia agents should be used and what should not, on an obese patient. Any unusual occurrence in the operating room should be noted on the anesthesia record as their occurrence may have an impact on the patient's condition. (For further information, see Volume 2, Chapter 21.)

Operative Reports

The surgeon is required by the Joint Commission to dictate or write the operative report immediately after surgery, recording the name of the primary surgeon and assistants, findings, technical procedures used, specimens removed, and postoperative diagnosis. If the operative report is not placed in the medical record immediately after surgery, a progress note should be entered immediately (TJC, 2007).

The preoperative diagnosis is sometimes contained in the operative report. In cases where the necessity of the operation is in question, the LNC should compare all the preoperative diagnoses, the operative findings, and the postoperative diagnosis with the H&P examination and the discharge summary for consistency. The LNC should be alert for operative reports that are brief and nonspecific, especially in commonly performed surgeries such as hysterectomies. He or she should note the date on which the operative report was dictated and look for a delay in dictation in cases that involve unrecognized surgical complications.

A good operative report also contains information about the types and locations of drains placed, estimated blood loss, detailed operative findings, and complications encountered during the procedure. The LNC should determine the names of any surgical assistants and types of specialized equipment used by the surgeon. He or she should pay close attention to the manner in which foreign bodies, such as hip and knee replacements, are described as being inserted, noting if the surgeon encountered any unusual bleeding that is not accounted for or if distorted or "difficult" anatomy is mentioned. This is especially important in cases where structures have been encroached upon improperly.

Surgical Pathology

In cases where biopsies are obtained, the LNC should look at the frozen section diagnosis and compare it with the surgery performed, the follow-up treatment, and the final pathology diagnosis. Sometimes the frozen section diagnosis differs from the final pathology diagnosis. Obviously, there are serious implications if a misreading of the frozen section results in unnecessary removal of tissue or body parts. If surgery was done to remove cancer, the LNC should note that the specimens removed have margins clear of tumor and note the size of each specimen removed. The LNC should determine whether the pathological diagnosis is consistent with the surgical diagnosis and the reason the surgery was being performed in the first place. It is important to be familiar with the standard of care in such situations. The LNC should consider the importance of adequate specimens for laboratory examinations.

Postanesthesia Recovery

Postanesthesia recovery records are of vital importance in cases involving immediate postoperative complications that are usually respiratory or cardiac in nature. The LNC should look for trends in vital signs, mental and neurological status, and the timeliness of the nursing staff's response to those changes.

Postoperative Anesthesia

The anesthesia staff, either an anesthesiologist or a nurse anesthetist, will see the patient post-operatively, usually on the day after surgery, and note the patient's response to the anesthetic delivered. In the case of epidural anesthesia, the anesthesiologist or nurse anesthetist will see the patient at least once daily and be available to respond to any complications with the epidural until the catheter has been removed and a determination has been made that the patient has not sustained any complications. In cases in which the patient received postoperative anesthesia, the LNC should review the progress notes of the anesthesia staff and the flowcharts corresponding to the anesthesia in question. The anesthesiologist is usually involved in monitoring the status of a patient on a PCA analgesia pump. Some larger facilities may use an anesthesia pain service for this purpose. If the PCA pump is used in a peripheral IV and not in the epidural, the RN and physician will monitor the pump as it is commonly used in services such as orthopedic surgery with hip and knee replacements.

Consultations

The LNC should determine whether the appropriate medical specialty consultations were ordered in a timely manner by looking at the date that the consultant was asked to see the patient and the consultant's response. Routine inpatient consultations with specialists such as with cardiologists have 24 hours for response unless the consultant is called or paged urgently for a life-threatening problem.

The consultant should review and consider all the pertinent patient history before coming to his/her conclusions. After the consultant has recommended a treatment plan, the consultant should then follow the patient as a team member with the attending physician and any other case specialists. If the attending physician is a family practice physician, the consultant may become the physician in charge of the patient's care while the acute condition is being resolved. The LNC should review the time relationships among consultants' examinations, the reports of diagnostic testing, and the entries on the order sheets.

Pay close attention to the number of consultants being used in complicated medical and surgical cases. Check to see whether the attending physician was coordinating the care among all the specialists, especially if any of the specialists appeared to have treatment regimens that might have been contraindicated by another. Determine whether each physician was looking at the patient as a whole or whether each was focused only on their specialty. Failing to put the entire clinical picture together in a complicated case can result in disastrous consequences for the patient.

If complications arose, the LNC may need to evaluate the timing and type of recommendations implemented to determine if the optimum treatment plan was instituted or errors were made. The timeliness of changes in the treatment plan may also need to be reviewed in order to determine if there were any unnecessary delays in appropriate care being provided to the patient.

Consult the hospital medical staff bylaws to determine whether they govern how the responsibility for total patient care is to be shared or transferred between primary physicians and consultants.

Physician Progress Notes

Progress notes should contain reference to the patient's test results and response to treatment and therapy, and should document objective and subjective signs and symptoms (Janulis, 2007). The LNC should look at how often the physician charted. The standard of care is every 24 hr; however, lack of an entry in the progress notes does not necessarily mean that the patient was not seen. When there is no daily note written, the LNC should check the physician's orders, the nurses' notes, and the notes of other health care providers for clues that the physician actually did examine the patient on a particular day.

The LNC should determine whether the physician's notes acknowledge other physicians' and health care providers' findings as well as the patient's complaint; the LNC should check the narrative parts of the medical record, looking at the time (if written) and date of all notes, for logical sequencing and progression; look for notes that may not have been written contemporaneously; and note if the entry ends abruptly or looks as if it was continued on the next page to detect potentially missing records. The LNC should determine whether each page, has the patient's hospital stamp plate on the corner and whether notes were written with lines drawn through the blank portion of the page so that no one else would write on that particular page. The LNC should analyze all notes written immediately after an incident, such as an unexpected cardiac arrest, with close scrutiny.

Radiology Reports

As with laboratory reports, the LNC should compare the date and times x-rays were ordered with the time the actual study was obtained. Many health care facilities do not list this on the radiology report, but the LNC may be able to piece the information together by looking at the remainder of the record, especially the nursing notes or at a preliminary report or note written by the physician or radiology department. If the dictated x-ray report does not specify the time the procedure was performed, the logs maintained within the radiology department may clarify the exact time the procedure was performed. He/she should find out whether relevant clinical information was provided with the request, as is required for x-ray and clinical interpretation (TJC, 2007).

They may also contain a preliminary or "quick read" report that may differ from the final radiologist's interpretation. Frequently, radiographic final reports only indicate the date in which the procedure was performed and not the time. Timing can be crucial in some medical negligence cases. Radiology logs will contain the date performed, preliminary and final read dates and time, date the report was dictated, and the date the report was transcribed.

The LNC should compare successive radiology reports looking for differences in the findings. Are there reports of air in the abdomen in a postoperative patient? Are accumulations of fluid noted? Does the report comply with the American College of Radiology (ACR) Standard for Communication: Diagnostic Radiology? (ACR, 2007) These standards define the minimum items needed for a diagnostic radiology report and the type of written communication and oral communication required from the ordering physician as a result of an urgent finding on such a diagnostic examination. If the technique of the radiology examination is in question, such as in diagnostic mammography, the LNC should compare the examination with that recommended by the ACR Standard for Diagnostic Mammography (ACR, 2007).

Laboratory Records

The LNC should determine whether the appropriate laboratory tests were done and reported in a timely manner. In cases where laboratory results are of importance, the LNC should ascertain whether or not all the laboratory results are in the chart. A final computerized summary of all the laboratory results gives the best assurance that this is so. The LNC should determine the time that the laboratory tests were ordered, the time the samples were obtained, and the time that the results were available. He or she should correlate the physician's progress notes and orders regarding specialized tests sent to outside laboratories and make sure that those results are on the chart.

In cases involving extremes in laboratory values, such as hyperkalemia and hypoxemia, the LNC should look for "critical" or "panic" values in the laboratory results and the documentation as to who was called regarding those values (usually the nursing staff) and the response to those critical values. The Joint Commission now requires physician notification of critical test values within a designated time period as outlined in the organizational policies. Various health care facilities use different normal parameters for various laboratory tests, but the results are always calibrated to that normal range.

The LNC should observe for trends in laboratory results such as reviewing the hemoglobin and hematocrit levels in a postoperative case or trending the platelet count in a case with heparin or suspected heparin-induced thrombocytopenia. If the LNC is doing this, then the clinical nurse caring for the patient should also have been doing so. In cases involving unrecognized infections, the LNC should ascertain the specifics of the white blood cell count and the differential. Cardiac enzymes should be monitored for result times and trends in cases involving failure to diagnose myocardial infarction and close attention should be paid to the arterial blood gas results in cases where there are progressive respiratory difficulties or respiratory arrest. These and many other reviews should be performed by the clinician as well as by the LNC when evaluating the care that was provided.

Transfusion Records

In cases involving transfusion reactions, the LNC should note the patient's and donor's ABO and Rh blood type, cross-matching tests, and antibody screening. The LNC should establish the events surrounding the blood transfusion, including the time the blood product was started and stopped, the amount given, and the documentation of the transfusion reaction. The LNC should review the transfusion records to determine if there are the signatures of the two nurses responsible for checking the blood, patient, and the time that the transfusion was started and completed. The LNC may wish to review the blood bank's log to determine exactly who picked up the units and at what time, when the record does not include this information. Complete typing and cross-matching may not have been done due to the acute need for blood transfusion; however, technical errors account for most transfusion accidents in nonemergency situations. Improper patient and donor identification remains the leading cause of transfusion errors (Janulis, 2007).

Physician's Orders

Physician's orders often provide invaluable clues about communication between the physician and the nurses caring for a patient and the care being rendered. For example, there may be a telephone order for pain medication in the order section of the chart but no mention anywhere else of a communication between the physician and the nurse. It is sometimes important to distinguish between orders written directly by a physician, verbal orders, and telephone orders in order to establish the whereabouts of a physician at a certain time. Additionally, the time that orders were written and the time that the orders were removed and countersigned by the nurse should be noted carefully, as well as whether or not the orders were transcribed correctly. The LNC should see whether the resident's or intern's orders were countersigned by the attending physician and pay particular attention to how orders were written in a case involving a medication error. The LNC should examine the record for orders such as "notify me of …," and determine whether the nurses followed through.

The physician's orders, when appropriate, must be carried out. Failure to do so can mean a deviation in the standard of care obtained, with only rare exceptions. Standing orders mandate certain actions when specific situations arise, for example, "O_2 2 liters/by nasal cannula for O_2 saturation <93%." Did the health care providers follow these orders? The LNC should check the physician's orders for items such as the frequency of vital signs, the patient's prescribed activity level, and other types of required monitoring. Often these are the basis for judging nursing actions in negligence cases. (Did the nursing staff monitor the patient with sufficient frequency as contemplated by the physician? For example, did the patient fall while going to the bathroom when he was supposed to be on bed rest?)

Medication Records

Medication records give the LNC a complete picture of the types of medications being given to the patient and when they were given. Joint Commission requires medication effects on the patient be continually monitored (TJC, 2007). The LNC should look for evidence of the patient's reactions to medications and the nursing response to those reactions. A delay between the writing of a drug order and the administration of the first dosage can be very important to a case. The patient's medication allergies should be prominently noted. With computerization of medication records, the pharmacy staff will enter allergies in the computer and the computer will alert the pharmacist if a drug is ordered that has cross-sensitivity with a drug that the patient is allergic to, such as antibiotics. This important safety feature may be negated when one-time medications, such as narcotics, are ordered; for example, administering Tylenol® #3 even when the patient is allergic to codeine because the nurse has access to this drug without going through the pharmacy.

"PRN" medications are of great importance to the LNC because they occasionally will not be mentioned in the nursing documentation. The LNC should compare the medications given and the doses of those medications with the physician's orders for discrepancies. He or she should note whether the site of administration of injection was recorded. This is important in nursing malpractice cases involving allegations of injuries due to injections.

Pharmacy bills can be helpful when the plaintiff alleges that a drug was not given, or given and not documented. Other sources of information for checking on the administration of narcotics include the pharmacy narcotic control slips, the pharmacy central narcotic record, and the pharmacy charge slips (TJC, 2007).

Graphics and Flow Sheets

Graphics and flow sheets, such as neurological check sheets, diabetic tests and pain assessments are all important in cases in which patient trends are not recognized and no follow-up action taken. The intake and output sheets may show a progressive positive fluid balance with diminishing urinary output in a patient who has congestive heart failure (CHF). Intake and output sheets may be of critical importance in cases involving infants and geriatric patients who are easily subject to dehydration.

The vital signs on the graphics sheets may be used as additional evidence to support the plaintiff's contention that shock was developing and was not recognized in a timely manner. Graphics and flow sheets may be of critical importance to the plaintiff, especially when the information required on the graphics and flow sheets has not been completely documented.

Nurses' Notes

As LNCs know, the nurses' notes are often the most valuable portion of the medical record, substantiating or contradicting evidence found elsewhere in the patient's hospital chart. Nursing care occurs 24 hr every day, 365 days a year. The nurse is the person who is at the bedside, and should be closest to the patient's condition every moment they are in the hospital. His/her notes should contain the detailed information that forms the foundation of this knowledge. As such, they are extensive, often repetitive, but of critical importance when the patient's condition deteriorates.

Admission History and Physical

The nursing admission assessment, while not a complete medical history and physical, does assess important considerations for nursing care during the patient's hospitalization. The LNC can determine the patient's physical limitations and functional status assessment when warranted by the patient's needs or conditions (TJC, 2007), mental status, understanding of his or her situation, special feeding problems, and allergies. Often, the admitting nurse will have ascertained and documented the most complete list of current medications. The LNC should compare the information in the physician's history with that written by the nurses for differences or contradictions that may have an impact on the case.

Nursing Care Plan

The nursing care plan is the basis for administering care to the patient and should be appropriate for the types of problems the patient is experiencing. The nursing care plan can be used in the legal setting as a barometer of the nurses' understanding of the type of care to be rendered to the patient and a standard by which that care is to be measured.

Ongoing Documentation

The LNC knows that the nursing notes represent an ongoing account of patient complaints, signs, and symptoms and the nursing responses to these matters. A determination of the status of the patient before and after diagnostic and surgical procedures can be made, as well as the patient's response to blood products, IVs, and medications. This documentation can be of utmost importance in some medical–legal cases. The nurses' notes may be the definitive clue to the timing of certain events, such as physician visits and adverse reactions, patient injuries, or respiratory or cardiac arrest.

The LNC should look specifically to see whether the nurses have followed through with their plan for nursing care of the patient and used appropriate judgment in complying with the standing orders. The LNC should look for trends in vital signs, wound problems, pain, and other patient complaints. (Did the nurses assess the patient adequately, and was the physician notified of adverse conditions and circumstances in a timely manner?) The nurses' notes may be invaluable for what they do not include as much as for what they do include.

Dietary Records

The LNC should examine dietary records to check ideal body weight recommendations versus the documented actual body weight, and check monitoring of albumin levels in a patient who develops pressure ulcers. Dietary records play a crucial role for patients with actual skin breakdown or any wounds upon admission to the hospital. Patients at high risk for skin breakdown can be targeted by a multidisciplinary approach to ensure an effective skin breakdown prevention care plan. The LNC can check for referral to dietary and the wound clinician upon admission, during the stay and when changes in condition develop and place the patient at risk for nutritional deficits. The LNC should evaluate whether the physician followed the dietician's recommendations concerning tube-feeding solutions, rate of administration, and so on.

Physical Therapy, Occupational Therapy, and Speech and Language Therapy Records

The LNC should examine physical therapy records to see whether the physical therapy staff is documenting the amount of assistance needed by the patient, and if this correlates with the nursing notes. LNCs should compare the outcomes and recommendations noted by the occupational therapy documentation with the nursing notes to determine whether they correlate. Speech and language therapy is responsible for providing swallowing evaluations, which are important for patients at risk for aspiration. The LNC should find out whether the health care providers followed these recommendations. The records should have communication between disciplines including physician and nursing when indicated. There was a case involving the patient returning to the unit after physical therapy was completed in the department. Upon arrival to the unit, the transporter left the patient, who was 1 day postknee replacement, in the bathroom unattended by any unit staff. The patient fell, with significant injury to her surgical limb. The records noted orthostatic blood pressure changes in the physical therapy department, but this information was not communicated to the nursing unit. The therapy departments have crucial documentation for the case manager to utilize in discharge planning. Collaboration between these parties can ensure appropriate planning.

Discharge Instructions

The Joint Commission requires that hospitals clarify responsibilities of patients and their families regarding the patient's ongoing health care needs and give them the knowledge and skills they need to carry out their responsibilities (TJC, 2007). The LNC should review these instructions for appropriateness when a posthospital complication is in contention, determine whether they are reasonable instructions applicable to the patient's diagnosis and treatment, and identify if the patient complied with the instructions. For liability purposes, many health care facilities now require that the discharge instructions given to a patient by the nursing staff be documented and signed by the patient and the nurse discharging the patient.

Review of Other Medical Records

Physicians' Office Records

Physicians' office records vary greatly from specialty to specialty. An internist who has seen a patient for many years may have extensively documented medical records, whereas an ophthalmologist may keep small index cards full of terms and acronyms unfamiliar to anyone without ophthalmology training. For maximum information to be extracted from these records, they should be placed in chronological order and logically sequenced.

The LNC should begin a review by determining how and why the patient came to see the particular physician. Was there a referral by another physician, and what problems were specifically to be addressed? Did the patient complete a history questionnaire that detailed his/her symptoms or problems? Did the physician complete a reasonable H&P examination that targeted the reported symptoms and/or problems? Were the appropriate diagnostic studies ordered? Did the physician communicate effectively with other health care providers concerning previous treatment regimens or proposed treatment regimens? Were consultations with other specialists obtained in a timely manner and were the recommendations of those specialists followed? The LNC should look for evidence of compliance on the part of the patient with the treatment regimen prescribed and analyze the types of drugs prescribed for the patient as well as the amounts, duration, and possible interactions of those drugs. The LNC can look for evidence of drug-seeking behaviors when the patient sees multiple physicians in the office setting. The attorney needs to be aware of all aspects and issues of the person's physical health and social habits.

Many clues regarding the patient's lifestyle, not evident in hospital records, can often be obtained from physicians' records, for example, drug abuse, psychiatric problems, stressful family situations, and aberrant social behavior such as domestic violence. The LNC should not overlook this type of information because of its potential impact on damages for the plaintiff.

Staff Model HMO Records

Staff-model-managed care records should be reviewed in the same manner as physicians' records, because staff model HMO records usually consist of a primary care physician's care and treatment of a patient with consultations obtained either "in-house" or outside the HMO or health care network. Given the incentive of HMOs to cut costs in health care delivery, the LNC should pay particular attention to the manner in which consultations are managed, that is, whether it appears that a consultation was obtained in a reasonable period of time, whether appropriate diagnostic and health maintenance tests (e.g., mammograms) were ordered, and whether abnormal diagnostic test results were investigated or followed. Since some HMOs require that their providers limit the types of treatment for certain diagnoses, the LNC should determine whether the plaintiff was given all reasonable options or choices for treatment currently available for the patient's diagnosis. (See Chapter 22 for more information.)

Managed Care Administrative Records

Health care health plans, unlike staff model HMOs, do not provide direct care to the patient, but instead, administer the care given by the enrolled providers in the plan. Nevertheless, administrative records are a great source for determining utilization patterns of care, a complete listing of providers and any grievances or difficulties that were encountered by the health plan in their administration of the care provided to the plaintiff.

Comparison of the Negligence Allegation(s) with the Medical Records

After systematically reviewing the medical records, the LNC should compare the complaints of the plaintiff (before a suit is filed) or the allegations of the lawsuit to determine consistencies and/or discrepancies from the medical records. Many well-meaning but ill-informed plaintiffs have drawn the wrong conclusions from their care and treatment experiences, and the medical records may substantiate this. If the complaint has been filed, the defense LNC should use the medical records to assist in determining the validity of the plaintiff's case. Review of the medical records may indicate that the plaintiff's allegations do not parallel the actual medical negligence that occurred, or that the allegations are not even focused on the proper potential defendant.

The LNC working for either the plaintiff or the defendant also identifies all alternative or potential causation theories and investigates the medical records for substantiation of these theories, in order to determine whether a case should be pursued by the plaintiff or, alternatively, vigorously defended or settled by the defendant.

Rereview of the Medical Records

After the initial review of the medical records and comparison with the allegations, especially in a complicated case, the central issues of the case will become clearer to the LNC. It is often helpful at this point to clarify some issues with the client, such as the timing of a certain symptom or the effect that a surgical complication has had on the client's life. A physician defendant could be asked why certain notes were made, and about their meaning. A preliminary medical literature review may also be helpful in clarifying natural history and pathogenesis of a disease or outlining information necessary to prove causation. In order to conduct a thorough medical record analysis, however, it is often necessary to review the medical records a second time, taking note of specific facts relevant to the case. The LNC should use these specifics to generate a written report as detailed later in this chapter.

Altered Medical Records

The plaintiff can use altered medical records to establish liability based on the defendant's conscious wrongdoing. Juries do not respond favorably to intentional record alteration, and exposing such actions frequently leads to an award of punitive damages. If a plaintiff can successfully show that a defendant is guilty of tampering with the record, the burden of proof in this case may shift to the defendant. The defense counsel may have to settle the case out of court even if no negligence occurred. Once the accuracy of the record is challenged, the integrity of the entire medical record becomes suspect.

Falsification of medical records can be the basis for both criminal indictment and civil liability for damages suffered (Pozgar, 2007). If the plaintiff can prove that the defendant altered the medical records, most insurance companies will strongly negotiate to settle the case.

Numerous types of alterations can be made to medical records. Because of the serious implications associated with altered medical records, the LNC should assess every relevant medical record entry for evidence of tampering or destruction of records as well as missing records. The LNC should be suspicious of any alteration and alert the attorney to the suspected nature and validity of the alterations.

Tampering or altering of the medical record involves any of the following: placing inaccurate information in the record, omitting significant facts, adding to an existing record at a later date without indicating that this addition is a late entry, rewriting or altering the record, omitting significant facts or events, dating an entry to make it appear as if this entry was written at an earlier time, adding someone else's notes, or destroying individual pages of the record or the entire file.

Late Entries

The most common alteration is the late entry. Hospitals usually have policies and procedures for entering later entries into the record. If the case is in litigation, and if a late entry exists, the LNC should obtain a copy of that policy. Ideally, the entry should clearly state the time and date when the late entry was written and the time and date to which the late entry refers. While late entries are not necessarily evidence of tampering, they are frequently self-serving and do not always portray an accurate complete picture of the events. In other circumstances, a late entry may have been made in order to portray a complete and accurate picture of the actual events. It is up to the LNC to determine the validity of the entry based on the context.

Falsified Entries

Falsification of records is rarely done, but when done, it is illegal, and physicians and nurses can be indicted and criminally prosecuted for such activity. Falsified entries include those that are backdated or changed at a later date. Detecting falsified entries demands a high level of attention by the LNC and requires that the entire record be heavily scrutinized for supporting information if the falsified entries are to be proven.

Fabricated Medical Records

Fabrication of medical records can be as damaging as falsifying entries. Fabrication occurs when a physician or other health care provider invents a set of circumstances, usually in retrospect, in order to justify the outcome of some of his or her actions.

Fabrication of the medical records also includes rewriting and replacing notes in the chart. Physicians' office records are the easiest to fabricate. New sheets can be added to the chart or copied over. The dictated notes may be inserted to replace handwritten ones that are then discarded. A whole new chart can be started and the original destroyed. Liquid correction fluid can be used on undesirable content and then the original photocopied. A common fabricated condition in the medical record is that of adhesions. A bowel or bladder perforation will be diagnosed postoperatively and the surgeon will then begin the second operative note discussing the numerous severe adhesions that were present during the first operation (which are not identified in the first operative note) and how the adhesions made the first surgery difficult.

Rewriting and replacing hospital progress notes or other health care provider notes is most commonly seen in catastrophic situations such as cardiac arrests and acute situations in a hospital that lead to a patient's untimely death due to acute and severe unrecognized postoperative surgical bleeding or progressive respiratory problems after anesthesia.

Destroyed Records or Medical Evidence

Each state has statutes or laws that address health care facilities' responsibility to maintain and protect patient records. These statutes impose a clear duty on these institutions not to lose or destroy records or medical evidence, such as radiology films or pathology specimens, within a specific time frame. Usually this time frame corresponds with the individual state's statute of limitations for medical negligence. Destruction of medical records or evidence includes loss and concealment of relevant x-rays, laboratory tests, and other evidence such as pathology slides and operative videotapes. The loss, concealment, or destruction may occur at the time of a potentially legally damaging incident or injury or at some later point when the health care provider anticipates becoming a defendant.

Omissions

Intentionally omitting a true entry or preventing one from being made, while not a written act, does constitute altering a record because the record fails to accurately reflect the care given to, and the response of, the patient. The LNC may note that the medical record conflicts with the client's testimony or memory of events. When reviewing the medical record, there is no documentation of the patient's complaints or symptoms. In reviewing some medical records, the LNC may find that there is no documentation on a specific incident or event when serious injury resulted. If the record is inconsistent with the picture of events, the LNC may wish to attempt to fill in the blanks by requesting incident or occurrence reports if the state allows access to them.

Illegible Entries

Although illegible entries rarely constitute negligence per se, the interpretation of illegible entries may contribute to negligence by others. When the LNC, after her best efforts, cannot read the record due to illegibility, this should be brought to the attention of the attorney. When the information is determined to be critical to the issues under litigation, the attorney may request a written transcription to be provided by the individual involved.

How to Identify Altered/Tampered Records

Identification of altered records requires a high degree of attention and a fair amount of skepticism on the part of the LNC. Recognition of the following findings can be the first step in proving record alteration: Long defensive narrations of facts that do not appear to be in sequence with the remainder of the medical record; pages that are written without the patient's stamp plate in one of the corners; notes that are written with the wrong date or time and may not correlate with the remainder of the chart; and additions to the notes, orders, or dictated summaries that are on the edge of the page. In addition, the LNC may notice laboratory records reflecting tests not done when orders and physician notes reflect that the tests were ordered; overwritten notes on top of a previous entry; a series of separate notes by any health care practitioner, over a long period of time, but are written one after the other; notes with times in sequence in a seemingly homogeneous handwriting pattern, with unusual neatness or consistency in the writing; medical charges for diagnostic or laboratory tests, medications, or equipment not referenced or seen in the chart; fresh condition of a single piece of paper compared to the general state of the medical record; unusual spacing of words or sentences or excessive blank spaces on a page; references to events that occurred after the purported date of the entry; and pathology or diagnostic findings that do not correlate with the H&P or stated need for a surgical or diagnostic procedure.

Minimizing Medical Record Alteration, Loss, or Concealment

When LNCs evaluate cases from a plaintiff's perspective, it is often wise to obtain the critical evidence or copies of the same at the earliest time possible by having the plaintiff obtain a copy of his or her own medical records (as opposed to having an attorney officially write for them).

This may reduce the possibility of alteration, loss, or concealment of potentially important evidence. The evidence should be conveyed in the safest manner possible, such as hand delivery by courier or another method whereby the package can be tracked.

When Tampering or Record Alteration is Suspected

If the LNC suspects medical record alteration or tampering, he or she should recommend that the attorney hire a document examiner. Document examiners use a myriad of techniques that can determine, among many things, whether all writing on a page was made at the same time and whether handwriting and pen inks match. Even when the client has supplied copies of the medical record to the attorney, the attorney will submit a request for the medical record. The client's copies of the records are compared with the attorney's copies to detect any alterations. Some attorneys send a second request for the medical record after the suit has been filed, and the two copies are compared for discrepancies that are due to alterations.

If record tampering is suspected, it will be necessary for the LNC to assist the attorney in developing this theory so that it can effectively be proven within the court. A forensic document examiner will be essential in proving the tampering. A forensic document examiner can be located by contacting the Board of Forensic Document Examiners. This document examiner will examine the physical characteristics of the original documents for authenticity; this examiner will scrutinize the handwriting to establish who wrote the entries, the examiner will examine the inks to determine if one or more ink was used as more than one ink in a single entry can be significant evidence of tampering. The document examiner will review the records to determine if it was written at one sitting or at different times and will look for obliterations or erasures as a means to decipher words that have been eliminated. As health care facilities move further toward complete computerization of medical records, these examination activities will decrease.

Event Chronology

A chronology should refer the reader to the exact location in the medical records of all the information presented. This can be accomplished by referring to the date and type of entry, or by page number of the entry if the records are paginated. An overwhelming amount of information can be simplified into a manageable sequence of events. Chronologies can be extremely useful in outlining a minimum of events to assist an attorney in understanding a sequence of events in a patient's history. Chronologies can be drafted into various formats. Appendix D reflects some different formats.

Alternatively, a chronology can encompass a myriad of details concerning the patient's medical history and treatment, and can be a very useful tool throughout discovery and even in the trial. However, during the course of discovery, additional facts concerning the plaintiff's medical history may become known, or additional theories of liability developed that the original chronology does not address. It is wise to date the chronology and update it from time to time as additional facts become known.

In cases in which the medical records are sketchy on details, yet there is an abundance of deposition testimony reflecting timing (such as in anesthesia-related cases) or dates, the LNC can take a chronology and incorporate only the information gleaned from the medical records into information obtained from the depositions.

Chronologies such as these, if done correctly, prove extremely useful during discovery and at trial in clarifying and delineating sequences of events and actions. The LNC and the attorney, or any other legal professional, should be cautioned not to rely on chronologies in place of the medical record itself, since a chronology is useful only to the extent that it includes all relevant information regarding the plaintiff's medical records.

The LNC may wish to consider adding an additional column to the chronology that will contain information only for the attorney. This column can contain medical illustrations to help educate and orient the attorney, definitions, information gleaned from the family's deposition, or other observations or suggestions such as requesting specific policies and procedures or questions to be presented to the specific caregiver during their deposition. When this chronology is passed on to the expert, this extra commentary column can be deleted, thus leaving the chronology clean and containing only direct excerpts from the medical record.

Charts and Graphs

In some cases, the most effective summary of medical information is a chart or timeline that communicates important facts of the case immediately. A chart or graph may be as simple as an inventory of laboratory results, or it may consist of more complicated graphic representations of certain facts. Figure 12.1 involves a woman with familial hyperlipidemia who was given subcutaneous estrogen pellets after a hysterectomy and oophorectomy. Her physician then gave her a prescription for Estrace to be taken in addition to the estrogen pellets, which the plaintiff alleged to have caused extreme hypertriglyceridemia resulting in severe acute hemorrhagic pancreatitis. Charts like Figure 12.1 can be used to incorporate a modicum of relevant events and actions and illustrate alleged cause and effect on some aspect of the patient's well-being.

Summary of the Medical Records

A short summary or outline of the facts of a case may be all that is necessary or desirable for an attorney, especially in a relatively simple medical malpractice or personal injury case. A plaintiff's attorney who is screening a case to decide whether to pursue it further will most likely want a brief summary that he or she can use to make decisions regarding the next step. The LNC's recommendations regarding the merits of the case should accompany this summary and will be useful to the attorney in the screening process. Personal injury attorneys usually have a large number of less complex cases and need the basics of who, what, when, where, and how from the medical records instead of meticulous physiological and standard-of-care detail. Their interest is the effects of an accident or event on the client compared with the client's pre-existing condition.

A defense attorney may want to use a short narrative type of summary when planning how to approach a case initially or when communicating with the insurance carrier, but will want an extensive timeline or chronology once the case is well in progress. Medical negligence cases usually require more extensive detail because the focus is on medical or nursing judgment and whether or not the professionals involved complied with the standard of care.

Alternatively, the attorney may have a good understanding of the facts of the case but want the LNC's input in determining discrepancies or problem points in the medical record (see Appendix E). In this situation, the LNC may want to provide an objective summary that discusses the facts of the case but adds the LNC's subjective comments, always in parentheses, to assist the attorney in understanding the context of the medical record findings and follow-up recommendations.

HGB HCT Chronology

Feb 14, 2008 1:30 a.m.	Feb 16, 2008 5:45 a.m.	Feb 18, 2008 5:50 a.m.	Feb 19, 2008 12:45 p.m.
HGB 12.2 HCT 35.3	HGB 9.8 HCT 27.6 RBC 2.83	HGB 9.1 HCT 25.7	HGB 3.6 HGB 10.5 RBC 1.06
Source(s): Laboratory report	Source(s): Laboratory report	Source(s): Laboratory report	Source(s): Laboratory report

Feb 14, 2008 8:52 a.m.	Feb 17, 2008 12:05 a.m.
HGB 12.0 HCT 34.7	HGB 9.2 HCT 26.3 RBC 2.69
Source(s): Laboratory report	Source(s): Laboratory report

Feb 15, 2008 12:01 a.m.
HGB 10.6 HCT 30.3 RBC 3.11
Source(s): Laboratory report

Feb 15, 2008 1:15 a.m.
HGB 10.6 HCT 31.6
Source(s): Laboratory report

Feb 14, 2008	Feb 15, 2008	Feb 16, 2008	Feb 17, 2008	Feb 18, 2008	Feb 19, 2008

Figure 12.1 Timeline of a HGB/HCT chronology illustrates a continuous and significant drop in both hemoglobin and hematocrit levels that was not treated in a timely manner with a transfusion.

Attorneys frequently utilize a concise overview of the facts and issues in settlement brochures. Appendix F reflects a sample settlement brochure. See Chapter 16, "Alternative Dispute Resolution: Settlement, Arbitration, and Mediation" for further information.

While there are many different LNC approaches and attorney preferences to medical record summaries, most attorneys want to read an analysis that not only gives a concise overview of the facts and issues, but also helps them to understand the bottom line quickly. With this approach, the LNC can begin with a concluding paragraph followed by substantiation of those facts and opinions. This could include review of the medical records in relation to the issues in contention in the case, as well as the standard of care (in a medical or nursing malpractice case) and the current medical literature on the subject.

Some summaries require total adherence to chronological order to be understandable. In such cases, the date and time of the care provided are of great importance. Other types of cases require that each health care provider's care be summarized chronologically and separately so that the attorney can see exactly what kind of treatment each provider rendered to the plaintiff. Yet another type of summary can be done in cases with multiple injuries or trauma. The records can be very briefly summarized by injury so that the attorney can quickly see the progress of each injury from the acute event through rehabilitation and final outcome. Each health care provider's records are reviewed specifically for the portion that addresses the specific injury or diagnosis.

An in-depth summary of the medical records may be best accomplished in narrative style that puts together all the records from various health care providers in chronological order or summarizes each separately. The most comprehensive approach to a medical record summary is a formulation that not only encompasses the facts of the case as reflected in the various medical records, but also provides an objective analysis of the implications for the attorney and the client and, in a medical malpractice or even a product liability case, an analysis of the standard-of-care issues involved (see Appendix G).

Whenever an LNC provides subjective commentary in any type of medical record summary, he or she should label the summary as "confidential attorney work product specifically requested by (the attorney in question)" to minimize the possibility for discovery in an adverse situation. The LNC should also be knowledgeable about discovery rules and recent court rulings regarding LNC work product in his or her state.

The LNC should write every report keeping in mind that this report may end up in the hands of another attorney, another LNC, or the client. The reality is that many attorneys share the LNC's work product with their clients. The LNC may wish to draft the report with this in mind and to explain how a juror might perceive this particular situation, or how a defense attorney may present this situation.

Conclusion

Medical record analysis is the cornerstone of LNC practice. It is the basis on which the LNC forms an opinion as to whether or not a case has merit. Every state differs as to who can or must sign an affidavit of merit. Many states have passed laws or have case law that now requires a nurse to sign an affidavit of merit, and have different rules as to qualifications to sign. The LNC needs to be aware of the laws of their state in regard to signing an affidavit of merit. The successful and effective LNC approaches the compilation, organization, review, and analysis of medical records with complete objectivity, providing his or her clients with analyses that are thorough and pertinent.

References

American Association of Legal Nurse Consultants. (2006a). *AALNC scope of practice for the legal nurse consultant*. Glenview, IL: American Association of Legal Nurse Consultants.

American Association of Legal Nurse Consultants. (2006b). *AALNC standards of legal nurse consulting practice*. Glenview, IL: American Association of Legal Nurse Consultants.

American College of Radiology. (2007). *Practice guidelines & technical standards*. Reston, VA: American College of Radiology.

American Society of Anesthesiologists. (2001). *Standards, guidelines and statements*. Park Ridge, IL: American Society of Anesthesiologists.

Electronic Communications Privacy Act of 1986, Pub. L. 99-508, October 21, 1986, 100 Stat. 1848, 18 U. S. C. § 25.10.

Health Insurance Portability and Accountability Act of 1996, Pub. L. No. 104–191 (1996).

Janulis, D. M. (2007). Medical records. In D. W. Louisell & H. Williams (Eds.), *Medical malpractice* (35.1–35.100, CD-ROM). New York: Matthew Bender.

Omnibus Budget Reconciliation Act of 1987, P/ L. 100–203, December 22, 1987.

Pozgar, G. D. (2007). Information management and health care records. In G. Pozgar (Ed.), *Legal aspects of health care administration* (10th ed., pp. 255–276). Gaithersburg, MD: Aspen Publishers.

St. Anthony's Hospital DRG guidebook. (2000). Salt Lake City: Ingenix Publishers: St. Anthony's Hospital.

Sartwelle, T. P. (1994, April). *Malpractice in nursing homes*. Syllabus of fifth annual conference of the American Association of Legal Nurse Consultants, Chicago.

The Joint Commission. (2007). *2008 Hospital accreditation standards*. Oakbrook Terrace, IL: Joint Commission Resources Publications.

Additional Reading

Beers, M. H., Berkow, R., & Burs, M. (Eds.) (1999). *Merck manual diagnosis and therapy* (17th ed.). Whitehouse Station: NJ: Merck Publishing Group.

Becker, S. (2000). Medical information and confidentiality. In S. Becker (Ed.), *Becker's Health care law: A practical guide* (8th ed.). New York: Matthew Bender.

Brunicardi, F. C., Anderson, D. K., Billiar, T. R., Dunn, D. L., Hunter, J. G., Matthews, J. B., Pollock, R. E., & Schwartz, S. I. (2004). *Schwartz principles of surgery*, (8th ed.). New York: McGraw-Hill Professional.

Buckner, F. (2001). Medical records and disclosure about patients. In S. Sandy Sanbar (Ed.), *Legal medicine* (5th ed.). St. Louis, MO: Mosby-Year Book.

Canale, S. T., & Campbell, W. C. (Eds.) (2004). *Campbell's operative orthopaedics* (10th ed.). St. Louis, MO: Mosby.

Candilio, G. (1988). The computer-based medical record: Analysis of problems in its implementation in a hospital. *Journal of Clinical Computing, 16*(5–6), 167–73.

Cecil, R. L., Goldman, L., & Bennett, J. C. (Eds.) (1999). *Cecil textbook of medicine* (21st ed.). St. Louis, MO: W. B .Saunders.

Cummingham, F. G, Williams, J. W., Leveno, K. J., Hauth, J. C., Gilstrap, L. C., Bloom, S. L., & Wenstrom, K. D. (2006). *William's obstetrics* (22nd ed.). New York: McGraw-Hill.

Dewitt, R. E., Harton, A. E., W. E., Jr., Keenan, R. M., Ill, & Ellis, M. B. (2001). Patient information and confidentiality. In A. Capron, & I. Birnbaum (Eds.). *Treatise on health care law* (pp. 1–131). New York: Matthew Bender.

DRG Expert, 2009: A comprehensive reference to the DRG classification system (2008). Salt Lake City: Ingenix/ Thompson Delmar Publishers.

Hudson, T. (1992). Medical record analysis can show legal risks. *Hospitals, 66*(22), 46–48.

Kee, J. K. (2001). *Laboratory and diagnostic tests with nursing implications* (6th ed.). Upper Saddle River, NJ: Prentice Hall.

Kliegman, R. M., Behrman, R. E., Jenson, H. B., & Stanton, B. F. (2007). *Nelson's textbook of pediatrics* (18th ed.). Philadelphia: Saunders.

Lewis, S. L., Heitkemper, M. M., Dirksen, S. R., Bucker, L., & O'Brien, P. G. (2007). *Medical–surgical nursing: Assessment & management of clinical problems* (7th ed.). St. Louis, MO: Mosby.

Perry, A. G., & Potter, P. A. (2001). *Clinical nursing skills & techniques* (5th ed.). St. Louis, MO: Mosby.

Roach, W., Jr. (1998). *Medical records and the law* (3rd ed.). Gaithersburg, MD: Aspen Publishers.

Stedman's Abbreviations, Acronyms & Symbols (3rd ed.). (2003). Baltimore, MD: Lippincott Williams & Wilkins.

Websites

American Academy Family Practice Physicians: http://www.aafp.org
American College Cardiology: http://www.acc.org
American College Emergency Physicians: http://acep.org
American College of Obstetricians & Gynecologists: http:// www.acog.org
American Health Information Management Association: http://www.ahima.org
American Institute of Medical Law: http://www.aimlaw.com
Center for Telemedicine Law: http://www.ctel.org
CPT Codes: http://www.ama-assn.org/ama/pub/category/3113.html
Digital Medical Library: http://www.telemedical.com/Telemedical/library.html
Guidelines Clearing House: http://www.guidelines.gov
Medical Malpractice Resource Page: http://www.helpquick.com/medmal.htm
Medscape: http://www.medscape.com
MD Consult: http://www.mdconsult.com

Test Questions

1. Which of the following statements is NOT true?
   A. Upon receiving a request for medical records, the facility copies and sends the entire medical record
   B. Although records of HIV testing are considered confidential, they are routinely contained within the standard medical record release
   C. Upon receiving a request for the release of medical records, the facility routinely sends copies of all typed reports
   D. When maternal and fetal records are ordered, fetal heart monitoring strips require a separate request form

2. Which of the following statements is true?
   A. The LNC should identify the type of medical record analysis necessary that will reflect the most accurate and complete summary of the medical records
   B. A comprehensive chronology of events is necessary in every medical record review
   C. Graphs and charts are always complex representations of the important facts of a case
   D. In-depth summaries are necessary for the medical record review of all cases

3. Which of the following statements is true?
   A. The attorney usually knows the strengths and weaknesses of the case that are evident in the medical record prior to the LNC review
   B. Personal bias is not a concern when LNCs provide medical record analysis
   C. It is important that the LNC have the ability to address the central issue of a case in a quick and decisive manner
   D. It is not necessary to review the entire medical record to obtain a complete overview for accusations, liability, or damages

4. Which of the following statements is NOT true concerning audit trails?
   A. Audit trails help reduce chances of tampering with the medical record as deletions are easily identified
   B. Most computer systems put a date and time stamp on each entry, making it easy to identify who entered information
   C. It is difficult to determine who altered data in a computerized medical record system because the final product will only show who last entered data
   D. Computer medical record systems have the ability to generate audit trails that identify who entered or altered data, and in which field the information was located

5. Tampering implications for the defendant in a medical negligence case includes:
   A. The defendant will probably lose credibility with the jury
   B. There is a strong probability that this case will settle because tampering is a difficult allegation to defend
   C. The defendant physician may lose his right to any insurance coverage if the jury answers "Yes" to the fraud issue
   D. All of the above

Answers: 1. B, 2. A, 3. C, 4. C, 5. D

Appendix A: Certification

I hereby certify that the attached is a true and complete copy of the medical records pertaining to
_____ (patient) kept in the office of _____ (health care practitioner) in my custody and that I am the custodian and keeper of said records.

I further certify that said records were made in the regular course of business of this office and that it was in the regular course of business for such records to be made at the time of events, transactions, or occurrences to which they refer or within a reasonable time thereafter.

Signed this _____ day of _____, 20____.

_____

CUSTODIAN OF MEDICAL RECORDS

Sworn and subscribed to before me on this

the _____ day of _____, 20____.

_____

NOTARY PUBLIC

My commission expires: _____

Appendix B: Sequences of Records

Hospital Records		
Adult	*Pregnancy*	*Baby*
Face sheet	Face sheet	Face sheet
Consents	Consents	Consents
Autopsy	Autopsy	Autopsy
Death summary	Death summary	Death summary
Discharge summary	Discharge summary	Discharge summary
Emergency medical services	Emergency record	Labor summary
History and physical	Prenatal record	Resuscitation record
Consultations	Labor admission H&P	Emergency record
MD progress notes	Labor record	History and physical
Code sheets	Obstetrical anesthesia record	Consultations
Anesthesia reports	Delivery record	Operative reports
Operative reports	Obstetrical operative report	MD progress notes
Radiology	Consultations	Radiology

continued

Adult	Pregnancy	Baby
EEGs	MD progress notes	EEGs
EKGs	Code sheets	EKGs
Laboratory/transfusion	Anesthesia records	Laboratory/transfusion
ABGs	Operative reports	Arterial Blood Gases (ABGs)
MD orders	Radiology	MD orders
Respiratory therapy	EEGs	Respiratory therapy
Physical therapy	EKGs	Physical therapy
Occupational therapy	Laboratory/transfusion	Occupational therapy
Speech therapy	Arterial Blood Gases (ABGs)	Speech therapy
Social worker notes	MD orders	Social worker notes
Dialysis	Respiratory therapy	Graphics
Graphics	Physical therapy	Medications
Medications	Occupational therapy	IV fluids/medications
IV fluids/medications	Speech therapy	Nursing assessment
Nursing assessment	Social worker notes	Nursing care plans
Nursing care plans	Dialysis	NICU notes
ICU notes	Graphics	RN notes
RN notes	Medications	Nursing discharge planning
Nursing discharge planning	IV fluids/medications	Nursing discharge summary
Nursing discharge summary	Nursing assessment	
	Nursing care plans	
	ICU notes	
	RN notes	
	Nursing discharge planning	
	Nursing discharge summary	

Physician or HMO Records

Office/clinic visit notes

Consultations

Radiology

continued

Adult	Pregnancy	Baby
Laboratory		
Other diagnostic tests		
Correspondence from other providers		
General correspondences—to patient, insurance company, etc.		
Hospitalization/emergency department records		
Phone messages		
Disability and insurance records		
Financial records		
Consents		

Appendix C: Sample Index

HARRIET SMITH
MEDICAL RECORDS
VOLUME I OF II

   A. Daniel Binder, MD (OB/Gyn)

      3/6/79–7/5/07
      1. Office notes/mammograms
      2. Laboratory

   B. John Henry, MD (Family practitioner)

      4/17/99–5/30/08
      1. Office notes
      2. X-ray/laboratory
      3. Echocardiograms/EKGs

   C. Michael Tillman, MD (OB/Gyn)
      8/1/07–4/3/08

   D. Northpointe Breast Care Center
      8/3/07

   E. Larry Goldstein, MD (Surgeon)
      9/21/07–6/29/08

   F. Dodge County Hospital
      3/2/08

   G. Northpointe Medical Center
      3/16/08

   H. Kevin Robards, Jr., MD (Oncologist)
      3/23/08–11/27/08

Appendix D: Medical Records Chronology

Sample Chrono 1

RICHMAN, JACK
OUR FILE NO. 07-037
COMPREHENSIVE CHRONOLOGY—NORTHERN MINNESOTA MEDICAL CENTER
3-20-08 WESTERN COUNTY EMS SYSTEM:

Time: 11:59, age: 79 years, female
Chief complaint: chest pain; diaphragm to shoulders
Vital signs: B/P 142/98 P 72 R 22 repeat vitals: B/P 166/102 P 80 R 20
Lungs clear. Pulse OX = 88 at room air (RA) O_2 per nonrebreathing mask (NRB)
Alert, conscious, oriented color = pink skin = warm and dry pupils equal and react
IV fluid started NaCl (normal saline)
Paramedic observations: while vacuuming #7 no nausea or diaphoresis, back pain
Medications = pain killers
MD orders: 2 ASA; 1 nitroglycerine (NTG) | #2 on 1–10; 1 NTG
Arrived hospital 5 min
(Interpretation: observations: while vacuuming experienced pain of #7 degree out of 1–10 scale.
Interpretation: MD orders: after the first dose of NTG pain had decreased to #2 out of 1–10 scale.)

3-20-08	EMS INCIDENT REPORT							
CC:	Chest pain							
HX:	Back pain for past few weeks							
MEDS:	Unknown pain medication							
Time B/P	P	R	Lungs	Pupils	Skin level consciousness			
1143	142/98	77	22	clear	PERL	W/D	A&O X 3	
1151	166/102	80	20	20				
1156	132/80	72						

SPO_2 88% on Rm Air 15 L NRB = 99%
EKG at 1142 = SR Rate 66
Drugs:
1142 O_2
1143 NS .9% 18 ga at TKO L AC (IV fluid at keep open rate L antecubital vein)
1145 2 ASA at 81 grains = 162 grains PO
1146 Nitro .04 SL
1151 Nitro .04 SL

Called because of chest pains. Arrived and found pt ambulatory j chest pain rate of 7–8 (1–10).

Stated she was vacuuming on her hands and knees when pain started. Pain started in diaphragm and radiated to both shoulders (sharp). Gave 2 ASA and 1 NTG. Pain after 3 min went to a 2 w/o radiation. Contacted Medical Center and obtained order for the second NTG. Pain after 1 min still about a 2. Also had pain upon palpation of abdomen. States it (abdomen) isn't usually this firm. Transported w/o incident.

3-20-08 EMERGENCY DEPARTMENT: (handwritten form)
> Arrived 1205
> CC: Chest & Abdominal Pain—Very Severe
> PMH: Hip & Back Pain
> Meds: Unknown Pain Medication; HTN; cancer pills
> Vitals: 1205 151/98 68 20 98.6
>   1502 146/92 64 26 98.3
> Time seen by MD: 1220

HPI: LBP X 2 wks; X-R's 3/19, Dr. Skip at NMMC. Bilateral shoulder pain, anterior neck - "touch of pain;" CP "squeezing," started about 1200, lasted X 5 min. Abdominal pain, onset about 1100, described as pressure. No N, V, D, C or UTI symptoms.

PE: Alert, good color, skin warm & dry, no acute distress. Chest clear to auscultation, heart normal. Abdomen w/+ bowel sounds, distended w/tympany in lower abdomen, + tenderness & guarding.

EKG: Normal sinus rhythm w/R bundle branch block. T waves inverted in $V_1–V_5$

IMP: L2 Compression FX; Abdominal distention, probably 2/FX

PT INSTRUCTIONS: Dulcolax suppository; Admit

ER NURSES RECORD:

1205: In pain mid abdomen 10/10 scale. Abdomen rounded, firm. Pt states "abnormal for her." SMV's good.
> 1330: Back from x-ray. **j** severe pain
> 1345: Toradol 30 mg IV
> 1515: States decreased pain after meds. Much more comfortable. Still some abdominal pain.
> 1525: Dulcolax suppository
> 3-20-08 EMERGENCY ROOM REPORT [dictated] Brian Burgeson, MD
> Seen at 12:20 p.m.

CC: Chest, abdominal & back pain

HPI: 78 yrs old, pt of Dr. Skip. Presents to ER & states she had back pain X last 2 weeks.

States she saw Dr. Skip yesterday & had x-rays done at NMMC. Husband thinks x-rays were of sacral area. Found pelvic films & there was no acute abnormality noted. States she has ongoing pain. Second complaint involves bilateral shoulder pain, w/some radiation to anterior neck & what she calls a "touch of pain." Describes chest pain as "squeezing," starting at 1200 & lasting X approximately 5 minutes. This does not appear to be a major component of her complaint at this time. Third complaint is worst, she is experiencing ongoing abdominal pain that started at approximately 1100 hours. She describes this as pressure pain. Did take a Dulcolax last night & has been having normal bowel movements for last two days. Denies, nausea, vomiting, diarrhea, constipation, or urinary tract symptoms. Husband confirms abdomen is larger than usual. She also states hearing increased bowel sounds.

MEDS: Unknown: Pills for pain; High B/P & Cancer & Dr. Skip has started her on what sounds like Medrol Dosepak.

PE: B/P 151/95, P 68, RR 20, T 98.6, Pulse Oximetry on Room Air = 98%

Awake w/ good color. Skin warm & dry. Appears to be in no acute distress. Lungs clear w/no retractions, wheezes, rales or rhonchi. Heart sounds normal, regular rate & rhythm. Abd w/good bowel sounds throughout, but w/some distention w/Tympany in lower abdomen; has tenderness w/ guarding; no rebound, no costovertebral angle tenderness. When pressing on abdomen appears to be comfortable.

LABORATORY DATA
WBC = 7300; HGB 12.8; HCT 35.8. Amylase and lipase NL. CPK, LDH & Troponin = negative. BUN = 26, total protein = 6; albumin = 3; PT = 11; PTT = 22; INR = 1.0. UA pending. EKG = normal sinus rhythm w/ R bundle branch block and some T-wave inversions in V_1–V_5; changes do not appear to be acute. X-rays including obstructive series & lumbar spine show only significant finding of crush-type fracture 2nd lumbar vertebra. Chest normal.

EMERGENCY DEPARTMENT COURSE
Remained essentially symptom-free in chest. Main complaint seemed to center on abdomen.
    Treated w/Toradol 30 mg IV w/some relief.

Impression

1. L2 Compression Fracture
2. Abdominal distention, possible due to #1

PLAN: Case discussed w/ Dr. Paul Groah (on call for Dr. Skip). Advised Dulcolax suppository, administered in ER. Admit to general medical bed for further care & evaluation

Sample Chrono 2

BRAGDON, BONNIE
OUR FILE NO.: 221
YOUR FILE NO.: 4586

Comprehensive Chronology

Date	Page	Source/Significant Information

Cardiovascular Associates—Clare McWilliams, MD

9/23/06	80–81	**MEDICAL CENTER:** Dr. McWilliams office records:
		CONSULTATION: Clare McWilliams, MD Attending: Kevin Nama, MD Chief Complaint: Precordial Pain, Shortness of Breath History Present Illness:
		... 67 yrs olf w/HX COPD, asthma, HTN presents to ... ED w/c.o increasing shortness of breath, dyspnea on exertion for approximately 2 wks ... DOE has been progressively worsening to point where she becomes SOB just walking from kitchen to bathroom ... several wks ago she developed sudden onset precordial pain described as pressure sensation rated 7/10 ... not radiating & occasionally exertional, relieved w/rest & sitting up ... has light headedness & dizziness, denies syncopal episode ... denies orthopnea, paroxysmal nocturnal dyspnea & has not noticed any unusual wt gain ... has lower extremity edema ... more in Rt lower extremity than in Lt ... placed on ABX & steroids w/o significant improvement in SOB, denies palpitations.

continued

Comprehensive Chronology (Continued)

Date	Page	Source/Significant Information
		Medications: Lasix, Mavik, Verapamil, Zantac, Advair
		Diagnostic Findings: EKG in ED demonstrates accelerated junctional rhythm, Lt ventricular hypertrophy w/repolarization abnormalities, cannot rule out lateral wall ischemia …
		Impression: 1. Precordial pain, SOB, R/O Pulmonary Embolus, MI 2. CHF—mild; suspect Diastolic Dysfunction 3. COPD
		Plan: … admit to telemetry … monitoring demonstrates sinus rhythm w/no tachy- or bradyarrhythmias … increase Lasix … follow wts & I&O … begin ASA … Lipitor … Verapamil … Mavik … 2DEcho w/Doppler ordered to assess any structural heart abnormalities … adenosine stress Cardiolite study to obtain in am to exclude obstructive coronary artery disease as possible explanation for symptoms … Carotid Duplex
9-23-06	54	**MEDICAL CENTER:** Dr. McWilliam's' office records: CAROTID DUPLEX STUDY: Ordered by: Dr. McWilliams 1. Calcified plaque disease Rt carotid bifurcation w/no flow abnormalities consistent w/less than 50% diameter stenosis … 2. Calcified plaque disease Lt carotid bifurcation w/moderate flow abnormalities consistent w/ 50–70% diameter stenosis … 3. Reverse flow noted Lt vertebral artery consistent w. Lt subclavian steal syndrome
9-23-06	51	**MEDICAL CENTER:** Dr. McWilliams office records: MYOCARDIAL PERFUSION SCAN w/DOBUTAMINE: Ordered by: Dr. Stathopoulos Apparent reversible perfusion defect involving inferior wall
9-23-06	56	**MEDICAL CENTER:** Dr. McWilliam's office records: BILATERAL LOWER EXTREMITY VENOUS DOPPLER ULTRASOUND: Ordered by: Dr. McWilliams No evidence lower extremity deep venous thrombosis …
9-23-06	49–50	**MEDICAL CENTER:** Dr. McWilliam's office records: DOPAMINE CARDIOLITE STRESS TEST: Attending: Ann M. Dilla, DO 1. Dopamine stress EKG negative for ischemia 2. No Chest pain 3. Rare Premature atrial contractions & rare premature ventricular contractions during infusion of dopamine 4. Cardiolite portion of dopamine Cardiolite stress … forthcoming …
8-8-07 1215 p.m.	449	**MEDICAL CENTER: Adm 8-3-07–8-10-07:** NURSING PROGRESS NOTE: (unable to read signature) … c/o pain 5/10, meds given, states relief …

Sample chrono 3

JOHNSON, LASHANA
OUR FILE NO: 07-095-18
YOUR FILE NO: 819-4563
May 26, 2008

American Women's Medical Center—Comprehensive Chronology

Date	Source/Significant Information
11-6-07	AMERICAN WOMEN'S MEDICAL CENTER:

HISTORY & PHYSICAL: Shannon Chen, MD

History Present Illness:

40 yr old G2, Para 0-0-1-0 w/last menstrual period of 2-25-07, estimated date of confinement 12-1-07 w/intrauterine pregnancy of 38.5 wks presented to office after ultrasound for growth & nonstress test: ultrasound revealed estimated fetal weight of $4\frac{1}{2}$ to 5#'s w/no fetal growth over last 3 wks & nonstress test showed reactivity w/atypical arrhythmia down to 100s; sent to labor & delivery for monitoring & continued to have irregular fetal heart rate & inability to assess fetal status; amniotomy performed releasing clear fluid & fetal arrhythmias continued & primary low transverse C-section done due to irregular heartbeat & non-reassuring fetal heart tones & inability to assess status

Past Medical & Surgical History:

Hypothyroid disease; Fibroids; S/P Thyroidectomy

11-22-07   AMERICAN WOMEN'S MEDICAL CENTER:
OPERATIVE REPORT:
Surgeons: Cathy M. Nabani, MD & Shannon Chen, MD
Preoperative Diagnosis:

1. Pregnancy at $38\frac{5}{7}$ w/non-reassuring fetal heart tones & inability to assess fetal status
2. Fibroids
3. Fetal Arrhythmias
4. Hypothyroid Disease
5. Primip [1st pregnancy taken to delivery]

Postoperative Diagnosis:

1 thru 5 same
6. Viable Female, Lt occiput transverse [fetal position at delivery]
7. Nuchal cord X1 [cord wrapped around fetus neck]
8. Multiple Uterine Fibroids

Procedure:

1. Primary Low Transverse Cesarean Section w/manual removal Placenta
2. Placement On-Q Pump
3. Amniotomy
4. Intravenous Antibiotic Therapy

continued

American Women's Medical Center—Comprehensive Chronology (Continued)

Date	Source/Significant Information
	AMERICAN WOMEN'S MEDICAL CENTER:
11-6-07	HISTORY & PHYSICAL: Shannon Chen, MD
11-24-07	AMERICAN WOMEN'S MEDICAL CENTER:
	DISCHARGE SUMMARY: Cathy M. Nabani, MD

Principal Diagnoses:
  IUP w/nonreassuring fetal heart tones; fetal arrhythmia; small for gestation age; fibroid uterus; hypothyroid disease; viable female; occiput transverse; malpresentation; tight nuchal cord

Procedure:
  Primary low transverse C-S w/manual removal of placenta; IV antibiotic therapy; Amniotomy; Placement of ON-Q Pump
  (40 yr old female who presented w/nonreassuring fetal heart tones; primary low transverse C-section performed, delivering viable female; Wt 5# 8 oz w/Apgar 91 & 95 [1 minute & 5 minutes of life]; 4 huge fibroids noted; postop remained stable ... D/C home (prescription for Ceftin & Darvocet [antibiotic & analgesic]; instructed to return to office in 1 wk....)

Appendix E: Sample Chronology 4: Work Injury Chronology

Sample provided by Liz Buddenhagen—all names, dates, and identifying information have been changed. Will send this as a pdf so that it can be printed in the original format of landscaped.

Liz Buddenhagen, RN112 Wood ok Avenue Bogart, Georgia 30622-1538; E-mail: zilbudd@yahoo.com; Phone: 770-725-2997; Fax: 770-725-4037.

Medical Chronology for Ryan Costa

Date	Provider	Synopsis	Cost
11/11/04	Plant Security and Emergency Services	Dispatched to site with arrival of 10:21 p.m. North side of "D" furnace for a report of two men down on that tope of the furnace. U/A [upon arrival] we found the pts on the ground, having been removed from the roof by coworkers using a man lift. The pts were moved to the ambulance for evaluation and treatment	[no bill]
		Stated bar struck his helmet ... had a rose harness that was cut off on the ground prior	

continued

Medical Chronology for Ryan Costa (Continued)

Date	Provider	Synopsis	Cost
		to the ambulance. Right arm was splinted to the body. No ROM with the right arm. Unable to make a fist ... pain 7 of 10. Some numbness and tingling to his right leg. Denies loss of consciousness.	
		IV started ... given 2 mg MS IV push. Vitals reassessed and given 2 mg IV push MS.	
11/11/04	Memorial Hospital	*Emergency Department* Dr. Hunt, emergency physician	$14,034.76 ED
		Nursing Notes: Arrival 11:12 p.m.	Physician $404.00
		1,000 lbs steel pole fell on pt R side. Pain to RUE, possible deformity just below R shoulder. N/V intact. States can't move shoulder/elbow. C/o numbness to RLE, abrasion below R knee w/knot BP 141/78, P = 68, R = 20, T = 97.1, Oxmtr = 100%. Pain 6–7, sharp. Vicodin PTA. Ht = 6' 3", Wt = 210# Allergies = nickel Physician Exam = 11:30 p.m. Right arm, piece of steel ~ 1000 lbs hit R side. C/o pain R arm, No hx fx, No LOC, Tingling/ numbness distally, [question mark over skin lac] SH: 1¹/2 pck/day Arm & shoulder: normal ROM, tenderness, soft-tissue/bony, swelling/ ecchymosis, deformity. Neuro-Vasc-Tendon: sensation intact, motor intact, no vascular compromise, tendon function normal. Chest tenderness	
11/11/04	Memorial Hospital	*Nursing Notes:* Toradol 30 mg IV Morphine 2 mg IV	
11/11/04	Memorial Hospital	*Radiology Department:* Chest: No active pulmonary disease Right Humerus: No fracture involving the right humerus	Radiologic Assoc of INDC: $30.00 $31.00

continued

Medical Chronology for Ryan Costa (Continued)

Date	Provider	Synopsis	Cost
11/12/04	Memorial Hospital	*Laboratory:* CBC: [abnormals] WBC 13.2, Hgb 12.4, Hct 37.7, Neutrophil 81.7, Lymphocyte 12.3, Absolute Neutrophil 10.78. Protime/INR = within normal	Pathology: $24.66
11/12/04	Memorial Hospital	*Emergency Department:* *Nursing Notes:* Pt placed in sling … Pt w/ strong radial pulse to R wrist before and after procedure	
11/12/04	Memorial Hospital	*Admitting physician*: Dr. Matson Diagnosis: R Scapula Fracture	
11/12/04	Memorial Hospital	*Radiology Department*: William Kelly, MD *CT of the right shoulder:* Comminuted fracture involving the inferior glenoid rim. There is approximate 2–3 mm distraction of the major fracture fragments. On the sagittal reconstruction images, the glenoid labrum appears angulated inferiorly, avulsed from the body of the scapula, with the humeral head in a cephalad relationship to the glenoid foss	Radiologic Assoc of INDC: $217.00
11/12/04	Memorial Hospital	*Orders:* IV LR KVO Morphine 2 mg IV Q 30 min prn severe pain Toradol 30 mg IV now … Q 6 hr prn. Morphine PCA 1 mg/mL, 1.5 mg initially, 10 minute lockout, Loading dose 2.5 mg	
11/13/04	Memorial Hospital	*Consultation:* Dr. Alan, orthopedic arm specialist … has some slight numbness and tingling to his right and small finger. This happened after the injury but appears to be returning. In no apparent distress … on oral pain medication … walking in room … finger abduction which was strong, finger extension, as well as wrist extension … appears to have a flicker of lateral deltoid still intact … ecchymosis in the axillary portion Impression: … stable tuberosity but there are concerns about the body and the inferior glenoid Awaiting CT scan Plans for surgery later in week	$274.00

continued

Medical Chronology for Ryan Costa (Continued)

Date	Provider	Synopsis	Cost
11/13/04	Memorial Hospital	*Radiology Department* *MRI Cervical Spine:* Larry Schnicke, MD Mild spondylosis at C5-6 *MRI Lumbar Spine:* Larry Schnicke, MD Broad-based disk bulge with superimposed central disk protrusion at L4-5 resulting in mild bilateral lateral recess stenosis. Minimal spondylolisthesis at L5-S1 resulting in bilateral neural foraminal stenosis	Radiologic Assoc of INDC: $285.00 $309.00
11/15/04	Memorial Hospital	*Discharge Summary:* G. Alan … stable fracture at this time due to pain level but has comminuted scapula with glenoid fracture … spine was cleared by Dr. Matson. Post discharge plan: … he is requesting another physician, a different hospital … will try to attempt to coordinate with his family and the work comp individual … discharge home with Ambien for sleep … work with pain medications	
11/16/04	The University Hospital	*Department of Surgery* *Section of Orthopaedic Surgery:* Daniel P. Morris, MD Letter to Catherine Chung … sustained an intra-articular glenoid fracture with a glenoid neck fracture … was at Memorial Hospital and Dr. Alan saw him and was going to operate on him, but he got unhappy with the hospital and came here on his own. … he is neurologically intact, he is very painful, and so we are changing his sling to a sling and swath-type to decrease his pain. … going to get new CT's of this fracture … provide written authorization … surgery next Wednesday, November 24, 2004	$89.00 $109.00 Immobilizer $90.00
11/16/04	The University Hospital	*Radiology Consultants:* *Rt GME Scapula:* Gregory Stand, MD Findings: There is a comminuted interarticular fracture of the scapula, with fracture lines extending to the articular surface of the glenoid and inferomedially along the lateral border of the scapula. There is 5 mm of inferolateral	Radiology $240.00 Radiologist $38.00

continued

Medical Chronology for Ryan Costa (Continued)

Date	Provider	Synopsis	Cost
		displacement of the distal fracture fragment; however, this fragment is also either displaced posteriorly or rotated, as see on the Y view. Additionally, there is a non-displaced fracture of the greater tuberosity. The distal clavicle is poorly visualized on the AP view, but the A-C joint appears slightly widened.	
11/18/04	The University Hospital	*Radiology Consultants* *CT Non-Infusion Upper Extremity:* Larry Dorn, MD Impression: Comminuted intra-articular fracture of the anteroinferior glenoid and fracture of the distal scapula	$1,481.00 Radiologist $233.00
11/24/04	The University Hospital	*Diagnosis: Scapula Fx:* Physician: Daniel Morris, MD Procedure: Open reduction internal fixation of right scapula with plate, screws, and k wire	Hospital $20,700.50 Surgeon: $1,944.00 $3,295.00
11/24/04	The University Hospital	*Physician Orders:* Adult Patient controlled Analgesia (PCA) Orders: Morphine, 2 mg every 10 minutes for total of 3 doses; PCA demand 1 mg; lock out 8 minutes Ancef 1 gm IV q 8 B × 3 Percocet 1-2 tabs po q 4-6B prn Morphine Sulfate 2–5 mg IV q 2-4B prn PolarCare to R Shoulder	
11/26/04	The University Hospital	*Discharge Instructions:* Follow up visits: Dr. Mun, DC AM 4B 12/9 9:45A. Percocet Arm sling	
12/9/04	The University Hospital	*Clinic Note:* Vishal Matta, MD *Orthopaedic Hand Clinic:* Follow up ... has no complaints. ... incision is healing well ... staples removed ... neurovascularly intact. X-rays were taken in clinic ... do not want his shoulder to moved around too much ... was difficult to obtain ... for the most part it appears that our fixation is unchanged	$89.00 Radiology $257.00 Radiologist $39.00

continued

Medical Chronology for Ryan Costa (Continued)

Date	Provider	Synopsis	Cost
		Assessment plan: … progress him to pendulum exercises of the shoulder and he is instructed to come out of the sling to do range of motion exercises to the elbow, wrist, and hand … not going to begin full range of motion to the shoulder … see him back in four weeks at which time we will re-evaluate him andprogress him to formal physical therapy …	
12/14/04	St. Andrews Medical Center	*Physical Therapy Department* Initial evaluation Pendulum exercises 2 visits	$133.00 $80.00
12/30/04	The University Hospital	*Department of Surgery:* *Section of Orthopaedic Surgery*: Daniel Matson, MD Office visit: … lying down about 90 degrees of passive forward elevation and about 10 degrees of external rotation. He still has significant discomfort in his shoulder and a lot of stiffness. X-rays demonstrate the fracture fragments to be in good alignment. Going to increase his exercise program by sending him to therapy to work on passive range of motion and then active range of motion over the next six weeks. Goal is to get full overhead function and to get the muscles working again … having a lot of nightmares and frights from his injury … recommended and gave a prescription for psychological counseling … referral to a rehab physician for evaluation and treatment of his neck, back and left leg pain and a pain management specialist	$89.00 Radiology $240.00 $257.00 Radiologist $77.00 $38.00 $39.00
1/6/05	Hudson Community Hospital	*Outpatient Physical Therapy* Initial Evaluation: RX from Dr. Matson for AAROM, Ice, isometric, sets + e-stim	$14,897.00 [through 9/05]
2/10/05	Hudson Community Hospital	*Outpatient Physical Therapy:* Progress Note: Judith Newton, PT 13 sessions Pain on the average is a 3/10 but goes as high as 10/10 at the end of available range. States he is able to function at 40% with moderate pain. Able to vacuum now and perform activities of daily living	

continued

Medical Chronology for Ryan Costa (Continued)

Date	Provider	Synopsis	Cost
2/10/05	The University Hospital	*Department of Surgery* *Section of Orthopaedic Surgery:* Daniel Matson, MD … three months status post ORIF … has now 135 degrees of active forward elevation.. improved external rotation, … can abduct 90 degree lying down in supination. I am going to move him to active resistant range of motion exercise program so he can build up his strength and see him back in six weeks. Because of his shooting pain … put him on Neurontin … seems to have a partial brachial plexis stretch injury … wean him off of Percocet	$89.00 $70.00
2/17/05	St. Marcy	*Behavioral Health Outpatient Center:* Initial Evaluation. Couples and med management.	$139.00
2/21/05	St. Marcy	*Behavioral Health Outpatient Center:* PTSD Symptoms accident at work … provided support, discussed concerns, ways to reduce anxiety/stress and improve outcomes	$108.00
3/1/05	St. Marcy	*Behavioral Health Outpatient Center:* PTSD Symptoms accident at work … provided support, discussed concerns, ways to reduce anxiety/stress and improve outcomes Non-compliant; pt discontinued Tx	$150.00
3/25/05	Hudson Community Hospital	*Outpatient Physical Therapy:* Progress Note Judith Newton, PT Seen 31 times States that on average pain is 1/10 and 3/10 is the worst … pain level during stretching is a 5/10 … does not have any pain during functional activities	
3/28/05	The University Hospital	*Department of Surgery* *Section of Orthopaedic Surgery:* Daniel Matson, MD … four months post open reduction and internal fixation pain is improved markedly with the Neurontin … significant atrophy of the anterior and lateral aspect of the deltoid … forward flex to roughly 140	$89.00 $70.00

continued

Medical Chronology for Ryan Costa (Continued)

Date	Provider	Synopsis	Cost
		degrees ... external rotation is somewhat limited to roughly 30 degrees actually with slight improvements with passive rotation. Internal rotation is somewhat limited, too. ... continue with therapy ... add some e-stim ... concentrate on the anterior and lateral aspects of the deltoids.	
4/13/05	The Point Clinic	*Office visit*: Amin Young, MD Chief complaint—back pain ~ 5 months ago a heavy object fell on shoulder which he then had surgery ... and had back pain at that time. L side of low back w/ burning sensation coming down leg to knee. Had MRI of back which he does i know results. Pain in back is constant 2–3/10. PE: spastic muscles at buttocks, swelling L back pain—s/p injury, most likely spasticity. Flexeril [RX] will obtain MRI results, if s will send to PT	$79.00
4/27/05	Hudson Community Hospital	*Outpatient Physical Therapy*: Has a ROM deficit and still lacks strength ... difficulty with stabilizing in supine at anything over that 90°	
5/24/05	The University Hospital	*Department of Surgery* *Section of Orthopaedic Surgery*: Daniel Matson, MD Letter to Ms. Williams ... six months post operative ... with significant postoperative pain and temporary axilliary nerve palsy ... because his job requires overhead holding activities, he cannot yet go back to work ...	$89.00 $70.00
5/23/05	Hudson Community Hospital	*Outpatient Physical Therapy*: doing a lot of work around the house ... quite difficult 2B to no strength overhead ... progressed to light resistance for prone scapular exercises	
6/13/05	Institute of Neurosurgery and Neuroresearch	*Initial Evaluation*: Mark Lewis, MD Referred by Dr. Young. Chief complaint of left-sided low back pain that radiates into the left leg with burning pain sensation. Pain is only present when he is lying ... pain 5/10 ... denies any weakness of the extremity, any numbness to the extremity ... on	$313.00

continued

Medical Chronology for Ryan Costa (Continued)

Date	Provider	Synopsis	Cost
		November 4, 2004, he had a work injury … the next day he started developing left leg burning pain … never had … prior to the work injury … he has not had any conservative treatment … Social history … admits to tobacco use … alcohol use - social Radiology … I reviewed the November 13, 2004 MRI scan of the lumbar spine … which revealed significant degenerative disc disease greater at L4-5 and L5-S1 and mild spondylolisthesis at L5-S1 with a small central L4-5 disc bulge but no herniated disc … Impression: Lumbar degenerative disc disease and a mild spondylolisthesis at L5-S1 Plan: order lumbosacral x-rays with flexion/extension views to check the stability of the spine … start a course of physical therapy … we will keep him off of work	
6/14/05	The University Hospital	*Department of Surgery* *Section of Orthopaedic Surgery:* Daniel Matson, MD … he felt a pop last week in the shoulder and since has noted decreased range of motion and increased pain … forward flexion to roughly 90 degrees and abduction to roughly 90 degrees … external rotation to 50 degrees … tender along the posterior inferior aspect of the incision … he is significantly decreased from his previous range of motion … Diagnostics: x-rays were taken today which did not show any significant interval change … hardware appears to be in good position. Treatment plan: … obtain and arthro-CT … go back to just doing pendulum exercises and isometrics as well as some passive range of motion exercises … wear a sling for comfort	$89.00 $70.00
6/14/05	The University Hospital	*Radiology Consultants:* Gregory Stevens, MD Rt GMI Scapula, Comp Findings: Two views of the scapula are provided. Again seen is intraarticular fracture along the lateral	Radiology $240.00 Radiologist $38.00

continued

Medical Chronology for Ryan Costa (Continued)

Date	Provider	Synopsis	Cost
		margin of the scapula extending through the inferior glenoid. There is attempted fixation of this fracture via two screws and a pin. The fracture line remains distinct, and there are no specific signs of healing when compared to the prior study.	
6/22/05	Hudson Community Hospital	*Outpatient Physical Therapy* pt requested not to perform lumbar evaluation since it was denied on Workers Comp and he can't afford deductible.	
7/1/05	The University Hospital	*Radiology Consultants:* Gregory Stevens, MD Rt GI Arthro Injection Shoulder Rt GI Shoulder Arthrogram Impression: Successful injection of Renografin and air into the right glenohumeral joint. CT Non-Inf Upper Extremity Impression: 1. Scapular fracture with little evidence of healing. 2. Poor visualization of much of the glenoid labrum … suggestive of tearing of the superior portions of the labrum.	Radiology $1,023.00 $211.00 Radiologist $362.00 Radiology $1,585.00 Radiologist $250.00
7/7/05	The University Hospital	Department of Surgery *Section of Orthopaedic Surgery:* Daniel Matson, MD Letter to Ms. Williams … big pop in his shoulder and we took him out of therapy and we got an arthro-CT … shows there is a lot of scar tissue in his shoulder … and a superior labral tear … not really excited about his shoulder motion and stability have actually gotten better … CT does demonstrate … cuts inside the fracture … and not fully healed … not symptomatic from this and the screws, are solid, not bent, broken or loose	$112.00 $96.00 EPI [stimulator] $2,442.10
7/11/05	Institute of Neurosurgery and Neuroresearch	*Office visit:* Mark Lewis, MD states no change in his symptoms ... complaining of left-sided low back pain that radiates into the left leg.. unable to get authorization through Workers Comp for the lumbosacral x-rays or the physical therapy Plan: … rewrite him a prescription for lumbosacral x-rays and physical therapy with a diagnosis of L5-S1 spondylolisthesis	

continued

Medical Chronology for Ryan Costa (Continued)

Date	Provider	Synopsis	Cost
8/8/05	Centers for Health	*Medical Evaluation:* Jonathan Jetson, DO Initial paperwork filled out for worker's compensation requested medical evaluation	
8/19/05	Centers for Health	*Medical Evaluation:* Jonathan Jetson, DO History: … presents for a medical evaluation concerning his lower back and left leg … was crushed by a 1000-pound weight, suffering severe injury to his right shoulder girdle area. This necessitated emergency hospitalization at Memorial Hospital … he has had multiple treatments for his right shoulder … states that prior to the incident he has some achiness in his back … did not seek treatment … occasionally would see a chiropractor … never lost any work as a result of his back and denies any previous left leg symptoms … the next day [after the accident] he complained of burning into his left … saw Dr. Morris for his back … was referred to Dr. Matson … performed surgery on his shoulder … he did discuss his leg and back with Dr. Matson … but he concentrated on his shoulder … was referred to Dr. Lewis by Dr. Young. Dr. Lewis recommended some PT for his back … he really just has a very small amount of back pain … major issue is burning thigh pain. Impression: Post-traumatic meralgia paresthetica left thigh. Recommendations: … his symptoms are causally related to the injury which occurred … some irritation of either the femoral nerve or the lateral femoral nerve cutaneous nerve at the anterior … Only treatment that may be of any benefit would be an attempt of a cortisone injection just medial to the anterior superior iliac spine … he will be a his maximum medical improvement … he needs no treatment for his lumbar spine	
9/12/05	Institute of Neurosurgery and Neuroresearch	*Office visit:* Mark Lewis, MD Went to see Dr. Jonathan Jetson for another opinion per the insurance company. I would agree of having him go to the pain clinic for injections of his lateral femoral cutaneous nerve, and possibly a lumbar epidural	$136.00

continued

Medical Chronology for Ryan Costa (Continued)

Date	Provider	Synopsis	Cost
		injection. Although he has had preexisting lumbar problems including degenerative disc disease and spondylolisthesis, I do feel that these conditions were aggravated by his work related injury	
9/2/05	The University Hospital	*Department of Surgery* *Section of Orthopaedic Surgery*: Daniel Matson, MD Letter to Ms. Williams … right shoulder remains in good position … but the CT demonstrated that he had a nonunion … must have micromotion because of a pop so started him on a bone stimulator … unfortunately I prescribed it in July but he did not get it until 2–3 weeks ago … too soon to get new x-rays … working on range of motion but	$103.00 $75.00
11/10/05	The University Hospital	*Department of Surgery* *Section of Orthopaedic Surgery:* Daniel Matson, MD Letter to Ms. Galliher Ryan's right shoulder is having much less pain after his glenoid fracture. … still has some clicks during therapy, but is not clicking in the office. X-rays still demonstrate a space but now motion at the fracture site. Treatment plan: … get a new CT scan … we are going to try to get him back to work …	$112.00 $96.00 Radiology $275.00 Radiologist $41.00
11/16/05	Centers for Health	*Consultation*: Jonathan Jetson, DO. … sent in for me to evaluate the meralgia parsthetica … Dr. Lewis has recommended a possible epidural injection. Still undergoing treatment with Dr. Matson concerning his right shoulder … may start a work conditioning program … slight amount of back pain … really hasn't been bothersome but he hasn't been very active … when he does increase his activity level the symptoms seem to be slightly worse in the low back … pain does not radiate … area of symptoms on the lateral thigh was diminished in size … burning pain has now resolved and he is now just left with some residual numbness	

continued

Medical Chronology for Ryan Costa (Continued)

Date	Provider	Synopsis	Cost
		Impression: 1. Status post right shoulder girdle injury 2. Resolving meralgia paresthetica 3. Minimal lumbosacral sprain with pre-existing spondylolisthesis and spina bifida occulta. Recommendations: … not recommend going with cortisone shot … not have an epidural injection	
11/17/05	The University Hospital	*Radiology Consultants:* Gregory Strong, MD Rt CT Non-Inf Upper Extremity Impression: Scapular fracture … with little evidence of healing compared to 7/1/05	Radiology $1,585.00 Radiologist $250.0
11/22/05	The University Hospital	*Department of Surgery* *Section of Orthopaedic Surgery:* Daniel Matson, MD Letter to Ms. Galliher Ryan's CT scan unfortunately demonstrates that his scapular fracture is well lined up but has not healed … risky for him to work with this fracture as he has a fibrous union and if he puts pressure through it, the screws could break. My recommendation is that he go to a permanent light duty job and/or even preferably have this reoperated on with bone grafting and re-screwing. He is not particularly interested in surgery … alternatives are to continue the bone stimulator to get him to see his primary physician to stop smoking …	$103.00 $75.00
1/31/06	St. Marcy	*Rehabilitation Services* Musculoskeletal Evaluation: Renata Plata, MS, PT … tenderness to palpation at the right supraspinatus area, posterior deltoid, and inferior aspect of right clavicle. … right clavicle is slightly more pronounced than the left Pt is going to participate in Functional Capacity Evaluation	
2/7/06	St. Marcy	*Rehabilitation Services* Functional Capacity Evaluation: Lisa Clarkson, OTR At this time, the worker's major limitations are: Decreased capabilities with lifting (especially	

continued

Medical Chronology for Ryan Costa (Continued)

Date	Provider	Synopsis	Cost
		shoulder height and above), carrying, pushing/pulling. There is decreased right upper extremity endurance with working in an overhead position. The worker did appear to tolerate light activity at table top level. He exhibited no difficulty with tool use, … worker reported burning and pain in the right anterior deltoid with material management tasks. There were rare reports of back, left hip, and right foot pain. There were good body mechanics with lifting and good overall endurance. He reported a pain level 6 in days following … Recommendations: … medium to medium-heavy physical demand level from floor to shoulder and light-medium from shoulder to overhead. The does not match the Heavy physical demand level of his job as a boilermaker	$1,269.00
2/28/06	The University Hospital	*Department of Surgery* *Section of Orthopaedic Surgery:* Daniel Matson, MD … mild-to-moderate discomfort in his right shoulder … 120 degrees of forward flexion and can lift about 50 pounds on an occasional basis at that level. Diagnosis: fracture of glenoid and scapula. Treatment plan: reached his maximal medical impairment as further surgery will not help him. Work Status: … needs to be on a permanent light duty job lifting below chest height, less than 50 pounds or he needs to go back to school or a rehabilitation program	$103.00 $75.00
3/25/06	The Point Clinic	Office visit: Amin Young, MD Chief complaint: 1. R shoulder Yarm Yhand pain. Now pain 4–5. Lower back pain 2. Depression Percocet was released by orthopaedic and was told i much more could be done for back. The Rt shoulder pain going to hand after injury and back pain is still present. Wants pain medication. lost job. Is restricted due to light duty forever	

continued

Medical Chronology for Ryan Costa (Continued)

Date	Provider	Synopsis	Cost
		Chronic shoulder and back pain—Percocet and pain specialist Depression—Lexapro	$83.00
	Walgreens Pharmacy	Refer to pharmacy binder for specific prescriptions	Total: $985.64

Appendix F: Settlement Brochure Sample

Date of review	*4/25/07*
Subsequent reviews	
CLIENT	Jamie Brewer
DATE OF LOSS	February 12, 2007

Personal Information:

Age: 62	Marital Status: Husband - Charles
Children	4 **1 dependent mentally challenged daughter, age 30 lives at home
Occupation	Retired accountant
Able to return to work	No
Educational background	Bachelor degree
Previous litigation	None

Past Medical History:

Allergies: Penicillin	Height: 5′ 4″ Weight: 142#
Medical & Surgical History:	Osteoporosis, Breast Cancer, Hyperlipidemia, Hypertension, Myocardial Infarction, Coronary Artery Disease, Depression, Fractured Arm, Mild Renal Insufficiency, Hypothyroidism, S/P Hysterectomy, Lumpectomy, Sinus Surgery
Current Medications:	Norvasc, Lipitor, Fosamax, Synthroid
Social habits:	Tobacco–quit five years ago after 30 years of two pack per day
Alcohol–socially	Illicit drugs–denied

Description of Accident/Event:

Rear-ended motor vehicle accident in which her vehicle was hit by a truck 2–3 times. She did not lose consciousness.

Treatment at Scene

East Martinsville EMS arrived at the scene at 11:19 a.m. with notation finding Jamie in the driver's seat of large sedan that was struck from behind by a semi. She was conscious and alert, complaining of back pain, chest pain, and left knee pain. No open wounds were noted, no LOC, had bruising to left lower rib cage and knee; c/o SOB. She was collared and boarded. The ambulance left the scene at 11:34 a.m.

Transported to:

St. Mary's Hospital–Emergency Department, arrival time 11:45 a.m. Jamie complained of pain to her head, back, chest, and bilateral hips. She was able to move all extremities without difficulty and was alert and oriented. BP was elevated at 228/95. She denied HA, LOC, N/V, abdominal pain, arm or leg pain, numbness, and/or tingling. She was a restrained driver of a car that was rear-ended by a semi, was pushed into side wall and "spun around." Per EMS, there was major damage to the driver side of car. Bilateral abrasions were noted over her knees with x-rays confirming fracture of left ileum and good position of left hip prosthesis. Cervical and thoracic spine x-rays were negative for fractures or mal-alignment. Dr. Raymond noted no distal pulses below the knee on both legs. She was noted to be slightly memory impaired. She was administered morphine 4 mg IV at 12:24 p.m. and again 2 mg IV at 3:13 p.m. A Foley was placed at 3:36 p.m. BP readings remained elevated, ranging between 132/48 and 219/92. The spine board was removed after x-rays were completed. Diagnosis: left ileum fracture, right radial fracture, cervical and lumbar strain, hypertension, and diabetes mellitus, new onset. Dr. Raymond was admitting physician with Dr. Zimmer for orthopedic consultation. [No consultation was found by Dr. Zimmer.] She had a nondisplaced fracture of the right distal radius.

Testing: Labs: abnormal values included: elevated BUN 45, Creatinine 2.7, Glucose 155, and WBC 12.67. Chest x-ray showed cardiomegaly, mild congestive changes, and chronic appearing ununited fracture of the proximal right humerus. Head CT scan was reported in physician notes as negative. [*She had no brain pathology such as bleed or hemorrhage but she would have met the criteria for brain trauma from the back and forth movement of the head that caused her head/brain injury. The brain is tossed inside the skull which caused trauma and mild swelling resulting in a concussion.* http://www.neuroskills.com/tbi/bfrontal.shtml *This site explains different lobe injuries. Symptoms would vary with the amount of injury; mild to severe. The multiple crash impacts with the semitrailer caused her to be tossed in many directions, leading to the head injury in more than just back and forth but side to side as well.*]

The nursing and therapy notes indicated the plan was to ambulate utilizing a walker with no weight bearing to her left leg if arm x-rays were negative. Rehab services [PT, OT] were to work on mobility with discharge plans for a short rehab stay and then nursing home if she was unable to be independent. Social worker notes indicated that she was the caregiver for her mentally challenged daughter and her husband was dependent for some ADLs and was unable to care for their daughter. During Jamie's recovery, adult children were assisting with care arrangements for their sister and father.

On 2/13/07, nephrologist Dr. Abram was consulted for her acute renal disease. He was not sure of her baseline creatinine level and her current labs indicated increased BUN and creatinine levels for several days. Her blood pressure medications were being held due to low BP readings. Dr. Abram noted that her dyspnea might be related to fluid overload. Jamie was on Lovenox as prophylactic for prevention of blood clots. Acute renal failure was considered as a new diagnosis. Dr. Smith, endocrinologist, was consulted for her hypothyroid and new onset of diabetes. His plan of treatment included thyroid medication and routine glucose monitoring with insulin supplementation.

On 2/15/07, Jamie's oxygen saturation was in low 80s and was placed on 3 L of oxygen. Pulmonary consult was called for acute hypoxemia, respiratory failure, and respiratory alkalosis with metabolic acidosis. She had abnormal arterial blood gases. Pulmonary infiltrates were noted but physician doubted it was CHF, but possibly pneumonia. A VQ scan ruled out pulmonary emboli (PE). Chest x-ray (CXR) showed cardiomegaly and right lower lung (RLL) infiltrate and was diagnosed with pneumonia and sepsis. Nephrologist noted anemia with hemoglobin of 7 g. She was transferred to ICU for more aggressive management of her unstable status and need for ventilator support.

On 2/18/07, Dr. Martin evaluated for recurring, intermittent atrial fibrillation and ordered IV Heparin, echocardiogram, and thyroid function tests. On 2/19/07, Dr. Jay ordered Perm Catheter placement for hemodialysis due to rising renal lab values. Dr. Ali, Infectious disease, consulted for progressive rise in WBC of 21.4 and felt it was possibly stress versus a pneumonia that might have developed from pulmonary contusion. Her previous treatment with zosyn and vancomycin were not improving her respiratory status, so Dr. Ali ordered Merrem (antibiotic) in an adjusted dose based on her renal failure. Her CXR was becoming worse and her hypothyroidism not well controlled.

By 2/20/07, Jamie was more lethargic and diagnosed with encephalopathy (many types of abnormality of the brain; it was not quantified by the physician). On 2/22/07, the Nephrologist noted improvement in renal function and noted rhabdomyolysis (destruction of skeletal muscles by the myoglobinemia, which can be fatal) and her acute renal failure was most likely related to acute tubular necrosis (ATN). (Since chart was incomplete, it is not clear how often hemodialysis was done.) On 2/24/07, her CXRs were improving (pneumonia) and atelectasis was present. She was coughing productively.

On 2/26/07, Jamie was transferred to the Rehabilitation Unit at St. Mary's Hospital. Her diagnosis included nontraumatic brain dysfunction and she was noted to be forgetful. She was using oxygen, was nonweight bearing to her right arm, and would be going to outpatient dialysis with DaVita. Complication of increasing shortness of breath on 2/27/07 resulted in her transfer back to the acute care level in IMCU. A cookie swallow, ordered for the possibility of aspiration, was refused by her.

CT of the chest showed right-sided pleural effusion. Dr. Raymond noted diagnosis of congestive heart failure, renal failure as additional diagnosis. Jamie had a thoracentesis done with 1500 cc removed from her right chest and then returned to the Rehabilitation side on 3/1/07. Her renal failure caused fatigue affecting her ability to perform therapy. Following dialysis treatment, most patients are unable to do anything but sleep. On 3/6/07, she was unable to tolerate 3 h of therapy, which is the minimal requirement for this level of care. On 3/7/07, she developed diarrhea. So, respiratory issues, cardiac and renal issues impeded her progress, so she was evaluated for skilled nursing facility (SNF). On 3/9/07, Jamie had another ultrasound guided thoracentesis with a collection of 650 cc of amber colored fluid and an echocardiogram. During her stay, Jamie was on a restricted diet with thickened liquids to prevent aspiration, a fluid restriction due to her renal failure, and restrictions in diet foods due to renal, cardiac, and diabetes. Nursing noted her refusal to eat, participate in personal care, and even some therapy sessions. On 3/15/07, Jamie was transferred to Crestlane Nursing Home by ambulance; this same ambulance transported her from the nursing home to Davitas for dialysis on 3/16/07 and 4/5/07. The social worker noted her family was struggling with care of Jamie's husband and daughter.

Treatment Follow-up: [await nursing home records]

Summary of Injuries: [if death and autopsy conducted, include findings]

1. Traumatic brain injury
2. Fracture of left ileum [pelvic fracture]
3. Nondisplaced fracture of right radius
4. Acute renal failure result of acute tubular necrosis
5. Respiratory failure with ventilator support
6. Pneumonia—aspirational
7. Sepsis
8. Anemia
9. Unstable diabetes
10. Unstable hypertension
11. Atrial fibrillation
12. Pulmonary contusion
13. Decubitus ulcer left hip
14. Nontraumatic brain dysfunction
15. Hypoxic encephalopathy
16. Cervical and lumbar strain
17. Congestive heart failure
18. Right-sided pleural effusion

*** as noted later, autopsy pending

Missing Records:

1. The records from St. Mary's were incomplete; Radiology reports, laboratory reports, therapy notes for PT,OT, ST.
2. Davita Dialysis notes missing for treatment at St. Mary's and nursing home.

Unrelated Records: None

Billing Review:

1. Billing complete for St. Mary's.
2. Billing needed for Davitas and Crestlane Nursing home.

Lost Wages: [current and future]

Have been requested; pending receipt.

Pharmacy Review:

Ordered; pending receipt.

Narrative Statement: Not indicated.

Strengths:

Functional loss: Totally independent prior to accident she will be unable to care for herself, her spouse, or her dependent adult child. Her previous health conditions were stable. The accident and trauma caused significant stress to her health conditions and caused new injuries. Her traumatic brain injury (TBI) contributed to her deterioration as she was resistant to some treatments based on her inability to grasp the concepts.

Future medical expenses: She will need to retire, change to medicare coverage at some point in time, and continue with skilled care until able to return to her home. At this point in time, her status will continue to be evaluated.

Need for life care planning: await her progress.

Weaknesses: None identified.

Follow-Up:

6/2/2007: Family notified office that Jamie was discharged from the nursing home on 5/17/07 and went to her home with arranged 24-hour care. She decided to stop dialysis treatments and she entered a hospice. She expired on 5/24/07. The family had an autopsy performed and will alert office when the report becomes available.

Appendix G: Sample Reviews

Sample Review 1

Preliminary Merit Review
MEMORANDUM—CONFIDENTIAL ATTORNEY WORK PRODUCT

To	Jch at Abc Insurance Company
From	Nancy Jones, LNCC
Date	November 25, 2008
Re	Ford, Charles–Claimant

Doctors Community Hospital
Claim No: 19127
Our File No. 08-248

As per your request, I have organized and reviewed the Doctors Community Hospital medical records, from 12-31-01 through 1-14-02, that pertain to the above-named client.

In general, the nursing documentation is very good. It is my belief that the fall that Mr. Ford experienced, on 1-5-02, was an unforeseen, unfortunate event. It is my belief that the actions of the nursing staff fell within the standards of care. Mr. Ford was identified as a potential fall risk; there were no preincident events that would have caused the nurses to be on high alert in monitoring this patient. While Mr. Ford was considered at risk for a fall due to his age, use of central nervous system depressants (pain medications) and his limited mobility due to the recent knee surgery left (total knee arthroplasty on 1-2-02) appropriate fall precautions are reflected in the documentation.

According to the documentation, Mr. Ford was asleep and dreaming and apparently attempted to get out of bed. This resulted in a fall that caused a fracture of the left distal femur. This fracture was located in the bone just above the knee prosthesis. After the fall, to prevent any further incidents, the nurses instituted the use of a Posey vest at night.

Prior to this incident, the nursing documentation reflects that Mr. Ford was alert and oriented, there were no periods of confusion, agitation, or other mental status changes. There were no documented events of either unsuccessful or successful attempts to get out of bed. Mr. Ford was receiving analgesics for postsurgery pain, that could "cloud" the mentation, but the only documentation of this possible medication effect is occasional drowsiness.

Specific nursing documentation, that reflects the nurses were cognizant of the possible fall risk factor, is seen on the "Detailed Documentation on Interventions" record. This documentation reflects that a fall risk was indicated and that the bed side rails were in the up position and there was an exit monitor in place. While central nervous system depressants (pain medications) were being utilized, he was alert and oriented, and there were no abnormal mental status changes.

On 1-5-02, in the Detailed Documentation on Interventions form, at 0923 (pg 15 of 56) is the first documentation of: "some periods of confusion." This statement is repeated at 1500 (pg 16 of 56). The documentation on 1–5 at 2130 does not mention confusion, stating "cooperative, speech clear, alert." This statement of "some periods of confusion" is again documented at 1538 on 1-6-02 (pg 17 of 56). These are the only statements pertaining to confusion and, until the discharge, there is no further documentation of occasional confusion.

According to the attorney's demand letter and the letter from Risk Management:

1. If the fall had not occurred, the length of stay would have been decreased by seven days.
2. If the fall had not occurred, the posthospital rehabilitation would have been dramatically decreased, maybe even to the point of in-home visits or out-patient daily visits versus the skilled rehab care that was necessary due to prolonged nonweight bearing status.

Our arguments will be:

3. Fall risk was initially identified and appropriate precautions were instituted.
4. There were no previous attempts at getting out of bed without assistance and there were no previous periods of confusion or diminished changes in mental status.
5. There was no indication that there should be a "sitter" with Mr. Ford at all times. There was no indication that night-time restraints were necessary (prior to event). If restraints had been utilized (prior to the event), this action would have been considered excessively restrictive and a violation of her basic rights.

While I do not believe the nurse's behavior or actions fell below the standard of care (and I believe are very defensible), an untoward event did occur. Looking at the bottom line, it may be less costly to offer to pay the medical bills as they are requesting versus the expense that would be encountered in defending this case.

Sample Review 2

Preliminary Merit Review—Letter Format
October 23, 2008
Samuel Gold, Esquire
425 Main Street Suite 1900
Denver, Colorado 80002

Mr. Gold:

As per your request, I have reviewed the medical records that pertain to your client, Cherry Adams. The following is a clinical fact summary and my observations pertaining to the medical care rendered. This is an abbreviated report as per your request.

Please call me once you have had an opportunity to review this report, so that we may discuss drafting a complete report that outlines a thorough analysis of the issues and deviations from the standards of nursing care.

Ms. Adams was 18 years of age at the time of her hospitalization at Mile High Hospital from 4-25-08 through her death on 4-28-08.

On 0315, 4-25-08 Ms. Adams called the Rock Hollow EMS with complaints that her "water broke." Upon arrival, the paramedics noted that Ms. Adams was in active labor and she had experienced a large volume of water leakage. Her contractions were 5–8 minutes apart and moderate in severity. She denied any urge to push. Transport to Mile High Hospital was accomplished in 8 minutes.

Upon arrival to the emergency department at Mile High Hospital, Ms. Adams was taken directly to the labor and delivery unit. The time of admission is documented as 03:30 a.m. She was immediately seen and evaluated by the on-call OB resident. Vital signs were obtained and were noted to be within normal limits. She was placed on an external fetal monitor which revealed abnormal fetal heart rate. A bedside ultrasound test revealed a singleton pregnancy with no amniotic fluid.

Ms. Adams related that she had not received any prenatal care and had a vaginal infection which had not been treated. She had a history of three previous cesarean sections and was refusing to undergo a trial of labor, requesting a repeat C-section. A workup including blood tests and an evaluation by anesthesia was performed and the attending physician, Jane Perez, MD, was alerted to the pending surgery.

At 0357, surgery was started with the delivery of a viable female infant with Apgar Scores on 7^1 and 9^5 at 0415. The dictated operative report by Dr. Perez stated the procedure was repeat low transverse C-Section for fetal distress. The operative findings revealed normal uterus, ovaries, and fallopian tubes. No intraoperative complications occurred. She was sent to the recovery room in stable condition. The surgical pathology report revealed a third trimester placenta with acute chorioamnionitis and three vessel cord.

While in the PAR unit Ms. Adams complained of significant pain and was given a total of 100 mg of Demerol and 25 mg of Vistaril. Her vital signs revealed an elevated pulse averaging

115–125 bpm and a decreased BP averaging 90/40–105/55, O$_2$ saturations were decreased ranging 85–89%. Ms. Adams was transferred from the recovery room to the postnatal unit at 0632. The PAR record indicates that Nurse Pope gave report to Nurse Mie at 0615. The PAR flowsheet indicates that Ms. Adams was transferred to the Postpartum Unit by the transport service at 0632.

The exact time that Ms. Adams arrived on the Postpartum Unit is unclear as there is no documentation. There is no admitting nursing assessment/evaluation. No admission vital signs were documented.

According to the nursing progress notes, at 0745 Ms. Lego, CNA, entered room #415 while refreshing the water in the patient pitchers. She noted that Ms. Adams was unresponsive and called Nurse Mie who proceeded to call a Code Blue.

The Emergency Response/Code Team responded and ACLS measures were instituted. Resuscitation at 0750 and lasted 30 minutes with no significant positive response, no return of a pulse or blood pressure. Ms. Adams was pronounced dead at 08:25 a.m.

A postmortem autopsy was performed by pathologist, J. McKluk, MD. The autopsy report reveals the following anatomic summary: (1) hemorrhage in pelvis due to ligated uterine artery with the evacuation of 1500 cc bloody fluid and hematoma; (2) postpartum C-section. The postmortem opinion was death due to hemorrhage due to abdominal incision due to C-section, no other significant conditions were noted.

It is my opinion, to a reasonable degree of nursing certainty, that had the nurses employed by Mile High Hospital appropriately evaluated Ms. Adams and provided appropriate nursing care, including notification of the physicians of abnormal physical findings the physicians would have been able to intervene in a timely fashion.

Examples of this opinion are as follows:

1. The PAR nursing staff did not notify the physicians of the abnormal vital signs consisting of low BP and low oxygen saturations and elevated pulse.
2. The nurses on the Postpartum Unit did not perform an admission assessment and evaluation and no admitting vital signs were obtained.
3. There were no postsurgical laboratory tests obtained, no postoperative hematocrit or hemoglobin.

It is my opinion that you will need an obstetric physician testifying expert to discuss the etiology of the arterial bleed and to discuss causation. You will need an obstetric-postpartum nurse to discuss the standards of care pertaining to the acceptance of a patient from the recovery room, performing admission assessments, and obtaining admission vital signs. You will also need a recovery room nurse to discuss notification of physicians when there are abnormal vital signs and acquisition of laboratory tests.

Please obtain the hospital policies and procedures that pertain to the care of a patient in the PAR as within the postpartum units.

As previously stated, please contact me so that we may discuss these findings. It has been a pleasure working with you.

Very truly yours,
Sandra Kingston, MSN, RN, LNCC
Legal Nurse Consultant
Kingston Consulting, Ltd.

Sample Report 3

Preliminary Merit Review
To: Gary McKern & Associates

Merit Review

Facts of the Case:
Admission #1:

Frances Long, 65-year-old female, presented to the Emergency Room at City General Hospital on 9/9/2005 at 9:26 a.m. She was transported from her home by paramedics due to complaints of "feeling weak/Bad gas." She stated she had abdominal cramping and bad gas for the last couple of days, then, last night she had weakness." Upon arrival to the ED her blood pressure was 140/80, pulse was 170, respirations were 20, her temperature was 96.7, and pulse oximetry was 90 (presumably on room air). She reported feeling like she was going to pass out; no blood in stool.

Her physical examination by the physician noted cool, clammy skin, lungs clear with good air entry, heart was irregular and tachycardic. Her abdomen was noted as obese, tender midline to deep palpation. She had trace edema to her extremities. She was short of breath (SOB) with atrial fibrillation.

Her admitting diagnosis was hypotension. During her stay in the ED her BP ranged from 54/21 to 102/47. She received fluid bolus, Unasyn (antibiotic) IV, phenylephedrine (inotropic for low blood pressure), digoxin (irregular heart rate and enhanced cardiac output). Her monitor showed rapid atrial fibrillation.

While in the department, she had a CT of abdomen/pelvis which was reported as no evidence of aortic dissection or aneurysm. There was a large pelvic mass with a lobulated extension into the left flank area and a large amount of ascites. This was noted as rather concerning for a pelvic malignancy. She had an echocardiogram that showed biatrial enlargement, hyperdynamic left ventricular systolic function with ejection fracture (EF) of 65–70% (normal range). The report noted a consideration of the hypotension as volume depletion as a cause secondary to the hyperdynamic function and small left ventricle (LV) cavity. Her chest x-ray showed cardiomegaly without pulmonary edema. No acute consolidation and no effusion.

On 9/10/2005, the CT of the abdomen was repeated and showed a large pelvic mass extending into the abdomen along with the previously noted ascites. The radiologist thought most likely a large uterine fibroid; ovarian neoplasm could not be completely excluded. The mass was causing mild obstruction of the right kidney, infiltrate in the right lung base, and nodularity of the left adrenal gland. There was also notation that the right hydronephrosis was not present in the previous study. The tissue density had a measurement of 17×21 cm (this a very large mass).

A repeat chest x-ray on 9/10/2005 showed a dense band of atelectasis at the right lung base and thin band of platelike atelectasis or scarring on the left.

Frances was admitted to ICU and had many consultations done. Her treatment included the phenylephrine for her hypotension and amiodarone for her atrial fibrillation with rapid ventricular response. She had a history of the A-fib and failed conversions. Her dobutamine stress test noted an EF of 65% (normal range); BNP was 77 (was normal, indicating she was not in heart failure). A Foley catheter was placed in the ICU (unable to place in ER). It was noted in the records, she had a UTI over the past month. Dr. Pang was a cardiology consult and oversaw the above treatments and diagnostic workup.

Dr. Noah was consulted for gynecological issue of the pelvic mass. He did not feel she was a surgical candidate due to her risk factors (morbid obesity, unstable cardiac status, weakness, anemia). He would re-evaluate at a later time as her condition improved. He ordered tumor markers of CA 125 (sensitive for ovarian cancer; her levels were not significantly elevated) and CEA was not elevated as well. Her pap smear was negative but it was noted by the physician of a poor sample due to speculum inadequate (again related to her size). She had a history of hormone replacement therapy (HRT) for 7–8 years. He noted she had irregular stools for 11/2 to two years with bloating. (Possibility of the mass presence for a period of time????)

Dr. Wise performed a colonoscopy on 9/12/2005 with results of colon polyps and tubular adenoma. This was essentially a normal test and did not identify any gastrointestinal bleeding.

Frances was anemic with a hemoglobin of 8.8 on 9/10/2005. She was transfused with 2 units of blood but her hemoglobin again dropped to 8.4 on 9/13/2005. She again received a unit of blood. The physicians were unable to determine the cause of the blood loss. It was not gastric or intestinal. There was no uterine bleeding and Frances denied any vaginal bleeding prior to admission. The source was undetermined but was possibly a hemorrhagic tumor.

On 9/11/2005, Frances had a pulmonary function test done that reported some restrictive pulmonary disease secondary to her obesity. Her CT of the chest reported a RLL infiltrate and possible pneumonia. Treatment with Avelox was initiated by the infectious disease physician consult. Her physician noted atelectasis secondary to decreased inspiratory effort and secondary to abdominal process (large abdomen pressing against diaphragm and restricting lung capacity).

Frances, 5″3″ and 350#, met the criteria for morbid obesity. Prior to admission it was noted she walked independently at home but only short distances. She admitted she was not active.

Allegations Brought by Daughter

1. The ER physician did not do an ultrasound of the abdomen but did anterior posterior (AP) abdominal x-ray and CT of abdomen.

   Standard of care was met for ordering CT test based on her presenting symptoms and level of care.

2. A second CT was done showing missed diagnosis from the first one.

   Hydronephrosis, not present in the first CT, is a result of a back up of urine flow, so the kidney enlarges with eventually a decrease in function. The pelvic mass was pressing on the ureters and kidney with noted reference of the mass being very near the uterus and bladder.

3. Daughter stated the problem of her pressure and heart rate was not present before and she suspected it was induced by this mass and was not addressed by the physician.

   The medical records clearly address her heart rate of A-fib was present in the past but was exacerbated at the time of admission. The notes do not state clearly of any correlation of her unstable BP, heart rate with the mass but the whole picture noted throughout the records demonstrates she had multi-system affect of most likely the pelvic mass. The significant size of the mass and the presence of ascites indicated the possibility of malignancy, and anemia with inability to confirm a source indicated the physicians were focused on the mass but were unable to confirm a diagnosis without surgery or an invasive procedure. Her medical condition prohibited surgery at this time.

4. The issue of the frequent stooling following her bowel prep, failure of staff to clean her perineal area in a timely manner, and the Foley area not being cleansed in a timely manner.

I agree these issues were risk factors for infection. A bedside commode was indicated to facilitate access for elimination. But her morbid obesity required a commode to meet her size. The staff did provide a commode but not in a timely manner. What is not clear in the records was there sufficient amount of equipment for her size. Sitting on the commode for several hours is not reasonable. Did she sit there continually? Or did Frances require being on and off the commode frequently for several hours? Bowel preps are challenging and the effects are different for individual patients. It is not uncommon to be on/off a commode multiple times for several hours.

The issue of UTI, perineal care, and skin irritation would not be a strong allegation alone. Rather it would demonstrate concerns of care. Frances had a need for a larger commode, there are individual responses to bowel preps, daughter providing the cleaning on her own were of most concern to daughter. The significant issue would be *lack of staff support to verify clean skin.* The placement of a Foley is a known risk for infection and would not have been a reasonable expectation during bowel prep. Foley catheters are a contributor to infection. More likely is the fact that the pelvic mass caused pressure on the urinary structures which did not allow them to function adequately resulting in urinary infection.

5. Daughter had issue with the timely initiation of the sequentials (pumps for her legs to prevent blood clots).

This physician order was not carried out timely. However, the nurse noted "patient refused." Also, the sequentials would have been a risk to use when Frances was up and down during the frequent stooling for her bowel prep. They should have been used prior to the bowel prep and again after the prep response eased. The fact that they remained in the plastic package does not demonstrate the staff made an attempt to apply the device to Frances or even give explanation of the reason for the sequentials. She had several risk factors for blood clots: atrial fibrillation, immobility, obesity, varicose veins, poor inspiratory ventilation. She was receiving Lovenox as well for prophylactic management. However, Frances did not have any complications from this issue so would be a care issue and not a negligence that caused an injury.

6. The issue of no solid food on 9/12/2005.

Physician orders were for clear liquid diet and this diet remained in place after the colonoscopy due to a possibility of surgery. The chart had orders for a "diet" and the nurse has a duty to ensure the patient has orders for diet and/or hydration of fluids in place. The daughter bringing her food from the cafeteria is risky and could have complicated her situation. A recommendation would be for family to meet with Patient Advocate representative at the hospital to address these care issues.

7. The urine bag looked dark and cloudy on 9/12/2005 but the nurses charted clear and yellow.

The nurses charting for this date was "clear, concentrated, yellow." Assessment of the urine is not by viewing the urine in the large bag portion of the urinary drainage system. Rather, the nurse is to assess the drainage tube that has the urine as it passes directly out of the bladder. The urine collects and mixes in the large bag and is then distorted. This would be difficult to prove. The physician did not see the need to repeat any urine testing (analysis or culture). A urine culture was done on 9/10 and was negative.

8. The IV fluids had been turned off and daughter felt Frances was not eating/drinking adequately.

The records did not have an order for the fluids to be discontinued. When the nurse did stop them, they also stopped recording intake and output. Thus, I am unable to determine her fluid and hydration status. Charting only noted "intake good" for her diet. This is an issue of concern and could have contributed to the confusion the daughter mentioned if Frances was indeed dehydrated.

9. The daughter noted on 9/14/2005, Frances had pressure and discomfort after the Foley was removed.

The records did not have any notation by nurse or physician of this complaint. Typically, there may be pressure and urgency after the removal of the Foley. This should resolve after a couple of times of voiding. But if Frances was not drinking fluids (as stated above by her daughter) and pressure and discomfort continued several hours after the Foley removal, then the nurse failed to monitor her condition postFoley removal for signs and symptoms of UTI. Hydration is important to ensure flushing of the bladder. The physician should have been contacted for ongoing discomfort. But the records did not even have any reference of her discomfort. Of note, urine culture was done on 9/10/2005 and was reported as negative. Also, the pelvic mass was noted in the CT report to be very near the bladder. "I cannot separate from the uterus or urinary bladder" was the radiologist's statement. So the pelvic mass was another possibility of her reported "pressure" and even having an effect on her voiding. The nurses charted "no voiding difficulties."

10. Confusion noted by daughter on 9/14/2005.

The medical records do not have any assessment of confusion. Her medications were reviewed and did not have indication of medications with this type of side effects. The charting noted alert, drowsy, oriented x4 by nursing. Occupational therapy noted drowsy but oriented x4. Her daughter discussed the confusion issue with the physician but he did not change his plans for her discharge/transfer to the skilled facility. The records did not have any notation of her nightmares, extreme confusion, or any other related issues.

Admission #2

Frances returned after only about 24 hr in the nursing home. Her condition deteriorated rapidly over the course of a few days. As noted by the daughter, Dr. Boyd admitted to not doing a urine test (urinalysis or culture?) prior to her discharge on 9/15/05. Her admission was for UTI. She was receiving Avelox and was noted on the nursing home records. This drug was prescribed by the infectious disease consult during her previous admission. It does cover *Staphylococcus aureus*, *Escherichia coli*, and others which is actually a good antibiotic. The possibility lies in the effectiveness of the anti-infective over time or the organism developing a resistance to the drug.

While in ICU, Frances continued to deteriorate. Her anemia continued and she was transfused. She developed more respiratory issues with eventual failure and the need for the ventilator. Even though Frances may not have had high fevers, she was septic. Her kidneys failed but again as noted previously, she had hydronephrosis from the pelvic mass. With the ongoing anemia, this was more of an indication of the mass bleeding but the intervention for this is removal of the mass. Of course, she was still unstable for any type of surgery. She was not even a candidate for dialysis.

Opinion

Frances had a very complex case involving a large pelvic mass. Her cardiac status was affected and eventually her respiratory and urinary status. The facts of the large pelvic mass along with ascites indicated a strong possibility of malignancy. Her physical condition of unstable heart, anemia, and respiratory status along with her morbid obesity prevented a complete diagnostic workup of the mass as she was not a surgical candidate during her first admission and even her second admission.

Frances had a negative testing for bladder infection during her first admission. Placing a Foley catheter is an increased risk for infection even with only being used for 3–4 days. Doing a urine culture after removal is not the standard of care as you would typically have colonized results. Testing is done for "symptomatic" conditions. But again the records do not have any reported/documented signs or symptoms. Even after the daughter spoke with the physician of her mother's confusion, the plan of care did not change. Therefore, the physician did not feel further testing was warranted. The pelvic mass was very close to the bladder (as noted in the CT scan) and another possibility for her "pressure feeling."

The care issues brought forward by the daughter are of concern. As I noted previously, care issues should be brought to the attention of the hospital through the patient advocate representative. In addition, the family can contact the state board of health to alert them of their concerns. They conduct investigations of these matters especially when they receive more than one report involving one facility.

The nursing care issues brought forward by her daughter do not have direct cause for the death of Frances. Sepsis was a result of the multiorgan failure most likely related to the pelvic mass.

Based on my review findings, the case does not have merit for nursing negligence that directly contributed/caused the death of Frances Long.

Jean Dworniczek, RN, BSN
September 17, 2006.

Chapter 13

Report Preparation
Principles and Process

Patricia Raya, RN-C, MBA;
Joahnna Evans Songer, RN, CCRN, CLNC; and
Cassandra Hall Valdivia, RN, BSN, LNC, CLNCP

Contents

Objectives

- Define attorney–client communication
- Describe the attorney–client report process
- Define the different types of reports, with examples provided

Introduction

Communicating thoughts, ideas, and recommendations regarding case analysis and case development in a concise, effective format is an essential skill for legal nurse consultants (LNCs). Good communication, whether oral or written, enhances case development and is an essential part of legal nurse consulting. Knowledge of the audience receiving the communication is one of the keys to successful communication. The LNC should develop effective report writing and communication skills in order to communicate information to the legal team and to enhance discovery, case development, and case outcomes.

The LNC–Client Communication Process

Communication between the LNC and the attorney/client is essential for the case development process. It is important to that communication process that the LNC research and become familiar with the report's audience. Use interviewing skills, the internet, firm websites, and personal references to learn as much as possible about the client to whom you will be presenting the report. Many attorneys list their education, legal experience, and additional personal information with online legal databases; more and more law firms are developing their own websites with mini biographies on the attorneys. This assists the LNC with additional knowledge regarding the attorney/client.

Researching the attorney/client audience also has professional implication for the LNC. If possible, research the reputation of the retaining attorney through local legal contacts or other LNCs who have had previous contact. The LNC must be responsible for his or her own professional integrity and professional reputation.

Understand your attorney/client audience. Good communication is essential again here, prior to the report-preparation process. Inquire regarding your audience's familiarity with medical terminology, and develop a format for explanation of unfamiliar terms (see Chapter 12, "Medical Record Analysis," for case report examples). Education of your audience on medical issues and medical terminology is an LNC responsibility essential to case development. Ask for the retaining attorney/client's report preferences: style, length, and content. Is a chronology preferable to a full-length written case summary? Will the report be verbal or written? As always, do not put anything into written form or send the attorney/client anything in written form without prior approval. See Appendix A for an example chronology.

Establish mutual timeframes, goals, and deadlines with your retaining attorney/client. Ensure a mutual understanding of the LNC work process and work product, and the estimated time expected for case review and report preparation. Establish your billing practices with the attorney/client; ideally the LNC should request and receive a signed fee schedule/letter of retainer and the retainer amount prior to beginning work on the case review and report. Understand the attorney's deadlines such as statute of limitations and the date that discovery will end. Stay within the retaining attorney/client's mutually agreed budgetary limitations, and notify the attorney/client immediately if additional time or cost is necessary.

Effective communication is a three-part process. The message is translated into words or written; the message is then delivered to the reader/audience (verbal report, letter, memo, report style of preference), and finally, the goal is achieved—the intended report audience understands the proposed message. Preparing the report with clear ideas and goals and understanding the audience's needs and knowledge level is essential. The writer should consider the audience knowledge, attitude toward and need for information that will be contained in the report.

Unfortunately there is always a chance that the report's message or intent may be misinterpreted. Garver-Mastrian and Birdsall (1986) note that "noise" such as poor grammar selection, misspellings, poor organization, and sloppy thinking can hinder communication. Such "noise" is in the control of the writer. If the reader is tired or distracted, does not like the topic, or has only skimmed, the report communication process will be ineffective. The writer must guide the reader toward the intended message. This can be done effectively only when the report topic, purpose, and audience need for information are considered.

Report Topic

Before beginning the case report process, the LNC should discuss the purpose of the report with the attorney/client to obtain the case theory and report purpose. How familiar is the attorney with the subject? Does he or she have preconceived ideas about the topic and case issues? What does the attorney hope to obtain through review of the report?

The Purpose of the Report

A written or verbal report may be requested following the LNC's completion of the medical record review, research, case analysis, and conclusion. The LNC should determine the purpose of the report: Is the report designed to educate, to inform, or to persuade the reader? What message will the report convey? Whether the objective of the report is to create a chronology of case events, or to inform and educate the attorney/client about the adherences to or deviations from the standard of care, the report's message should be clearly and concisely conveyed to the reader, the LNC's audience.

An alternative purpose for a report may be to present and substantiate an alternative point of view or case issues identified by the LNC during review of the medical records and documents. The LNC has been consulted by the attorney for his or her knowledge of medically related issues. A thorough review of case medical records and documents may reveal additional information and alternative case theory that is important to communicate to the attorney. The LNC's honest review and opinions are essential to case integrity.

Ask the attorney/client who will be reviewing your report. Is the report intended for the attorney alone or for additional members of the legal team such as cocounsel and paralegals? Will other retained experts or expert witnesses be reviewing the report as part of their own case research process? This could affect the discoverability of your report. Will the report be made available to opposing counsel? These considerations are essential knowledge to obtain prior to report preparation. LNC rule of thumb: Never put anything into writing that you are not prepared to be presented with and answer to at a later time.

Once the audience and purpose of the report have been determined, the LNC should organize the information received to date and then expand it through medical research and identification of additional discovery. The LNC should allocate approximately 30% of the document preparation time to organization and case issues research, 40% to composing the report text, and the remaining 30% to editing and refining the final report LNC work product.

Plan and Development of the Report Document

The document plan should be brief and to the point. The LNC should review the purpose of the report, for example, to determine whether a case is meritorious or to prepare a case analysis outlining standards of care and noted deviations from and adherences to those standards. The LNC should develop a theory and define the purpose and objectives of the report. For example, is the purpose to convey a deviation from the accepted standards of care, to explain the injuries sustained and correlate those to the documentation, or to present a chronology or timeline of case events? Each case is different and requires its own unique form of presentation for effective impact.

Document Organization

Organize your outline to address the case issues, and to present the information in the most effective format. Is the case issue code blue procedure or medications and timing of code events? Then a timeline with explanation of events would be an effective style of report for this case.

Case Research

A review of the medical records will provide a guide to the case-relevant topics that require research. If the attorney has not yet obtained the medical records, or if the LNC determines that the medical records and documents received to date are incomplete, the LNC should present the attorney with a list of additional discovery necessary to review the case. It may be necessary for the LNC to write to the institution or physician's office requesting a true and complete set of the records. The attorney may choose to either name the LNC in the request for additional discovery, or to simply designate that persons working with the attorney on the case will also be reviewing the medical records and documents. Obtain permission from the attorney prior to any direct communication between the LNC and the medical facilities, as this may have discoverability implications for the case and for the LNC work product. The institution should require an authorization for release of the information from the patient or patient's authorized representative prior to release of the information. The LNC should be aware of and abide by Health Insurance Portability and Accountability Act (HIPAA) guidelines while requesting medical information. Usually a fee is required to duplicate the records, and is paid prior to the facility's release of the records. This fee is most often paid by the attorney. The sample letter follows:

> Dear Dr. Brown:
>
> Please provide a complete and certified copy of any and all medical records, chart notes, documentation, x-ray results, laboratory values, memos, etc. regarding any and all treatment and care of John Doe by you and your partners. We are in dire need of these medical records and request that you forward them to our office as soon as possible. Enclosed you will find a fully executed authorization for the release of this information to our office.
>
> If there is a fee for the copying of this material to our office, kindly send an invoice along with the requested records and documents and we will send a check promptly.
>
> Thank you for your prompt attention to this matter,
> Very truly yours,

Once the medical records are received, the LNC should use research time effectively. Before beginning the case research, the LNC should define the purpose and the best source(s) for obtaining the needed information: is the purpose to establish or to obtain new information, to locate a specific document or text, to locate names and information of potential witnesses, or to obtain research articles and information relevant to the case issues? Search engines and databases on the internet are excellent information sources, as well as the extensive selection of textbooks and articles available at a local hospital or university library. The LNC should consider subscribing to online database vending services for additional research information and articles. Other research information resources include professional publication subscriptions, professional organizations, the board of nursing, and other LNCs.

Prepare the Report Outline—Organize the Information Effectively

Whether the report is verbal or written, an effective outline format ensures the most effective information delivery to the attorney/client audience. The general rule for preparing a report outline is "tell them what you plan to tell them; tell them; then conclude by telling them what you just told them."

The outline should contain

a. Introduction
b. Body
c. Conclusion/summary
d. List of research resources used to prepare the report

Edit and proofread the report for grammatical and spelling errors. Use the spell check function on your computer to identify words and phrasing that your eyes may have missed. Review the report for clarity of information, again with your attorney/client audience in mind. Does the report convey the information intended? Does it convey the information in a concise, logical presentation style with the information building to the summary and conclusion?

Revising the Outline

Additional medical records and documents, as well as research findings and additional information render document revision necessary, at times even after the report has been delivered to the attorney. Throughout the report process, it is imperative that the LNC identify the medical records and documents reviewed in preparation for the report, then designate the report as being based on review of the "medical records and documents received and reviewed to date." This is important for report integrity in the event that additional documents and information are identified and reviewed that might alter opinions and findings presented in the report. The writer should constantly be asking whether the initial case theories were correct, and consciously looking for new information that requires these case theories be updated or revised. When satisfied that review and research have revealed sufficient information to draw a conclusion, the LNC then drafts the formal case report outline.

Report Format

The way in which information, facts, and ideas are organized and presented can influence a reader's comprehension. When writing a report, albeit a memo, analysis, chronology, or an expert report, the LNC should set aside a sufficient uninterrupted block of time to accomplish as much as possible. The LNC should:

- Begin by organizing a framework to assist the reader, that is, an introduction, body, and conclusion
- Develop a theme and support it with facts and case research, identifying and leaving out irrelevant information
- Present facts in a format that is clear and concise
- Clearly identify and back up personal opinions, using professional literature and published standards of practice
- Draw a conclusion based on the scientific evidence and professional standards of care

If "writer's block" occurs, the LNC should take the time to refocus. Reorganization of thoughts and ideas may be needed to be more effective. If satisfied with the format and contents, the LNC should rewrite the report, using a recognized publication manual as a guide for presenting the final report.

The 5th edition of the *Manual of the American Psychological Association* (APA) (2001) provides a guide for documenting text citations. Sources should be acknowledged in the text of the chapter itself and in an alphabetical list at the end of the text. A parenthetical citation should contain the author's last name, the date of the publication, and often the page number from which the material is borrowed. Numerous textbooks and guides on the APA format are available online, as well as in local libraries and bookstores.

The final LNC report product should look neat and professional. You never get a second chance to make a first impression with your written LNC work product. It should be written in a font and a type size that are easy to read and allows the attorney to make notations directly on the report if needed. Prior to submitting the report, the LNC should proofread and edit it, preferably several times, including the spell check and grammar check used by his or her computer program. Spelling and grammatical errors will detract from the efficacy of the report. Have a colleague review the report if possible for clarity and communication of information prior to sending the report to the attorney.

Discoverable and Nondiscoverable Reports

A report that is written by the testifying LNC or expert witness is considered a discoverable report. The attorney and other experts involved with the case, as well as opposing counsel and his or her experts, will read the report; the report may also be referenced in another expert's work or as a source of case research. Reports written by LNCs working "behind the scenes" as consulting experts (as opposed to testifying experts) are generally considered nondiscoverable, as these are part of the attorney's education and case development process. The LNC should always check with the attorney before putting anything into writing, and should ask the attorney whether the report is considered discoverable or not. A nondiscoverable report may contain opinions that a nurse expert witness could not express, such as the negligence of other healthcare providers, or suggestions for additional discovery and case development strategy. It is important to mark each page of the report with "attorney work product" so that it does not inadvertently get identified as a discoverable document. One exception would be if a testifying expert uses a consulting expert's report as part of their case research—this could make the report discoverable. The general rule of written reports is never put anything into writing that you are not prepared to see again at some point in the future!

Do not assume that e-mail communications between the LNC and the attorney will be nondiscoverable.

Types of Reports

Memo

The word "memo" is short for "memorandum"; it is perhaps the most frequently used form of communication in any situation (Acerbo-Avalone & Kremer, 1997). Memos are usually used to communicate to people with the agency or institution and follow the basic format given here:

Date:
To:
From:
Subject:

The memo is a very basic piece of communication. It is usually shorter than a letter and quickly summarizes the message in an introduction, body (discussion), and conclusion. To be effective, it should be concise, clear, interesting, and "user-friendly."

Informal Report

The informal report may be either a written or a verbal report. Sometimes attorneys prefer a verbal report prior to receiving a written report from their consulting experts or expert witnesses.

A written informal report is essentially a three- to four-page piece of information. It does not require a title page, a table of contents, and so on. The informal report does include the three basic report elements: introduction, body, and conclusion. The goal is to educate or to persuade the readers regarding the written opinion.

Formal Report

Medical Research

Often an attorney will ask the LNC to summarize a piece of medical literature. It is the responsibility of the LNC to summarize the article into language that is easy to understand for the attorney and other laypersons. It may be necessary for the paralegal, the client, or other persons less knowledgeable about medical terminology to understand a medical issue, so the summary must be in "user-friendly" prose.

Chronology or Timeline

A chronology is the sequential listing of pertinent case events related to the incident in question. The chronology may be day by day, week by week, or even as intense as minute by minute. The LNC should determine what time frame is appropriate for the chronology and then list the medical incidents in chronological order (see Appendices A and B). There are several computer programs available to LNCs that assist with case chronology and timeline development and format. The chronology must be objective, listing only the facts. The LNC may add a column for clinical commentary if the explanation would benefit understanding the case events. When completed, both the chronology and the timeline should be like road maps, leading from one medical fact to another. See Appendices A and B for a sample case chronology and a sample timeline.

Medical Record Analysis

Medical record analysis provides the attorney with a complete account of the events, alleged potential malpractice, potential witnesses and involved parties, and an evaluation of the significance of those events in relation to the injury (APA, 2001). These facts are then presented in an organized, logical manner in a written report. The report should "tell the story" in chronological order so that the attorney can use the information to construct a fact pattern relative to the occurrence or injury.

The report should review and address the central issues of a case; these issues should be clearly presented to the reader. Include direct quotes or citations from the medical record. Avoid introducing distracters or irrelevant case information that might cloud the case issues. The first page of the report should include the following:

- Date of report
- Patient/client name or case name
- Name of the attorney for whom the report was written
- File number given to the case by the attorney
- Treatment dates
- Listing of medical records, expert reports, depositions, and interrogatories that were reviewed for the analysis

The LNC should prepare an objective and factual chronology or medical records summary that includes all materials that are relevant to the case (e.g., nurses' notes about an incident, physician progress notes). Abnormal patient findings are especially important to include and explain. The analysis should present facts of the case, followed by LNC clinical commentary and recommendations, identifying any relevant missing records or additional discovery items.

Expert Report

The expert report provides an analysis of the alleged malpractice. It attempts to prove or disprove deviations in acceptable standards of care and practice. The expert report addresses only facts relating to the expert's area of expertise. The nurse expert comments on issues within the scope of nursing. Medical issues are addressed by physician experts. The expert report should contain a summary of the expert's qualifications, a brief summary or chronology of the event, a discussion regarding the standards of care, and a professional opinion and thoughts on whether or not deviation from acceptable standards of care occurred.

Summary of Independent Medical Examination

The Independent or Insurance Medical Examination (IME) provides an overview of a client's history and a detailed evaluation of the client's treatment, recovery, and prognosis. It is generally requested by the defense to determine the actual extent of the plaintiff's injuries. An IME may also be requested by a plaintiff attorney, insurance company, employer, or the court. The IME is conducted by an impartial physician or medical specialist to prevent undue influence by the interested parties. (See Chapter 19, "Defense Medical Evaluations," for more information.)

The defense may require that the plaintiff submit to a physical or mental examination by a physician chosen by the defense. The plaintiff has the right to refuse an IME, but refusal may be viewed unfavorably by the court. The examining physician reports on the extent and possible causes of the injuries, and may render an opinion as to the merits of the plaintiff's allegations (APA, 2001). The LNC should be prepared to write notes and, if allowed, to audiotape the examination if asked to accompany the plaintiff to the IME. The LNC should note when the examination began and ended. The LNC should note the physician's and the plaintiff's gestures and body language. For example, if the doctor asked the plaintiff to bend over and touch his toes, did the plaintiff do it hesitantly? The LNC should write down things not picked up on tape. Did the doctor appear to lead the plaintiff to answer "yes" or "no" by his or her facial expression? After the IME, the LNC needs to prepare a written "transcript" of the examination. Attorneys will want the actual audio file sent to them, also. Incorporate notes into a detailed chronology and report of the assessment.

Client Intake Interview

An LNC may be asked to conduct an initial client interview to gather facts from the client about what happened and the issues involved. The LNC should do the following:

■ Note the date of the interview, the interviewee's name, address, and contact numbers
■ Obtain the interviewee's recollection of the event and his or her role in it
  – Ask the interviewee to recall any significant dates and times of incidents: Were any contributing factors involved? Does he or she remember the physician's orders, lab work, treatments, or physical therapy that was done? Did the healthcare provider say anything to a family member regarding the care or treatment?

After gathering the information, the LNC should prepare a written report objectively documenting the facts that the interviewee revealed. The report should also include the date and time of the interview, and whether it was conducted in person or on the phone. It should note whether the interviewee "recalled," "confirmed," or "speculated" about different issues when relating the incident.

Conference with Potential Expert

Both the plaintiff and defense are entitled to have a physician review the medical records and prepare an opinion as to the allegations regarding standards of care. The physician expert should be board-certified and have experience in the area of medicine under review. The LNC should review the physician's curriculum vitae, noting any published articles, speaking presentations, involvement in academics, and attendance at seminars in the expert's area of expertise. The expert should be current in his or her field, render an opinion as to the standards of care provided, and note and discuss any deviations from standards. A verbal report is usually undiscoverable unless the opinion is to be used in court. A written report is discoverable. Therefore, it is important for the attorney to meet with the physician expert, if feasible, so that the medical and legal portions of the case can be discussed and reviewed.

Interrogatories

Interrogatories are written questions from one party to the other. Written interrogatories are generally used to obtain information not readily available during trial or depositions. The LNC may be utilized to help the attorney formulate questions to be posed. After the responses are received, the LNC may be asked to write a summary of the responses, as well as to explain complex medical issues.

Conclusion

LNCs write numerous reports, chronologies, summaries, memos, and other types of correspondence. Effective communication requires that the LNC considers the scope of the topic, the purpose or objective of the communication, and the audience's need for the information. The final product should be clear, concise, and professional.

Acknowledgment

The authors wish to acknowledge Research Assistant: B. Roderick Jarrett RN BSN CCRN LNC for his assistance in developing this chapter.

References

Acerbo-Avalone, N., & Kremer, K. (1997). *Medical malpractice claims investigation: A step-by-step approach.* Gaitherburg, MD: An Aspen Publication.

Garver-Mastrian, K., & Birdsall, E. (1986). *Writing on the job: A guide for nurse managers*. New York: Wiley.

American Psychological Association (APA). (2001). *The Publication Manual of the American Psychological Association* (5th ed.). Washington, DC: Author.

Additional Reading

Aaron, J. E. (2000). *The Little, Brown compact handbook*. Reading, MA: Pearson Custom Publishing.

Garner, B. A. (2001). *Legal writing in plain English: A text with exercises*. Chicago: University of Chicago Press.

Goldstein, T., & Lieberman, J. (1989). *The lawyer's guide to writing well*. Los Angeles: University of California Press.

Poirrer, G. (1997). *Writing to learn: Curricular strategies for nursing and other disciplines*. New York: NLN Press.

Shelton, J. H. (1994). *Handbook for technical writing*. Chicago: NTC Business Books.

Zilm, G. (1998). *The smart way: An introduction to writing for nurses*. Orlando: Harcourt Brace.

Test Questions

1. "Noise" that can interfere with effective written communication includes
   A. Thoughtlessness
   B. Misspellings
   C. Television
   D. Current newspaper articles

2. A writer should be sensitive to the audience reading the document. Readers may need to read to
   A. Locate information
   B. Order supplies
   C. Review additional literature
   D. Set up an interview with the attorney

3. A common style guide that provides ways of documenting text citations is
   A. PAR
   B. SKR
   C. APA
   D. KFC

4. The nurse attending an IME will present an audiotape, as well as a prepared written report that includes
   A. Body language and gestures of the nurse recording the IME
   B. Comments made by the receptionist
   C. Body language and gestures of the physician or the plaintiff
   D. Fee charged by the physician to conduct IME

5. In the client intake interview, the LNC should NOT include
   A. Interviewee's recollection of the event
   B. Interviewee's recollection of contributing factors
   C. Interviewee's recollection of the physician's orders
   D. What the plaintiff had for lunch before arriving at the IME

Answers: 1. B, 2. A, 3. C, 4. C, 5. D

Appendix A: Sample Case Chronology

P ———— v. ————, et al. (Case No. ————)

Summary of Medical Records and Deposition for Noneconomic Damages

Date	Event/ Care Provider	Source	Event/Description	Legal Nurse Consultant Clinical Notations (Article ref. #'s)
5/23/2003	Motor vehicle accident (MVA) EMS	Accident Report	South-bound on 101, turned wheels to R. Struck from behind by trash truck, vehicle pushed to R shoulder across a lane of traffic. Treated and released by paramedics on scene	Air bag would not have normally deployed with rear-end collision. Front of vehicle did not suffer any impact
5/28/2003	Initial treatment for back/neck symptoms after MVA	Chiropractic Office; Initial Visit	PT C/O [Complaints of]: Constant/mod/ sha** low back pain (LBP), stiffness radiating down L hip; Neck pain radiating to both shoulders; HA [head ache] w/light sensitivity	C-Spine x-ray [cervical spine] Negative for fracture, Break in Georges line [indicates a sprain, possible fracture of neural ring] @ C4-5, C5–6
	Chiropractic Dr. H___	Patient Data Form **0373-0376	**: "Neck pain, head aches, back spasms" and dizziness, "whiplash" symptoms began 5/23/2003 Dr.'s Notes: (**0375) (1) Neck pain and tension, had headache every day "6" [0–10 pain scale], shoulder pain, arms ache (2) R sided LBP and spasms "4" (3) Headache, sensitive to light "8" "Before accident felt fine" Chiropractic Treatment: 3 ×/week	Article 2A Anatomy of a Normal Spine Article 2B Cervical Lines of Menstruation Article 2C Numerical Pain Rating Scale Denies taking any medications, so was not taking any pain meds after her lumpectomy (3/03, **0088) than would have affected her driving or judgment

continued

P ——— v. ———, et al. (Case No. ———)

Summary of Medical Records and Deposition for Noneconomic Damages

Date	Event/Care Provider	Source	Event/Description	Legal Nurse Consultant Clinical Notations (Article ref. #'s)
5/30/2003	Follow-up chiropractic treatments Dr. H ———	Treatment Notes (Hole was punched through **#…)	** (S = subjective, patient's own words recorded by care practitioner): LBP and tension, very sore; L and R neck pain, having headaches	Article 4A Cervical Pain: Description and Diagnosis Article 4B Evaluation of Patient With Cervical Spine Disorders, p. 5 Article 5A Low Back Pain
6/2/2003	Follow-up chiropractic treatments Dr. H ———	Treatment Notes	** (S) "LBP improved" Notes upper back pain and tension	Improvements in pain were temporary. Her pain fluctuates according to her need for movement and daily activities as a mother, wife and working adult
6/5/2003	Follow-up chiropractic treatments Dr. H ———	Treatment Notes	(S) LBP and tension, L arm pain and tension, muscles tight R lower back	First noticed/mentioned L arm tingling and pain, approx two weeks after accident *Article* 4C Cervical Sprain and Strain
6/9/2003	Follow-up chiropractic treatments Dr. H ———	Treatment Notes (Hole was punched through **#)	(S) Upper back pain and tension, Lower back pain Dr.'s notes: "Patient stopped treatment seeing MD."	Almost three weeks after the accident, a simple muscle strain should have been improving, and ——— sought further treatment Article 4B, p. 3 Article 6A, p. 2

Appendix B: Sample Case Timeline

18:35	Patient received from the operating room to PACU s/p (R) carotid endarterectomy
18:40	Left arm weakness noted; paged surgeon
18:50	Surgeon returned call; informed of patient's left arm weakness
19:05	Surgeon and anesthesiologist at bedside; discussed plan of care with patient's wife—patient remains partially sedated
19:30	Patient returned to operating room

Chapter 14

Trial Preparation and the Trial Process

Diane L. Reboy, MS, RN, LNCC, FACFEI DABFN, CFN, CNLCP

First Edition
Barbara Loecker, MSEd, BSN, RN; Judy Ringholz, BSN, RN; and Adella Toepel Getsch, BSN, RN, LNCC

Second Edition
Jane Barone, BSN, RN, LNCC; Lucille Evangelista, BS, RN; Barbara Loecker, MSEd, BSN, RN; Patricia Raya, BS, RNC, MBA; Judy Ringholz, BSN, RN; and Adella Toepel Getsch, BSN, RN, LNCC

Contents

Objectives

Upon reading this chapter, the legal nurse consultant (LNC) will be able to

■ Describe the purpose of well-organized trial and witness notebooks and identify eight to ten items to include in each
■ Explain the difference between admissible and inadmissible medical records
■ State one issue to be concerned when preparing each type of evidence—deposition testimony, documents, and physical evidence—for trial
■ List three examples of demonstrative evidence
■ Identify three points to keep in mind with regard to how a witness may feel about testifying, and the purpose of preparing for trial testimony
■ Identify one way to put a witness more at ease
■ Name and describe the major portions of a civil trial
■ Identify the role of the LNC during jury selection and presentation of testimony
■ Discuss the important issues involved in determining the verdict
■ Discuss jury awards, including comparative and contributory negligence and punitive damages
■ Evaluate post-trial activities
■ Discuss ethical considerations at trial

Introduction

Trial preparation and the trial are the culmination of all the efforts put forth in developing a case. Depending on the nature of the case and its jurisdiction, the LNC and the trial team may have spent years working on a particular case. Thorough preparation is the key to a successful outcome. The attorney must be able to rely on the LNC to assist him/her in presenting the case in an organized fashion. The jury can easily detect a lack of preparedness in the trial team, and this will reflect on the team's competence. "Nothing so undermines the confidence of a court or jury in an attorney as his or her constant groping and fondling" (Appleman, 1952). The ultimate outcome of the case is influenced by how well the attorney has learned his client's story and how he or she is able to convey that story to the jury.

The role of the LNC may vary during trial preparation and trial due to variations of practice settings, talent and training of the LNC, and the practice patterns of the trial attorney. Variations in the role of the LNC can occur in different areas of the country and even within a law firm. The LNC who combines nursing expertise with creative, independent thinking soon becomes an essential member of the litigation team. The LNC's role is different from the trial attorney, so the LNC should not expect the trial attorney to teach the LNC what he or she needs to know in order to accomplish a particular task.

An experienced LNC is the new LNC's best resource. The LNC may be expected to assume responsibility for tasks a paralegal routinely performs, tasks that the LNC is best prepared to perform, and now, in the technologically advance courtroom, tasks that also include electronic trial presentation. Another valuable resource is the experienced litigation paralegal who has worked with the trial attorney. When both legal assistants (formerly known as legal secretaries) and "LNCs" are working together on the trial team, a clear division of responsibilities should be established. All members of the team need to be aware of what tasks each professional is to perform in order to eliminate duplication of efforts and prevent an important task from being overlooked. The successful trial team must display the true meaning of the word "team" in that a cooperative effort is necessary in order for things to run as smoothly as possible during trial.

The common theme is anticipation—anticipation of courtroom procedure, anticipation of witness testimony, anticipation of witness scheduling, and anticipation of anything else expected to arise in the courtroom setting. The LNC must be familiar with trial procedure and should be comfortable in the courtroom whether as a formal expert, or as an informal expert behind the scenes assisting the attorney.

Preparation for the LNC's role in the courtroom begins well before the trial. It begins during the discovery phase of the case. Trial strategy, testimony, and exhibits are developed during discovery in anticipation of the trial. The legal preparation for trial may be done by an associate attorney who has not had any trial experience. Therefore, it is important for the LNC to understand the trial attorney's strategy, which may differ from the associate's attorney as well as the venue of the court (federal or state). The trial is the showcase for the case, and barring appeals, it is the culmination of years of work for all the parties involved. Meticulous preparation and presentation are vital for success in the courtroom. Juries do not decide cases on the merit of the claim alone. Cases are often won or lost by the presentation from the trial attorney, the experts, and the litigation team. An attorney who fumbles for exhibits, forgets key information, and backtracks when presenting testimony is not viewed as a winner, and is not successful in the courtroom. The presentation must be a well-orchestrated work of art.

The LNC is a key member of the litigation team in a medical malpractice case. The LNC participates in the development of the trial strategy, testimony, and preparation of the trial exhibits. Having the testimony and exhibits organized is essential. The trial is the opportunity for the plaintiff and defense to tell their story, and the party who convinces the jury will prevail. The LNC's role is to develop the medical side of the story while the trial attorney concentrates on the legal side, with constant communication between the two. Neither develops one part of the case in isolation from the other.

The LNC may share responsibilities with a legal assistant or a paralegal in case preparation. Although a paralegal frequently attends the trial and takes notes during the voir dire and testimony, the LNC is uniquely qualified to appraise the medical testimony. LNCs are the ideal nonattorney member of the trial team because they can perform all of the routine duties, provide on the spot analysis of the medical testimony, and in many instances operate all the equipment necessary to present a case electronically. The LNC at trial must therefore be prepared to perform a wide variety of tasks as the primary trial assistant to the attorney.

The key elements of a trial include the following:

- Motions in limine
- Voir dire
- Opening statements
- Presentation of testimony by witnesses through direct and cross-examination
- Rebuttal
- Closing arguments
- Receipt of the verdict
- Interviewing the jury on behalf of the attorney

Trial Notebooks

Paper Notebook

Trial notebooks may take on many different forms, ranging from simple manila file folders by subject to thin three ring binders with tabbed subject divisions, all the way to a large, legal size, self-sealed, predivided, five-holed punched binders, specifically prepared for trials. Common section headings may include case analysis, proof checklists, voir dire, opening statement; pretrial orders, stipulations, witnesses; deposition index, document index, memoranda, closing argument, and jury instructions. Specifically for any cases involving medical records, these may be in a separate notebook possibly divided by a health care provider, medical chronology or timeline, and any pertinent medical literature (supportive or nonsupportive).

Trial notebooks, whether paper or electronic, are used to compile all the pertinent information that will be needed at the time of the trial in a convenient format. As trial courts, whether federal or state, are renovated for technology the LNC needs to be aware as to the type of electronic technology the specific court uses and whether or not the trial judge will allow electronics to be used. Many judges still rely on paper formats in their courtrooms, thereby making it necessary for the trial team to prepare both traditionally, with hard copies of everything, as well as electronically.

Electronic Trial Notebooks

According to Robert Claus in his paper entitled, "The Electronic Trial Preparation" (Claus, 2002), the advantages of electronic trial preparation have grown with the development of large complex cases, whether the nature of the cases are criminal or civil. An example of this would include large class action suites. Advantages to the use of electronic trial notebooks include the convenience of having the entire file in one place such as a CD or flash drive, the ability to organize and retrieve documents by using a find or search feature with the software, and the ease of transferring documents from paper to computer and vice-versa. As always, this may be a problem if not all documents are organized prior to the transfer process.

396 ■ *Legal Nurse Consulting Principles*

Professor McElhaney (1994) also discussed the electronic trial notebook. This "virtual" notebook should provide the user the same organization as the "traditional" notebook but can provide better flexibility, greater accessibility, and organization in a compact size. He also reported when changes need to be made, such as a last minute witness or report, it is just a click away. Another good resource to familiarize the reader with this concept is the article by Ronald C. Morton, called The Electronic Trial Notebook (2005).

Many software packages have been currently developed for this purpose, such as Lexis Nexis' Concordance and Summation (http://www.summation.com). In Data/Trial Director, the software provides electronic discovery, trial preparation, and video services (http://www.indatacorp.com). Coupled with the advances in programs such as Microsoft Office (Word, Excel, Access, and PowerPoint), Adobe, and others, electronic developments just keep growing. By using the "virtual" process, documents can be moved around, added, deleted with just a key stroke. Unfortunately, with the traditional style, if there are any additions, deletions, and so on, then it will require changes such as the Table of Contents and/or Index each time there is a change.

There are two schools of thought regarding when to create the trial notebook. One school of thought is to wait until you know the case is going to trial. In many states and law firms, trials are double and triple booked with the court to start on the same day, in the anticipation that most will settle before that date arrives. Therefore, to start a trial notebook for every case would be a waste of human, electronic, and paper resources.

The other school of thought is to start creating the trial notebook from the very beginning of litigation in order to avoid last minute pretrial crunches. This can be especially critical when the LNC may be responsible for several trials, which may be scheduled to start on the same date. The LNC needs to be aware of each of the trial attorney's practice preferences and the general type and percentage of cases the attorney litigates which will settle or go to trial.

The trial notebook is best organized in a three-ring binder with tabs to include the necessary documents for each section of the notebook and is consistent with the attorney's needs. Color coding various sections may be helpful. The LNC should prepare a concise Table of Contents with an index and organize the notebook with enough detail to allow the attorney or anyone working at his or her side instant access to pertinent documents. If there are several trial notebooks, a Table of Contents and/or Index should be included in each notebook. Trial notebooks commonly contain pleading and discovery documents for both plaintiff and defense. This should be clearly marked for easier access.

The LNC may also wish to incorporate some, or all, of the following materials into the trial notebook or have these items available in the courtroom in some other form:

- Motion in limine
- Proposed jury instructions
- Notes on voir dire examinations
- Notes on opening statement
- Notes on final argument
- Pretrial order
- Court's docket control order
- Designation of witnesses by plaintiff
- Designation of witnesses by defendant
- Order of proof (order in which witnesses will be called)
- Plaintiff's list of exhibits to be admitted at trial
- Defendant's list of exhibits to be admitted at trial
- Relevant portions of medical records at issue

- Summaries of medical records and medical chronologies
- Pertinent medical literature
- Definitions of pertinent medical terminology
- Relevant portions of other significant records (education, employment, etc.)
- Expert reports
- Opposing experts CVs, prior testimony, impeachment documentation
- Opening statement
- Final argument
- Medical timeline or chronology

Witness Notebooks

In addition to a trial notebook, the attorney may require a separate notebook or file folder for each witness. The notebooks or folders should include:

- Contact information
- Copies of correspondence sent to or pertaining to the witness
- Notes taken during meetings with witness
- Any written item or statement prepared by witness
- Compressed transcript (mini script) of deposition with concordance
- Errata sheet with revisions to deposition testimony and signature page
- Summary of deposition or line and page outline
- Outline of direct or crossexamination
- Copy of report (for experts)
- Copy of curriculum vitae and bibliography (for expert)
- Other pertinent document (e.g., medical literature authored, notes regarding significant entries made by witness in medical records)
- Pertinent investigative reports

Burden of Proof

Negligence

In Chapter 4, "Elements of Triage: Effective Case Screening of Medical Malpractice Claims" the concept of negligence was discussed. Recall that the burden is on the plaintiff to prove each of the four elements of negligence. Both sides prove their respective cases through the evidence that they present at trial. This proof is a huge burden for the plaintiffs as they must prove ALL four elements of negligence. For the defense, it is easier in that strategy-wise, the defense must only punch a clear hole in one of the four elements in order to defeat the plaintiff's efforts.

In addition, the reader must recall that the burden of proof differs between a civil and criminal case. In a civil case, the plaintiff has to prove on the preponderance of the evidence, whereas in a criminal case it is beyond a reasonable doubt. Some states now use "clear and convincing evidence" as the standard for civil trials. That is, the scales must tip only slightly toward one party or the other for the jury to find in favor of that party. In many jurisdictions, the jury may find the defendant negligent but also find the plaintiff to have been negligent.

Under comparative negligence statutes or doctrines, negligence is measured in terms of percentage, and any damages allowed should be diminished in proportion to the amount of negligence attributable to the person for whose injury, damage, or death recovery is sought. Many states have replaced contributory negligence acts or doctrines with comparative negligence. Contributory negligence is the act or omission by the plaintiff that, along with the defendant's negligence, was the proximate cause of the plaintiff's injury. Where negligence by both parties is concurrent and contributes to injury, recovery is not barred under such a doctrine, but the plaintiff's damages are diminished proportionately, provided that the plaintiff's fault is less than the defendant's and that, by exercise of normal care, the plaintiff could not have avoided consequences of the defendant's negligence after it was or should have been apparent.

Most jurisdictions allow the jury to find either comparative or contributory negligence by the plaintiff. An example is when a worker slips in a hole and fractures his leg. The employer should have taken action to cover the hole so as to avoid an employee from falling and sustaining a serious physical injury. However, the worker was aware of the hole but did not see it as he was carrying a piece of lumber and talking to his fellow workers. As a result, the comparative negligence might be 80% employer and 20% employee. If the award was $1000.00, then the employee's award would only be $800.00 or 80%.

A querulous or contentious plaintiff can lose a case. A plaintiff who the jury concludes was exaggerating or lying can lose a case. The best position for the plaintiff to be in is that of a litigant who describes the same course of events as is recorded in the medical records, avoids controversy, and prevents himself or herself from being the focus of the case (Fisher, 1994). The defense counsel will make every effort to shift the focus of the trial from the conduct of the defendant to the conduct of the plaintiff.

Evidence

Status of Admissibility of Records

Evidence comes in many forms, including testimony of parties and witnesses as well as various types of ancillary materials. In addition to preparing parties and witnesses for trial (which will be discussed later in this chapter), the LNC plays a crucial role in obtaining, reviewing, analyzing, and summarizing records, especially medical records (see Chapter 12, "Medical Record Analysis"). Medical records must be in admissible form in order to be introduced into evidence at trial.

The LNC must understand what makes medical records admissible. Admissibility is determined by the method through which the records are obtained (see Chapter 4, "Elements of Triage: Effective Case Screening of Medical Malpractice Claims") and the fact that they are disclosed properly in the litigation. In Texas, for example, medical records can be obtained in admissible form by subpoena duces tecum or with an affidavit that is accompanied by a current medical authorization executed by the client. If records are obtained with affidavits, they are not admissible unless the affidavits are filed with the court at least 14 days before the trial begins. In New Jersey, for example, hospital records must be certified by the hospital as a complete copy of the records in order for them to be admissible.

When records are obtained by subpoena, the ordering party receives the original or court copy of the records. In some states, the records ordered for trial must be sent directly to the court. If the records are sent to the party requesting the records, the LNC should contact the party and return the records with the corrected court address. This is to avoid possible inadmissibility of the records. It is the responsibility of the LNC to check with the trial attorney should this happen. If a codefendant ordered records and settles before trial, the LNC must remember to obtain the court copies from that party. If the codefendant obtained the records by affidavit with an authorization, the LNC must obtain proof that the affidavit was filed in a timely fashion. When working with a codefendant, it is always best to determine which records to request, as cost sharing helps to keep trial preparation expenses in check.

Procedures for obtaining records vary from state to state. A reputable record-retrieval service should be able to explain the difference between admissible and inadmissible records. Imagine the potential result of not learning until after trial has begun that the most significant medical records are not admissible and, as a result, cannot be used as evidence or referred to during the trial. This information should be easily accessible and updated as additional medical records are received. There are computer databases that are designed for this purpose. The LNC may wish to design a database for specific needs with programs such as Word® and Excel®. Appendix A displays an example of how the information can be recorded in a computer database.

Deposition Testimony

For witnesses who are not called to the stand to testify live at trial, each side identifies the portions of the witness's deposition testimony that they wish to offer into evidence and the portions to which they object. These offers and objections are exchanged with opposing counsel prior to trial. Particularly if the witness is a health care professional, the LNC may be asked to review the transcript or videotape of the witness's deposition and to draft proposed offers and objections. In addition, the LNC may then be the trial team member who edits the electronic synchronized video transcript (when used) to ensure that only agreed upon testimony is presented in the courtroom.

In order to do this, the LNC must be aware of and note on the amendment page or errata sheet any revisions the witness makes to the deposition testimony, and indicate the page number and line number referenced in the transcript where each section being offered or excluded by objection begins and ends. The reason for any objection must be indicated with the reason why as related to the rules of court. Once the offers and objections have been exchanged and, if necessary, ruled on by the court, the videotape can be edited to include only the testimony that will actually be offered. If the videotape is not available, the portions to be offered are read from the transcript at trial. The LNC may be asked to role-play the witness and read the responses contained in the deposition transcript of the witness from the witness stand. When doing role-playing, the LNC should keep in mind the transcript needs to be read as objectively as possible with no vocal inflections.

Preparing Exhibits

The LNC is frequently the trial team member who drafts the trial exhibit list. Then, the attorney must determine, in advance, which documents he or she intends to use as exhibits. The LNC should then review the list to establish the order for it to reflect the order in which the attorney plans to use the exhibits. The LNC should do the following:

- Create a separate folder for each exhibit.
- Groom the document to ensure it has no highlights, underlines, or attorney-made marks on it other than those which were a part of the original document.
- Mark the document as "Plaintiff or Defense Exhibit _____" (the blank will be filled in by a letter or number according to the local court rules, generally by the court reporter), and prepare a corresponding exhibit list. Familiarity with the local procedural rules will assist in marking the exhibits properly for identification during trial.
- Whenever possible, use the original document and have a copy available in the exhibit folder.
- If the original document is not available, insert a note in the folder regarding where it is kept and how it can be obtained. This will allow for trial use by the certified medical records sent to the court as described above.

In some jurisdictions, the actual exhibits are exchanged between the parties before the trial begins. Some court clerks prefer that exhibit lists be submitted on computer disks (CD) so that they can input the data into their files. During the pretrial conference, as well as during the trial, it is necessary to keep the exhibit list (and the opposing party's exhibit list) available at all times, noting directly on the list when each exhibit is offered into evidence, objected to being admitted, or withdrawn. The trial attorney must be able to know at a glance which exhibits have been properly introduced into evidence and which exhibits have not been properly introduced. The LNC must also be aware of whether or not the attorney intends to introduce specific documents, records, or other exhibits into evidence through a particular witness by having that person authenticate them while under oath. In some states, the medical record may be certified by a notary, to be accepted by the court so the record keeper does not have to appear in court to authenticate the medical records. If so, the LNC should be certain that the documents are organized before the witness takes the stand. This is why it is helpful to prepare witness notebooks. If the LNC is coordinating the offering of exhibits with a codefendant, the LNC should be certain to determine ahead of time which party will be responsible for which exhibit. This prevents the submission of duplicate exhibits and helps to minimize trial preparation costs.

Physical Evidence

Physical evidence is any tangible item that may be used or displayed as an exhibit during trial. An example of physical evidence is a medical device (e.g., intravenous infusion pump or fetal monitor) that has been positively identified as the one used, or is representative of the one used, during a procedure at issue. The item must be appropriately marked by the court reporter and identified on the exhibit list. The LNC needs to remember that any demonstrative device used in a trial may not be released by the court until conceivably years after the trial is over. Therefore, the attorney, client, and LNC must carefully consider whether a specific item or, alternatively, a duplicate should be placed into evidence instead.

Demonstrative Evidence

Demonstrative evidence allows the attorney to demonstrate certain issues to the jury in a way that facilitates their understanding of the complex concepts being presented. The LNC, as the person on the litigation team who is most familiar with the medical records, can be particularly helpful in identifying issues that can best be presented through the use of demonstrative evidence.

Demonstrative evidence can be in the form of a chart, table, diagram, illustration, or animation. The LNC can blow up a document contained in the medical records that illustrates a specific point which the trial attorney wants the jury to visualize. Medical models and/or illustrations are often helpful in explaining an anatomical matter. Computer-generated animation can be used to reconstruct an accident. This is often done when an accident reconstructionist wants the jury to see the dynamics of how the accident occurred. The LNC should consider what the trial attorney is trying to prove (plaintiff) or disprove (defense) in order to determine how best this information can be presented. The LNC should then make certain to have the necessary equipment available in the courtroom for the presentation.

Discussing with the clerk what the court's preferences are making a trip to the courtroom to personally determine what audiovisual equipment is/is not available are invaluable before the start of the trial. (See Volume 2, Chapter 18, "Ambulatory Care Settings," for more information.) It is also helpful to check with the court clerk as to what type of demonstrative evidence the trial judge will permit. For example, a blown-up Excel graph illustration was brought in for use by the toxicology expert during his testimony. Unfortunately, the judge would not allow the chart to be viewed by the jury.

Many companies can create medical illustrations, courtroom graphics, animation, and so on. to be used as demonstrative exhibits. Some may provide the necessary equipment and assist with the actual presentation. The LNC should plan for the possibility that an outside vendor may take more time than anticipated to create a desired exhibit. The LNC may need to weigh the high cost of an elaborate exhibit against its benefit—that is, successfully communicating his/her client's position to the jury. Experts may also need to approve any demonstrative evidence they will reference during their testimony. This approval process is needed to authenticate the exhibit and eliminate any errors, but will also take additional time to coordinate.

Example 14.1

Emily Smith, an elderly woman, aspirated a piece of solid food while eating lunch at home with her husband. Her lower airway was partially obstructed and she was brought to Lakeside Hospital for treatment to remove the obstruction. Ms. Smith had been diagnosed with Parkinson's disease 10 years earlier. It was alleged that her deteriorating condition was caused by treatment delays by the defendants. The hospital, the emergency room physician, and the pulmonologist were sued. In this instance, the defendants claimed Ms. Smith's condition was a result of the progression of her Parkinson's disease. Appendix B quotes excerpts from multiple medical records in an effort to establish the progression of her disease prior to the time of the incident in question. Appendix B displays the chronology of events that took place at the defendant hospital on the day of the incident in an effort to controvert the plaintiff's claims that there were extended periods of time during which Ms. Smith was not attended to by the hospital staff. Appendix B was enlarged to 30 by 40 in. for display at trial.

Medical Literature

Chapter 11, "Researching Medical Information and Literature," discusses medical literature research. The focus in this section is on the organization of medical literature research for purposes of trial preparation. A medical literature notebook, organized in a three-ring binder, may be useful or research articles may be placed within a particular witness's trial notebook. Sometimes, having both a medical literature notebook and duplicate articles in the witness notebook is helpful so as to avoid a problem should one or the other notebooks not be available. The LNC should begin to collect and organize medical literature during the discovery phases of case development. The medical literature should be reviewed by the attorney as it may assist and/or direct the development of plaintiff or defense theories.

The LNC should include pertinent journal articles, articles from newspapers or periodicals, and chapters or excerpts from medical textbooks that support the trial attorney's theory of the case. The items can be organized chronologically by topic, or alphabetically by author. Each item should be tabbed to correspond with a concise index. If more than one notebook is needed, each notebook needs to contain the concise index with the outside of the notebook marked clearly as to what is contained within that particular notebook. The LNC should always include identifying information for each item, such as a copy of the title page with the date of publication.

Once the LNC has obtained and organized pertinent medical literature, it is equally important that he/she review it thoroughly. An article that includes statements that support the case may also say something that is quite damaging to the case. For that reason, the LNC may wish to consider a color-coded method for literature review. The LNC may use three differently colored highlighters (e.g., pink, yellow, and green) similar to the colors of a stop light with pink for red.

Information highlighted in pink (stop) signals the attorney that it may be damaging to the case. Statements highlighted in yellow (make note) are significant to the case in some way, but neutral in nature. Highlighted portions in green (go) are supportive of the theory of the case and potentially damaging to the other side.

If the LNC chooses instead to highlight with only one color, then the potential damaging information should be brought to the attention of the attorney with a Post-it note or color tab with key words. The LNC should insert the highlighted copy in the notebook in order to help the attorney find the information he or she needs, and also insert an unmarked copy (used during trial as described above). An unmarked copy is submitted to the court when applicable. The attorney may find it helpful to have a concise summary of the article to use as an easy reference.

When preparing medical literature to be used at trial, the LNC must be aware of the rules regarding admissibility. For example, in some jurisdictions it is permissible to refer to literature that speaks to issues pertaining to standard of care only if it was published prior to the date of the alleged incident. However, articles that speak to causation issues, and were published subsequent to the occurrence, may be allowed, as long as they refer to the condition at the time of occurrence. The LNC should also be aware of major court decisions that have an effect on what may be submitted, such as *Daubert v. Merrell Dow*, which limits "junk science" (see Chapter 15, "Locating and Working with Expert Witnesses").

Witness Preparation

The effective preparation of a witness before testimony at trial is absolutely necessary. It is the responsibility of the trial attorney to perform witness preparation. Preparation requires both time and patience. In many cases, the witness may have never seen the inside of a courtroom, and may be anxious or frightened. The LNC should try to alleviate the witness's anxiety by helping him or her understand what will take place at trial. The experienced LNC may be asked to assist the lawyer in, or to be solely responsible for, preliminary preparation of the witness.

The LNC may also be responsible for scheduling the witness for trial preparation and testimony on the attorney's request. If this is the case, letters informing the witness of deposition and/or anticipated trial testimony dates should be sent out as early as possible in order that scheduling conflicts can be resolved early. The LNC should contact the witness to obtain availability for witness preparation and coordinate with the attorney's schedule. Preparation may take several hours and/or days, so the witness needs to be aware of this possibility. The more thoroughly the witness is prepared, the better the trial presentation.

The first step is to establish a rapport with the witness and to put the witness at ease. The LNC should NOT role-play the attorney for the opposite side. Initially asking tough questions may increase the witness's anxiety and make the preparation more difficult. The purpose of preparing witnesses is to make certain they are calm and anticipates the types of questions they may be asked and how they need to answer those questions. The LNC should explain that the attorney will ask questions (direct examination) that may be followed by questions from one or more opposing counsel(s) (crossexamination), which may again be followed by redirect and re-crossexamination. The LNC should make certain that the witness clearly understands the theory of the case.

Also by preparing a witness for trial, the attorney gets a "preview" of how the witness will appear to the jury. Nonverbal appearance can convey a possible undesirable view of the witness to the jury. Physical appearance will also play an important visualization. In instances where witness mannerisms or appearance is of concern, in addition to the efforts made by the attorney and LNC, an informal testifying consultant may be brought in to assist prepping the witness.

If requested by the attorney, the LNC may want to counsel the witness to some, or all of the following:

■ Maintain a demeanor that is polite and sincere. On crossexamination, the attorney may make an effort to make you angry or defensive. Do not lose your composure or be condescending. It might be better for the witness to take a few seconds before answering the question to help formulate a nondefensive or nonangry answer.

■ Be aware of body language. Maintain eye contact with the trial attorney when he or she is asking you a question. Shift your glance between the attorney and the jury when responding. The attorney may use certain signals, such as a blinking eye, as a clue regarding a question.

■ Do not cross your arms, put your hands over your mouth, or near your face. It is easier to keep your hands on your lap.

■ Dress appropriately for the courtroom and make sure that any family members or friends who may accompany you dress appropriately as well. An example is: would you rather hear from a witness in jeans and T-shirt or someone who appears in neat business or business casual attire?

■ Be aware of the techniques that attorneys use in an effort to get you to answer the question in a certain way, such as hook, compound, and hypothetical questions.

A hook question is one that incorporates or implies facts that, if not corrected by the witness prior to the time that he or she responds, will be assumed to be true by virtue of the witness's silence regarding the issue.

Example 14.2

Nurse Wilson, you testified that the nurse is not responsible for assessing blood pressure after surgery. Isn't it true that the nurse does not have to check the pulse either?

A compound question is one that incorporates two or three questions into one. If the witness responds, the same answer may be assumed to apply to each component of the question.

Example 14.3

Is it true that the Post Anesthesia Care Unit nurse does not have to check the blood pressure every 15 min and to observe for airway obstruction?

A hypothetical question usually begins with, "Assume with me . . ."

Example 14.4

Nurse Webster, I'd like you to assume for the purposes of this question that the following are true.

• It is most important to listen *very* carefully to the question and answer only what is directly being asked. Do not offer additional information.
• Never answer a question that you do not understand. Ask the attorney to repeat it or rephrase it. The witness can state he or she does not understand the question. Do this as many times as is necessary until you understand the question.
• If you perceive the attorney is asking a question that you have answered previously, but he or she is wording it differently, give the same answer that you gave earlier.
• Always be certain the attorney has finished asking the question before you begin to answer. Pause for a few seconds (maybe count to 5 is helpful). This allows you time to reflect on your response. It also allows the opposing attorney time to object if they choose to do so. Do not

attempt to answer if an objection is made. Wait for the judge's ruling and respond accordingly. Usually the judge will indicate to "answer the question."
- Speak clearly and slowly. Speak loudly enough for each juror to hear your answers without straining.
- Use your own words. Do not adopt the attorney's language. If you disagree with a portion of the question or would phrase it differently, do so before you answer.
- If the attorney references a specific document in the question (e.g., a medical record or journal article), request a copy of the document and read it carefully *before* responding.
- If instructed to answer the question "yes" or "no" and you cannot limit the answer this way, state that you cannot provide an accurate answer using only yes or no.
- If you do not know the answer to the question being asked or you do not recall, say so. *Never* guess or speculate.
- Always tell the truth based on your personal knowledge. Give brief and concise answers.
- After practicing repeatedly, you will begin to memorize the answers to anticipated questions. Do not let your responses sound as though they were rehearsed.

The LNC should adequately review with the witness any materials that could be used for impeachment purposes. These include prior deposition testimony, answers to interrogatories, answers to requests for admission, and any oral or written statements that were made previously. Also, any public or electronic documents may impact the possibility of impeachment. The LNC should make sure the witness understands all information, reports, prior testimony, and literature that may be utilized by opposing counsel for impeachment.

Discuss the probable testimony of other witnesses in order to ascertain whether or not there is a potential for inconsistencies in testimony at trial. The LNC should advise the attorney of any such inconsistencies as soon as possible. The LNC should review and discuss any exhibits the trial attorney has determined that he or she will prove or authenticate through the witness.

An attorney may prefer on some occasions to have a deposition videotaped or video conferenced rather than take a live deposition. Videoconferencing is done in real time as opposed to taped, and interaction takes place between the parties and the witness. This may be done when the witness is unable to be present at the time of trial. Videoconferencing may be used to prepare a witness for testimony or for a deposition, or at the time of trial. The witness should be prepared as previously described, and also be made aware that the videoconferencing equipment will be present in the room.

Even if all parties are in agreement about who will appear at trial, the attorney may prefer or it may be necessary in a particular jurisdiction that all witnesses and parties be served with a subpoena or notice to appear at trial. The LNC should determine what the local rules require and discuss with the trial attorney what his or her wishes are in reference to the witness subpoena process. If the attorney plans to serve a subpoena on a friendly witness (one who agrees to testify and is supportive of the theory of the case), the LNC should discuss the matter with the witness ahead of time, explaining the rationale for issuing a subpoena even though the witness has agreed to testify. The LNC should also alert the witness's office staff, if applicable, so that they are not surprised when the process server arrives.

Supply Box

The LNC may organize the case materials, box them securely, and supervise that the box is safely transported to the courthouse. Items for the supply box include:

- Various types and colors of pens and pencils
- Easel
- Colored markers (for easel)
- Thick black permanent marker

- Highlighters
- Legal pads
- Extra folders
- Two-hole and three-hole punches
- Post-it® notes and tabs in various sizes
- Correction fluid and correction tape
- Transparent tape
- Stapler and staples
- Paper clips and binder clips
- Ruler
- Pointer (maybe a laser pointer)
- Exhibit stickers
- Envelopes
- Business cards (attorney's and LNC's)
- Rolls of quarters (for pay phones and copy machines)
- List of phone numbers of people the LNC will need to contact
- Medical dictionary and relevant medical textbooks
- Copy of the rules of civil procedure and rules of evidence that apply in your jurisdiction
- Acetaminophen, ibuprofen, and aspirin
- Antacids
- Adhesive bandages
- Facial tissues
- Energy snacks
- Extension cords
- Luggage cart
- Cellular phone
- Umbrella
- Breath mints
- Water
- Electronic equipment
  - CD
  - Extra computer battery
  - External hard drive with back up of trial information
  - Projector
  - Screen
  - Extension cords
  - Connector cords
  - Duct tape
  - Mouse with mouse pad
  - Portable scanner/printer
  - Laser pointer

Packing Up and Heading Out

Numbering each box (i.e., 1 of 25, 2 of 25, etc.) will benefit the LNC greatly in the trial if he or she takes the time to do it with precision while packing. Then, he or she should list the contents of each box. The list may be placed on the top of the box for easier assessment. If any of the contents are removed, the LNC should note what supplies were used and replace them as soon as possible. This will prevent the LNC from having to rummage through boxes and appear disorganized during trial. The LNC should remember that he or she is being observed and monitored by the jury and others from the moment that he or she walks into the courtroom until the trial ends. When the trial is over, the LNC might go through the contents and add missing supplies so the package is ready for the next trial. Sometimes, trials may be simultaneous or back to back, so having the box ready for the next trial will help with trial preparation.

Ethical Propriety

The conduct of attorneys applicable during the trial process is governed by the Code of Professional Responsibility, also referred to as the Canon of Ethics. Although these are mandated for attorneys, LNCs are bound by the same ethical code. These rules and disciplinary guidelines concern expected professional conduct, integrity, competency, and compensation practices; prohibition of unauthorized practice of law by nonlawyers; exercise of competent professional judgment; preservation of the client–lawyer relationship; conflict of interest; communication restraints; trial publicity; avoidance of even the appearance of impropriety; and contact between parties, witnesses, and jurors during an ongoing trial. For more information, the American Bar Association has numerous articles on this topic and may be found at http://www.abanet.org/. Also check your state-specific Bar Association for any updates.

Initial Trial Proceedings

Motions in Limine

A motion in limine is a written statement that is usually made before or after the beginning of a jury trial for a protective order against prejudicial questions and statements. The purpose of such a motion is to avoid injection into the trial of matters that are irrelevant (immaterial), inadmissible (evidence that according to law cannot be entered, evidence that was illegally seized, and certain types of hearsay), and prejudicial (a preconceived opinion). Should a motion in limine be granted, then records need to be revisited and exhibits need to be altered or information removed from the records. The assisting LNC performs this function in order to be in compliance with the judge's ruling. Failure to adhere to the motion in limine may result in sanctions (punitive measures) or a mistrial.

Voir Dire—Jury Selection

Voir Dire is a process where the judges, attorneys for both the plaintiff and defense, along with the plaintiffs and defendants, have the opportunity to examine prospective jurors from the jury pool, assessing jurors' attitudes toward trial issues. Voir dire comes from a Latin phrase, *verum dicere*, meaning to give a true verdict. Voir is French for truth. In this legal process, the participants are able to see the perspective juror and talk to him/her personally during this evaluation process.

The Sixth Amendment of the U.S. Constitution guarantees the right of an individual to a public trial. Rule 47 of the Federal Rules of Civil Procedure provides for the selection of jurors. Cases may be tried before the court (involving just the judge known as a bench trial) or before a jury. Most malpractice suits are presented to a jury. The rationale behind this is the belief that the jury will be more sympathetic to the injured party (the plaintiff) and provide a substantial verdict award.

Prospective jurors are randomly chosen from the community, known as the jury pool, using a random method of selection. The most common sources of selection are community voter registration lists, driver's license lists, tax rolls, public utility consumers, or a combination of all jury pools who at one time had automatic exemptions for individuals from certain occupations from being called. Some of these occupations include doctors, firefighters, politicians, and people who worked within the criminal justice system such as police officers. The skills these people possessed were considered indispensable to the local community such that absences for an extended period could cause community hardships. Other exemptions included sole caregivers to young children, incompetent adults, persons holding religious/ideological beliefs such as Jehovah's Witnesses, because their beliefs precluded them from swearing oaths.

However, it was found in some people more than others; therefore, exemptions in some regions were eliminated. For example, President Clinton was called for jury duty and presented himself as required although he was subsequently exempted.

The jury selection process has become a science, with a host of trial and jury consultants available to the trial team. A jury consultant is a skilled observer who may be trained in behavioral science, psychology, and possibly law or criminal justice. When a jury consultant is used in the voir dire process, the consultant is observing the dress, actions, and responses of the perspective juror in order to determine who has the ability to influence the jury for either side. As part of the trial team, the jury consultant may assist the team in developing questions to be asked during the voir dire process.

A jury consultant has the ability to make generalizations on the perspective jury. Generalizations may include areas such as socioeconomic, race, venue of the trial (such as east vs. west, north vs. south), life experience, educational levels, marital status, and more. For example, if the case was medical malpractice, a juror with a medical background would be ideal for either side. However, other factors such as socioeconomic background or demographics may limit this potential juror. The jury consultant uses both verbal and nonverbal communication assessments during the voir dire process. Body language, facial expressions, dress, and mannerisms, all provide the experienced jury consultant with clues to the prospective juror's ability to listen, visual responses, and more. Attorneys use jury focus groups and trial simulations to identify jurors who would be beneficial to their case.

When the jury consultant is present during a trial, the consultant will observe the jury for their reaction as to how the attorney is presenting the case. Not only does the consultant observe the jury but he/she also observes the witnesses and how the jury reacts during each witness's testimony. The consultant makes note of any emotional reactions or discomfort by the jury, as this may influence deliberations on the verdict, possibly leading to a hung jury, and causing a mistrial. Jury consultants have the ability to influence the length of testimony of a witness. The consultant may render an independent decision, as to whether the case might be won or lost once all testimony and closing statements have been completed, while awaiting the verdict.

The field of jury consulting is not an exact science as by nature, people and their behaviors are not always predictable. Jury consultants are used in more high-profile cases, both civil and criminal, for both sides.

The oral examination of prospective jury members is performed by the judge and/or the attorneys (plaintiff and defendant). In addition, a "silent voir dire" may be employed in which written questions are answered by the perspective juror and then analyzed prior to the oral examination. The voir dire process varies widely depending on whether the case is being tried in the federal or in a state court. The attorney's search for the ideal juror, one who will openly listen to testimony and render an impartial judgment, can take different avenues.

Disqualification for Cause

The preliminary voir dire is conducted by the judge, who shares some general information relating to the case with the jurors. Having done this, the judge may ask the jurors as a whole if they are unable to render a fair and impartial verdict. Those responding positively are often excused. Following this, a judge and/or the attorneys might ask specific questions of the individual jurors. The questions posed vary widely depending on the case, but may include the prospective juror's connection to any one of the parties or legal counsel, any financial interest in the case or outcome, or any prejudicial or biased belief on the prospective juror's part. Disqualification of a prospective juror for cause is referred to as a causal strike. There is no limit on the number of causal strikes allowed.

Peremptory Challenges

The initial voir dire is directed toward elimination of prospective jurors for cause. Following this, each side's attorney is entitled to strike additional jurors in order to secure a jury more harmonious to his or her side. The trial team reviews the notes of the voir dire and ranks the jurors in order of compatibility with the juror profile previously obtained. These peremptory challenges are limited to three strikes for each side, and the attorneys are not obligated to offer any reason for invoking these privileges.

Detailed notes by the assisting LNC are crucial to this process. The note-taking method must be accurate and detailed. The note-taking system should allow space for identification and separation of responses that do and do not fit the jury profile. One system that has been effectively used lists demographic information followed by the attorney's questions with sections for responses perceived as positive or negative (see Appendix C, at the end of the chapter, for a sample jury voir dire).

In addition to taking notes during the voir dire, the LNC may draft questions beforehand for the attorney's use and should observe the jurors' reactions to the questions posed. Once the voir dire process is completed, the notes taken during the process should be kept in a separate notebook. If for any reason during the trial the attorney may need to refer to these notes, having the notebook readily available will be essential for reference.

Nurses are trained to be detailed observers. Therefore, the presence of the LNC during trial is often invaluable to the attorney not only for reading the jurors, but also for monitoring the behavior of all other participants in the courtroom, as the attorney will be too occupied to do so himself.

Opening Statements

According to Polchinski (2000), the opening statement is an argument to the jury within the rules of evidence and professional ethics. It is not an outline, preview, or inventory of evidence. The purpose of the opening statement is to advise the jury of facts relied upon and of issues involved, to give the jury a general picture of the facts so that the jury will be able to understand the evidence. The opening statements are made by the plaintiff's attorney at the beginning of the trial just before the presentation of the first witness. The defense counsel may give his or her opening statement following the plaintiff's statement or may elect to wait until the opening of the defense portion of the case.

The opening statement of a medical malpractice case is extremely important. The opening statement is not evidence; it familiarizes the jury with the essential facts that each side expects to prove. The lawyers inform the jury of the facts they expect to prove and of the witnesses they expect to call to make such proof (Corley & Reed, 1999).

It is the responsibility of the LNC to take notes of the opening remarks and be able to discuss them with the attorney. The LNC should be able to analyze the opposing counsel's remarks and identify whether any new theories may require a change in trial strategy, emphasis, or additional follow-up.

Order of Proof

Presentation of Witnesses

Witnesses take center stage in a trial; through their testimony, a story is told to the jury. Three types of witnesses testify in a civil trial: expert, fact, and lay witnesses. An expert witness is one who, by reason of education and/or specialized experience, possesses superior knowledge about specific subjects in which jurors have no particular education or training and about which therefore, jurors would be incapable of forming an accurate opinion or deducing correct conclusions without the expert's testimony. An expert witness is a witness who has been qualified as an expert prior to giving testimony by the court. (Refer to *Daubert or Frye*, which is state specific for expert testimony determination depending on your state.)

In a professional negligence trial, the role of expert witnesses is to explain the medical facts of the case to the jury. Plaintiff experts describe deviations from accepted standards of care and the care that should have been provided to the plaintiff. Plaintiff damage experts describe the injuries to the plaintiff and project the impact on his or her life in the future. These witnesses describe the financial, emotional, and physiological changes that the plaintiff can expect.

Defense witnesses also testify to standard of care and causation, but do so in support of the defendant. Defense damage experts usually rebut the plaintiff's expert testimony as it relates to the financial, emotional, and physiological damages sustained by the plaintiff. An example of an expert witness would include a life care planner who has been asked to develop (for the plaintiff) a life care plan as a result of the claimed negligence. The life care planner for the defendant will review the plan disclosed by the plaintiff, looking for errors or costs which were included but which are contested, based on the testimony previously provided by the causation experts.

Medical expert witnesses also testify in other types of personal injury cases not involving professional negligence as cause of the claimed injury. These experts do not testify about standard-of-care issues, but do explain the plaintiff's injuries, treatment, and projected impact of the injuries in the future. Defense expert witnesses present rebuttal testimony concerning the impact of the plaintiff's injuries, and highlight other possible causes of the injuries; including pre-existing conditions that alternatively could have caused or exacerbated the claimed injury.

Fact witnesses are individuals who are not the focus of the negligence claim but who may have been present and who testify to the facts surrounding what actually occurred. The nurse observing a delivery, when the obstetrician is the defendant, would be an example of a fact witness. Lay witnesses are often family members or close friends who have observed the care provided to the plaintiff and witnessed the impact of injuries on the plaintiff and how it has changed the plaintiff's lifestyle. They may also include employers or coworkers, ministers, and so on. The attorney may ask the LNC to summarize previous testimony and review anticipated testimony with the witness (see Table 14.1).

Table 14.1   Sample Notes for Witness Testimony

Examination	*Follow-Up*
1. Board certification	How many times taken?
2. Hospital privileges	Any revoked?
3. Informed consent	Plaintiff given any narcotics before discussion of risks?

The LNC is usually responsible for ensuring the witness is available when called for testimony. This may mean meeting an expert at the airport and transporting him/her to the hotel or courtroom. This transportation time is an opportunity to discuss testimony and consult with the expert about issues that have arisen in the course of the trial. The LNC may have to coordinate local transportation for a fact witness or simply greet the witness as he or she arrives outside the courtroom. Many witnesses are nervous about testifying before a jury and are not familiar with courtroom etiquette or appropriate attire. It is the responsibility of the LNC to explain courtroom procedures and etiquette, and provide reassurance and information to the witness. The witness should always be reminded not to discuss any aspect of the trial while in the halls or restrooms of the courthouse. The witness should also be reminded never to speak to the jurors outside of the courtroom.

At the conclusion of the testimony, the LNC may be responsible for transporting the expert witness back to the hotel or airport or coordinating transportation for local witnesses. She or he may be asked to correspond with expert witnesses regarding their testimony or the outcome of the trial. If the case settles prior to the witness testimony, it may be the responsibility of the LNC to notify the witness of this and to provide other information as allowed in the settlement agreement.

Trial Examination of Witnesses

Following opening statements, the judge instructs the plaintiff's attorney to begin the presentation of his or her case. It is the responsibility of the plaintiff to prove his or her case to the jury. The case is proved by examination of expert and fact witnesses and the introduction of exhibits that assist the witnesses in telling their stories to the judge and/or jury. After the plaintiff has presented his or her case to the jury, the defense has the opportunity to present their case in rebuttal to that of the plaintiff. The defense does not have to disprove the entire plaintiff's case. The defense simply needs to disprove one of the four negligence claims leveled against the defendant: duty, breach of duty, causation, and injury. Like the plaintiff, this is accomplished by the defense through the examination of expert witnesses, including but not limited to the defendant themselves.

Although the plaintiff's case and the defendant's case are presented separately, examination of each witness is performed by both parties. Examination of witnesses has three primary phases:

■ Direct examination
■ Crossexamination
■ Rebuttal

Redirect and re-crossexamination may also be warranted if the trial attorney wants to clarify or dispute the witness' testimony. In summary, presentation of trial testimony occurs in the following order: direct examination, crossexamination, redirect examination, re-crossexamination, and rebuttal.

Direct Examination

Direct examination is conducted by the party who calls the witness. Leading questions are generally not allowed. A leading question gives the witness clues about the response expected by the attorney. An example is "Tell the jury what you did when you approached the intersection and saw the red light." Direct questions may be open-ended to allow the witness to elaborate on an answer or may be close-ended and require a brief response, such as yes or no. A direct examination question may ask "What happened when you approached the intersection?" Close-ended questions are used often for adverse or hostile witnesses from whom a simple answer without elaboration or explanation is desired. An example of a direct close-ended question is "Did you step on the brake when you saw the red light?"

Crossexamination

Crossexamination is conducted by the adverse party at the conclusion of direct testimony. Examination is limited to the subject matter of the direct examination. Crossexamination focuses on proper questions so that the elicited testimony and evidence are accurate and simple for the jury to understand. At the same time, the crossexamination attempts to undermine or discredit the witness. The tone of the questioning is often intentionally adversarial. Questions may be leading, such as "You did not step on the brake, correct?" Through counsel's aggressive questioning, witnesses may become intimidated, angered, and confused. The jury may perceive this response in a negative light and decide in favor of the opposing party. Therefore, the jury's perception during crossexamination is relevant to the case. An effective crossexamination can make or break the case, especially in medical malpractice trials in which large sums of money are involved.

Redirect and Re-Crossexamination

Crossexamination (of a witness) may be followed by redirect (further examination of a witness following cross examination by the defense) examination. The attorney uses this examination to clarify or reinforce previous testimony. This questioning may be followed by re-crossexamination (further examination of a witness by the defense following redirect examination). Again, this testimony is used to clarify or emphasize specific testimony. New subjects cannot be introduced during redirect or re-crossexaminations.

Rebuttal

Rebuttal testimony is offered after the close of the defendant's case. The plaintiff may wish to call additional witnesses to contradict or dispute specific testimony given by a defense expert witness. The same rules for direct and crossexamination of witnesses are in effect for rebuttal witnesses. Rebuttal testimony provides an opportunity to respond to the testimony of the defendant's witnesses other than through crossexamination. Attorneys may also reserve the right to recall any witness after their initial testimony.

Deposition Transcripts in Trial

Computer programs are available that store prelitigation depositions by transcript and/or by synchronized video/transcript formats. This allows prior deposition testimony to be easily accessed from a laptop computer during trial. Searches can be made by a key word for reference information that may be quickly needed.

In addition, many courtrooms today have real-time court reporting, which allows all parties to immediately access testimony transcripts during trial and even more importantly, save and review them later for trial strategy analysis.

The LNC's Role during Trial Testimony

In a traditional courtroom, the LNC follows the planned testimony as the attorney questions each witness, making detailed notes of the witnesses' responses and noting additional areas for examination by the attorney. In this setting, detailed and accurate notes are imperative. Traditional hardcopy court transcripts are not generally available on a daily basis unless the attorney pays for them. The trial team may need to rely on only memory and notes for its review of testimony and planning for additional witnesses.

However, modern courtroom technology also allows access to real-time court reporting via the Web. In an electronic courtroom, a live-feed electronic recording of the testimony can be made and referenced both during the trial proceedings as well as later in the day after the trial session has concluded. Since the O.J. Simpson trial in 1994, remote access to transcripts has been possible and transcripts can be researched, indexed, and managed immediately. The attorney often consults with the LNC in the courtroom before concluding his or her examination of the witness.

At that time, the LNC must be prepared to suggest specific questions, or further areas of questioning, or point out inconsistencies in previous testimony. If an expert has quoted from an article or textbook, the LNC must be prepared to advise the attorney if the testimony is incorrect or incomplete. The LNC should also be very familiar with the relevant medical records and can point out inaccuracies in testimony regarding the records. The LNC may need to provide this information in written form if the court discourages verbal conferences in the courtroom. Throughout the trial, the LNC should listen to each witness's testimony to analyze its impact on the case as a whole. Trial strategy is dynamic and may change during the trial.

The LNC as a member of the trial team must always be cognizant of the fact that this is a one-time opportunity for the plaintiff or the defendant to tell the story. Critique and discussion of the testimony and exhibits following the trial does not help win the case. Inconsistencies in testimony must be noted immediately for effective impeachment. If jurors do not appear to be listening to specific testimony or do not appear to understand testimony, alterations in questions or demeanor of the attorney or witness must be made immediately.

Each LNC will develop his or her own method of note-taking. A legal pad with a vertical line dividing the page in half allows notes for testimony on one side and areas for follow-up on the other side. Notes to be handed to the attorney in the courtroom should be written legibly on a small note card. The cards should be unobtrusive and written clearly to avoid lengthy discussions in the courtroom while the jury is present. Alternatively, a notebook or laptop computer can also be used for note-taking and provides the ability to store and retrieve information.

Trial testimony can be frustrating for the LNC who is primarily an observer to the process. Witnesses may not respond as planned, and new theories may be considered by the opposing party. The LNC may need to conduct additional literature searches on specific topics during the trial to develop new theories or expand on earlier ones. New theories need to be communicated by the attorney to witnesses in preparation for their testimony.

Trials can be exhausting and invigorating at the same time. Long hours may be necessary to ensure that the client's case is presented as clearly and convincingly as possible. It can be rewarding to see the years of work by the trial team and the client come together to tell the complete story to the jury.

Evidentiary Issues

The Federal Rules of Evidence (*www.uscourts.gov/rules/Evidence_Rules_2007.pdf*) regulate how the facts may be proved at trial. This is applicable in all civil and criminal cases in federal court. In order for real evidence (physical, documentary, and demonstrative evidence) to be properly submitted into the trial proceeding, it is imperative that it be accountable from the discovery phase through the trial phase. The object's whereabouts as well as the names of individuals to whom its care has been entrusted are paramount. This is referred to as the chain of custody and cannot be broken. The condition of the item at trial must be the same as at the time of the incident.

Exhibits

Trial exhibits are used to help the attorney tell the story to the jury. An exhibit is a document, model, or computer presentation exhibited to the court during the trial to present proof of facts. After being accepted and marked for identification, the exhibit is made a part of the case. Exhibits may be admitted as evidence and sent with the jury for deliberation. Exhibits that are not admitted are used for demonstrative purposes only and are not viewed by the jury during deliberations. In this case, witnesses use the exhibits to demonstrate a point of their testimony. Medical records are generally admitted as evidence, but enlargements of specific portions of the record may be used as demonstrative evidence. Anatomical models or scale replicas of equipment may be used as demonstrative evidence to assist the jury in understanding an expert's technical testimony. Scale drawings of an accident site, or photographs of the site or equipment, can help the jury to "see" the event.

Exhibits help the jury to understand and retain key elements of the testimony through visual media (photographs, chalkboards, whiteboards, computer graphics, etc.). Often jurors become tired and distracted when technical testimony is presented without the visual element offered by exhibits. Exhibits are used to enhance the memory of witnesses for details of complex records. The LNC may be responsible for transporting exhibits to the courtroom and for securing them at the close of each trial day. The LNC may have to coordinate audiovisual equipment, such as overhead projectors, slide projectors, computer projection equipment, and easels for charts or enlargements. The LNC should keep a record of each trial exhibit so that it is easily recoverable by the attorney (see Table 14.2). Also, most courts require each piece of the trial exhibits to be marked prior to the trial or at the time of testimony. The LNC can assist with that task.

Table 14.2 Sample List of Exhibits

Exhibit No.	Exhibit	Date	Introduced	Offered	Accepted
1	ER report	1/1/98	11/4/98	11/4/98	11/4/98
5	Consent	1/2/98	11/4/98	11/4/98	11/5/98
8	Consent	1/10/98	11/5/98	11/5/98	11/5/98
14	Autopsy report	2/1/98	11/6/98	11/6/98	11/6/98
15	Death certificate	2/1/98	11/4/98	—	—

The LNC can assist the attorney in preparing trial exhibits and presentations of evidence. The following demonstrates several evidentiary issues with which the LNC can become involved.

Medical Literature

Medical journal articles are not admissible in court as evidence. The same is true for the use of a Physicians' Desk Reference to establish the standard of care in relation to the administration of medication. In one case in which a defendant physician based his expert opinion that he had not been negligent upon medical literature, the appellate court refused to admit the articles as evidence (Shandell & Smith, 1996).

Medical Bills

The plaintiff has to prove that the damages occurred as a result of negligence. Hence the burden of proof lies on the plaintiff. A plaintiff must be able to prove what medical bills are related to the malpractice incident. For example, an Illinois case alleged failure to diagnose a postsurgical complication. The plaintiff failed to introduce testimony, explaining what portion of the medical bills had been incurred as a result of malpractice. Thus there was no way to distinguish which of the medical charges was the direct result of negligence and which charges were incurred regardless of any negligence. Therefore, it was determined that the medical bills should not have been admitted as evidence (Shandell & Smith, 1996).

Hospital Policy and Procedure

Hospitals, clinics, nursing homes, and other health care facilities have policies and procedures for surgical, emergency, and routine activities. Failure to abide by the facility's policies and procedures may be evidence of a lack of ordinary and prudent care.

Hearsay Rule

There are exclusionary rules of evidence. Among the most noted is hearsay. This form of evidence is ordinarily inadmissible in court unless one of the exception rules prevails (refer to Federal Rules of Evidence 803 and 804). According to Fisher (1994), hearsay is a statement made outside the courtroom to establish the veracity of matter contained in the statement. It is considered second-hand information by the declarant, the person making the statement. It may be oral or written. Not all out-of-court statements by nonwitnesses are hearsay. Some examples of exceptions to the hearsay rule include statements for purposes of medical diagnosis or treatment, public records, and reports and statements made under belief of impending death.

Summation

Closing Arguments

Closing arguments are the summation of the testimony by the attorney for each party. These final statements are made by attorneys to the jury or court to summarize the evidence they think they have established and the evidence they think the other side has failed to establish. These statements are the final words from the attorneys before the judge's charge to the jury. The arguments by the attorney do not constitute evidence and may be limited in time by the court. The LNC should note any areas for rebuttal or areas that require further clarification by his or her party. Generally, each party may allot a brief time for rebuttal.

Jury Instructions and Deliberations

Jury instructions are written explanations of the laws that jury members must follow when determining the outcome of the case. Proposed jury instructions are presented to the judge by each party before the start of the trial. At some point before or during the trial, the attorneys and the judge discuss the proposed instructions. The judge determines which instructions will ultimately be presented to the jury. At the conclusion of closing arguments, the judge reads the instructions to the jury and provides any necessary explanations or clarifications.

In most civil trials, the jurors are not sequestered; that is, they are allowed to go home each evening during the presentation of evidence and during deliberations. The jury is escorted to the jury room by the bailiff and deliberates during the hours established by the judge. During deliberations, the jury may request clarification of the jury instructions by the judge or may request that portions of the transcript be read to them. Sometimes the jury will ask to see any trial evidence to assist with the deliberation process. (See Appendix D for Samples of Malpractice Jury Instructions at the end of the chapter.)

Jury Ballot

A ballot is prepared by the plaintiff's attorney and submitted to the jury. The ballot requires several questions to be answered by the jury before deliberations are completed. The first question requires the jury to determine whether the plaintiff has proved negligence by one or more of the defendants. The next question asks the jury to determine the percent of negligence attributed to each defendant. In jurisdictions with comparative or contributory negligence, the jury must then determine what percent, if any, the plaintiff was negligent.

Damages

In order for monetary damages to be recovered, a victim must prove that some specific injury has occurred. This financial reparation for a tortuous act may be awarded as a consequence of the harm—loss of body parts or function, lost wages, inability to continue in an occupation, emotional impairment, and related damages. The jury may also award damages for pain and suffering, although these awards may have statutory limits in some jurisdictions. In negligence cases, compensatory damages are common (i.e., out-of-pocket costs including medical expenses, lost wages, and mental anguish).

Punitive or exemplary damages, as the name implies, are awarded over and above compensatory damages. These are granted to punish or make an example of the defendant. Punitive damages are often requested in product liability cases. When punitive damages are demanded, the trial may be bifurcated, that is, divided into two separate phases: liability and damages.

The jury hears testimony on liability and causation, and then deliberates on these issues. If it finds negligence by the defendants and that the negligence caused the plaintiff's injuries, then the damage phase of the trial begins. Evidence is presented to prove physical damages as well as the economic worth of the defendant. Expert testimony may be presented by a life care planner whose life care plan is developed on present-day values and an economist, who uses the life care planner's data to project future costs associated with medical and economic trends.

Punitive damages are almost nonexistent in negligence cases, although they are awarded in gross negligence cases in which willful and wanton disregard for the standard practices is proven.

In wrongful death cases, the statutes allow the surviving family members of the deceased to recover damages for projected income. Computation is based on insurance actuarial tables and takes into consideration the victim's life expectancy with adjustments for projected living expenses. The income projections are generally developed by economists.

In cases (wrongful death, medical malpractice, etc.) in which a judgment is anticipated to be excessive, a high–low agreement may be considered as an alternative. The high–low agreement is similar to a typical settlement agreement, with some added features. The theory behind the agreement is that the plaintiff and the defendant insure the other against an excessive verdict. The plaintiff and defendant agree that the outcome of the case will be no less than X dollars (the low) and no more than Y dollars (the high). If the verdict is in favor of the plaintiff, and exceeds Y dollars, the plaintiff gets Y dollars. If the verdict is in favor of the defendant, and lower than X dollars, the plaintiff gets X dollars (Connelly & McGivney, 1999).

Verdict

After receiving instructions from the judge, the jury retires. In all cases, jury deliberations are secret. In both state and federal courts, jurors must reach a unanimous decision. However, previously arranged agreements may preclude a unanimous verdict and make a vote of the majority of jurors acceptable. Some state courts permit a majority vote after 6 hours of deliberations. The time a jury takes to reach a verdict usually depends on the complexity of a case. In all, 3–6 hours is considered average time, but great variances may occur.

When a verdict has been reached, it may be given to the parties by the judge by telephone, but in most instances the jurors will re-enter the courtroom. The foreperson then reads the verdict after the judge sees the verdict. The different sides may request a polling of each juror's verdict. If the judge suspects an error, the jury may be retired to deliberate again, or a mistrial may be declared.

Judgment is the verdict of the case signed by the judge. The prevailing party can prepare this, or it may be in a form document. It will usually state a monetary amount. The judge has the authority to accept the verdict as presented, to set it aside, or to reduce the amount of money awarded to the plaintiff. Unless sealed by a judge, this information is public record.

Post-Trial Activities

Jury Interviews

The LNC may be assigned the task of interviewing the jurors after the trial is concluded. The jurors are under no obligation to talk to any party but are free to do so provided that state laws are not violated. Valuable information for future trials may be gained from juror interviews. Questions regarding the presentation by the attorney, including demeanor, the exhibits, or the witnesses, may yield areas for change or improvement in the attorney's next trial. The opposing party's attorney should question the jurors about their presentation as well.

The LNC is the perfect individual to conduct post-trial juror interviews as he/she is usually approachable and does not intimidate the jurors as the attorney would. Generally, when encouraged to do so, the jurors are more than willing to criticize the attorney's courtroom performance when the nurse explains the importance of their feedback to improving the attorney's performance in future trials. When the attorney conducts such interviews, the jurors will frequently refuse to be interviewed and/or will not be as candid in their feedback.

Bill of Costs

Most jurisdictions allow the prevailing party to be reimbursed for court costs by the opposing party. This is referred to as the Bill of Costs. The items in which relief can be sought vary between federal and state courts. The usual court costs include filing fees, fees for service of process, printing and copying expenses, and costs associated with subpoenaed witnesses. In federal court an affidavit attesting to the accuracy and necessity of the costs is required. The deadline for filing the Bill of Costs is usually 10–30 days from judgment. A copy of the bill must be served on all other parties. The LNC may be asked to calculate the amounts of the medically related costs, such as expert witness fees, medical exhibit fees, and time spent on case presentation by the LNC.

Motion for a New Trial or Appeal

The jury's verdict can be set aside through the process of post-trial motions. The most common is a motion for a new trial or a motion for judgment as a matter of law after trial (JMOL). The trial court judge who heard the case usually decides post-trial motions. The judge grants a JMOL when it is believed that the jury rendered a wrong decision as a matter of law. In situations in which the JMOL is granted, the original verdict is overturned with a new judgment in favor of the other party.

Motions for a new trial are based on the principle that a prejudicial error occurred at trial that ultimately affected the outcome. These motions are not granted lightly.

Another venue for relief of the verdict is the post-trial appeal. An appeal is made to a higher court to review the lower court's decision. Different codes and rules are applicable during the appeal process.

Throughout the post-trial period, the LNC assists with researching and drafting post-trial motions or assists in preparation of an appeal.

Conclusion

Meticulous preparation and presentations are vital for the LNC who prepares the discovery phase of a case or engages in strategic legal analysis (with the attorney) prior to entering trial. Cases are won or lost by the presentation set forth by attorneys and expert fact witnesses; those who fumble for exhibits or key pieces of information are not seen as winners, and their success in the courtroom may be limited. The LNC's role, whether for the plaintiff or defense, should be a work of art providing an opportunity for the attorney to tell a story that will convince the jury which party should prevail.

Assisting at trial can be challenging and stressful, but it can also be exciting and rewarding. An LNC who has done everything possible to assist the trial attorney in presenting a case effectively will have a feeling of ownership in the trial's outcome and will enjoy a feeling of personal satisfaction (not to mention job security).

References

Appleman, J. A. (1952). *Successful jury trials: A symposium*. Indianapolis: Bobbs-Merrill.

Claus, R. (2002). *The electronic trial preparation*. Retrieved July 28, 2008, from http://www.searchlight.ca/resources/download/THE ELECTRONIC TRIAL PREP.pdf

Connelly, R., & McGivney, L. L. C. (1999). *High–low agreements: A viable settlement alternative*. Retrieved July 28, 2008, from library.findlaw.com/1999/Aug/1/128425.html

Corley, R. N., & Reed, O. L. (1999). *The legal and regulatory environment of business*. Boston: Irwin McGraw-Hill.

Fisher, K. (1994). *The process of civil litigation with contract and tort law* (Vol. 2). Atlanta: The National Center for Paralegal Training.

McElhaney, J. W. (1994). *McElhaney's trial notebook* (4th e-ed.). Chicago: American Bar Association.

Morton, R. C. (2005). *The electronic trial notebook*. Retrieved July 28, 2008, from http://www.mortonelderlaw.com/articles/TrialNotebook.pdf

Polchinski, P. D. (2000). *Elements of trial practice*. Tucson: Lawyers & Judges Publishing Company, Inc.

Shandell, R. E., & Smith, P. (1996). *The preparation and trial of medical malpractice cases*. New York: Law Journal Seminars Press.

Additional Reading

Hegland, K. (2005). *Trial and practice skills in a nutshell*. Eagan, MN: West Publications.

Kadame, J. B. (2002). Anatomy of a Jury Challenge. *Chance, 15*(2). Retrieved July 28, 2008, from http://www.amstat.org/publications/chance/pdfs/152.kadane.pdf

Mauet, T., & Maeroweitz, M. (1996). *Fundamentals of litigation for paralegals* (2nd ed.). Boston: Little, Brown.

Parke, A. (2001). Planning cross examination. *For the Defense, 43*(9), 20.

Sanbar A. A., Firestone M. H., Fiscina S., et al. (Eds.) (2007). *Legal medicine* (7th ed.). Philadelphia: Mosby Elsevier.

Scheeman, A. (1995). *Paralegals in American Law*. Albany, NY: Delmar Publishers, Inc.

Singer, A. (1996). Trial consulting: A much-in-demand, highly effective, and nicely profitable professional subspecialty for legal nurse consultants. *Journal of Legal Nurse Consulting, 7*(2), 2.

Statsky, W. (1997). *Introduction to paralegalism* (5th ed.). Eagan, MN: West Publishing Company.

Trimm, H. H. (2005). *Forensics: The easy way*. Hauppauge, NY: Barrons Educational Services, Inc.

Weishepple, C. (2001). *Introduction to legal nurse consulting*. Albany: West Thompson Learning.

Test Questions

1. Motions in limine are used to
    A. Highlight the key points of the trial strategy
    B. Prohibit introduction of certain testimony into trial
    C. Determine the order of witnesses
    D. Object to the other party's witnesses

2. An attorney may use a peremptory challenge to
    A. Dismiss a potential juror without specific cause
    B. Object to a question by the opposing attorney
    C. Question the qualifications of an expert witness
    D. Attempt to remove a judge from the case

3. Demonstrative evidence is
    A. Evidence used by the jury to show how they reached a verdict
    B. Evidence used to assist a witness in explaining his or her testimony
    C. Sent to the jury room with the jurors for deliberation
    D. Evidence used only in opening statements or closing arguments

4. Crossexamination
    A. Reinforces the credibility of the witness
    B. Is a process by which leading questions are not permitted
    C. May appear to be theatrical
    D. Is of little consequence to the outcome of the trial process

5. When a plaintiff is assessed with comparative negligence, it means that his or her
    A. Award is compared with other awards for similar injuries
    B. Negligence is compared with the defendant's and his or her award reduced proportionately
    C. Injuries are compared to those of individuals in similar cases
    D. Negligence is compared to the defendant's but his or her award is not changed

Answers: 1. B, 2. A, 3. B, 4. C, 5. B

Appendix A: Excerpts from Medical Records Pertaining to Emily Smith

Date	Doctor	Page	Entry
11/14/80	Brown	17	(History and Physical-Lakeside Hospital) Hospitalized January 1980 with arthritis
11/17/80	Brown	14	(Discharge summary-Lakeside Hospital) Ms. Smith is a 63-year-old lady with history of arthritis; over the past year has had difficulty with mobility; noticed a tremor in right hand. She has difficulty initiating movement, but denies any specific paralysis. Her neurological exam was suggestive of probable Parkinson's disease; admitted to work up other possible problems
			Final Diagnosis: Probable Parkinson's disease
			Ms. Smith to be discharged on Sinemet 10/100 mg
01/18/83	Stevenson	1	Reported has had arthritis in the back for past three years, complains of low back pain, upper back pain, and neck pain, some decreased strength in her hands, but no real peripheral arthritis
02/18/85	Brown	9	Complains of slowness of movement
02/10/86	Brown	10	Very upset … depressed
05/28/86	Brown	11	Exam: Speech much slower; slurs; shuffles more
07/16/86	White	41	(History and Physical-Lakeside Hospital) Ms. Smith has become very stiff, immobile-like with a heavy weight pulling her down toward the ground. She reports has Parkinson's disease. This morning she had an unusually severe episode of this, associated with severe, excruciating, unbearable back pain. The patient is stiff and rigid, almost statue-like, very immobile, has to be helped to do anything
			Impression: Parkinson's disease with off-on phenomenon and Severe back pain
07/16/86	White	36	(EEG Report) Interpretation: Abnormal indicating diffuse cerebral dysfunction. The record is abnormal by virtue of increased amounts of slow activity consistent with a mild diffuse encephalopathy

continued

Date	Doctor	Page	Entry
07/31/86	Feldman	50–52	(Initial Neurological Evaluation) Ms. Smith has noted increasing difficulties with gait becoming slow and shuffling, and has difficulties turning, difficulty arising from a chair and, in fact, occasionally has to get down on her fours in order to get up from a chair. She occasionally spills liquids when she brings them to her mouth. She notes some insomnia, which she attributed to generalized body discomfort during the night. In fact, she sleeps on the floor. Has a seven-year history of slowly progressive Parkinson's disease. Amitriptyline will be substituted. This latter medication should improve her insomnia as well as mild depression
09/23/87	Feldman	46	Ms. Smith occasionally stammers and has increased forgetfulness. According to husband, she is less alert and has occasional visual hallucinations; most recently, a month ago, she "saw mice in her bed"
07/27/88	Feldman	43	There has been some deterioration in her symptoms since her last visit. She seems to stutter more and is frequently mixed up, occasionally having hallucinations. Her balance also has deteriorated and she has fallen on two occasions … possibly developing into PSP (progressive supranuclear palsy)
04/24/89	General	10–12	Intermittent bouts of confusion and irrational pain for approximately six months; spells are described as forgetting her surroundings, believes she is in different places with different people. These spells have been increasing in intensity and duration occasionally lasting an entire day. There is question of a stroke eight years ago, although husband refutes this
04/25/89	General	63	(EEG Report) Impression: abnormal record, characterized by the following: (1) Diffuse slowing of background activity, indicating diffuse disturbance in brain function. (2) A focus of very slow (Delta) activity in the left temporal region, indicating presence of a lesion involving that region
04/27/89	General	57	[Magnetic Resonance Images (MRI) of the brain] Impression: Mild to moderate age-related and/or atrophic changes as described with peri-ventricular white matter ischemic change

continued

Date	Doctor	Page	Entry
08/15/89	Benton	21	(History and Physical-Lakeside Hospital) Initially had a little tightness in the chest, then later on began to notice a fluttering in the chest
			Impression: Ventricular tachycardia; parkinsonism; degenerative arthritis
08/18/89	Stevenson	5	Her arthritis is stable. Her parkinsonism is progressing
09/27/89	Feldman	32	During the last month her condition clearly has deteriorated. She has developed more dyskinesias, particularly after 11 AM, which interferes with eating; has become more nervous and depressed; has had period of palpitations lasting 5 to 10 minutes, associated with a smothering feeling. She continues to have some anxiety and phobias, particularly phobias of crowds
08/14/90	Benton	6	47-pound weight loss over two years. Now 100 pounds. Parkinson's
12/17/90	General	256	(EEG Report) Impression: compared to the previous EEG of 4/25/89, there continues to be diffuse slowing of background activity, indicative of a diffuse disturbance in cerebral function
12/18/90	General	255	(MRI of the brain) Impression: (1) Small focal ischemic insults (2) The ischemic changes have appeared since the last study dated
12/20/90	Feldman	23–26	(Discharge Summary-General Hospital) Discharge Diagnosis: 1. Right subcortical stroke. 2. Parkinson's disease … evidence of left nasolabial droop with drooling from left corner of mouth, wide-eyed stare with decreased blinking and hypermetric. The patient's stance was stooped. EEG was done and compared to the previous EEG April 1989. There continued to be diffuse slowing in the background and activity indicative of a diffuse disturbance in cerebral function. MRI scan done showed small focal ischemic insults with ischemic changes not seen on the last MRI of April 1989
	General	(235–238)	
12/26/90	Feldman	27	Ms. Smith recently discharged from hospital after suffering a mild stroke producing swallowing difficulties. At this time, she is very frozen and has difficulty moving about. This improves after taking Sinemet, but she becomes quite confused and begins hallucinating
04/12/91	Feldman	21	According to patient and husband, she is clearly worse. She has more fluctuations

Appendix B: Demonstrative Exhibit

June 17, 1999

Time	Description
3:00 p.m.	Ms. Smith arrives in emergency room; is assessed by Carol Jones, RN. Cardiac monitor applied. Dynamap applied and oxygen begun by Ms. Jones
3:05 p.m.	Examination by Dr. Green. Order received by Ms. Jones. IV started, arterial blood gases obtained, and pulse oximeter applied by Ms. Jones
3:08 p.m.	Dr. Benton notified. Portable chest x-ray obtained. Dr. Ross notified by Dr. Green
3:30 p.m.	Blood gases redrawn and oxygen changed to 100% per face mask
3:45 p.m.	Ms. Smith continuously monitored by Nurse Jones, who describes respirations as easy and nonlabored. Dr. Green speaks with Dr. Ross
4:05 p.m.	Nurse Jones speaks to Dr. Ross. Orders received. Consent signed for bronchoscopy
4:25 p.m.	EKG obtained
4:30 p.m.	Ms. Smith is transferred to pre-op holding area on continuous monitors accompanied by orderly and Carol Jones RN; patient received by Susan Lewis RN, report given and continuous monitors exchanged
4:40 p.m.	History and assessment by John Carter, CRNA. Preoperative assessment by Nurse Lewis
5:00 p.m.	Ms. Smith is continuously monitored by Nurse Lewis, who notifies Dr. Ross that she is ready for bronchoscopy
5:45 p.m.	Dr. Ross arrives to OR holding area. Receives report from Nurse Lewis
6:00 p.m.	Ms. Smith is transferred to MICU. Continuous monitors are exchanged. Report received by head nurse who admits Ms. Smith to unit
6:30 p.m.	Amanda Parker, RN receives report from head nurse and assumes care of Ms. Smith. Dr. Ross and respiratory therapist at bedside upon her arrival. Assessment performed by Nurse Parker. Flexible bronchoscopy initiated

Appendix C: Sample Voir Dire

State of Michigan in the District Court, __th Judicial District
Name and)
Name,)
                      Plaintiffs,)

v.

Automobile Company,)
a State Corporation,)

Dealer Ford, Inc.,)
and Automobile Credit)
Company, a Delaware)
Corporation, Jointly and Severally,)
                    Defendants.)

Plaintiffs' Requested Voir Dire

Plaintiffs, by their attorneys, [*Attorney for Plaintiff*], requests the following voir dire:

Personal/Employment Information

1. Where do you work?
   a. What do you do there?
   b. Do you like your job?
      (1) If not, why?
2. Where does your spouse/significant other work?
   a. Does he/she like his/her job?
3. Do any of you, your family or close friends work in the automobile industry or a related industry?
   a. If so, please tell us about your/their work.
4. Do any of you, your family or close friends work for Automobile Motor Company, Dealer Ford and/or Automobile Motor Credit Company?
5. Do you or any of your family or close friends hold or own any stock in Automobile Motor Company?

Prior Jury/Litigation Experience

1. Do any of you watch any of the legal shows on TV, for example, "The Practice," "Ally McBeal," or "Law and Order"?
   a. If so, which ones do you watch?
   b. For those of you who watch "The Practice," do you know what "Plan B" is?
2. Has any member of the jury, or a family member or close friend ever been involved in a lawsuit?
   a. If so, please give details.
   b. Were you/they satisfied with the outcome?
      (1) Do you feel that the outcome was fair?
      (2) Why or why not?
   c. What do you think of the job that your/their lawyer did?
3. Has any jury member, or a family member or a close friend ever had to testify in Court or at a deposition?
   a. What were the circumstances?
   b. How did you/they feel about testifying?
4. Do any of you, or your family or close friends work or have experience in the legal field or court system?
   a. Please tell us about your/their experience?

5. Have any of you ever sat as a juror before?
    a. If so, how many times and when?
        (1) Please give details of each occasion, such as whether it was a civil or criminal trial, and so on.
    b. What did you think about your experience as a juror?
        (1) What did you like best?
        (2) What did you like least?
    c. Is there anything about that experience that you think might influence the way you think about this case?
    d. Do you think that there was anything that could have been done to improve your experience? (by the court, lawyers, or others?)
6. Has any member of the jury had any unpleasant associations with lawyers, judges or the courts?
    a. If so, would that experience interfere with your ability to decide this case?
7. Do any jurors believe that it is wrong, or improper for a person to bring a lawsuit?
8. This is a civil trial. It is not a criminal trial. The standards of proof in a civil trial such as this one are not as strict as in a criminal case. The person bringing the suit need only produce evidence that preponderates in her favor. If she does, then she can recover. She does not have to prove the claims or her damages beyond a reasonable doubt.
    a. Does any jury member have any ideas or opinions that would interfere with your ability to apply this lower standard of proof that is required in a civil trial?
9. At the conclusion of this trial, the judge is going to instruct you on the law as it pertains to this case and, under our system, you *must* follow the law in deciding this case.
    a. Is there any member of the jury who feels that he or she cannot follow the law for any reason, even if he or she personally may disagree with the law?

General Background

10. Do any of you subscribe to a newspaper or magazine—or even if you don't subscribe, is there a publication you read pretty regularly?
    a. Which ones?
    b. What do you enjoy about that publication?
11. How do you prefer to get your news?
    a. TV, newspaper, radio, or word of mouth?
12. Any of you belong to any clubs or organizations? (Including block clubs, neighborhood watch, sport or racquet clubs, business associations?)
    a. How active are you?
13. Have any of you seen any articles about Ford or any of Ford's cars or trucks?
    a. What was the substance of the article?
    b. What was your reaction?
    c. Would this affect how you would look at this case?
        (1) Do you think you could follow the judge's instructions and look only at the evidence in this case and follow the law as the judge gives it to you?
        (2) Do you think you could make a fair decision in this case?
14. Do any of you have any background in mechanics or engineering?
15. Do any of you have any background in fire investigation, fire fighting or arson investigation?

16. Have any of you or members of your family or close friends ever had a vehicle or house fire?
    a. If so, what happened?
    b. Did you ever learn what caused the fire?
    c. If a vehicle fire, was the vehicle repaired?
       (1) Was the repair covered under warranty?
    d. Do you believe your experience would influence how you might look at this case?
17. Have any of you ever done any of your own maintenance on a car or truck?
    a. If so, how did you learn how to do this?
    b. What kind of car was it?
18. Do any of you read any automotive magazines or papers?
    a. If so, which ones?
19. How many of you are familiar with what a vehicle shop manual is?
    a. Ever use one?
       (1) Which one(s)?
20. Are any of you familiar with Chilton's Auto Repair manuals?
    a. Ever use one?
21. Are any of you familiar with what a Technical Service Bulletin is?
    a. How did you learn about Technical Service Bulletins or TSB's?

Product Experience

22. Have any of you ever purchased a new car or van?
23. What made you decide to buy new instead of used?
24. Would you go back to the particular dealer that you bought from?
    a. Why or why not?
25. Has anyone purchased a new car or truck on any kind of manufacturer's discount program—like an A-Plan/Option I or employee discount?
    a. Which program?
    b. How did you qualify for the program?
26. Have any of you ever owned a vehicle?
    a. Buy new or used?
    b. How long did you keep it?
    c. What year was it?
    d. What made you choose that van?
    e. Did you have any problems with it?
    f. Did you sell it or trade it in?
    g. What made you decide to get rid of it?
27. Have any of you ever owned any kind of Ford car, truck or van?
    a. What year and model was it?
    b. Buy new or used?
    c. How long did you keep it?
    d. What year was it?
    e. What made you chose that car?
    f. Did you have any problems with it?
    g. Did you sell it or trade it in?
    h. What made you decide to get rid of it?

28. Have any of you ever dealt with Dealer Ford?
    a. When?
    b. What were the circumstances?
29. What is your opinion of Ford products in general?
    a. Do you think Ford products are better or worse than average?
30. Have any of you ever been dissatisfied with the service you've received at a dealership?
    a. Please tell us what happened.
    b. Would you be able to set that experience aside and decide this case based only on the evidence and the judge's instructions in this case?
31. Have any of you ever been dissatisfied with a vehicle that you owned or leased?
    a. What was the problem?
    b. Did you take any action to try to resolve the problem?
       (1) Please tell us what you did?
    c. Were you able to get the problem resolved to your satisfaction?
    d. Do you think these experiences would unfairly influence your decision in this case in any way?
32. Is there anyone here who has never had to take a vehicle into a dealer for service?
33. Have any of you ever been dissatisfied with any type of product—not necessarily a car or truck—and tried to return it?
    a. What kind of product?
    b. Why did you want to return it?
    c. What happened?

Closing Questions

34. Does anyone on the jury know any of the following individuals:
    a. Name or Name?
    b. Any of the Defendants?
    c. Any of the Attorneys?
    d. Any of the witnesses (see pretrial order)?
35. Do each of you feel you are the kind of person that you would want as a juror if you had your own case in court?
    a. If not, why not?
36. Is there any member of the jury who does not wish to sit on this jury for any reason whatsoever?
37. Does anyone have a reason that they would prefer not to sit, but wants to keep the reason private?

Thank you.

This sample pleading is adapted from a recent case by Dani Liblang, Attorney at Law, 165 North Old Woodward Avenue, Birmingham, Michigan 48009–3380. Because the pleadings are from an actual case, they are quite fact specific, and are presented solely for the purposes of demonstration. All sample pleadings must be adapted by practitioners to meet actual needs and practices. This sample may be found with other sample trial documents at: http://www.consumerlaw.org/publications/manuals/content/samples/M9warr_891–893.pdf

Appendix D: Samples of Malpractice Jury Instructions

BAJI 6.00.1

Duty of Physician

In performing professional services for a patient, a physician has the duty to have that degree of learning and skill ordinarily possessed by reputable physicians, practicing in the same or a similar locality and under similar circumstances.

The further duty of the physician is to use the care and skill ordinarily exercised in like cases by reputable members of the profession practicing in the same or a similar locality under similar circumstances, and to use reasonable diligence and [his] or [her] best judgment in the exercise of skill and the application of learning, in an effort to accomplish the purpose for which the physician is employed. A failure to fulfill any such duty is negligence.

BAJI 16.02

Medical Perfection not Required

A physician is not necessarily negligent because [he] [or] [she] errs in judgment or because [his] [or] [her] efforts prove unsuccessful. The physician is negligent if the error in judgment or lack of success is due to a failure to perform any of the duties as defined in these instructions.

BAJI 6.03

Alternative Methods of Diagnosis or Treatment

Where there is more than one recognized method of diagnosis or treatment, and no one of them is used exclusively and uniformly by all practitioners of good standing, a physician is not negligent if, in exercising [his] [or] [her] best judgment, [he] [or] [she] selects one of the approved methods, which later turns out to be a wrong selection, or one not favored by certain other practitioners.

BAJI 6.20

Duty of a Hospital

[Defendant _____, a hospital, has a duty to use reasonable care in furnishing a patient the care, attention and protection reasonably required by the patient's mental and physical condition.]

[Defendant _____, a hospital, [also] has a duty to use reasonable care in [selecting a competent medical staff] periodically reviewing the competency of its medical staff.]

The amount of caution, attention and protection required in the exercise of reasonable care depends on the known condition and needs of the patient, and must be appropriate to that condition and those needs. The standard of reasonable care required of a hospital is the care, skill and diligence ordinarily used by hospitals generally in the same or a similar locality and under similar circumstances.

A failure to fulfill any such duty is negligence.

BAJI 6.21

Liability of Hospital for Negligence of Physician or Nurse

If you should find that the plaintiff was injured as a result of the negligence of defendant, (doctor) or (nurse), you then must determine whether the defendant (hospital) is liable for that negligence.

If the defendant (doctor) or (nurse) was employed directly by the plaintiff or by someone on the plaintiffs behalf', the defendant (doctor) or (nurse) was not the agent of defendant hospital and the hospital is not liable for the negligence, if any, of the [doctor] [nurse].

A hospital may, as an accommodation to a patient, procure for the patient the services of a physician or nurse, without assuming any control over the services. Also, a hospital may, as an accommodation to both patient and [doctor] or [nurse], collect from the patient for the [doctor's] [nurse's] [fees] [wages]. Any such accommodation on the part of the hospital does not, in and of itself, make the [doctor] [nurse] the agent of the hospital.

If, however, the defendant hospital undertakes to provide [medical] [or] [surgical] [or] [nursing] service to the plaintiff by [a doctor or doctors] [a nurse or nurses] in its employ and under its control, then that person was the agent of defendant hospital and the hospital is liable for the negligence, if any, of the [doctor] [nurse], occurring within the scope of the employment.

BAJI 6.25

Duty of a Nurse

A person who undertakes to perform the service of a trained or graduate nurse owes a patient duties of care, namely (1) to have the knowledge and skill ordinarily possessed, and (2) to exercise the care and dill ordinarily used in like cases, by trained and skilled members of the nursing profession practicing their profession in the same or a similar locality and under similar circumstances. A failure to fulfill either of these duties is negligence.

Steps in Malpractice Lawsuit

1. Receipt of Notice of Intent to Commence Action (Code of Civil Procedure §364.65)
2. Filing of Complaint
3. Service of Summons and Complaint
4. Answer to Complaint
5. Investigation & Discovery
   (a) Meeting with Defense Counsel
   (b) Formal Discovery
       (1) Interrogatories
       (2) Depositions
   (c) Input from Medical Experts
6. Settlement Conference
7. Jury Trial

Chapter 15

Locating and Working with Expert Witnesses

Mary Lou Hazelwood, RN, LNCC

First Edition
Doreen James Wise, EdD, MSN, RN

Second Edition
Patricia A. Fyler, BS, RN, CEN

Contents

Objectives

- Describe the role of the expert witness in medically related civil litigation
- Differentiate the types of expert witnesses
- Identify the qualifications of the expert witness
- Describe the characteristics of an effective expert witness
- Provide an effective approach to locating an appropriate expert witness
- Provide guidance in the support of the expert witness
- Familiarize the reader with key legal decisions affecting expert witnesses

Most jurisdictions require the use of an expert witness during the litigation process to educate the judge and jury about specialized knowledge. In medical litigation, one key component that may make or break a case is the medical expert witness. Today's health care delivery system contains very specialized knowledge and is not easily understood by the layperson. An expert witness is an individual qualified by his or her experience, training, or education to opine about a specific subject, such as standards of practice, anatomy, or physiology. This chapter addresses the selection and support of nursing and other medical-provider expert witnesses. Because legal nurse consultants (LNCs) are instrumental in identifying, selecting, and developing experts, they often play an important role and make a critical difference in medical litigation outcomes. Discussion will be directed toward the following:

Qualifications and characteristics of the expert witness
Resources for locating qualified experts
Elements involved in working with experts
Legal rulings affecting the expert witness and the admissibility of expert testimony

Role of the LNC

The LNC serves many roles in the legal arena. One role in litigation support may be identifying, selecting, and supporting expert witnesses, whether nurses, physicians, ancillary personnel, or administrative staff and managers. Another role may be as a testifying expert nurse witness. To succeed in either role, the LNC must understand the medical issues involved in the case, the strategy or theme of the case he or she is representing, and the expertise and qualifications of the opposition experts (if known). It is also essential to know the laws relating to expert witnesses in the jurisdiction in which the case is to be tried. LNCs often prepare an expert witness, who may lack courtroom experience for trial or deposition. While it would be preferable to review all cases while unaware of whether the attorney represents the plaintiff or defense, in the real world this is usually not possible. Some physicians, nursing administrators, and ancillary personnel will testify only for the defense. At some point the expert must know the litigation orientation of the attorney to be able to offer advice regarding liability and to advise how best to develop or defend the case.

The consulting LNC works behind the scenes with either a plaintiff or a defense attorney. In this confidential process, the LNC may perform a constellation of activities. These may include the opportunity to interview potential clients, review medical records, locate missing or required documents, and identify medical issues in the case. They may also include educating the attorney regarding medical terms and procedures, policies or procedures, preparing visual aids and exhibits, and assisting in determining which types of experts will be needed and assisting in locating them. When the LNC consults on a case requiring a medical expert witness, the consultant may not be expected to testify in the case. The consulting LNC's name and work products are usually nondiscoverable because, by law, they are considered "attorney work product." If a testifying expert relies on the work product of the consultant to formulate an opinion, the LNC's work product may then be discoverable by the opposing party only upon request.

Types of Expert Witnesses

Expert witnesses play the most valuable, crucial role in civil litigation. An expert mainly educates the attorneys, judges, and juries. Two main types of experts work as members of today's litigation teams: standard of care and teaching witnesses. Without the benefit of instruction and illustration on relevant medical and nursing issues, most jurors find it very difficult to render informed verdicts. Experts also assist many judges in the preparation to rule on admissibility of relevant medical evidence. Each expert must be educated, trained, and experienced in one or more specialty practice areas. In several states (e.g., Arizona, Texas, and Oregon), attorneys are required by law to consult an expert before a medical malpractice case is filed with the court. Truthfulness is essential and misrepresentation or exaggeration of clinical facts or opinion to establish an absolute right or wrong may be harmful, both to the individual parties involved and to the profession as a whole.

Standard of Care Expert Witness

The Standard of Care Expert witness performs a serious, knowledgeable review of the records involved, and arrives at a conclusion and opinion regarding the outcome. Following the expert's independent review and formulation of opinion, they may assist the attorney in developing the case theory, and then may be selected to support that theory in the courtroom. When qualified to do so, this expert may be called on to testify regarding any deviation from the standard of care and whether this breach caused the alleged injury. The attorney chooses this expert to teach and explain issues because anatomy and physiology are not necessarily common knowledge and issues may be complex. If identified and chosen, the expert's work product becomes discoverable. For this reason, the attorney's decision either to request written reports or analyses or to keep all communications verbal must be made at the time the expert is engaged. The Standard of Care Expert witness provides trial testimony, based on standards in effect at the time the alleged event took place, and explains how the defendant did or did not adhere to those standards. In order to qualify a person as an expert, the court must recognize and give serious weight to his or her testimony. The litigation team must take care that such expert testimony does not reflect the expert's own views in isolation, but are based on applicable standards, as well as evidence-based medicine. The opinions may not be shared by all providers, but should not be excluded from other acceptable and perhaps more realistic choices.

Standards of Care

Standards of care can be national, local, community-based, or specific to an agency. National standards are found in nursing textbooks, laws, journal articles, and pharmacology books (e.g., the Physicians' Desk Reference or Drug Facts and Comparisons). Nursing specialty organizations, for example the American Nurses Association (ANA), have published comprehensive standards of care. The standards that have been established by the U.S. Department of Health and Human Services in the Agency for Healthcare Research and Quality (AHRQ) are excellent sources. The Joint Commission has established standards in the Accreditation Manual for Hospitals that are used to evaluate and monitor the clinical and organizational performance of health care facilities. Local standards are found in the facility's policy-procedure manuals and internal instructional documents. Standards of care will be discovered only if requested by the attorney; however, the expert witness should identify to the retaining attorney any of these that will be needed to support the proposed testimony.

Community Standards

The concept of "community standards" is controversial. It is generally believed in the medical field that the standards are consistent throughout the nation because doctors and nurses use the same textbooks, read the same journals, and attend the same symposia. However, within the medical community it is unrealistic and improper to expect the providers at a rural facility to recognize and intervene in an obscure neurological syndrome that might be commonplace in the neurological intensive care unit at a tertiary center. There is less of a "community" standard than a standard relating to the practice of a reasonably prudent medical provider with similar education, skill, and experience.

Legally, however, the principle of community standard is still applied in some states and jurisdictions. Some states have a requirement that the expert witness must practice in the state where the incident occurred or in an adjacent state, an apparent application of the "community standard" rule. State laws are a source of community standards (e.g., Title 22 in California). The potential expert witness should be prepared to describe their familiarity with and how they know, the community standard, particularly if he or she has been employed at one facility for many years.

Trial preparation includes many hours of discussion with the testifying expert. If the expert's opinion cannot support the retaining attorney's case, the issues must be discussed and explained with supportive literature. This is equally important in either a plaintiff or defense case. The difficulties of the case facts must also be made known, and the plaintiff's attorney, the insurance company, or defense attorney must be informed of the significant issues that are likely to be addressed by the opposition. It is important not to write a report for either the attorney or the insurance company until you have discussed your findings and opinions and have determined that a written report is requested.

Expert Teaching Witness

The role of the expert teaching witness is strictly instructive, which excludes rendering an opinion on the applicable standard of care, and is not asked to give an opinion regarding the defendant's conduct the witness or its effects. A fact witness may be retained by an attorney or appointed by the court. The expert teaching witness reviews and summarizes the medical records and relevant professional literature, then provides the Trier of fact with relevant factual information using layperson's terminology.

Qualifications and Selection of the Expert Witnesses

Rule 702 of the Federal Rules of Evidence states that if specialized knowledge (e.g., medical, nursing, or technical) will assist the Trier of fact to comprehend the evidence on facts at issue in a case, then an individual who is qualified as an expert by knowledge, skill, experience, training, or education may provide testimony in the form of an opinion. The explanations need to be easily understood by juries and judges.

Minimum legal credentials for a health care expert include a current professional license and clinical expertise in the area at issue. Professional credibility, education, and skill may be enhanced by other credentials, such as graduate degrees, refereed journal publications, research, and certification in the specialty. These professional credentials reflect the highest level of expertise and knowledge of the appropriate standard of care (see Table 15.1). Professional credibility may also be damaged by any past history, including any type of disciplinary action by the licensing board or criminal indictment. A curriculum vita will usually be offered as an exhibit at the time of trial and includes the entire expert's educational background, experience, published materials, and speaking experience.

Table 15.1 Expert Qualifications

Education

Current professional licensure[a]

Clinical expertise[a]

Current clinical practice

Concurrent clinical practice in the specialty (usually)

Specialty certification

Graduate degrees

Professional refereed publications and research

Honors

[a] Indicates minimal legal requirements.

Selection of the Medical Expert Witness

The medical expert may be a Medical doctor, chiropractor, podiatrist, dentist, psychologist, or other provider who practices medicine in some form and who is addressed as "Doctor." Table 15.2 lists the desirable characteristics for medical experts.

Resources

Resources for finding medical experts are much like those that can be used to find nursing experts. Expert and consultant directories published by the local bar association are rich sources of qualified individuals. Other directories are frequently included in the annual membership guide of the local bar association. Some directories are published by legal organizations such as Martindale-Hubbell and in publications that report jury verdicts (e.g., Legal Expert Pages). Both directories of experts and specialty membership lists can be found online. Characterization of the expert witness as a "hired gun" is a risk when the expert is found in these publications.

Personal contacts are valuable resources. A physician whom the LNC has utilized as an expert witness in the past may be able to provide a referral to a colleague. Many physicians who are associated with medical schools will do medical–legal work. One can find them by accessing the physician referral service. If the contacted specialist does not testify, he or she can usually refer you to a colleague who does.

It is important to look for specialists in the right places. The local medical association may refer callers to an appropriately specialized physician or list of physicians. If this medical or surgical specialist is unable to assist, he or she may be a good source of referral to one who may be valuable. As an example, the pediatric neuroradiologist will probably be found at a children's hospital. The chiropractor can be found at the chiropractic college. The physiatrist who specializes in physical rehabilitation will be found as the director of a hospital rehabilitation department, or as one of many physiatrists at a rehabilitation (not convalescent) hospital. The clinically active LNC who works with an appropriate specialist can ask whether he or she does this kind of work. The LNC

Table 15.2 Qualifications for Medical Experts

Board certification in the specialty

History of achievement in the specialty (e.g., fellowships, awards, and recognition)

Medical school teaching appointments

Clinical experience with the medical activity in issue

Publications in refereed journals

Staff privileges at prestigious hospitals

Experience as an expert witness (preferably reviewing cases for both plaintiff and defense attorneys)

A sincere, believable affect

The ability to explain complex medical issues in lay terms

should be aware of agency policies and avoid drawing attention to part-time work with attorneys if the employing agency frowns on it.

Selection of the Ancillary Expert

The ancillary expert category encompasses all medically related disciplines that do not fall under medicine or registered nursing. These include pharmacologists, x-ray technologists (including CT or *computerized tomography*, MRI or resonance imaging, and radiation-therapy technicians), laboratory technicians (including blood bank technologists), licensed practical nurses (LPN/LVN), human resources administrators, biomedical engineers, and more. Their qualifications and characteristics mirror those of nursing and medical experts, and they require the same support.

These specialists can often be found among the clinically active LNC's coworkers. Their specialty organizations may be found online. As for nursing and medical experts, a contact at a major medical malpractice firm, whether plaintiff or defense, may be able to direct the LNC to an appropriate expert and provide an assessment of that person's work as an expert witness. Less often, they can be found in the expert and consultant directories that are published in print or online.

Selection of the Nurse Expert Witness

Sullivan v. Edward Hospital., 806 N.E. 2d 645 (Ill. 2004) determined that a physician was not qualified to testify to nursing standards (see Chapter 2, "History, Entry into Practice, and Certification," Appendix F). The selection and use of the Nurse Expert may be more challenging than other provider witness selection. While some courts have held that the only requisite qualification to testify as an expert witness is knowledge that is greater than that found in the general community, other courts have challenged testimony by a professional in the nursing science. Several jurisdictions disallowed testimony by nurses and others they deemed to be inadequately qualified. The most common accepted criterion of an appropriately educated or experienced nursing expert seems to be current and relevant clinical practice. While courts have occasionally allowed expert testimony by people who no longer practice in the specialty at issue, more commonly, such testimony may be excluded. A safe practice in selection of an expert witness is to insist on current clinical practice or teaching in the specific area at issue in the case. For example in one case, a nurse who had worked in a law firm office for several years was listed as an expert witness regarding nursing practice about which she felt absolutely qualified to testify. The judge refused to qualify her as an expert because of her lack of current clinical practice in the issue under litigation and her lack of clinical practice at the time of the alleged incident, which left the attorney without an expert witness in the matter.

Selection within a Specialty

Nursing Science created numerous specialties and subspecialties within the nursing profession, of which the attorney should be made aware. Table 15.3 is a partial listing of nursing specialties to help in identifying the nurse specialist who will be required for specific case issues. Institutions vary in size, function, and specialty area. The selected expert needs to be familiar with the functions and work activities being reviewed. For example, hospital care, medication, and treatment guidelines differ not only from state to state, but also from county to county, and care in a tertiary teaching center may significantly be different from that in a community hospital. Not all emergency nurses deal with trauma, which affects not only the level of medical care provided, but also the qualifications of the person doing triage. Many general emergency departments rarely care for

Table 15.3   Nursing Specialty Areas

Abortion	Emergency (including prehospital)
AIDS, AIDS-related complex	Endoscopy
Alzheimer's	Enterostomal therapy
Anesthesia	Epidemiology
Angioplasty	Ethical issues
Assisted living	Evidence location and preparation
Behavioral disorders	Eye surgery
Bill auditing	Genetic counseling
Board and care homes	Geriatrics
Bone marrow transplant	Hemophilia
Burns	HMOs
Cardiac care	Home health care
Cardiac rehabilitation	Hospice
Cardiac special procedures	Hospital regulations and standards
Case management	Infection control
Chemical dependency	IV insertion and monitoring
Chemotherapy	Laparoscopic surgery
Claim management	Life care planning (adult and pediatric)
Clinical specialist	Long-term care
Clinics	Managed care
Coagulation disorders	Med/surg (medical and surgical)
Complex home care	Mobile intensive care nurse (MICN)
Convalescent care	Neonatal (including NICU)
Critical care (all types)	Nephrology
Critical care transport	Neurology
Defense medical exam (DME/IME)	Nurse practitioner (all specialties)
Diabetes	Nursing administration
Diabetes education	Nursing standards of care
Dialysis (hemo- and peritoneal types)	Obstetrics (labor and delivery, postpartum)
Discharge planning	Oncology

continued

Table 15.3   (continued) Nursing Specialty Areas

Orthopedics	Resuscitation
Pain management	Risk management
Paramedic care	School nursing
Pediatrics	Sexual assault
Physician assistant	Shunts
Plasmapheresis	Skilled nursing facilities
Psychiatric nursing	Surgery (all types)
Pulmonary care	Surgicenter
Quality improvement	Toxic exposures
Radiology (including special procedures)	Transplants
Recovery (postanesthesia)	Trauma
Rehabilitation	Urgent care
Research	Ventilators

a child with a complex chronic illness or life-threatening injury when a children's hospital is available in the area, and will usually simply stabilize and transfer the patient. It would be impossible to identify the subsets of knowledge and experience for every nursing specialty; it is essential for the LNC and attorney to be aware that they exist, and select accordingly.

Qualifications of the Expert Witness

The Standard of Care Expert witness must have at least the educational background of the person whose practice is under review. In practice, the more profound the educational background of the expert, the greater his or her credibility. In nursing, a registered nurse (RN) with a bachelor of science in nursing may have greater credibility than a nurse with an associate of science in nursing degree. Usually, the more academically advanced nurse will have greater impact. A doctorate confers a constellation of credibility, whether it is in nursing, education, or some other discipline. Board Certified physicians will be afforded more testimony weight than one who does not hold that distinction. Graduates of the more prestigious centers of higher learning hold more esteem than lesser known institutions; a Harvard or Stanford medical graduate, for instance, is usually held in very high regard.

Certifications, even an unrenewed certification obtained by examination, provide more credibility than never having taken a certification examination. There is also an important distinction between American Board of Nursing Specialties certification on the one hand, and certificates of completion of hospital or seminar programs. The latter certificate is open to denigrating cross-sexamination because it merely shows course hours without competency testing. The authors have seen curricula vitae (CVs) in which the nurses have listed as certifications the hospital in-service requirements of their employers. While this will tend to support the premise that the nurse is well prepared for her nursing tasks, attendance at such required developmental programs and educational seminars should be clearly described and not appear to be an attempt to inflate the CV for deceptive purposes.

The expert witness who has published, has additional credibility, particularly when the subject matter relates to the case under scrutiny. The best authoritative persons are those who author text-books, writes articles in refereed journals, or serve on a journal review panel. Refereed journals publish materials that have undergone a peer-review process by eminent consultants with diverse professional backgrounds. Examples of refereed journals include the *American Journal of Nursing* (AJN) and the *Journal of Legal Nurse Consulting* (JLNC). These publications are available to the opposing counsel, and the expert witness can be sure they will be obtained. They will be carefully reviewed for evidence of a conflicting opinion contrary to the one the expert now professes, and any other adversary content.

Honors awarded to the expert can cause the jury to be predisposed to like or accept the expert. If the expert was named outstanding educator, for example, or employee of the quarter, or a nominee for the excellence award at the employing hospital, it adds to credibility. In all areas of expertise, awards convey the appearance of excellence in the field and recognition of meritorious conduct.

Characteristics of the Desirable Expert Witness

In addition to legally required licensure and practice requirements, advanced education, certification, teaching and publication activities, personal characteristics may be of great importance. The expert witness should be poised, articulate, and able to explain complex concepts or procedures in simple language. A neat physical appearance, good grooming, and wholesome general demeanor are desirable, as are a warm personality and sincere, believable effect. The expert witness should be able to absorb hostile questioning without taking offense, and rebound. An excellent memory will enable the expert to identify misquotations of testimony and correct them in a timely fashion. Ideally, the expert possesses verbal skills and ability to explain complex or specialized issues in every-day language. Jury appeal remains one of the overall objectives for successful outcome.

Balance

An expert's opinion is viewed by the Trier of fact as impartial and unbiased. Although in the past it was common for an expert to work exclusively for defense firms or plaintiff firms, such one-sidedness is now considered a negative. The more closely the expert's work is evenly divided between plaintiff and defense, the more objective the expert will appear to be, and in all probability, the more objective the expert will be.

The following are key characteristics for successful trial outcome and working relationships.

Compatibility

Attorneys who hire expert witnesses will be working closely with them, so it is important for the attorney and the expert to have a comfortable working relationship. It is safe to assume that if the attorney does not like the expert, it is entirely possible that a judge or jury may have the same reaction. If the LNC has the key role of locating the expert, the impressions the LNC forms while interacting with the expert are important. The courteous, responsive expert who readily provides information in the initial contact is likely to have an edge over the expert who reacts sluggishly or egotistically.

Presentation Skills

Most medical providers, including physicians and nurses, are expert at presenting complex medical issues in language understandable to unsophisticated lay people. This skill is essential to the testifying expert. Occasionally, an LNC may encounter a nurse or other expert, who cannot easily make the transition from professional language to common language. Asking the expert to explain a medical issue that the expert does not understand can test this. A tendency to use medical terms or graduate school-level vocabulary is not enough to disqualify the nurse, but it does signal a need for significant preparation time. The trial preparation LNC can be valuable in assisting in the preparation of such experts in their testimony.

Specific Knowledge

The expert witness must have current knowledge of the illness, injury, procedure, or equipment at issue in the case. It is possible to work in the operating room, for example, but have no experience with open-heart surgery, or to work in pediatrics but never to have encountered the illness from which a litigant has suffered. To believe that any nurse or doctor can testify to virtually all medical issues is a recipe for disaster.

Example 15.1

In one case involving the sudden and unexpected death of a young oncology patient, the plaintiff nurse expert had never worked in oncology and had, in fact, been working in chemical dependency for the previous five years. At a deposition she testified to causation, blaming the chemotherapy that had been administered, apparently because Drug Facts and Comparisons indicated that the drug was nephrotoxic, and ignoring that the reference also stated that symptoms of toxicity appear approximately three weeks after treatment. She not only lacked specific knowledge, but also exceeded her scope of practice in testifying to medical causation. She left the deposition in tears, and the attorney was left to attempt to find a qualified witness immediately. The chosen expert was absolutely unqualified to testify in the case. The plaintiff attorney said that she had "held herself out to be qualified," which may have left her vulnerable to a charge of malpractice.

Practical Experience

The testifying expert should have absolute command of the clinical area. A physician or nurse who has worked in a specialty area for 20 years, but now works only part time in that area, is an entirely satisfactory witness. A practitioner who has worked in the specialty area part time for the past three years may lack the requisite command of the specialty. The trial team must ensure the qualifications of the testifying expert.

Experience as an expert witness is desirable because testimony experience in deposition, arbitration, or trial improves the likelihood that the person will be an effective witness. Some attorneys prefer the novice witness, believing that people who have no history of providing expert testimony are somewhat immunized against characterization as "hired guns" (experts who do extensive testifying, particularly representing only plaintiff or only defense, and from which they derive the bulk of their income). Expert witnesses may be required by the court to provide evidence of the amount of revenue they obtain from reviewing, consulting, and testifying in court cases.

Practical Hints and Working Resources

To ensure organization, it is advisable for the supportive LNC to have an intake questionnaire and case form that addresses all requisite information (see Figure 15.1). The elements should include the issues in the case; the case caption or name; the facility, nurses, and doctors involved; the attorney's name and any other contact at the law firm or insurance company; the firm name, address, and telephone and fax numbers; whether plaintiff, defense, personal injury, or other; important dates; materials to be mailed or faxed; expert or consultant assigned; date and time the information was sent; and the source of the referral and the date.

While some elements of the intake format form are self-explanatory, others are best explained to all users. Issues in the case should be as comprehensive as is necessary to enable the LNC to determine the appropriate expert for the case. Elements should include the allegations of negligence; the alleged damage from that negligence; the locale in which the event or events took place

---

Case Name

Issues:

Facility/Personnel Involved:

Attorney:

Contact:

Firm Name:

Address:

Telephone: (_____) Fax: (_____)

Plaintiff, Defense, PI, Other:

Date of medical procedure or other action complained of:

Date of the injured party's awareness of his or her injury or loss there from:

Date of filing of the complaint with the court:

Dates on which the summons and complaint were served on each of the defendants:

State, County and Court title in which the litigation is filed:

Specialty Required:

Potential Expert:

Materials to Be Mailed or Faxed:

Date & Time Information Sent:

Source of Referral:

Comments:

Date: Signature

Figure 15.1   Sample case form.

(acute hospital, skilled nursing facility, board and care facility, surgicenter, psychiatric facility, or other); and the department within the facility in which the alleged negligence occurred.

Identification of the facility and personnel involved enables the LNC to screen for conflicts with the potential expert witness. This information is not always available at intake, but every effort should be made to obtain it.

The case form includes spaces for important dates. The dates of the medical action complained of and the injured party's awareness of the effects, as well as the dates of filing the complaint and service on defendants, all relate to statute of limitations issues, as well as to court-claimed notice requirements in actions against many governmental bodies. These are important because care must be taken that the expert's testimony does not, in some unintended way, relate adversely to the client's position on these legal issues.

Many jurisdictions require disclosure of experts and their opinions to adverse parties. In such jurisdictions, there will usually be some type of schedule or timetable applying to the process of that disclosure. The dates expected for disclosure of reports and adverse deposition of experts are therefore of critical importance to the potential expert early on.

The date or general time of an expected trial date is likewise a matter of critical importance to the expert in relation to his or her availability.

Identification of Expert

Identifying and locating an effective and appropriately qualified expert can be a daunting task. Here, networking skills are invaluable. The local American Association of Legal Nurse Consultants (AALNC) chapter is a rich source of nurses of varied clinical backgrounds. The in-house nurse at a large medical malpractice or malpractice defense firm may be an excellent source of highly recommended experts. If the LNC is clinically active, many qualified experts can be identified through the LNC's place of employment. Some LNCs prefer not to draw attention to their work with attorneys, and it may be the best medical practice not to recruit experts from a personal employment site.

The local bar association may publish a directory of experts and consultants, including nurses, particularly in heavily populated areas. The AALNC membership data may lead the LNC to precisely the required nursing expert. The AALNC nurse locator site may provide many qualified testifying nurse experts. When an exceptionally well-qualified Standard of Care expert is required, the best resource may be an expert at one of the major university centers or center of excellence. Often this person can provide referrals to others in his or her network. Online registry sources such as http://www.ExpertPages.com, nursefinders.com, and the state board of registered nursing (BRN) can also be accessed. An expert witness screening form (see Figure 15.2) can be utilized when making contact with an expert to elicit details about experience and fees.

Support for the Expert

Even the most experienced expert witness needs some support. The relative newcomer to this function requires a great deal of support, background, preparation, and coaching. At minimum, the LNC should be certain that the expert is confident in the following areas:

- ■ Elements of liability
- ■ Understanding the litigation process
- ■ Standards of care

Expert name: Date: _____

Specialty:

Office address: Mailing address: where to send records

_____

Phone #: Fax #:

Best time to call:

(Day or evening)

Name of office contact:

Current CV on file: yes or no Entered into database: yes or no

Signed contract: yes or no Date of contract: _____

Rate for review: _____ Typed fee schedule: yes or no

Rate for deposition: _____

Rate for trial: _____

Cancellation fee: _____

Time cancellation fee will be effective:

Retainer required: yes or no Amount of retainer: _____

Number of cases reviewed per year:

Number of times testified at deposition:

Number of times testified at trial:

Number of plaintiff cases # vs. defense cases #

Percentage of plaintiff cases % vs. defense cases %

Comments:

Expert name: Date: _____

Specialty:

Office address: Mailing address: where to send records

_____

Phone #: Fax #:

Best time to call:

(day or evening)

Name of office contact:

Current CV on file: yes or no Entered into database: yes or no

Figure 15.2 Expert witness screening form.

Signed contract: yes or no Date of contract: _____

Rate for review: _____ Typed fee schedule: yes or no

Rate for deposition: _____

Rate for trial: _____

Cancellation fee: _____

Time cancellation fee will be effective:

Retainer required: yes or no Amount of retainer: _____

Number of cases reviewed per year:

Number of times testified at deposition:

Number of times testified at trial:

Number of plaintiff cases # vs. defense cases #

Percentage of plaintiff cases % vs. defense cases %

Comments:

Figure 15.2 (continued)

Elements of Liability

The elements of liability are as follows:

- There must be a duty to provide care. (Good Samaritans, e.g., have no such duty.)
- There must be an act or failure to act that falls below applicable standards of care.
- There must be damages.
- The breach of the standard of care must have caused or contributed to the damages.

It is possible to provide medical and nursing care that was substandard, but incurred no liability because the care and treatment neither caused nor contributed to any damages suffered by the plaintiff. The four elements required for the breach in the standard of care must be met.

Understanding the Litigation Process

The testifying expert must understand that litigation proceeds in a standardized format. The expert's file is discoverable. All materials utilized in reaching the conclusion and the opinions expressed are valuable. Occasionally, an expert witness will be directed to relinquish the entire file relating to a case, including notes on the outside, Post-its®, notes regarding conversations with the attorney, and anything else that was written. The novice expert may innocently write both the favorable and unfavorable impressions that he or she derived from reviewing the medical record, depositions, policies, and procedures. The more experienced expert should know that all impressions may be communicated to the attorney verbally, but that all written work is potentially discoverable.

The supporting LNC should proofread written reports several times, avoid criticisms of other personnel, and submit reports in a timely fashion. Figure 15.3 provides one example of format guidelines.

DATE:

TO: (claim adjuster, attorney, contact person)

FROM: (your name, title, degrees, certifications)

SUBJECT: Medical Record Review

FILE NO.:   (Insurance company or law firm file number)

CASE CAPTION: (Case name: Fyler v. St. Agatha Medical Center)

CO. FILE NO.:   (your personal filing system)

NURSING MEDICAL RECORD REVIEW

[Brief statement:] At your request I have reviewed the … records of … to ascertain …

RECORDS REVIEWED

[Listing of each segment of each chart:]

Office Records Dr. Walsh, 4/16/75 to 6/6/00

Paramedic Report 1/3/99

Prehospital Report, Mission Hospital 1/3/99

University of California Irvine Medical Center 1/3/99 to 3/1/99

Emergency Department Record, 1/3/99

Radiology Reports

Laboratory Reports

Intensive Care Nursing Record

Interdisciplinary Progress Record

Physical Therapy Evaluation, 1/5/99

Occupational Therapy Evaluation, 1/5/99

etc. Give dates, when multiple.

SUMMARY OF FINDINGS

Mrs. Williams is a 45-year-old lady who was struck by a car while crossing Harbor Blvd. in Costa Mesa at 1700 on January 3, 2006. She was treated at the scene by Orange County Paramedics, Unit 59, and taken to UCIMC where she was treated in the Emergency Department by the trauma team, headed by Dr. Smith and found to have multiple injuries. Following surgery she was admitted to the Trauma Intensive Care Unit. She made satisfactory progress, and was transferred to the orthopedic unit three days later. Physical therapy and occupational therapy were started and she continued to make good progress. However, she has many injuries, which can be expected to require treatment for some time and which may cause permanent disability.

CHRONOLOGY

This should provide a chronological record of relevant data. It is not always required, but when it would be valuable to the attorney or claims representative it should be included. The length of the summary or chronology should be discussed with the requesting attorney. Some attorneys prefer a shorter three page summary to a 53 page table-type chronology. It is wise to discuss this task and obtain permission before providing a chronology because it can be time-consuming (and thus expensive). It is most often needed in complex cases and long-term care, and may prove invaluable as a minute-to-minute record of an emergent surgical or obstetrical episode.

Figure 15.3 Sample report format.

Data might include: day of injury or illness, x-ray findings, abnormal laboratory or cardiology results, significant progress notes, physical therapy notes—anything that should be identified, noting its place in the progression of care.

DISCUSSION

There is a concern that … diagnosis was not made until … Additionally, there are numerous nursing notations describing the patient as "uncooperative," "resistant," "demanding," and "distraught." Nursing care appears to have met most standards of care. There were missed medications [describe medicine, date, and time], failure to document output [times, dates], and an incomplete day of admission assessment. None of these deviations would have caused or contributed to a less than satisfactory outcome in this case. [OR: the failure to monitor and record circulation in the right leg may have contributed to …]

CONCLUSIONS

It is very important that the standard of care expert come to some conclusions and state clearly if there is or is not any consequential deviation from the standard of care. These should include both general and specific deviations and associated damage. The expert must believe in his or her opinion strongly enough to testify in a court of law, under oath that a breach in the standard of care occurred and the supportive reasoning for this opinion. The testifying witness will cite the standards, specifics of the opinion, and the harm that did result or may have resulted from this deviation from the standard of care. It is important to cite official standards of care various nursing specialty organization, AHRQ [Agency for Healthcare Research and Quality] and hospital policy and procedure relating to the issue of care. The expert's opinion must be as honest, as objective as possible, and easy to articulate.

RECOMMENDATIONS

[Identify missing records that should be obtained.

Identify relevant policies and procedures that should be obtained.]

REFERENCES

[Appropriate standard or standards

Books or magazines reviewed, noting edition and pages

Copies of articles]

DEFINITIONS

[If few in number, terms can be defined in the body of the text. If many, do a definition (glossary) page. Keep the vocabulary simple. Some attorneys and claims representatives are quite sophisticated. Some know virtually no medical terminology. Err on the side of caution.]

ANATOMICAL DIAGRAMS

[Clear visual aids to describe the system and organs involved]

THANK YOU

[A simple statement of thanks for providing you the opportunity to review this interesting case (or whatever fits).]

Figure 15.3   (continued)

Depositions

An expert witness may be called to give a deposition if the case is proceeding toward arbitration or trial. Some states (e.g., Pennsylvania, Oregon, and New York) do not require depositions.

Occasionally, an attorney will choose not to depose an expert, to save on costs. This deposition may be used in a future trial for impeachment purposes.

The novice expert witness should receive some preparation for the deposition experience. The process should be explained, with emphasis on the fact that this is not an environment in which the nurse is a teacher. Rather, each question, and only that question, should be answered. The response should be fairly concise and should not include information that the attorney has not requested. In this venue the opposition is the "enemy," who may attempt to lead the expert to express opinions either that the expert does not hold or that conflict with previous testimony.

The expert should know that a break may be requested at any time, so long as there is no question then pending for answer; in that event, only the attorney may request a break, and many jurisdictions may insist as a general matter that the pending question be answered before the break is taken. If there is a question pending answer, and the expert wants a break for some reason, the expert should convey that thought to his or her attorney for a decision and action. The expert should pause before answering any question, to give the retaining attorney time to object. The expert may declare that a question is not clear, and may ask that complex questions be broken down into their elements. Any misquotation on the part of the opposing attorney should be corrected. The expert must be conscious of the limitations of his or her expertise and must not exceed them, for example, by testifying to medical causation.

When the deposition has been transcribed, the expert witness should request a copy of it to review and sign. This is the time to make any corrections that are necessary, but the expert should be aware that a change of opinion will damage credibility, and may result in further deposition of the expert witness.

Many publications address the deposition process. It is advisable to refer the novice expert witness to one of them or even to supply the desired material. Chapter 14 explores the process in greater depth.

Preparation of the Expert for Trial

The LNC who assists in the expert's trial preparation must take an organized approach to this task. Review the testimony experience of the expert witness. The thoroughly experienced expert will need little preparation; the novice will require intensive preparation, coaching, and guidance.

Here is a long list of preparatory items to consider and address with the expert:

- Attire.
- Arrival time, place, and parking.
- Documents or exhibits that the expert is expected to bring with him or her.
- Material that should not be brought to court.
- Review the testimony with the expert witness to express, briefly, the facts he or she intends to provide. If there is any variation from your understanding, contact the attorney immediately for discussion.
- Evaluate the effectiveness of the presentation, and work with the expert witness to present more effectively, if needed.
- Practice using any visual aids, diagrams, or drawings, or even power point presentation.
- Emphasize the need to answer only the question that is asked for opposing counsel.
- Remind the expert not to begin an answer before the question is completely finished, so as to allow the attorney for whom the expert is working an opportunity to object. If the expert

is hopeful of an objection being interposed, the expert should nevertheless *not* look at the attorney as if for help.

- Review the expert witness's right to ask to have a question repeated if it is unclear, and to ask to have complex, multiple-focus questions broken into individual components.
- Practice responses.
- Develop sample questions of the type that the opposing attorney may ask.
- Ask the expert witness to respond only to the questions put forth.
- Focus the expert on only the issues put forth.
- Emphasize honesty. Questions are often asked in several forms and when the answers are always honest, there should be no inconsistency.
- Watch for distracting mannerisms, such as finger tapping, knee jiggling, diverted eye contact, or eyebrow movement, and work with the expert to eliminate them.
- Remind the expert witness that most answers should be addressed to the jury, but that the response can be to the attorney when it seems more appropriate.
- Warn the expert witness about attorney tactics, such as
  - Attack on the expert witness's qualifications
  - Attack on the expert's testimony by using amazement, sarcasm, or disbelief
  - The "best friend" approach
  - Misstating the expert witness's previous testimony.

Videotape a practice testimony, if possible. This is very beneficial because the expert witness can view it to critique his or her responses and mannerisms. The witness may view real trial proceeding, a mock trial, or video of a mock trial.

Resources

This text provides guidance on many issues that confront the expert witness. The internet has many websites for specialty medical organizations, which may contain their standards. One can research the specific specialty physician board certifications. The ANA publishes comprehensive standards for clinical nursing, which serve as a template for specialty standards and standards for nursing administration. Every nursing specialty organization publishes standards of care as they relate to that specialty. All states will provide a copy of their Nurse Practice Act on request, and many are available on the internet.

Legal Rulings on Expert Testimony

In medical malpractice litigation, negligence is established through expert testimony as to the applicable standard of care for the specific circumstance at issue, a deviation from that standard, and an injury proximately caused by that deviation. Standards are referenced to demonstrate that the medical professional did or did not breach the duty of care owed to the client. If the provider failed to meet the standard of care and breached his or her duty, by definition the provider is negligent.

Before 1980, physicians served as the expert witnesses at trials regarding nursing standards of care. Two landmark court cases, *Avret v. McCormick* (Ga.1980) and *Maloney v. Wake Hospital Systems* (N.C. Ct. App. 1980), set the stage for acceptance by the court system of nurse experts, defining roles and standards of care for nursing practice. In *Avret v. McCormick*, a trial court excluded a nurse expert from rendering an opinion as to standards of care in keeping sterile a needle used to draw blood from a client. At trial, the physician against whom the medical malpractice suit was brought testified that blood-drawing is not a procedure exclusively limited to the professional skills of physicians. The Georgia Supreme Court held that the nurse was qualified as an expert witness in that a "nurse duly graduated from a school of nursing and licensed in this state and who has drawn blood and given intravenous injections in numbers exceeding two thousand, is qualified to testify as an expert witness." A Georgia Supreme Court ruling followed by a Georgia appellate court case distinguished Avert on the facts.

A similar ruling was made in *Maloney v. Wake Hospital Systems*. The North Carolina Court of Appeals held that the trial court had erred in disqualifying a nurse expert who was certified in intravenous therapy from stating an opinion as to the cause of a physical injury. The plaintiff suffered burns on her hand due to an intravenous administration of undiluted potassium chloride into the tissues. The appellate court held that an expert witness is not disqualified from giving an expert opinion as to the cause of a physical injury simply because she is not a medical doctor. The nurse's expertise is different from, but no less exalted than that of a physician. *Maloney v. Wake Hospital Systems* (N.C. Ct. App. 1980)

Judicial decisions have restricted the scope of nursing expert testimony relative to causation on injury issues and medical diagnosis issues. In *Dikeou v. Osborne* (1994) and *Kent v. Pioneer Valley Hospital* (1997), the Utah appellate court concluded that a nurse expert could opine on the nursing standards but was not qualified to opine on proximate causation of injury. In *Stryczek v. Methodist* (1998), the Indiana Court of Appeals held that the nurse expert could render an opinion as to the standard of care for administering cardio toxic medications by nurses, but not medical diagnosis, because nurses do not have the same education, training, and experience as physicians. *Stryczek* was cited in an Oklahoma Supreme Court case, which expressed no adverse opinion. Similar rulings were found in *Chadwick v. Nielson* (1988) and *Taplin v. Lupin* (1997).

With the emergence of advanced nursing practice, judicial decisions traditionally held the duty of care owed by the advanced practice nurses to the medical (physician) standard (Harris, 1979; Hendry, 1969). More recent court findings have disagreed with the preceding case rulings and have found that advanced practice nurses are not subject to the same standards as physicians.

In *Ewing v. Aubert* (1988) and *Fein v. Permanente Medical Group* (1985), the courts found that the nurse practitioner was held to the standard of care for an advanced nurse practitioner in diagnosis and treatment and not to the physician standard of diagnosis and treatment. Court decisions have also allowed advanced practice nurses to testify as expert witnesses against physicians when the services provided by the physician were the same as those that could legally be provided by an advanced practice nurse (*Samii v. Baystate Medical Center*, 1979). In courts the breach in the standard of care is proven through the expert witness testimony, and generally nurses are held to standards applicable to their specialty practice area and level of qualifications (O'Keefe, 2001). *Fein* was cited by Northern District of Texas, the Ohio Supreme Court, the Illinois Supreme Court, and Ohio court of common pleas. Each of those cases cited *Fein* with regards to the tort recovery limitations issue presented.

Legal Rulings on Medical Expert Testimony

Frye v. United States (1923) established the "general acceptance" standard for opinion testimony. In *Frye*, trial counsel for the defendant offered as an expert witness a scientist who had conducted a blood pressure deception test on the defendant. The court disallowed the testimony, holding that the systolic blood pressure deception test had not yet gained such standing and scientific recognition among physiological and psychological authorities as to be "generally accepted" in that branch of medicine, and would not justify the admission of expert testimony based on it.

A more liberal approach to admission of expert opinion testimony was followed by the courts with the adoption of Federal Rule of Evidence 702 in 1975. The federal rule makes no reference to the "general acceptance" standard, in stating as follows:

> If scientific, technical, or other specialized knowledge will assist the Trier of fact to understand the evidence or to determine a fact at issue a witness qualified as an expert by knowledge, skill, experience, training or education, may testify thereto in the form of an opinion or otherwise.

Daubert v. Merrell Dow Pharmaceuticals, Inc. (1993) involved two children and their parents as petitioners who alleged that the children's birth defects had been caused by the mothers' prenatal ingestion of a prescription drug for nausea (Bendectin) marketed by Merrell Dow Pharmaceuticals. The trial court determined, and appeals court held, that the evidence presented by the petitioners' experts did not meet the "general acceptance" test. The Supreme Court reversed the decision, holding that the "general acceptance" standard was superseded by the 1975 adoption of the Federal Rules of Evidence intending to liberalize the admissibility of expert testimony, the Court placed responsibility for deciding admissibility on the trial judge, who was given the role of "gatekeeper," allowing admission of reliable scientific evidence and excluding less reliable evidence. *Daubert* set forth a nonexclusive checklist for trial courts to use in assessing the reliability of scientific expert testimony. The specific factors explicated by the decision are (1) whether the expert's technique or theory can be or has been tested, (2) whether the technique or theory has been subject to peer review and publication, (3) the known or potential rate of error of the technique or theory when applied, (4) the existence and maintenance of standards and controls, and (5) whether the technique or theory has been generally accepted in the scientific community. *Frye* has been cited at least 356 times and *Daubert* at least 179 times. More details of these cases can be found by doing extensive legal research. The Court articulated four nonexclusive criteria that were to be considered when evaluating expert testimony:

■ Whether the theory is tested
■ Whether the theory or technique has been subjected to peer review and publication
■ The potential error rate
■ The existence and maintenance of standards controlling the technique's operation

In *General Electric Company v. Joiner* (1997), the Court ruled that appellate review of admitted expert testimony is limited to the sole issue of "abuse of discretion" by the trial judge in admitting the evidence.

In *Kumho Tire Company, Ltd. v. Carmichael* (1999), the plaintiff expert intended to testify that by virtue of his experience he knew that a tire had failed because of a manufacturing defect. He based his opinion on the absence of certain criteria that he believed would be present if the tire had failed due to abuse. His testimony was disallowed because the Court held that the admissibility criteria of *Daubert* and Rule 702 apply to all experts providing testimony at trial, not just to novel scientific theories, and that the proposed testimony did not meet those criteria. The Court in *Kumho* held that these factors might also be applicable in assessing the reliability of nonscientific expert testimony, depending on the "particular circumstances of the particular case at issue" (199 S.Ct at 1175). No attempt has been made to codify these specific factors.

The Court, in *Weisgram v. Marley Company* (2000), determined that under Federal Rule of Civil Procedure 50(a), "appellate courts have the power to direct a district court to enter judgment notwithstanding the verdict against a winning plaintiff if the appellate court determines that admitted testimony was unreliable and inadmissible under *Daubert.*" This case has been cited by the 9th Circuit, but not selected for publication.

The advisory committee for the Federal Rules of Evidence deemed it necessary to amend Rule 702 on the basis of the Court's recent decisions on expert testimony and the disparate treatment of Rule 702 by the district courts. The new rule adds that expert testimony is admissible "if (1) the testimony is based on sufficient facts or data, (2) the testimony is the product of reliable principles and methods, and (3) the witness has applied the principles and methods reliably to the facts of the case."

In *Chambers v. Dr. Ludlow* (1992), the Indiana Court of Appeals held that every element of a prima facie case of medical malpractice need not be satisfied by a single expert opinion; a number of expert opinions on various issues may be combined to meet the burden of a prima facie case. Generally, in order to establish a claim of medical malpractice, the plaintiff must establish by means of expert medical testimony the applicable standard of care; the manner in which the defendant doctor breached that standard of care; and that the breach in the defendant doctor's standard of care was the proximate cause of the injuries noted in the complaint.

The evidence code as applied also states that for a witness to qualify as an expert, the subject of opinion or implication must be so related to the profession, trade, business, or occupation as to be beyond the understanding of the layperson, and the witness must have sufficient skill, experience, or knowledge in that field to make it appear that his or her opinion or inference will aid the Trier of fact in arriving at a just conclusion.

In *Broders v. Heise* (1996), the Supreme Court of Texas held that the witness called by the plaintiff was not qualified as expert on the issue of cause in fact. The case involved failure to diagnose a head injury in the emergency department, and the disqualified witness was an emergency physician. The court held that the mere fact that the witness was a medical doctor did not qualify him as expert in a medical malpractice action against other doctors. The fact that the witness possesses knowledge and skill not possessed by people generally does not in and of itself mean that such expertise will assist the Trier of fact (Rule 702). This case was cited a number of times by Texas appellate courts and once in a later Texas Supreme Court case. One Texas appellate court case observed that Broders was limited to determining the qualifications of the expert and did not extend to determining whether the methods used by the expert were reliable. All of the other cases did not squabble with the law stated in Broders, but distinguished it based on the facts of each case.

In *O'Connor v. Commonwealth Edison Company* (1992), the district court held that the physician was not qualified to render an expert opinion that radiation cataracts are pathognomic or that the plaintiff's cataracts could be caused only by exposure to radiation. The physician was a board-certified ophthalmologist who specialized in contact lenses and had no experience in the field of radiation-induced cataracts, nor had he studied published literature on the subject. A Central District of Illinois case has been cited in New York and the Northern District of Illinois dealing with procedural issue and not distinguished on its facts.

Idiosyncratic State Laws on Expert Testimony

All LNCs must be knowledgeable about the Nurse Practice Act in their states, legal opinions and case law that set precedent, and legislation regarding testimony that may affect the ability of the chosen expert to testify. A few examples follow.

In Texas, no side may examine or crossexamine an individual witness for more than 6 hours. Breaks during the depositions do not count against this limitation (Texas Rule 199.5©).

In California, it is illegal for anyone to be called "nurse" who is not licensed as an RN or LVN. The activities comprising the practice of nursing are outlined in the Nursing Practice Act, Business and Professions Code Section 2725.

In California, the attorney general issued an opinion that a nurse may not take orders from a physician assistant (PA). The PA may transmit orders from the physician but may not, himself or herself, institute such orders, as submitted in California Section 2725(a). In some states, the expert must have been practicing in the identified clinical environment, and in some cases in the year in which the incident occurred.

Other states have their own idiosyncratic laws. It is not sufficient to assume that the attorney will know all laws governing nursing and medical practice in the state in which he or she practices.

The LNC should study the Nurse Practice Act in his or her own state, and should regularly access any source of legal rulings affecting nursing practice in that state. It is the attorney's responsibility to know the law, and it would be unreasonable to expect the LNC to assume legal responsibility for knowing each idiosyncrasy of the law in his or her state. The attorney bears the final responsibility in this matter, but the more in-depth knowledge the LNC brings to the table, the greater his or her value to the attorney.

Compensation and Fees

The independent LNC should be compensated for all supporting activities and tasks. These include locating an expert. There are three commons types of billing: a flat fee, hourly rate, or billing the expert through the LNC directly and adding the LNC fee.

A common method of billing for expert identification is to charge a flat fee for the expert location service. The advantage to a flat fee charge is that it is readily understood by the attorney. This charge must be clearly identified prior to service, so that it does not lead to a conflict regarding billing. One disadvantage is that the LNC must make certain that the expert located is actually utilized in the case because attorneys usually refuse to pay for the location of an expert whom they do not retain.

An LNC may also charge for billable time spent on this activity, keeping hourly accounting of the activity. The advantage to charging only the time spent for expert location is that, usually, it will be viewed as fair and as a charge that is easily justified to the client.

A larger LNC firm may include this fee as an hourly rate and add to the expert's charges, if the expert is billed through the LNC services. The LNC needs to be aware of laws governing billing charges. An LNC who chooses to charge a flat fee for expert location must be acutely aware of any laws governing this activity. The LNC should determine if the state's laws forbid charges that exceed the actual time spent in locating the expert.

The LNC should be advised that the potential expert has been engaged. If the LNC has a large base of potential experts, this method may limit the return to an hour or less of time charged, despite the extensive time and resources that were expended to develop the expert base. If extensive time and money are required, for example when unusual expertise or credentials are needed, the attorney should agree to some overcharges in advance or may dispute the charges after the fact. In such situations, the LNC should notify the attorney if a search is taking more than 2 hours and obtain permission to continue.

Some LNCs obtain compensation by adding a fee to each hour of activity billed by the expert. On average, this provides a more appropriate level of compensation than charging either a flat or hourly location fee. Disadvantages to this approach are that it requires a contractual relationship with the expert and that it slows the collection time and payment to the expert because the expert bills the LNC, who then bills the attorney. Payment is made to the LNC, who then pays the consultant.

In some states it is legal to add a fee to each hour the expert bills, as long as the client is aware that this is the method by which the LNC will be compensated. Fees obtained by this method are generally adequate to provide for marketing activities, to compensate the LNC for expert-finding activities that do not result in an engagement, and to provide a fair return for services rendered.

Regardless of the method chosen, the LNC should inform the attorney at the time expert search is requested that there will be a charge for this service, and should provide a clear explanation of the manner in which it will be done. Failure to inform the attorney can lead to inappropriate expectations and a conflict over fees.

Conclusion

Like all other expert witnesses, the medical expert witness must be familiar with the elements of liability; sources of practice standards; local, state, and national legislation that governs practice in the specialty under litigation; community standards; and legal rulings on the admissibility of expert testimony (e.g., *Frye v. United States*, 1923; Federal Rule of Evidence 702; *Daubert v. Merrell Dow Pharmaceuticals, Inc.*, 1993; and Kumho Tire Company, Ltd. V. Carmichael, 1999).

Preparation for trial or deposition should follow a carefully orchestrated scenario similar to that described in this chapter regarding nurse expert witnesses. The physician may need extra coaching to avoid an affect that will be perceived as either arrogant or "thin-skinned." The physician, like the nurse, will be well served by viewing himself or herself in a practice testimony session and by watching a tape of a mock trial.

Physicians have been allowed to testify to nursing standards of practice. While this is now much less commonly allowed than in the past, if the LNC finds himself or herself working with a physician who is expected to do so, some very comprehensive preparation will be required. Most physicians know nothing of nursing standards; they just know what they want the nurses to do, which is not at all the same thing. Preparation for physician testimony regarding nursing practice will require considerable education in the sources of nursing standards, the laws that direct nursing practice in that locale, and the existence of policies and procedures that may govern the nurse's action.

An LNC may play an important role in identifying, locating, selecting, and supporting an expert witness. This opportunity is one of the more challenging activities in this chosen field. The LNC who approaches the task in an organized fashion will succeed in this endeavor. Maintaining a database of useful contacts and sources is a valuable tool. However, it is not enough to locate a qualified expert if that expert is unfamiliar with the legal process or is a novice at testifying. In that case, the LNC can apply skills that he or she developed as a clinical nurse to support the expert witness and achieve a successful outcome. LNCs provide critical support in the lifeblood function of developing expert witness participation in medical litigation.

References

Avret v. McCormick, 271 S.E.2d 832 (Ga. 1980).
Broders v. Heise, 924 S.W.2d 148 (Tex. 1996).
Chadwick v. Nielson, 763 P.2d 817 (Utah Ct. App. 1988).

Chambers v. Ludlow, 598 N.E.2d 1111 (Ind. Ct. App.1992).

Daubert v. Merrell Dow Pharmaceuticals, Inc., 509 U.S.579 (1993).

Dikeou v. Osborne, 881 P.2d 943 (Utah Ct. App. 1994).

Ewing v. Aubert, 532 So. 2d 876 (La. Ct. App. 1988).

Fein v. Permanente Medical Group, 38 Cal. 3d 137 (1985).

Frye v. United States, 293 F. 1013 (D.C. Cir. 1923).

General Electric Company v. Joiner, 522 U.S. 136 (1997).

Harris v. State through Huey P. Long Hospital, 371 So. 2d 1221 (La. 1979).

Hendry v. United States, 418 F.2d 744 (2d Cir. 1969).

Kent v. Pioneer Valley Hospital, 930 P.2d 904 (Utah Ct.App. 1997).

Kumho Tire Company, Ltd. v. Carmichael, 526 U.S. 137 (1999).

Maloney v. Wake Hospital Systems, 262 S.E.2d 680 (N.C. Ct. App. 1980).

O'Connor v. Commonwealth Edison Company, 807 F. Supp. 1376 (C.D. Ill. 1992).

O'Keefe, M. (2001). *Nursing malpractice and the law: Avoiding malpractice and other legal risks.* Philadelphia: F.A. Davis.

Stryczek v. Methodist Hospital, Inc., 694 N.E.2d 1186 (Ind. Ct. App.1998).

Taplin v. Lupin, 700 So. 2d 1160 (La. Ct. App. 1997).

Testimony by Experts, Federal Rule of Evidence 702 (1998).

Weisgram v. Marley, 528 U.S. 440 1001 (2000).

Additional Reading

Aiken, T., & Catalano, J. (1994). *Legal, ethical and political issues in nursing.* Philadelphia: F.A. Davis.

American Academy of Pediatrics. (2002). Policy statement guidelines for expert witness testimony in medical malpractice litigation. *Pediatrics, 109*(5), 974–979.

Anderson, R. (1997). *Legal boundaries of California Sacramento.* California: Nursing Practice.

Babitsky, B., & Mangraviti, J., (1997). *How to excel during cross-examination: Techniques for experts that work.* Falmouth, MA: Seak, Inc.

Babitsky, S., Esq., Mangraviti, J. J. Jr., Esq. (2002). *Writing and defending your expert report: The step-by-step guide with models.* Cape Cod, MA: Seak, Inc.

Bogart, J. (Ed.). (1996). *Legal nurse consulting: Principles and practice.* Boca Raton, FL: CRC Press.

Federal Rule Changes. (2000). Part B: Rules 701–703. Opinion Testimony, http://www. depo.com/ Evidence2000.htm.

Guido, G. (2000). *Legal and ethical issues in nursing.* New York: Prentice-Hall.

Iyer, P. (2001). *Working with expert witnesses in nursing malpractice.* In P. Iyer (Ed.) (2nd ed.). Tucson, AZ: Lawyers & Judges Publishing Company.

Kluwer, W. (2009). *Drug facts and comparisons.* Springhouse, IL: Lippincott Williams & Wilkins.

Pierson, E. (Ed.). (2000). *Wiley expert witness update: New developments in personal injury litigation.* New York: Aspen Law & Business.

Purver, J. (Ed.). (2002). *Expert witness update: New developments in personal injury litigation.* New York: Aspen Law & Business.

Report of the Advisory Committee on Evidence Rules. (1999). In Federal Rule Changes 2000 Part B: Rules 701–703. *Samii v. Baystate Medical Center*, 395 N.E.2d 455 (Mass. 1979).

Salovesh, C. (2000). *Presentation of evidence: A survival guide for nurses.* Cypress, CA: West Haven University.

Smith, J. (2000). *Hospital liability.* New York: Law Journal Seminars Press.

Stedman, A. (2005). *Stedman's Medical Dictionary,* 28th ed. Baltimore, MD: Wolters Kluwer.

Testimony by Experts, Federal Rule of Evidence 702, 1998.

Weber, E. (Author), Iyer, P. (Editor) (2001). *Asthma in a pediatric patient: An expert witness perspective.* Glenview, IL: American Association of Legal Nurse Consultants.

West's Legal Thesaurus/Dictionary. (1985). New York: West Publishing Company.

Online Resources

Code of Federal Regulations: Title 22, http://lula.law.cornell.edu/cfr/cfr.php?title=22
http://www.chiropractor-finder.com
http://www.dentist.com
http://www.ilnd.uscourts.gov/LEGAL/frcpweb/cvev98.htm
http://dir.yahoo.com/government/law/journals
http://www.alllaw.com/journals_and_periodicals/legal
http://www.expertpages.com
http://www.legalexpertpages.com
http://www.locateadoc.com

Test Questions

1. Which of the following statements is NOT true?
   A. Current licensure is requisite for an RN expert witness
   B. Clinical expertise in the specialty is usually required
   C. Old disciplinary action by the BRN is of no significance
   D. Certification in the specialty is desirable

2. Place the following actions in the best sequence when locating an expert
   A. Notify the attorney of the potential expert and send a copy of his or her CV
   B. Identify one or more potential experts
   C. Obtain comprehensive information about the issues in the case
   D. Contact the potential experts to determine availability and conflicts

3. Which of the following statements is NOT true? Criteria for admission of evidence according to Daubert include
   A. Whether the theory or technique has been subjected to peer review and publication
   B. The potential error rate
   C. Whether the theory is tested
   D. Whether the theory meets the "general acceptance" test

4. Which of the following statements is true?
   A. An RN without advanced practice credentials may opine as to physician standard of practice.
   B. The RN credential, in and of itself, qualifies the nurse to opine as to nursing standards of care in any department.
   C. It is unnecessary to know the laws restricting nursing practice in the expert's state. The attorney is expected to know them and advise the expert.
   D. It is important to know the sources of nursing standards.

5. Which of the following statements is NOT true?
   A. Once an individual has been qualified as an expert by a trial court, he or she may give opinion testimony in any jurisdiction
   B. The "general acceptance" test establishes admissibility based on scientific evidence
   C. An in-house LNC at a medical malpractice firm may provide a good referral to an appropriately qualified expert witness
   D. An effective expert witness will have good personal as well as professional characteristics

Answers: 1. C, 2. CBDA, 3. D, 4. D, 5. A

Chapter 16

Alternative Dispute Resolution
Settlement, Arbitration, and Mediation

Madeline C. Good, MSN, RN, LNCC

First Edition
Tracey Chovanec, BSN, RN; Janet Kremser, BS, RN, C-SN, CDON/LTC; and Barbara J. Levin, BSN, RN, ONC, LNCC

Second Edition
Tracey Chovanec, BSN, RN; Janet Kremser, BS, RN, C-SN, CDON/ LTC; Barbara J. Levin, BSN, RN, ONC, LNCC; Eileen Watson, EDD, MSN, RN, ANP, LNCC; and Nancy Wilson-Soga, BS, MS, RN

Contents

Objectives

- Define "alternative dispute resolution (ADR)"
- Define "arbitration" and compare and contrast the processes of binding arbitration and nonbinding arbitration
- Discuss the role of the legal nurse consultant (LNC) in the arbitration process
- Define "mediation"
- Identify the steps in the mediation process
- Discuss the role of the LNC in the mediation process
- Identify the steps used in the preparation of a settlement brochure to be used at mediation
- Discuss other settlement methods

Introduction

Alternative dispute resolution (ADR) has become an increasingly popular process within our justice system and is a method used to aid in resolving lawsuits outside of the courtroom. The United States Code defines "ADR" as any procedure that is used, in lieu of adjudication, to resolve issues in controversy [15 USC § 571(3) (Suppl. 1993)]. This includes, but is not limited to, settlement negotiations, conciliation, facilitation, mediation, fact-finding, minitrials, and arbitration, or any combination thereof. While ADR may be used in cases involving many types of issues, it is perhaps most useful in those cases involving personal injuries, medical malpractice, employment issues, financial institutions, and contract disputes. With court dockets becoming more and more overcrowded, judges are ordering the participants in lawsuits to attempt to resolve their disputes through ADR. In some states, litigation filed in court is automatically assigned before trial to ADR resolution. The advantages to ADR are that both sides might avoid the cost of continuing litigation, and that it allows a claim or dispute to be resolved in a timely fashion and without a lengthy and expensive trial. Arbitration and Mediation are two of the most common methods of ADR and this chapter focuses on those two types and the LNC's role in the process. There has been a general increase in all forms of ADR in recent years because of the advantages offered such as reduced cost, fast resolution, and privacy.

Arbitration

Arbitration is a legal technique for the resolution of disputes outside the courts, wherein the parties to a dispute agree to chose a third party, that is, a person or panel of impartial persons (the "arbitrators" or "arbitral tribunal") by whose (written) decision (the "award") they agree to be bound. Arbitration is an option for a lawsuit ready to go to trial in order to avoid clogged court calendars and/or a court trial (Garner, 1999). It may be voluntary, it may be required by a provision in a contract for settling disputes, or may be compulsory as provided under state statute or court order. The parties select a retired judge or a respected lawyer to serve as the arbitrator or panel member, or rely on an organization, such as one provided by the American Arbitration Association which has a specific set of rules to provide these services.

The AAA is a private enterprise in the business of arbitration and one of several arbitration organizations that administers arbitration proceedings. The International Centre for Dispute Resolution (ICDR), established in 1996, administers international arbitration proceedings initiated under the institution's rules. ICDR currently (as of 2007) have offices in New York City, Dublin, and Mexico City and is scheduled to open an office in Singapore (International Centre for Dispute Resolution, 2007). Many contracts include an arbitration clause naming the AAA as the organization that will administer an arbitration between the parties. The AAA does not itself arbitrate disputes, but provides administrative support to arbitrations before a single arbitrator or a panel of three arbitrators. The arbitrators are chosen in accordance with the parties' agreement or, if the parties do not agree otherwise, in accordance with the AAA rules.

There are two categories of arbitration—binding arbitration and nonbinding arbitration—each of which can be either mandatory or voluntary. Mandatory arbitration involves cases in which contractual relations are present, such as labor–management disputes; insurance claims (personal injury); securities industry disputes; and auto accident injury cases in no-fault states such as New York, New Jersey, Minnesota, Hawaii, and Oregon. Trade associations and professional insurance liability carriers utilize arbitration to resolve conflict.

Binding Arbitration

In binding arbitration, the parties submit the dispute to one or more impartial arbitrators who have both expertise and knowledge of the case as well as a substantive basis for rendering informed decisions and awards. Once the arbitration decision is rendered, this leads to finality, in which the award is contractually based and imposed.

Binding arbitration is an agreement between the parties in advance to abide by an arbitrator's decision. The process usually takes place when a contractual agreement states that the conflicts will be resolved by binding arbitration. In the United States, many large corporations are requiring individuals to submit to mandatory binding arbitration.

Although arbitration was originally intended to be used for disputes between commercial entities of similar sophistication and bargaining power, it has increasingly been extended to disputes between parties of greatly disparate bargaining power such as consumer disputes and civil rights and other employment disputes. Numerous courts in the United States had ruled that mandatory arbitration clauses in contracts are unenforceable, at least in the early 1900s. By the year 2000, it was well accepted that the Federal Arbitration Act (FAA) preempts state law and is binding except in extreme circumstances. At present, everything from your credit card to your employment is subject to arbitration. Some states allow hospitals to place arbitration clauses in hospital admission agreements, thus the LNC should inspect all signed hospital admission forms to determine whether they include such clauses. Doctor's offices utilize patient information forms and contractual service forms which include such clauses and the LNC should request and inspect all such signed forms.

Because there is a finality to decisions under binding arbitration, the process is generally covered by state statutes that outline specific guidelines and require explicit warnings to the participants about the consequences of entering into arbitration. In Texas, for example, Vernon's Annotated Statutes, Article 4590i, § 15.01(a) states as follows:

> No physician, professional association, or health care provider shall request or require a patient or prospective patient to execute an agreement to arbitrate health care liability claims unless the form of agreement delivered to the patient contains a written notice in 10-point bold-face type clearly and conspicuously stating: UNDER TEXAS LAW, THIS AGREEMENT IS INVALID AND OF NO LEGAL EFFECT UNLESS IT IS ALSO SIGNED BY AN ATTORNEY OF YOUR OWN CHOOSING. THIS AGREEMENT CONTAINS A WAIVER OF IMPORTANT LEGAL RIGHTS, INCLUDING YOUR RIGHT TO A JURY. YOU SHOULD NOT SIGN THIS AGREEMENT WITHOUT FIRST CONSULTING WITH AN ATTORNEY.

The Texas statute also states that violations of the above section by a physician or professional association of physicians constitute violations of the Medical Malpractice Act. This action would be subject to enforcement provisions and sanctions.

The binding arbitration process usually involves submitting a contested matter to a three-member panel. Appeals to the binding arbitration decision are very limited. As a result, this process is the least desirable in personal injury or medical malpractice cases. Binding arbitration is more commonly used in contract disputes.

Nonbinding Arbitration

Nonbinding arbitration usually involves one arbitrator, yet the decision is not final. If either the plaintiff or the defendant is dissatisfied with the arbitrator's decision, the case remains on the court's docket. The nonbinding arbitration process is often preferred over the binding arbitration process because the nonbinding type is less final.

Many states provide for mandatory arbitration of cases on a nonbinding basis in the hope that these minitrial proceedings conducted by experienced attorneys will give the parties a clearer picture of the probable result and lead to acceptance of the arbitrator's decision. An individual can still have his or her day in court if arbitration does not produce any resolution.

The Arbitration Process

The AAA provides procedural guides to dispute resolution as a method to resolve claims in an inexpensive manner. Examples of types of claims submitted to the AAA include slip-and-fall cases that are in suit for several years, auto accidents, swimming-pool accidents, false arrests, and medical malpractice. Often the role of the LNC employed at a law firm is to initiate the process of preparing the submission to an arbitration board. This can be easily carried out by the following:

1. Logging on to http://www.adr.org, the Web site for the AAA, to determine where a local state office can be found.
2. Submitting names and addresses of the insurer, claimant, and their attorney or representative, along with contact phone numbers.
3. Completing case, claim, or docket numbers.
4. Providing a brief synopsis of the claim along with the dollar amount involved in the case.

5. Adding any additional information that may assist the AAA in arranging the case for arbitration or mediation. Here it should be stipulated whether the decision will be binding or nonbinding.

The AAA office then contacts all parties to gain approval for submission to arbitrate (binding) or mediate (nonbinding). Once agreement to arbitrate is unanimously established, the AAA appoints an experienced arbitrator from its panel of neutral attorneys. A biographical sketch of the arbitrator is sent to all parties to review and, if necessary, to object if a conflict of interest is identified. Following the appointment of an arbitrator, a hearing is scheduled at a convenient location. The LNC assists in preparing medical documentation of the case as well as gathering evidentiary material such as x-ray reports, highlighted medical documents, photographs of the injured area, and anatomical charts. These materials serve to educate the arbitrator. Under most states' arbitration laws, arbitrators have the right to subpoena witnesses and documents. Attorneys may choose to have witnesses and experts interviewed prior to the arbitration hearing to make certain that these individuals understand the format of arbitration and the importance of their testimony.

Although the arbitration hearing is less formal than a court trial, the process is as important to the parties as a trial. Hearings are conducted in a manner that affords a fair presentation of the case by both parties. Opening statements are made to describe the case and to detail what each party is seeking. This aids the arbitrator in understanding the relevance of the testimony that will be presented and the decision being sought. The arbitrator decides what evidence or testimony is relevant in understanding the issues and can reject evidence that he or she deems less than useful. The claiming party customarily presents first, each party states its position, trying to convince the arbitrator of the correctness of his or her position. This is not the strict "burden of proof" that would have to be outlined in a civil court trial. Witnesses are utilized to clarify issues and identify documents and exhibits. Crossexamination is permitted. Closing statements include a summary of the facts and arguments as well as refutation of points made by the opposing party.

The arbitrator closes the hearing and usually has approximately 30 days to review all the evidence and testimony in order to determine an appropriate decision and award. The award is a brief statement detailing which party will be providing a specific relief. This decision must be adhered to in a binding arbitration.

The appendix includes the plaintiff's formal demand for arbitration, the defense's arguments in response to the plaintiff's allegations as well as the exhibits prepared for utilization during the arbitration proceedings, and the arbitrator's award.

The Mediation Process

By far, mediation is the preferred process for most litigants considering ADR. Mediation is a voluntary and confidential means of dispute resolution without handing over the decision-making power to someone else (such as a judge). It is an attempt to settle a legal dispute through active participation of a third party (mediator) who works to find mutually agreeable points between the participants in order to facilitate an agreed resolution. The mediator does not make findings nor does the mediator tell the opposing parties what to do, nor will they judge as to which party is right or wrong. Control over the outcome of the case remains with the involved parties who agree to resolve their differences through a negotiated settlement agreement.

Mediation has become very common in the resolution of domestic relations disputes (divorce, child custody, and visitation for example) and is often ordered by the judge in such cases. Mediation has also become more frequent in contract and civil damages cases. In this forum, the plaintiff and defendant agree to conduct a settlement conference before an impartial third party known as a mediator. The case needs to have reached a mature status—exhibits having been collected and discovery nearing completion—to be ready for mediation.

Retired judges and lawyers with special expertise and training offer services as mediators. In some states, nonattorneys with training in mediation proceedings and expertise in a specific field of practice (for example, physicians, nurses, psychologists, educators) make excellent mediators. The mediator's fee is agreed upon in advance by all parties. Average daily mediation fees vary, ranging from approximately $600 to $1500 per party. Sometimes, mediators charge fees on an hourly basis. The financial cost is less than fighting the matter in court and may achieve early settlement and an end to anxiety.

Mediators use appropriate techniques and/or skills to open and improve dialogue between disputants. Normally, all parties must view the mediator as impartial. Although the mediator is an impartial third party, it is important to educate and inform him or her about the issues of the case prior to the settlement conference. One tool frequently used by the plaintiff is a settlement brochure, which is discussed in depth later in this chapter. The mediator can study the brochure and then develop an opinion. Such brochures are confidential submissions of the separate parties to the mediator, which ideally will emphasize the parties' strengths and the opponents' weaknesses that is likely to reflect the potential outcome in the courtroom. Naturally, the plaintiff hopes to convince the mediator to the possibility of a large jury verdict. Alternatively, the defense will focus on educating the mediator to the opposite opinion The ideal result of mediation is for the mediator to persuade both sides to meet somewhere on middle ground, thus resolving the claim absent a jury trial.

Agreements to mediate, mediation rules, and court-based referral orders may require disclosure of information by all parties. Mediators may also have express or implied powers to direct the parties to produce certain case-related documents or reports. In court referred mediations, the parties are usually required to exchange all material normally available through discovery or disclosure rules were the matter to proceed to a court hearing.

During mediation, the settlement conference itself often has a friendly atmosphere. At the beginning of the settlement conference, all parties meet together with the mediator, and counsel for each side presents a brief oral synopsis of the case. The parties then proceed to separate conference rooms for confidential caucuses between the mediator and the respective parties. Meeting privately with each party, the mediator strives to influence the opposing parties to adjust their respective expectations, focusing on the strengths and weaknesses of each party's claim. The ultimate goal is to resolve the differences between the parties and reach a settlement that is satisfactory to both sides. For successful mediation to occur, the presence of party representatives who possess authority to finalize settlement agreements is a prerequisite.

The following activities and discussions can assist in preparing for the mediation process; however, not all will apply for every mediation:

- Is mediation the right dispute resolution process at this time? Are the parties ready to settle?
- Readiness has great importance. Overwhelming emotions may render objective decision-making extremely difficult. In some cases, an injury may not have had sufficient time to heal, making any residual loss difficult to quantify. Precise diagnosis and enlightened prognostications and, frequently, ample expert support enable the parties to more accurately determine the "value" of the matter.
- Although entering into a mediation to settle the entire dispute may seem inappropriate, it may be appropriate for some of the issues.

- Identify who should participate in the mediation. Laws give decision-making power to certain individuals. These individuals are essential to the mediation and their attendance at the proceedings is crucial. Other important participants may include lawyers, accountants, experts, interpreters, or spouses.
- Convening a mediation session requires as much care as convening any other important meeting. Consider a location that best fosters settlement. Do any participants have special needs? What date and time works best? How much time might a mediation take?
- The task of selecting the right mediator occurs more readily when participants allow time to analyze the dispute. What is the dispute about? By identifying disagreements, parties clarify the issues in dispute. Is it possible that there is missing information which, if shared by all parties, the matter would quickly settle?
- What information do participants require in order to make good decisions?
- Do pictures, documents, corporate records, receipts, medical records, bank statements, expert reports, and so on exist that parties need to gather, copy, and bring to the mediation?

With all of the information at hand at the mediation, one may avoid the need to adjourn the meeting to make another at a later date while the parties gather other information.

The LNC's Role in Mediation

The LNC often plays a very visible role in mediation, both before and during the settlement conference. In a medical malpractice case, for example, an LNC could be employed by either the plaintiff or defense, to audit the presentation during mediation, to detect discrepancies or inaccuracies. The LNC would, of course, privately relay such information to the employing attorney. The LNC can also serve as an informed educator at the mediation forum. When complex medical issues are introduced, the mediator sometimes needs more information on the standard of care, the medical issues in dispute, or explanations of medical terminology. The LNC can be a resource liaison to the mediator.

An LNC can offer valuable assistance in mediations as an educator regarding the medical issues of a malpractice or personal injury case. The following outlines the medical aspects of a mediation presentation:

1. Overview of the case
2. Health history of the plaintiff
3. Injuries sustained and definitions
4. Questions and clarifications

Figure 16.1 describes the vital role that an LNC played in the successful outcome of a mediation in a personal injury case. Figure 16.2 provides an example of demonstrative evidence created by an LNC in a nursing home case. The mediator and parties were able to gain a comprehensive understanding of the medical issues and damages, which helped move the case to settlement.

Production of a Settlement Brochure

Prior to the settlement conference, the LNC is a major contributor to the production of a settlement brochure. The term "brochure" is somewhat of a misnomer. Brochures, as the term is typically used,

---

Mrs. Smith, a 41-year-old married woman with two children, was in a motor vehicle accident on a snowy February 1, 1995 at 2:30 p.m. While Mrs. Smith was driving north, Mr. Jones' car was driving south and crossed over the median strip and hit Mrs. Smith's car head-on at 30 mph.

Mrs. Smith's injuries included a left open grade 3B tibia fracture, a left shoulder dislocation, and a four-inch laceration to the parietal area of the head. She required emergent open reduction internal fixation (ORIF) surgery to stabilize the tibia fracture, and 20 sutures to the left parietal area. A week later, she underwent a Bankart procedure to stabilize the left shoulder.

Approximately eight months after the surgery, a nonunion of the tibia was diagnosed on x-ray. A second ORIF with right iliac crest bone graft was performed. A month later, the hardware in the tibia fractured due to the nonunion of bone. Another surgical procedure was required to replace it.

Mrs. Smith's health history included a history of smoking two packs per day for 20 years and adult-onset diabetes mellitus treated with insulin, both of which contributed to ineffective healing. At approximately seven months after the accident, Mrs. Smith showed signs of osteomyelitis. Intravenous and oral antibiotics were administered. Within five months and following multiple irrigation and debridements, she required a left below-the-knee amputation.

Three long-term goals for Mrs. Smith were identified and presented:

1. Return to previous level of function
2. Bipedal ambulation utilizing a prosthesis
3. Return to her job as a corporate secretary

During the presentation, the LNC provided detailed information regarding the grade of the fracture, surgeries, effects of diabetes and smoking on the healing process, and definitions of medical terminology, such as osteomyelitis and the Bankart procedure.

Figure 16.1   A successful outcome of a mediation in a personal injury case. (Courtesy of Barbara Levin.)

are often simple trifold documents. Frequently, such documents are referenced as "Confidential Submission of Plaintiff [Defendant] to the Mediator." A brochure used as a settlement tool is several inches thick and is bound with dividers. The settlement brochure can vary in size depending on the issues and evidence to be presented. Both plaintiff and defense counsels prepare brochures, although the plaintiff's brochure is usually more extensive. A settlement brochure serves three purposes:

1. It aids the trial team in focusing on specific medical issues that may later be used for trial of the case in the courtroom
2. It educates the mediator as to the strengths and weaknesses of the medical aspects of the case
3. It presents evidence that the parties are prepared for trial

The Plaintiff's Brochure

A number of formats are used in preparing an effective brochure from the plaintiff's perspective. The appendix provides a sample of a portion of an LNC's contribution to a settlement brochure. Also, the guidelines below can be incorporated into a brochure format. The LNC should begin by dividing the document into six sections titled Table of Contents, Brief Statement of the Case, Detailed Discussion of Medical Management Issues, Damages and Injuries and Negligence, and Exhibits.

1. The Table of Contents refers the reader to the pages where specified information is located.
2. The Brief Statement of the case is a precise statement of position. An example is: "John Doe collapsed and died from cardiac arrest while waiting to be attended to at ABC Hospital."

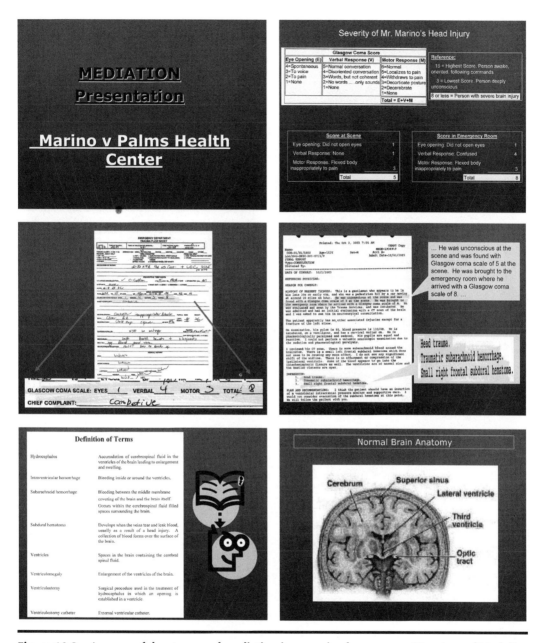

Figure 16.2   A successful outcome of mediation in a nursing home case. (Courtesy of Madeline Good and Renato Inacio.)

Avoid conveying a description of the case in the statement. The theme of the case can sometimes be used in the brief statement.

3. The Detailed Statement of Medical Management Issues should be prepared by the LNC in consultation with the attorney. An in-depth study of medical records and medical references enables the LNC to prepare a detailed synopsis of the medical issues.

4. The LNC may also have input into the section on damages and injuries. The one purpose of this section is to humanize the plaintiff, showing the impact of the injuries on the plaintiff

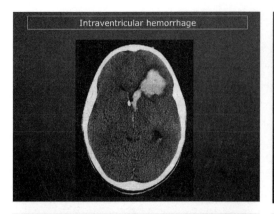

Tracking of CT Scan Findings	
10/1/03	Blood noted in the right ambient cistern and to the left of the superior cerebellar vermis. Small bilateral subdural hematoma in the frontal regions in the frontal region.
10/2/03	No hydrocephalus. Now ventricular blood in the fourth ventricle and in both occipital horns which may be secondary to insertion of intracranial pressure monitoring device. Bifrontal subdural hematomas again seen measuring 4.0 mm on right and 6.0 mm on left. Subarachnoid blood in the sylvian fissures. No evidence of new bleed.
10/6/03	Parenchymal, subdural, subarachnoid, and intraventricular hemorrhages. No significant change noted.
10/8/03	Interval decrease in size of the ventricular system. Interval decrease in size of hemorrhage. Area of contusion noted in the right frontotemporal lobe.
10/13/03	Increasing size of the ventricles. Small amount of blood in the ventricles. Improved subarachnoid hemorrhage. New area of hypodensity in left frontal region and left parietal area.
11/13/03	Worsening hydrocephalus. Intraventricular hemorrhage resolved. Remote bifrontal contusions. Resolution of subdural hematomas.
11/15/03	Interval placement of right parietal ventriculostomy catheter. Ventricles diminished in size but remained dilated.
12/30/03	Diffuse ventriculomegaly. Right sided ventriculostomy catheter. Probable arachnoid cyst identified in the left anterior temporal region. Low attenuation areas identified in the periventricular and subcortical white matter felt to reflect either ventricular seepage of cerebral spinal fluid versus small vessel ischemic changes.

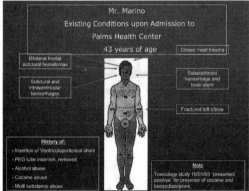

Mr. Marino's Diet and Feeding Abilities

Date	Diet	Notes
10/23/03	Peractive Tube Feedings	Tolerated well.
11/7/03	Mechanical Soft Diet Boost supplement	Consumed 50 - 75% of meals.
11/17/03	Mechanical Soft Diet	Tolerated well but coughed on eggs. Delayed coughing with thin liquids.
11/19/03	Pureed Diet. Nectar thickened liquids	No aspiration with applesauce consistency. Inconsistent penetration to vocal folds with nectar consistency. Transient penetration with thin consistency, cleared with swallowing, no aspiration.
11/21/03	Regular Diet with Thin Liquids	Consumed 75% of meals and 100% supplement.
12/4/03	Regular Diet.	Diet tolerated well.
12/15/03	Mechanical Soft Diet.	Vomited undigested food. Diet changed.
12/17/03	Mechanical Soft Diet.	Intake declining. Did not have swallowing delay. Took fluids well.
12/21/03	Pureed Diet.	Coughed on scrambled eggs but ate oatmeal without difficulty. Diet changed.

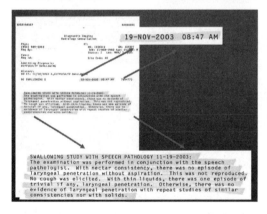

Mr. Marino's Physical and Mental Abilities Did Not Change

Mental and Physical Abilities	Present upon discharge from on 12/4/03	Present upon discharge from Center on 12/22/03	Present upon discharge from Center on 1/16/04
Decreased alertness and orientation	Yes	Yes	Yes
Mumbling	Yes	Yes	Yes
Poor insight and safety awareness	Yes	Yes	Yes
Decreased memory and cognitive deficits	Yes	Yes	Yes
Inconsistent following of commands	Yes	Yes	Yes
Awake but inconsistent response to questions	Yes	Yes	Yes
Required extensive assistance with mobility and ADL activities	Yes	Yes	Yes

Figure 16.2   (Continued)

and his or her family—what they can and cannot do anymore. An example is John Doe, whose left leg was amputated. An avid skier, he and his two daughters used to take yearly vacations to Colorado at Christmastime to ski, snowboard, and cross-country ski. The reader is referred to photographs of the last year's vacation in Tahoe. Poetic license is often used to dramatize the plaintiff's injuries and damages. The damage section should include an itemized accounting of the economic losses (e.g., medical expenses, lost earnings, property damage, etc.). An offer of settlement is also noted.

5. Negligence or gross negligence can also be addressed by the LNC. Violations of standards of care or deviations from policies and procedures fall within the area of the LNC's expertise. Expert reports and experts' curricula vitae are also presented in this section. Authoritative papers, guidelines, and standards written by specialty or other organizations should also be included.
6. The section for exhibits consists of pertinent medical records (appropriately highlighted), medical expense invoices, funeral and burial expense invoices, photographs, greeting cards, letters, school records, employment records, certificates, graphs, charts, and so on. This section contains references to supporting data for the brochure. These exhibits are numbered and may be referred to in the narrative of the brochure by number.

The Defendant's Brochure

A defense brochure can be divided into five similar sections:

1. The brief statement of the case from the defendant's viewpoint.
2. The detailed statement of medical management issues may or may not be addressed by the defense; in its place, the defense may wish to insert the defendant doctor's qualifications, experience, and a listing of professional and community services.
3. The section for damages and injuries could be used by the defense to address any mitigating factors.
4. The negligence or gross negligence issue may be addressed by the defense by discussing the defense expert's opinions about the standard of care or any contributing negligence of the plaintiff. The exhibits section may or may not be applicable for defense brochures. In general, a settlement brochure may present any factor or aspect of a case on which either side wishes to focus. There are no rules or requirements. This is a place where the evidence can be presented creatively for effect.
5. Mediators generally are experienced in trial tactics and strategies and while creativity may be helpful and appreciated, one should avoid hyperbole and overreaching, as mediation is a process of narrowing rather than expanding differences.

Other Settlement Modalities

Minitrials

A minitrial is not a trial, but rather, a settlement process that goes beyond the ADR. The parties (defense and plaintiff) present highly summarized versions of their respective cases to a panel of officials who have authority to settle the dispute. The presentation generally takes place outside of the courtroom, in a private forum. After the parties have presented their best case, the panel convenes and tries to settle the matter. The process is particularly suitable for larger, more complex disputes where there are points of law or substantial issues of fact. Typically, a case that might last several weeks or months in a courtroom would be dealt with in a minitrial within two or more days.

A minitrial represents a pretrial alternative attempt to settle the matter before lengthy trial begins. It is usually conducted after formal litigation has been undertaken and involves the presentation of each side's case, usually without live testimony, with opening and closing statements and an outline of evidence intended to be produced at trial. Parties of a lawsuit generally stipulate to "stay" pending litigation (to put a hold on further advancement of the litigation) until the minitrial is concluded. The outcome of the minitrail is generally confidential and advisory only. The parties may proceed to trial if settlement negotiations fail (Bennett, 2001).

Trial Consultants

A variety of consultants aid trial attorneys in developing the themes of a case, sometimes using mock jury presentations or focus groups before entering into settlement discussions or going to trial. Mock juries and focus groups can give the trial team valuable information about what a disinterested third party feels about the facts of a case, the plaintiffs, the defendants, and the experts. This information can be crucial to strategic planning and development of the case. Such sources of information can help to determine the overall chances of obtaining a satisfactory verdict or judgment. This impartial information can assist the LNC in evaluating complex medical issues in the case to see whether additional explanations or evidence are necessary.

The mock trial begins where the actual trial begins—with a conflict or a dispute that the parties have been unable to resolve on their own. Most mock trials use some general rules of evidence and procedure, an explanation of the basic facts, and brief statements for each witness.

Some LNCs have developed a specialty practice providing jury consulting. Mock jury trials are usually used in cases that involve either large dollar demand or multiple parties, such as class action suits. The LNC specializing in organizing mock jury trials or focus groups works with marketing firms that gather a sample of 50–80 persons representative of the demographic area where the trial is to be held. These individuals, who may be randomly selected, receive payment for spending one or two days listening to and observing a "mock trial." Simplified steps in a mock trial are as follows:

- Opening statement: First the prosecutor (in a criminal case) or the plaintiff's attorney (in a civil case) presents what the evidence will be and what the evidence will show. The defendant's attorney follows with an explanation of what their evidence will be and what is their side of the case and what the evidence will show.
- Prosecution's or plaintiff's case: Witnesses are called to testify and other physical evidence is introduced. Each witness called is cross examined by the defense.
- Defendant's case: Witnesses are called to testify and other physical evidence is introduced. Each witness called is cross examined by the plaintiff.
- Closing statements: An attorney for each side reviews the evidence presented and asks for a decision in their favor.
- Jury instructions: The Judge explains to the jury appropriate rules of law that they are to consider in weighing the evidence. The prosecution or plaintiff's attorney must meet the burden of proof in order to prevail.

The jurors may record their responses on a computerized handheld device and the information is entered into a database for future statistical analysis by the trial team. Often members of the trial team sit behind one-way mirrors to determine how the "jurors" discuss the testimony. The LNC may be involved with the statistical analysis of the material or may role-play the expert witness to the jury.

After the closing arguments, the mock jury breaks into smaller groups for deliberation. Each group renders a decision (verdict). The verdicts are important because they provide a representation of what an actual jury may render at trial. If all deliberating groups render a higher dollar amount than the defense firm is requesting, then the insurance company will likely be compelled to settle the case.

Jury Research

Jury research is an umbrella term for various methods of research associated with jury trials including (but not limited to) prospective juror demographic research, jury selection, shadow jury (acts as a surrogate for the real jury by sitting in a courtroom whenever the real jury is present and agrees to be interviewed at regular intervals during a trial), or posttrial jury interviews. The goals of research vary from assessing the case to discovering the primary juror-defined issues, to help plan the case presentation, to develop the trial theme that will resonate most strongly with jurors, and to determine with the maximum degree of probability the most likely trial outcome. Jury research is similar to test marketing of products that companies conduct before they introduce them to the public. The research is conducted to understand how juries operate rather than to give one side or the other an edge in a specific trial. Generally, jury research is a part of trial strategy in high-profile cases in civil or criminal litigation (Jury Research, n.d.). It is extremely important for a legal team member to adequately research jury verdicts on similar case scenarios prior to the offer of settlement. Reference sources include databases kept by insurance companies, the Association of Trial Lawyers of America, and special reports that are usually compiled by private sources that work through the local courthouse records of verdicts rendered. Jury research firms include First Court, Inc. and the National Legal Research Group.

The Medical Review Panel

Many states have adopted variations on the medical review panel to provide for resolution of medical malpractice cases outside of a formal trial. Goals of such panels are as follows:

- Reduction of the court's caseload
- Reduction of the costs of medical malpractice litigation
- Prevention when possible of the filing of court actions against health care providers and their employees for professional liability situations where the facts do not permit at least a reasonable inference of malpractice
- The panel's evaluation of a case provides an objective expert view for both plaintiff and defense counsel. The panel's decision may induce a settlement or convince a plaintiff to reconsider filing a lawsuit. Expensive litigation in court is thus avoided.

States that have adopted the utilization of a medical review panel include Louisiana, Wyoming, and Indiana. Figure 16.3 describes Louisiana's panel system.

The LNC contributes to preparation of the case for presentation to the panel in the same way that he or she prepares for mediated settlement conferences or for trial. The LNC attends the panel presentations and plays a vital support role for the attorney in helping to detect errors in the opposition's case presentation and analyzing the strengths and weaknesses of the case. The LNC may also serve as a panel member in nursing malpractice cases.

Strengths and Weaknesses of ADR

Research continues to be conducted to test the efficacy of ADR use in the private or court system. According to David Sellinger, a Washington, DC attorney and mediation proponent, "Litigators in today's economic environment have to think about ADR in most every case they handle" (Hoffman,

Louisiana permits its health care providers to become qualified. The advantage of being a qualified health care provider is that all medical malpractice claims must go through a medical review panel prior to filing suit. To become qualified, the participant health care provider must pay an annual premium that supplements the malpractice insurance premium paid to the patients compensation fund.

Once the provider is qualified, there is a cap on the amount awarded in a malpractice claim. The health care provider, or its insurer, is responsible for the first $100,000. The maximum amount awarded by the patient's compensation fund is $400,000, for a total award of $500,000 plus medical costs.

Prior to filing a lawsuit, a case is reviewed by a medical review panel. This panel consists of an attorney chairman and three health care providers, usually physicians: one chosen by the plaintiff, one chosen by the defendant(s), and one chosen by the two selected health care providers.

All parties involved submit evidence to support their positions to the members of the medical review panel. After reviewing the information, the medical review panel attorney chairman convenes a meeting to discuss the information. The panel delivers one of three decisions:

1. The evidence supports the conclusion that the defendant or defendants failed to comply with the appropriate standard of care as charged in the complaint
2. The evidence does not support the conclusion that the defendant or defendants failed to meet the applicable standard of care as charged in the complaint
3. There is a material issue of fact, not requiring expert opinion, bearing on liability for consideration by the court

In rendering an opinion, the panel provides typed reasons to support its decision. The plaintiff has a specified period of time following the panel decision in which to file a lawsuit.

Figure 16.3   Louisiana's panel system. (Courtesy of Janet Kremser.)

1999). Choosing to utilize one of the various methods of ADR can be a matter of achieving the right results for all parties economically, thereby creating a win–win outcome. Lawyers must decide with their clients how best to proceed with a case, while at the same time evaluating their clients' satisfaction with the desire to create solutions and to participate in the ADR process.

Arbitration has been widely accepted as an enforceable alternative to the civil justice system for decades. The FAA was signed into law by President Calvin Coolidge back in 1925. Now, years later, issues surrounding arbitration are being hotly debated in many courts around the country. Probably the most hotly debated issue regarding arbitration is the waiver of the parties' right to trial by jury (Lowe, 2008).

Currently pending before Congress is the Arbitration Fairness Act of 2007, which was introduced by Senator Russell Feingold (D-WI). He has introduced a bill aimed at equalizing the bargaining powers of the parties who agree to arbitration and to ensure that Americans are not "forced" into mandatory arbitration agreements. Senator Feingold said that his bill will "prevent a party with greater bargaining power from forcing individuals into arbitration through a contractual provision. It will insure that citizens once again have a true choice between arbitration and the traditional court system" (Feingold, 2007).

An April 2008 article in the Wall Street Journal by Nathan Koppel noted that nursing home patients and their families are increasingly giving up their right to sue over disputes about care, including those involving deaths, as the nursing homes write binding arbitration clauses into their standard contracts. The nursing home industry's arbitration strategy is part of a much broader response by U.S. companies to consumer lawsuits. Physicians, surgeons, and other medical practitioners, as well as businesses from restaurants to banks have increased their use of arbitration agreements in recent years to reduce litigation costs and sidestep emotion-laden juries, often requiring patients or consumers to give up their rights to a trial as a condition of receiving services. Nursing homes have been among the biggest converts to the practice since a wave of big jury awards in the late 1990s. Critics say the binding agreements are determining the outcome of high stakes cases of vulnerable patients that should instead be handled by the courts. There is concern that people do not understand whether the clauses are either binding or mandatory or that they are signing away their right to sue. The AAA frowns on agreements requiring disputes over nursing home care and often refuses such cases. Defense attorneys for the nursing homes comment that they prefer arbitration in place of a jury of six laypeople who do not know medicine. On the other hand, plaintiff attorneys believe that an arbitration panel consisting of seasoned attorneys are much less likely to have a "how could they" attitude as compared to a jury (Koppel, 2008).

The LNC together with the attorney can provide the best representation for the client. Working to achieve a win–win outcome can be a rewarding experience for a nurse preparing a case to be presented before an alternative forum of adjudication.

References

15 USC § 571(3) (Suppl. 1993).

American Arbitration Association. (2007). Retrieved http:www.adr.org

Bennett, N. (2001). *Mini-trials and summary jury trials.* Retrieved from http://gov.news/press/2001pres/01fsprivacy. html

Feingold, R. (2007). *Fact sheet regarding Arbitration Fairness Act of 2007.* Retrieved from http"//www.govtrack. us./congress

Garner, B. A. (Ed.). (1999). *Blacks Law Dictionary* (7th ed.). St. Paul, MN: West Group.

Hoffman, E. (1999). The impact of the ADR Act of 1998, Trial, 30.

International Centre for Dispute Resolution. (2007). Retrieved from http://www.adr.org/about_icdr

Jury Research. (n.d.). Retrieved from http://en.wikipedia.org/wiki/Jury_research

Koppel, N. (2008, April 11). Nursing homes in bids to cut costs, prod patients to forgo lawsuits. *The Wall Street Journal*, A1.

Lowe, C. (2008). Mandatory binding arbitration: Is anyone really getting their day in court? *Medical Malpractice Law and Strategy*, 25(9).

Additional Reading

Craver, C. (June 1999). *Mediation: A trial lawyer's guide*. 35 Trial 37.

Emery, J., Edwards, L., & Edwards, J. (2000). *Civil procedure and litigation*. New York: West Legal Studies.

Hechler, D. (June 25, 2001). ADR finds true believers companies make the leap—and save tens of millions of dollars. *The National Law Journal*.

Meek, S. (1996). *Alternative dispute resolution*. Tucson, AZ: Lawyers and Judges Publishers Inc.

State statutes by topic: Alternative dispute resolution. (2001). Retrieved from http://gov.news/press/2001pres/01fsprivacy. html

Tex. Rev. Civ. Stat. Ann. art. 4590i, § 15.01.

List of litigation research firms found at http://wwwdomoz.org/Society/Law/SErvices/ligiation_Support/

Test Questions

1. What is the most widely used format of ADR that issues a binding decision?
   A. Mediation
   B. Arbitration
   C. Negotiations
   D. Minitrials

2. An LNC's role in arbitration may include all of the following EXCEPT:
   A. Preparing evidentiary material
   B. Interviewing experts
   C. Educating the litigation team and arbitrator about medical issues
   D. Discussing the facts of the case with the arbitrator after the hearing ends and before the award is rendered

3. Components of a settlement brochure include
   A. Brief statement of the incident
   B. Facts of the dispute
   C. Damages
   D. Demand

4. During mediation, what role does the LNC carry out?
   A. Negotiates the mediator's fee
   B. Is a resource liaison to the mediator
   C. Prepares written negotiated agreement
   D. Develops questions for crossexamination

5. A decision rendered by an arbitrator or a tribunal of arbitrators is referred to as
   A. Award
   B. Decision
   C. Verdict
   D. Memorandum of understanding

Answers: 1. B, 2. D, 3. D, 4. B, 5. A

Appendix: Nursing Home Case*
Arbitration Presentation: Plaintiff

Comes now John Smith, by and through his undersigned counsel, hereby demands arbitration with Palm Harbor Nursing Care Center pursuant to the terms of the Admission Agreement, and states as follows:

1. That John Smith was admitted to Palm Harbor Nursing Care Center from November 18, 2006 through December 8, 2006.
2. During the time of John Smith's admission, Palm Harbor Nursing Care Center violated John Smith's nursing home resident's right and was negligent under Florida Statue 400.022 and 400.023 as follows:
   a. Failed to adequately inform the resident, his family, and physicians of changes in his condition, to allow proper intervention and care
   b. Failed to render adequate and appropriate health care and protective services
   c. Failed to keep him free from mental and physical abuse
3. These rights were violated and actual negligence committed in the following respects:
   a. John Smith was admitted for rehabilitation following hip surgery
   b. Coumadin therapy was reinstituted at Palm Harbor Nursing Care Center following its discontinuation for surgery
   c. Palm Harbor Nursing Care Center failed to properly monitor his Coumadin levels, allowing him to develop a Coumadin coagulopathy causing a severe hematoma and nerve damage
4. As a result, John Smith suffered significant nerve damage impairing his ability to ambulate.
5. Additionally, Palm Harbor Nursing Care Center failed to provide adequate outside care on or about December 4, 2006 when he developed excruciating pain and requested transportation to the hospital.
6. As a result of the delayed treatment, John Smith's Coumadin coagulopathy progressed to the point where it caused permanent impairment.
7. As a further direct and proximate result, John Smith had to be hospitalized and has suffered continuing long-term care.
8. John Smith has sustained mental and physical pain and suffering, loss of enjoyment of life, medical bills, and other compensatory damages. The plaintiff plans on calling Mr. Smith and his expert nurse as live Witnesses during the arbitration proceedings. The remainder of his evidence will be presented through medical records.

Arbitration Presentation: Defense

Mr. Smith, 88 years of age, was admitted to Palm Harbor Nursing Care Center on November 18, 2006 by Dr. McMurray with the diagnosis of atrial fibrillation, degenerative disease, deep venous thrombosis, sick sinus syndrome with pacemaker, dyspnea, hypothyroidism, status post knee replacement, esophageal reflux disease, and cardiac disease. His immediate prior history included a total hip replacement on November 15, 2006 secondary to a failed hip surgery. He was described as alert and oriented, had intact skin, and was continent of bladder and bowel function. Mr. Smith

---

* Courtesy of Madeline Good and Susanne Reidhammer, Esquire.

required assistance with dressing, bathing, ambulation, transfers, toileting, and feeding. He planned to return home with physical therapy after his rehabilitation.

The nursing admission assessment noted that the patient had clear speech and was able to communicate his needs, had pedal pulses present bilaterally, was independent with eating, and complained of mild pain at the right hip operative site. In addition, Mr. Smith required one to two person assistance for bed mobility, transfers, and toileting. According to the fall risk assessment, he had a history of one to two falls in the past three months, was chair bound, and required the use of assistive devices. A side rail assessment was completed and revealed that Mr. Smith used side rails for positioning. The nursing staff noted that Dr. McMurray was in to see the patient and ordered physical therapy to evaluate the patient's weight bearing as well as ambulation abilities.

The initial care plan was created on November 19, 2006 and identified patient problem areas related to psychological well being, nutrition, falls and safety risk, altered activity pursuits, discharge planning, pain management, ADL decline, and anticoagulant therapy. Interventions regarding nutrition included monitoring the patient's food intake, serving the diet as ordered by the physician, weekly weights, and determining the patient's food preferences. Interventions regarding falls and safety risk included encouraging the patient to use the call light to request assistance, referring Mr. Smith to the appropriate therapies, and providing adaptive assistive devices. Interventions regarding the administration of anticoagulation therapy included monitoring for signs of bleeding, protecting the patient from injury, and monitoring the PT/INR results.

Mr. Smith also received skilled occupational and physical therapy services. An occupational therapy evaluation was completed on November 19, 2006 which noted that the patient was able to bathe and dress himself with limited assistance. He was provided with a long handled sponge, reachers, and sock aide as well as given instructions for their use. Therapy was to include instructions regarding total hip precautions and assistance with ADL activities. The physical therapist noted that Mr. Smith had been using a rolling walker for the past three months secondary to a deteriorating right hip. The assessment revealed weakness of the patient's right lower extremity following the total hip replacement and pain to the area. The therapist noted that the patient's rehabilitation potential and safety awareness were good. Therapy included bed mobility training, transfer training, gait training, pain management, range of motion and therapeutic exercises, and balance re-education.

As of November 22, 2006, Mr. Smith was able to perform his own sponge bath and able to dress himself using adaptive equipment while sitting in the wheelchair. His standing tolerance and balance were improving, but he continued to have difficulty with sitting to supine transfers.

On November 30, 2006, the physical therapist noted that the patient was utilizing the parallel bars to improve his standing balance and dynamic exercises to promote his stability. Mr. Smith was able to ambulate well with a rolling walker for 200 feet and navigated stairs with stand by assistance. Although he still had some weakness of the right hip, he was progressing well towards walking independently with a rolling walker. Mr. Smith continued to make progress through December 4, 2006. On that date, Mr. Smith refused physical therapy because he felt nauseated and complained of right hip pain. The therapist documented that there was some decline in his functional abilities, especially in performing exercises. On December 7, 2006, both the patient's sessions with the physical therapist and occupational therapist were withheld. On December 7, 2006 at 3:00 p.m., Mr. Smith complained of severe leg pain, which extended from his right buttock to his calf. Darvocet had been administered without relief so he was given a dose of Morphine 1.0 mg IM. Dr. McMurray's PA examined Mr. Smith and noted that there was minimal swelling to the right hip area, that the right hip incision was healing well, and that he had no edema of his lower extremity. A lower extremity ultrasound was negative for deep venous thrombosis. The following day on December 8, 2006, the nursing staff timely reported the patient's complaints of pain to Dr. McMurray who ordered an x-ray of the hip and knee as well as an approval to transfer Mr. Smith to Health Park for evaluation in accordance with the patient's request.

In conclusion, Mr. Smith was admitted to the facility for rehabilitation and was provided with appropriate health care and treatment. It does not appear at this time that the staff deviated from the standard of care in any aspect of the care rendered during his residency. He was sent to the hospital due to a significant change in condition where he recovered and then was discharged to Health Park.

We believe the care and treatment provided by the staff of Palm Harbor Nursing Care Center was appropriate and did not compromise his existing status or outcome in any way. The defense is supported by the following facts.

That Mr. Smith was seen by a PA the day before he was sent to the hospital and Dr. McMurray gave orders that evening.

The PT/INRs were drawn as ordered and results were reported to Dr. McMurray in a timely manner. Mr. Smith also had a Doppler study performed on 12/7/06 which came back as negative for a deep venous thrombosis.

With respect to the alleged fall, there is no reference or description of any incident that could be described as a fall in our chart. Moreover, Mr. Smith was doing quite well in physical therapy in the December 2–3, 2006 time frame, when the alleged fall occurred.

The staff also utilized a Coumadin flow sheet which reflects that labs were drawn as ordered and reported to the physician.

Mr. Smith's medical history and subsequent medical treatment reflect that he had several problems in the past and after Palm Harbor Nursing Care Center that would affect his ability to walk and would cause pain in his leg, that is, spinal stenosis, hip and knee replacements and back problems.

Our facility chart makes no mention of an EMS call on 12/7/06 but there is an EMS report reflecting that a call from Mr. Smith's room was cancelled by the facility staff. No one at the facility has recollection of this event. Nurse Ecklund did testify, however, that it would be a violation of a resident's rights to prohibit them from going to the hospital. Other than the EMS report which states that the call was "cancelled by Palm Harbor Care Staff," there is no evidence that the staff refused to allow him to go to the hospital. We will argue that while this cancelled call may have occurred based on the EMS records, there is no evidence that this cancellation effected Mr. Smith. Mr. Smith was seen by a PA that day, who did not order a transfer. Nor did his physician, Dr. McMurray, order a transfer that evening. The next day he was sent out.

The defense will be calling several live witnesses including the Executive Director of Palm Harbor Care Center as well as expert witnesses in the specialty areas of long term care nursing, geriatrics, and hematology. Additional evidence will be presented through medical records and deposition testimony. In addition, the defense will be presenting several exhibits during the arbitration hearing including:

Calendar exhibit demonstrating Coumadin orders, PT/INR orders, Coumadin administered, and the PT/INR results per date.

Calendar exhibit demonstrating pain medication orders and administration of pain medication.

Exhibit listing medical history by year including significant surgeries such as knee replacements, hip replacements, and insertion of a vena cava filter.

Calendar exhibit touch chart identifying types of care givers who saw the patient each day.

Calendar exhibit touch chart identifying different types of care provided and number of times care provided during the care.

Arbitration Presentation: Arbitrator Award

A hearing was held in the presence of an arbitration panel over a two day period. After consideration of the evidence, the panel finds as follows:

1. Liability is found against the Respondent for a violation of the Claimant's Nursing Home Resident's Rights under Florida Statues Chapter 400. During the initial stay from November 18, 2006 until early December 2006, Claimant's pain complaints were readily treated with minimal dosages of Darvocet. Beginning on December 3, 2004, the dosage began to increase as the Claimant began complaining of more pain. He also refused to participate in physical therapy on occasion. By December 7, 2006, he indicated that his pain level was at its highest 10/10. Claimant himself called 911.

    According to the evidence, someone on Respondent's staff "cancelled" the 911 personnel. It is unclear whether the EMS personnel actually examined the Claimant or whether they merely learned of his room number as noted on the report without actually seeing him. Regardless, respondents experts and staff all testified that the Claimant or his health care surrogates had the right to call 911 and there was no clear explanation for the staff canceling the call. It was discovered a little over 24 hours later, on December 8, 2006, that the Claimant was suffering from a hematoma that formed near his right iliac region where he had previously undergone a second hip revision procedure that was the basis for his admission to the facility on November 18, 2006 for rehabilitation.

2. Damages: Claimant contended that the delay in treatment for the Coumadin coagulopathy resulted in a femoral neuropathy due to the internal bleeding diminishing his ability to ambulate. The chart from Respondent indicated that the Claimant had progressed in ambulating during his stay to 200 feet by November 30, 2006. Furthermore the treatment administration record had a note that a PT/INR was to be taken on December 6, 2006. This test was never done.

However, the uncontroverted testimony of even Claimant's nursing expert, Nancy Moorland, was that the Respondent's staff followed all physician orders. Respondent's nursing expert, Allison Clark, and both medical experts Dr. Robert Steinman, a hematologist, and Dr. Richard Patrick, a gerontologist, indicated that a treatment administration record entry is superceded by a physician order. Claimant's admitting physician Dr. McMurray had been in contact with Respondent's staff and ordered that the next PT/INR should be done in two weeks from November 29, 2006 or on December 13, 2006. Therefore, the failure to do the Coumadin test on December 6, 2006 was not a violation of a physician's order and Respondent's staff was within full compliance even when the Claimant left the facility for Memorial Hospital on December 8, 2006.

Regarding the escalating pain complaints in early December 2006, the evidence reflected that each time Claimant was given Darvocet, a mild prescription pain medication, he got complete relief. Dr. McMurray had authorized up to 12 Darvocet per day for Claimant before his order would be exceeded. Even though Claimant did say his pain increased between December 3, 2006 and December 6, 2006, on each occasion, the pain reduced to 0/10 after no more than four Darvocet on any of those days. Claimant required only one Darvocet during the whole day of December 5, 2006. It was not until December 7, 2006 that Claimant's pain was not relieved by the Darvocet and on that day, Respondent contacted an ARNP and a medical doctor to increase the pain medication. Although the ARNP incorrectly suggested that Percocet be used, before Claimant received any, Morphine and later Talwin was prescribed for the pain level again.

Additionally, the uncontroverted testimony of Dr. Steinman indicated that Respondent's staff would not have suspected there Claimant was suffering from an internal Coumadin coagulopathy on December 7, 2006 since there was no evidence externally of "black and blue" marks on his skin. Also, Respondent had a Doppler study performed on Claimant on December 7, 2006 that was normal. As Claimant responded well for almost three weeks with simply Darvocet for pain management, the staff would have little evidence of the Coumadin imbalance. Claimant may have told occupational therapy that he could not participate on December 7, 2004 because he did not feel well, but according to nurse expert Clark, Claimant had been able to ambulate in his room up until December 6, 2006. Although Dr. Steinman noted that the Memorial Hospital Emergency Room found Claimant's PT/INR to be incalculable on December 8, 2006, he testified that PT/INR readings can "go high real quick." Even Dr. Green who saw the Claimant at Memorial Hospital described Claimant's retroperitoneal hematoma as "spontaneous." There did not appear to be any evidence that Claimant had injured himself in a fall six days earlier as he claimed at the hospital. In fact, Claimant was not complaining of pain by December 9, 2006 at the hospital and on December 10, 2006 Dr. Patrick testified that the Coumadin therapy was re-instated after being incalculable two days before. Dr. Patrick also noted that a "second bleed" may have occurred at the Memorial Hospital on December 12, 2006 based on Claimant's pain level dramatically increasing on that date and from hospital testing results.

The panel also notes that Claimant suffered from chronic spinal stenosis well before his admission to Respondent's facility. Dr. Dillard in 2003 conducted EMG testing and described Claimant as suffering from a "florid" or extensive deneravation. Well after Claimant's Coumadin coagulation episode, Dr. Enrique on August 23, 2007 again noted Claimant's extensive degenerative disc disease with disc bulges at multiple levels. He pointed out that Claimant's right total knee replacement was not the main problem limiting ambulation even though it was "worn somewhat." Rather, Claimant's spinal stenosis was the cause of his right leg pain and decreased ambulation.

Dr. Steinman noted that Claimant's mild to moderate bleed was centered in his lower back and diagnosed as a lumbar plexopathy. He testified that Claimant had suffered from blood clots before and after this episode on December 8, 2006. However, Dr. Steinman did admit that there may have been some nerve damage to Claimant as a result of the bleed being untreated on December 6, 2004 and/or December 7, 2006. To the extent the Coumadin coagulopathy aggravated his femoral neuropathy, the panel finds that Claimant is entitled to damages. Yet the uncontroverted testimony of Dr. Steinman and Dr. Patrick is that a common condition from spinal stenosis is femoral neuropathy.

Therefore the panel feels the incident of Coumadin coagulopathy at Respondent's facility only minimally impacted the overall ambulation ability of Claimant and awards $60,000.00.

Chapter 17

Nursing Home and Subacute Rehabilitation Litigation

Laura A. Conklin, MSN, MSA, RN, ONC, CWS, LNCC, FCCWS, Dip. AAWM

Second Edition
Patricia W. Iyer, MSN, RN, LNCC and
Mary Lubin, BS, MA, RNC, NHA

Contents

Objectives

- Identify common areas of nursing home litigation and defense strategies
- Identify common areas of subacute rehabilitation litigation

Introduction

The complexion of nursing homes has changed dramatically over the years. The recent changes in long-term care, including the growth of subacute rehabilitation in the nursing home environment, have provided attorneys with a growing source of litigation possibilities. Nursing homes are no longer a repository for the aged but now have seen many younger residents admitted for a variety of subacute rehabilitation needs. Subacute care reaches beyond the aging population and focuses on restoring the resident to a full and independent life, within the limitations of their disease process. The legal nurse consultant (LNC) may be asked to evaluate nursing home medical records, to identify if and where applicable standard of care (SOC) have been breached. Knowledge of common negligence or malpractice issues in long-term care and subacute rehabilitation will facilitate this endeavor. This chapter will assist the LNC in looking at specific areas that differ from the acute care setting and are unique to the nursing home or long-term care environment.

The Changing Environment of Long-Term Care

Today's nursing homes provide a variety of services that were not available years ago. In addition to nursing care and assistance with activities of daily living (ADLs); many nursing homes now provide traumatic brain injury (TBI) support, ventilator care, rehabilitation, hospice, and respite care. It is no surprise that as the population is living longer and is able to contend with a variety of disabilities, there is an increased need for rehabilitation services. In the state of Ohio alone it is estimated that by the year 2020 there will be an increase of 71.8% to 1.5 million people between the ages of 60 and 69. In addition, the 90 and older age group is expected to also increase by 72.6% adding to the demands for additional services (Tramer, 2007).

Changes in Resident Acuity

The nursing home environment has changed from that of a facility dedicated to meet the needs of the elderly to a comprehensive multiservice resource committed to a variety of special needs and expectations for assistance to achieve independent function. Subacute rehabilitation has expanded from the acute hospital setting to nursing homes, to meet the demands for physical, occupational, speech, and language services, eliminating the need for extended hospital stays and thereby decreasing costs. The new nursing home resident may be a 25-year old in rehabilitation from a traumatic amputation or a middle-aged resident recovering from joint replacement surgery. After several weeks of physical therapy, they are expected to return home. Traumatic brain injured patients offer a variety of challenges requiring a variety of methods of rehabilitation services, depending on the severity and location of the injury. Potential areas for litigation will expand as the continuum of care evolves into different community-based settings.

The LNC reviewing medical records from a facility that offers a focused subacute rehabilitation program along with skilled nursing care must be aware of the SOC as it relates to the variety of diagnoses presented. Whether the LNC is working with plaintiff or defense counsel, the focus of the review must evaluate whether the SOC was met and expected outcomes were obtained. If preprinted care plans are used, the LNC will need to determine if the care plan addressed the resident's current needs based on the assessment. The care plan may be similar to one from an acute care setting since the acuity of long-term care residents is increasing.

Staffing Issues

Title 42: Code of Federal Regulations (CFR) Part 483.30 outlines nursing services requirements for states and long-term care facilities as follows: "The facility must have sufficient nursing staff to provide nursing and related services to attain or maintain the highest practicable physical, mental, and psychological well-being of each resident, as determined by the resident assessment and individual plans of care" (Code of Federal Regulations, 2008). These guidelines are often open to interpretation as to how nursing staff is defined. Over and above the federal guidelines, state statutes and regulations may differ, and must be taken into consideration when reviewing staffing patterns. Each state describes minimal staffing standards according to their Public Health Code or similar compiled laws (Harrington, 2008). Besides nursing, other health care professionals may include physicians, nurse practitioners, physiatrists, physical therapists, occupational therapists, recreational therapists, speech and language pathologists, respiratory therapists, psychologists, social workers, clergy, case managers, pharmacists, and dieticians. The services available may depend on the affiliation with other health care institutions and size of the nursing home.

As the acuity level of residents changes, so does the mix of caregivers needed to provide care. Staffing issues surface in light of allegations of abuse, neglect, malnutrition, dehydration, pressure ulcers, and sepsis. Norris Cunningham, Esq., an Indiana attorney, reports that the trend toward litigation will continue to increase with a shift from general negligence to a focus on issues of understaffing and underbudgeting (Cunningham, 2006). The LNC will be instrumental in recognizing the impact of staffing on substandard care. Factors such as age, length of illness, comorbidity, and functional ability have a bearing on unavoidable negative outcomes and must be considered during any review of medical records. The LNC will be asked to determine if residents with higher acuities were segregated from custodial residents and assessed by licensed professionals or mixed with the general population.

Staffing patterns are made available during discovery, after the case is filed in court, and should be matched to documentation and signatures by time and date. Looking at the date and time of signatures on the Medication Administration Record or Treatment Record will assist the LNC to determine if documentation was added at a later time, once an incident occurred and litigation was anticipated.

Prior to filing, information regarding staffing patterns standards can be obtained through the Medicare and Medicaid website (Nursing Home Compare, 2008) where research can be conducted by state. Information regarding other violations and quality of care issues are also available for review. Local and state advocacy groups like American Association of Retired Persons (AARP), National Council of Senior Citizens, and Council for Aging also track nursing home performance data. The attorney and the LNC should review any brochure or advertisement of the nursing home for references to staffing mix. Another area of interest is the annual report. Juries do not look favorably on nursing homes that make a sizeable profit but do not staff adequately to provide safe and compassionate care.

Example 17.1

The plaintiff was a 75-year-old female admitted to Beverly-Manhattan Nursing Home in Jackson, Miss. for long-term rehabilitation and care after suffering several strokes. During several visits her daughter began to notice signs of poor hygiene, loss of weight, dehydration, pressure ulcers and contractures. Due to chronic staffing shortages, no one was available to provide her mother with fresh water to drink, assist with feeding, turn to prevent the pressure ulcers, and maintain proper hygiene. In addition, the resident suffered lacerations, pressure ulcers, and contractures that resulted from avoidable falls. The parent company and the administrator were sued for negligence and medical malpractice. The defendants claimed staffing was adequate but concealed staffing records during the discovery process. The court deemed the records irrefutable to the issue of staffing shortage. The jury found in favor of the plaintiff and awarded $1.5 million in compensatory damages and punitive damages of $8.2 million, for a total of $9.7 million (*Groves v. Beverly Enterprises*, 2004).

Current Trends in Settlements

Society and its needs are changing opening potential areas of litigation. Nursing homes are accepting residents at a younger age and with a mix of comorbidities. Elderly, no longer part of an extended family and separated by distance and/or a family member's work location and requirements, school, or other circumstances, may opt to live in residential facilities. Such moves, often influenced by the perception that good care will be rendered as promised to loved ones, may be later challenged if unexpected events such as falls and fractures occur.

No one really knows what final acts or omissions bring a family to pursue litigation against a nursing home. The decision can be influenced by the hope of improving care to others in the same facility, the expectation of compensation for substandard care, or the desire to increase the estate of the loved one who suffered at the hands of an uncaring care giver. Nursing homes can be an easy target for opportunistic families and the abundance of attorneys advertising large settlements against nursing homes may influence the final decision. Medical subrogation rights or medical liens against the settlement may decrease the expected windfall considerably. In Ohio a law passed mandating any judgment first goes to paying back Medicaid (Zinn, 2003).

Another suggested reason for the sustained increase in litigation is the attitude of the baby boomers. Their parents are living longer and are approaching an age when many will be residing in nursing homes and, assisted living arrangement, rather than with their children. Often this leads to guilt, with the realization that they may be next (Reibstein & Figueroa, 1998). The baby boomer generation is said to be more vocal regarding demands for services and are typically more litigious with a greater sense of entitlement when something goes wrong. They are not ready or willing to suffer inconveniences as their parents did. With the advertisement of large rewards, they often see the opportunity for litigation as a means of collecting easy money (Smith, 2006).

The surge in litigation has impacted the liability costs of long-term care with a 400% increase over the past 11 years (Data Trend, 2005). This has led to tort reform legislature in several states designed to lessen the burden of rising costs. Providers have made operational changes reflecting quality of care initiatives and stronger defenses. In spite of these efforts, frequency of claims continues to climb from 5.5/1000 occupied beds in 1995 to 11.1 in 2006 (Long Term Care, 2007). In the state of Ohio, for instance, tort reform legislation focused on three issues: the awarding of punitive damages for malpractice, use of surveys and plans of correction (POCs) as proof of substandard care, and changes in the statute of limitations to within one year after the alleged cause of action occurred in the hope of eliminating frivolous claims. Criteria established by the Ohio General Assembly aided judges and juries in awarding punitive damages. The nursing home's ability to pay was determined based on its net worth, whether the punitive damages would deter substandard conduct and if finances retained would be sufficient to provide care. Criteria further prohibited the use of any investigation by a state survey agency or POC to be used as evidence in a malpractice case since these issues focused on licensure and certification requirements (Schabes, 2002). These legislative changes focus on the major concerns regarding nursing home malpractice and negligence issues.

Jury Verdicts and Damage Awards

The greatest exposure for nursing homes is in the area of punitive damages. Unlike compensatory damages, juries are often given no guidelines to assist in determining punitive damages. They often lack sympathy for large corporate-owned operations that are perceived to post large profits yet deliver substandard care to the often frail and defenseless elderly entrusted to their care.

The defense attorney must educate the jury on what really occurs in a nursing home setting and the challenges faced by workers providing care to confused and sometimes combative residents. The LNC can be instrumental in defining standards of care and pointing out the many successes the organization has had in the past. Often the litigated incident is an isolated case that was unavoidable for many reasons. It is important for the defense counsel to emphasize the fact that most employees set out to do the best job they can under the circumstances. These large sums awarded with punitive damages are often reduced substantially or overturned on appeal (Brady, 2001).

From the plaintiff side the LNC can be helpful in assisting attorneys to determine if the defendant acted maliciously, threatened bodily harm, caused the plaintiff to suffer mental anguish, violated health and safety standards, or practiced fraud. Were there similar complaints or disciplinary actions against the defendant? Is there evidence of substandard practice? Are there records missing? Looking at state survey results will substantiate allegations of substandard care.

Even with the best trial strategies planned, juries can be very unpredictable. Therefore, jury selection will be critical to success. The LNC is valuable in helping the attorney understand clearly the issues involved and if the incident is isolated or a pattern in a particular nursing home. Questions to ask potential jurors that reveal prejudice or guilt regarding placement in a nursing home can also be developed by an LNC. Some attorneys resort to mock trials or focus groups to get a feel for the attitudes towards long-term care in general and in a specific community (Trial Behavior Consulting, 2008). The following example points to how juries can find for the defendant in spite of seemingly overwhelming evidence of neglect.

Example 17.2

The decedent was an 80-year-old woman who was confined to her bed after numerous falls. She had been a resident in the nursing home from August 18, 1997 until her death in June 20, 2004 from sepsis, gangrene, and osteomyelitis that developed from infected stage IV pressure ulcers on her hips. She also suffered from malnutrition and dehydration. The plaintiff's counsel argued that the decedent was not properly protected from falls nor was she fed properly. The defense counsel argued that the falls sustained by the decedent were due to her Alzheimer's diagnosis and the staff was not able to feed her. The physician suggested a feeding tube but the family refused, thereby adding to her malnourished state. The jury found for the defense citing that under the circumstances, the nursing home did all they could (*Billy Wayne Paige v. Mariners Health Care, Inc.*, 2008).

Establishing the SOC

SOCs cover a wide variety of expected practices that are carried out by any nurse who has a similar license and similar background and training such as a registered nurse, license practical nurse, or licensed vocational nurse. The state boards of nursing guarantee that basic nursing education requires some form of competency evaluation prior to practice. An SOC in nursing is established through external and internal guidelines taught in all basic nursing education programs.

The external standards of care are set by state boards of nursing, nurse practice act, public health codes and may vary from state to state. Internal standards of care are set by policies and procedures within an organization and reflect the minimum standard of current and acceptable prevailing practice. Any deviation from current and prevailing practice or in following the policies and procedures of the organization may lead to an incident.

Establishing where, when, and who breached the SOC is key to successful litigation of medical malpractice cases. This is where the LNC can be most instrumental in pointing out areas where the breach occurred. The LNC will be able to review the circumstances surrounding the incident and will be able to determine if policy and procedure were followed as written in that particular organization.

The American Nurses Association's Standards of Clinical Nursing Practice (American Nurses Association, 2004) and Scope of Standards of Gerontological Nursing Practice (American Nurses Association, 1995) set standards for nursing in a long-term care environment. Careful review of the nursing home policies will help the LNC determine if a breach in the standard occurred. Other contributory issues like understaffing or environmental safety concerns also need to be explored.

State and Federal Guidelines

The Centers for Medicare and Medicaid Services (CMS) and the Department of Health and Human Services (HHS) set forth the requirements for long-term care facilities. These can be found in Title 42 of the Code of Federal Regulations Subpart B, §483.1 through §483.75. Every aspect of long-term care is addressed including:

- Resident rights
- Scope of services
- Resident behavior
- Resident assessment and monitoring
- Quality of care
- Nursing responsibilities
- Physician services
- Dental services
- Specialized rehabilitation
- Physical environment

While some of these regulations seem stringent, they are designed to meet the needs of nursing home residents regardless of age or infirmity. Providing the minimal SOC should not be interpreted as a burden for anyone advertising and promising quality care while collecting Medicare and Medicaid funds.

State regulations governing long-term care may vary based on local legislation. They do, however, support all CMS guidelines. State survey teams inspect and assure quality of care mandates are carried out. Penalties are assigned for infractions causing potential or actual harm, based on the severity. These penalties range from fines to actual closure of a facility.

Certifications

The Joint Commission

The Joint Commission is committed to improving health care safety and inaugurated its certification program for nursing homes in 1966. Since then over 1300 institutions offering long-term care services have been certified. The program concentrated on assisting management to provide quality care in a cost-effective manner. Areas of focus include:

- Ethics, Rights, and Responsibilities
- Provision of Care, Treatment, and Services
- Medication Management
- Surveillance, Prevention, and Control of Infection
- Improving Organization Performance
- Leadership
- Managing the Environment of Care
- Management of Human Resources
- Management of Information

The Joint Commission accreditation is voluntary and covers approximately 30% of long-term standards not covered by Medicare/Medicaid conditions of participation (The Joint Commission, 2008). There is a fee associated with accreditation. The advantage of accreditation offers the organization a means of analyzing survey results and obtaining insight into root causes of deficiencies.

The LNC can access the CMS Nursing Home Compare website for performance histories. The Joint Commission is currently working on developing a similar database.

Commission on Accreditation of Rehabilitation Facilities

The expanding rehabilitation services imbedded in long-term care facilities are certified by the Commission on Accreditation of Rehabilitation Facilities (CARF). When diagnostic related groups (DRGs) restricted length of stays in acute care settings, the use of beds in nursing homes for rehabilitation was an easy transition as some acute care hospitals also owned skilled nursing homes. Residents who could not tolerate physical therapy in the hospital were offered therapy at a slower pace in the long-term care environment. The role of CARF is one of a consultant rather than an inspector, working with the organization to develop policies and standards reflecting quality initiatives. Like the Joint Commission and CMS, CARF accreditation provides the benefits of resident-focused standards, accountability for funding resources, marketing tools, and guidance for management to assure quality outcomes in rehabilitation efforts (CARF, 2008). Knowing a facility has accreditation from Joint Commission and/or CARF will assist the LNC in determining if the standards of care adopted were upheld.

Areas of Typical Liability and Common Defense Strategies

Nursing Home Issues

Falls

Fear of falling is one of the greatest concerns of the elderly. Complications such as lacerations, bruising, hemorrhage (internal or external), subdural hematomas, fractures, or sprains decrease independence and can lead to significant morbidity and mortality. Deaths resulting from falls rose from 4.8 per 100,000 to 6.4 between 1999 and 2005 in the general population (QuickStats: Percentage Changes, 2008). When you add in weakness, comorbidities, and age, it is easy to appreciate the fact that the numbers of falls are increasing in a nursing home setting.

Fall prevention becomes essential in avoiding serious complications, and starts with the admission assessment. There are many fall risk assessment tools available through published forms and on the internet. The key to successful use is to adapt a simple form and back it up with a policy and procedure to hold the staff accountable for its use. The form should be comprehensive enough to address the common risks for falls and should include definitions of any rating scale used on the form itself. Any tool used should include the more common risk factors or falls, such as the following:

- History of previous falls
- Effects of medications, including diuretics, narcotics, antihypertensives, hypoglycemics
- Mental status changes, dementia, altered cognition, diminished decision-making capacity
- Stroke, Parkinson's, or other neuromuscular diseases, neuropathies, impaired functional status
- Visual changes, vertigo, hypoglycemia, orthostatic hypotension
- Incontinence
- Use of assisted devices for ambulation

Environmental factors can also play a crucial role in fall prevention. Issues such as poor or dim lighting, slippery or wet surfaces, inappropriate footwear, uneven flooring, loose carpeting, lack of safety railings/grab bars, and malfunctioning call systems all contribute to fall potential. The LNC reviewing records in a fall case must determine what existing and potential contributing conditions were taken into consideration in formulating a plan of care for fall prevention.

Because falls can be devastating, interventions to prevent falls should take into account individual needs based on a thorough assessment. Multiple factors placing residents at risk must be shared with all caregivers to increase awareness of risk potential. Even with the best plan of fall prevention, some falls and their consequences are unavoidable. Once a fall occurs, the focus shifts to performing a postfall evaluation and adjusting the plan of care accordingly. The LNC should look for evidence of interventions to prevent future falls. Were bed alarms used and functioning? Was the call light functioning and within reach? Was the resident left unattended and unable to summon help? Were other departments such as physical or occupational therapy involved in a root cause analysis of the fall? Were recommendations made and implemented? All these factors will have a bearing on litigation outcome.

The physician and family/significant others must be notified in the event of a fall. The resident must be thoroughly assessed, which may include sending the resident out of the facility to an emergency room for more extensive evaluation for injuries. Documentation should include time and date of the fall and all the specific data including what happened in the resident's own words in quotes, who was called, when and what was done. Was the family or significant other notified? If the resident was not evaluated as to the cause of the fall nor the physician notified, the LNC should note any reason documented as to why this was not done (Michigan Department of Community Health, 2001). An incident report should also be filed with the essential data, but its existence should not be reflected in the medical record. An incident report may or may not be protected under a peer review privilege, depending on the state statutes regarding such documents and how they are reviewed by management.

Example 17.3

Billy Hughes, 82, resided at Childress Healthcare Center from January 1, 1998 until his death on December 26, 1999. According to his son, Mr. Hughes fell over 50 times of which 37 falls were unwitnessed. The falls resulted in fractures, lacerations, and ultimately led to his decline and death. The family alleged that in spite of his multiple injuries, the staff failed to monitor his pain level or offer medication. The allegation of failure to monitor, prevent falls, and adequately train staff were substantiated. The case settled for $2.5 million (Marks, 2003).

Pressure Ulcers and Skin Concerns

The aging process causes complex changes in the skin to take place. Adding comorbidity, decreased activity, poor nutrition and decreased mobility, and the potential of pressure ulcer development should be obvious to the nursing staff. As skin ages, the elasticity decreases and the base membrane and epidermis thin. In addition, mechanical protection, skin barrier function, and sensory perception decline (Beers, 2006).

Risk assessment for pressure ulcer development includes the following:

- Age of resident
- Nursing assessment on admission and after any significant health changes

- Evaluation of the resident's ability to reposition in bed
- Identification of all potentially contributing risk factors (mental status, medication, incontinence, friction/shear, immobility, inactivity, moisture, and nutrition)
- Documentation of risk assessment scores and implementation of a plan of care (National Pressure Ulcer Advisory Panel, 2007)

Unfortunately, once the potential for pressure ulcer development assessment is completed, the Registered Nurse infrequently sees the resident. Care, bathing, turning, and ambulation are carried out by certified nursing assistants (CNAs). It is, therefore, paramount that CNAs are taught to recognize early signs of pressure ulcer development potential and other skin care issues. A minimal competency for skin assessment should include knowledge of normal aging skin characteristics, effects of moisture and incontinence on the skin, positioning options and schedule, nutritional and hydration impact on the skin and healing, and identification of risk factors. Caregivers need to be educated on the staging process and suspected deep tissue injury characteristics. Pressure ulcers can have mixed stages or be totally unstageable due to a thick covering of necrotic tissue, making it impossible to measure depth.

Many families and plaintiff attorneys jump at the opportunity to initiate litigation when a nursing home resident is diagnosed with a Stage III or Stage IV pressure ulcer that involves layers of skin, subcutaneous tissue, muscle, and bone. These ulcers are deep, often infected, foul smelling, and have a significant impact on quality of life. Relatives and friends may be repulsed at the sight and smell, and feel nothing was done to prevent the ulcer from forming. Juries often do not understand the nursing home environment and are quick to award large settlements based on perceived neglect. Neglect may not be the only contributing factor. When reviewing the records, the LNC should look for factors that may contribute to pressure ulcer formation such as:

- Chronic diseases like diabetes, cancer, peripheral vascular disease, stroke, heart disease
- Inability to perceive pressure, mental impairment
- Incontinence, excessive moisture
- Inability to reposition, fractures, contractures
- Poor nutritional intake, friction/shear
- Sleeping and seating surfaces (National Pressure Ulcer Advisory Panel, 2007; Berlowitz, Bezerra, Brandeis, Kader, & Anderson, 2000)

Knowing which factors may make pressure ulcer formation unavoidable, the medical record should include interventions for prevention such as:

- Team conference notes identifying all risk factors, including old healed ulcers
- Admission and weekly documented skin assessments and measurements including a risk assessment scale (like the Braden Scale), (Ayello & Braden, 2001)
- Existing photographs of wound healing progress
- Individualized and timely updated care plan
- Devices used to relieve pressure
- Nutritional assessments and interventions
- Weight records, including monitoring and analysis of weight gain/loss
- Evaluation of edema

- Significant lab value analysis
- Physician orders and progress notes regarding skin issues and treatment

Every effort should be made to protect skin from injury and skin tears. This traumatic injury causes a separation of the dermis and epidermis, and occurs most frequently in the hands affecting a resident's ability for self-care. Skin tears in the sacral region can be mistakenly classified as Stage II pressure ulcers. It is important to distinguish these two wounds since the etiology is different for both. Protecting the skin with clothing, avoiding strong soaps, caution when removing tape, and moisturizing will help prevent skin tears (Reddy, 2008). Other skin issues, such as pruritis, rashes, or cellulitis, need to be evaluated by a physician and a plan of care established.

Staffing patterns become important when considering whether appropriate staff was available to give care. If the facility was chronically understaffed, it would be difficult to implement even the basic plan of care to prevent pressure ulcers. Staffing patterns become available during the discovery phase and should reflect a skill mix appropriate to the facility size and resident acuity. Registered nurses are required to assess and evaluate a plan of care (Dorr, Horn, & Smout, 2005).

Example 17.4

Having suffered three strokes, Frances Gross, 72, was admitted to Heritage Park Nursing Home. She was totally dependent on the home for her care and had a small pressure ulcer on her coccyx. In just 30 days, the pressure ulcer grew to 11 × 9 cm and developed into a Stage IV, necrotic and infected. An additional Stage III pressure ulcer developed on her right gluteal fold. She was grossly dehydrated and had lost 21 pounds in spite of having a percutaneous endoscopic gastrostomy (PEG) feeding tube and was totally dependent on the staff to meet her nutritional needs. She was transferred to Vencor Hospital. The wounds were on their way to healing after 600 days of repeated debridement and proper nutritional support. The plaintiff alleged that the catastrophic injuries were caused by not turning and repositioning, a lack of sufficient water and tube feeding, and no protection of the skin surface from contact with urine and feces. The defense contended that the weight on admission to the nursing home and the weight on admission to Vencor Hospital were incorrect and that Mrs. Gross did not lose 21 pounds in a month. In addition, they alleged that the pressure ulcers were unavoidable due to comorbidities and an allergic reaction to the Duoderm applied. The case settled for the plaintiff in the amount of $5,000,000 prior to trial (Marks, 1999).

Dehydration and Malnutrition

There are numerous reasons why residents succumb to dehydration and malnutrition. Altered nutritional status is common in nursing home residents and should be evaluated as soon as possible on admission. The total caloric requirements and food likes and dislikes (including allergies) need to be calculated and documented, with a plan developed to provide adequate nutrition and prevent weight loss. Factors such as weight, ability to participate in basic hygiene, poor dentition, swallowing difficulty, appetite, limited vision, constipation or diarrhea, medical diagnosis, infections, and pain are risks to nutritional impairment and should be identified and documented. Is the resident on medication that alters the flavor of foods? What is the cognitive status? Is the resident blind? One of the most significant factors contributing to malnutrition is the availability of staff to feed or assist residents at mealtime. Untrained staff may not recognize signs of dysphagia such as throat clearing, coughing, or having a wet voice putting the resident at risk for aspiration pneumonia. When staffing is short and many residents need to be fed, large amounts of food are given at a fast pace to accommodate a typical 1 hour meal service (Shipman & Hooten, 2007).

Oral hygiene is often overlooked as a cause of malnutrition. Does the resident have teeth and are they in good condition? Are dentures properly fitted or loose? Can the resident safely chew food? Often weight loss will affect denture fit and some residents literally eat with one hand and hold their dentures in their mouth with the other (Kayser-Jones, 2000, October). Trying to drink liquids with no teeth produces a poor seal and causes liquids to spill out of the mouth.

During document review, the LNC must consider all factors and clinical conditions affecting dehydration and malnutrition. Food intake records may not be a part of the medical record and may be documented in a CNA care plan kept elsewhere in the facility. Consideration must be given to risk factors such as medical diagnoses of anorexia, cancer, renal disease, behavior disorders, or other cognitive impairment. Is there a written plan of care reflecting current and prevailing treatment modalities? Does the plan of care reflect interventions to prevent weight loss? Does cultural diversity play a role? Is food from home a viable alternative to encourage intake? Were the dietician's recommendations followed and reflected in the progress notes? Were there speech and language pathologist's consults, evaluations, and recommendations in the medical record? Were laboratory results of albumin levels, electrolytes, and other pertinent diagnostic tests addressed by the physician? Was there a nutritional plan of care? These questions, once answered, will provide important information regarding the comprehensive efforts to meet the resident's nutrition and hydration needs.

Nutrition and hydration have a significant bearing on the body's ability to heal pressure ulcers and other skin conditions. Protein intake must be adequate, and the body must be able to use nutrients effectively. The use of feeding tubes and parenteral feedings may supply needed calories for tissue repair.

When residents refuse to eat, reasons must be explored and interventions added to the plan of care. Physicians or psychologists may explore and treat signs of depression. The LNC must look for appropriate facility responses to nutritional issues brought up by family members during team conferences.

End of life care issues often surface in the nursing home setting. Hospices may offer an organized approach to end of life care. Clarification on the difference between hunger and thirst, and nutrition and hydration, when the resident is placed in hospice care, will eliminate guilt feelings of family members who believe their loved one is being starved to death. Experienced health care professionals are available to counsel family members and offer support during this difficult time.

Example 17.5

A resident was choked to death after receiving the wrong tray, delivered by an agency CNA covering for striking workers. The resident was blind and had no teeth and was served a regular diet instead of mechanical soft and thickened liquids. He choked and was resuscitated but died 10 days later in the hospital. The plaintiff argued that the resident was served his roommate's tray. The defendant nursing home argued that they were not at fault and that the blame rested solely with the CNA and the agency that sent her. A posttrial settlement was reached for $4,047,232 paid by the defendant CNA and the agency. The jury found that the nursing home had vicarious liability for the acts of the agency CNA. This was a moot point since the agency had sufficient insurance to cover the verdict (Sussman, 2008).

Resident Rights

The basic rights of residents in nursing home environments have long been a concern of society. In 1974 Congress passed the Nursing Home Bill of Rights (NHBR) (Long Term Care, 2007) and tied reimbursements to meeting federal standards on quality of care focused on the right of every resident to maintain dignity in the nursing home setting. The passage of the Omnibus Budget Reconciliation Act of 1987 (OBRA) added new regulations emphasizing resident rights to lead a full and dignified life within the limitations of their medical condition. The residents were entitled to a full evaluation on admission and yearly thereafter. The evaluation must determine their ability to walk, talk, eat, dress, bathe, and communicate their needs. The greatest impact came from the resident's right to be free of restraints, both physical and chemical. Nursing homes have a history of housing the elderly and medicating them to control activity and behavior. The resultant inactivity can lead to immobility and corresponding complications. Taking into consideration the impact of anti-psychotic drugs on mobility has led to a 28–36% decline in the use of psychotropic drugs and reduced physical restraint use by 40% (Turnham, 2001).

The right to privacy and confidentiality, a basic human right, was denied in a nursing home setting prior to enactment of the NHBR act. Residents now have a right to complain without reprisal and participate in decisions affecting their environment through resident council meetings. OBRA provided a minimum set of standards that established protocols to provide for a resident's happiness and well-being. Policies, reflecting compliance, provided for access to services outside the nursing home. The resident has a right to inspect all records pertaining to them, including charges for services and financial records of personal funds. These much needed changes arose from a growing concern regarding poor quality of care. Residents are now informed of their rights upon admission, and the Bill of Rights must be posted in the facility.

While residents do have the right to refuse treatment, this does not negate the responsibility of the facility to provide needed care. When a resident refuses to be repositioned or turned, it is not sufficient for the nurse to document "refused." It becomes the obligation of the nurse to educate the resident on the ramification of the refusal and to document the resident's verbalized understanding. It is the responsibility of the nurse to notify the physician, family members, and adjust the plan of care accordingly when refusal of care, treatments, or nutrition becomes habitual. In a review of records for litigation, the LNC must be alert to documented attempts to advocate on behalf of the resident. What interventions were utilized to address the refusal? Was the refusal justified or in conflict with a medical plan of care? Did the resident understand the ramifications of the refusal and what was done to clarify the course of action? Was there a cultural or communication barrier? Were there safety issues? What other disciplines offered resolution? Answering these questions will assist in determining liability.

The right to be free of restraints does not extend to the resident's right to wander liberally into harm's way. Facilities have the right to set safety limits regarding use of the grounds, smoking, visitation, and leaving the facility without notice. Supervisory responsibility extends to all residents, including the mentally challenged. Where there is a lack of communication or understanding, wander guard devices can be employed to potentially alert the staff to unsafe activity.

Resident Abuse and Neglect

Resident abuse and neglect are some of the more serious issues leading to litigation, with juries often imposing staggering punitive damage awards when a facility attempts to conceal potentially incriminating facts. Society has an obligation to protect the frail and elderly and criminal background checks are required on all nursing home employees, especially direct care givers such as CNAs. The LNC can be instrumental in verifying licensing and background checks of employees involved in an incident. Names can be misspelled or nicknames used to hide criminal backgrounds, as evidenced in the following example:

Example 17.6

In 1991, Texas Health Enterprises hired a 6-foot, 200 pound man with a criminal history of forgery and robbery. When the background check was conducted, the gender was entered as female and the record was returned as clean and he was hired. Three weeks later he was fired by the Assistant Director of Nursing for repeatedly slapping an 87-year-old female resident. He went to another nursing home where another background check was conducted. Again his last name was entered incorrectly leading to his hire and a repeated episode of resident abuse and rape of a 65-year-old stroke victim. Questionable body fluids on the victim alerted other care givers to report the abuse. The reports were dismissed at first but the insistent reporting by other aides led to an arrest and conviction of the abusive aide. The jury found the nursing home grossly negligent and awarded $4,650,000 in damages, of which $1,900.000 were punitive damages (*Martha Fough v. Texas Health Enterprises*, 2008).

Residents who have Alzheimer's or are mentally challenged are often the victims of abuse since they cannot defend themselves nor can they voice a complaint. The abuse is often at the hands of other residents. The LNC can determine if any effort was made by the facility to segregate residents with known abusive tendencies. Staffing must be adequate to monitor behavior and intervene in a timely manner to prevent abuse.

Example 17.7

Will Barr, a 73-year old, wheel chair bound resident with dementia, was beaten to near death by Gerald Bradford, his 49-year-old paranoid schizophrenic roommate. Bradford had kicked Barr in the head repeatedly for almost an hour. Barr died 3 weeks later as a result of his injuries. The nursing home was sued by the family, claiming the roommate should never have been admitted to the facility due to his history of aggressive behavior and criminal background. The Director of Nursing had expressed an opinion that Bradford should not be admitted, but that assessment was ignored by the Medical Director. Bradford had a history of aggressive behavior toward the staff and other residents, resulting in several room changes and emergency calls to the police. Testimony revealed that the nursing home attempted to suppress any knowledge of Bradford's criminal background or behavior issues. The nursing home agreed to a $1.3 million settlement 2 months prior to trial (Andrews Publication, 2000).

Example 17.8

An 87-year-old resident was ordered sitz baths for labial cysts. The resident sustained second and third degree burns on her buttocks and perineal area when scalded by extremely hot water, leading to a decline in her health and death. The nurses admitted to obtaining hot water from the kitchen industrial coffee urn, with the rationale that steam would be better than the lukewarm water soaks that were ordered. The water temperature was tested by the Illinois Department of Public Health the following day and was in excess of 185°F. The jury found gross negligence and awarded $1.5 million dollars to the plaintiff's family (Andrews Publication, 2002).

Understandably, failure of a facility to provide a safe environment is paramount in the decision to litigate. Verdicts are often dependent on what efforts were documented to support or refute a plan of care reflective of an individual resident's needs assessment. The Plan of Care becomes the primary source to evaluate the efforts to prevent harm once potential injury is foreseeable. Adjustments to the Plan of Care need to be made in a timely manner based on a current and ongoing assessment.

Wandering and Elopement

Like abuse, neglect takes on many forms. Residents with limited mental capacity must be protected from wandering out of a facility and into harm's way. Wander guard alarms are available to alert staff to wandering residents. Doors to the outside should have working alarm systems in place and alarms should be responded to as soon as activated. Alarms on all exit doors should be operational and responded to immediately when activated. Failure to do so may result in injury or death of a resident. Residents with any form of diminished mental capacity may attempt to elope in search of familiar surroundings.

Example 17.9

Tyrine Wilson placed her 87-year-old husband Gilbert in a nursing home on December 31, 2005 due to his Alzheimer's diagnosis and her inability to keep him from wandering. The nursing home assured her they would watch him and provide a safe environment. Gilbert wandered from the facility and was struck by a paving company truck on January 3, 2006. Due to heavy rains, the truck driver was unaware of what he hit and returned to the scene of the accident with his supervisor, where they discovered the body of Gilbert Wilson submerged in a ditch at the roadside. Gilbert was in the morgue as a "John Doe" for 6 weeks from January 3 to February 22 before Tyrine Wilson was notified of her husband's death. He had apparently wandered off January 2 and was struck nine miles from the nursing home. No one had made an attempt to look for him or notify the police. The plaintiff contended that the nursing home should have known they were unable to watch Mr. Wilson based on his diagnosis and wandering tendencies. The defendants argued that they met the standards of care and that Mrs. Wilson knew the nursing home did not have a locked unit. The jury found the defendant negligent and awarded $1,480,000 to the estate of Gilbert Wilson (Wrongful Death: Alzheimer's, 2008).

Other Areas of Negligence

Other areas of negligence litigation include:

- Burns
- Urosepsis
- Equipment failure
- Insect infestation
- Choking
- Failure to notify physician in a timely manner
- Failure to monitor
- Fecal impaction

Example 17.10

An Alabama jury awarded a resident $5.35 million as a result of a fire ant attack. Employees noticed fire ants in the facility and alerted management several weeks prior to the attack. Lucille Devers, a 79-year-old resident, was discovered to be covered with a swarm of fire ants so severe that ants were coming out of her mouth, nose, ears, and vagina and she suffered hallucinations as a result of the attack. Employees testified that the nursing home had previously supplied them with cans of bug spray to use if more ants were noted and failed to contact an exterminator in a timely fashion. The defense argued that the attack was not foreseeable and the exterminator was responsible for ridding the facility of the fire ants. The daughter sued the nursing home and Terminex. As a result of evidence presented at trial, the jury awarded compensatory damages of $1,850,000 jointly for each defendant and $1,756,000 punitive damages for each defendant (Jovanovic, 2002).

Another common area of neglect is the failure to monitor medication effects and laboratory data. Residents admitted from an acute care setting are often on anticoagulation therapy. Dosing of Coumadin is based on laboratory International Normalized Ratio (INR) results, which need to be reported to the physician as soon as they are known in order to obtain correct dosage for Coumadin administration. Failing to do so may leave the resident with clotting problems, leading to the formation of emboli or over anticoagulation leading to hemorrhage. A plan of care should be in place for any resident on anticoagulation medication, including aspirin, indicating interventions to monitor effect of medication and to observe for excessive bleeding or escalating bruising. The LNC will be able to determine if physician orders, lab results, monitoring, medication, treatment, and administration records reflect the policies and procedures of the organization and met the SOC.

Monitoring should also include other medications such as antihypertensive drugs. Are blood pressures taken and recorded prior to administration? Are medications held for low blood pressures and the physician notified to adjust the dosage? Are pain medications given in a timely manner and relief recorded? Often residents cannot ask for pain medication verbally so facial expression, body language, or behavior need to serve as a guide for administration of medication. All monitoring interventions should be part of the plan of care.

Subacute Rehabilitation

Resident Rights and Participation in Care

Reflecting the push for patient discharge based on DRGs, many individuals are transferred from acute care facilities to a nursing home environment for the purpose of rehabilitation and restoring or maximizing functional capacity after an injury or illness. Rehabilitation residents require a longer period of physical therapy than can be accommodated in a hospital setting. The rehabilitation team sets short-term and long-term goals after evaluating the resident. Refusal to participate may find the resident discharged to a long-term facility for custodial care. Rehabilitation goals are discussed and care is directed by a physician specializing in rehabilitation and physical medicine, known as a physiatrist. Rehabilitation team members may include the following: rehabilitation nurse, physical therapist, occupational therapist, speech pathologist, social worker or case manager, clinical psychologist, pharmacist, and dietician. The resident must participate to the extent of their ability to keep the plan viable. The team meets weekly and discusses progress towards goals. The resident may be invited to participate in the discussion and agree to adjustments in the plan of care.

The LNC reviewing the medical record must be aware of the evaluations and goals set by participating therapists. It becomes important for information discussed at the team meeting to filter down to the lowest classification of caregiver. How this occurs varies with the facility. Adjustments to the care plan and resident responses to treatment and therapy must be recorded. If there was a refusal to go to therapy or participate in the plan of care, what was the resident told regarding the ramifications of the refusal? Was the information clear? Was there a voiced understanding and was that documented?

Falls

Falls occur in the subacute rehabilitation population for many reasons. Lack of awareness of physical limitations, equipment issues, lack of trained personnel, use of assisted devices, or unfamiliarity with prosthetics increases the potential for falls in this resident population. Based on the evaluations of the rehabilitation team, the staff must adhere to recommendations for assistive devices and hands-on or standby assistance for ambulation; failing to do so may result in a fall and possible serious injuries. All caregivers need to be aware of the plan goals and understand common abbreviations such as

- CGA = contact guard assist, required to physically have a hand on the resident
- FWB = full weight bearing
- NWB = nonweight bearing
- PWB = partial weight bearing
- SBA = stand by assist, be ready to help if needed
- I = independent
- WFL = within functional limits
- WNL = within normal limits

Within the functional Independence Measure (FIM), SBA also refers to supervision and cuing or prompting. This will be discussed later in the chapter. Additional FIM abbreviations are Min A = minimal assistance from 1% to 24%, Mod A = moderate assistance from 25% to 49%, and Max A = maximal assistance from 50% to 75% with TA = total assist (Therapy Abbreviations, 2006). Understanding a resident's limitations prior to initiating activities or ambulation can prevent falls and injury.

Spinal Cord Injury

Residents with spinal cord injury (SCI) present a unique challenge for caregivers. An assessment of sensory and motor functions will alert the caregiver to the resident's ability to participate in therapies and care. Quadriplegia, or tetraplegia, refers to paralysis of all four extremities. Paraplegia refers to paralysis of the lower extremities. Because of the inability to move independently, residents with SCI are at greater risk for the development of complications resulting from immobility, such as pressure ulcer development and respiratory problems. Bladder and bowel function is compromised and can lead to chronic urinary tract infections and bowel obstruction. The plan of care must reflect an understanding of the potential for complications and must identify preventative interventions. Evaluation of the plan and adjustments are made at the team conference or as problems arise.

Pressure relieving or reducing surfaces should be used on sleeping and sitting surfaces. Residents with SCI are taught pressure relief in the acute setting and reinforcement of teaching is a must. Skin inspection during bathing will alert the caregiver to intervene early to prevent breakdown. CNAs must be taught to recognize early signs of potential problems and alert the licensed care provider. Institutional policy and procedures should cover all aspects for care of the SCI resident. Review of the medical record and policies regarding care will assist the LNC in determining a breach in the SOC.

From a defense perspective, attorneys often argue that the predisposition to breakdown and complications cannot be avoided. The burden of proof will lie in the plan of care and its reflection of all possible means to avoid anticipated complications based on a specific diagnosis. The foreseeability of SCI complications compels the LNC to identify specific interventions to meet the SOC. Consideration must be given to areas such as timely resident assessment, seating and sleeping surfaces in place prior to tissue breakdown, nutritional needs met, bladder and bowel protocols in place, resident compliance with care, and documented educational efforts. This is a partial list of the basic quality of care issues often addressed in litigation. While some complications may be unavoidable, the defense lies in the efforts of all involved in the resident's care. Not all nursing home facilities are equipped to offer rehabilitation services to SCI residents.

Example 17.11

A $1 million verdict was awarded to Jerzy Warydrag, a 51-year-old quadriplegic for negligent care received at the defendant nursing home. Mr. Warydrag was admitted to Alden North Shore Nursing Home for rehabilitation in June 2001. Within 6 months, he developed severe pressure ulcers on his tailbone, right and left hip, and both heels. The nursing home argued that the pressure ulcers were unavoidable due to his quadriplegia. Mr. Warydrag was transferred to another facility where the ulcers healed within 1 year (Levin, 2007).

Traumatic Brain Injury

Like the SCI resident, the resident with a TBI has a specific set of needs, beyond basic care, dependent on the location and severity of the brain injury. Characteristics of TBI behavior are classified by the seven level Ranch Los Amigos scale and define cognitive functioning (Rancho Los Amigos National Rehabilitation Center, 1990). Sensory stimulation is started with low-level residents (Levels I through III). Levels IV and V pose the greatest challenges to care since the residents are confused and agitated. They are often fearful, cannot comprehend what has happened to them, and will strike out. TBI residents are highly focused on basic needs and are often sexually and verbally inappropriate depending on the location of the brain injury.

Families and caregivers need to understand that the behavior and language are not directed at anyone in particular and represents a lack of inhibition due to the site of the injury. Residents with TBI are easily agitated and have very limited attention spans. Monitoring behavior and setting consistent consequences to behavioral issues will assist in advancing the resident to a higher level of functioning. Sources of stimulation must be limited, including visitors. Residents with higher levels of functioning exhibit a lack of safety awareness but are redirected more easily. Consistency in following a plan of care is imperative to safe rehabilitation of the TBI resident.

Litigation surrounding TBI residents falls into similar categories as Alzheimer and dementia residents, with falls, malnutrition, dehydration, and wandering emerging as leading causes of legal action. Restorative services may work with the TBI resident to maintain achieved parameters and prevent decline in physical and mental functions, once physical therapy goals are met or the resident has plateaued in therapy efforts. Careful review of the records will reveal if a plan of care was established and followed. Policies, procedures, and marketing information about the facility will alert the LNC to its stated ability to accept and treat TBI residents.

Example 17.12

A 35-year old suffered a TBI from a car accident, leaving him in a persistent vegetative state. The plaintiff suffered first-, second-, and third-degree burns when left unattended in a shower by a CNA. The water-mixing valve malfunctioned causing 135°F water to fall on his scalp, ear, back, neck, and shoulder. He was returned to bed and no report of the injury was made. A licensed practical nurse noted redness and blistering and notified the registered nurse on call who, without assessing the resident, ordered antibiotic cream to be applied, according to a standing order for minor burns, without assessing the resident. Neither the family nor physician was notified until 48 h after the burns occurred. The defendant was negligent in leaving him in the shower unattended and not notifying a physician. A confidential settlement was reached (McVeigh, 2007, January 26).

The Bariatric Resident

The National Institutes of Health estimates that 11–15 million Americans are morbidly obese. Bariatric weight reduction surgery centers have increased 40% since 2002 and many have turned to the advances of science in the hope of overcoming obesity (Bariatric Surgery.info, 2004). While bariatric procedures are becoming increasingly common, hospital recovery has extended into the long-term care environment. Comorbidities linked with obesity often require additional time for healing and regaining mobility. The nursing home environment and subacute rehabilitation offer a solution.

Equipment needs of the bariatric resident must accommodate weight restrictions. If the nursing home attempts to save money by using an equipment not rated for the weight limits of the resident, injury will occur. Rental of bariatric beds, mechanical lifts, commodes, and shower equipment can be costly. A review of medical records for litigation should include billing records reflecting equipment rentals.

Direct care staff will also require education in lifting and repositioning techniques to prevent injury to staff and residents. A rehabilitation plan of care will require input from a physiatrist, a nutritionist, a nurse, a pharmacist, a case manager, and a clinical psychologist to develop a behavior modification approach to recovery. Resident and family support is vital to success of any bariatric rehabilitation attempt.

Analysis of the Nursing Home Medical Record

Whether electronic or paper, the medical records in the nursing home environment differ from acute care settings. The medical record is separated similarly to a hospital record, with the exception of forms such as Minimum Data Sets (MDS), Resident Assessment Instrument (RAI), Resident Assessment Protocol (RAP), Resource Utilization Group (RUG), and, if the facility has subacute rehabilitation FIM and Functional Assessment Measure (FAM).

The MDS are a part of the federally mandated clinical assessment of all residents in a certified Medicare or Medicaid nursing home. Currently, Version 2.0 is in use with Version 3.0 expected to make its debut in March 2009 (Centers for Medicare and Medicaid Services, 2008a, 2008b). The MDS is a very comprehensive assessment covering:

- Demographics
- Customary routines
- Background information
- Cognitive patterns
- Communication/hearing patterns
- Vision patterns
- Mood and behavior
- Psychosocial well-being
- Physical functioning and structural problems
- Continence in last 14 days
- Disease diagnosis
- Health conditions
- Oral/nutritional status
- Oral/dental status
- Skin condition

- Activity pursuit patterns
- Special treatments and procedures
- Discharge potential and overall status

Many disciplines contribute to sections of the MDS as the assessments are completed. MDS assessments must be completed by the 14th day after admission, annually, and after any significant change in the resident. Problems identified on admission need to be addressed with a temporary plan of care during completion of the MDS. Once the MDS is entered into the computer, the RAI and RAP forms are generated. These documents form the basis of the resident plan of care and are transmitted electronically to the CMS database. Information is then compared with local, regional, and national participating nursing homes for the purpose of tracking quality indicators and other trends. During record review, the LNC should compare MDS data with documentation in the nurses' notes. Often the MDS is completed by individuals who do not evaluate the resident and depend on second-hand information. When this occurs, the discrepancies in documentation may make it difficult to determine liability regarding whether the applicable SOC was met. The RUGs category determines reimbursements based on the MDS and medically complex cases including rehabilitation services (Centers for Medicare and Medicaid Services, 2008a,b).

In nursing homes where subacute rehabilitation is offered, FIM measures the resident's independent function level as it pertains to 18 categories. The categories are eating, grooming, bathing, dressing upper body, dressing lower body, toileting, bladder management, bowel management, bed/chair/wheelchair transfer, toilet transfer, tub and shower transfer, walking/wheelchair locomotion, stairs, comprehension, expression, social interaction, problem solving, and memory. The numbers assigned to each scale range from 1 = total assist to 7 = completely independent.

FAM items were developed by the different disciplines in the acute rehab setting and support FIM measurements. These items are swallowing, car transfer, community access, reading, writing, speech intelligibility, emotional status, adjustment to limitations, employability, orientation, attention, and safety judgment (Wright, 2000). Both of these measures are used most commonly with the brain-injured population. Not all facilities that have rehabilitation programs use FIM or FAM measurements.

Summary

Nursing home environments have changed drastically, and as acuity levels rise, so does the potential for litigation. Reimbursements from Medicare, Medicaid, and private insurance companies are often inadequate to cover the cost of necessary services, and increased litigation and the cost of defending nursing homes can have a negative impact on the quality of care. Money spent on defense is not available for staffing or other needs. Residents are often evaluated and treated by licensed personnel with little experience or knowledge of medically complex admissions, and the least educated level of care giver providing majority of the care. The ramifications of knowledge deficit in care are staggering. Litigation may be brought about out of guilt, greed, and inability to deal with the loss of a loved one, regardless of advanced age. The LNC involved in nursing home litigation must remain objective during the review process, keeping in mind that there are always two sides to every allegation.

References

American Nurses Association. (1995). *Scope and standards of gerontological nursing practice.* Washington, DC: Nursebooks.org.

American Nurses Association. (2004). *Standards of clinical nursing practice.* Washington, DC: Nursebooks.org.

Andrews Publication. (2000, February). Fatal attack on resident results in $1.3 million settlement. *Nursing Home Legal Insider, 1*(6). Retrieved October 18, 2009 at http://www.levinperconti.com/files/nursing_home_legal_insider_022000.doc.

Andrews Publication. (2002, March 8). Illinois court approves record 1.5M settlement in nursing home burn case. *Nursing Home Litigation Reporter, 4*(14), 1–2. Retrieved October 18, 2009 at http://www.levinperconti.com/files/pease2.doc

Ayello, E., & Braden, B. (2001). Why is pressure ulcer risk so important? *Nursing, 31*(11), 75–79.

Bariatric Surgery.info. (2004). Statistics and statistical surveys of weight loss surgery. Retrieved September 22, 2008, from http://www.bariatric-surgery.info/statistics.htm

Beers, M. (Ed.). (2006). *Aging and the skin. Merck manual of geriatrics.* Whitehouse Station, NJ: Merck & Co.

Berlowitz, D., Bezerra, H., Brandeis, G., Kader, B., & Anderson, J. (2000). Are we improving the quality of nursing home care? The case of pressure ulcers. *Journal of the American Geriatric Society, 48*(1), 59–62.

Billy Wayne Paige, individually and as administrator of the estate of Mary Paige, deceased, v. Mariner Health Care, Inc.. f/k/a/ Mariner Post Acute Network, Mariner Health Group, Inc. National Heritage, Inc. Mariner Health Care Management Co. and those operating subsidiaries of Yazoo City Health and Rehabilitation Center. (2006). No. 5:06 CV 162-DCB-JMR, U.S. District Court for the Southern District Mississippi, Western Division. Retrieved September 9, 2008, from http://www.websupp.org/data/SDMS/5:06-cv-00162-13-SDMS.pdf

Brady, M. (2001). Avoiding or mitigating punitive damage exposure in nursing home litigation. *FDCC Quarterly/Fall.* Retrieved June 13, 2008, from EBSCO Host database.

CARF, Commission on Accreditation of Rehabilitation Facilities. (2008). *The value of accreditation to the provider.* Retrieved September 12, 2008, from http://www.carf.org/providers.aspx?Content=content/Learning/SurveyToolBox/TheValue.htm&ID=15

Centers for Medicare and Medicaid Services. (2008a). *MDS 3.0 for nursing homes.* Retrieved September 12, 2008, from http://www.cms.hhs.gov/NursingHomeQualityInits/25_NHQIMDS30.asp

Centers for Medicare and Medicaid Services. (2008b). *RUG refinement.* Retrieved September 12, 2008, from http://www.cms.hhs.gov/SNFPPS/09_RUGRefinement.asp

Code of Federal Regulations. (2008). Title 42: Public Health. Part 483, subpart B—requirements for long term care. 483.30, Nursing services.

Cunningham, N. (2006, September). Recent developments in long-term litigation: Trends, verdicts, decisions and legislation. Nursing Home ALF Litigation Seminar.

Data Trends. (2005, June). Long term care sector sees 400% increase in liability cost. *Healthcare Financial Management, 128.* Please provide page number in Data Trends (2005, June).

Dorr, D., Horn, S., & Smout, R. (2005). Cost analysis of nursing home registered nurse staffing times. *Journal of the American Geriatric Society, 53*(5), 843–845.

Groves v. Beverly Enterprises. (2004). *Wilkes and McHugh, P.A., Notable Verdicts and Overview.* Retrieved October 6, 2008, from http://www.wilkesmchugh.com/florida-nursing-home-neglect/index.html

Harrington, C. (2008). *Nursing home staffing standards in state statutes and regulations.* California: University of California San Francisco, Department of Social and Behavioral Sciences.

Jovanovic, R. (2002, July 22). Ant-bite case yields $5.35M award. Elderly woman in nursing home swarmed by fire ants. *The National Law Journal Features.* Retrieved October 18, 2009 at http://fly.hiwaay.net/~tsmlaw/nlj.htm

Kayser-Jones, J. (2000, October). Improving the nutritional care of nursing home residents. *Nursing Homes: Long Term Care Management, 49*(10), 56. Retrieved September 21, 2008, from MasterFILE database.

Levin, S. (2007, June 15). $1 million settlement for quadriplegic against North Shore Nursing Home. Levin & Perconti Press Release. Retrieved 10/10/08 from http://www.levinperconti.com/docs/press_release_-_wazydrag_-_6.15.2005.pdf

Long Term Care. (2007). The impact of patient rights laws. *Aon Global Risk Consulting* (24). Columbia, MD: AON Global Risk Counseling.

Marks, D. (2003). Father fell 50 times in two years, son alleged. *Hughes v. Senior Living Properties*, LLC d/b/a Childress Care Services, et al. *Marks, Balette & Giessel. About our cases.* Retrieved October 10, 2008, from http://www.marksfirm.com/articles/hughes.htm

Marks, D. (1999). Frances Gross and Annette Miller, a/n/f of Frances Gross vs. Horizons/CMS Healthcare Corporation. *Marks, Balette & Giessel. About our cases.* Retrieved October 12, 2008, from http://www.marksfirm.com/articles/gross.htm

Martha, F., Representative of the Estate of Dorothy Cooper v. Texas Health Enterprises, Inc. and HEA Management Group, Inc. Denton County District Court, 362nd, TX. (2008). Retrieved September 9, 2008, from http://www.marksfirm.com/PDF/Agreement.PDF

McVeigh, K. (2007, January 26). Wyo. Nursing home sued for scalding of vegetative patient. *Nursing Home Litigation Reporter, 9*(16).

Michigan Department of Community Health. (October, 2001). *Process guideline for evaluation of falls/fall risk.* Retrieved September 20, 2008, from http://www.michigan.gov/documents/mdch/bhs_CPG_Falls_Process_206279_7.pdf

National Pressure Ulcer Advisory Panel. (2007). *Pressure ulcer prevention points.* Retrieved October 12, 2008, from http://npuap.org/PU_Prev_Points.pdf

Nursing Home Compare. (2008). *Center for Medicare & Medicaid Services, US. Department of Health and Human Services.* Washington, DC. Retrieved December 31, 2008, from http://www.medicare.gov/Download/DownloaddbInterim.asp

QuickStats. (2008). *Percentage change in death rates for leading causes of unintentional injury, by mechanism of injury—United States, 1999 to 2005.* Center for Disease Control and Prevention (CDC), Morbidity and Mortality Weekly Report (MMWR Weekly), (June 27, 2008). Atlanta, GA. Retrieved September 20, 2008, from http://www.cdc.gov/ncipc/factsheets/nursing.htm

Rancho Los Amigos National Rehabilitation Center. (1990). *Family guide to the Rancho levels of cognitive functioning.* Downey, CA: Rancho Los Amigos National Rehabilitation Center. http://www.rancho.org/patient_education/bi_cognition.pdf

Reddy, M. (2008). Skin and wound care; Important considerations in the older adult. *Advances in Skin and Wound Care, 21*(9), 424–436.

Reibstein, L., & Figueroa, A. (1998, July 27). Nursing-home verdicts: There's guilt all around. *Newsweek, 132*(4), 34. Retrieved May 18, 2008, from Academic Search Alumni Edition database.

Schabes, A. (2002, September). Liability: Hints of 'sweet reason' from the Midwest. *Nursing Homes: Long Term Management, 51*(9), 52. Retrieved February 1, 2009, from MasterFILE Premier database.

Shipman, D., & Hooten, J. (2007, July). Are nursing homes adequately staffed? *Journal of Gerontological Nursing, 13*(7), 15–18.

Smith, L. (2006). Another health care time bomb…Baby boomer values drive growth in nursing home litigation. *Of Counsel, 25*(4), 18–19.

Sussman, P. (Ed.). (2008, February). Theresa Dalessio, Administratix, v. Lexington Health Care Group Inc., et al., *Personal Injury Yearbook, 2007, The Connecticut Law Tribune*, 4–6. Retrieved September 9, 2008, from http://www.ctlawtribune.com/Supplements/PIYBK_2007.pdf

The Joint Commission. (2008). Facts about long term care accreditation. Retrieved September 3, 2008, from http://www.jointcommission.org/AccreditationPrograms/LongTermCare/AccreditationOptions/ltc_facts.htm

Therapy abbreviations. (2006). Theramax Therapy Services, PC. Retrieved September 22, 2008, from http://theramaxtherapyservices.com/therapyabbreviations.aspx

Tramer, H. (2007, September 17). Graying population turns attention on nursing homes. *Crain's Cleveland Business, 28*(37), 15–15. Retrieved from MasterFILE Premier database.

Turnham, H. (2001). *OBRA '87 summary, National Long Term Care Ombudsman Resource Center.* Retrieved September 20, 2008, from http://www.ltcombudsman.org/ombpublic/49_346_1023.cfm

Trial Behavior Consulting. (2008). When prevention isn't enough using jury research for nursing home litigation. Retrieved September 9, 2008, from EBSCO host database.

Wrongful death: Alzheimer's patient left nursing home, was fatally hit by car. (2008). Sample case report. *Verdict Search*. Retrieved October 10, 2008, from http://www.verdictsearch.com/index.jsp?do=news&rep=recent&art=152703

Wright, J. (2000). *The functional assessment measure. The center for outcome measurements in brain injury.* Retrieved September 22, 2008, from http://www.birf.info/home/bi-tools/tests/fam.html

Zinn, L. (2003, October). Riding out the rising tide of litigation. *Nursing Homes: Long Term Care Management*, *52*(10), 34–39. Retrieved June 13, 2008, from Academic Search Premier database.

Test Questions

1. Which of the following statements regarding documentation in long-term care is NOT true?
   A. MDS assessments have input from nutritional services
   B. Nurses must document in the medical record each shift
   C. Physical therapy will develop a plan of care based on their evaluation
   D. CNAs are allowed to document in the medical record

2. Resident abuse and neglect can be attributed to
   A. Limited mental capacity of a resident
   B. Interference from family members
   C. Comorbidities
   D. Lack of training of caregivers

3. Subacute rehabilitation litigation may include the following
   A. Establishing short-term goals in therapy
   B. Failure to notify the physician in a timely manner
   C. Failure of family members to participate in team conferences
   D. Participation of CNAs in developing a plan of care

4. The LNC with an understanding of the long-term care environment will assist the attorney with all of the following EXCEPT
   A. Determining trial strategy
   B. Identifying where a breach in the SOC occurred
   C. Assisting with development of deposition questions
   D. Interpreting the MDS, RAI, RAP, and RUG scores

5. Information on nursing home quality of care issues can be obtained from
   A. Bureau of Vital Statistics
   B. Centers for Medicare and Medicaid (CMS)
   C. State Bureau of Health Professionals
   D. Center for Aging Studies

Answers: 1. B, 2. D, 3. B, 4. A, 5. B

Chapter 18

Personal Injury and Accident Reconstruction

Pat G. Carroll, RN, BSN, LNC, CAISS; Cheryl Gatti, RN, BSN, LNCC; Jude Lark, RN, BSN, CCRN; and Linda Luedtke, RN, MSN

Second Edition
Arlene King Klepatsky, JD, BSN, BA, RN

Contents

Objectives

- Define the elements of personal injury (PI) litigation
- Differentiate the role of the plaintiff and defense legal nurse consultant (LNC) in PI litigation
- Identify appropriate experts to establish negligence, liability, causation, and damages
- Discuss the role of accident reconstruction in motor vehicle accident (MVA) litigation
- Identify and describe common injuries in the PI case

Introduction

LNC roles have expanded in the area of PI litigation. Whether consulting for plaintiff or defense, the LNC's role typically includes the conversion of voluminous medical record data into a user-friendly chronology and education of the attorney or professional claims handler regarding the nature and extent of injury. The plaintiff LNC functions focus on defining the severity, residual effects, long-term outcome, and costs or losses associated with an injury. The defense LNC role assists in determining the reasonableness of the alleged mechanism of injury and medical expenses, and investigation of nontraumatic etiologies of the alleged injury and residuals. Both the plaintiff and defense LNC need a working understanding of negligence, liability, causation, and damages. The LNC's unique ability to apply general information regarding mechanisms of injury, accident reconstruction, and common injuries to a specific case makes the LNC a valuable member of the PI litigation team.

PI litigation serves a number of purposes in our legal system. For example, it

- Provides a mechanism for awarding compensation to those who are injured as a result of the wrongful conduct of others (with the goal of making the injured party "whole" again)
- Provides an incentive to act safely in conduct that affects others
- Allocates accountability to the party with the most control over the conditions that cause risk of the injury
- Spreads the risk through the liability insurance system

PI litigation involves many different types of incidents leading to injury. Examples include motor vehicle collisions and incidents involving other modes of transportation, such as airplanes, trains, and ships. PI cases also include premises liability involving falls, elevator and escalator accidents, and other dangerous conditions on property. There are also workplace injuries (often litigated in the state workers' compensation system), product liability cases (injuries due to defective products), injuries caused by animals or toxic substances, and other miscellaneous incidents. Almost any condition or situation that leads to human injury or suffering may be the subject of a PI lawsuit.

PI litigation involves the law of torts. A tort, which comes from the Latin word "torquere," meaning "to twist," is a civil wrong committed against a person, property, entity, or relationship. The plaintiff, the injured or complaining party, sues the defendant to obtain remedy for the injury. Of note, generally, the injured party is first a claimant, meaning that a claim has been filed with the insurance company of the defendant. The claimant becomes a plaintiff when legal action is commenced.

There are many different torts, each with its own set of elements and defenses. Some examples of torts include assault, battery, false imprisonment, negligence, strict liability (including products liability), intentional and negligent infliction of emotional distress, defamation, invasion of privacy, nuisance, and trespass.

Each tort has its own set of elements that must be proven to state a cause of action as well as its own set of defenses. The plaintiff's attorney must present sufficient evidence to satisfy the burden of proof for each one of the elements of the tort. The burden of proof in a torts case is the "preponderance of the evidence" standard. The preponderance of the evidence means that it is more probable than not. When just over 50% of the evidence is in favor of a party, that party has met the burden of proof by a preponderance of the evidence.

Conversely, the defense attorney needs to present evidence to refute the plaintiff's claims regarding the elements of the cause of action (or at least one of the elements). The defense argues that the plaintiff has not met the burden of proof on any one or all of the elements. The defense attorney may also present evidence of one or more affirmative defenses (discussed below). The defense has the burden of proof when asserting the affirmative defenses. It is the role of the LNC to identify the facts within the medical records that support and refute the elements of the tort and affirmative defenses.

The Tort of Negligence

PI litigation frequently involves the tort of negligence. Negligence is the failure to act as a reasonable person, under the same or similar circumstances, which causes harm. This definition, when broken down into its component parts, determines the elements of negligence. These elements are derived directly from the definition of "negligence." The attorney needs to know whether there is information in the medical records that supports or refutes these required elements.

Defenses to Negligence

Once a PI case is filed and served, the defendant asserts defenses by disputing the existence of any one of the elements of the cause of action, or by presenting evidence of an affirmative defense. This section will discuss just a few of the affirmative defenses to negligence, including comparative negligence, the seat belt defense, and assumption of risk.

Comparative Negligence

With this defense, the defendant alleges that it was the plaintiff who caused the injury. This may be a complete or a partial defense. The trier of fact (jury or arbitrator) may find the plaintiff 100% liable for the incident, may find the defendant 100% liable, or may allocate some fault to the defendant and some to the plaintiff. The rule varies from state to state, but in general, the plaintiff's award is decreased in proportion to the plaintiff's own negligence. This defense, formerly known as contributory negligence, bars any recovery when there is any negligence by the plaintiff. The doctrine of comparative negligence allows partial recovery by the plaintiff.

Example 18.1

A young woman slipped and fell in a grocery store. In the subsequent lawsuit, the defendant claimed that the woman had been negligent in wearing shoes that she knew were too slippery. If the jury were to find the plaintiff 40% liable for the injuries, the plaintiff would receive 60% of the award.

The LNC should be aware of the defense of comparative negligence and look for any facts that suggest that the plaintiff's conduct contributed to the incident. The LNC who reviewed the above case was aware of the significance of the statement given to the nurse regarding the shoes' being too slippery and brought it to the attorney's attention.

The Seat Belt Defense

The seat belt defense is one form of comparative negligence defense. In motor vehicle cases, if the plaintiff was not wearing a seat belt, the defense wants to know what damages the plaintiff would have avoided had he been wearing one. This requires the opinion and testimony of an expert witness. The defense argues that it should not have to pay for any damages that occurred because of the failure to wear a seat belt.

Example 18.2

The plaintiff was an unrestrained passenger in a vehicle without airbags on the passenger side. The vehicle in which the plaintiff was riding was involved in a moderate-speed frontal collision. The plaintiff struck her head on the windshield and suffered a subdural hematoma. The defense hired a biomechanics expert, who testified that if the plaintiff had been wearing her seat belt, her head would not have come in contact with the windshield. In fact, her head would not have struck anything. The defense declined to pay for treatment and sequelae of the head injury since it was caused by the plaintiff's failure to buckle up.

Assumption of Risk

Assumption of risk is an interesting defense, though it is unlikely that the LNC will work on these cases. Plaintiff's attorneys are aware of this defense and decline to take cases in which the defense is likely to apply. This defense applies in cases involving recreational activities that cannot be made entirely safe without materially altering the activity. Some of these activities are skiing, golfing, water-skiing, river rafting, rock climbing, horseback riding, and martial arts. The defense of primary assumption of risk is based on the notion that these activities, by their nature, have inherent risks. The defendant has no duty to protect the plaintiff from the inherent risks of the activity. For example, the owner of a ski resort has no duty to remove trail markers because the markers are an inherent part of the sport of skiing. Thus there is no negligence when a skier runs into such a marker. The ski resort owner does have a duty to adequately maintain equipment, such as the tow cables. Injury from a broken tow cable is not inherent to the sport of skiing.

Liability

Liability is responsibility or accountability. In a PI case, it is presumed the defendant in some way caused the injury and therefore has financial responsibility for the treatment of the injury and other losses associated with the injury. LNC record review may uncover information that supports the liability of the defense, such as exam findings of jaw bruising and tenderness in an individual alleging temporomandibular joint (TMJ) syndrome resulting from a side impact MVA. Conversely, in a food poisoning case, liability of the defendant would be questioned if review of the records found reports of family members (who did not eat the same food as the plaintiff) becoming similarly ill.

Causation

Simply, cause is what brings about an effect. The term causation, however, takes on different meanings depending on the context. A legal opinion of causation is deductive, considering the opinions of experts, anecdotal and case-specific information, as well as liability. There are several sources of information regarding scientific and legal definitions of causation. One such source is the *Guides to the Evaluation of Disease and Injury Causation* (Melhorn & Ackerman, 2008).

The LNC is not directly responsible for determining causation, but rather uncovering the information within the medical record that speaks to the scientific and legal definitions of causation. The PI LNC is often called upon to research medical literature (studies and anecdotal accounts), which address etiology of disease and mechanism of injury. The LNC identifies the facts within the medical record that correlate with the scientific or legal definitions of causation.

Example 18.3

The defense questioned blunt head trauma as the etiology of a subdural hematoma in a case of an eight-week-old infant. On the date of injury, CT scan revealed bilateral extra-axial fluid with no bleeding. Approximately one month later, the infant was found to have a possible small acute subdural bleed. The LNC was able to identify several facts relative to the etiology of abnormalities seen on imaging scans. Review of medical literature found that bilateral extra-axial fluid is an anatomic variant in a number of infants, which increases the risk for subdural hematoma.

Damages

Damages refer to the loss or harm suffered by the claimant/plaintiff as a result of the injury. Damages are the primary incentive for plaintiff and defense actions. The monetary value of damages is what drives the need for PI LNC assistance. Generally, the greater the dollar damages, the greater the monetary settlement. The plaintiff is motivated to identify all incurred and potential costs related to an injury. The defense is motivated to scrutinize and question the veracity of the damages. Evidence of damages is documented in the medical billing records (special damages) and in the medical records (general damages).

Special Damages

Special damages are the quantifiable or "out-of-pocket" costs related to the medical care for the injury. This includes both the care received up to the time the case is settled or litigated and the costs of predictable future care. Some components of special damages may include

- All inpatient and outpatient treatment
- Therapies
- Medications
- Medical supplies
- Home care services
- Costs of travel to and from appointments
- Durable medical equipment
- Modifications to the environment (such as ramps and safety bars)
- Costs of help with services to assist with necessary household functions (shopping, house-cleaning, lawn cutting, and even snow removal when appropriate)

Other out-of-pocket expenses may be involved depending on the particular circumstances. Special damages also include wages lost as a result of the injury. Documentation of lost wages is demonstrated through pay slips before and after the injury; employment records; income tax records; and business records, such as profit and loss statements for the self-employed person.

To assist with the calculation or verification of damages, the LNC identifies and requests all billing records for medical care related to the incident. The LNC knows that one visit to the emergency department will often yield separate bills from the ambulance company, the hospital, the emergency physician's group, the outside laboratory, and the radiologist. The LNC's ability to comprehend ICD-9 and CPT coding on billing is an asset in determining whether treatment is related to the injury in question.

No discussion of special damages would be complete without mentioning the collateral source rule. This rule prevents the defendants from telling the jury that the plaintiff had health care insurance (including Medicare and Medicaid) that covered all or part of the damages. This suggests the plaintiff could get a double recovery—having the bills paid and then obtaining the money from the lawsuit. This generally does not happen because the insurance companies and the government subrogate or file a lien against any recovery for reimbursement of the costs of care needed as a result of the defendant's wrongful conduct. Plaintiff's attorneys may negotiate with the insurance companies regarding what they are willing to accept on the lien. Of note, both plaintiff and defense need to pay particular attention when Medicare is the injured party's primary health insurance. There are rules for notification of Medicare of PI claims, settlements, and recovery.

General Damages

General damages are not easily quantifiable, but a monetary figure is determined based on the severity of the damages and the impact on the plaintiff's life. General damages (also referred to as noneconomic damages) include

- Pain and suffering (both physical and emotional)
- Loss of function
- Loss of enjoyment of life
- Inconvenience
- Fear (such as fear of driving) resulting from the incident
- Embarrassment
- Emotional pain of disfigurement

One of the functions of the LNC is to extract evidence of pain, suffering, loss of function, and other indications of general damages from the records. The roles of the plaintiff and defense LNC regarding evaluation of pain and suffering and reasonableness of special damages are discussed later in this chapter.

Loss of Consortium

Loss of consortium is an independent claim that can be made. The spouse of an injured party may sue the defendant for loss of consortium. This involves the loss of love, comfort, companionship, affection, sexual relations, assistance in maintaining the household, and other components of the relationship. The loss of consortium must be directly related to the injuries suffered in the accident.

Settlement/Payment of Damages

The insured party receives reimbursement for damages either through an alternative dispute resolution (such as settlement) or from jury or judge award as a result of trial. More information regarding this topic can be found in Chapter 16.

Most of the time, the defendant's insurance company pays the damages. The liable party's auto insurance company pays damages arising from MVAs. Damages arising from premises liability cases are paid by the property owner's insurance or from commercial general liability (business) policies. In addition, there may be excess coverage that covers losses above a certain amount. In exchange for the premiums collected, the insurance company promises both to defend and to indemnify (pay damages on behalf of) the insured. The insurance company chooses the defense attorney. The insurance company generally retains a measure of control over the litigation. It is the duty of the defendant to cooperate.

Uninsured/Underinsured Coverage

When a driver and passengers are injured by an uninsured or underinsured driver, damages may be paid by the driver's own insurance company. When the liable driver has no insurance, uninsured motorist coverage comes into play. When the liable driver has a policy limit that is not large enough to cover the proven damages, then the underinsured motorist coverage applies. (The amount of uninsured/underinsured coverage available may depend on the plaintiff's own policy limits.) Payments under uninsured and underinsured motorist coverage are not automatic. These cases are often litigated. The injured person often must prove the case with respect to liability, causation, and damages. In some states, these cases are litigated by binding arbitration as opposed to trial by jury.

Lack of Insurance

In a situation where no valid insurance coverage is found to apply to an incident, a liable party may have to pay damages from personal assets. However, occasionally the liable party is judgment proof. This means that there are no substantial assets to satisfy a judgment. Some attorneys prefer not to take a case when there is no valid insurance coverage. Very often, one of the initial inquiries by a plaintiff's attorney is regarding the existence and amount of an insurance policy.

Self-Insured Entities

Some large companies or other entities, such as universities, may decide to self-insure. In other words, they set aside funds to cover the costs of defense and indemnification. Sometimes entities that are self-insured purchase excess coverage. This is insurance coverage that applies once the value of a case reaches a certain amount.

No-Fault Insurance

In 2008, Puerto Rico and 12 states: Florida, Hawaii, Kansas, Kentucky, Massachusetts, Michigan, Minnesota, New Jersey, New York, North Dakota, Pennsylvania, and Utah had no-fault insurance for automobile accidents (http://www.iii.org/media/hottopics/insurance/nofault). In general, under a no-fault system, each party's own insurance covers the damages (up to policy limits) regardless of which party is at fault. This system was created in an attempt to avoid the costly litigation that took place in order to determine who was at fault in accidents. While special damages are covered under the no-fault system, an injured party may still sue for general (noneconomic) damages under certain circumstances as determined by state law and the insurance policy. In general, these cases involve the more serious accidents. More information regarding no-fault insurance can be obtained from the Insurance Information Institute.

Wrongful Death Cases

In wrongful death cases, the damages are not based on the grief of the survivors, but on the loss of the benefits of the relationship, such as the economic support of the deceased person. In some states, there is no recovery for pain and suffering in a wrongful death case. Only certain heirs as outlined in a State's statute are able to sue under the wrongful death statute.

Reasonable Medical Expenses

Should the claimant or plaintiff be found eligible to receive reimbursement for special damages for medical care rendered or anticipated, this is done on the basis of reasonable (usual and customary) fees. The defendant is only responsible for medical specials that are reasonable. The LNC working for defense reviews medical specials to see if charges are within the expected fee range. The LNC working for the plaintiff organizes information regarding the cost of ongoing or anticipated future care.

Role of the Plaintiff LNC in PI Litigation

Discovery

Discovery consists of various legal processes used to gather evidence to determine the facts of a case. Chapter 6 discusses the process in detail.

The intake interview is the initial contact between the attorney and the potential client. The purpose of the interview is to obtain the client's story. The LNC's participation in the initial interview is helpful in a number of ways. The LNC has the knowledge to ask specific questions regarding past medical history, the injury and continuing complaints, and treatment. Many attorneys have their own methodology in conducting intake interviews. Consequently, the LNC should communicate with the attorney to understand the expectations as to her role in the interview process. This can vary considerably. It is helpful if the client has prepared some type of narrative by way of diaries, time lines, or event logs. After the interview, the LNC is a valuable resource to the attorney when discussing the merits of the case. One method to assist in this situation is for the LNC to prepare a work product including the following information:

- Vital statistics
- Mechanism of injury
- Injuries
- Past medical history
- Diagnostics related to injury
- Past and current treatment
- Ongoing problems related to injury
- LNC's comments and analysis
- Records needed

This work product will provide the attorney with an overview of the facts to date, and what is needed to go forth.

After it is determined what records are required, the attorney will proceed with discovery by obtaining those records. It may be important to request, in addition to the medical records, prehospital reports, such as police and ambulance reports. In some cases, employment records may also contain vital information. The LNC may also be responsible for the organization and filing of the medical records, depending on the amount of office support staff. The medical records are then reviewed to establish if any are missing, or if additional records are needed.

A chronology is one of the most useful tools to help the attorney and LNC analyze the data contained in the medical records. A list of all records reviewed should be included, and updated as more records become available. It is important to note that the chronology should be identified as a confidential attorney work product. This ensures that the document is nondiscoverable. The LNC's role in this case is one of attorney support, rather than testifying expert. The chronology should include date/time, Bates stamps if applicable, factual data (test results, progress notes, etc.), provider, and LNC commentary/analysis. The commentary should include definition of terms, explanation of significant test results and critical comments. Again, the attorney may have a particular format or methodology that he or she prefers to incorporate. The chronology is useful in establishing causation and identifying potential weaknesses in the case. A well-formatted chronology often becomes a pivotal part of the case documents.

Example 18.4

Records obtained from prior hospitalization for carpal tunnel surgery with residual weakness were paramount in the defense of a case where the alleged injury was right-hand weakness alleged to have resulted from a cervical disc injury.

The LNC's analysis of medical records and other case-related documents involves issue spotting, identifying facts or statements that may suggest the liability of other parties, inconsistencies of the plaintiff's complaints, and the consistency between the mechanism of injury and the claimed versus documented injuries. The LNC analysis is to identify any issues that require further exploration by the appropriate experts.

In certain computer software programs, the medical chronology takes on sophisticated capabilities such as filtered searches, and the ability to transfer data into timelines and summary judgment reports. A timeline is helpful in certain cases because it shows, at a glance, the type and frequency of care. It is also helpful when timing is an issue in the case.

The LNC involved in a PI case becomes invaluable to the attorney by her use of a thorough literature search regarding medical conditions: anatomy and physiology, injuries suffered by the plaintiff (see Example 18.5), and explanation of medical terminology. As referenced in Chapter 11, the LNC is responsible for educating the attorney on what may be a difficult and complex medical injury for a layperson to grasp. Often in PI cases, the experienced attorney will have become quite well versed in understanding the injury as well as in treatment options. Conversely, there may be cases in which there are unusual injuries and sequelae. The attorney who demonstrates a true understanding of the plaintiff's injuries and resulting treatment has greater success in the litigation proceedings, from filing the complaint to case settlement.

Example 18.5

A 64-year-old seatbelt restrained driver was involved in a MVA where she was hit from behind. She incurred no external head trauma or loss of consciousness (LOC). Her initial complaint in the emergency room was of a headache. A CT scan showed a left parenchymal contusion. She also complained of neck soreness. The physical examination was essentially benign. Her past medical history included anxiety disorder, hypertension, and hypothyroidism.

The plaintiff developed some mild cognitive alterations and increased anxiety following the accident. The attorney had heard of mild traumatic brain injury (MTBI) but needed additional information regarding the correlation of the plaintiff's current somewhat benign injuries and the accident in which a restrained driver had not experienced head or visual injuries.

The literature search on traumatic brain injury (TBI) and MTBI as well as posttraumatic stress disorder (PTSD) provided the framework and understanding necessary for the attorney to successfully settle this case.

In a case that involves a catastrophic injury, a "Day in the Life" video may be a useful tool for settlement or trial purposes. The LNC may be asked to participate in the production of the video. This is often contrasted with a video of the plaintiff prior to the injury to illustrate how the incident has changed the plaintiff's life.

Identification and Location of Experts

Once the plaintiff attorney has agreed to take a case, the LNC in conjunction with the attorney determines the type of liability, causation, and/or damages experts needed. The attorney may request the LNC to assist with location of an expert. This would include obtaining CVs, fee schedules, and discussion of the facts of the case with the expert.

The LNC who chooses to locate experts for plaintiff attorneys for PI cases should begin compiling a database of experts. The LNC should make it clear that the attorney retains the responsibility for ensuring that the chosen experts are providing opinions that are legally sound according to the laws of the particular jurisdiction. See Chapter 15, "Locating and Working with Expert Witnesses," for more details.

A forensic anatomist may testify regarding causation of injury. Some of the factors considered by the forensic anatomist in reaching a conclusion regarding causation involve information contained in the medical record (Figure 18.1). An LNC may be asked to summarize these data from the medical records for this type of expert. In addition to rendering an opinion on the causation of injury, this expert may also be able to unravel disputed facts such as who was driving the vehicle at the time of the accident. This can become an issue when the driver and the passenger are both ejected from the vehicle. A close look at the types of injuries suffered by the occupants provides important clues as well. Usually, the driver suffers injuries that differ from those of the passengers due to contact with the steering wheel. In a side impact, the side of the body that the injuries are on may suggest who was driving.

- Mechanism of injury (e.g., forces of direction of impact, seat, position, use of restraint devices, vehicle specifications)

- Anatomy of the particular plaintiff (e.g., height, weight, congenital anomalies, position of plaintiff at impact – head, hands, arms, torso)

- Data from radiology/imaging studies

- Clinical data (past medical history, postincident medical care)

- Surgical findings (if any)

Figure 18.1 Factors considered by a forensic anatomist in determining the causation of injury in a personal injury case. (Reprinted with permission of Dr. Lawrence Elson.)

Biomechanical/biomedical engineers analyze the effects of various forces on the human body. They apply engineering principles to the biological systems of the human body.

Accident reconstructionists calculate important data regarding the forces involved in a particular motor vehicle collision. Accident reconstruction is discussed in detail later in this chapter. Human factors engineers analyze the interactions of humans with their environment. This type of expert may be used when the possibility of human error is a factor in a case.

Physicians may also serve as causation experts in PI cases. For example, a neuropsychiatrist may be able to testify that a certain type of head injury was the cause of certain cognitive deficits or emotional changes. A neurosurgeon may be needed to testify that injury to the spinal cord at C2 caused the plaintiff's paralysis. A neuroradiologist may be hired to reinterpret diagnostic studies such as magnetic resonance imaging and CT scans.

Forensic pathologists render opinions regarding the cause of death. For example, a pathologist may be used to testify how a blunt head trauma caused intracranial bleeding, leading to increased intracranial pressure, tentorial herniation, and brain death. The pathologist may also be able to determine which of many injuries actually caused the death. This can be important in PI cases.

Vocational experts determine whether a plaintiff can perform specific job functions given the disabilities from an injury. They can determine the degree of impairment and disability. They may also determine the need for vocational rehabilitation if the person is not able to return to duties of his customary job.

A life care planner, usually a registered nurse with certification in life care planning or related specialties, evaluates the future needs of a severely injured plaintiff and determines the cost of those products and services over the life of the plaintiff. The life care planner then drafts a life care plan for use in calculating damages in the case. An economist may be utilized to calculate damages in terms of the future value of the medical costs, adjusted for inflation. Economists may also help determine the loss of future income, or the amount of income the client would have earned had there been no accident and related injuries. (See Volume 2, Chapter 2, "The Expert Fact Witness: Non-economic Damages Testimony.")

Life expectancy experts are actuaries, PhDs, and occasionally, medical doctors who render opinions regarding the plaintiff's life expectancy, taking into account many factors unique to that plaintiff. Predicted life expectancy is important when future damages are to be calculated for the rest of an injured person's life. As one would expect, the defense life expectancy expert often predicts a shorter life expectancy than a plaintiff's expert in these situations.

Defense Medical Examination (DME) Attendance

In a PI case, the state code of civil procedure provides for an examination by a physician of the defendant's choosing. This is called the independent medical examination (IME). Some states allow the plaintiff's attorney or a representative of the plaintiff's attorney to attend this examination. This is a perfect role for the LNC.

The LNC accompanies the client to the exam on a prearranged date, time, and location. Depending on the discovery code of the state, an LNC may be allowed to audiotape or videotape the examination in addition to observing it and taking notes. The LNC then reviews the IME physician's report. The LNC will, if necessary, testify regarding what she observed. For example, the LNC may have documented that the client grimaced during the shoulder range-of-motion examination, but the physician reported that there was full range of motion without pain. Also, the LNC can be called to testify (without being disclosed in advance) as an impeachment witness to refute the testimony of the IME physician. Generally, the LNC who is attending the IME is not the same LNC who is reviewing the other aspects of the case. The role of attorney's representative at the IME compromises the LNC's behind-the-scenes, nontestifying role. For more information on the IME, see Chapter 19, "Defense Medical Evaluations."

Preparation of Documents

The LNC may assist the attorney in drafting documents used for settlement negotiations. Prior to filing a lawsuit, the attorney often sends a demand letter to the insurance company. This letter sets out the liability of the tortfeasor (the person committing the tort) as well as the injuries suffered by the attorney's client. The LNC will review the medical records and extract, interpret, and summarize important information to persuade the insurance company to settle with the injured party. The LNC is also adept at suggesting exhibits from the medical records to illustrate the points made in the demand letter. The LNC may also list and calculate the medical care costs to date.

After the case is filed, the attorney will often put together a settlement package for the insurance company. This may be more complex than the demand letter. The LNC is able to assist the attorney in preparation of this package as well. These settlement documents need to paint a picture of the injured client. The LNC's skill in extracting key information from the medical records and effectively communicating this information adds heightened clarification to what are often complexities in the client's scenario. See Chapter 16, "Alternative Dispute Resolution: Settlement, Arbitration, and Mediation," for more information.

There are a number of other legal documents, including Opinion Statements and Bills of Particulars that the LNC may assist in preparing, depending on individual state law. These documents are prepared with the testifying expert to memorialize their opinions related to causation, liability, and the injury.

Deposition Preparation

The LNCs role in depositions is defined in detail in Chapter 6, "Discovery and Disclosure." Initially, the LNC can assist with question preparation focused on discovery of facts supportive of the allegations. The plaintiff attorney will be deposing the defendant(s), defense experts, and any identified witnesses.

Trial

The LNC can assist the attorney in preparing for trial in many ways. The LNC, as a trained patient educator, possesses the skills to assist the attorney in creating or obtaining the demonstrative evidence that will best illustrate the points of the case to the jury. The LNC may identify entries in the medical records that may be "blown up" for presentation to the jury. The LNC may suggest items, diagrams, or charts that would help to educate the jury about the case.

Example 18.6

In a case involving an accident resulting in quadriplegia, the plaintiff LNC demonstrated use of a Hoyer lift to the jury to explain how the plaintiff must be transferred.

The LNC can assist a graphics artist in creating charts, diagrams, and timelines that can make information and associations clear. This type of demonstrative evidence assists the jury in understanding the nature of the injury.

The LNC may review the depositions of medical witnesses and suggest further questions to be asked during trial. In addition, the LNC will perform research on issues arising before or during trial. The LNC is also skilled in preparing the testifying experts as well as providing emotional support to the client prior to their testimony. See Chapter 14 for more information.

With a solid clinical nursing background, the LNC is well suited to the unique role of expert fact witness. The expert fact witness reviews the medical records and medical literature relevant to the case. The LNC then explains this factual material to the jury in "layperson's" terms. This LNC gives no opinion regarding the standard of care (which is not usually an issue in a PI case). This role of expert fact witness is one that will serve the attorney well in a PI case, especially when the medical records are voluminous or confusing. This LNC role is also valuable to the defense attorney when there is a significant amount of past medical history that may weaken the plaintiff's claims of injury.

Role of the Defense LNC in PI Litigation

The Defense Clients

Unlike the plaintiff LNC who has a single client, the plaintiff's attorney, the defense-oriented LNC may have different types of clients. A primary client is the insurance claims adjuster. Claims adjusters evaluate claimed injuries and the associated damages. The defense LNC may work with claims adjusters employed by the defendant's insurance company or the defendant company. Self-insured companies or organizations may handle some or all of PI claims in-house, within a risk management department. In other cases, the self-insured company may outsource evaluation and processing of claims to a third-party administrator (TPA), which employs the claims adjuster.

Depending on the monetary exposure, claims adjusters have the authority to settle claims on liability cases. The claims adjuster contracts the defense LNC for assistance in understanding the nature and extent of injury and to determine whether medical specials are reasonable. The claims adjuster may contract the LNC because of suspicion that the defendant did not cause the injury as alleged, or when then the severity of the alleged injury is questioned. The claims adjuster may also engage the LNC services because of the volume, complexity, or illegibility (to a layperson) of the medical records. Particular to the insurance company, the claims adjuster may handle a mix of property and PI claims. Given that, the defense LNC may encounter a claims adjuster with limited medical knowledge.

A rare type of medical records review from a claims adjuster is a first-party claim, in which the claimant is also the insured. For instance, it may be questioned whether the admission for chest pain following the accident was related to the accident or a pre-existing cardiac condition.

Once alleged damages have reached a certain dollar demand, or should a suit be filed, there may be a change in the assignment of the case from a claims adjuster in a liability unit to a claims adjuster in a litigation-only unit. The LNC will generally find the claims adjuster in the litigation unit to have more than average general medical knowledge. At this point, the LNC may become involved with the defense attorney hired by the defendant's insurance company. The claims adjuster generally forwards the LNC's findings to the defense attorney. The LNC may be asked to discuss findings with the defense attorney and/or perform a review of additional medical records as these become available via subpoena. Depending on the insurance company, the claims adjuster may or may not have contact with the LNC once a defense attorney is involved. Regardless, the LNC needs to be astute in keeping the claims adjuster apprised of all LNC activity on the file; the claims adjuster is the LNC's primary client.

The defense LNC needs to be aware of the potential for animosity from the defense attorney. The claims adjuster may utilize the LNC's cost-effective expertise in preparing a chronology and summary of the medical records instead of having this completed by the defense attorney or a non-nurse paralegal in the attorney's office. In other words, defense LNC services are somewhat forced upon the defense attorney in order to reduce defense attorney costs. Not dissimilar to dealing with disagreeable patients or physicians, the defense LNC can develop a working relationship with the somewhat reluctant defense attorney through provision of an excellent chronology and analysis of the medical records and meeting the attorneys informational needs and deadlines.

Defense attorneys knowledgeable of the benefits of LNC consulting services may directly engage the LNC. In this case, the LNC may be an employee of the defense attorney's office or be hired as an independent consultant. The defense attorney often contacts the independent defense LNC for an estimation of the cost of the medical record review prior to asking for permission of the defendant (defendant's insurance company) to use LNC consulting. The benefit of LNC services needs to outweigh the cost of LNC services. The cost of LNC services needs to be budgeted for by the defendant; the insurer also needs to consider the costs of LNC and other consulting services as part of the total cost of settling or litigating a claim.

Clients of the defense LNC also include governmental agencies. State and local governments may be self-insured, processing their own PI claims. Examples of such claims include MVAs involving government-owned vehicles, injuries sustained on the premises of governmental property, or allegations of injuries by incarcerated prisoners. In such cases, the LNC may be working with government employed claims adjusters, city attorneys, assistant attorney generals, or government hired defense attorneys.

Excellence in Defense Analysis

Excellence in analysis by the defense LNC requires integration of three domains of information: the medical records, current medical literature, and utilization review/current treatment practices. The LNC's unique ability to wield this information is what creates the distinct role for the defense LNC.

The typical defense client, the experienced claims adjuster or the defense attorney, can read and understand a large part, but not all, of the medical records. It is natural for the layperson reading a medical record to focus on what is easily understood. That being the case, the layperson can unknowingly miss a critical case fact and area of defense. The LNC has the proficiency to interpret and comprehend the entire medical record, insuring that all potential medical-related defenses are gleaned from the medical record.

It may be argued that a physician would be better able to understand the medical records than the LNC. However, a physician performing a medical record review tends to focus on physician-written records, paying less attention to ancillary records which may contain critical information regarding the plaintiff's functional status and credibility. Further, the LNC review costs much less than a physician review. In most circumstances, it is a defense work product, meaning that the defense LNC's findings do not have to be disclosed to the plaintiff's attorney prior to trial.

Example 18.7

A plaintiff alleging injury to a shoulder joint from an MVA presented with anterior shoulder pain and reduced shoulder range of motion when examined by the treating physician. Defense LNC review of subsequent physical therapy treatment notes found references to indicate the plaintiff had been painting a ceiling at home, which provided an alternative explanation for the complaints and examination findings.

With Internet access, it is easy for the claims professional or defense attorney to obtain current medical information. However, the defense LNC can discern the authority and quality of the information source. In addition, the defense LNC's nursing education and clinical experience assist the LNC in identifying critical connections between record facts and allegations that the layperson may not make.

Example 18.8

The plaintiff alleged cervical disc herniation requiring surgery and neurogenic bladder resulting from MVA. The claims adjuster contracted the defense LNC because of the allegation of neurogenic bladder and concern that the plaintiff had sustained a permanent spinal cord injury. The LNC's review found that the symptoms of neurogenic bladder did not onset until months after the accident. There was also no evidence the plaintiff had been compliant with urinary diagnostics tests, and the plaintiff was taking several medications with a potential side effect of urinary retention.

Utilization review refers to the determination that appropriate care has been delivered for a given diagnosis. Utilization review is the reason for precertification for nonemergency hospital admissions and outpatient procedures. Aspects of utilization review are present throughout the health insurance delivery. This is largely concurrent, meaning that it occurs when the care is being delivered, either through the Health Insurance Company or internal monitoring by the health care provider.

With the exception of worker's compensation injuries, there is generally no concurrent utilization review for PI cases. Therefore, there can be a tendency for the health care provider to recommend more treatment for the plaintiff than what would typically be rendered if a health insurance company was the payer.

With PI cases, there is no incentive for the injured party to be frugal with medical treatment. The settlement for pain and suffering (general damages) is often based on the medical specials. Therefore, the plaintiff may have the incentive to treat more, not less.

The defense LNC evaluates retrospectively whether the treatment rendered in a PI case was in line with current treatment practices at the time the injury occurred. The defendant's insurance company is responsible for the usual and customary treatment for the injuries found to be related to the accident in question. The plaintiff and defendant will likely have different opinions as to what was reasonable, usual, and customary. The defense LNC's findings relative to the course and cost of treatment are valuable to the claims adjuster and defense attorney for planning and negotiating. There are several publications that the LNC may utilize as resources regarding treatment practices and expected treatment cost. These include *The Medical Disability Adviser* (Reed, 2005), *Physicians' Fee and Coding* Guide (MAG, 2007), and *Managing Physical/Occupational/Speech Therapy & Rehabilitation Care* (Apollo Managed Care, 2008).

ABCs of Report Writing for the Defense

The LNC primarily communicates with the claims adjuster or the defense attorney via a written report. Well-written reports meet the client's educational needs and can provide the basis for defense strategy. By consistently applying the ABCs (Accuracy, Brevity, and Completeness) of reporting writing, the LNC can produce a quality report, which ultimately serves to build one's defense LNC's practice. More information regarding report writing can be found in *Report Preparation*, Chapter 13.

A is for Accuracy; no statements are made within the report to the defense client that are not consistent with the facts in the provided medical records or literature consulted for the analysis.

B is for brevity, stating facts and completing analysis in as few as words as possible without loss of meaning. Defense attorneys and claims adjusters are almost always pressed for time. Writing a succinct report often takes no less time than a long cumbersome report. In fact, the reverse may be true.

C is for completeness; no pertinent information relative to the allegations, record review, or defense client request can be omitted from the LNC's written report. The report's value to the defense is diminished when all pertinent facts have not been included.

Defense LNC Analysis Tactics

Adherence to the ABCs is the basis for D, the best defense-oriented report. There are other tactics the defense LNC can use to facilitate the process. Of particular importance is *facts first*. Facts first refers to writing the report summary in such a way that the defense client can easily distinguish facts in the case from the LNC's opinion. The LNC may briefly report knee operative findings in a single paragraph and then provide the reader information regarding the anatomy and clinical significance of the findings in the next paragraph.

Follow format is another way for the LNC to include potential areas of defense. Almost all medical disciplines follow SOAP (subjective, objective findings, assessment, plan) or similar charting format. The defense LNC should do the same when presenting case facts and when analyzing facts for potential areas of defense. Of particular importance to large medical record reviews for complex personal injuries is the concept of the *big fish*. The big fish is the injury of most financial importance to the defense client. This may or may not be the injury for which the plaintiff has received the most treatment; it may be the injury with the most potential impairment or disability.

Example 18.9

An older plaintiff sustained sprain/strain injury to the neck and back and tibial plateau fracture as a result of an MVA. Bills for primary physician and chiropractic treatment were greater than for the tibial plateau fracture that was treated conservatively. However, the tibial plateau fracture was the big fish, because anticipated total knee joint replacement was part of the alleged damages.

The defense LNC needs to know the *cut off*, or that point at which treatment no longer appears related to the respective accident or injury. The defense client may use this information in calculating a settlement offer. The cutoff may be easy to identify in a young person sustaining a femur fracture; it would likely coincide with the date the treating orthopedist released the plaintiff from treatment. The cutoff however, may be difficult to identify in an elderly person sustaining a hip fracture because of the morbidity and long-term effects associated with this injury.

There are PI cases reviewed by the defense LNC in which obvious patterns of inconsistent reporting are noted. These may include treatment noncompliance, prescription abuse, symptom magnification, etc. Once identified by the defense LNC, the discussion of these patterns in the report to the defense client is *extra gravy*. The LNC may not need to discuss in detail each of the incidents, but may provide an overview in a chart or table format. This information can be powerful during settlement negotiations or trial.

The defense LNC needs to be aware of the *eggshell* plaintiff, the fragile plaintiff with significant pre-existing conditions that affect the risk as well as the recovery from injury. An eggshell plaintiff will generally allege greater injury and damages. Particularly with the eggshell plaintiff, the defense LNC needs to look for the *banana peel effect*. The banana peel effect refers to the possibility that progression of the pre-existing condition(s) could be primarily responsible for the plaintiff's postaccident health status, not the alleged injury. Such an example would be a poorly controlled diabetic with a history of peripheral neuropathy alleging lumbar nerve root compression from a herniated disc.

The defense LNC needs to avoid *slippery slopes*. In this situation, the defense LNC may place too much emphasis on a finding that leads the LNC and the defense client away from more important issues. For example, in the case of a plaintiff with multiple previous compensable injuries, the LNC may find reason to question the veracity of previously offered impairment ratings because of incomplete preaccident medical records. However, instead of questioning the degree of the plaintiff's preaccident impairment, the defense LNC may better serve the defense client by discussing the implication of the impairment rating. The impairment rating implies that the individual is expected to have symptoms or abnormal physical exam findings despite further medical or surgical treatment.

Response to Plaintiff Demand Letter/Package

The defense LNC's responsibilities may involve assisting the claims adjuster or defense attorney with a response to the plaintiff's demand letter. The plaintiff's demand letter is read prior to review of the medical records, but is not specifically dealt with until after completion of the defense client report. At this time, the defense LNC will know the content of the medical records better than the defense client. Therefore, the defense LNC can objectively respond to statements made in the plaintiff's demand letter, paying particularly attention to any statements that do not appear completely consistent with the provided records.

Motor Vehicle Accident

The LNC should be knowledgeable in the mechanisms of various injuries. One of the most common mechanisms of PI cases for the LNC is the MVA.

Vehicles involved in PI claims may be motorized, such as cars, trucks, motorcycles, golf carts, boats, all terrain vehicles, snowmobiles, jet skis, amusement park rides, buses, motorized wheel chairs, and airplanes, or nonmotorized, such as bicycles, skis, and snowboards. With regard to the motor vehicles operated on roadways and highways, there are various categories of MVAs. Motor vehicles can be rear-ended, side-swiped, hit head-on, rolled over, involved in a chain reaction event, or a combination of two or more of these events.

Mechanisms of Injury

Knowledge of the occupant kinematics (from the Greek *kinein*, which means to move) is utilized to determine if the mechanism of the claimed injury existed in the subject incident (i.e., did the person move in such a way that this injury could be generated?). To better appreciate the occupant kinematics of a specific event, one must first be familiar with the principles of basic physics, as dictated by Newton's Laws of Motion. Newton's first law states that a body at rest will remain at rest and a body in motion will remain in motion unless acted upon by an external force. In other words, a body that is standing still will stay immobile unless acted upon by a force and, likewise, a body that is moving will continue to move at that rate unless acted upon by an external force. An occupant in a motor vehicle travels at the same speed as the motor vehicle. Force is defined as the cause or instrument that alters the motion of an object. Forces are defined by two characteristics: magnitude (intensity) and direction, and both of these properties influence the motion of the body and thus the mechanism of injury.

Newton's second law explains the association between the force applied to the body to initiate its change of motion, the length of time that the force is applied, the extent of velocity change (commonly called delta V) that the body experiences, and the body's mass. For example, assume that two vehicles of the same mass are traveling at the same speed and both decrease their forward velocity to zero, but by different methods. The first vehicle slows down when the brake is applied, generating a force at the tire/road boundary that acts on the vehicle, and causes it to decelerate and come to a stop. The second vehicle collides with a stationary object (such as a wall), generating a force at the wall/vehicle interface that acts on the vehicle and causes it to rapidly decelerate. The first experiences a *small* force over a *long* period of time and the vehicle that collides with the wall experiences a *large* force over a *short* period of time. When the vehicle hits the wall, the wall does not move, and thus the majority of the energy is dissipated through deformation (e.g., crushing) of the vehicle structures (e.g., bumper, hood, etc.). The occupant of the braking vehicle will slow as the vehicle slows, resulting in minimal motion of the body relative to the vehicle interior. When the vehicle hits the wall and stops suddenly, the occupant continues moving at his initial speed (e.g., the speed of the vehicle before impact). The restrained occupant moves forward at his initial speed within the compartment until he is slowed by interaction with the seatbelt and/or airbag, whereas the unrestrained occupant continues his forward motion within the compartment with little reduction in speed and strikes the interior surfaces (steering wheel, dashboard, windshield) that have slowed due to impact. These interactions with the seatbelt, airbag, or interior structures can cause injuries that provide insight into the occupant's state of restraint use (e.g., belted or unbelted).

Newton's third and final law states that for every force there is an equal and opposite force or response. This law is demonstrated when two cars hit each other head-on. Each vehicle experiences the force from the other pushing against its front bumper. Neglecting deformation in both vehicles, these forces are equal. Also, when an unrestrained occupant contacts the vehicle interior, the force causing the injury to the body is matched by an equal and opposite force on the vehicle structure. This may result in physical evidence of contact, which is revealed by inspection of the vehicle after the accident.

Experts

The accident reconstructionist and the biomechanical engineer are two experts with whom the LNC may work. The LNC assists these experts in the investigation of the PI claim by reviewing and analyzing the medical records to find relevant information regarding the type, severity, and location of the alleged trauma. Additionally, the LNC must ascertain prior medical injuries and illnesses that may impact the current claimed injuries. Detailed reports of these findings are valuable to assist the engineer in determining body position at the time of injury, quantifying the forces that produced the injuries, and facilitating the reenactment of the event.

Biomechanics is the application of the principles of engineering and physics to the human body. The biomechanical engineer studies the movements of the body and the forces that act upon the musculoskeletal system. These data are instrumental in determining the mechanism of injury. Biomechanical engineers consider the medical diagnoses in a given injury, when calculating accelerations, forces, or torques (twisting effort applied to an object that makes the object turn about its axis of rotation) that may apply.

The accident reconstructionist analyzes the damage to the vehicle and evidence from the scene to determine how the event happened and the motions of the vehicle during the event. The reconstructionist often inspects an exemplar (similar body type) vehicle as part of his analysis, pays meticulous attention to the details of the crash regarding the scene topography and specific conditions present at the time of the accident, and may utilize three-dimensional computer simulation and analysis software to recreate the accident.

Records

The LNC will find it extremely beneficial to review several different types of reports prior to completing the work product for the biomechanical engineer or accident reconstructionist. Police reports offer information that is important in evaluating the PI case. In general, police reports provide personal information of the victims, aberrant conditions at the time of the accident, vehicle data, diagrams, as well as airbag and seat belt status.

Eyewitness reports contain observations by those who were in the vicinity of the accident at the time of the event. Eyewitnesses may provide information regarding actions that occurred prior to, during or after the event, or the nature of the injuries sustained by the occupants. These individuals are usually deposed and may be called for testimony at trial.

Medical records for the claimant prior to the event provide valuable information regarding health and medical conditions up to the date of the subject incident. Many past and current illnesses and injuries may influence the extent of the claimant's current injuries. For example, if the claimant has a history of diabetes and receives an open wound during the accident, prolonged wound healing or nonhealing may be attributable to the medical condition.

First responder reports contain valuable information regarding the activity at the scene. They contain data regarding the position of the vehicle occupants, the position of those ejected from the vehicle, safety restraint usage, airbag deployment, complaints of those involved, estimated or stated weights, description of visible injuries, information regarding possible use of alcohol or drugs, vital signs, and medical interventions performed in the field. Data regarding the position of the occupants, especially those who are ejected, as well as estimates of the intrusion distance into the compartments of the vehicle, the use of the Jaws of Life or other extrication equipment on the vehicle, and other vehicle damage information (such as steering wheel deformation) are extremely important to the engineer and reconstructionist in simulating the event (e.g., determining the motion of the vehicle and the response of the occupants).

Emergency Department records are valuable in providing descriptions of the external injuries (e.g., ecchymosis, abrasions, lacerations, redness, swelling, deformity, open fractures), as well as related diagnosis. Bruises that are noted laterally on the neck, diagonally across the chest, and horizontally across the iliac crest area may be referred to as "seatbelt sign" by the medical staff. Seatbelt sign refers to bruising caused by the occupant loading the seatbelt restraint system during the event. These are particularly important for the LNC to document, since use of the restraint system may be a key factor in the legal claim. The victim's height and weight are used when locating surrogates (substitute persons) for reconstruction of the event.

The engineer utilizes information the LNC has obtained from the hospital records. When the engineer performs a vehicle inspection armed with knowledge of the documented injuries and their specific body locations, he/she will examine the vehicle for "witness marks" (evidence on the vehicle indicative of occupant contact and/or location of injury). For example, in the case of an injured driver with lacerations on the right side of his forehead and scalp, the engineer will examine the windshield's rearview mirror to see if it is cracked and askew with hair embedded in the glass fragments. Based on similar findings, the rearview mirror would thus be a possible cause of the laceration to the driver's head.

Radiological imaging studies are useful in determining the forces that caused the injuries. Specific types of forces applied to the human body at different angles produce specific types of injuries. For example, if the driver of a vehicle has a dislocated hip from a head-on collision, the engineer knows that a specified amount of force against the patella can cause the hip to dislocate from the acetabulum. Imaging studies are reviewed to see if the acetabulum shows evidence of dislocation, the medical records are reviewed for evidence of knee bruising or discoloration, and the vehicle is inspected for evidence of knee contact to the lower dash or other forward structures.

Operative reports frequently contain details of the injuries that cannot be found elsewhere. Well-written operative reports contain very explicit descriptions of the internal injuries encountered, such as areas of internal lacerations, ruptures, and contusions, and detailed descriptions of fractures. On occasion, photographs will be taken by the surgeon. These are excellent resources for the LNC to provide to the biomechanical engineer and reconstructionist since they are the visual documentation of the actual injuries, not merely descriptions.

Pathology reports contain detailed descriptions of body parts removed and are often beneficial in the investigations of injuries involving amputated limbs. Autopsy reports include information regarding all of the body systems and the internal and external injuries. The autopsy report frequently includes photographs taken prior to the procedure, allowing the LNC to visualize the injury that the pathologist describes.

LNC medical record review for accident reconstruction extends beyond the initial ER and hospital treatment.

Accident Reconstruction

Type of Event

To determine the type of event that occurred, the biomechanical engineer and/or the reconstructionist performs a thorough investigation of the accident to develop a chronological account of the incident that is consistent with the known physical evidence. The investigation consists of a systematic review of documents, identification of technical issues, documentation of the accident site, and inspection of the vehicles involved. Vehicle inspections are frequently performed years after the actual event occurred. The vehicle is rigorously examined and numerous photographs are taken. After all of the information has been collected and analyzed, the event can be recreated on a vehicle test track or in a computer simulation.

Reports Reviewed

As previously mentioned, the LNC reviews many relevant reports (both medical and nonmedical) to provide vital information to the biomechanical engineer and the accident reconstructionist. The LNC composes a chronology to include information from the police report, the emergency medical services report, postaccident medical records, and prior medical records, if available.

Other expert reports from the opposing side of the case should be reviewed to ascertain the opposing points of view. Review of the opposing reports provides insight into their approach to the case and possible rebuttal points.

Injury Information

The biomechanical engineer applies basic engineering principles and the scientific method to the analysis of the factual information acquired from the investigation of the event. Medical records and radiological imaging studies are critical evidence utilized in the biomechanical analysis. Human injury tolerance data, including bone fracturing strengths, joint movement and injury thresholds, and soft tissue characteristics, provide additional evidence in the analysis of the injuries.

Specific claimant data are important when performing a surrogate analysis in an exemplar vehicle. A surrogate analysis usually involves a surrogate of the same height and weight as the claimant, seated in an exemplar vehicle. The purpose of the study can range from determining distances from specific body points to internal vehicle components to visualizing how the seatbelt fits around the surrogate's body and corresponds to the evidence.

The following is an illustration of how the injuries are used as data to analyze a case.

Example 18.10

The driver of a van claimed that a young child was inside the rear compartment of the van when the rear lift gate door opened and the child fell out onto the ground. The child died as a result of the injuries sustained in the accident. The child's injuries, as described in the autopsy report, were diffuse subarachnoid hemorrhage, bilateral parietal skull contusions, fracture of the right femur, contusion of the right thigh, fractures of the left parietal and temporal bones, scalp detachment on the left side of the head, and fractures of the left ninth and tenth ribs. The biomechanical engineer was able to demonstrate by the bilateral distribution, location, and severity of the injuries that the injuries were not consistent with a child falling out of a van, but were caused by the driver backing into the child while he was walking behind the van and knocking him to the ground with substantial force. The contusions on the right parietal skull and the right shoulder were determined to be from contact with the closed rear lift gate door of the van, the fracture of the right femur and the contusions of the right thigh were caused by contact with the rear bumper of the van, and the left-sided head injuries and fractured ribs were determined to be caused by contact with the ground as the child fell.

Event Reconstruction/Re-Enactment

A simulation or re-enactment of the subject incident may be performed to assess the body position, movement, and contacts prior to and at the time of impact, and to determine the injury mechanism present. The event can be re-enacted in the form of a crash test or via computer modeling. This includes utilizing instrumented exemplar vehicles (recording vehicle accelerations and other parameters) and anthropomorphic test devices (ATDs), frequently referred to as "crash test dummies" (recording the loads acting upon the occupant). The crash test dummy acts as a mechanical surrogate of the human and is used to evaluate occupant motion and injury potential during collisions.

Premise Liability

Investigation of other types of PI cases proceeds in a manner similar to the analysis of vehicular accidents. Premise liability is an area of litigation in which the LNC may be requested to assist in reviewing medical records. Allegations may include slips due to wet floors or carpet defects, trips due to uneven steps or holes in the sidewalk, and falls due to uneven walkways or poorly placed decorative features.

The LNC will review the medical records for evidence of factors that may have contributed to the incident, such as current medical conditions, or the ingestion of specific medications, alcohol or drugs, which could possibly cause impaired reasoning or unsteady gait. The LNC would also look for details regarding the specific sidewalk conditions (as reported in the police report and/or the EMS report) and include this information in the chronology.

Others (Pharmacy Errors, Food Poisoning)

Another type of PI case in which the LNC may become involved is prescription error litigation. In this type of PI case, the claimant alleges injury as a result of receiving the wrong medication, an incorrect dosage, or experiencing a dangerous drug reaction that was missed by the pharmacist. Generally, LNC services are requested in these cases if the reported pharmacy error results in significant symptoms and medical bills, such as those requiring hospitalization.

Example 18.11

A pharmacy error resulted in the plaintiff receiving an incorrect dosage of Coumadin (5 mg tablets instead of 2 mg tablets) causing a gastrointestinal bleed requiring hospitalization.

Another area in which the LNC is a valuable asset is reviewing the records in cases of food-borne illness or injury claims. There are a number of different types of illnesses/injuries in this category. Injury claims may include trauma to the gastrointestinal tract due to the ingestion of foreign substances in food or drink, such as glass or metal. The LNC performs a thorough review of the medical records to determine if the symptoms are consistent with the alleged exposure or injury as other means of contact may have caused the illness or injury.

Common Injuries

Head Injuries

According to Langlois, Rutland-Brown, and Thomas (2004), the four most common causes of TBI are falls, MVA, struck by/against events, and assaults. Significant injuries, such as skull fracture or subdural hematoma, have abnormal structural imaging and in most cases have more significant permanent sequelae; therefore damages are usually evident and more severe. The definition of MTBI was developed by the Mild Traumatic Brain Injury Committee of the Head Injury Interdisciplinary Special Interest Group of the American Congress of Rehabilitation Medicine. A patient with MTBI is a person who has had a traumatically induced physiological disruption of brain function, within defined criteria. Concussion is now defined as MTBI (www.cdc.gov). With MTBI there is usually normal structural imaging, therefore damages are often not as evident. Neuropsychological, psychiatric, and vocational evaluations are often helpful in assessing damages. A neuropsychological evaluation is a comprehensive assessment of higher cognitive abilities performed in order to identify deficits in brain function. In addition, new neuroimaging techniques are being utilized to identify injury.

Psychiatric Injuries

Plaintiff and defense LNCs are increasingly becoming involved with psychiatric injuries. Examples of psychiatric injuries include PTSD and depression or adjustment disorder, anxiety, and depression often related to sexual harassment in the work place. Psychiatric injuries may be alleged in conjunction with physical injuries. The LNC proceeds with the review using the same process followed for a physical injury. Of particular importance in psychiatric cases is the plaintiff's pre-existing psychosocial history and level of function in the social, academic, and occupational settings.

Chest and Abdominal Injuries

MVAs and motorcycle accidents account for the majority of chest trauma seen in PI litigation. The severity of the injury is directly related to the mechanism of trauma. Researchers have determined that minor chest injuries occur in 30% of people involved in MVAs. This is in fact due to the "seatbelt syndrome." The injury occurs as a result of the restraining loads exerted on the restrained occupant by a seatbelt during a collision (Hill, 2004). Rib fractures and their sequelae are the most common result of blunt chest trauma. Blunt trauma may cause a myriad of intrathoracic injuries including pneumothorax, hemothorax, cardiac and pulmonary contusions or an aortic tear (Bradley, 2001).

Spinal Injuries

Common types of spinal injuries alleged in PI claims are herniated discs, fractures, and spinal cord injuries. Cases involving disc problems and fractures may require many months of ongoing therapy, and the LNC may review voluminous medical records. The medical documents must be scrutinized to determine other possible causes of the ongoing and/or changing complaints, such as falls, workers compensation events, or MVAs that may have occurred before or after the subject incident. Severe spinal cord injury cases will often utilize a life care planner (frequently an LNC) who will provide a report containing the types and monetary value of treatments, medications, and therapies required by the claimant over the remainder of his/her life. This report will also include psychosocial environment modification and equipment necessary for activities of daily living. This report is an integral part of the plaintiff attorney's case, as the monetary damages considered for settlement are based on an accurate depiction of the ongoing needs derived from the facts presented in the report.

Orthopedic Injuries

Sprains, strains, fractures, and dislocations occur frequently in accident situations. The LNC thoroughly reviews the medical records for evidence of prior injuries and similar complaints that may affect the current symptoms. Claimants with orthopedic injuries may undergo ongoing therapies, examination for impairment ratings, functional capacity evaluations, workers compensation evaluations, and IMEs. With long-term orthopedic complaints, the plaintiff LNC concentrates on the claimant's disabilities and the effect on the claimant's ability to earn a living, family life, personal relationships, and recreational activities. The defense LNC attempts to determine whether the claimed disabilities were pre-existing and whether the reported level of functioning is compatible with the symptoms reported. Both the defense and plaintiff LNC closely examines the medical records for evidence of prior activity levels, including recreational activities, and other events that may have contributed to the current allegations.

Soft Tissue Injury/Chronic Pain Syndromes

Soft tissue injuries of the spine also referred to as whiplash, sprain/strains, and hyperflexion/hyper-extension injuries are some of the most common claim-related injuries. With this type of injury, it is not uncommon for the plaintiff to seek untraditional treatment, such as massage or acupuncture. A challenge for the LNC in reviewing this type of case is the monotony of the subjective complaints; there may be limited objective physical examination and diagnostics findings.

Often related to soft tissue injury are allegations of chronic pain syndromes, which may include fibromyalgia, myofascial pain syndrome, and reflex sympathetic dystrophy [RSD, also known as complex regional pain syndrome (CRPS)]. With any of these conditions, the plaintiff LNC focus is on the plaintiff's suffering and how the condition has affected the plaintiff's activities of daily living. In contrast, the defense LNC's review focuses on possible nontraumatic factors contributing to complaints and whether there are inconsistencies in the reported symptoms and functioning.

Conclusion

The role of the LNC in PI investigation and litigation has expanded. LNCs are making significant contributions in the PI litigation process as well as in accident reconstruction.

References

Apollo Managed Care. (2008). Managing physical/occupational/speech therapy & rehabilitation care (6th ed.). Santa Barbara, CA: Apollo Managed Care.

Bradley, J. P. (2001). Traumatic rupture of the thoracic aorta; endoluminal approach. *The Internet Journal of Thoracic and Cardiovascular Surgery*, 4(1). http://www.iii.org/media/hottopics/insurance/nofault/

Hill, J. R. (2004, February). Chest and abdominal injuries caused by seat belt loading. *Accident, Analysis & Prevention*, 11.

Langlois, J. A., Rutland-Brown W., & Thomas K. E. (2004). *Traumatic brain injury in the United States: Emergency department visits, hospitalizations, and deaths*. Atlanta: Centers for Disease Control and Prevention, National Center for Injury Prevention and Control.

MAG Mutual Healthcare Solutions, Inc. (2007). *Physicians' fee and coding guide 2008*. Duluth, GA: MAG Mutual Healthcare Solutions, Inc.

Melhorn, J. M, & Ackerman, W. E. (2008). *Guides to the evaluation of disease and injury causation*. Chicago, IL: American Medical Association.

Reed, P. (2005). *The medical disability adviser: Disability duration guidelines* (5th ed.). Boulder, CO: Reed Group Ltd. www.cdc.gov

Additional Reading

http://.www.exponent.com

Melvin, J. W., & Nahum, A. M. (Eds.). (2002). *Accidental injury biomechanics and prevention* (2nd ed.). New York: Springer.

Test Questions

1. Which statement *is not* true regarding the purpose of PI litigation?
    A. It provides a mechanism for awarding compensation
    B. It provides an incentive to act safely in conduct that affects others
    C. It determines criminal charges against those found liable
    D. It allocates accountability to the party with the most control over the conditions that cause risk

2. The burden of proof in a tort case is the preponderance of evidence standard. This means
    A. It must be proven beyond a reasonable doubt
    B. When just over 50% of the evidence is in favor of the party
    C. When less than 50% of the evidence is in favor of the party
    D. None of the above

3. The LNC working for the plaintiff attorney may assist in preparing documents. They would include all of the following *except*
    A. The accident report
    B. Bill of Particulars
    C. Demand Letter
    D. Opinion Statement

4. The defense LNC may work directly with the following, *except*
    A. The insurance claims adjuster
    B. The claimant's attorney
    C. The claims adjuster in the litigation unit
    D. The defense attorney

5. Which of the following documents *does not* provide important information for the accident reconstructionist?
    A. The traffic collision report
    B. Eye witness accounts
    C. An informed consent form
    D. An injury diagram

6. When the medical provider documents that the patient had a "seatbelt sign," what three body areas may be included?
    A. Neck, chest, and back
    B. Chest, abdomen, and thigh
    C. Neck, chest, and iliac crests
    D. Chest, iliac crests, and back

Answers: 1. C, 2. B, 3. A, 4. B, 5. C, 6. C

Chapter 19

Defense Medical Evaluations

Lorraine E. Buchanan, RN, MSN, CRRN and
Thomas H. Anderson, RN, BSN, BC

First Edition and Second Edition
Karen L. Wetther, BSN, RN

Contents

Objectives

Upon completion of the chapter, the reader will be able to

- State the purpose of a defense medical examination (DME)
- List two reasons why a plaintiff's attorney might request the presence of a legal nurse consultant (LNC) at the client's DME
- Describe the LNC's recourse if the examiner will not permit his or her attendance at a DME
- List two things that the LNC should do to prepare for the examination

Purpose of Defense Medical Evaluations

During the discovery phase of litigation, opposing parties often disagree about physical or mental health claims. The defense may be unwilling to offer a settlement. The plaintiff may be unwilling to accept the settlement offered by the defense, while the defense is unwilling to offer a greater amount, frequently based on the belief that the claims of the plaintiff or the medical opinions of the plaintiff's treating physicians or experts are erroneous or exaggerated. The law allows the defense to have the plaintiff undergo a medical examination and, under certain circumstances, a mental examination, by a health care practitioner of its choice, generally referred to as a DME or independent medical examination (IME).

Plaintiff attorneys rarely use the term "IME" because they often feel that it is a misnomer. The examination is not really independent or necessarily unbiased, because it is performed by a health care practitioner whom the defense selects and pays. Plaintiff attorneys generally refer to such examinations as "DMEs." The term "independent" is used to designate the examination as independent of the plaintiff's case. For those who prefer the term "IME," perhaps a better definition would be *insurance medical evaluation*.

The term IME is used to describe the examination performed in the context of any litigation in which the defendant is entitled to examine the claimant/plaintiff—workers' compensation or personal injury. In some instances, the term used to describe the examination is "agreed medical examination," but it is a misnomer because, typically, the reason for the examination is not "agreed upon." In some circumstances, plaintiff and defense counsels "agree" upon the examiner chosen in the worker's evaluation. However, the defense counsel reserves the right to choose the examiner to evaluate the injured worker.

Workers' compensation cases are governed by different, though similar, rules and vary from state to state. Examinations may also be done in the context of Social Security Disability claims, which are governed by federal guidelines. This chapter is focused on a discussion of DMEs. (The reader is referred to Volume 2, *Legal Nurse Consulting, Practices*, 3rd ed. for information regarding workers' compensation, social security disability cases, and insurance review cases.)

An LNC may be asked by the plaintiff's counsel to attend and observe the DME as the attorney's representative. This chapter will discuss some of the legal requirements relating to these examinations and the role of the LNC who attends DMEs. Rule 35 of the Federal Rules of Civil Procedure governs the use of DMEs in federal cases; therefore, in federal cases, DMEs are consistent from state to state. In cases filed in state court, statutes governing DMEs vary by state. The LNC retained to attend a DME is responsible for clarifying with the attorney his or her role at the examination. Regardless of the type of litigation, the LNC's role is the same—to observe and document what takes place during the evaluation.

Major Advantages and Disadvantages of the DME

Advantages of the DME from the defense perspective are having the plaintiff examined by a physician of choice who may find the plaintiff lacks any signs or symptoms of the alleged physical injury.

The only potential advantage for the plaintiff is the potential that the examiner will support the claimed injuries and that they are related to the incident involved in the lawsuit.

Disadvantages of the DME from the defense perspective include the following:

- Costs, such as the examiner's fees for reviewing medical records, performing the examination, and preparing a report.
- Necessity of obtaining cooperation from the plaintiff's counsel with regard to obtaining medical records and x-rays prior to the examination.
- Necessary reliance on the examiner to review medical records and x-rays prior to the examination.
- The examination may have a reverse effect, for example, the risk that the examiner's findings and report may support or even magnify the plaintiff's claims. Therefore, the examiner's testimony in court may weaken the defendant's case.

Disadvantages from the plaintiff perspective include

- Concern that the examiner will be biased
- The plaintiff will give mixed or incomplete messages
- The plaintiff will fail to appear for the examination and a cancellation fee will be charged
- The LNC is late or does not appear for the examination, causing forfeiture of examination or examination without representation

Role of the LNC

The role of the LNC is to be the eyes and ears of the attorney client during the DME. Astute observation and careful documentation are necessary to record the elements of the history and/or physical examination, as well as the verbal and nonverbal responses of the plaintiff. Attorneys may not always specify what they expect of the LNC. It is the responsibility of the LNC to determine the expectations of the attorney client for each examination observed. The LNC should clarify the following with the attorney client:

- Who will be preparing the plaintiff? If the LNC, does the attorney have guidelines indicating the attorney's preferences?
- Should the client complete any paperwork at the DME office?
- Can diagnostic tests be performed?
- Are case managers or any other persons allowed to be present for the exam?

It is critical for the LNC not to be late for the DME. The examiner can offer a limited late allowance for either patient or observer. If the LNC is not present for the exam, then the examination either proceeds without an observer or is cancelled. Neither of these situations is helpful to the attorney client or good for the LNC's business.

Guidelines

Communication with the Plaintiff Attorney

Prior to the examination, the LNC should clarify the plaintiff attorney's expectations for his or her participation in the DME, since expectations may differ among attorneys. Discuss communication with the plaintiff attorney. Being aware of the details of the case may not be pertinent to the observer but some benefit may be derived from knowing the physician's specialty and/or the part of the body that is affected.

Plaintiff Preparation

Prior to the examination, the LNC should establish a set time to meet the plaintiff at the examiner's office prior to the examination. The LNC should ask the plaintiff's attorney to instruct his or her client not to agree to enter an examination room prior to the arrival of the LNC. The LNC should plan to arrive at the examiner's office 15 minutes before the plaintiff arrives. The plaintiff and the LNC should converse briefly outside the examiner's office and make introductions if this is their initial meeting. The attorney should have told the plaintiff that a registered nurse would attend and observe the examination. This is the time for the LNC to put the patient at ease and to help the patient understand what to expect of the examination.

The plaintiff should be prepared for the DME by the attorney (some use pamphlets or videotapes) but the attorney will expect the LNC to speak directly with the client. The LNC should remind the patient that if any part of the examination hurts, he or she should say so aloud and not assume that the doctor is watching for facial expressions or other nonverbal signs of discomfort. The LNC and plaintiff should be aware that the office receptionist may have been asked by the physician to observe the plaintiff's actions and behavior in the reception area to determine whether they are different from those observed in the examining room.

Permissible Conduct

The examining physician may ask questions about how the accident occurred, such as "how fast were you going" or "were you drinking?"—which would reflect on liability issues in question. It is important for the LNC to recognize which questions are inappropriate and learn to object to inappropriate questions in a professional manner. If available and appropriate, the LNC may wish to review the Demand and the Response to Demand, the objections, and the stipulations, and discuss these with the plaintiff attorney prior to the DME.

The LNC may politely introduce himself or herself to the examiner as the attorney's representative retained as an observer to the examination. Family members who have accompanied the plaintiff to the examination may be invited into the examination room by the patient. They should be instructed not to interfere or participate in the examination unless they are consulted directly. An exception may be made if the family member is needed to translate; however, the LNC should be aware that in many states, if a plaintiff does not speak or understand English, the Evidence Code requires that a professional interpreter must be present.

If the examiner has any dispute concerning the presence of the LNC during the examination, or what is disallowed in that particular case (such as intrusive tests or x-rays), or audio taping, the prudent way to handle such a situation is to call the plaintiff's attorney. The doctor or plaintiff attorney may contact the defense counsel to resolve a dispute. Or, the plaintiff's attorney may instruct the LNC to terminate the examination and to leave the examination site with the plaintiff immediately. In most cases, the problem is simply a lack of communication or knowledge of the law that can be clarified with a telephone call, if necessary. If the examiner does not let the LNC attend the examination and the lawyer or his staff cannot be reached, then the LNC should have a predetermined course of action.

Notes and Observations

Most plaintiff attorneys do not want the client to fill in forms. If the plaintiff fills out any paperwork, request a copy and attach it to your report. If a copy is refused, note that in your report. Generally, the LNC will be asked to keep a detailed written account and time log of what occurs from the time the plaintiff arrives until he or she leaves the office. This should include the following:

- Time spent filling out forms in the waiting room prior to the examination (not allowed by most plaintiff attorneys)
- Time spent sitting in the waiting room, having x-rays taken, or blood drawn (if authorized)
- Time spent being escorted to the examining room
- Time spent waiting in the examining room
- Time that the examiner or any staff member enters or exits the examining room
- What transpires in the examining room
- Anything that happens once the examination is completed prior to leaving the office
- If the examiner exits the room for any reason, exit and reentry times should also be recorded
- At least the start and stop times for the history and physical portions should be noted

Depending on the type of examination, observations *may* include

The Patient

- Use of assistive devices (crutches, cane, walker, and wheelchair)
- Gait (slow, antalgic, and limp)
- Limitation of movements
- Ability to tolerate sitting (duration without position changes)
- Position changes (frequency)
- Verbal and nonverbal responses during the examination (e.g., grimacing if no verbal response is made)
- Clothing worn
- Visible scars in the area of injury

The Examiner

- Interaction with patient
- Examination technique (gentle, moderate, or forceful palpation)
- Components of examination
- Use of examination tools (reflex hammer, pinwheel, dynamometer, etc.)

■ Presence of medical records or x-rays in the examination room (does the examiner indicate whether they were reviewed prior to the examination?)

"Other" Evaluations

The most common defense medical evaluations are orthopedic and neurological—and the third most common evaluations are psychiatric. These evaluations are different in that they are mostly verbal, but the same guidelines apply. Observation is still key in order to document the nonverbal aspects of the patient's and the examiner's behaviors.

Defense Psychiatric Evaluations

Defense psychiatric evaluations can be time consuming, because the history portion of the evaluation can be extensive—dating back to childhood experiences and family relations. The interview questions and objective psychological testing should specifically address the claimant's psychological status and functional capacities and may include the following:

■ Detailed background information of the client
■ Past psychiatric history
■ Medical history
■ Substance abuse history
■ Present mental status examination
■ Description of the functioning of the client prior to becoming disabled
■ Description of the functioning of the client after becoming disabled
■ Severity of impairment
■ Relationship of present impairment to client's ability to work (in specific occupation and general or related fields)
■ Client's historical interest in the specific occupation
■ Personality, psycho-social, and other factors contributing to disability
■ Summary of previous treatment
■ Need for additional treatment

Psychiatric evaluations, neuropsychological evaluations, and vocational evaluations may also include extensive testing that includes

■ Neuro-Psychological Test Battery
■ Wide Range Achievement Test-4 (WRAT-4)
■ The COPSystem Interest Inventory (COPS)
■ The Career Ability Placement Survey (CAPS)
■ The Purdue Pegboard of Manual Dexterity
■ The Bennett Hand Tool Test
■ The Slosson Intelligence Test Revised (SIT-R)
■ The Gates-MacGinitie Reading Test—Level AR

Prior to the appointment, the LNC should ascertain whether or not the attorney client wants the consultant to observe the testing (as well as the interview portion of the evaluation)—because it is nonverbal and can be lengthy and costly for the attorney client to pay for the LNC's time.

Whether or not the LNC is directed to stay for the testing portion of the evaluation, a list of the tests administered should be obtained at the time of the evaluation.

Ophthalmologic, Dental, and Otolaryngologic Defense Evaluations

The LNC should be prepared to use common sense and professional ingenuity for some examinations. Most nurses have never participated in eye, teeth, or ear, nose, and throat (ENT) examinations—except as patients. These examinations do not lend themselves to the observer being able to see what the examiner sees. For example, in ophthalmologic examinations, the examiner generally turns out the lights—and the observer is left in the dark, literally. In dental and ENT examinations, there is no way that the observer can get close enough to watch.

There are a few ways around these problems. Dentists often dictate their findings to a dental assistant. The LNC can listen and take the same notes. The eye examination and the ENT examination are tougher—but then it is most important to note what the examiner tells the patient as accurately as possible. If all else fails, it is most important to report the truth—and, sometimes, that is, "I couldn't see and he didn't say."

"I Couldn't See a Thing!" and Other Problems

The LNC may encounter numerous pitfalls when accompanying a patient to a DME. The physician may not let the LNC attend the examination at all—or he or she may make every effort to block the LNC's view of the patient during the physical examination. In the worst case, the LNC may need to contact the attorney and possibly terminate the examination. At best, the report of the evaluation should reflect the examiner's efforts to be obstructive.

A hostile doctor is generally not a new phenomenon for a professional nurse. A hostile patient may be more problematic. A patient who curses the doctor may need the LNC to intercede and strongly suggest alternative behavior. Ideally, issues of anger, hostility, and decorum are addressed with the plaintiff by the attorney client and LNC observer prior to the actual examination.

More anticipated difficulties relate to the initial problems of taking notes, checking the time, listening, writing, and observing simultaneously. If a battery-powered tape recorder is used, the clarity of the recording should be checked before leaving the LNC's office to ensure that the batteries are strong. Digital recordings may be used if the LNC and attorney have the necessary system in place for sending and receiving the data. Bringing extra pens, paper, tapes, and batteries to the examination is a good idea.

Given time, the professional nurse will develop her own style, and the facility of multitasking improves considerably with experience. The community of physicians who perform DMEs is relatively small, and, over time, each one's style will be apparent to the LNC. With familiarity, the LNC will become more proficient.

Report Preparation

The LNC should not be expected to be a stenographer who takes verbatim notes throughout the examination. However, with practice, the LNC should be able to record contemporaneous notes

Table 19.1 Report Pitfalls
Avoid real or the appearance of bias
Avoid opinions or judgments
Avoid jargon and "techno-speak"
Avoid synonyms that are new to you

that reflect the substance of the history portion of the examination and the elements of the physical examination, along with a time log of events as they take place.

It is highly advisable to write the report of the examination the same day as it takes place in order to ensure that recall can assist in deciphering notes taken during the examination. If you cannot write the report immediately after the examination is concluded, at least read over your notes, clarify your shorthand and familiarize yourself with what will be your report content. Then, write the report as soon as possible.

Always make sure that the reader understands who is "speaking" in your report. Every complaint, comment, or description should be appropriately attributed to the patient—or to whomever else it applies. Be careful not to just make a statement—which would sound as though you knew something to be true. Sometimes that means you must use the patient's name and similar sentence structure repetitively.

The format of the report should be consistent from one DME to the next. This ensures that the attorney client will understand what to expect of the report when he or she retains an LNC to accompany the client to a medical examination. The report should be arranged chronologically, reflecting the notes as they were taken. Unless requested by the attorney, the written report is not an appropriate place for the LNC's opinions (see Appendices A and B for sample report).

Always put your best effort into your work to be sure it is well written. It is important to ensure that grammar and spelling are correct and appropriate. Errors are 100% avoidable! It is a great idea to have someone else review and edit your reports before they are submitted.

If the examination is audiotaped, the tapes should be submitted with the written report. The attorney's secretary is more likely to be proficient at transcription, so the LNC should determine whom the attorney would like to transcribe the audiotape (Table 19.1).

Billing Considerations

The LNC may charge either an hourly fee for services rendered or a flat fee. Fees should allow for travel time, waiting time, observing the examination, and report preparation. A policy regarding "no-shows" and "same-day cancellations" must also be considered. The fee schedule and terms of payment should be clarified with the attorney client prior to the examination. Formal written contracts between the attorney and the LNC and retainer requirements are recommended.

It is courteous (and good business) to clarify with the plaintiff's attorney in advance how the LNC should handle excessive waiting time at the examiner's office. If the attorney does not provide time parameters, it is courteous to call the attorney after waiting for more than 30 min beyond the scheduled appointment time. The LNC's time is the client's money, and acknowledging that fact openly helps to ensure goodwill and future business.

Benefits of Using an LNC

Traditionally, plaintiff attorneys have attended DMEs themselves or have sent a paralegal or secretary to observe the examination. In order to market this service effectively, the LNC should be prepared to explain the advantages of using a nurse. The LNC should emphasize that the plaintiff is apt to be more comfortable with a nurse than with a nonmedical person. A nurse can assist the plaintiff with changing into an examination gown and redressing without embarrassment.

A nurse is considerably more familiar with a medical environment than a nonmedical observer and often creates rapport that may not occur between medical and legal professionals. More important, a nurse is knowledgeable about what may be included in the examination of various body parts, and therefore may be able to alert the plaintiff's counsel (verbally) to important omissions in the examination.

An example of an important observation by a nurse that may not have been noticed by a nonmedical person occurred in a case in which the physician examiner repeatedly asked his office nurse for a *Jamar* dynamometer to test a patient's grip strength. When he was unable to find the device he sought, he used a bulb dynamometer instead. The LNC was able to note the use of the alternative device in her report—and to testify later as to the specific device used, even though the physician had documented and testified that he made his measurements with a *Jamar* dynamometer.

Court Testimony Relating to DMEs

An independent LNC may testify at trial regarding the report generated from the examination and about any discrepancies between his or her report and that of the examiner. Because the LNCs compensation is not dependent upon the outcome of the litigation, his or her report and testimony are more credible.

When testifying about observations at a DME, whether in court, deposition, or arbitration, the role of the LNC is to serve as a fact witness, not as an expert witness. While the LNC may, indeed, be an expert in nursing—or at least some aspects of nursing—that clinical expertise does not apply when testifying about his or her observations. The DME fact witness provides fact based testimony on observations, unlike the liability expert who provides opinions on how the examination was conducted. The testimony must relate to specific observations contained in the original report, unless the specific examination at issue is recalled clearly. The LNC may be asked specific questions regarding the length of the examination or particular observations made during the physical examination. Sometimes, the LNC is asked to read his or her report into the record verbatim.

The LNC is expected to describe the events that took place, not to judge the examination. During testimony, the LNC will often be told what the examiner reported that conflicted with the LNC's report. Argument is the purview of the attorneys. It is the LNC's job to report only what he or she saw and heard. Even when pushed to offer an opinion, the LNC should not comply.

Conclusion

The goal of a DME should be to obtain objective, accurate information about the patient's physical or mental status at the time of the examination relating to the subject injury that can be used to effect a fair settlement or verdict. Regrettably, some examiners' reports reflect some bias. For this reason, many attorneys now retain LNCs to assess, observe, monitor, and report detailed objective information to facilitate the accurate disposition of a case.

Additional Reading

Babitsky, S., Mangraviti, J. J., & Melhorn, J. M. (2004). *Writing and defending your IME report: The comprehensive guide.* Falmouth, MA: SEAK, Inc.

Pollock, D. A. (2000). The LNC's vital role in a defense medical examination. *Journal of Legal Nurse Consulting, 11*(8).

Seidel, H. M., Ball, J., Benedict, W., & Dains, J. E. (2007). *Mosby's guide to physical examination (6th ed.).* St. Louis: Mosby-Year Book, Inc.

Skidmore-Roth Publishing. (1997). *Expert 10-minute physical examinations* (1st ed.). St. Louis: Mosby-Year Book, Inc.

Strunk, W., & White, E. B, (2000). *The elements of style.* New York: Longman.

Swartz, M. H. (2001). *Textbook of physical diagnosis: History and examination.* Philadelphia: W.B. Saunders.

Wood, B. A. (2001). Legal and ethical considerations of patient/provider communications. *Journal of Legal Nurse Consulting, 12,* 10–13.

Test Questions

1. The purpose of a DME is
   A. To give the defense an opportunity to evaluate the plaintiff's claims of injury, illness, or incapacity
   B. To determine the impact of preexisting illnesses of injuries on the subject complaints and claims
   C. To allow the plaintiff to prove that he or she is injured
   D. To show the client that his or her attorney is earning his fee

2. Which of the following is not part of the LNC's role at a DME?
   A. To determine whether an adequate examination is performed
   B. To ensure that the examiner does not abuse the client
   C. To ensure that no x-rays or diagnostic tests are performed unless they have been agreed to previously
   D. To determine the opinion of the examiner with regard to the plaintiff's diagnosis and treatment

3. Which of the following would an LNC NOT be allowed to do at a DME?
   A. Audiotape the examination
   B. Videotape the examination
   C. Question the examiner about omissions in the examination performed
   D. Assist the patient with removing his or her shoes and socks

4. A potential disadvantage to the defense attorney who orders a DME is that
   A. The examination may be videotaped by the opposing party
   B. The examiner's findings and report may be detrimental to the defense of the case
   C. The patient may divulge the circumstances of the injury
   D. The LNC is considered to be an expert witness for the plaintiff

5. If the physician refuses to have the LNC observe the examination, the LNC should
   A. Leave the office without the plaintiff
   B. Call the defense attorney to explain why the LNC is allowed to be present
   C. Cancel the examination and leave with the plaintiff
   D. Call the plaintiff's attorney from the examining room to explain the resistance that is being encountered

Answers: 1. A, 2. D, 3. C, 4. B, 5. D

Appendix A: Orthopaedic "DME" Sample Report

December 21, 2008
John Doe, Esquire
123 Main Street
Anytown, New York 12345

RE: John Smith

Dear Mr. Doe:

On December 21, 2001, I accompanied your client, John Smith, to his scheduled 1:00 p.m. defense medical evaluation with James Jones, M.D., at General Hospital Medical Arts Building, Rm. 110, 100 E. First Avenue, Your Town, NY. The following is a report of the evaluation.

Mr. Smith was present in the waiting room when I arrived at 12:30 p.m. He was called to the examination room by the office receptionist at 1:16 p.m. Dr. Jones arrived at 1:18 p.m. , introduced himself, and commenced the history portion of the evaluation immediately.

Mr. Smith confirmed his age of 73 years and that he is right-handed. Mr. Smith said that he is a retired postal worker. In response to Dr. Jones' question, Mr. Smith said that he was injured on 02/15/00, when he fell on a patch of ice. Mr. Smith said that he hurt his right wrist and the left side of his back, and that he cut his head. Mr. Smith confirmed being unemployed at the time of the accident. Mr. Smith said that he went to the emergency room at General Hospital.

When asked about his treatment, Mr. Smith said that Dr. Williams was his treating physician and that he was discharged from his care in July 2001. He said that Dr. Williams inserted an internal fixator into his right arm. Mr. Smith said that he was also referred to General Hospital from ABC Rehabilitation Center regarding the dermatitis on his right forearm. He said that he was also treated at General Hospital for varicose veins.

Mr. Smith related that he had broken his right arm as a child and is hyperglycemic, but not diabetic. He said that he is otherwise in good health, takes no medications, does not smoke, and has had no other accidents or surgeries. In response to Dr. Jones' questions, Mr. Smith said that he is 5 feet, 11 inches tall and weighs 180 pounds.

When questioned about current symptoms, Mr. Smith said that he has trouble rotating his right wrist and closing his right hand completely. He said that the strength in his right wrist is decreased; and although the pain in his shoulder has greatly improved, he still experiences difficulty in raising his right arm completely. Mr. Smith said that he cannot bear weight on his right arm or wrist, and he offered the example of lifting himself out of bed. Mr. Smith said that his back has healed completely, and the dermatitis, resulting from the use of the machines from ABC Rehabilitation Center, healed when therapy was completed. Mr. Smith responded affirmatively when asked whether he currently does home exercises.

Dr. Jones concluded the history portion of the evaluation at 1:30 p.m. and instructed Mr. Smith to remove his outer shirt and T-shirt. Dr. Jones returned at 1:32 p.m. and commenced the physical examination immediately.

Dr. Jones measured both forearms without comment. He tested tip-to-tip prehension by asking Mr. Smith to bring his right thumb into opposition with the other five fingers. Mr. Smith performed this maneuver without difficulty. Dr. Jones tested the grips of both hands using three widths without comment.

Cervical range of motion was assessed and appeared to be full and painless in flexion, extension, and rotation. The foramina compression test was performed with Mr. Smith bending his head to both sides and applying pressure. Mr. Smith denied pain bilaterally with this maneuver. Lumbosacral flexion was performed and appeared full and painless.

Manual muscle testing of the deltoids, biceps, triceps, and fingers was performed. The right arm appeared noticeably weaker with testing. Mr. Smith complained of soreness with testing of the right deltoid. With Mr. Smith's hands in supination, Dr. Jones asked that he abduct and adduct his wrists bilaterally. Mr. Smith exhibited difficulty with abduction and adduction of his right wrist. The Phalen's, Reverse Phalen's, and Tinel's tests were performed bilaterally with negative results.

With Mr. Smith seated on the edge of the examination table, knee extension was performed with no apparent gross weakness noted and no complaints offered. Mr. Smith was wearing TED stockings to control his varicosities. Shoulder range of motion was assessed and appeared full and painless in overhead extension and elevation through forward flexion. Dr. Jones assessed medial rotation and adduction and lateral rotation and abduction by requesting that Mr. Smith touch his hands behind his head and to his lower back. Range of motion in these areas was limited. Mr. Smith complained of pain with both of these maneuvers. Mr. Smith was asked to draw circles in the air with both arms, which he did without difficulty. Mr. Smith was then asked to touch his hands to his shoulders bilaterally. He seemed to experience difficulty touching his right hand to his right shoulder.

The deep tendon reflexes of the upper extremities (biceps, triceps) were tested with positive results. Dr. Jones checked the radial pulses without comment. Mr. Smith denied pain with palpation of both wrists.

Dr. Jones measured the distance between the thumbs and forefingers bilaterally without comment. Dr. Jones also measured the angles of the fingers bilaterally when at rest and when bent at the joints and knuckles. Dr. Jones assessed movements of the fingers by asking Mr. Smith to open and close his fingers and to cross his fingers. Mr. Smith complained of soreness in his right fingers with these movements.

Dr. Jones concluded the physical examination at 1:52 p.m. and left the examination room. Mr. Smith redressed, and he and I left the doctor's office together at 2:00 p.m.

Thank you for using the services of LNC DME, Inc.

Very truly yours,
Mary Smythe, RN,
Legal Nurse Consultant

Appendix B: Psychiatric "DME" Sample Report

January 30, 2009
Michael Waters, Esquire
202 Current Road
Rapid City, PA 17000

RE: Mr. Ebb

Dear Mr. Waters:

On January 25, 2009, I accompanied your client, Mr. Ebb to his 11:00 a.m. scheduled defense medical evaluation with Dr. Flow at 21 River Road, Tidewater, PA. The following is a report of the evaluation.

I was seated in the waiting room when Mr. Ebb arrived at 10:50 a.m. Dr. Flow invited us **into her office at 11:06 a.m.**, explained her role, and **commenced the evaluation immediately**. Dr. Flow mentioned that she had evaluated Mr. Ebb twice before, but Mr. Ebb said that he didn't remember Dr. Flow.

In response to initial questioning, Mr. Ebb said that he is "not doing great," while explaining that he "almost lost it last week" before he received a nerve block that usually decreases his pain for five or six days. Mr. Ebb went on to say that his pain has increased since the electroconvulsive therapy (ECT) was discontinued and he's not sure if he can handle the pain, which also prevents him from sleeping and causes him to cry a lot. Mr. Ebb said that if it wasn't for his wife, he probably wouldn't be here today and "would have done something stupid." He said that he attempted suicide in the past. Mr. Ebb said that he understands that the ECT will help him mentally, but he feels that it also takes the pain away.

Regarding his current symptoms, Mr. Ebb explained that he experiences neck pain that radiates down his right arm and right side to his waist, which affects his right hand, causing a difference in temperature and color of that extremity and restricts his finger movements.

Mr. Ebb provided an extensive list of his medications, which included a morphine pump, but didn't appear certain about the dosages or the purposes of some of his medications. Dr. Flow noted that Mr. Ebb removed the medication lists from his wallet with his left hand, but he indicated he was right hand dominant. She also noted that he stood and rocked during portions of the evaluation. When asked about this behavior, Mr. Ebb said that he is in pain. He also indicated that he suffers short term memory loss, reflex sympathetic dystrophy (RSD), and has "violent nightmares."

During the *Mini-Mental State* test, Mr. Ebb appeared to do well except for the recall portion. He could only remember two out of the three words previously mentioned by Dr. Flow.

Regarding his daily routine, Mr. Ebb said that he usually awakens between 7 a.m. and 8 a.m., except for nights when he is unable to sleep because of the pain, when he will sleep to noon. He indicated that he spends his day reading the newspaper, watching television, and walking his dog. He said that he lives with his wife, who leaves the house at 8 a.m. for work and returns at 6 p.m., his daughter, 24 years of age, who works and attends school, and his 20-year-old son who is unemployed.

Mr. Ebb described his appetite as being "all right," while indicating that he will have a cup of coffee or two in the morning, but doesn't usually make lunch and usually doesn't eat in the middle of the day. He said that he occasionally has a beer or two, but denied alcohol or drug abuse. He also mentioned that he was previously misdiagnosed with hepatitis.

Mr. Ebb said that he is aware that the electroconvulsive therapy causes short-term memory loss, but he feels the pain reduction outweighs the short-term memory loss. He also expressed that he is unable to cope with the pain and is fearful of harming himself or others, and described episodes of angry outbursts towards his son. Mr. Ebb verbalized that he loves his wife too much to hurt her, but doesn't want her to be "forced to take care of a weirdo."

When asked to elaborate about his suicidal ideation, Mr. Ebb denied current thoughts of suicide, but said that increased pain may cause him to stab himself or cut his veins. Mr. Ebb related that his current medication and the morphine pump control the pain to a point, but when the pain increases, they don't seem to help.

Mr. Ebb described his desire to eliminate the pain which would enable a return to a normal life—including work, having a good time, and enjoying his family and friends. He commented that he has a few friends and that his best friend usually stops over on Sundays, which he finds enjoyable.

In response to final questioning, Mr. Ebb said that his hope for the future is that his family would be okay and he will be able to cope with his symptoms. He also indicated that he is fearful that the ECTs will continue to be denied.

Dr. Flow **concluded the evaluation at 12:12** p.m. and Mr. Ebb and I left the office together at that time.

Thank you for using the services of *Independent Allied Health Consultants, Inc.*

Very truly yours
Thomas. H. Anderson BSN, RN, BC
Allied Health Consultant

Chapter 20

Pharmaceutical and Medical Device Product Liability Litigation

Paula Windler, MS, RN, LNCC and Sue Barnes, MSN, MSHCA, RN

First Edition
Mary Baldwin; Shirley Cantwell Davis, BSN, RN, LNCC; Nathan Dean; Joan E. Miller; and Patricia L. Pippen, BSN, RN, LNCC, OCN

Second Edition
Shirley Cantwell Davis, BSN, RN, LNCC; Pamela M. Linville, RN, CCRC, CPBT; Rosie Oldham, BS, RN, LNCC; and Patricia L. Pippen, BSN, RN, LNCC, OCN

Contents

Objectives

- State the difference between the legal theories of strict liability and negligence in a product liability case
- Describe hypothetical instances of defective design and defective manufacturing of a medical product
- Discuss three criteria used to determine the adequacy of manufacturer warnings
- Formulate a request for an adverse drug reaction report or medical device report under the Freedom of Information Act
- Describe the informed consent process for pharmaceutical clinical trials

- Knowledgeably rule out professional medical negligence and establish clear causation in a medical product liability case
- Research and maintain a current knowledge base of new drugs in product liability cases

Introduction

Few areas of litigation are as fascinating and complex for the lawyer and the legal nurse consultant (LNC) as pharmaceutical and medical device product liability litigation. In order for LNCs to successfully work in product liability litigation involving drugs and devices, they must have a basic understanding of legal theories regarding strict liability and negligence as well as design defects, manufacturing defects, and failure to warn. LNCs must also be cognizant of the steps involved in Food and Drug Administration (FDA) approval of a new drug or device and the postmarketing process. A good working knowledge of the standard of care practiced by health care practitioners who use prescription drugs and medical products is essential so that a differentiation can be made between a medical malpractice and a product liability matter.

Theories of Liability*

Product liability is a concept in the law holding a manufacturer, distributor, or merchant liable or responsible for the product they have on the market. The underlying legal theories of product liability stem from common law, which is based on old English law and is established through precedent rather than statutory laws. Common law comprises the principles of law that are generally recognized in the United States. Restatement of the Law Third, Torts: Products Liability published by the American Law Institute (ALI) in 1998, enumerates the rules on a wide variety of issues for product liability law. Although the restatements do not have the force of law, they have traditionally been influential in the courts.

The key provision in the Restatement of the Law Third, Torts: Products Liability, Section 2, is that "a product is defective when, at the time of sale or distribution, it contains a manufacturing defect, is defective in design or is defective because of inadequate instructions or warning." Instead of standard categories of negligence, strict liability, and breach of warranty, it provides a functional definition of product defect in terms of design, manufacturing, and warning. It further defines each category of strict liability as follows:

- A product "contains a manufacturing defect when the product departs from its intended design even though all possible care was exercised in the preparation and marketing of the product" (Section 2a).
- A product "contains a design defect when the foreseeable risks of harm posed by the product could have been reduced or avoided by the adoption of a reasonable alternative design by the seller or other distributor, or a predecessor in the commercial chain of distribution and the omission of the reasonable alternative design renders the product not reasonably safe" (Section 2b).
- A product "is defective because of inadequate instructions or warnings when the foreseeable risks of harm posed by the product could have been reduced or avoided by the provision of reasonable instructions or warnings by the seller or other distributor, or a predecessor in the

---

* Restatement of the Law Third, Torts: Products Liabaility. Copyright 1998 by The American Law Institute. Reprinted with permission.

commercial chain of distribution and the omission of the instructions or warning renders the product not reasonably safe" (Section 2c) (The American Law Institute, 1998).

Because there is no federal product liability law, product liability claims are based on applicable state laws, and brought under the theories of negligence, strict liability, or breach of warranty. In addition, a set of commercial statutes in each state, modeled on the Uniform Commercial Code, contains warranty rules affecting product liability. The attorney will determine whether the product falls under the purview of the consumer Product Safety Improvement Act of 2008. The legal field is a dynamic area of practice with court decisions setting new precedence. A Supreme Court ruling on February 20, 2008 has far-reaching impact on this area of law and is discussed later in this chapter under the Medical Devices section.

Strict Liability

The Third Restatement, Section 2d, provides for *strict liability without fault* for a manufacturing defect. The liability is based on the fact that a defect existed at the time the product left the manufacturers, wholesalers, or retailers and that the defect caused an injury. There is no need to prove that it was unreasonably dangerous or not reasonably safe. The intent of strict liability for manufacturing defects is to encourage manufacturers to place greater emphasis on product safety and for retailers to deal with reputable manufacturers and distributors.

This places the responsibility for the safety of the drug or device on the pharmaceutical or medical device company that manufactured, distributed, or sold a product that harmed a person. They may be held strictly liable. In a strict liability analysis, it is assumed that the defendant knows the dangerous propensity of the product to potentially cause injury; under a negligence theory, the plaintiff must prove that the defendant knew or should have known of the danger. This makes the plaintiff's burden of proof less difficult under a strict liability theory than under negligence. By eliminating the issue of manufacturer fault, the concept of no fault or strict liability allows plaintiffs to recover where they otherwise might not. However, under strict liability the plaintiff must still establish proximate cause between the product defect and the harm suffered by the plaintiff.

When trying to prove that a product is defective or unreasonably dangerous, the LNC must remember that some products simply cannot be made safer without losing their usefulness. For example, an electric knife that is too dull to injure anyone would also be useless for its intended purpose. In every case, drugs and devices used for medical purposes must be examined and analyzed from a risk/benefit ratio in order to assess whether or not they are unreasonably dangerous in the first place. It is important to examine the question whether the desired and foreseeable actions of the drug or device are sufficiently beneficial to justify the risks of adverse reactions. Manufacturers and suppliers of unavoidably unsafe products must give proper warnings of the dangers and risks of their products so that consumers can make informed decisions regarding whether to use them. In the area of manufacturing defects, plaintiffs have gained a reduced burden of proof with the implementation of strict liability, while defendant manufacturers will face the burden of proving that the alleged defects were not in existence when the product left their possession.

Example 20.1

Although as many as 25 known pathogens may be present in blood (Rueda, 2001), only human immunodeficiency virus (HIV), hepatitis C virus (HCV), hepatitis B virus (HBV), and a few others are required to be screened after collection. Detection tests are not yet developed or implemented for all recognized pathogens, including parasites. Four percent of patients who receive the average amount of blood during a transfusion are at risk of being infected with a contaminated unit and exposed to the danger of serious adverse reactions, including future debilitating conditions. People who develop transfusion-related diseases generally have been unsuccessful when making claims against the vendors of blood products because of blood shield statutes that were initially enacted in response to unknown pathogens that made the blood an *unavoidably unsafe* product (Wade, 2004).

Example 20.2

Another good example of an unavoidably unsafe drug is the broad-spectrum antibiotic chloramphenicol, which is a wide spectrum antibiotic used for Gram-positive and Gram-negative cocci and bacilli (including anaerobes), rickettsia, mycoplasma, and chlamydia. This drug has been linked to aplastic anemia in a small percentage of users. Because of bone marrow toxicity, the availability of alternative antibiotics, and the emergence of resistance, as of 2005 chloramphenicol is no longer a drug of choice for any infection, except serious infections due to a few multidrug-resistant pathogens that retain susceptibility to this antibiotic (Porter, 2008). The manufacturer clearly denotes this association in all products labeling in order to provide adequate warning of this potentially fatal adverse reaction to the drug.

Negligence

The doctrine of *res ipsa loquitur*, when translated, means *the thing speaks for itself* and shifts the burden of proof in some product liability cases to the defendant because the defect would not exist unless someone was negligent. If the doctrine is used successfully, the plaintiff is no longer required to prove how the defendant was negligent; rather, the defendant is required to prove that they were not negligent. A manufacturer, distributor, or merchant is liable for a negligent act when they had a duty to another person and breached that duty by failing to take ordinary care in producing a product that causes the harm. Strict liability, on the other hand, is liability without negligence and there is no need to show fault. Strict liability is most often found in product liability cases but it is also found in some other cases.

The Third Restatement uses the theory of negligence for design defects. To prove a design defect, the plaintiff must demonstrate the existence of a reasonable alternative product design (RAD). A risk-utility balancing test asks "whether a reasonable alternative design would, at reasonable cost, have reduced the foreseeable risks of harm posed by the product and, if so, whether the omission of the alternative design by the seller ... rendered the product not reasonably safe" (Ruff & Jurado, 1999). To establish a prima facie case of defect, the plaintiff must prove the availability of a technologically feasible and practical alternative design that would have reduced and prevented the plaintiff's harm (Ruff & Jurado, 1999).

A drug company has a duty to act prudently, and a breach of this duty would include, for example, not performing an investigation, after several unexplained deaths in the first three months after FDA approval of a new drug. FDA approval does not in and of itself provide an adequate defense for a manufacturer when negligence is alleged. Alternatively, a product manufacturer may have breached its duty to act prudently by employing someone who is not qualified to run the clinical trials. Both of these are examples of a pharmaceutical or medical device manufacturer's failure to exercise ordinary care, diligence, or prudence, breaching its duty to the consumer or user of the product.

Example 20.3

On September 30, 2004 the FDA (FDA, 2004a, 2004b) acknowledged the voluntary withdrawal of Vioxx (chemical name rofecoxib) from the market. Merck withdrew Vioxx from the market after the data safety monitoring board overseeing a long-term study of the drug recommended that the study be halted because of an increased risk of serious cardiovascular events, including heart attacks and strokes. Dr. Topol (2004) noted that the recall came after more than 80 million patients had taken this medicine and annual sales had topped $2.5 billion, when the company withdrew the drug because of an excess risk of myocardial infarctions and strokes. According to Dr. Topol, for five-and-a-half years, from 1999 to late 2004, neither Merck nor the FDA fulfilled its responsibilities to the public (Topol, 2004). The pivotal trial for rofecoxib involved 8076 patients with rheumatoid arthritis and demonstrated that this coxib had lower gastrointestinal toxicity than naproxen. Even though the drug was approved in 1999 on the basis of data submitted to the FDA, the data were not submitted to a peer-reviewed journal until the following year and did not appear in print until November 23, 2000, one and a half years after commercial approval had been granted. The cardiovascular data reported in that article were incomplete, in part because of incomplete ascertainment: the design and execution of the trial had not anticipated that untoward cardiovascular events might occur. It was not until February 8, 2001, that the FDA's Arthritis Advisory Committee met to discuss concern about the potential cardiovascular risks associated with rofecoxib. Over the course of the five-and-a-half years, many epidemiologic studies confirmed the concern about the risk of myocardial infarction and serious cardiovascular events associated with rofecoxib. These studies considered large populations, up to 1.4 million patients, tracking the use of various nonsteroidal anti-inflammatory medications or coxibs to determine the risk of adverse events. Each time a study was presented or published, according to Dr. Topol, there was a predictable response from Merck, which claimed that the study was flawed and that only randomized, controlled trials were suitable for determining whether there was any risk. As of September 2008, the class-action securities lawsuit brought by investors who claimed the drug maker failed to disclose info concerning the Vioxx painkiller was reinstated by a three-judge panel of the Third Circuit Court of Appeals.

Consumer misuse is a defense to a design defect claim that was developed through case law and is adopted by the Third Restatement. In this situation, the plaintiff is injured when he or she misuses the product in a manner unforeseeable to the manufacturer. The evidence of foreseeable product misuse, alteration, and modification must also be considered in deciding whether an alternative design should have been adopted. Foreseeable misuses do not constitute a complete defense (Ruff & Jurado, 1999).

Example 20.4

In February 2008, the FDA issued a communication about an ongoing safety review regarding Botox and Botox Cosmetic. The FDA had received reports of systemic adverse reactions including respiratory compromise and death following the use of botulinum toxin types A and B for both FDA approved and unapproved uses. The reactions reported were suggestive of botulism, which occurs when botulinum toxin spreads in the body beyond the site where it was injected. The most serious cases had outcomes that included hospitalization and death, and occurred mostly in children treated for cerebral palsy-associated limb spasticity. The use of botulinum toxins for treatment of limb spasticity (severe arm and leg muscle spasms) in children or adults is not an approved use in the United States (FDA, 2008a).

While critics have labeled the revisions as *pro-defendant* and *anticonsumer*, the Restatement provisions, in fact, have created difficulties and improvements for litigants on both sides of a product liability action. The Third Restatement has substantially altered the landscape of product liability law. In the area of design defects, plaintiffs now face the added hurdle of proving that a reasonable alternative design existed and was feasible at the time the product was designed. On the other hand, manufacturers have been harmed by the loss of the *state of the art* and *open and obvious* defenses (Ruff & Jurado, 1999).

Warranty

Warranty is an assurance by the manufacturer, either expressed, which is an overt assurance, or implied, that the goods are merchantable and of average quality. These warranties can be found in the Uniform Commercial Code, which is followed by every state. A manufacturer implies a warranty of fitness by selling a product that the manufacturer contends is merchantable and reasonably fit for a particular purpose. For example, a prosthetic hip should not fracture after implantation. If it does fracture, a breach of warranty may exist because the prosthetic hip is not, by definition, merchantable or fit for the purpose for which it was sold. Some warranties may also be implied due to the nature of the sale. An implied warranty of merchantability is a promise that a product sold is in good working order and will do what it is supposed to do. An implied warranty of fitness for a particular purpose is a promise that a seller's advice on how to use a product will be correct. Warranty and breach of warranty are concepts used in both strict liability and negligence.

Vaccine Liability

In 1986, Congress passed the National Childhood Vaccine Injury Act (NCVIA) in response to a liability crisis and public health concerns about the safety of diphtheria and tetanus toxoids and pertussis vaccines that caused supply shortages, and vaccine prices to skyrocket (Evans, 2006). It requires physicians to notify all parents and/or patients of the benefits and risks of vaccines listed in the Vaccine Injury Table through the use of Vaccine Information Statements (VIS). For more information, see http://www.cdc.gov/vaccines/pubs/VIS/vis-facts.htm. The NCVIA mandates that all health care professionals report certain adverse events after a vaccination using the Vaccine Adverse Events Reporting System (VAERS) at http://vaers.hhs.gov/. Anyone can file a VAERS report: health care providers, manufacturers, and recipients or their parent/guardian.

Individuals can request compensation for injury from a vaccine through the National Vaccine Injury Compensation Program (VICP). VICP is a "no-fault" compensation program for resolving vaccine injury claims based on the Vaccine Injury Table and covers all vaccines recommended by the Centers for Disease Control Prevention (CDC). The Table summarizes medical conditions and the time interval of onset following the receipt of a covered vaccine. More information is located at http://www.hrsa.gov/Vaccinecompensation/.

Example 20.5

McDonal v. Abbot Laboratories (2005), a CA5 Thimerosal/vaccine liability suit over mercury poisoning from the vaccine preservative Thimerosal. The plaintiffs brought a state court action against the makers of Thimerosal, the makers of the vaccine, and health care professionals who had given the vaccine, on the theory they had not made adequate warnings. Thimerosal is an inorganic mercury compound that is metabolized to ethyl mercury and thiosalicylate and has been present since the 1930s as a preservative in some vaccines and pharmaceutical products to prevent bacterial and fungal contamination. An appeal involved issues of improper joinder and the Vaccine Act, 42 U.S.C. §§300aa-1 et seq. Abbot Laboratories appealed to move the case to federal court, alleging that the health care professionals were *improper joinded* and, alternatively, that the Vaccine Act gave rise to *federal question jurisdiction*. On April 27, 2005, the federal district court dismissed the health care professionals and therefore refused to remand it to state court, and then dismissed all claims based on the Vaccine Act (Appellate Law & Practice, 2005).

Example 20.6

The parents of a four-month-old infant filed a compensation claim under NVIA for brain injuries allegedly occurring following a vaccination for diphtheria, pertussis, and tetanus. A pediatric neurologist found that the infant had seizures within three days of the vaccination. However, the neurologist also found that the infant had significant pre-existing microcephaly and concluded that the seizures were not the first symptoms of brain injury. Therefore the claim was rejected under the rules of NVIA.

Important Concepts Used to Prove Liability in Product Liability Litigation

Three theories of recovery are used in product liability litigation, regardless of whether negligence or strict liability is alleged. These theories are defective design, defective manufacture, and failure to warn.

Defective Design

Defective design exists when a drug or device is not reasonably safe for its intended use or a use that can be reasonably anticipated. This may occur when a drug or device is formulated to specifications, but is not efficacious for the intended purpose or is a product with massive side effects. If the product's design is found to be defective, all the products manufactured using that same design are considered to be defective. Sometimes, the designer has not performed adequate and appropriate testing of the product. A defective design may not be discovered until after the product has been sold. When that happens, the manufacturer will usually issue a product recall.

Example 20.7

In 2006, a manufacturer of cold therapy units was found to have problems with the warnings regarding the temperature control of its product. This company had prior notice of 38 injuries over the 12-year use of the unit. Five were reported to the FDA. These injuries included severe frostbite and necrotic-type injuries. The manufacturer did not tell the sales force about the potential for injury. At trial, it was brought out that the manufacturer did not test how cold the pad could get. The recommended use for continuous flow was 45–55°F. The device had a dot on a plastic dial to indicate a "safe" temperature with "colder" and "warmer" on opposite ends. Colder temperatures below the dot was not to be used. The manufacturer apparently knew there was a risk to patients, and yet made no attempt to change the device to prevent patients or health care providers from using it at a temperature that might cause injury.

Example 20.8

In the silicone breast implant litigation, the plaintiffs have alleged defective design of silicone-gel breast implants, claiming increased risk for connective tissue disorders, immune system illnesses, and implant rupture due to the faulty design of the implants. The plaintiffs claim that the manufacturers knew or should have known that the defective design of the implants would cause them to leak or rupture, with consequent migration of silicone that might ultimately result in systemic effects. In June 1999, an independent committee of scientists, who did not review past information and apparently did not conduct any new research (Brooks, n.d.), concluded that although silicone breast implants may be responsible for localized problems, such as hardening or scarring of breast tissue, implants do not cause any major diseases (e.g., lupus or rheumatoid arthritis). An

FDA study (FDA, 2001) collected data from 334 women via a questionnaire and noted a 2.8% association between extracapsular silicone gel and fibromyalgia. The issue of silicone breast implants has not ended, as the concern continues in the public mind. A few legal claims remain, even though a vast majority of breast implant cases have been completed, and in the meantime the use of saline implants continues. The FDA (November 17, 2006) approved silicone gel-filled breast implants for sale in the United States. However, the FDA requires manufacturers both to continue their long-term studies of women who received the implants before 2006 and to conduct a 10-year postapproval study that will involve 40,000 women to evaluate complications, connective tissue disease, neurological disease, rupture rates, and cancer.

Defective Manufacture

Defective manufacture can be alleged if the product is defective as a result of the manner in which it is manufactured and the defect existed when the product left the manufacturer's control. Defective manufacture is usually alleged when there is a one-time mistake (e.g., when one batch of a drug is tainted such that the flawed product differs from the manufacturer's intended design and manufacturing).

Example 20.9

In April 2008, a voluntary recall of a single lot of morphine sulfate 60 mg extended release tablets occurred because of a report of a tablet with twice the appropriate thickness. Oversized tablets possibly contained as much as two times the labeled level of active morphine sulfate. Opioids such as morphine have life-threatening consequences if overdosed. Consequences can include respiratory depression and low blood pressure. Patients who are highly debilitated with reduced strength or energy as a result of illness may be less likely to determine that a tablet is overweight or oversized. Another product recall with oversized tablets included Digitek (digoxin) used to treat heart failure and abnormal heart rhythms.

Example 20.10

In 2006, numerous eye centers throughout North America reported an increased incidence in the occurrence of toxic anterior segment syndrome (TASS) following outpatient cataract surgery. This was very similar to an outbreak that occurred in the late fall of 2005, which was found to be related to endotoxin contamination of ophthalmic solutions. TASS is an acute sterile anterior segment inflammation following generally uneventful cataract and anterior segment surgery. One of the main factors in differentiating TASS from an infectious endophthalmitis is the rapid onset. Most patients with TASS will develop symptoms within 12 to 24 hours of the surgery.

Failure to Warn

The duty of the manufacturer to warn of the dangers associated with the use of a product is crucial in any drug or device case, whether the case encompasses strict liability, negligence, or both. The key issue when failure to warn is alleged is the adequacy of the product label. It is assumed that when a warning is given, the manufacturer may reasonably expect that it will be read and heeded. While that presumption operates to the benefit of the manufacturer, when an inadequate warning is found, the presumption operates to the benefit of the plaintiff as if there were no warning, and the product can be presumed to be defective.

Drug and device companies routinely warn of adverse reactions in the labeling and package inserts that accompany each bottle or single package of the product or device or, in the case of drugs, in the *Physicians' Desk Reference* (PDR, 2008). The FDA requires a labeling revision, supplementation to the package insert, and in some cases direct notification to the physicians prescribing the product as soon as there is reasonable evidence of an association between a newly recognized serious hazard and a drug or device. A causal relationship does not need to be proven (Shulman & Ulcickas, 1989). The argument by a defendant drug company that it was not bound to provide a warning until the occurrence of the side effect was frequent and clearly defined will often be rejected by the courts (*Wooderson v. Ortho Pharmaceutical Corp*, 1984).

Example 20.11

DonJoy, a manufacturer, has changed its label because of frostbite injuries and necrotic injury associated with its Iceman Cooler cold therapy units (FDA, 2008b). The original product labeling did not have the specific type warning of these types of injuries.

Example 20.12

Vioxx was part of a class of nonsteroidal anti-inflammatory drugs (NSAIDs) called COX-2 inhibitors that was approved by the FDA in 1999. In June 2000, Merck submitted to FDA a safety study called Vioxx Gastrointestinal Outcomes Research (VIGOR) that found an increased risk of serious cardiovascular events, including heart attacks and strokes, in patients taking Vioxx compared with patients taking naproxen. After reviewing the results of the VIGOR study and other available data from controlled clinical trials, FDA consulted with its Arthritis Advisory Committee in February 2001 regarding the clinical interpretation of this new safety information (Villalba, 2001). In April 2002, FDA implemented labeling changes to reflect the findings from the VIGOR study. The labeling changes included information about the increase in risk of cardiovascular events, including heart attack and stroke (FDA, 2004a). On September 30, 2004 the Vioxx recall was announced (FDA, 2004b). The day of the Vioxx recall, acting director of the FDA's Center for Drug Evaluation and Research (CDER), Steven Galson said the announcement was not a total surprise and the agency had been concerned and aware of cardiovascular safety concerns linked to Vioxx for the previous several years. These cardiovascular events, surfacing just after Vioxx was approved, have been heavily scrutinized in light of the Vioxx recall. Critics have questioned the FDA for failing to take these initial warning signs seriously and requiring that further studies be performed, and Merck has been accused of spinning the data (Rosenberg, 2008).

Learned Intermediary

In the case of prescription drugs and medical devices, the manufacturer's duty to warn goes to the physician rather than the patient, since the patient can obtain the product only through the physician. The learned intermediary stands between the manufacturer of a medical device or product and the person who uses the product. The physician acts as the *learned intermediary* with regard to the drug and is expected to convey to the patient the labeling information provided by the manufacturer. The plaintiff, as the patient and consumer, has to rely on the health care expertise of the physician to read and be cognizant of the warnings. This doctrine has been a part of product liability law for years.

Example 20.13

In *Cowley v. Abbott Laboratories* (2007), the claim alleged that a neurological disorder was caused by taking Humira (Abbott) and by the manufacturer's failure to adequately warn about certain neurological side effects. The defendant moved for summary judgment, arguing that under North

Carolina's learned intermediary doctrine, it had no duty to warn the plaintiff directly and that it had discharged its duty to warn by adequately warning plaintiff's prescribing physician (the learned intermediary) of the possible side effects (Prince, 2007).

Example 20.14

Schering Corporation, which manufactures Garamycin (gentamicin), cannot be expected to warn patients directly concerning the potential effects this drug can cause (e.g., nephrotoxicity and neurotoxicity). The burden falls on the learned intermediary, the person with knowledge who prescribes the drug, to be informed and to monitor the patient for these potential problems. Schering Corporation has warned of these adverse reactions through such sources as the package insert and the Physicians' Desk Reference (PDR, 2008).

By providing adequate information to the physician, the manufacturer in effect erects a barrier to liability. To the extent that the labeling information is inadequate, that barrier is weakened, and the manufacturer becomes more vulnerable.

Over-the-Counter Products

FDA Class II devices, which are available for purchase over the counter (OTC) without a prescription, must carry adequate warnings of potential hazards written in language that consumers can understand, since there is no learned intermediary when using these products.

In March 1999, the FDA announced that a new labeling regulation would be available for OTC drugs (*Over-the-counter human drugs; labeling requirements*, 1999). The regulation called for a standardized format that would improve the labeling on drugs that Americans use most—nonprescription or OTC drugs. By clearly showing a drug's ingredients, dose, and warnings, the new labeling would make it easier for consumers to understand information about a drug's benefits, risks, and proper use. The FDA indicated that the new labeling would be in effect two years from the date of the announcement and that all OTC medications would have to adopt the new labeling within six years. Since March 17, 1999, FDA has published six additional major final rules on OTC drug monographs and several minor amendments to existing final monographs (*Agency information collection activities*, 2005). Except for OTC sunscreen drug products and a small number of other OTC drug products, the effective date for relabeling the OTC drug products in the new format occurred by the end of 2004. There continues to be ongoing review and changes of labeling by the FDA.

Conduct of the Manufacturer

Whether the cause of an action is negligence or strict liability, there are criteria that the conduct of a manufacturer will be judged (21 U.S.C. §321, 1982). These criteria focus primarily on three factors:

1. Knowledge of the risk
2. The nature and timing of the duty to warn
3. Language used to convey the warning

Knowledge of the Risk

The drug company may not be held liable for failure to warn of adverse effects unless the adverse effects were known or reasonably scientifically knowable at the time the product was distributed by the manufacturer. The manufacturer is held to the standard of an expert in the field and is charged with actual knowledge of adverse drug reactions arising from both its own research and knowledge of reported reactions from outside sources, such as the scientific literature.

Example 20.15

The FDA is investigating a possible association between the use of Singulair and behavior/mood changes, suicidal thinking/behavior, and suicide. Singulair is a leukotriene receptor antagonist and is used to treat asthma, symptoms of allergic rhinitis, and prevent exercise-induced asthma. In 2007 and 2008, the maker of Singulair (Merck & Co, Inc.) updated the prescribing information and patient information to include the following postmarketing adverse events: tremor in March 2007, depression in April 2007, suicidality (suicidal thinking and behavior) in October 2007, and anxiousness in February 2008. In February 2008, FDA and Merck discussed how best to communicate these labeling changes to prescribers and patients. Merck will highlight the changes in the prescribing information in face-to-face interactions with prescribers and provide prescribers with patient information leaflets about Singulair (FDA, 2008c).

The Nature and Timing of the Duty to Warn

The determination whether the manufacturer acted reasonably regarding warnings depends on the company's knowledge of the risks associated with the product at the time the product was distributed to the plaintiff. The duty to warn does not expire when the product is placed on the market, but is continuous. This imposes an obligation on the manufacturer to seek out information regarding its product. If information becomes available indicating that a certain danger is associated with the use of the drug, then the manufacturer cannot disregard the information in drafting or altering its warning simply because the manufacturer feels the evidence is unconvincing. The onus is on the company to communicate and warn physicians regarding a new risk as soon as it is reasonably practical. The drug or device manufacturer is not allowed to wait until a statistically significant number of people have been injured or until a causal relationship has been established by epidemiological studies.

In previous cases, the courts have rejected the defendant manufacturer's argument that it was not bound to provide warnings until the occurrence of side effects was so frequent and the evidence of causation was so clear-cut that the manufacturer itself was convinced that the drug caused or contributed to such problems (*Wooderson v. Ortho Pharmaceutical Corp*, 1984). On this issue, the court's view agrees with the FDA regulations requiring a labeling revision as soon as there is reasonable evidence of an association of a serious hazard with a drug. A causal relationship need not have been proved.

Example 20.16

A case in point was a problematic defibrillator manufactured by Marquette Electronics, Inc. The defibrillator used a special battery pack, which was found to wear out prematurely, manifesting as a rapid loss of charge capacity after being removed from the battery charger. The FDA eventually initiated a Class I recall (complete recall) of the battery charger. However, FDA Medical Device Reports (MDRs) revealed that Marquette had been on notice of this problem for a significant period of time prior to recall. A Freedom of Information Act (FOIA) request to obtain information on a certain drug or device revealed a number of reports of the defibrillator's failure to work due to rapid loss of charge capacity in the batteries, causing death in some instances, for a substantial period of time prior to Marquette's warning to users of this association. The FOIA can be found in Title 5 of the United States Code, section 552 (Title 5, section 552, 2000 & Supp. III 2003). It was enacted in 1966, and provides that any person has the right to request access to federal agency records or information. Additional information about the FOIA can be found at the United States Department of Justice web site, http://www.usdoj.gov/oip/index.html.

Language Used to Convey the Warning

The FDA regulates all prescription drug and medical device promotional activities that fall within the definition of labeling and advertising (21 C.F.R. §201.56, 201.57, 1988). Once a determination has been made to include a warning in the drug or device labeling, it is incumbent upon the manufacturer to adequately convey the warning to the doctor. Product labeling includes written material both physically on the product and accompanying the product. Labeling has been widely interpreted to include the package insert, exhibits, brochures, product-detailing pieces, press releases, speeches by company officials, and other promotional materials (e.g., "Dear Doctor Letter") that are sent to medical providers with information regarding problems with different medications or devices.

The format and content of drug labeling is rigidly controlled by the federal regulations. Labeling must include indications, precautions, warnings, contraindications, and dosage, among other information. The product label is approved by the FDA during the drug approval process; the label is not a document arbitrarily designed by the drug manufacturer. All subsequent promotional materials must conform to the language in the approved labeling. The FDA labeling regulations impose a continuing obligation on the manufacturer, and new data must be incorporated in the label as it becomes available. The regulations permit the manufacturer in specified instances to change its labeling without prior authorization of the FDA. A failure to share new information could result in the drug's being improperly labeled or misbranded. This would constitute evidence for the plaintiff in a product liability suit.

The adequacy of the warning included in the labeling is measured not only by what is stated, but also by the manner in which it is stated.

Example 20.17

In an FDA alert of August 2008, the FDA notified health care professionals of the risk of muscle injury, rhabdomyolysis, which can lead to kidney failure or death, when simvastatin (drug to lower cholesterol) is used with amiodarone (controls heart rhythm problem). This risk is dose-related and increases when a dose of simvastatin greater than 20 mg per day is given with amiodarone. Although a revision of the simvastatin labeling in 2002 described this increased risk of rhabdomyolysis in reference to the above dosage, FDA continued to receive reports of rhabdomyolysis in patients treated concurrently with amiodarone and simvastatin. Prescribers should be aware of the increased risk of rhabdomyolysis when simvastatin is prescribed with amiodarone, and they should avoid doses of simvastatin greater than 20 mg per day in patients taking amiodarone.

A warning can be found inadequate if the facts are insufficient, the response unduly delayed, or the manner of the words reluctant or lacking in intensity. The warning must be expressed in a tone congruent with the nature of the risk.

Example 20.18

On July 3, 2007, U.S. District Judge Eldon Fallon opined that the FDA approval of a drug label does not exonerate the manufacturer from claims of inadequate warning. Had Fallon sided with Merck, the drug company could dispute lawsuits alleging that Vioxx caused plaintiff's heart attack and other cardiovascular problems. The judge rejected Merck's attempt to throw out lawsuits brought by two people who began taking Vioxx after April 2002, when the FDA approved a label warning that the drug might increase the chance of such problems (Fallon, 2007).

There are several important considerations in the review of warnings. Warnings must be conspicuous and prominent. Warnings can be considered ineffective and insufficient if they are printed in a body of other information of the same size and color. This means that it is incumbent upon the manufacturer to make the warnings conspicuous and prominent. As the result of litigation involving toxic shock syndrome associated with tampon use, the warnings are now usually printed on the top of the box or prominently located in a package insert placed on top of the product. In the Physicians' Desk Reference (PDR, 2008), drugs with particularly dangerous side effects have special warnings, sometimes referred to as "black box warnings," with bold print and placement at the beginning of the labeling.

To be adequate, warnings must convey the risk of the danger associated with the use of the product. The question of adequacy depends upon the language used and the impression that such language might reasonably be calculated to make upon the physician or consumer. The wording used must be simple and straightforward. If a warning with reference to a particular side effect is labeled *rare*, the physician might be more inclined to recommend the product than if the side effect were labeled as *common* or *occasional*.

Warnings must also not be ambiguous or lack of clarity or narrowness. The risks and types of possible adverse reactions must be clear and straightforward. Over-promotion and activities such as direct consumer advertising may dilute the warnings or even render them insufficient.

Example 20.19

In May 2007, Medicis received an allegation regarding their medication Loprox that they targeted at pediatricians and urged them to use as a treatment for diaper rash. The drug is approved as a fungicide and not for treating children less than 10 years of age (U.S. Government Accountability Office, 2008).

Example 20.20

In June 2004, GlaxoSmithKline, the makers of Paxil CR received a warning letter that cited a television ad that suggested that anyone experiencing anxiety, fear, or self-consciousness in social or work situations was an appropriate candidate for Paxil CR (U.S. Government Accountability Office, 2008). Paxil CR is indicated for the treatment of major depressive disorder, panic disorder, social anxiety disorder, and premenstrual dysphoric disorder.

A manufacturer has a duty to keep abreast of the current state of knowledge regarding their products as gained through research, medical literature, and adverse reaction reports. The subsequently acquired knowledge may necessitate a further duty to notify both physicians and potential consumers of this new information. Manufacturers have a duty to warn of all potential dangers either known or that should have been known in the exercise of reasonable care.

Example 20.21

A large verdict was returned in Georgia regarding the failure of Ortho Pharmaceutical to warn about the potential for teratogenicity of Ortho-Gynol contraceptive jelly. The plaintiff showed that substantial research proved a connection between spermicidal jelly and birth defects and that the manufacturer had failed to include this information in the warnings. The failure to change the warnings to reflect this knowledge meant that the warnings were inadequate, and the product was deemed defective (*Wells v. Ortho Pharmaceutical Corp*, 1985).

Example 20.22

Zyprexa, the brand name for olanzapine, was approved for the treatment of schizophrenia and bipolar mania. It is one of a type of drugs called psychotropics, which are believed to reduce symptoms of some mental disorders by balancing chemicals in the brain. Zyprexa was approved in 1996 by the FDA. In March 2004, the FDA notified health care professionals of the increased risk of hyperglycemia and diabetes in patients taking these medications. In a Dear Doctor Letter, the FDA informed the providers of the changes made to the drug label describing these risks (FDA, 2004c). Since that time, Ely Lilly has settled thousands of lawsuits based on allegations that Zyprexa caused problems with high blood sugar and the drug labels failed to adequately warn of these risks.

On January 18, 2006, the FDA unveiled a major revision to the format of prescription drug information, commonly called the package insert, to give health care professionals clear and concise prescribing information. In an effort to manage the risks of medication use and reduce medical errors, the newly designed package insert will provide the most up-to-date information in an easy-to-read format that draws physician and patient attention to the most important pieces of drug information before a product is prescribed.

Some of the most significant changes include (1) a new section called Highlights to provide immediate access to the most important prescribing information about benefits and risks; (2) a Table of Contents for easy reference to detailed safety and efficacy information; (3) the date of initial product approval, making it easier to determine how long a product has been on the market; and (4) a toll-free number and Internet reporting information for suspected adverse events to encourage more widespread reporting of suspected side effects. This stems from several widely publicized safety problems, most notably an increased risk of heart attacks and strokes that led manufacturers to pull the painkillers Vioxx and Bextra from the market (Zwillich, 2006).

U.S. Food and Drug Administration

The purpose of the U.S. FDA, formulated under the auspices of the Food, Drug, and Cosmetic Act of 1938, was to strengthen government regulation of medications and required evidence of safety prior to the marketing of a new drug. This act introduced the use of prescriptions for the majority of drugs and established a regulatory agency, the FDA, to oversee the marketing and set the policies for the sale of new drugs (Food, Drug and Cosmetic Act of 1938). Due to the grave adverse reactions associated with thalidomide, the Kefauver-Harris Amendments of 1962 to the Food, Drug, and Cosmetic Act imposed strict guidelines regarding drug safety and labeling and resulted in 7000 drugs being removed from the market. Since that time, the FDA's role has been centered on identifying and communicating adverse reactions associated with pharmaceuticals, medical devices (21 U.S.C. §360c, d, e, & i, 1982), or biologicals such as vaccines, insulin, blood product, or gene therapy.

The main consumer watchdog group is the FDA's CDER created in response to the FDA Modernization Act of 1997, who evaluate new drugs before they can be sold. They ensure both brand names, generic, and OTC drugs work correctly and the health benefits outweigh their known risks. This not only helps to curtail quackery, but also provides information needed to use medicine wisely. In 2005 the FDA established an independent Drug Safety Oversight Board (DSOB) to oversee the management of drug safety issues and communication to the public about the risks and benefits of medicines. They conduct evaluations of emerging drug safety issues and select drugs to be placed on a Drug Watch Web site.

The Food and Drug Administration Amendments Act (FDAAA) of 2007 was signed into law and was a significant addition to FDA authority. FDAAA reauthorized and expanded the Prescription Drug User Fee Act (PDUFA) to ensure that CDER has the resources needed to conduct complex and comprehensive drug reviews and to provide more resources for drug safety activities. Two other important laws were reauthorized; the Best Pharmaceuticals for Children Act and the Pediatric Research Equity Act. Both laws encourage more research into developing treatments for children. On June 4, 2007, the FDA established a Risk Communication Advisory Committee (RCAC), as suggested by the Institute of Medicine (IOM) and endorsed in the FDAAA. The committee comprises practitioners and experts in risk communications.

Example 20.23

In July 2008, the FDA informed health care professionals of the possibility that x-rays used during computed tomography (CT) examinations may cause some implanted and external electronic medical devices to malfunction. Most patients with electronic medical devices undergo CT scans without any adverse consequences. However, the agency has received a small number of reports of adverse events in which CT scans may have interfered with electronic medical devices, including pacemakers, defibrillators, neurostimulators, and implanted or externally worn drug infusion pumps (Schultz, 2008).

Clinical Trials/Studies of Pharmaceuticals

The drug approval process is constructed to theoretically minimize the possibility that drug errors will make their way to consumers. Before approving a new drug for marketing, the FDA must ascertain the drug's safety and efficacy. This verification process requires the drug manufacturer to put the drug through a lengthy experimental protocol. The FDA approves a drug based on these premarketing evaluations, or clinical trials, performed by the drug company to determine the safety and effectiveness of the drug.

Clinical trials are considered the gold standard of pharmaceutical research, but the results apply to only a small range of questions and cannot be applied to the general population. Clinical trials compare outcomes among two or more groups: one group is deliberately exposed to the new therapy, while the others receive standard or alternative treatment or a placebo. These trials are used to test the efficacy of new treatments (Inman, 1980). An Investigational New Drug (IND) application must be submitted to the FDA and a local institutional review board (IRB) for review before a clinical trial/drug study begins. To demonstrate the safety and efficacy of a new drug, there are three phases of testing. Phase 1 trials are typically carried out in a small number of healthy subjects to determine the most frequent side effects, how often, and how the drug is metabolized and excreted (FDA, 2002). Phase 2 trials evaluate the drug's safety and efficacy in the target population. This phase is typically done in small samples of 50–100. Phase 3 studies are randomized, blind, and, many times, placebo controlled.

Randomization is a mechanism of assigning the study patients to treatment arms, like tossing a coin or throwing a dice. The chance of being put on the study drug is usually 50%. The study researcher is not allowed to choose who receives the study drug and who receives the comparison study therapies. Blinding the studies means that both the study participants and the investigators who carry out the protocol and collect the data do not know which study subjects are receiving the study drug. Both of these elements are used to prevent researcher bias when treating and evaluating the study patients.

The FDA closely regulates all three phases of the clinical trial process in cooperation with the drug manufacturer. Safety is maintained by giving the drug under controlled circumstances with careful monitoring by physician experts in the treatment of the particular disease under consideration. The experts give meticulous attention to reporting adverse consequences of all types (Avorn, 1989). The results of all the clinical studies are submitted to the FDA for review. After sufficient research and review have been completed, the FDA grants a New Drug Application (NDA) and the drug can be manufactured.

As a result of the FDA regulatory process, when the average drug is marketed, consumers have a reasonable expectation that serious adverse effects are unlikely to occur when the drug is used

- For its approved indication
- At its recommended dose
- For limited periods
- In medically uncomplicated, nonpregnant young or middle-aged adults who are medically compliant

Because of limited sample sizes and duration of clinical trials, these studies often cannot detect or measure serious adverse effects that are infrequent or related to long-term use. Additionally, the effects of a new drug on a frail elderly patient with multiple illnesses may be difficult to predict even after the completion of the clinical trials (Dukes & Swartz, 1988).

Example 20.24

In July 2008, the FDA reminded health care professionals who treat patients with mitoxantrone (Novantrone and generics) about recommendations that left ventricular ejection fraction (LVEF) be evaluated before initiating treatment and prior to administering each dose of mitoxantrone. FDA offered additional recommendations for cardiac monitoring to detect late-occurring cardiac toxicity, and provided information for patients with multiple sclerosis (MS) who receive the drug. These recommendations were established in 2005 in response to postmarketing reports and case reports in the medical literature that described decreases in LVEF or frank congestive heart failure in patients with MS who had received cumulative doses of mitoxantrone that were lower than 100 mg/m^2. Since that time, the FDA has received information from a post-marketing safety study that demonstrated there is poor adherence to these recommendations in clinical practice. FDA is working with the manufacturers to educate health care providers to adhere to cardiac monitoring recommendations for patients with MS (FDA, 2008d).

Example 20.25

The FDA notified health care professionals in June 2008 that both conventional and atypical antipsychotics are associated with an increased risk of mortality in elderly patients treated for dementia-related psychosis. In April 2005, the FDA notified health care professionals that patients with dementia-related psychosis treated with atypical antipsychotic drugs are at an increased risk of death. Since issuing that notification, the FDA reviewed additional information that indicates the risk is also associated with conventional antipsychotics. Antipsychotics are not indicated for the treatment of dementia-related psychosis. The prescribing information for all antipsychotic drugs will now include the same information about this risk in a BOXED WARNING and the WARNINGS section (FDA, 2008e).

Informed Consent in Clinical Trials

Protection of human research subjects in the field of clinical trials has been a key issue since the reported abuses of human subjects in biomedical experiments, especially during World War II. Some of the significant guidelines regarding the safety of human subjects and proper research conduct that have been developed since the reported abuses include The Nuremberg Code (1949), The Belmont Report (1979), The Declaration of Helsinki (1964), and Good Clinical Practice (GCP) Guidelines. The Nuremberg Code encompasses the directives for human experimentation and voluntary consent. The Belmont Report summarizes the basic ethical principles and guidelines for research involving human subjects. The Declaration of Helsinki is an ethical principle to guide physicians and other medical personnel regarding human subject medical research.

The Office for Human Research Protections (OHRP) in the Department of Health and Human Services (HHS) now heads the department's programs for the protection of human research participants and oversees human protection in HHS-funded research. GCP Guidelines are used as standards for all aspects of clinical trials. The Code of Federal Regulations (Title 21 CFR, Part 50, and Subpart B) explains the requirements, eight basic elements, and documentation of informed consent (Code of Federal Regulations, 2000a, 2000b).

Obtaining an informed consent that is voluntarily signed, dated, witnessed by an investigator or designee, and approved by the IRB from the human research subject is required by law for the subject's protection. It must be obtained before research procedures are performed. The informed consent can be obtained from the subject's legally authorized representative. The informed consent process involves providing the research subject with adequate and understandable study information, including possible risks, and sufficient time and opportunity for discussion (with the investigator or designee and others, such as family, when appropriate), including the opportunity to ask questions for comprehension. If the subject voluntarily chooses to participate, then they must sign the informed consent document. A copy of the document is part of the permanent medical record, and a copy is given to the subject (Code of Federal Regulations 2000c). Chapter 4, "Informed Consent," discusses the informed consent process in greater detail. Frequently found deficiencies or violations involve inadequate informed consent and failures of the health care facility's IRB.

Example 20.26

There are numerous reports accusing FDA and other scientists of breaches of ethics: retractions in peer-reviewed journals, sales forces told to lie, and product liability lawsuits (Cezanne, 2007). Darren McDaniel, CEO of the Lake Forest, CA, for-profit IRB, concluded that the process of enrolling subjects should be to obtain consent, give subject time to decide, do not coerce, and use understandable language, do not waive legal rights, give subject a copy, and answer his or her questions. This vagueness around issues such as time (how long is long enough to decide?), coercion (what precisely constitutes coercion?), and language (how do you know whether or not the subject "understands"?) are what makes the current requirement inadequate. He further said there is provision for audiotaping in the regulations, and such a tape will provide objective evidence in the case of a later lawsuit (Cezanne, 2007).

Example 20.27

According to Avitzur (2005) *Lett v. Zahenk* was based on a patient's complaint that she was tricked into participating in a clinical study at Ohio State University Medical Center (OSUMC) when she sought treatment for Charcot-Marie-Tooth syndrome (CMT). Although it was acknowledged that a nerve biopsy would be performed for research purposes and not for diagnostic purposes, the consent form was allegedly not presented to the patient until she was on the operating table. Counts in the patient's lawsuit included breach of the right to be treated with dignity in which the Nuremberg Code, the Declaration of Helsinki, and the Code of Federal Regulations (that established the law with respect to the protection of human research subjects at institutions such as OSUMC) were alleged to be violated (Avitzur, 2005).

Current Trends in Pharmaceutical Trial Conduct

Phase IV of a drug trial is post marketing clinical research. The pharmaceutical industry has had a great deal of negative publicity as a result of high-profile product withdrawals caused by inadequate safety profiles. A changing regulatory environment, growing concerns about the safety of new medicines, and various uses for large-scale, real-world data on marketed drugs' safety and efficacy are primary drivers of the growth seen in the Phase IV research environment today. Postmarketing research is an important element of commercialization that enables companies to expand existing markets, enter new markets, develop and deliver messaging that directly compares their products with the competition, and secure a niche position in crowded markets. What's more, payer groups and regulators are both requiring more postmarketing data from drug companies.

Implications for the LNC

One of the first issues to be considered by the LNC in pharmaceutical liability case reviews is whether or not the patient was involved in a clinical trial with a study drug. If not, then other product liability issues would need to be evaluated, as described below. During medical record review of a case, the LNC may discover a reference to a study someplace within the medical records. This should be researched further for possible areas of liability.

If the patient was involved in a clinical trial of a study drug, the LNC should look for a clinical trial consent form document found within the medical records. If not found, the LNC should search for evidence within the medical records that the patient was involved in a clinical trial with a study drug: is the consent form signed, dated, and witnessed? Is it signed by the patient or the patient's legal representative? The consent form would need to be closely evaluated for all the required elements as regulated by law. Other areas to consider for review are possible protocol violations regarding enrollment of an ineligible subject and dosage administration errors.

Example 20.28

A fraud theory was used in a New York lawsuit against GlaxoSmithKline ("Glaxo") for its dissemination of results of clinical trials of Paxil (paroxetine) on children and adolescents with Major Depressive Disorder. It was claimed that Glaxo misled the public and the medical community by providing information concerning the drug's clinical trials that yielded positive (or partially positive) results, but not those in which the results were negative or inconclusive. Shortly after the complaint was filed, Glaxo voluntarily posted full results of all clinical trials of Paxil on its web site. On August 26, 2004, the case was settled on terms requiring a continuation of this practice, establishment of an online "Clinical Trial Register," inclusion of safety and efficacy data in Medical Information Letters to physicians concerning off-label uses of drugs, and a payment of $2.5 million (Nagle, 2004).

Medical Devices

A medical device is any health care product that does not use a chemical action or is metabolized to achieve its primary purpose. Medical devices also include diagnostic aids such as reagents and test kits (FDA, 2006). Medical devices were not subject to extensive FDA regulation until 1976, when the Medical Device Amendments to the Food, Drug, and Cosmetic Act were passed. Before 1976 and the Safe Medical Devices Act of 1990, medical devices could be marketed without review by the FDA. Under the Medical Device Amendments, medical devices have been subject to the regulatory process that is similar to that utilized for pharmaceuticals. There are important differences.

The statutory definition of a medical device is all-encompassing. Essentially, any item promoted for a medical purpose that does not rely on chemical action to achieve its intended effect is considered to be a medical device. *In vitro* diagnostic tests are also regulated as medical devices. Medical devices are classified and regulated according to their degree of risk to the public. Devices that are life-supporting, life-sustaining or implanted, such as pacemakers, must receive agency approval before they can be marketed (Rados, 2006).

Unlike the regulation of new drugs, in which standards of safety and effectiveness are applied uniformly, the regulation of medical devices is based on risk. Securing FDA approval of a new medical device before marketing requires that the manufacturer provide reasonable assurance that the device is safe and effective when used for the purpose for which the approval is sought. Safety and effectiveness are assessed with specific reference to the uses for which the device is intended, as set forth in the labeling on the device. Safety is evaluated by weighing the probable benefits to health against the probable risks of injury. The risk/benefit ratio must be acceptable, but proof that the product will never cause harm or will always be effective is not required.

There are three different regulatory classes for medical devices. Only devices classified as "Class III" undergo the strict scrutiny of a premarketing approval (PMA) process. This class is reserved for devices deemed critical, such as heart valves, that are implanted within the body or whose failure would be life-threatening. PMA applications may take nine months or more to be processed and may include a hearing before a panel of outside experts.

Class II devices do not undergo the PMA process but are subject to special controls, which usually take the form of additional quality control requirements imposed during the manufacturing process. Manufacturers of devices classified as Class I need only comply with good manufacturing practices in the manufacture of such products. Most medical devices are not subject to FDA scrutiny (Code of Federal Regulations, 2000d).

The Supreme Court made a ruling on February 20, 2008 that protects many types of medical device makers from personal injury lawsuits in *Riegel v. Medtronic* (2008). In *Riegel* the Supreme Court concluded that Congress, based on interpretation of a flawed clause ruled that it intended that the premarket approval process would bar patients from filing lawsuits that in effect, second-guess regulators' judgments about the safety and effectiveness of devices they have reviewed. The Supreme Court ruling also presumed that the labels companies develop to warn of side effects and limitations are adequate because they, too, receive FDA review. The majority of Class III devices submitted for FDA consideration are variants on products like standard pacemakers that were already in the market when the main law covering devices was passed by Congress in 1976 (Feder, 2008).

Example 20.29

The Supreme Court in *Riegel v. Medtronic, Inc.* (2008) denied a plaintiff an award for damages when his balloon catheter ruptured during heart surgery due to over-inflation. The man sued the manufacturer of the catheter, alleging that the device violated New York state law and that the defective product caused him to suffer from severe and permanent injuries. After hearing the facts, the Supreme Court found that the federal Medical Device Act prevented the man from seeking remedies based on his state common law claims of strict liability, breach of implied warranty, and negligence (Greenberg & Rudman, 2008).

Example 20.30

Now plaintiffs with injuries they attribute to devices like heart valves, artificial hips, and defibrillators may no longer have valid cases. Medtronic is asking courts to dismiss their lawsuits. In December 2007, Medtronic announced an agreement to pay $114.1 million to settle 2682 injury lawsuits related to its 2005 recall of defibrillators with a defective battery. In November, Boston Scientific agreed to pay up to $240 million to settle 8550 claims stemming from recalls of defibrillators made by a subsidiary, Guidant. Plaintiffs in those cases are free to stay out of the settlements and try to continue suing the companies, but the chances of a verdict in their favor is doubtful (Feder, 2008).

FDA's Adverse Events Reporting System

Adverse Events Reporting System (AERS) replaced the Spontaneous Reporting System in October 1997. The Adverse Event Reporting system flags safety issues and identifies pharmaceuticals or therapeutic biological products (such as blood products), for further epidemiological study. It may ultimately prompt regulatory responses such as drug labeling changes, letters to health care professionals, or market withdrawals.

The agency requires product manufacturers and distributors to report adverse events regularly in accordance with 21 CFR §310.305 and §314.80. Mandatory reports for drugs in clinical trials and newly marketed drugs are submitted in various forms: 15-day alerts, quarterly or annual updates. The MedWatch program also collects voluntary reports from health care professionals and consumers. Adverse drug events include any serious and unexpected consequences of human drug use in a medical practice such as failure of expected pharmacological action, as well as accidental or intentional overdoses or abuse (Karceski, 2008).

A Serious Adverse Event (SAE) is to be reported when the outcome is any of the following:

1. Death
2. A life-threatening adverse event with a substantial risk of dying
3. An event that results in initial or prolonged hospital stay
4. A congenital anomaly/birth defect
5. A persistent or significant disability, incapacity, or damage
6. A medical product that might result in a condition that required medical or surgical intervention to prevent permanent impairment or damage (refer to http://www.fda.gov/medwaTCH/how.htm)

Example 20.31

The FDA issued a Class I Recall of Medtronic Inc. Sprint Fidelis Defibrillator Leads, model numbers 6930, 6931, 6948, and 6949 manufactured from September 2004 through October 15, 2007. Medtronic voluntarily suspended distribution because a small number of fractures had been detected (FDA, 2007).

In order to document adverse effects not readily or reliably uncovered by clinical trials, federal regulations require adverse drug reaction (ADR) reporting to the FDA. The central focus of the regulations, which are directed to drug manufacturers, is the timely collection, analysis, and reporting of the adverse drug reaction data to the FDA. An adverse drug reaction is defined in the regulations as any adverse event associated with the use of a drug, whether or not it is considered drug-related. Regulations require that a manufacturer submit a report to the FDA within 15 days of learning of any serious event, death, or hospitalization. Compliance with these regulations will constitute important evidence for a manufacturer in the course of a product liability suit and may be a key element in avoiding liability (Code of Federal Regulations, 2000d).

Once adverse events are known to occur in association with specific products, combination of products, or specific diseases, the drug may be taken off the market or recalled either at the request of the FDA or voluntarily by the pharmaceutical manufacturer. A few drugs have been taken off the market by their manufacturers after intense media attention based on anecdotal reporting. Examples of recent product recalls include Vioxx, Fen-Phen, Redux, Baycol, PPA (phenylpropanolamine), Propulsid, and Rezulin. Examples of medical devices recently taken off the market are the Guidant defibrillator, knee replacement prosthesis, Sulzer hip implant, Ortho Summit Processor Instrument used for screening infectious diseases in human blood, and Baxter dialyzers.

The Adverse Reporting System plays an important role in the litigation process. Physician reports, which are the mainstay of the system, are voluntarily made mainly to manufacturers, who are required by regulation to summarize and forward the data to the FDA in a timely manner. Some physicians report an ADR directly to the FDA, as do some pharmacists, patients, nurses, and others. Any death or hospitalization associated with the use of a vaccine must be reported directly to the FDA by a physician. This is the only type of product for which physicians are legally responsible to report an ADR. The burden of reporting an ADR for nonprescription drugs falls on the consumers.

Meeting the standard of the reasonably prudent manufacturer with respect to ADR reporting requires a considerably greater allocation of resources today than it did in the past. The obligation to analyze and categorize each ADR report to ensure timely and appropriate reporting falls, for the most part, on the manufacturer. The manufacturer is responsible for analyzing adverse reaction reports from multiple sources, including foreign and domestic reports, commercial marketing experiences, postmarketing clinical evaluations, postmarketing epidemiological surveillance studies, scientific and medical literature, and unpublished manuscripts.

While an efficient compilation of ADR reports is necessary to meet the regulatory requirements, these same documents may provide the plaintiff with important evidence regarding when the manufacturer became aware of the risk in question. A crucial element in the drug manufacturer's litigation control program is the establishment of procedures for timely internal investigations of ADR reports from the moment the data are first received. The drug company that is compliant with the regulations and has excellent documentation will have a better inherent defense in a product liability suit. Since the manufacturer is responsible for keeping abreast of all written articles or letters to the editor reporting observed adverse effects of its product, the plaintiff should certainly address the issue regarding the length of time between the first reports in the medical literature and when the product label was changed to include an adverse reaction.

The plaintiff can then follow the paper trail from the manufacturer, including, for example, the date on which a "Dear Doctor" letter was sent to notify prescribing physicians of reported serious side effects, as well as when the product-detailing literature changed to reflect the inclusion of the side effect. The reporting system of the FDA is no guarantee of drug safety; it serves public health as an early warning system to monitor possible drug risk. In fact, it may be the most efficient and the only affordable method of detecting serious clinical events that occur less frequently than 1 in 10,000 drug exposures.

There are contributions and limitations to the adverse drug event reporting system. One contribution is that a signal is generated from the field of clinical use as to unacceptable, even rare, drug toxicities. The limitations are many, including reports laden with opinion, overreporting, misinterpretation, and underreporting. The most serious drawback to the system is the rate of underreporting. In several studies, a physician's perceived legal liability correlated with his unwillingness to report adverse reactions. The reporting may be biased and cluttered with events that are not attributable to the drug, causing false negatives and false positives in the system. Thus, the system must not be used for calculation of specific rates of adverse reactions. Only with proper epidemiological studies, where biases can be detected, can the true rates of adverse reactions and the nature of the causation of those reactions be appropriately determined.

In June 1993, the FDA instituted a new adverse event reporting system called MedWatch, the Medical Products Reporting Program, to ensure that health providers identify and report adverse events (see Appendices A and B). The premise for emphasizing the health care provider's responsibility in reporting is that only by the reporting of events to the FDA or drug manufacturer can the FDA ensure the safety of drugs and biological and medical devices. Even the large clinical trials of a new drug may study only several thousand persons. If an adverse event occurs for 1 in 1000 users, these trials may miss identifying a potentially harmful side effect. Only when the drug is released to the mass market and hundreds of thousands are using the product, will a large number of incidences of the potentially harmful side effect be detected. Additionally, when the drug is taken with other medications or OTC products, interactions may occur that were not previously identified in the limited study populations of the clinical trials (Kessler, 2003; Kuc, 1995).

The MedWatch system was developed to make it easier for the health care provider, including doctors, nurses, and pharmacists, to report to the FDA serious events, which are defined as death, risk of death, hospitalization, significant disability, congenital anomaly, or events requiring intervention to prevent impairment or damage. Under this system the FDA should also be notified about medical device problems, such as defects, inaccurate or illegible product labels, package or product mix-ups, drug contamination, or drug stability problems. In the past, the notification of adverse reactions has resulted in critical FDA action on several occasions. It is hoped that MedWatch will increase the ease of reporting, resulting in higher numbers of reports for the FDA to analyze. LNCs can review current and past information for medications and medical devices from MedWatch at http://www.fda.gov/medwatch/.

Example 20.32

The FDA reviewed 30 postmarketing reports of acute hemorrhagic or necrotizing pancreatitis in patients taking Byetta® (exenatide), a drug used to treat adults with type II diabetes. An association between Byetta and acute pancreatitis was suspected in some of these cases. All patients required hospitalization, two patients died, and four patients were recovering at the time of reporting. Amylin Pharmaceuticals, Inc. agreed to include information about acute pancreatitis in the precautions section of the product label. On August 18, 2008 the FDA notified health care professionals to be alert to the signs and symptoms of acute pancreatitis and instruct patients taking Byetta to seek prompt medical care if they experience unexplained, persistent, severe abdominal pain that may or may not be accompanied by vomiting. If pancreatitis is suspected, Byetta should be discontinued. If pancreatitis is confirmed, Byetta should not be restarted unless an alternative etiology is identified (FDA, 2008f).

The LNC's Role in Case Analysis

Rule Out Medical Negligence

The LNC has a large role in working on the pharmaceutical and medical device litigation team. The first and foremost responsibility of the nurse consultant when evaluating a medical product liability claim is to examine the standard of care practiced by the medical practitioner who prescribed the drug or medical device. If the health care practitioner has not prescribed the drug or used the device in accordance with the manufacturer's recommendations, common sense would dictate that the manufacturer might not be held liable for any injury that occurred as a result of the use. Findings of medical malpractice may shift liability in part or completely to the health care practitioner. Review of the plaintiff's medical records will be helpful in establishing clear causation and should be examined to confirm whether there is misdiagnosis, below standard medical treatment, or inadequate follow-up by any of the health care providers. In previous years, drug manufacturers marketed almost exclusively to health care professionals. A large allocation of advertising dollars is now spent marketing to consumers. The ever-increasing number of prescriptions filled is proof that this type of marketing is successful. The downside of the equation is that less informed physicians coupled with greater pressure from patients who desire more control of their own health care equals a new arena of prescribing errors.

Develop the Plaintiff's Medical History

The LNC must also obtain and thoroughly review all the records pertaining to the plaintiff. This includes medical, pharmacy, insurance, mental health, employment, education, criminal, and military records. The LNC should be aware that it is sometimes difficult to recognize drug-induced illness in a person who has multiple coexisting illnesses, such that the appearance of a drug-induced symptom may be difficult to distinguish from the plaintiff's pre-existing problems or conditions. An LNC will deal with all age groups, but as life span is increasing, we will see an increasing amount of cases involving the elderly. These cases can be very challenging and involve a lot of different medical records and could include interviews with medical staff and family members.

Example 20.33

Patients over 65 years old bear the greatest burden of illness and thus are the greatest beneficiaries of drugs to prevent, ameliorate, or treat conditions; they consume an ever increasing proportion of all prescribed drugs (Avorn & Shrank, 2008). The use of anticholinergic drugs presents risks of additional drug side effects; the use of dopaminergic drugs, generally not appropriate for drug-induced Parkinsonian syndrome, suggests that extrapyramidal neuroleptic side effects may often be mistaken for idiopathic Parkinson's disease in older patients (Avorn, Bohn, Mogun et al., 1995). The elderly experience a great impact of clinical iatrogenic illness. More than 1,900,000 adverse drug events occur each year among 38 million Medicare enrollees; estimates based on our study suggest that there are in excess of 180,000 life-threatening or fatal adverse drug events per year, of which more than 50% may be preventable (Gurwitz, Field, Harrold et al., 2003). Any new symptom in an older patient should be considered a possible drug side effect until proved otherwise (Avorn & Shrank, 2008).

It is imperative that the LNC fully delineate the plaintiff's pharmaceutical history, including use of vitamin or herbal supplements, and other OTC medications. There are a growing number of prior prescription medications that are now sold OTC. The history will identify possible drug interactions, contraindications for prescribing the drug in question, prior use of the alleged drug or a drug in the same family without injury, or "physician-hopping" and obtaining multiple prescriptions resulting in overusage. Also, the LNC should not overlook references to alcohol in the review, as alcohol can potentiate or interact with some drugs. In some cases, it may also be necessary to review food intake and some medications may be affected by different foods the patient ate.

In alleged negligence matters, the plaintiff is bound to the statute of limitations, or the period of time within which the plaintiff must initiate an action against the defendant. First, the LNC must know the statute of limitations for the product liability cases in the state where the matter has been filed. Second, the LNC must review the medical records, cross-checking the dates of the prescriptions, product use, or device implantation and failure against the date on which the suit was filed to ensure that it falls within the statute of limitations.

A sample product liability narrative report (medications) is found in Appendix C. A report for a medical device claim may have to be written somewhat different to include key information. Each law firm may have specific requirements for the type of medical information placed in the format. The sample summary shows the relationship of medical facts, provides a condensed analysis of the medical facts of the case, highlights crucial medical information, references the medical records, identifies additional information needed, and recommends physician experts for the case. If the law firm requires a more detailed analysis of the medical records, a detailed chronology with analysis would be submitted.

Identify Possible Third-Party Counterclaims

A counterclaim is a separate cause of action that a defendant asserts against a third person or party. In the answer to the plaintiff's petition, defendants may allege a separate claim against the third party they believe is at fault in the matter. If an orthopedic surgeon purposefully bends a metallic plate to make it conform to the patient's spine and the plate subsequently fractures, the plate manufacturer may counterclaim for improper use of the device against the orthopedic surgeon, if he is not already a defendant in the case. The plate manufacturer would state in its counterclaim that any negligence found by the judge or jury occurred as a result of the orthopedic surgeon's actions.

Establish Clear Causation

It is also important that the LNC make the causal link between the injury and the drug or device therapy. The medication in question must be shown to be the active cause that sets in motion a chain of events that brings about a result without the intervention of any other source. The plaintiff's LNC should utilize the medical records to show that the drug given or device used caused the ensuing injury and should exclude other contributing events or conditions. Causation can be formulated by the "but for" rule, which states that one event is a cause of another when the second event would not have occurred but for the first event.

Example 20.34

A patient was found to have heart rhythm abnormalities and died as a result. If the plaintiff can show that he was not taking any other drug but Propulsid® (Janssen Pharmaceutica) and had no other history of cardiac arrhythmias, the plaintiff could easily prove that but for the consumption of Propulsid, no cardiac arrhythmia would have occurred and the patient would not have died.

Finding supportive evidence clearly proving that the drug caused the symptoms/illness alleged in the suit, when the drug-induced illness mimics the very condition for which the medication is prescribed, can be very difficult. The LNC may recommend the attorney obtain the service of a physician or clinical pharmacist with expertise related to the drug use or incurred injury.

Example 20.35

Many antiarrhythmics, such as quinidine and Procainamide, have the well-known property of generating arrhythmias in certain doses in some patients. Instead of decreasing the frequency of cardiac irregularities, the drugs may actually make them worse. Another paradoxical side effect is akathisia, or restlessness and an inability to sit down or be still, associated with many antipsychotic drugs. As restless behavior is often a clinical symptom of psychoses, there may be a failure to recognize this adverse reaction as a drug event associated with antipsychotic medication.

Research for Discovery

The LNC must perform thorough medical literature searches concerning the product prior to and during discovery. Before beginning this task, the LNC must know about the complete circumstances of the use of the drug or device, including the indications for the product and patient outcome.

The LNC involved in pharmaceutical litigation will find that the drug or device label in the case will be the most referred to exhibit during the discovery and trial process. The LNC should be intimately familiar with this document and any changes made in it from year to year. Most important, the LNC should review the warnings for the year or period in which the medication or device was prescribed. The LNC should review not only the package insert, but the language and content of the advertisements published by the drug company. In addition, the LNC should review any type of labels on a medical device that reflects usage, warnings, and precautions.

Since the early 1970s, the National Library of Medicine (NLM) has made searching the biomedical literature faster and easier by providing online information retrieval on the Medical Literature Analysis and Retrieval System (MEDLARS) family of databases. MEDLINE (Medical Literature Analysis and Retrieval System Online) is the NLM premier database, having more than 16 million references of journal articles in life sciences with a concentration on biomedicine. The LNC should execute a computer online search, using a service such as MEDLINE, ensuring that the drug and similar drugs are cross searched with the resultant injury and similar injuries. (See Chapter 11, "Researching Medical Information and Literature.") Thorough research of the scientific literature has tremendous benefit to both case development and case strategy. The LNC must discover everything, both positive and negative, for a full understanding of the plaintiff's theories and defense positions in the case. A search engine may be useful in finding web sites with references to specific drugs. Sometimes the LNC will be able to identify law firms seeking clients who have been allegedly injured by a product, consumer web sites, and the manufacturer's web site. All may contain useful information about the issues involved.

Research material can be crucial in establishing exactly what the manufacturer knew or should have known and when that knowledge was or should have been acquired. Additionally, pinpointing this information can be essential in determining when certain data were known by medical researchers and experts in the field. The literature can be used to establish "duty" because the manufacturer has a duty to keep up with current information about the product in the medical literature. All information should be indexed and catalogued for use during discovery.

Obtain Adverse Reaction and Medical Device Reports

As mentioned previously, adverse effects of drugs and devices are reported in the postmarketing surveillance period of a particular product or device. The MDR and ADR are required by the FDA when an injury is linked to a medical product, drug, or device. Under the FOIA, every citizen is entitled to request this information from the FDA. LNCs may want to exercise their right under the FOIA and write to the FDA requesting information regarding ADR or MDR for a particular drug or device. To submit an FOIA request, write to the Federal Communications Commission, 445 12th Street, S.W., Room 1-A836, Washington, DC 20554. You can also submit a request via electronic means to FOIA@fcc.gov. FOIA searches can be fruitful, although it often takes a long time to receive a response. There may be various fees and/or charges involved with the request. If the drug has not been approved and is still investigational, the FDA will not give out information regarding the drug, and the LNC will have to rely on medical literature and computer databases.

In response to an FOIA request, the LNC may receive a literal copy of the FDA's computerized tabulations of the various adverse reports for the requested drug or device. (Older data are not organized or computerized, but may be sent in an unorganized state.) Specific requests can be made for edited (confidential patient information removed) copies of the actual reports themselves. These reports are often impossible to validate, and the adverse effects can be a result of excessive doses or too frequent use of the drug. Through FOIA responses, some plaintiffs have identified extremely compelling reports of a drug's association with similar symptoms as those alleged in their claims. The LNC should remember that these reports do not represent cause and effect, and the plaintiff cannot prove his case with adverse reaction reports.

Identify Epidemiological Studies and Epidemiologists

The final outcome of a pharmaceutical product liability case can depend on the court's acceptance or rejection of epidemiology evidence. Epidemiology is the study of disease in people, and epidemiologists are educated specialists in the science of defining and explaining the various factors that determine the frequency and distribution of disease (Hallberg, 1995). For example, epidemiological studies have been pivotal in identifying the causal relationship between smoking and lung cancer.

To provide meaningful conclusions, the epidemiology study must meet certain criteria of scientific method to avoid bias and error. The epidemiology expert can speak to the reliability of these studies and validate whether or not the study can demonstrate cause and effect. The data considered by the epidemiologist in a product liability lawsuit include epidemiology studies that show statistically significant evidence that the plaintiff is a member of the group that has been exposed to a drug or toxin at the required level and duration to cause an adverse effect. The epidemiology expert is able to show the interrelationship between scientific information, including laboratory, clinical, and experimental studies, and the plaintiff's alleged injuries. In any drug or device product liability case, the plaintiff has to prove that the product could cause the alleged injury and did cause the injury in the particular matter. Since the courts have recognized that epidemiology studies provide evidence on both sides of these issues, the LNC should ensure that the enlisted experts have knowledge of the strengths and weaknesses of the epidemiology data pertinent to the case.

Evaluate All the Evidence to Prove or Disprove the Legal Basis for the Plaintiff's Case

The LNC should review all the available data, including medical and other records concerning the plaintiff, medical literature, drug and device labeling, and adverse reaction and medical device reports, for clues as to the feasibility of the legal basis for the plaintiff's and the defendant's cases. The LNC, in conjunction with the attorney, should analyze all the evidence that does or does not support a strict liability or negligence claim against the manufacturer. A checklist might include the following questions:

1. Did the defendant sell the product?
2. When and where was the product manufactured?
3. Did the product reach the user or consumer without substantial change from the condition in which it was sold?
4. When and where was the product consumed or used and for how long?
5. Was the device unreasonably dangerous at the time it was manufactured?
6. Is the product unreasonably unsafe based on the type of warnings given by the manufacturer?
7. Did the manufacturer exercise ordinary care in manufacturing and distributing the product?
8. Does the product have a design or manufacturing defect?
9. Did the defendant know of the danger of the defect in the product at the time it was manufactured or sold?
10. Was there a learned intermediary?
11. Did the learned intermediary use the product correctly?
12. Did the manufacturer adequately warn of the dangers associated with the use of the product in its labeling, package insert, and advertising?
13. When should the manufacturer reasonably have known of the risk of danger and warned of it?
14. Did the manufacturer act reasonably regarding the manner in which the warnings were formulated?
15. Did the manufacturer change its product warnings without undue delay when the information of new risks became available?
16. Is the language used to express the warnings adequate to convey the risk of danger associated with the use of the product?
17. Are the warnings conspicuous and prominent?
18. Are the warnings ambiguous?
19. Was the product excessively promoted?
20. Did the advertising falsely create high expectations on the part of the consumer such that the warnings were disregarded?
21. Have the warnings been changed since the time of the events alleged in the case?
22. What was the basis for the change in the warnings?
23. Have there been any FDA enforcement actions regarding the product? If so, did the manufacturer comply with the FDA enforcement rulings?

The answers to the above questions may not be readily apparent, especially to the plaintiff's LNC prior to filing a lawsuit, but the LNC should keep all of these questions in mind as the lawsuit proceeds since the answers will form the basis for the outcome of the litigation.

Obtain Medical Experts

An additional critical task for the LNC is obtaining qualified medical and technical experts who can explain to the jury not only the medical issues of the case, but also the issues surrounding the design and manufacture of a product, development of warnings, epidemiological studies, and, perhaps, marketing. An attempt should be made to utilize experts who have done research, performed clinical trials, or written medical articles regarding the medication or device in question. A review of all generally available scientific literature may assist both in determining the elements of causation and in the identification of potential expert witnesses. The enlisted experts should be extremely familiar with the drug (e.g., physicians, pharmacologists, and clinical pharmacists) or the device and its indications, adverse reactions, metabolism, and method of action. Experts must be able to demonstrate that their testimony has a reliable basis in the knowledge and experience of their own discipline. Experts should be able to cite literature to support their conclusions.

Example 20.36

The defense enlists one of the plaintiff's treating physicians as a defense expert to provide testimony that the plaintiff was diagnosed with the alleged symptoms before the drug in question was ever prescribed. However, on cross-examination by plaintiff's counsel regarding whether or not he utilizes or prescribes the suspect drug, the physician responds negatively. The fact that the expert does not use or prescribe the drug may have a devastating effect on the defense of the case.

Through a series of court rulings, the trial judge has been designated as the gatekeeper for determining the admissibility of expert evidence. The courts are to examine the basis of an expert's opinion to assess its scientific reliability before allowing the evidence to be presented before a jury. The trial judge's role as gatekeeper is to keep out unscientific and speculative testimony in favor of pertinent evidence based on scientifically valid principles. The U.S. Supreme Court has ruled that judges are advised to take into account whether or not expert testimony is based on published data contained in peer-reviewed journals (Annas, 1994; *Daubert v. Merrell Dow Pharmaceuticals, Inc*, 1993; Oldknow, 2001).

In *Kumho Tire Co. Ltd. v. Carmichael* (1999), the U.S. Supreme Court expanded the application of the *Daubert* rule. The Court's ruling in *Kumho* determined that the criteria set forth in *Daubert* apply to nonscientific or applied science testimony as well. Although all criteria may not specifically apply to an economist, actuary, or accountant, as examples, the judge is still to ensure that testimony is reasonable, credible, and relevant, whatever the discipline. Together the rulings in *Daubert* and *Kumho* challenge *junk science* from entering the courtroom. In 2000, these standards on admission of expert testimony were incorporated into the Federal Rules of Evidence (FED. R. EVID. 702; FED. R. EVID. 703). Although the Federal Rules of Evidence do not apply to state courts, the cases are often cited in state court decisions, and more states are electing to follow these guidelines. Either side has the option to challenge whether the named experts are qualified to testify and whether their opinions are based on published scientific data. These federal guidelines have been revised and took effect on December 1, 2006 for the year 2007.

It is imperative for the LNC to locate medical experts who can substantiate and support the legal theories of the case. The medical expert's role is primarily that of educating the jury, rather than acting as an advocate for the client. The LNC has a pivotal role in ensuring that prospective experts have completely reviewed the entire records, medical and otherwise, in the matter prior to being designated; that they understand all the issues; and that they feel strongly about their opinions in the case.

Example 20.37

At trial, plaintiff's counsel enters into evidence of multiple ADR reports received in response to an FOIA request regarding a toxic side effect not mentioned in the product labeling. The plaintiff would benefit substantially from placing an FDA regulatory expert on the witness stand who could testify that spontaneous reports of adverse experiences in association with pharmaceutical use represent the most potentially powerful signal for early detection of rare but unacceptable drug toxicities.

Conclusion

Due to the complexity of today's world, especially in advanced medical science, much of the current theories driving drug and device suits are based on case law. Although many lawsuits are unique and applying legal theories can be difficult, case law is increasingly important, with precedent-setting cases occurring daily.

When consulting on drug and device product liability matters, the LNC will be challenged to utilize both legal knowledge and medical expertise. The LNC must perform periodic research to remain current and knowledgeable regarding various drugs and devices that fall under the product liability statutes. A complete understanding of manufacturers' responsibilities and regulatory processes is essential to a thorough review of the case. The LNC has the opportunity to be a valuable asset to the litigation team once these are learned and employed in the consulting process.

References

21 CFR §201.56, & 201.57 (1988).

21 CFR 310. §314.80.

21 CFR §310.305.

21 U.S.C. §321 (1982).

21 U.S.C. §360c, d, e, & i (1982).

Agency information collection activities; submission for office of management and budget review; comment request; format and content for over-the-counter drug product labeling, 70(59) Notices, Federal Register (29 March, 2005) pp. 15864–15865. Retrieved October 18, 2008, from http://www.fda.gov/OHRMS/DOCKETS/98fr/05-6088.htm

Annas, G. (1994). Scientific evidence in the courtroom: The death of the Frye rule. *New England Journal of Medicine, 330,* 1018.

Appellate Law & Practice. (2005). *CA5 thimerosal/vaccine liability.* April 27, 2005. Retrieved October 18, 2008, from http://appellate.typepad.com/appellate/2005/04/ca5_thimerosalv.html

Avitzur, O. (2005). Clinical research trials in private practice: Under legal scrutiny in practice. *Neurology Today, 5*(1), 72–74.

Avorn, J., Bohn, R. L., Mogun, H., Gurwitz, J. H., Monane, M., Everitt, D., & Walker, A. (1995). Neuroleptic drug exposure and treatment of Parkinsonism in the elderly: A case-control study. *American Journal of Medicine, 99,* 48–54.

Avorn, J., & Shrank, W. (2008). Making a difference adverse drug reactions in elderly people: A substantial cause of preventable illness. *British Medical Journal, 336,* 956–957.

Avorn, J. (1989). Detection and prevention of drug-induced illness. *Journal of Clinical Research and Drug Development, 3*(5).

Brooks, M. (n.d.). *History of breast silicone implant litigation: 1977–1999.* www.goarticales.come/publisher.html

Cezanne, J. (2007). Audio taping consent sessions seen thwarting lawsuits (Informed consent). *BioResearch Compliance Report,* October.

Code of Federal Regulations. (2000a) *Title 21 CFR, Part 50, and Subpart B U.S. Food and Drug Administration.* Washington, DC: U.S. Government Printing Office, 2000. Retrieved March 6, 2009, from https://www.accessdata.fda.gov/scripts/cdrh/cfdocs/cfCFR/CFRSearch.cfm?CFRPart=50&showFR=1&subpartNode=21:1.0.1.1.19.2

Code of Federal Regulations. (2000b). *Title 21, Part 50.25, U.S. Food and Drug Administration.* Washington, DC: U.S. Government Printing Office. Retrieved March 6, 2009, from http://www1.va.gov/oro/apps/compendium/Files/21CFR50.htm#fda21cfr5025

Code of Federal Regulations. (2000c). *Title 21, Part 50.20, Part 50.27, U.S. Food and Drug Administration.* Washington, DC: U.S. Government Printing Office, 2000. Retrieved March 6, 2009, from https://www.accessdata.fda.gov/scripts/cdrh/cfdocs/cfCFR/CFRSearch.cfm?CFRPart=50

Code of Federal Regulations. (2000d). *Title 21, Part 312.32, U.S. Food and Drug Administration.* Washington, DC: U.S. Government Printing Office. Retrieved March 6, 2009, from https://www.accessdata.fda.gov/scripts/cdrh/cfdocs/cfCFR/CFRSearch.cfm?fr=312.32

Cowley v. Abbott Laboratories, Inc., 476 F.Supp.2d 1053 (W.D. Wis. 2007).

Daubert v. Merrell Dow Pharmaceuticals, Inc., 509 U.S. 579 (1993).

Dukes, M., & Swartz, G. (1988). *Responsibility for drug induced injury.* Amsterdam: Elsevier Science Publishers.

Evans, G. (2006). Update on vaccine liability in the united states: Presentation at the national vaccine program office workshop on strengthening the supply of routinely recommended vaccines in the United States, 12 February 2002. *Clinical Infectious Diseases, 1*(42) (Suppl. 3), S130–S137.

Fallon, E., Hon. (2007). *Order & Reasons dated July 3, 2007.* Retrieved March 4, 2009, from http://vioxx.laed.uscourts.gov

FED. R. EVID. 702.

FED. R. EVID. 703.

Feder, B. J. (2008). Medical device ruling redraws lines on lawsuits. *New York Times,* February 22.

Food and Drug Administration (FDA). (2001). *Study of silicone gel breast implant rupture, extracapsular silicone, and health status in a population of women.* Retrieved March 9, 2009, from http://www.fda.gov/cdrh/breastimplants/extracapstudy.html

Food and Drug Administration (FDA). (2002). The FDA's drug review process: Ensuring Drugs are safe and effective. *FDA Consumer Magazine,* July–August 2002 Issue Pub No. FDA05-3242. Retrieved March 6, 2009, from http://www.fda.gov/Fdac/features/2002/402_drug.html

Food and Drug Administration (FDA). (2004a) Merck withdraws Vioxx; FDA issues public health advisory. *FDA Consumer Magazine,* November–December 2004 Issue, http://www.fda.gov/fdac/features/2004/604_vioxx.html

Food and Drug Administration (FDA). (2004b). *Issues public health advisory on Vioxx as its manufacturer voluntarily withdraws the product.* Retrieved March 4, 2009, from http://www.fda.gov/bbs/topics/news/2004/new01122.html

Food and Drug Administration (FDA). (2004c). *2004 safety alert: Zyprexa (olanzapine).* Retrieved March 6, 2009, from www.fda.gov/medwatch/SAFETY/2004/zyprexa.htm

Food and Drug Administration (FDA). (2006). FDA approves silicone gel-filled breast implants after in-depth evaluation. *FDA News,* November 17. Retrieved March 4, 2009, from http://www.fda.gov/bbs/topics/news/2006/new01512.html

Food and Drug Administration (FDA). (2007). *Medtronic spring Fidelis Defibrillator Leads.* Retrieved March 6, 2009, from http://www.fda.gov/Medwatch/SAFETY/2007/safety07.htm

Food and Drug Administration (FDA). (2008a). *Botox and Botox Cosmetics.* Retrieved March 6, 2009, from fda.gov/medwatch/safety/2008/safety08.htm#botox

Food and Drug Administration (FDA). (2008b). Cold Therapy Unit; DonJoy Iceman Cooler Modell #1100. Lot #112907-01B. *Medical Product Safety Network Newsletter #27.* Retrieved March 4, 2009, from http://www.accessdata.fda.gov/scripts/cdrh/cfdocs/medsun/news/newsletter.cfm?news=27

Food and Drug Administration (FDA). (2008c). *Early communication about an ongoing safety review of montelukast (Singulair).* Retrieved March 4, 2008, from http://www.fda.gov/Cder/drug/early_comm/montelukast.htm

Food and Drug Administration (FDA). (2008d). Information for healthcare professionals mitoxantrone hydrochloride (marketed as Novantrone and generics). *FDA Alert* 7/29/08. Retrieved March 6, 2009, from http://www.fda.gov/cder/drug/InfoSheets/HCP/mitroxantroneHCP.htm

Food and Drug Administration (FDA). (2008e). Information for healthcare professionals Antipsychotics. *FDA Alert* 6/16/08. Retrieved March 6, 2009, from http://www.fda.gov/CDER/drug/InfoSheets/HCP/antipsychotics_conventional.htm

Food and Drug Administration (FDA). (2008f). Information for healthcare professionals Exenatide (marketed as Byetta). *FDA Alert* 8/18/08. Retrieved March 6, 2009, from FDA.gov/CDER/drug/InfoSheets/HCP/exenatide2008HCP.htm

Food and Drug Administration Amendments Act (FDAAA). (2007). Retrieved on March 4, 2009, from http://frwebgate.access.gpo.gov/cgi-bin/getdoc.cgi?dbname=110_cong_public_laws&docid=f:publ085.110

Food, Drug and Cosmetic Act. (1938). Ch. 675, Pub. L. 75–717, 52 Stat. 1040. Drug Amendments of 1962, 102, Pub. L. 87–871, 76 Stat. 781.

Greenberg, D., & Rudman, J. (2008). Medical malpractice/products liability: Supreme Court denies claims of negligence, strict liability and breach of implied warranty on Medtronic medical devices. *Los Angeles Injury Lawyer Blog*, February 29.

Gurwitz, J. H., Field, T. S., Harrold, L. R., Rothschild, J., Debellis, K., Seger, A. C., Cadoret, C., Fish, L. S., Garber, L., Kelleher, M., & Bates, D. W. (2003). Incidence and preventability of adverse drug events among older persons in the ambulatory setting. *JAMA, 289*, 1107–1116.

Hallberg, M. (1995). The use of epidemiological studies and epidemiologists in proving or disproving causation, *Network, 5*(1), 19.

http://vaers.hhs.gov

http://www.fda.gov/medwatch/

http://www.hrsa.gov/Vaccinecompensation/

http://www.usdoj.gov/oip/index.html

Inman, W. H. W. (1980). *Monitoring drug safety.* Philadelphia: Lippincott.

Karceski, J. (2008). *FDA adverse events reporting system.* National Institute for Computer-Assisted Reporting, 6/27/08. Retrieved March 6, 2009, from http://data.nicar.org/node/25

Kessler, D. (2003). Introducing MEDWatch: A new approach to reporting medication and device adverse effects and product problems. *Journal of the American Medical Association, 269*, 2765.

Kuc, J. (1995). A progress report on the FDA's MEDWatch. *Journal of Legal Nurse Consulting, 6*(5), 5–8.

Kumho Tire Co., Ltd. v. Carmichael, 526 U.S. 137 (1999).

McDonal v. Abbot Laboratories 408 F.3d 177, 184 (5th Cir.2005).

Nagle, M. E. (2004). State "fraud" suits over drug clinical trial results tread on free speech rights. *Washington Legal Foundation, 19*(30), 1–4.

Oldknow, P. F. (2001). *Daubert*, the scientific method, and the legal nurse consultant, *Journal of Legal Nurse Consulting, 12*(4), 3–9.

Over-the-counter human drugs; labeling requirements; Final rule (64 FR 13254): Federal Register (1999, March 17).

Porter, R. (Ed.). (2008). Chloramphenicol. *Merck Manual Online.* Retrieved March 6, 2009, from http://www.merck.com/mmpe/sec14/ch170/ch170d.html

Physicians' Desk Reference (PDR). (2008). *Prescription and over-the-counter drug product list*—19th Edition Cumulative Supplement Number 3: March 1999, *Physicians' Desk Reference* (62nd ed.) 2008 (www.PDR.net).

Prince, J. (2007). Learned intermediary doctrine provides basis for summary judgment in two cases. *Products Liability ProfBlog.* Retrieved March 6, 2009, from lawprofessors.typepad.com/products_liability/2007/03/learned_interme.html

Rados, C. (2006). Medical device and radiological health regulations come of age. *FDA Consumer Magazine. The Centennial Edition.* Retrieved March 4, 2009, from fda.gov/fdac/features/2006/106_cdrh.html

Riegel v. Medtronic, Inc., No. 06-179, 2008 WL 440744 (U.S. Feb. 20, 2008).

Rosenberg, M. (2008). Burying clinical data, spinning journal articles, selling bad drugs. *CounterPunch: Weekend Edition January 19/20, 2008.* Retrieved March 4, 2009, from http://www.counterpunch.org/rosenberg01192008.html

Rueda A. (2001). Rethinking blood shield statutes in view of the hepatitis C pandemic and other emerging threats to the blood supply. *Journal of Health Law, 34*(3), 419–459.

Ruff, E., & Jurado, S. (Spring 1999). The restatement (third) of torts and its effects on products liability law. *Federation of Insurance & Corporate Counsel Quarterly, 265.*

Schultz, D. (2008). *FDA preliminary public health notification: Possible malfunction of electronic medical devices caused by computed tomography (CT) scanning.* Food and Drug Administration. Public Health Notification, FDA, July 14, 2008. Retrieved March 6, 2009, from http://www.fda.gov/cdrh/safety/071408-ctscanning.html

Shulman, S., & Ulcickas, B. (1989). Update on ADR reporting regulations: Products liability implications. *Journal of Clinical Research and Drug Development, 3*(2), 91.

The American Institute. (1998). *Restatement of the law third, torts: Products liability,* St. Paul, MN: American Law Institute Publishers.

Title 5 of the United States Code, section 552 (2000 & Supp. III 2003).

Topol, E. J. (2004, October 10). Failing the public health. *New England Journal of Medicine, 351*(17), 1707–1709.

U.S. Department of Health and Human Services. (n.d.). *MedWatch: The safety information and adverse reporting program, Form FDR 3500.* Retrieved March 4, 2009, from fda.gov/medwatch/safety/FDA-3500_fillable.pdf

U.S. Department of Health and Human Services. (n.d.). *MedWatch: The safety information and adverse reporting program, Form FDR 3500.* Retrieved March 4, 2009, from fda.gov/medwatch/safety/FDA-3500A_fillable.pdf

U.S. Government Accountability Office. (2008). *Report to the ranking member, Committee on Financing, U.S. Senate, Prescription Drugs: FDA's Oversight of the Promotion of Drugs for Off-Label Uses, July 2008.* Retrieved March 6, 2009, from http://www.gao.gov/new.items/d08835.pdf

Vaccine Act, 42 U.S.C. §§300aa-1 et seq.

Villalba, L. (2001). *VIOXX™ gastrointestinal outcome research (VIGOR).* Retrieved March 4, 2009, from fda.gov/ohrms/dockets/ac/01/slides/3677s2_02_villalba.PPT

Wade, J. (2004). *Blood shield statutes.* Retrieved March 6, 2009, from http://www.noblood.org/general-discussions/1212-blood-shield-statutes.html

Wells v. Ortho Pharmaceutical Corp., 615 F. Supp 262 (N.D. Ga. 1985).

Wooderson v. Ortho Pharmaceutical Corp., 681 P.2d 1038, 1051 (Kan. 1984).

Zwillich, T. (2006). FDA to simplify drug safety labels. *WebMDHealth: WebMD Health News.* WebMD Inc.

Additional Reading

Federal Register and Federal Register Abstracts: Daily publication of the U.S. government providing notification of official agency actions, regulations, proposed rules, and legal notices, such as when the FDA requests that a drug company change its warning.

Freedom of Information Act: http://www.usdoj.gov/oip/index.html

Health Devices Alert®: Reports problems with diagnostic and therapeutic medical and implanted equipment.

Health Devices Sourcebook®: Current information regarding diagnostics and therapeutic medical devices.

Lenzer, J. (2004). FDA bars own expert from evaluating risks of painkillers. *British Medical Journal, 329,* 1203.

Pharmaceutical News Index PNI®: Current news about drugs and medical devices.

Trade Journals

Devices and Diagnostics Letter (weekly) and Clinical World Medical Device & Diagnostic News (weekly): updates on what is new in research and development, legislation, and recalls of drugs and devices.

Pharmaceutical Litigation Reporter (monthly): summaries of the latest verdicts in pharmaceutical litigation.

Web Sites

http://classaction.findlaw.com/: Provides information from the FindLaw Class Action and Mass Tort Center.

www.hhs.gov/ohrp/policy: Provides information from the Office for Human Research Protections.

http://ohsr.od.nih.gov/: Provides information from the Office of Human Subjects Research.

http://www.fda.gov: Provides information from the Food and Drug Administration regarding current drug and product liability links to MedWatch.

http://www.law.cornell.edu/topics/products_liability.html: Provides information regarding product liability from the Legal Information Institute.

http://www.usdoj.gov/oip/index.html: Provides information from the United States Department of Justice regarding the Freedom of Information Act.

Test Questions

1. The plaintiff must prove all of the following in a strict liability cause of action EXCEPT
   A. The defendant sold the product that was defective
   B. The product was the proximate cause of the plaintiff's injuries
   C. The plaintiff has damages
   D. The user made a mistake in the use of the product

2. The drug manufacturer's duty to warn
   A. Expires when the product is placed on the market
   B. Obliges the manufacturer to seek out information regarding its product
   C. Is not required until a causal relationship between the drug and adverse effect is proved
   D. Can wait until a statistically significant number of people have been injured

3. As a result of the Food and Drug Administration's regulatory process, when the average drug is marketed, consumers have a reasonable expectation that serious side effects are unlikely when the drug is used EXCEPT
   A. For its approved indication
   B. Above the recommended dose
   C. For limited periods
   D. In medically uncomplicated, nonpregnant, compliant, young to middle-aged adults

4. The accuracy and reliability of the scientific evidence presented in the courtroom is the responsibility of the
   A. Jury
   B. Attorneys representing each side
   C. Judge
   D. Product manufacturer

5. An informed consent form is signed and dated by the participant
   A. Before any study procedures are performed
   B. At the end of the study
   C. Before the Institutional Review Board provides final approval
   D. When the study drug is administered

Answers: 1. D, 2. B, 3. B, 4. C, 5. A

Appendix A: FDA MedWatch Form for Voluntary Reporting of Adverse Events and Product Problems by Health Professionals (FDA MedWatch 2008)

U.S. Department of Health and Human Services

MEDWATCH

The FDA Safety Information and
Adverse Event Reporting Program

For VOLUNTARY reporting of
adverse events, product problems and
product use errors

Page ____ of ____

Form Approved: OMB No. 0910-0291, Expires:10/31/08
See OMB statement on reverse.

FDA USE ONLY

Triage unit
sequence #

A. PATIENT INFORMATION

1. Patient Identifier	2. Age at Time of Event, or Date of Birth:	3. Sex	4. Weight
In confidence		☐ Female ☐ Male	____ lb or ____ kg

B. ADVERSE EVENT, PRODUCT PROBLEM OR ERROR

Check all that apply:

1. ☐ Adverse Event   ☐ Product Problem *(e.g., defects/malfunctions)*
   ☐ Product Use Error   ☐ Problem with Different Manufacturer of Same Medicine

2. Outcomes Attributed to Adverse Event
   (Check all that apply)

   ☐ Death: _____ *(mm/dd/yyyy)*   ☐ Disability or Permanent Damage
   ☐ Life-threatening   ☐ Congenital Anomaly/Birth Defect
   ☐ Hospitalization - Initial or prolonged   ☐ Other Serious (Important Medical Events)
   ☐ Required Intervention to Prevent Permanent Impairment/Damage (Devices)

3. Date of Event *(mm/dd/yyyy)*	4. Date of this Report *(mm/dd/yyyy)* 01/13/2009

5. Describe Event, Problem or Product Use Error

6. Relevant Tests/Laboratory Data, Including Dates

7. Other Relevant History, Including Preexisting Medical Conditions *(e.g., allergies, race, pregnancy, smoking and alcohol use, liver/kidney problems, etc.)*

C. PRODUCT AVAILABILITY

Product Available for Evaluation? *(Do not send product to FDA)*

☐ Yes   ☐ No   ☐ Returned to Manufacturer on: _____ *(mm/dd/yyyy)*

D. SUSPECT PRODUCT(S)

1. Name, Strength, Manufacturer *(from product label)*

   #1
   #2

2. Dose or Amount	Frequency	Route
#1		
#2		

3. Dates of Use *(If unknown, give duration) from/to (or best estimate)*	5. Event Abated After Use Stopped or Dose Reduced?
#1	#1 ☐ Yes ☐ No ☐ Doesn't Apply
#2	#2 ☐ Yes ☐ No ☐ Doesn't Apply

4. Diagnosis or Reason for Use *(Indication)*	8. Event Reappeared After Reintroduction?
#1	#1 ☐ Yes ☐ No ☐ Doesn't Apply
#2	#2 ☐ Yes ☐ No ☐ Doesn't Apply

6. Lot #	7. Expiration Date	9. NDC # or Unique ID
#1	#1	
#2	#2	

E. SUSPECT MEDICAL DEVICE

1. Brand Name

2. Common Device Name

3. Manufacturer Name, City and State

4. Model #	Lot #	5. Operator of Device
Catalog #	Expiration Date *(mm/dd/yyyy)*	☐ Health Professional ☐ Lay User/Patient ☐ Other:
Serial #	Other #	

6. If Implanted, Give Date *(mm/dd/yyyy)*	7. If Explanted, Give Date *(mm/dd/yyyy)*

8. Is this a Single-use Device that was Reprocessed and Reused on a Patient?
   ☐ Yes   ☐ No

9. If Yes to Item No. 8, Enter Name and Address of Reprocessor

F. OTHER (CONCOMITANT) MEDICAL PRODUCTS

Product names and therapy dates *(exclude treatment of event)*

G. REPORTER *(See confidentiality section on back)*

1. Name and Address

Phone #	E-mail

2. Health Professional?	3. Occupation	4. Also Reported to:
☐ Yes ☐ No		☐ Manufacturer ☐ User Facility ☐ Distributor/Importer
5. If you do NOT want your identity disclosed to the manufacturer, place an "X" in this box: ☐		

PLEASE TYPE OR USE BLACK INK

FORM FDA 3500 (10/05)   Submission of a report does not constitute an admission that medical personnel or the product caused or contributed to the event.

ADVICE ABOUT VOLUNTARY REPORTING

Detailed instructions available at: http://www.fda.gov/medwatch/report/consumer/instruct.htm

Report adverse events, product problems or product use errors with:

- Medications *(drugs or biologics)*
- Medical devices *(including in-vitro diagnostics)*
- Combination products *(medication & medical devices)*
- Human cells, tissues, and cellular and tissue-based products
- Special nutritional products *(dietary supplements, medical foods, infant formulas)*
- Cosmetics

Report product problems - quality, performance or safety concerns such as:

- Suspected counterfeit product
- Suspected contamination
- Questionable stability
- Defective components
- Poor packaging or labeling
- Therapeutic failures (product didn't work)

Report SERIOUS adverse events. An event is serious when the patient outcome is:

- Death
- Life-threatening
- Hospitalization - initial or prolonged
- Disability or permanent damage
- Congenital anomaly/birth defect
- Required intervention to prevent permanent impairment or damage
- Other serious (important medical events)

Report even if:

- You're not certain the product caused the event
- You don't have all the details

How to report:

- Just fill in the sections that apply to your report
- Use section D for all products except medical devices
- Attach additional pages if needed
- Use a separate form for each patient
- Report either to FDA or the manufacturer *(or both)*

Other methods of reporting:

- 1-800-FDA-0178 -- To FAX report
- 1-800-FDA-1088 -- To report by phone
- www.fda.gov/medwatch/report.htm -- To report online

If your report involves a serious adverse event with a device and it occurred in a facility outside a doctor's office, that facility may be legally required to report to FDA and/or the manufacturer. Please notify the person in that facility who would handle such reporting.

If your report involves a serious adverse event with a vaccine call 1-800-822-7967 to report.

Confidentiality: The patient's identity is held in strict confidence by FDA and protected to the fullest extent of the law. FDA will not disclose the reporter's identity in response to a request from the public, pursuant to the Freedom of Information Act. The reporter's identity, including the identity of a self-reporter, may be shared with the manufacturer unless requested otherwise.

-Fold Here-   -Fold Here-

The public reporting burden for this collection of information has been estimated to average 36 minutes per response, including the time for reviewing instructions, searching existing data sources, gathering and maintaining the data needed, and completing and reviewing the collection of information. Send comments regarding this burden estimate or any other aspect of this collection of information, including suggestions for reducing this burden to:

Department of Health and Human Services
Food and Drug Administration - MedWatch
10903 New Hampshire Avenue
Building 22, Mail Stop 4447
Silver Spring, MD 20993-0002

Please DO NOT
RETURN this form
to this address.

OMB statement:
"An agency may not conduct or sponsor, and a person is not required to respond to, a collection of information unless it displays a currently valid OMB control number."

U.S. DEPARTMENT OF HEALTH AND HUMAN SERVICES
Food and Drug Administration

FORM FDA 3500 (10/05) (Back)   Please Use Address Provided Below -- Fold in Thirds, Tape and Mail

---

DEPARTMENT OF
HEALTH & HUMAN SERVICES

Public Health Service
Food and Drug Administration
Rockville, MD 20857

Official Business
Penalty for Private Use $300

NO POSTAGE
NECESSARY
IF MAILED
IN THE
UNITED STATES
OR APO/FPO

BUSINESS REPLY MAIL

FIRST CLASS MAIL   PERMIT NO. 946   ROCKVILLE MD

MedWatch
The FDA Safety Information and Adverse Event Reporting Program
Food and Drug Administration
5600 Fishers Lane
Rockville, MD 20852-9787

Appendix B: FDA MedWatch Form for Mandatory Reporting of Adverse Events and Product Problems by User Facilities, Distributors, and Manufacturers (FDA MedWatch 2008)

Form Approved: OMB No. 0910-0291, Expires: 10/31/08
See OMB statement on reverse.

U.S. Department of Health and Human Services
Food and Drug Administration

For use by user-facilities, importers, distributors and manufacturers for MANDATORY reporting

MEDWATCH

FORM FDA 3500A (10/05)   Page ____ of ____

Mfr Report #

UF/Importer Report #

FDA Use Only

PLEASE TYPE OR USE BLACK INK

A. PATIENT INFORMATION

1. Patient Identifier	2. Age at Time of Event: or ——— Date of Birth:	3. Sex ☐ Female ☐ Male	4. Weight ___ lbs or ___ kgs
In confidence			

B. ADVERSE EVENT OR PRODUCT PROBLEM

1. ☐ Adverse Event   and/or   ☐ Product Problem *(e.g., defects/malfunctions)*

2. Outcomes Attributed to Adverse Event *(Check all that apply)*

☐ Death: _____ *(mm/dd/yyyy)*   ☐ Disability or Permanent Damage

☐ Life-threatening   ☐ Congenital Anomaly/Birth Defect

☐ Hospitalization - Initial or prolonged   ☐ Other Serious (Important Medical Events)

☐ Required Intervention to Prevent Permanent Impairment/Damage (Devices)

3. Date of Event *(mm/dd/yyyy)*   4. Date of This Report *(mm/dd/yyyy)*

5. Describe Event or Problem

6. Relevant Tests/Laboratory Data, Including Dates

7. Other Relevant History, Including Preexisting Medical Conditions *(e.g., allergies, race, pregnancy, smoking and alcohol use, hepatic/renal dysfunction, etc.)*

Submission of a report does not constitute an admission that medical personnel, user facility, importer, distributor, manufacturer or product caused or contributed to the event.

C. SUSPECT PRODUCT(S)

1. Name *(Give labeled strength & mfr/labeler)*

#1 _____

#2 _____

2. Dose, Frequency & Route Used

#1 _____

#2 _____

3. Therapy Dates *(If unknown, give duration) from/to (or best estimate)*

#1 _____

#2 _____

4. Diagnosis for Use *(Indication)*

#1 _____

#2 _____

5. Event Abated After Use Stopped or Dose Reduced?

#1 ☐ Yes ☐ No ☐ Doesn't Apply

#2 ☐ Yes ☐ No ☐ Doesn't Apply

6. Lot #   7. Exp. Date

#1 ___   #1 ___

#2 ___   #2 ___

8. Event Reappeared After Reintroduction?

#1 ☐ Yes ☐ No ☐ Doesn't Apply

#2 ☐ Yes ☐ No ☐ Doesn't Apply

9. NDC# or Unique ID

10. Concomitant Medical Products and Therapy Dates *(Exclude treatment of event)*

D. SUSPECT MEDICAL DEVICE

1. Brand Name

2. Common Device Name

3. Manufacturer Name, City and State

4. Model #	Lot #	5. Operator of Device
Catalog #	Expiration Date *(mm/dd/yyyy)*	☐ Health Professional ☐ Lay User/Patient
Serial #	Other #	☐ Other:

6. If Implanted, Give Date *(mm/dd/yyyy)*   7. If Explanted, Give Date *(mm/dd/yyyy)*

8. Is this a Single-use Device that was Reprocessed and Reused on a Patient? ☐ Yes ☐ No

9. If Yes to Item No. 8, Enter Name and Address of Reprocessor

10. Device Available for Evaluation? *(Do not send to FDA)* ☐ Yes ☐ No ☐ Returned to Manufacturer on: _____ *(mm/dd/yyyy)*

11. Concomitant Medical Products and Therapy Dates *(Exclude treatment of event)*

E. INITIAL REPORTER

1. Name and Address   Phone #

2. Health Professional? ☐ Yes ☐ No   3. Occupation   4. Initial Reporter Also Sent Report to FDA ☐ Yes ☐ No ☐ Unk.

MEDWATCH

FORM FDA 3500A (10/05) *(continued)*   Page ____ of ____

FDA USE ONLY

F. FOR USE BY USER FACILITY/IMPORTER *(Devices Only)*

1. Check One
☐ User Facility   ☐ Importer

2. UF/Importer Report Number

3. User Facility or Importer Name/Address

4. Contact Person

5. Phone Number

6. Date User Facility or Importer Became Aware of Event *(mm/dd/yyyy)*

7. Type of Report
☐ Initial
☐ Follow-up #

8. Date of This Report *(mm/dd/yyyy)*

9. Approximate Age of Device

10. Event Problem Codes *(Refer to coding manual)*
Patient Code [   ] - [   ] - [   ]
Device Code   [   ] - [   ] - [   ]

11. Report Sent to FDA?
☐ Yes ____
☐ No   *(mm/dd/yyyy)*

12. Location Where Event Occurred
☐ Hospital
☐ Home
☐ Nursing Home
☐ Outpatient Treatment Facility
☐ Other: ____
(Specify)
☐ Outpatient Diagnostic Facility
☐ Ambulatory Surgical Facility

13. Report Sent to Manufacturer?
☐ Yes ____
☐ No   *(mm/dd/yyyy)*

14. Manufacturer Name/Address

G. ALL MANUFACTURERS

1. Contact Office - Name/Address *(and Manufacturing Site for Devices)*

2. Phone Number

3. Report Source *(Check all that apply)*
☐ Foreign
☐ Study
☐ Literature
☐ Consumer
☐ Health Professional
☐ User Facility
☐ Company Representative
☐ Distributor
☐ Other:

4. Date Received by Manufacturer *(mm/dd/yyyy)*

5.
(A)NDA # ____
IND # ____
STN # ____
PMA/ 510(k) # ____

6. If IND, Give Protocol #

7. Type of Report *(Check all that apply)*
☐ 5-day   ☐ 30-day
☐ 7-day   ☐ Periodic
☐ 10-day   ☐ Initial
☐ 15-day   ☐ Follow-up # ____

Combination Product   ☐ Yes
Pre-1938   ☐ Yes
OTC Product   ☐ Yes

9. Manufacturer Report Number

8. Adverse Event Term(s)

H. DEVICE MANUFACTURERS ONLY

1. Type of Reportable Event
☐ Death
☐ Serious Injury
☐ Malfunction
☐ Other:

2. If Follow-up, What Type?
☐ Correction
☐ Additional Information
☐ Response to FDA Request
☐ Device Evaluation

3. Device Evaluated by Manufacturer?
☐ Not Returned to Manufacturer
☐ Yes   ☐ Evaluation Summary Attached
☐ No *(Attach page to explain why not)* or provide code:

4. Device Manufacture Date *(mm/yyyy)*

5. Labeled for Single Use?
☐ Yes   ☐ No

6. Evaluation Codes *(Refer to coding manual)*
Method   [   ] - [   ] - [   ] - [   ]
Results   [   ] - [   ] - [   ] - [   ]
Conclusions [   ] - [   ] - [   ] - [   ]

7. If Remedial Action Initiated, Check Type
☐ Recall   ☐ Notification
☐ Repair   ☐ Inspection
☐ Replace   ☐ Patient Monitoring
☐ Relabeling ☐ Modification/ Adjustment
☐ Other: ____

8. Usage of Device
☐ Initial Use of Device
☐ Reuse
☐ Unknown

9. If action reported to FDA under 21 USC 360i(f), list correction/ removal reporting number:

10. ☐ Additional Manufacturer Narrative   and / or   **11.** ☐ Corrected Data

The public reporting burden for this collection of information has been estimated to average 66 minutes per response, including the time for reviewing instructions, searching existing data sources, gathering and maintaining the data needed, and completing and reviewing the collection of information. Send comments regarding this burden estimate or any other aspect of this collection of information, including suggestions for reducing this burden to:

Department of Health and Human Services
Food and Drug Administration - MedWatch
10903 New Hampshire Avenue
Building 22, Mail Stop 4447
Silver Spring, MD 20993-0002
Please DO NOT RETURN this form to this address.

OMB Statement:
"An agency may not conduct or sponsor, and a person is not required to respond to, a collection of information unless it displays a currently valid OMB control number."

Appendix C: Sample Format for Product Liability Narrative Report

Privileged and Confidential—Attorney Work Product
Date
Firm Name:
Attorney:
Address:
City/State/Zip:

Subject: (Name) Case Number if available
                DOB:
                SS#:
                DOD: (if applicable)
                State (e.g., Texas)
                (Introductory paragraph here)

Case Impressions:
1.
2.
3.

    A. Family History
    B. Other pertinent history

        1)

Pre-exposure Medical History:

Pre-exposure Medications:
Summary based on the pharmacy and medical records provided.

Date	Physician	Medication Prescribed	Medication Dispensed

History of Exposure:
Summary based on the pharmacy and medical records provided.

Date	Physician	Medication Prescribed	Medication Dispensed

Total Amount of Medication:

Please note that the information provided is based on records available at the time of review.
Records reviewed were: PROVIDERS.
Please obtain the following additional records: PROVIDERS.

An in-depth medical chronology would provide you with greater detail in this case. Thank you for allowing our firm to assist you with this most unfortunate case.

LNC name & credentials.

Chapter 21

Evaluating Toxic Tort Cases

Michelle Cannon, BSN, RN, CRNI and
Elisabeth Ridgely, BS, RN, LNCC

First Edition
April Clemens, MSN, RN; Marva J. Petty, MSN, RN, LNCC; and
Kathleen Woods Araiza, BA, RN

Second Edition
April Clemens, MSN, RN; Marva J. Petty, MSN, RN, LNCC;
Jan Smith Clary, BSN, RN, LNCC; and
Kathleen Woods Araiza, BA, RN

Contents

Objectives

■ Define the concept of a toxic tort
■ Differentiate between pharmaceutical and occupational/environmental toxic exposure cases
■ Describe the relationship between the Claimant's risk factors and exposure history
■ Describe the importance of a complete review of medical, educational, social, and occupational records in the preparation of a toxic tort case
■ Identify the types of experts that may be required in preparing the toxic tort case
■ Identify resources for researching chemical substances and environmental substances

Introduction

Toxic torts are civil actions asserting a demand for recovery of damages where there was an exposure to a chemical substance, emission, or product that allegedly resulted in physical and psychological harm. During the last two decades, world news has been inundated with stories of toxic tort cases involving thousands of plaintiffs, many of whom allege repeated exposures to one or more toxic substances. Even the occasional news watcher is aware of the Chernobyl radiation leak, complaints of groundwater contamination resulting in spontaneous abortion and birth defects, and asbestos litigation that can last for years. Events such as these have raised public awareness of individual and collective vulnerability to toxic substance exposures in the home, workplace, and global environment.

Toxic tort cases have their origin in product liability litigation, and much of the case law is still found there. A toxic tort case shares many of the properties of other tort cases: negligence theories; causation issues; insurance coverage issues; and the determination of fraudulent, possibly even criminal, behavior of involved parties.

In a toxic tort case, the plaintiff must prove that an injury or the potential for injury has occurred and will result because of an exposure to substances or products. The plaintiff's discovery involves the development of both medical causation issues and scientific proof that the alleged injury or injuries occurred as the result of exposure to the substances or products. Conversely, the defense will attempt to disprove plaintiff's theories. This is paramount and will be the crux of the legal nurse consultant's investigation. The defense will develop strategies related to the following:

■ The exposure was insufficient to result in the alleged damages.
■ The substance or product did not cause the alleged injury.
■ The alleged condition was incorrectly diagnosed.
■ There are other causes for the alleged injury (e.g., familial disorder, pre-existing condition, and other unrelated exposures).

The challenge for the legal nurse consultant reviewing toxic tort cases is gaining familiarity with the special circumstances of toxic tort litigation. Typically, there are multiple plaintiffs and the records to review can be voluminous. This is difficult for the solo practitioner, as research, review, and summary of hundreds of plaintiff records are time consuming. In recent years, litigation companies have spawned to fulfill this role. In a large amount of toxic litigation, the legal nurse consultant will not work independently *per se*, but will work for a firm that performs these functions using many legal nurse consultants. This helps to streamline the process and provides the most comprehensive review of the particular litigation in question.

Generally, toxic tort cases center on efforts to prove or disprove the relative safety of one or more chemical substances or products. These cases offer the legal nurse consultant an exciting opportunity to combine nursing and medical knowledge with research, pure science, and regulatory law. During the preparation of such a case, the legal nurse consultant may have an opportunity to work with experts in toxicology, industrial hygiene, occupational health, neuropsychology, pulmonology, and other medical specialties.

This chapter is not intended to be an exhaustive description of toxic tort litigation, but rather, is a general framework for the legal nurse consultant preparing a toxic tort case for the plaintiff or defense attorney.

Toxic Tort Cases: A Complex Subject

Whether the legal nurse consultant is working from a plaintiff or defense standpoint, similar procedures will be followed in developing the case. The first step is the identification of the type of case. It is not uncommon for a toxic tort case to involve multiple plaintiffs and defendants, each with their attendant attorneys, experts, and consultants. The plaintiffs may allege single or multiple exposures to single or multiple toxic substances.

These types of cases can be extremely complex. The legal nurse consultant should participate in the early planning processes for managing the case. Without adequate planning and budgeting for file management, data acquisition and document storage, it becomes nearly impossible to manage the thousands of pages of depositions, opinions, scholarly papers, as well as medical records that will accrue throughout the life of just one of these cases. Multiple legal firms specializing in toxic tort, mass tort, and product liability litigation exist to handle these types of complex claims.

It is uncommon for a single legal nurse consultant to be the only nurse working on these types of cases. Law firms utilize the legal nurse consultant to assist in a particular aspect of the litigation process. This may change as the needs of the litigation change. An example would be in the recent Merck Vioxx® litigation in which the plaintiffs contended that the drug Vioxx® caused cardiovascular conditions and other significant morbidity as a result of its use (Findlaw.com, 2008). (See Chapter 20, "Pharmaceutical and Medical Device Product Liability Litigation" for more examples of Vioxx® cases.) The legal nurse consultant who participated dealt with a specific portion of the litigation which included the extrapolation of information from medical records. This nurse was also involved in the summary analysis of these records.

Not all toxic tort cases are complex. A single-claimant case may involve an individual exposed to one or more substances in a single (acute) exposure or over a long period of time (chronic). Multi-litigant cases typically involve many individuals with similar exposure but with medical claims differing in type and severity. In some cases involving multiple litigants, attempts may be made for the court to certify as a class action suit. Class action suits involve multi-plaintiff litigation. Certain standards established by the court must be met in order for the group of cases to be certified as a class action. Often a representative, or Bellwether group, is selected to represent the class. As defined by this type of litigation, a Bellwether group is a representative group that meets specific criteria against which each of the litigants is judged (Rudlin, 2007).

Learning the Language of the Toxic Tort Case

The legal nurse consultant must first learn the basic language of this specialized area of litigation before tackling a toxic tort case. This language deals with how the exposure occurred, how it is measured, the acronyms of measurement, and the acronyms for the regulatory agencies. Appendix A lists and defines the basic terms used in describing how an exposure is measured (Gots, 1991).

Often in the early stage of a case, only a portion of the chemical or compound is identified. The discovery process will reveal whether the plaintiff was exposed to a single chemical, a chemical compound, or numerous chemicals and compounds. Recalling previous chemistry courses, the legal nurse consultant will be reminded that there is an important distinction between a single element and a combination of elements resulting in a compound. For example, in the Tom's River case, the legal nurse consultant helped to determine that the chemical source was through exposure in the water system. The plaintiffs may allege that injury occurred as the result of synergistic effect between two chemicals in a compound. Such an effect can render two relatively "harmless" chemicals more potent and able to cause dramatic afflictions that the individual chemicals are not known to produce alone. The legal nurse consultant should work with designated consultants to determine the validity of any such assertion. This is where it is helpful in working through or with a litigation management company. Multiple experts will be required, and the nurse should not be expected to handle each aspect of the litigation.

Measuring Exposure

The most important determination to be made during the preparation of the case is the confirmation that an exposure occurred. Exposure is measured in terms of the route or means of exposure. Discovery will reveal facts as to whether the plaintiff sustained an exposure by inhalation, oral ingestion, or cutaneous absorption, including ophthalmic exposure.

Once the type of exposure is known, one must look carefully at the duration of the exposure. How long was the plaintiff exposed? Various advisory panels and regulatory agencies (Appendix B) set forth guidelines for safe exposure time to many chemicals and compounds. The legal nurse consultant will find that most of the experts in the toxic tort cases have a formal association with these advisory bodies.

Not only must one know the duration of the exposure in understanding the event and alleged injuries, one must also know the frequency of the exposure. Did the individual experience a single sustained exposure, also known as an acute exposure, or was it an exposure that occurred repeatedly during the day, over the course of weeks or years, or intermittently over an extended period of time, producing a chronic exposure?

An excellent example is the case made famous by Erin Brokovitch regarding Pacific Gas and Electric Company in Hinkley, California. The allegations involved the exposure of chromium-6 into water supply that was linked to certain medical conditions. The suit blamed this chemical for multiple symptoms including breast cancer, miscarriages, nosebleeds, Hodgkin's disease, and spinal deterioration. During the investigation, it was discovered that workers in the plant who inhaled chromium-6 over extended periods had an elevated risk of developing lung and sinus cancers. Conversely, it was argued that Brochovich's theories were considered "junk science" (Jaroff, 2003).

Another example of exposure involved a coincidental elevation of pediatric cancers in Tom's River, New Jersey, as mentioned above. An oncology nurse discovered a common link between her pediatric oncology patients and their home locations. With two "Superfund" sites surrounding Tom's River, New Jersey, there was speculation that the elevation of childhood cancers was a direct result of the contaminated drinking water. After investigation, no link was statically concluded except the environmental link between prenatal exposure to contaminated drinking water and pediatric female leukemia (Medscape General Medicine, 2002).

When information regarding the route, frequency, and duration of exposure has been obtained, the legal nurse consultant can work with toxicologists and industrial hygienists to estimate the dose of the exposure. The process used to quantify the relationship between the level of exposure and increased risk of adverse effects is termed the dose–response (Gaba, 2001). It is important to determine whether the plaintiff experienced a sustained or repeated exposure and whether the amount ingested, inhaled, or absorbed was at a minimum or maximum dose.

The Mechanics of Chemical Exposure

In preparing toxic tort cases, consideration must be given to how the exposure actually occurred. This could be through ingestion, inhalation, or cutaneous exposure. Many chemicals are absorbed through the lungs. Inhalation exposures are not only limited to gaseous chemicals, such as chlorine, solvents, and isocyanates, but also include particulate matter such as fiberglass, asbestos, animal dander, silica dust, bacterial pathogens, and viral pathogens.

Inhalation exposures can occur in the home, workplace, or global environment. Noxious fumes from carpets, glues, and paints are typically found in the home. Environmental exposure cases include tobacco cases, surface and groundwater contamination cases, and sick building syndrome. The term "sick building syndrome" is used to describe the cluster of symptoms found to occur in office environments, particularly in sealed buildings with centrally controlled mechanical ventilation (Fauci & Braunwald, 1998).

In the past few years, it has become evident that inhaled pollutants do not solely result in respiratory effects, but affect other systems such as cardiovascular, renal, and neurologic (Yeates & Mauderly, 2001). As an example, the solvent benzene, which is found in gasoline, paint removers, and many commercial solvents, is easily inhaled but causes little damage to the respiratory system when inhaled at low doses, even over a long period of time. However, chronic exposure even at low doses can result in hematopoietic system injury. Prior to 1963, it is estimated that several hundred cases of fatal aplastic anemia resulted from chronic benzene exposure [Agency of Toxic Substances and Disease Registry (ATSDR), 2000].

Inhalation exposures are also alleged to be associated with changes to the immune and nervous systems. It is important to realize that the practice of immunology is relatively new. Many diagnostic immunology tests, which determine dysfunction of the immune system, are experimental and may be performed in nonstandard laboratories. Such tests may be considered outside the mainstream of general medical practice, and the legal nurse consultant should seek reputable professionals as experts and information sources concerning these tests (Exponent, 2007).

Toxic tort cases involving immune system dysfunction may include complaints of allergies, hay fever, hives, and asthma. Autoimmune disease has been alleged as a response to a variety of drugs, vaccines, and bacterial toxins. These disorders must be looked at carefully for the determination of idiopathic autoimmune diseases such as lupus and scleroderma. While certain immune deficiencies are congenital, others are acquired, such as radiation sickness and radiation-related cancers. Others occur as the result of exposure to environmental toxins such as pesticides, nuclear waste, and groundwater contaminants.

Ingestion exposures may occur anywhere. The plaintiff may have accidentally swallowed solvents or other substances in the workplace or at home, or may have ingested unwashed fruits or vegetables contaminated with pesticides or fertilizers. Even handling food or other items with unwashed hands may transmit undesirable substances via ingestion. It may be difficult to quantify the dose of an ingested substance. A toxicologist or pharmacologist may be required to use simulation to calculate how much chemical was ingested, metabolized, and/or excreted (Food and Drug Administration, n.d.).

Cutaneous exposure results from direct skin contact with a substance. Because of the protective function of the skin, cutaneous exposures may often be limited to local reactions such as irritation, pruritus, and urticaria. The popular press has recently carried stories relating to the purported increase in generalized reactions to dermal exposure to substances such as newsprint, latex, detergents, and other substances commonly found in the home and work environments. Since a chemical may enter the body via skin, hair follicles, sweat glands, and sebaceous glands, particular attention should be paid to determining the pre-exposure condition of the skin. Was more chemical absorbed because of rashes, cuts, or other skin breaks?

Product Labeling Information

Strict interpretation of exposure guidelines presents other challenges for both the plaintiffs and the defendants. Issues of accurate labeling, storage, proper use of protective equipment and clothing, and the proper disposal of the chemical substance must be examined.

Proper labeling and safe use guidelines are important in cases of chemical exposure. The material safety data sheet (MSDS) describes what is in a compound, any health hazards, fire hazards, first aid, optimal use, storage, and disposal. MSDS forms are found in the home and workplace. Anyone changing a toner cartridge in a printer or copier will find an MSDS in the box. In the workplace, MSDS forms may be found in or on the packaging container. Because the MSDS of a product may change over the years, all the MSDS forms for the relevant time periods are likely to become exhibits in the litigation. The MSDS can also provide a quick reference for delineating changes in exposure guidelines over a period of time.

In 1989, the Occupational Safety and Health Administration (OSHA) set permissible exposure limits (PELs) for nearly 500 hazardous chemicals in the United States. The American Conference of Governmental Industrial Hygienists (ACGIH) is an association composed of occupational health professionals employed by government and educational institutions. The Threshold Limit Value Committee and Ventilation Committee of the ACGIH publish guidelines annually, which are used worldwide. In some cases, the ACGIH exposure limits are lower than the OSHA PELs. When a case involves a workplace exposure, it is important to determine which exposure limits the workplace relied on at the time of the alleged exposure.

The Legal Nurse Consultant's Role in the Toxic Tort Case

Establishing the Presence or Absence of Causation

Causation requires a relationship between the exposure and the alleged adverse outcome. Generally, plaintiffs have the burden of showing by a "preponderance of the evidence" that the exposure resulted in the injury or a significant likelihood to produce the injury at a later time because of the exposure (Gaba, 2001). Proving that a toxic substance caused a physical injury is very complicated and requires the proof of scientific causation. Scientific causation is established using statistical methods to determine a high-confidence or statistically significant relationship between exposure and illness. The illness or injury must be substantiated in the medical and social records, and the substance at issue must be proved to cause the alleged injury. Of utmost importance is careful evaluation for the presence of unrelated disease or other pathological processes.

A significant problem in proving injury includes a long period of time between exposure and illness (latency period). If the plaintiff has developed a disease such as cancer, it can be very difficult to prove that the exposure caused the disease. A long latency period gives rise to increased probability of exposure to multiple deleterious or toxic substances, complicating the causation issue. In regard to low-level toxic substance exposures, the "scientific" evidence is generally very limited. Epidemiological studies may show a statistical association between the exposure and increased rates of disease. Unfortunately, there may not be any existing studies, and it can be extremely expensive to perform them (Gaba, 2001). This is an excellent example of why social history, occupational history, and regional habitat are important. These details will provide insight into alternative causation and risk.

At toxic levels, all chemicals attack a target organ or organ system. For example, benzene, a well-known solvent, is known to be linked to specific types of leukemia; it is not known to be associated with colon cancer. Through the use of the timelines and comparative charts, the defense team could easily demonstrate the lack of a causal link between the alleged exposure (e.g., benzene) and the symptom cluster (e.g., colon cancer symptomatology).

The legal nurse consultant must be mindful of the alleged specifics of the exposure during the initial review of medical records. Legal nurse consultants working for either the plaintiff or defense team are likely to follow the same process in their goal of advancing the client's case. Both will be establishing the extent of the injury and trying to prove or disprove the causal link between exposure and injury.

Epidemiology studies already established related to the toxin's effects on medical injury as well as scientific opinions based on previous studies are essential in determining a causal link. It is important for the legal nurse consultant to be proficient with research retrieval and understanding study criteria when researching articles and studies to support their side (see section "Reviewing the Literature").

The legal nurse consultant working for the defense team may or may not be able to visit the worksite or other location where the alleged exposure occurred. If such a site visit is not possible, the legal nurse consultant reviews the materials produced during discovery for references to the presence or absence of the client's product at the site. The manufacturer's defense team will want to show that their product cannot be traced to the plaintiff's alleged exposure. If it is established that the product was available in the workplace at the time of exposure, the defense team will try to prove that the product was not actually in use in an area where the plaintiff could experience an exposure, that the substance was not properly stored and maintained by the plaintiff, or that it was not used in accordance with suggested and required guidelines.

The defense will try to show that the claimed injuries were not caused by the client's product, or that any alleged injuries are not consistent with those known to be caused by the subject product. Finally, the defense position in mitigating damages may be to show the plaintiff's contributory negligence by failing to seek timely treatment, failure to use available safety equipment, or misusing the product. This is considered alternative causation and is an important factor in review of these types of cases.

The legal nurse consultant working with the plaintiff team may have unlimited access to the injured party. The plaintiff must prove product tracing and plaintiff exposure. The team will try to prove that despite the plaintiff's appropriate storage and care in the use of the defendant's product, their client sustained a measurable exposure to that product, resulting in injury to person and property.

Example 18.1

A high school student assisted his friend one weekend at a full-service gas station. One week later, he presented to the doctor with fatigue, fever, bone pain, and multiple bruises. A bone marrow study confirmed the diagnosis of acute myelomonocytic leukemia. Knowing that the young man had worked with gasoline, a diagnosis of benzene-related exposure was made and he filed suit. The literature reveals that acute myelomonocytic leukemia can be linked to chronic benzene exposure (latent period of 5–15 years). The legal nurse consultant advises the attorney that in the absence of the temporal relationship described in the literature, it would be unlikely for a young man with a single exposure to a small amount of benzene to develop leukemia, particularly this quickly. However, the process of evaluating these types of cases may reveal that there are no alternative causative factors and that this single exposure was significant. In this particular study, the legal nurse consultant would be reviewing social history, occupational history, and regional history of the plaintiff to assist in determining alternative causation.

Reviewing and Analyzing the Records

The importance of obtaining a complete set of medical records, along with other information about the plaintiff (e.g., school records, occupational records), cannot be overemphasized. Detailed information about the plaintiff is the crux of establishing the validity of the injury. Close examination of the relationship among the exposure, claimed injury, and pre-existing medical condition is essential. The complete social and medical records should provide the necessary information.

The social history can be obtained from school records and occupational records. Records from childhood may describe congenital problems, debilitating childhood illnesses, or traumatic events that affected the plaintiff. Neurological or IQ testing may confirm that the plaintiff has a reduced earning capacity based on limited intellectual and learning abilities. The plaintiff's occupational records may yield valuable information about other sources of exposure and other risk factors for disease that are not the responsibility of the defendant.

The litigation of workplace exposure cases depends heavily on a thorough employment history. For example, did the plaintiff ever work in a shipyard or in an environment where there was asbestos? Does the plaintiff currently work in an environment where other substances or conditions might adversely affect him? Was the alleged exposure in an enclosed area or outdoors? Ventilation and atmospheric dispersion will impact an inhalation exposure case and need to be thoroughly investigated. A former mechanic may have been exposed to airborne concentrations of chlorinated fluorocarbons, cleaned machine parts in other solvents, and inhaled endless amounts of lead- and benzene-laden exhaust, yet his claim may arise out of his current employment in a film laboratory. Which chemical or compound caused his illness?

Obviously, exhaustive deposition questioning must be used to obtain a complete history of chemical exposures sustained over a plaintiff's lifetime. Occupational health records may contain some of these information. These same records are likely to include pre-employment physical examinations, regular medical screenings, laboratory results, and employee attendance records. Efforts should be made to determine whether each place of employment was in compliance with state and federal laws designed to assist workers in protecting themselves from such hazards. These laws are known as the "right-to-know" legislation.

Lifestyle habits of the plaintiff and others who live with him are also important. Is the claimant living with a smoker or doing laundry for someone whose clothing may be contaminated with pathogens or carcinogenic chemicals? Does the plaintiff pursue hobbies that involve exposure to chemicals? Avid gardeners may be exposed to pesticides, fungicides, and rodenticides, in addition to organic and inorganic fertilizers. Crafters may be exposed to solvent-laden paints and glues, phenols, ketones, and other dangerous substances. Does the plaintiff spend long periods of time in a manicure salon inhaling noxious chemicals used in preparing and painting fingernails? Does the plaintiff use "harmless" household chemicals to keep the bathroom sparkling clean? Furniture polish, bleach, ammonia, spot removers, and pine cleaners are solvents known to produce a variety of transient symptoms.

Example 18.2

A 58-year-old man presents to an attorney inquiring about filing suit against his employer. He points to a rash around his face, neck, and chest and says that he works in a warehouse "around a lot of chemicals." He believes that as the result of his exposure, he has become sensitive to the sun and burns easily. The legal nurse consultant is asked to review the medical aspects of the case.

The legal nurse consultant takes an extensive history from the client, attempting to obtain a complete list of exposures that might have been sustained at the workplace and at home. Eventually, the claimant brings in a list of the chemicals and a notebook full of MSDS forms from his workplace. Upon research, the legal nurse consultant learns that most of the chemicals are inert liquids and not used by the plaintiff. The potential plaintiff's doctor has confirmed a diagnosis of contact dermatitis and attributes the cause to the chemicals in the work environment. Since a workplace exposure has been ruled out, the legal nurse consultant must look to the social history. She visits the claimant's home, making an extensive list of products in use there. The client shows her his bathroom, and she sees many bottles of aftershave cologne. When she begins to make a list of the product names, the claimant tells her that he no longer uses those products as they irritate the pruritic areas on his face and neck.

Research reveals that a number of the claimant's aftershave products contain musk ambrette and two preservatives, methylparaben and Quaternium-15. The literature reports that musk ambrette is known to cause not only contact dermatitis but also photosensitivity. The legal nurse consultant also learns that members of the paraben family are the most commonly used preservatives in cosmetics and generally considered to be among the safest. Quaternium-15 has been identified as an antibacterial preservative belonging to a family of formaldehyde-releasing chemicals. Further research reveals that combining preservatives can cause sensitivity, characterized by localized dermatitis, to develop. The would-be plaintiff is advised that he does not have a good exposure case against his employer and any product manufacturer of the workplace chemicals.

It is easy and dangerous to overlook other sources of exposure. Because everyone is exposed to chemicals and substances every day, most individuals do not consciously consider the variety of daily exposures to which they are subject. Both the defense and plaintiff teams must construct questions and deposition outlines that will prompt the individual to confront these alternative exposures.

Medical Records

All parties must obtain the medical records as soon as possible from the plaintiff's health care providers. Individuals are often unprepared for the degree of invasion of their privacy when entering litigation. Many are embarrassed about certain medical treatments, including treatment for sexually transmitted disease, plastic surgery, psychiatric treatment, and alcohol or chemical dependency, and may conveniently "forget" or even refuse to identify the relevant providers. Other plaintiffs may simply be poor historians and genuinely unable to remember all of their health care providers. Records of payments by the plaintiff's insurers to providers may reveal the otherwise unidentified providers.

Plaintiffs often allege neurological or central nervous system (CNS) injury in toxic tort cases.

In no other area of the case preparation is the legal nurse consultant likely to face more challenges than in the evaluation of the medical and social records for pre-existing and concurrent psycho-emotional disorders. Neurological or CNS complaints are often subjective, vague, and difficult to measure or disprove. Some neuropsychological testing is poorly standardized, and results are directly related to the effort put forth by the test subject. Some tests are sensitive to the subject's efforts to falsify present physical and mental conditions (see Appendices C and D).

The legal nurse consultant should work with expert neurologists, neuropsychologists, neuro-psychiatrists, and others skilled in measuring cognitive functions when evaluating claims of toxic encephalopathy, organic brain syndrome, and convulsions. Claimed injuries to the peripheral nervous system may include allegations of neuropathy and sensorimotor dysfunction.

The medical record establishes the plaintiff's pre-existing health status, defines the existence and extent of the injury, describes the treatment rendered, and often gives a prognosis for recovery. This information not only provides an outline, but also provides a focus as the case develops.

The legal nurse consultant compares postexposure complaints with pre-existing problems to determine whether or not there is a relationship. Pathological processes are dynamic in nature, sometimes resulting in a "natural" and progressive decline in health. Such declines may be completely unrelated to the exposure although the plaintiff may allege that his condition developed or worsened as a result of the exposure. Such allegations require the defense to prove either that the underlying disease did not worsen, or that the pathology is simply the product of age. The defense may also seek to prove that the plaintiff sought medical care because he thought he was affected or because he was anticipating litigation. If it is determined that an exposure caused an exacerbation of a pre-existing condition, such an injury is usually compensable.

As the legal nurse consultant develops chronologies, summaries, and timelines concerning the facts of the case, information will be added from the literature that describes symptoms known to be associated with a particular substance. With those additions made, one can readily compare the plaintiff's symptoms with those known to be associated with exposure. Further comparison can be made between the pre-existing ailments and the postexposure complaints.

Chronologies are essential to the legal nurse consultant, who must assimilate and explain the medical and scientific elements of the case to the attorney. When the financial, personnel, and equipment resources are available, computerized databases are recommended for cataloguing specific information about the plaintiff's symptom history, such as when each symptom appeared, what events were related to the symptom, what precipitants were identified, and what treatment was given. This information can be used to create a sophisticated timeline to show the presence or absence of causal links between exposure and injury. Summaries should document the date of each contact with health care providers, the complaint, physical findings, diagnosis, treatment, diagnostic test results, and anecdotal information entered by the health care provider.

In addition, it is advantageous to paginate the medical records and cite the pages in the summary. Keep in mind that all charts, chronologies, and demonstrative evidence should be user-friendly for the nonmedical professionals, such as attorneys, insurance adjusters, and workers' compensation panels.

Evaluating the Corporate Defendant's History

When the defendant is a corporate entity, it will have to reveal corporate practices and how those practices may or may not relate to the allegations made against it. The legal nurse consultant may be asked to evaluate "in-house working papers" or other documents prepared by the client during the research, development, manufacturing, and marketing of the product in question. These papers are likely to include both *in vivo* and *in vitro* studies conducted with cellular, animal, and human subjects. These internal documents are generally considered to be proprietary and should be handled as confidential material.

Since the relative safety of the subject product is important to the case, the defense must demonstrate that their product was properly labeled and packaged with instructions for safe use. The legal nurse consultant may be asked to compare MSDS inserts with their contemporaneous package labeling and any other packaging information in an effort to evaluate claims of proper labeling. Litigants in the past have tried to show that internal corporate studies were fraudulent, leading to misrepresentation to the governing body and the public.

Despite organization, diligence, and persistence, it may be difficult for the plaintiff to prevail in attempts to prove that a corporate defendant showed reckless disregard and conspired to defraud the public regarding the safety of the product. This is not to say that litigants are not successful in proving these claims. In many instances, when it can be demonstrated that a corporate entity has committed a civil wrong, executive and supervisory staff not only may be found civilly liable, but may face criminal charges as well.

Identifying and Working with Experts

The legal nurse consultant may participate in the selection of experts for the preparation of the case. It should be noted that these complex cases tend to require specialized experts, such as epidemiologists, toxicologists, industrial hygienists, safety engineers, and physicians practicing in such specialty areas as occupational medicine, neurology, oncology, immunology, and pulmonology.

Epidemiologists evaluate causal links based on observations of the relationships between a disease entity and its presence in the general population. Like other scientists and researchers, epidemiologists must have a well-defined research hypothesis, a well-defined and adequate cohort, high-quality data, analysis of attributable actions, and minimal bias or skew in the data.

Like the epidemiologist, the toxicologist also contributes significantly to the case. The toxicologist may be the best expert to describe or refute the soundness of methods used in evaluating or testing a chemical substance. The toxicologist evaluates "poisonous" materials and their effects on living organisms. This is known as the "dose–response effect." A chemical considered "harmless," "safe," or "nontoxic" in small doses can be toxic in higher doses. For example, two aspirin can relieve pain, but a full bottle is lethal. Simply put, "the dose is the poison."

Because the toxicologist must evaluate dose–response when assessing any chemical substance at issue, the discovery process must obtain the most accurate possible data regarding the exposure and the environment in which the exposure occurred.

Various medical experts may be called on to evaluate the medical and psychosocial data in a toxic tort case. Neuropsychologists and other cognitive experts may offer testimony about any changes or lack of changes in cognition or perception in the postexposure plaintiff. Early school records may become important as the only objective baseline data available that delineate the subject's ability to process cognitive and sensory information.

The search for the experts may be pursued through the writings found in the literature search and through various professional organizations, such as the ACGIH, the American Institute of Chemists, and other organizations like the National Environmental Law Center. Appropriate experts may include practitioners, researchers, and academicians from universities, the National Institutes of Health, the Environmental Protection Agency, the Food and Drug Administration, the Centers for Disease Control, and other research facilities. The appropriate experts must be identified for trial testimony. In researching possible experts, the legal nurse consultant must consider whether the candidates could be deemed biased if a defendant company funded any of their research.

The legal nurse consultant is often the person on the litigation team who interacts directly with the experts as the case develops. The attorney must be able to rely on the legal nurse consultant to summarize the findings of the various experts, to assess the expert's suitability as a witness, and to determine the relevance of the expert's testimony. Moreover, as the liaison between the experts and the attorney, the legal nurse consultant is in the best position to coordinate the efforts of the various experts, often preventing costly overlap of research and testimony.

Reviewing the Literature

Along with collecting data about the plaintiffs and the defendants, both sides will perform literature searches. Gathering factual data in an effort to support toxicological and medical findings and conclusions is required to substantiate or refute claims. In some instances, the legal nurse consultant will perform this task for the experts. At other times, the attorney may prefer to have the experts perform their own searches for purposes of strategy. When experts perform their own searches, they will be free of any accusation that conclusions were drawn and opinions formed on the basis of another's bias in how the literature searches were conducted.

Ideally, the legal nurse consultant will have access to a library with such basics as references on occupational health, toxicology, chemistry, and medicine. The Internet is a valuable tool for locating specialized online databases and for providing access to the various regulatory and advisory agencies.

The authoritative literature discusses and describes the illnesses and symptoms known to be caused by the product at issue. Detailed information may be found about signs and symptoms of illness as the result of acute and chronic exposures in humans and animals. In the area of solvent toxicity, for example, Sweden has conducted long-term studies of individuals exposed to various solvents. These studies address findings ranging from serious illness to subtle changes seen only at the cellular level.

As in other areas of legal nurse consulting, attention must be paid to gathering data relevant to the time frame of the case. In addition, the literature search should also include the most current information. Where possible, it is suggested that research specialists and librarians familiar with scientific databases be consulted in conducting searches of widely accepted and peer-reviewed literature.

Often, the toxic tort case requires a jury to sit through tedious testimony regarding biochemistry, pharmacology, toxicology, and physics, subjects they may be unable to understand. As a result, attorneys may present as evidence "studies" with jury appeal, that were not conducted by proper scientific method. These "studies" may have had inadequate numbers in their study population, may not have been subject to peer review, or may have been published in the popular literature rather than in scholarly journals.

In some venues, courts have been very generous in allowing spurious findings to be accepted into evidence in the toxic tort case, believing that because the subject matter is complex, it is better to allow all literature and expert testimony. New case law severely limits the ability to include such material as evidence. Standards established as the result of *Daubert v. Merrell Dow Pharmaceuticals* (1993) have resulted in the trial judge's role as a gatekeeper. In this role, the judge evaluates the basis of the methodology, reliability, and relevance of expert opinions. If the judge determines that the expert opinions are not based on valid scientific methodology, the expert opinions are not admitted as evidence in the courtroom.

Although *Daubert* standards are not utilized in all courts, they are becoming more widely recognized. The legal nurse consultant should understand how these standards are interpreted and applied to medical evidence. Equipped with the awareness of *Daubert* standards, the legal nurse consultant will be able to better analyze the medical records, medical expert reports, and medical literature (Oldknow, 2001).

The literature search may include obtaining journal articles and abstracts published in foreign journals. The legal nurse consultant who overlooks or disregards materials simply because they are in another language may be missing articles published by distinguished researchers from well-respected institutions. Articles published in a foreign language may have English abstracts that will provide a clue to the articles' usefulness. Certified translators may be used to provide authentic translations. The legal nurse consultant may be asked to obtain a translator and should be aware that translators can be costly.

Ultimately, the literature search will yield such diverse items as doctoral dissertations, medical journal articles, textbook reference materials, regulatory position papers, and even "letters to the editor," making anecdotal reports of findings. From this eclectic assembly, each side will find relevant materials to prove its own and dispel the opposition's causation theories. The legal nurse consultant has a core knowledge and understanding of medical conditions, pathophysiology and expertise as a registered nurse to assist the legal team with PowerPoint and video presentations as well as working with trial support companies to assure an understanding of the medical information and issues presented before the jury during the trial phase.

Summary

It is insufficient for a litigant to merely profess that he is ill as the result of chemical exposure. The plaintiff's trial team must prove that the client sustained a sufficient period of exposure to a substance at a dose high enough to cause the alleged harm, or the significant and likely potential that the exposure will cause future harm or damage. The defense team will attempt to prove otherwise.

Undoubtedly, work experience in specialty areas of nursing may assist legal nurse consultants in preparing the toxic tort case. Experience in occupational health or in pulmonology may be helpful. For other types of cases, nurses who are knowledgeable about immunology, neurology, or oncology may find it easier to master the reading material. There is no requirement that legal nurse consultants be experts in occupational medicine or other specialty areas in order to assist in preparing these cases. The basic requirement includes a willingness to use one's nursing and general science backgrounds in preparing cases with objectivity and careful analysis.

Whether legal nurse consultants are working for attorneys or consulting firms, they must possess the ability to review and analyze information from a variety of sources. Legal nurse consultants must be able to work with experts and act as liaisons between the experts and the attorneys in order to bring a powerful, proficient multidisciplinary team approach to this novel area of litigation.

References

Agency of Toxic Substances and Disease Registry (2000). *Benzene toxicity: Physiologic effects*. Retrieved October 1, 2008, from http://www.atsdr.cdc.gov/csem/benzene/physiologic_effects.html

Exponent. (2007). *Respiratory toxicology*. Retrieved October 5, 2008, from http://www.exponent.com/Respiratory-Toxicology-Capabilities

Fauci, A. S., & Braunwald, E. (1998). *Harrison's principles of internal medicine* (14th ed.). New York: McGraw-Hill.

Findlaw.com. (2008). *Vioxx overview*. Retrieved October 5, 2008, from http://injury.findlaw.com/vioxx/vioxx-overview.html

Food and Drug Administration (FDA). (n.d.). *Metabolism and pharmacokinetic studies*. Retrieved October 5, 2008, from http://www.cfsan.fda.gov/~acrobat/red-vb.pdf

Gaba, J. M. (2001). *Environmental law* (2nd ed., pp. 48, 196). St. Paul, MN: West Group.

Gots, R. E. (1991). *Seven steps to toxic tort analysis and defense*. Chicago: The Defense Research Institute.

Jaroff, L. (2003). *Erin Brockovich's junk science. Time Magazine*. Retrieved October 5, 2008, from http://www.time.com/time/columnist/jaroff/article/0%2C9565%2C464386%2C00.html

Medscape General Medicine. (2002). *Why are investigations of potential environmental cancer clusters so often inconclusive?* Retrieved October 1, 2008, from http://www.medscape.com/viewarticle/442554_5

Oldknow, P. F. (2001). The scientific method, and the legal nurse consultant. *Journal of Legal Nurse Consulting,* 12–14.

Rudlin, D. A. (2007). *Toxic tort litigation* (pp. 185, 186). Gale Group, Farmington Hills, MI: American Bar Association, ISBN 1590317343, 9781590317341.

Yeates, D. B., & Mauderly, J. L. (2001). Inhaled environmental/occupational irritants and allergens: Mechanisms of cardiovascular and systemic responses. *Environmental Health Perspectives, 109*, 4.

Additional Reading

Adams, R. M. (1999). *Occupational skin diseases* (3rd ed.). Philadelphia: W.B. Saunders.

Baselt, R. C. (2000). *Disposition of toxic drugs and chemicals in man* (5th ed., p. 79). Foster City, CA: Chemical Toxicology Institute.

Bass, R., & Vamvakas, S. (2000). The toxicology expert: What is required? *Toxicology Letters, 112–113,* 383–389.

Food and Drug Administration (FDA). (2000). *An FDA overview: Protecting consumers, protecting public health*. Retrieved October 1, 2008, from http://www.fda.gov/oc/opacom/fda101/sld001html

King, R. (2008). *Toxic mold litigation* (2nd ed.). Chicago, IL: American Bar Association. ISBN 1590318838, 9781590318836.

Lewis, R. J. (2000). *Sax's dangerous properties of industrial materials* (10th ed.). New York: Wiley.

McElhaney, R., & Beare, P. G. (1998). Expert witness/legal consultant: The importance of data collection, clinical nurse specialist. *Clin Nurse Spec, 12*(3), 117–120.

Occupational Health and Safety Administration. (2001). *Permissible exposure limits*. Retrieved through previous author from http://www.osha-slc.gov/SLTC/pel/index.html

Patnaik, P. (1999). *Comprehensive guide to the hazardous properties of chemical substances* (2nd ed.). New York: Wiley.

Test Questions

1. All of the following agencies or advisory bodies have informational resources on chemical exposures EXCEPT:
   A. Natural Resources Conservation Service
   B. Environmental Protection Agency
   C. American Conference of Governmental Industrial Hygienists
   D. Occupational Safety and Health Administration

2. You are working for the plaintiff's attorney in an environmental exposure case and are asked to obtain information about the health of the plaintiff's neighbors. Why?
   A. The plaintiff and his attorney care about those around the plaintiff and want to be assured that they are healthy.
   B. If the neighbors are sick all the time, the plaintiff's case will look better to the jury. If many of the neighbors have a variety of symptoms, it will prove that the chemical in the groundwater has made everyone sick.
   C. The attorney wants to prove that his client's illness is part of a cohort of individuals who have been made ill by the exposure. Similar symptoms in the neighbors may strengthen the claim.
   D. This is a great opportunity for the plaintiff to find out more about his neighbors.

3. Mrs. Jones has alleged that since she had breast implants, she has developed a tendency to develop rashes and rhinitis. You review the medical and social records. All of the following are items of importance in your review, EXCEPT:
   A. Mrs. Jones has had saline implants for 10 years. She has her hair colored every 4 weeks at the same salon where she has her nails done.
   B. Mrs. Jones has eight children, six of whom are being treated for eczema and multiple food allergies.
   C. Mrs. Jones had silicone implants until one of them broke and was replaced with saline.
   D. Mr. Jones' sister has lupus.

4. A worker had a single, acute exposure to formaldehyde and claims that as a result he has elevated liver enzymes. He has approached a plaintiff attorney regarding the merits of his claim. You are asked to do a literature search and compare it against the medical record. You find that the worker has had intermittent liver enzyme elevations over the last few years. The employer's occupational health clinic notes make a reference to his being referred to a chemical dependency treatment program. Your first step is
   A. To advise the plaintiff attorney not to accept the case because the plaintiff is an alcoholic
   B. To consult the databases for information on liver injury as the result of exposure to formaldehyde
   C. To ask what the route of exposure was before starting the reviews
   D. To request the plaintiff's childhood medical records

5. The defense attorney has asked you to assist in an alleged ammonia (inhalation) exposure case. The plaintiff, a 30-year-old female, works for the defendant janitorial service and states that the use of household concentration ammonia products over the past year has resulted in

her progressive development of emotional problems, clumsiness, uncoordinated movement, fatigue, paresthesias, and urinary incontinence. All of the following information is critical and will be beneficial in the mitigation of this case EXCEPT:

A. The plaintiff's family physician referred her to a neurologist 2 years ago for a multiple sclerosis workup
B. Inhalation of household ammonia products causes few effects unless they are in large quantities
C. The plaintiff had mononucleosis as a teenager
D. The plaintiff's condition has rapidly deteriorated since the birth of her baby 4 months ago

Answers: 1. A, 2. C, 3. D, 4. C, 5. C

Appendix A: Measuring Exposure

- Immediately dangerous to life and health (IDLH)—The maximum concentration from which one could escape within 30 minutes without experiencing irreversible health effect or impairing self-rescue.
- MSDS—Form included with shipment of products containing chemical substances. The MSDS lists the chemical ingredients, their Chemical Abstracts Service registry identification information, and information related to exposure and handling. Manufacturers and vendors are legally required to include this with each shipment of product.
- PEL—Similar to threshold limit value (TLV)/time weighted average (TWA).
- Personal protective equipment (PPE)—Includes protective garments, masks, goggles, and respirator.
- Short-term exposure limit (STEL)—A short exposure added to the TLV/TWA. STEL exposures may not exceed 15 minutes more than four times daily, with each exposure separated by at least 60 minutes. Workers must not suffer irritation, chronic tissue damage, or inability for self-rescue.
- TLV—Also known as TWA. The daily exposure that a worker can sustain to airborne concentrations 8 hours per day, 40 hours per week without adverse effect. These exposures may be described in parts per million (ppm) or billion (ppb), or in the case of dermal exposure, in milligrams per cubic meter (mg/m^3).

Appendix B: Advisory and Regulatory Agencies

- American Conference of Governmental Industrial Hygienists (ACGIH) http://www.acgih.org/
- American Industrial Hygiene Association (AIHA) http://www.aiha.org/
- Environmental Protection Agency (EPA) http://www.epa.gov/
- Food and Drug Administration (FDA) http://www.fda.gov
- Occupational Safety and Health Administration (OSHA) http://www.osha.gov/
- National Academy of Sciences (NAS) http://www.nas.edu/
- National Research Council (NRC) (not to be confused with the Nuclear Regulatory Council) http://www.nas.edu/nrc/
- National Institute for Occupational Safety and Health (NIOSH) http://www.cdc.gov/niosh/homepage.html
- Society of Toxicology (SOT) http://www.toxicology.org/

Appendix C: Toxic Tort Treasures

1. Obtain all medical records, mental health records, school records, and employment records. [Special authorizations may be required for sensitive information (e.g., HIV status). Separate authorizations are also required for mental health records.]
2. Obtain missing records (e.g., billing records indicate that an office visit occurred, yet office records for that date are missing; EMS run sheet, lab results).
3. Prepare a list of additional health care providers mentioned in the records, so that the attorney can obtain these records.

4. Review past medical history carefully. For example, a plaintiff states that leukopenia was first diagnosed following the exposure in question. With careful review of the records, the legal nurse consultant learns that a hematologist was consulted 6 years prior to the incident in question for leukopenia. The plaintiff failed to share this history with the attorney or current physicians.

5. Family medical history (e.g., asthma) should not be ignored. The defense team will address genetic influences versus exposure.

6. Note current medications listed in the health care providers' records. Often, you may see a current medication not previously mentioned. Who prescribed this medication? This may lead to identification of yet another treating health care provider.

7. In preparing the chronological summary, you may become aware of time lapses in which there are no medical records. Question this! Why are there large time gaps? Did the plaintiff live elsewhere during this period? Was the plaintiff healthy and not in need of medical care?

8. Pharmacy records provide another source of identification of additional treating physicians.

9. Note conflicts in the records. Sometimes the plaintiff is simply a poor historian, or will carefully select what he shares with a particular health care provider. This will become evident to the prudent legal nurse consultant in preparing the chronological summary. Often it is clear that a particular physician may not have been made aware of some previous events, such as motor vehicle accident resulting in neck and back injuries. For example, a neurologist diagnosed a plaintiff with neuropathies and related them to the alleged toxic exposure. The physician was unaware of the plaintiff's history of neuropathies related to a motor vehicle accident.

10. Question the existence of other lawsuits. The plaintiff may be alleging the same injuries in more than one case.

11. Note the absence of a physician's physical examination or appropriate diagnostic tests. For example, the plaintiff's alleged symptoms included watery eyes, stuffy nose, congestion, wheezing, and shortness of breath as a result of the exposure in question. The plaintiff stated that his symptoms began immediately following the incident and continued for several months. Although the treating physician saw the plaintiff within 2 h of the alleged exposure, the physician failed to document any physical findings. One week later, the plaintiff was seen by his physician on follow-up. Again, no physical examination was documented. Because there were no documented physical findings, it is not clear whether diagnostic tests should have been ordered. Question this lack of documentation. Is this treating physician a hired gun?

12. Finally, be suspicious and be inquisitive!

Appendix D: Medical Records Summary Excerpt

Many different formats may be used in summarizing medical records. Some key bullets that should be included in the summary would include the following: the date of the medical record reference, usually in month/day/year format. A description of what the information is, for example, office records, nurse's notes, or hospital records. The chief complaint or background information should be documented. The current complaint as well as any current medication should be included. Typically, physician physical examination findings as well as impression and plan would be included. In some cases, the attorney will ask for your impression and recommendations, which should also be included. Finally, depending on particular attorney preference, bates references may be included.

- Example: 02/10/01
- Office records of John Doe, MD (Dermatologist)
- Chief complaint/Background information
- Current complaint
- Current medication
- Physical examination findings
- Physician's Impression and Plan
- Other pertinent information
- Your conclusions and recommendations
- Bates reference

Chapter 22

ERISA and HMO Litigation

Susan van Ginneken, RN

Second Edition
Cynthia Dangerfield, RN, CPN and William J. Scott, Esq.

Contents

Objectives

After the review of this chapter, the legal nurse consultant (LNC) will be able to

■ Discuss different types of managed care products
■ Define terms related to the Employee Retirement Income Security Act (ERISA), health maintenance organizations (HMOs), health insurance coverage, and litigation issues involving these topics
■ Identify how the ERISA has affected HMO litigation cases in the past and how legislative changes will impact future cases
■ Assist in the development of cases involving HMOs covered under the ERISA.

Introduction to ERISA and HMO Litigation Issues

The ERISA is a law enacted by the Congress in 1974 as a way of ensuring that employees of companies that provide retirement and pension benefits receive the promised benefits. ERISA's main focus is to provide the framework through which the benefit plans are administered. According to information given in a lecture at Georgetown University, "Upwards of 160 million Americans obtain health coverage through the workplace and are thus affected by ERISA" (Bloche, 2008). This includes HMOs.

Health care costs have risen drastically in the past 20 years. The passage of Medicare and Medicaid in the 1960s initiated the rapid rise, and by 1993 health care expenditures accounted for about 13.4% of the gross domestic product (GDP); this had risen to 15.3% by 2003, and are expected to be about 18% by 2013 (Smith, Cowan, Sensenig, Catlin, & the Health Accounts Team, 2005). As was common practice in the early 1980s, many companies looked at HMOs as a type of "health care reform," a financially manageable way to help cover the expense of providing health care coverage for their employees. HMOs and various other forms of managed care were viewed as the panacea to spiraling health care costs and mismanagement.

Millions of Americans are covered by HMOs and other types of managed care health plans. Hegyvary reports that "In 2004, 39% of Americans were enrolled in managed care organizations, about one third of them in managed HMOs and two thirds in preferred provider organizations (PPOs) (Mason, Leavitt, & Chaffee, 2007)." HMOs provide many employers with an affordable means of providing health care coverage to their employees.

As the growth of the managed care industry developed, so too have the issues associated with this model of health care delivery, such as utilization review decisions that appeared to be acts of limitation by the HMO. The fear among health care providers and the public, who were unfamiliar with guidelines and "critical pathways" for treatment of the more common diseases, was that managed care arbitrarily withheld health care and followed some secret code of denial. Another example of the HMO "strategy" that quickly fell under the light of suspicion was the belief that HMOs offered financial incentives to the physicians and health care providers to limit care which would raise ethical concerns. The latter seemed very unethical. Some of these incentives were limitations of referrals to specialists. It was believed that any competent internist or general practitioner could treat almost every illness with the exception of the most dire and complicated ailments. Referrals to specialists were no longer the norm for the treatment of conditions. The money that was saved by "withholding" care was distributed to the physicians. Frustration with managed care decisions seems to have led to a shift away from HMOs. This may account for PPOs having more than doubled the amount of subscribers in the HMO plans in the last 10 years (Kaiser Family Foundation, 2007).

Decisions by HMOs today do not appear to have the adverse impact on patients that was previously reported. According to a recent journal article, "Health maintenance organizations (HMOs) are a major and growing source of health insurance for the near-elderly (those aged 55 to 64) in the United States. Many people have questioned the use of capitation by HMOs (doctors are reimbursed a set fee per patient, regardless of services provided), saying it motivates providers to order fewer tests or perform fewer procedures and puts the patient's needs last. However, a new study, supported by the Agency for Healthcare Research and Quality (HS13992), found no ill effects of HMOs decisions on the health status of the near-elderly. In fact, those with chronic health conditions actually fared better upon enrolling in managed care plans" (Xu & Jensen, 2006).

Early on, the managed care industry was concerned that it would never be able to get a fair hearing in medical malpractice and negligence suits, as a result of the commonly held perception that HMOs provide substandard care. With the advent of ERISA, however, employer-sponsored HMOs became immune from the state law causes of action. The ERISA generally preempts all state laws that "relate to" an ERISA plan (29 U.S.C. §1144) in matters resulting in negligence and medical malpractice. This means that employer-funded HMOs could only be sued for violations of the ERISA. Claimants cannot recover punitive or compensatory damages under the ERISA. Rather, they are only entitled to benefits payable under terms of the plan or other appropriate equitable relief in the case of a breach of fiduciary duty (see 29 U.S.C. §1132).

"In the mid 1990's, the Supreme Court limited the scope of the ERISA preemption, which afforded greater opportunities to enrollees to sue their health plans in state courts, where they could seek compensation for lost wages, medical expenses, and pain and suffering in addition to seeking compensation for the cost of medical services not provided" (Hellinger, 2005). ERISA is no longer the safe harbor for the managed care industry. Today, with the advent of patients' rights, patients' bill of rights, and the focus on results-oriented quality care, HMOs must take the responsibility for their design and administration of benefits. Also, HMOs are responsible for the appropriateness of their utilization decisions, structuring of health care options under the practice of case management or disease management programs, and coverage decisions. These issues must be handled within the new framework of rising health care costs and less legal protection under the law.

Overview of ERISA

As described in the Introduction, Title 1 of ERISA was developed to provide the minimum standards and the framework by which voluntary employee benefit plans would be administered. Employee benefit plans are generally established and offered by an employer, an employee organization (such as some types of unions), or a combination of both. Different types of employee benefit plans include pension plans (defined benefit and defined contribution) and "welfare" plans, such as health, disability, and life. ERISA governs most private-sector employee benefit plans, but does not cover plans created or maintained by government bodies, churches, and/or benefit plans, maintained for the sole purpose of complying with workers' compensation, disability, and unemployment laws. In addition, ERISA does not apply to benefit plans that are maintained outside the continental United States, regardless of the plan type.

ERISA essentially ensures that employee benefit plans are established and maintained in a financially sound manner. It mandates that once established, the employer is obligated not only to provide promised benefits but also to do so according to the ERISA fiduciary rules guidelines. These guidelines include the following:

- The plans are provided for the exclusive benefit of plan participants (employees) and their dependents/beneficiaries
- The plan fiduciaries discharge their duties in "a prudent manner," while avoiding transactions that appear to be a conflict of interest
- The plan fiduciaries comply with limitations in employer investments in securities and property
- The plan funds benefits according to legal requirements and plan rules
- The plan discloses information on benefits, management, and the financial condition of the plan to the appropriate government entities and plan participants (e.g., financial reports and summary plan descriptions [SPDs])
- The plan provides documents required by government regulations to validate compliance with ERISA guidelines (Employee Retirement Income Security Act, 1974)

The government agency with primary jurisdiction over Title 1 of ERISA and the entity that administers and controls benefit plans is the United States Department of Labor, along with the Pension and Welfare Benefits Administration and the Internal Revenue Service (U.S. Department of Labor, 2008).

ERISA's preemptive provision has a significant impact on medical malpractice and negligence claims that involve care provided through an ERISA-governed plan. ERISA preempts any and all state laws that "relate to" an ERISA-governed plan (29. U.S.C. §1144). The courts have consistently applied this doctrine to claims arising under HMOs, which means medical malpractice, negligence, and personal injury claims are generally preempted. Claimants challenging care administered through an HMO are generally limited to benefits payable under the terms of the plan (20 U.S.C. §1132(a)(1)(B)). There have been numerous changes in the way the law looks at ERISA's impact on insurance, due to litigation issues. In the late 1990s, a number of states attempted to enact laws that held health plans liable for damages due to treatment decisions made by employees of the health plans. The passage of these laws began with Texas in 1997, followed by Georgia and California in 1999. In 2000, four more states passed laws of this type: Washington, Arizona, Maine, and Oklahoma. Finally in 2001, three more states joined the group: West Virginia, New Jersey, and Oklahoma (Hellinger, 2005). These laws were intended to address the problem of patients being wrongly denied care, and to allow them to recover legal remedies other than just getting the treatment (which was often too little and too late). However, the insurance companies challenged the legality of these state laws. In 2004, the Supreme Court addressed the issue of whether these types of laws were preempted by ERISA. The Supreme Court ruled that ERISA preempted these types of state law and any verdict found under those state laws must be overturned. Despite the Supreme Court's decision, the question of to what extent ERISA preempts medical malpractice claims that challenging the care administered under an HMO continues to be litigated in the courts. It was suggested by Justice Ruth Bader Ginsburg that obtaining legislation by the Congress "may be the only mechanism available to provide patients with adequate compensation for damages incurred as a result of coverage decisions made by employer-sponsored health plans" (Hellinger, 2005).

Overview of HMOs

In order to understand how litigation in an HMO case can be affected by ERISA, the LNC needs to understand the structure of the different managed care plans. Managed care organizations

(MCOs) provide active coordination of, arrangement for, and delivery of health care within a network of contracted providers (physicians, nurse practitioners, physician assistants, and other health care professionals) who receive monetary compensation for agreeing to provide services for patients who are enrolled in the plan. Often, contracting providers lower their usual fee substantially in exchange for the assurance of a consistent patient population, thereby creating a steady income. Providers may contract with several plans at once or may contract with only a select few. In some situations, providers work only for one HMO and do not treat private, or nonmember, patients.

Managed care operates on three basic principles: (1) oversight of medical care given (utilization review); (2) contracts with care providers and organizations; and (3) benefits furnished in accordance with the employer's health plan terms, which can vary from employer to employer or even member to member. Among the types of managed care are HMOs, PPOs, point of service providers (POS), exclusive provider organizations (EPOs), newer, hybrid consumer-directed health plans (CDHPs), physician-hospital organizations, and independent practice associations (IPAs).

The best known model in managed care is the HMO. Some HMOs are known as "staff model" HMOs. The plan, or HMO, actually employs the physicians and ancillary health care providers for the sole purpose of providing care to its members. A "group model" HMO involves contracts with physicians in a group or professional association or a professional corporation. The health plan pays the group, and the group manages compensation of the individual provider group members (arranging contracts with hospitals and other health care providers, such as home health agencies and durable medical equipment [DME] companies) who provide these services to the patients assigned to the group.

Managed care plans also include PPOs, POSs, and EPOs. Authorizations and referrals are generally not required for these three types of organizations as long as the member utilizes contracted providers for services. In addition, the members' costs and financial responsibilities will increase if they utilize out-of-network providers. This also applies if patients require the services of specific disciplines that are not provided by the PPO, POS, or EPO because they have failed to or were unable to contract with that type of provider. Monetary compensation for contracted providers may take the form of capitation, a per-member/per-month payment, or a flat fee for contracting with the plan.

Other forms of remuneration include bonuses that were previously based on the lack of referrals to specialists, reduced inpatient hospital care, low pharmacy utilization, and other similar scenarios. The physician was financially rewarded when utilization of these services was low, but was financially penalized when usage was high. This is often referred to as an "incentive." Currently, the focus has shifted in the industry to rewarding physicians for high levels of patient satisfaction and quality service, as health care has shifted to the evidence-based practice (EBP) model.

HMOs have been a source of health care benefit management since the early 1980s, and some pioneer forms of HMOs existed prior to that time. The general premise behind the HMO was the prevention of illness and catastrophic health conditions. A person's health could be maintained through preventive services, rather than caring for conditions that resulted from physical neglect and lack of appropriate medical attention prior to the illness.

These preventive services took the shape of programs, such as vaccinations for infants and children, influenza and pneumonia vaccination programs for the elderly and at-risk populations, prenatal care and "well baby" visits, smoking cessation programs, and community health fairs. Over time, the HMOs observed that few members availed themselves of these "added-value" benefits. What became evident was that on average, participants in HMOs experienced illness, injury, and chronic medical conditions as much as the participants in other types of managed care and traditional insurance plans did.

For HMOs to remain competitive in the health care marketplace, the savings that HMO models promised their administrators, members, and employers had to be found elsewhere in the plan. Utilization review and case management seemed to be the answer to this dilemma.

Cost Control for the HMO

The main focus of utilization management is to monitor and control several aspects of a patient's care. Some plans focus on utilization from a quality-driven perspective: care is monitored to ensure that patients receive everything they need to recover, as expeditiously as possible, with the intent that maximum care would provide the fastest results. This would save money by reducing the length of hospitalization or recurrent illnesses. This was a rarity since few plans had the capital to offer this approach and remain competitive in the insurance market.

Ten years ago, most utilization plans were opposite in nature: only the most necessary procedures, supplies, and days in the hospital were "authorized," or approved, by the plan's utilization review department. Decisions for benefit denial, or nonauthorization of medical care, were generally initiated by a nurse who was employed by the plan and reviewed the patient's records to determine the procedure, service, hospital stay, or supply was medically necessary. These decisions were then reviewed by a medical authority, usually a physician or the plan's medical director, and a final disposition was made. Not only does this process apply to hospitalization and utilization of expensive equipment and supplies, but it also applies to referrals to specialists, home health care, and customized equipment and supplies. Utilization review continues today, but in a less restrictive manner than before.

In standard HMO models, the money that is paid to the plan from member premiums is "pooled" after administrative expenses and plan costs are removed. The pool may then be equally divided among the contracted providers or left in one unit. For any "extra" care that is provided to a member outside of routine office visits, such as an emergency room visit or a referral to and treatment by a specialist, the value of the pool is diminished. For the provider who has his own pool, the incentive would be to preserve the balance in order to receive the money in the pool.

Although the incentives appear to motivate providers to refuse referrals to specialists, deny emergency room treatment, and discharge patients prematurely from hospitals in order to retain their pools, the original impetus to providers was to eliminate any unnecessary or extraneous referrals and services. The intent was to avoid prolonged hospitalizations, for example, or situations such as referring a patient to an otolaryngologist for treatment of a sore throat when the patient's physician (who may be a pediatrician or internal medicine physician) was quite capable of treating the condition. A newer incentive for physicians has emerged in the recent years: the high-performance network. Quality indicators are collected from insurance companies, evaluating the past performance of physicians. This may be based on cost per episode of care or measures such as preventive care testing. Insurers then encourage subscribers to choose those physicians who score higher on efficiency and quality. The belief here is that physicians may lose enough patients to colleagues who scored better than them, and they, in turn, would improve their efficiency and quality in order to compete (Ginsburg, 2006).

Example 22.1

The following is an illustration of a prolonged hospital stay scenario: A patient is admitted to the hospital for surgery. The physician and patient agree to a hospitalization of six days. The intensity of service/severity of illness criteria utilized by the HMO indicate that the average hospital stay for this particular type of surgery, barring any severe complications, is three days, and that is what is "pre-authorized" by the plan. Unless there was a medical reason for the patient to remain in the hospital after the approved three-day stay, the patient would be financially responsible for any additional days over the initial three days. Also, the physician would more than likely be responsible for the "overutilization" of inpatient days and penalized by the plan.

When a joint pool is shared by many providers, some felt that providers may attempt to influence each other by recommending the authorization of fewer referrals and services, thereby creating a larger balance to share. This concept is known as "risk sharing." One of the benefits of a shared pool applies to doctors who are in the same group and practice together, or professional organizations or partnerships. In this situation, patients could be referred to different specialists within the group practice, thereby controlling extraneous referrals and maintaining the pool money within the group. All of these incentives and health care delivery models are a type of utilization management.

Another type of utilization management is performed by a case manager. A case manager is usually a nurse or social worker employed by the HMO (or other insurance provider), who is experienced in a variety of medical conditions. This person can anticipate most of the patient's needs and treatment requirements, making cost-effective arrangements for delivery of these services by providers within the HMO network. The case manager is usually familiar with clinical pathways, or usual and predictable courses for the treatment of a given condition. Based on the criteria set, medical necessity is determined and care and services are authorized and delivered in a controlled, closely monitored environment.

This model of utilization management falls short of delivering promised savings when the patient's medical condition does not follow the normal course of resolution. In addition, not all HMOs are capable of contracting every type of provider that a patient may potentially require, and in these situations, the case manager must consider out-of-network arrangements while still attempting to provide savings to the plan.

Currently, the style of case management has progressed to "care management," a sort of hybridized or refined case management program of coordinating the patient's care from a proactive viewpoint. There is more of a partnership with both the provider and the patient, and the care manager is not only a liaison for the health plan, but may also perform patient advocacy and physician/service coordination. This type of case management is usually restricted to specific and often common disease processes, and has been found to reduce costs in some patient diagnoses that utilize the largest amount of health care services: diabetes, congestive heart failure, and asthma. Case managers have "care maps" that they use to guide the care of patients with these chronic conditions, and the success with these chronic conditions have encouraged the use of this tactic for the treatment of obesity, tobacco addiction, and depression (Mason et al., 2007). Additionally, innovative ideas for encouraging wellness participation by subscribers are emerging. "They include, for example, small cash payments for the completion of a health risk assessment, gift cards, gym membership discounts, and reimbursement for weight management programs, such as Weight Watchers" (Draper, 2008).

Volume 2, Chapter 7, "The Legal Nurse Consultant as a Case Manager," provides more information on case/care management. It was once assumed that benefit denial decisions were arbitrarily determined by HMO accountants and financial officers as well as nonmedical clerical staff based solely on cost. In fact, most ethical and prudent HMOs leave the decision-making power to the medical staff, which usually includes nurses, social workers, physicians, and a committee of a variety of health care workers as a backup system.

Medical decisions are generated by a comparison of the patient's symptoms and physical condition to a national data set, or utilization guidelines, often referred to as intensity of service/severity of the illness criteria. Two of the more popular sources of this information are InterQual Criteria and Milliman Care Guidelines. Both of these criteria sets and others similar to them give general guidelines for lengths of stay and the appropriate time during the progression of an illness to perform diagnostic tests or decide which ones are needed. The criteria that a patient must meet in order to be considered appropriate for discharge from care are also considered.

Decisions independent of these guidelines are made when a patient appears to progress at a rate faster than that outlined in the criteria and when treatment may end sooner than expected. On rare occasions, making an accelerated decision turns out to be disastrous for both the patient and the plan. Early discharges sometimes result in a relapse of the condition, or unseen complications that may have been evident had the patient remained hospitalized under a watchful clinical eye or undergone more diagnostic studies.

Data published in the *Journal of the American College of Cardiology* reported that compared with other types of health benefit plans, HMOs historically authorized fewer procedures, but reported longer hospital stays for acute myocardial infarction admissions (Every et al., 1995). This could be due, in part, to the lack of access to the appropriate facilities, providers, or specialists, and even diagnostic equipment and procedures within the HMOs network. In some situations, this policy results in cost savings to the HMO. In other situations, the cost of patient care is significantly higher because the patient was denied access to necessary and needed care.

With the advent of the patients' rights movement in 1999, plans turned to compliance and quality programs. One of the more popular "watchdog groups" to review plan activity according to higher industry standards is the National Committee for Quality Assurance (NCQA). This is a not-for-profit organization independent of other insurance organizations and health care plans whose main function is to monitor various types of plans in order to ensure quality of services. This is done through member surveys, strict credentialing guidelines, and monitoring of Health Plan Employer Data and Information Set Data (HEDIS), a "report card" that indicates how a plan is performing compared with its peer group.

Organizations of this type generally will accredit or certify a plan after a rigorous on-site review of administrative and clinical practice processes and verification of contracting practices. "Quality health care can be defined as the extent to which patients get the care they need in a manner that most effectively protects or restores their health. This means having timely access to care, getting treatment that medical evidence has found to be effective and getting appropriate preventive care" (National Committee for Quality Assurance, 2008). These organizations and others like it are holding the current standard of health plans at a more patient-friendly level. Although meticulous and painstaking to undertake, successful accreditation or certification reviews also serve the plan by increasing its marketability and credibility as a quality health plan.

HMO management has been dissected and re-evaluated in many superior court cases. With each case, the opportunity has presented itself for the public to understand how to administer an HMO as well as how to maneuver within the managed care system. In addition, it appears that HMOs may be evolving into a more user-friendly, cost-effective answer to the coverage of health care benefits.

Role of the LNC in HMO Litigation

Under ERISA guidelines, the plaintiff, during litigation, could expect to recover an amount equal to the denied benefit, receive authorization to utilize the benefit, or obtain the requested medical care (when it was not originally a covered benefit). The plaintiff also could have the opportunity to potentially recover attorneys' fees as long as the administrator of the plan was found to have made the denial in bad faith, or to have breached a duty to the plan participant. State laws enacted since 1997 have attempted to award punitive damages to the plaintiff, but a deciding opinion by the Supreme Court in 2004 ruled that these state laws are preempted by ERISA (Duffy, 2004).

When approached to review records and apply medical expertise, the LNC should be alert to potential issues involving HMOs. The primary issue will be to determine whether or not the client is covered by an ERISA plan. This is generally confirmed by the attorney prior to the case or medical record review, but the LNC should be familiar with how this is determined.

As a general rule, ERISA applies to any employer-provided health insurance coverage that is provided to the employer's employees. ERISA does, however, provide a "safe harbor" for certain insurance coverage offered directly to employees. To fall within the safe harbor, and thus be exempt from ERISA coverage, the coverage must satisfy four criteria: (1) premiums must be paid 100% by the employee; (2) coverage must be entirely voluntary; (3) employer can collect and remit premiums, but cannot profit; and (4) employer cannot endorse. Endorsement has a fairly low threshold, for example simply putting the company name on a policy may be enough to constitute an endorsement.

All ERISA-governed plans must adopt reasonable claim procedures for the processing of claims (29 C.F.R. §2560.503-1). When an administrator denies a claimant's request for benefit coverage, the steps for requesting and obtaining a review are set forth in the plan document (usually the insurance policy) and "SPD" and must be followed. In order for this process to be appropriately initiated, the claimant must have knowledge of this process. ERISA requires that the plan provides notice of the denial in writing, and clearly delineates the steps that must be followed for a review. The claimant must also have enough time for the claim review. The time period for deciding the initial claim and appeal is prescribed by statute/regulations and varies based on the type of claim under review. For example, an urgent care claim must be decided within 72 hours; a preservice claim must be decided within 15 days; and a postservice claim must be decided within 30 days (29 C.F.R. §2560.503-1). In other words, the plan should not delay the review for such an extended period of time that the claimant suffers ill effects simply because of the delay in the review.

In addition, the persons deciding the claim are generally subject to ERISA's fiduciary provisions. Plans are permitted under the law to administer their own benefits structure. A conflict-of-interest situation is innate in this arrangement. However, the law also clearly defines how the fiduciary (responsible plan administrator) must conduct business for the exclusive purpose of providing benefits to the plan participants. The law also states that the fiduciary should be

> Acting solely in the interest of plan participants and their beneficiaries and with the exclusive purpose of providing benefits to them; carrying out their duties prudently; following the plan documents (unless inconsistent with ERISA); diversifying plan investments; and paying only reasonable plan expenses (Meeting Your Fiduciary Responsibility, 2008).

The LNC Checklist

The primary role of the LNC involved in assisting with HMO litigation cases is to determine whether the HMO delivered promised health care benefits to the claimant. The attorney will most likely have ascertained the nature of the administrative issues associated with the case, such as scope of benefit coverage and the type of benefits selected by the claimant. It is helpful for the LNC to be familiar with some of the legal nuances that distinguish this type of litigation from other types. The following is a checklist of helpful issues for the LNC and attorney to investigate:

1. Request the certificate of insurance, plan document, SPD, explanation of benefits, or the actual contract signed by the HMO member when the plan was elected. The LNC will also want any policies, procedures, or rules that were relied on in making the claim determination and should also ask for a copy of the claim file. Familiarity with the benefits selected by the

member (known as election of benefits) will help to determine whether the denied benefit was elected by the member and should be a covered benefit to which the client is entitled. Good sources to review for this type of information also include any pharmacy benefit plans, formularies, and DME coverage plans. This information should be available either in the contract or as an addendum to the contract.

2. When an exception to the contracted benefit plan has been requested by the HMO member and denied by the plan, it is necessary to determine whether or not the benefit is of an industry standard. This is something that is routinely provided by comparable HMOs and MCOs. Many national and well-noted HMOs provide access to their benefit plans on a website's home page or even make them available upon request. The Internet may also provide a veritable gold mine of information related to standards of care through the managed care association, medical association, and insurance association websites.

3. Determine whether or not the SPD information is decisive and clearly understood by the reader. Although this can be a subjective judgment, it should be stated that a medical procedure/service/supply is not covered. Language demonstrating this would be similar to what "is considered experimental and therefore not a covered benefit," or "is not a covered benefit under this plan due to the lack of medical evidence that this is a required procedure." Consider for whom the information is written. For example, if the HMO member speaks Spanish, the information should be available in Spanish. The plan should contain language that specifically grants the plan administrator the discretionary right to interpret benefits.

4. When changes occur to the client's plan, the member normally should have been notified in a timely manner, such that the impact of the change could be evaluated in time for the member to possibly choose another plan or make other arrangements for coverage. A stipulated timeline is usually established and documented in the plan with language and amendments describing the time limitation. As a general rule, these changes occur and are presented immediately prior to the annual enrollment period.

5. Inquire whether the member has exhausted all remedies under the terms of the plan. The plan's claim procedures should include an initial claim followed by an appeal, with some plans providing for a second-level appeal.

6. If a member fails to exhaust the plan's claim procedures, they are generally foreclosed from filing suit in court. The courts have unanimously held that the claim procedures under ERISA are mandatory. The LNC and attorney should be aware that fairly rigid timelines may be associated with the steps necessary to comply with an appeal process or grievance hearing.

7. Determine whether the claim at issue is an "urgent care claim," which is generally one involving emergency-type care. If the claim is an urgent care claim, the plan must render its initial decision within 72 hours and any appeal must also be decided within 72 hours (29 C.F.R. §2560.503-1(f)(2)(i)). If a participant decides to receive treatment before the plan renders a decision, he or she may be responsible for the charges.

8. Obtain a copy of the document outlining the denial and any supporting information. It will be necessary to understand and be familiar with the criteria (such as InterQual Criteria [InterQual Length of Stay Criteria©, 2008]) or plan policies that are the basis for the denial. If the denial appears to be based on language that is clearly stated in the SPD, a copy of the full and complete contract of coverage, in addition to any amendments, should be requested. If the member has a copy of the denial letter, it must include specific information as cited under ERISA: the reason for denial, notification to the client on the specific steps that can be taken in order to have the request reviewed, and a list of any information that the member may be able to submit that supports the appeal and claim.

9. Obtain a copy of an authoritative source for the standards of care related to the member's condition and benefit request. In these days of EBP, many physicians are following a kind of "care map" for patient care. These can include managed care, nursing and medical standards, and standards for specialty fields that some specialists (physicians and nurses) are held to above and beyond the more common standards of general medical and nursing practice. Ask whether the standards were adhered to in this situation. Supporting information can also be obtained from governmental or authoritative agencies such as the Food and Drug Administration (FDA), the National Institutes of Health (NIH), and the Centers for Disease Control. In some cases, the HMO member may never receive a letter, or the letter may be deficient or vague in the information required by ERISA. A referral to the specific area of the health care plan language that applies to this denial should be addressed and cited in the denial letter. When there are differences between the language in the SPD or benefits coverage information that the client received and actual plan or contract language, the plan or contract should carry the greater weight. Alternatively, if the SPD appears to be conferring benefits that are not included in the plan, the SPD usually prevails. Assessment skills and knowledge of medical terms and procedures equip the LNC with the ability to notice the subtle differences in the contract language. Attorneys will find the LNC's knowledge base helpful to clarify medical terminology and to review the SPD for needed areas that may not be covered.

10. Gather any and all documents, sources, and information possible to support or refute the member's claim. When the information is submitted to the plan for the reconsideration of the denial, the aim is to provide enough information for the plan administrator to make an informed, well-supported, and well-substantiated decision. Close attention must be paid to procedural errors, conflicting or questionable language in the documents, and "arbitrary or capricious" behavior in the administration of the plan benefits.

11. The opinions of the treating physician are generally allowed significant weight by the court; however, in the Nord decision, the US Supreme Court held that the plans are not required to give deference to the treating MD's opinion. Still, the value of a face-to-face meeting with the treating physician cannot be overestimated. The LNC can bring the most value to case development as he/she will communicate very differently with the physician than the attorney will.

12. Gathering documentation to pursue a case involving ERISA and HMOs is not that different from the standard record requests as far as the medical record is concerned. The LNC will need to obtain a copy of the SPD, however, and that may require a particular release form. Many resources are available via the Internet with sample forms. Also, medical and legal libraries provide examples of forms that can be used for requesting information from HMOs, physicians, and medical facilities. These provide details of items that will assist the LNC and attorney in gathering necessary documentation in order to support or refute a case. In addition, networking with other LNCs and professionals will provide some of the support necessary to understand this complex situation.

13. There is a fine line of distinction between the HMO representative suggesting a less expensive alternative versus making a medical decision by denying an intervention (test, procedure, medication). The LNC must determine which of these was done. The primary indicator of this is denial of a service without reference to alternative resources for intervention in the situation. Understanding the distinction between making a medical decision and an administrative decision is key to this determination. An example of medical decision-making by the HMO could be denying the necessary medical treatment or refusing to provide the needed medical devices. If this is the case, it must be determined whether or not the member suffered any harm as a result. Moreover, if this determination is made, the attorney must

decide whether the HMO has made a medical decision and, in effect, is practicing medicine as opposed to administering medical benefits.

Evaluating HMO Liability

In analyzing a managed care case, a number of preliminary questions must be addressed to determine what remedies are available to the client and how the attorney must plead the remedies. Three fundamental questions must be addressed by the legal team:

1. Is it a case involving significant injuries?
2. Does the case involve an ERISA plan, or is the HMO coverage/insurance coverage provided by a nonERISA entity or an ERISA-exempt entity? The answer to this question in most cases controls the causes of action that the client may bring as well as what remedies are available.
3. Is the managed care entity an HMO, PPO, traditional indemnity insurance, or point of service contract?

Medical Malpractice

A medical malpractice claim must be investigated in order to identify duty, liability, damages, and proximate cause. The LNC should obtain a copy of or have access to authoritative sources or standards of care related to the member's condition and benefit request. These can include managed care standards, nursing and medical standards, or standards that some specialist physicians are held to above and beyond the more common standards of general medical practice. Ascertain that the standards were or were not adhered to in this situation. Supporting information can also be obtained from such entities as the FDA and NIH. (See Chapter 4, "Elements of Triage: Effective Case Screening of Medical Malpractice Claims," for more information about the evaluation of medical malpractice cases.)

Significant Injury

The first step in the analysis is to determine whether the client has suffered significant injuries because of the managed care plan's actions. Cases involving managed care plans have many varied legal issues that will invariably result in lengthy appeals. Consequently, only those cases involving serious long-term injuries or potentially significant long-term consequences resulting from the denial of care justify the considerable financial expense and substantial time commitment required to pursue or defend the claim.

ERISA and HMO Coverage

ERISA does not apply when the client's claim is governed by the state law. The potential causes of action to consider against an insurance/PPO company not involving an ERISA plan include breach of contract, medical malpractice, fraud in the inducement, intentional infliction of emotional distress, breach of fiduciary duty, common law negligence, and insurance bad faith.

HMOs are generally not subject to state insurance bad faith laws because they are not considered health insurance carriers. Consequently, the potential causes of action against an HMO include breach of contract, medical malpractice, breach of fiduciary duty, common law negligence, fraud in the inducement, intentional infliction of emotional distress, and state statutory causes of action. They may also include claims for vicarious liability as well as agency theories against the HMO for the actions of its doctors.

If the managed care claim involves an ERISA plan, then the client has no right to personal injury damages. The only right available to the client who has an ERISA-based plan is the option of an administrative remedy (i.e., an in-house review by the insurance carrier or the HMO). If the client disagrees with the findings of the in-house review, then an appeal to the federal court can be made, arguing that the in-house review was arbitrary and capricious. The only remedy to be obtained from an appeal to the federal court is payment of the benefit being sought or an interpretation of the contract. In states where the laws hold insurance companies liable for the harm they cause, this should be reviewed on a case-by-case basis, since the area is very gray and is still being argued in court today.

When a client's claim arises from an ERISA-based plan, the potential causes of action against a managed care provider must be analyzed by the attorney and are beyond the scope of the LNC's analysis. It would be appropriate for the LNC to alert the attorney that the managed care plan may be employer provided, and thus invoke ERISA.

Type of Entity

The final question to be determined is whether the managed care entity is an HMO, PPO, traditional insurance, point of service contract, or other such insurance plan. If the coverage is provided by an insurance carrier such as a PPO, point of service, or traditional health insurance contract, then the claim is a basic "denial of coverage" dispute. If the managed care plan is an HMO, then other standards will also apply.

Conclusion

HMOs are generally subject to statutory and regulatory duties. The LNC can assist the attorney by identifying the type of managed care provider at issue. If the managed care provider is an HMO, then the attorney will determine what statutes and regulations apply. The LNC can be an invaluable asset to the legal team when determining potential injuries, long-term effects of the denied benefit, and the ultimate effects on the client's life.

References

20 U.S.C. §1132(a)(1)(B)

29 U.S.C. §1132

29 U.S.C. §1144

29 C.F.R. §2560.503-1

29 C.F.R. §2560.503-1(f)(2)(i)

Bloche, M. G. (2008, August). Professor of Law, Georgetown University; Adjunct Professor, Bloomberg School of Public Health, Johns Hopkins University. *How do law & politics shape health systems change?* Georgetown, Washington, DC: Johns Hopkins University Press.

Draper, D. A. (2008). *Health and wellness: The shift from managing illness to promoting health.* Washington, DC: Center for Studying Health System Change.

Duffy, S. (2004). 3rd Circuit Boots Theory Allowing Bad Faith ERISA Legislation. Incisive Media US Properties. http://www.law.com/jsp/law/LawArticleFriendly.jsp?id=900005540339

Employee Retirement Income Security Act of 1974. (2008). U. S. Department of Labor. http://www.dol.gov/dol/topic/health-plans/erisa.htm

Every, N., Fihn, S. D., Maynard, C., Martin, J. S., & Weaver, W. D. (1995). Resource utilization in treatment of acute MI: Staff model HMO versus fee-for-service hospitals. *Journal of the American College of Cardiology, 26*, 401–406

Ginsburg, P. B. (2006). *High-performance health plan networks: Early experiences.* Washington, DC: Center for Studying Health System Change.

Hellinger, F. J. (2005). Health plan liability and ERISA: The expanding scope of state legislation. *American Journal of Public Health, 95*, 217–223.

InterQual Length of Stay Criteria©. (2008). InterQual Products Group, McKesson Corp., San Francisco, CA. Retrieved from http://www.mckesson.com/en_us/McKesson.com/For%2BPayors/Private%2BSector/InterQual%2BDecision%2BSupport/InterQual%2BDecision%2BSupport%2Bfor%2BPrivate%2BPayors.html).

Kaiser Family Foundation and Health Research and Educational Trust. (2007). Employer health benefits 2007 annual survey. Health care market place project. Retrieved from http://www.kff.org/insurance/7672/

Mason, D., Leavitt, J., & Chaffee, M. (Eds.). (2007). *Policy and politics in nursing and healthcare* (5th ed.). St. Louis, MO: Saunders.

Milliman Care Guidelines©, Milliman, Seattle, WA. Retrieved from http://www.careguidelines.com/.

National Committee for Quality Assurance. (2008). *Health plan report card.* Retrieved from http://www.ncqa.org/tabid/60/Default.aspx

Smith, C., Cowan, C., Sensenig, A., Catlin, A, & the Health Accounts Team. (2005). Health spending growth slows in 2003. *Health Affairs, 24*, 185–194.

U.S. Department of Labor. (2008, 9 March). Employee Benefits Security Administration. *Meeting your fiduciary responsibilities.* HYPERLINK "http://www.dol.gov/ebsa/publications/" http://www.dol.gov/ebsa/publications/fiduciaryresponsibility.html

Xu, X., & Jensen, G. (2006). Health effects of managed care among the near-elderly. *Journal of Aging and Health, 18*, 507–533.

Additional Reading and Resources

Baumberger, C. (1998). Vicarious liability claims against HMOs. *Trial 34*(5), 30–35.
Connette, E. (1998). Challenging insurance coverage denials under ERISA. *Trial 34*(5), 20–29.
Kongstvedt, P. (1996). *The managed care handbook* (3rd ed.). New York: Aspen Publishers.
Websites: The following Web sites can offer more information on the subject of managed care:
http://my.abcnews.go.com
http://hr.blr.com/
http://www.dol.gov/dol/topic/health-plans/index.htm
http://www.harp.org
http://www.hcfa.org
http://www.hiaa.org
http://www.ncqa.org
http://www.managedcaremag.com
http://www.mcareol.com
http://www.truemanlaw.com

Test Questions

1. The following are examples of MCOs:
    A. HMO, PPO, and SSA
    B. HMO, PPO, and POS
    C. NCQA, SSI, and POS
    D. IPA, SDP, and PWAB

2. ERISA is a law that
    A. Describes how to perform utilization management
    B. Stipulates that lawsuits involving HMOs are to be argued in the state court
    C. Denies benefits when they are too costly
    D. Governs the administration of certain employee benefits plans

3. Utilization management is a form of
    A. Health care cost containment
    B. Documenting the use of healthcare services
    C. Healthcare statistics
    D. Keeping a record of what physicians do

4. When a health care provider is paid by the health plan to administer health care services to a group of members, it is known as
    A. Capitation
    B. Per member/per month
    C. IS/SI (intensity of service/severity of illness)
    D. Per capita

5. "SPD" is an acronym for
    A. Standard pertusis/diphtheria
    B. Summary plan description
    C. Start percutaneous dialysis
    D. Superior portal ductus

Answers: 1. B, 2. D, 3. A, 4. A, 5. B

Chapter 23

Evaluating Forensics Cases

Diana Faugno, MSN, RN, CPN, SANE-A, SANE-P, FAAFS;
Sandra Higelin, MSN, RN, CNS, CWCN, CLNC; and
Anita Symonds, BSN, RN, CFC, CFN, SANE-A, SANE-P, MS

First Edition
Joseph R. McMahon, JD and Patricia Ann Steed King, RN

Second Edition
Doug Davis, BSN, RN, DABFN; Joseph R. McMahon, JD; and
Patricia Ann Steed King, RN

Contents

Objectives

- Provide an overview of specific areas of criminal law, procedure, and evidence
- Review the basic constitutional protections afforded to those accused of criminal offenses in connection with the collection and admission of evidence
- Address the admissibility of scientific evidence in criminal proceedings
- Discuss how the burden of proof for a criminal case differs from that for a civil case
- Describe the roles and responsibilities of law enforcement, the prosecuting attorney's office, and the sexual assault nurse examiner (SANE) or sexual assault examiner, medical examiner or coroner in the investigation of a criminal case
- Identify three ways in which the legal nurse consultant (LNC) can assist the attorney in the prosecution or defense of a criminal case
- Describe how the processes of evaluation, assessment, and implementation are ongoing in a criminal case and why this is important

Introduction

Criminal law is a field that, by itself, is extremely broad and continues to grow broader with each passing legislative session or appellate decision. The practice of criminal law encompasses the application of law, procedure, and evidence. The information in this chapter will provide the LNC with the basic principles of criminal law and the criminal justice system as they relate to the analysis of criminal cases.

There are inherent differences between civil and criminal cases. Civil cases involve wrongs that are personal in nature, such as property, contracts, and torts. Civil actions are considered private matters between individual parties (Aiken, 2004). Criminal cases involve wrongs against society. A crime is defined as any act that is forbidden by law or as the omission of an act required by law. Criminal law is statutory and will vary from municipality to municipality. Crimes are generally divided into misdemeanors and felonies. Legislatures enact criminal codes that distinguish between the two basic types of crimes (Swanson, Chamelin, & Territo, 1999). Generally, a misdemeanor is a crime punishable by imprisonment of up to one year, and a felony is a crime punishable by imprisonment of more than one year or death. The same criminal act may give rise to both civil and criminal causes of action. For example, O. J. Simpson was prosecuted under both criminal and civil law after he was accused of murdering his wife. Although the law applying to criminal and civil cases is different, the basic concept of determining the truth based on evidence is common to both.

Criminal Law

Criminal law is the body of law by which all human conduct is judged. Although laws that make conduct criminal vary widely from community to community, state to state, and country to country, each system of laws is based on the social mores and values of the society that establishes them. Laws are the enactment of social, political, and moral viewpoints of a society.

Unlike the consequences under civil law, rarely are criminal consequences attached to negligent acts. Although some jurisdictions have enacted statutes that penalize the consequences of a negligent act, these damages are more commonly than not addressed in the civil courts of our country where monetary damages are at issue. In the rare incidences where criminal law considers the effects of negligence, wanton disregard of human safety is a general issue that must be considered, and prosecutorial discretion has great flexibility.

Although each of us is familiar with a variety of terms used within the context of criminal law and evidence from entertainment and the media, our understanding of the topic is generally flawed by inaccuracies inherent in the media. For instance, many of us have heard the television prosecutor argue that the murder was premeditated; in some jurisdictions there is no requirement that the prosecutor prove that a killing was premeditated to support a conviction for murder. Several of the everyday inaccuracies in criminal law will be addressed while exploring criminal law, procedure, and evidence in this chapter.

Violations of criminal law generally require some level of intent to commit the crime charged. General criminal intent is present whenever there is specific intent and also when the circumstances indicate that the offender, in the ordinary course of human experience, must have expected the prescribed criminal consequences as reasonably certain to result from his act or failure to act. In a general intent crime, the criminal intent necessary to sustain a conviction is shown by the very doing of the acts that have been declared criminal. Specific criminal intent is that state of mind that exists when the circumstances indicate that the offender actively desired the prescribed criminal consequences to follow his act or failure to act.

An example of a general intent crime is simple possession of narcotics. The prosecutor in Louisiana who seeks to convict a defendant of simple possession of narcotics must prove that the defendant possessed a narcotic substance that has been classified as illegal.

An example of a specific intent crime under the common law is burglary. Burglary requires the breaking and entering into a dwelling of another, but in addition to the general intent to commit the trespass, it must also be established that the defendant acted with intent to commit a felony within the premises. The prosecutor is required to establish that the offender had "specific intent" to commit a felony in addition to the breaking and entering in order to secure the conviction.

In Louisiana, the law defines "second-degree murder" as the killing of a human being when the offender has the specific intent to kill or cause great bodily harm. In order to successfully prove the elements of this crime and obtain a conviction, the prosecutor must prove to the jury that the defendant killed the victim and that the defendant possessed the specific intent to kill or inflict great bodily harm upon the person of the victim. If the prosecutor is unable to prove that specific intent existed, the jury should not find the defendant guilty of second-degree murder.

Because criminal law statutes differ from state to state, the LNC must be familiar with the statutes that are specific to the jurisdiction in which the case is being tried.

Criminal Procedure

The prosecutor is required to prove the level of intent along with each and every element of the crime to support a conviction for any crime, whether it is a felony or misdemeanor. The criminal defense attorney is not required to prove anything in a criminal prosecution, whereas the defense attorney in a civil trial has an equal and opposite responsibility to present evidence supporting the defense position. The Fifth Amendment to the U.S. Constitution grants the accused the right to be silent and not to testify or to self-incriminate. Specifically, the amendment provides, "No person . . . shall be compelled in any criminal case to be a witness against himself." The prosecution bears the entire burden of proof. After the prosecution has presented its case, the accused may present witnesses on his behalf or rest upon the presumption that a person is innocent until proven guilty. If a defendant elects to present a defense in a criminal case, his counsel will generally seek to disprove the facts presented by the prosecution that support the elements of the crime, or the attorney will attempt to create doubt in the mind of the judge or jury. For example, a person charged with a crime may present alibi witnesses who place the person in a different location at the time of the offense or may attack the reliability of evidence used by the prosecution.

The prosecution in a criminal case bears the burden of proof. Just as in a civil case, the party bringing the action is required to prove the case. Civil and criminal cases differ in the standard by which they are to be judged. Civil cases are generally judged by the preponderance of the evidence standard. This standard requires the finder of fact to listen to the evidence and render a verdict based on a finding of which side presented the best evidence to support its position. In criminal law, the prosecutor is required to prove his case beyond a reasonable doubt in the eyes of the trier of fact. While it is generally agreed that reasonable doubt is doubt based on reason and common sense, the Supreme Court has affirmed "Reasonable doubt" is defined as follows: it is not a mere possible doubt; because everything relating to human affairs, and depending on moral evidence, is open to some possible or imaginary doubt. It is that state of the case which, after the entire comparison and consideration of all the evidence, leaves the minds of the jurors in that condition that they cannot say they feel an abiding conviction, to a moral certainty, of the truth of the charge [App. in No. 92-9049, p. 49 (emphasis added) Sandoval App.]. The trier of fact is called upon to listen to the evidence as presented by the prosecution or defense to determine whether the facts as presented are logical, credible, and worthy of belief. If so, the facts should be used as a basis for reaching a verdict. If they are not logical, credible, and worthy of belief, then they should be used to reach the opposite verdict.

Should the prosecution fail to prove the allegations beyond a reasonable doubt in the eyes of the trier of fact and an acquittal or "not guilty" verdict is rendered, the prosecution may not subject the accused to another trial. The Fifth Amendment to the U.S. Constitution further provides, "nor shall any person be subject for the same offense to be twice put in jeopardy of life or limb." This provision, commonly referred to as double jeopardy, is more far reaching than the amendment or its name implies. Not only is the prosecution barred from bringing an action for the same offense against an accused who has been acquitted, it is also barred from pursuing criminal charges against an accused for crimes that require proof of the same elements. For example, although an accused may be charged with theft and possession/receiving stolen things, the accused may be neither tried nor convicted of both offenses in most jurisdictions under double jeopardy.

The Sixth Amendment to the U.S. Constitution provides that in addition to the right to a speedy trial, an accused has the right to confront his accusers and to be represented by counsel. This amendment allows the accused to take advantage of the subpoena power of the court to require witnesses to appear and to testify. It also secures competent counsel for an accused to assist in his defense. The test for determining whether or not counsel was competent was outlined in *Strickland v. Washington* (1984). In order to prove ineffective assistance of counsel, the defendant must show that counsel's performance was deficient and that this deficiency prejudiced the outcome of the trial. To show that counsel was deficient, the defendant must demonstrate that counsel failed to meet the level of competency normally demanded of attorneys in criminal cases. The U.S. Supreme Court has held that the benchmark for judging a charge of ineffectiveness is whether the attorney's conduct so undermined the proper functioning of the adversarial process that the trial cannot be considered to have produced a just result (*U.S. v. Cronic*, 1983). Decisions of counsel regarding trial strategy are generally not considered as the basis for an ineffective-assistance-of-counsel claim under the Sixth Amendment and the holding of *Strickland v. Washington*.

Evidence

In criminal law, prosecutors and defense counsel rely on three types of evidence: testimonial evidence, physical evidence, and scientific evidence. Within each of these three types of evidence, there is direct and indirect evidence. Before discussing the three types of evidence, direct and indirect evidence should be defined. Direct evidence is evidence that, taken alone, is designed to establish a fact or element. For example, a witness can testify that he observed a defendant point a gun at a convenience store clerk and demand money, or a videotape could be introduced showing a robbery that took place. This would serve as direct evidence that an armed robbery had occurred. Indirect evidence is competent evidence that establishes a fact or element by reference. This evidence, although competent, must be viewed by the trier of fact to eliminate all other reasonable explanations.

For example, as the trial progressed, evidence was presented that revealed that a search of the defendant's residence had uncovered a handgun similar to that described by the clerk. Although this is competent evidence and should be considered by the jury, it does not conclusively establish that the defendant committed the armed robbery. Equally true is the following example: When the jurors walked into the courtroom, it was a sunny spring day. During the trial, a man wearing a wet raincoat and carrying a wet umbrella walks into the courtroom. This is indirect evidence that it may be raining outside. If there are no other reasonable explanations or evidence presented, indirect evidence can be used to establish that it is or has been raining.

Whether LNCs work for the defense or prosecution, they play a significant role in reviewing and analyzing the evidence to ensure that proper evidence collection protocols are followed as it relates to the issues of the case.

Testimonial Evidence

Testimonial evidence is best defined as that evidence which is presented through the words of victims, witnesses, and parties to a criminal case. This evidence amounts to the words of those who were present when a crime was committed, those who investigated the crime after it took place, or those who dispute the accuser's involvement. Although a defendant is not required to testify at trial, the words of a defendant prior to trial may be used against him. In *Miranda v. Arizona* (1966), the court held that before the state may introduce into evidence what purports to be a confession or statement of a defendant, it must first affirmatively show that the statement was freely and voluntarily given and was not made under the influence of fear, duress, menaces, threats, inducements, or promises. In addition, if the statement was made during custodial interrogation, the state must prove that the accused was advised of his *Miranda* rights and intelligently and voluntarily waived those rights. It is not sufficient for the words to be read to an accused; officers and prosecutors looking to use the accuser's words against him must prove to the court that the accused understood the rights as explained and voluntarily waived the rights.

Physical Evidence

Physical evidence consists of objects or tangible items that are used to demonstrate or establish facts or elements of the crime charged. Physical evidence generally consists of drugs, money, guns, photographs, or other objects found or discovered in conjunction with the investigation of the crime. Objects that are taken from the person or control of a defendant are subject to constitutional protections. The Fourth Amendment to the U.S. Constitution provides as follows:

> The right of the people to be secure in their persons, houses, papers, and effects, against unreasonable searches and seizures, shall not be violated, and no Warrants shall issue, but upon probable cause, supported by Oath or affirmation, and particularly describing the place to be searched, and the persons or things to be seized.

This amendment seeks to protect individuals against unreasonable search and seizure. The prosecution is required to prove that seizure of items from an accused was done in a manner so as to enforce the constitutional protections granted to the defendant. Property that is abandoned by a defendant is not constitutionally protected. Therefore, the subject who flees from the police while discarding narcotics does not enjoy constitutional protections over the narcotics; however, officers must meet constitutional safeguards when serving search warrants or taking property from an accused person. These safeguards include those provided by the amendment. A police officer must provide to the court by affidavit or oath sufficient facts to establish probable cause for the issuance of the search warrant. Probable cause exists when the facts and circumstances within the officer's knowledge and of which the officer has reasonably trustworthy information are sufficient to cause a person of reasonable caution to believe that an offense has been or is being committed.

Evidence may also be seized by officers without the necessity of a warrant under certain jurisprudentially approved circumstances. For instance, officers may seize evidence from the person of an accused when the search is performed incidental to a lawful arrest. Property may be seized from a vehicle when that vehicle is being impounded. Evidence may be seized when it is in the plain view of an officer. For example, a police officer walking through a neighborhood observes a marijuana plant growing in the front room of a home. The officer may seize the plant as evidence. Equally true, an officer conducting a traffic stop who observes a weapon or narcotics on the floorboard of the stopped vehicle may seize the evidence. The officer may not shuffle through the vehicle to uncover the contraband or place it in plain view. These are a few examples of issues common to the constitutional questions involved in searches and seizures by law enforcement officers. This area of the law is extremely broad and cannot be completely covered here.

Scientific Evidence

Scientific evidence is that field of expertise in which physical objects and technology merge to establish facts or elements or to disprove facts or elements. Scientific evidence includes fingerprint analysis, ballistics, blood testing, and DNA testing in buccal swabs, feces, vaginal secretions, urine, vomit, dead skin tears, ear wax, tissues and organs, bone marrow, dental pulp, skin cells, sweat, blood, saliva, and semen.

The Federal Rules of Evidence provide the basis for most rules of evidence that have been adopted by individual states and that determine the admissibility of scientific evidence. Federal Rule of Evidence 702 provides: If scientific, technical, or other specialized knowledge will assist the trier of fact to understand the evidence or to determine a fact in issue, a witness qualified as an expert by knowledge, skill, experience, training, or education may testify thereto in the form of an opinion or otherwise.

Subsumed in the requirements of Rule 702 is the premise that expert testimony must be reliable to be admissible (*State v. Cressey*, 1993). A U.S. Supreme Court case, *Daubert v. Merrell Dow Pharmaceuticals, Inc.* (1993), set forth a means for determining reliability of expert scientific testimony and answered many questions as to proper standards for admissibility of expert testimony. The standard for admissibility of evidence in criminal cases is equally applicable to civil litigation and should not be thought of as a separate or distinct standard.

In *Daubert*, the Court was concerned with determining the admissibility of new techniques as the basis for expert scientific testimony. Formerly, the test for admissibility of expert scientific testimony was based on a short, citation-free 1928 decision of the District of Columbia Court of Appeals, *Frye v. United States* (1923). In Frye, the rule for admissibility of expert testimony was delineated as requiring "general acceptance" of a technique in its respective scientific field before the technique would be considered admissible. Finding that "a rigid "general acceptance" requirement would be at odds with "the liberal thrust of the Federal Rules," the Court in *Daubert* concluded that Frye's "austere standard, absent from and incompatible with (this liberal thrust), should not be applied in federal trials." (Subsumed in the requirements of Rule 702 is the premise that expert testimony must be reliable to be admissible [*State v. Cressey*, 1993].) U.S. Supreme Court case, *Daubert v. Merrell Dow Pharmaceuticals, Inc.* (1993), set forth a means for determining the reliability of expert scientific testimony and answered many questions as to proper standards for admissibility of expert testimony. The Supreme Court, in *Kumho Tire Co. v. Carmichael* (1999), broadened the criteria for admissibility of scientific evidence from nonscientists. Admissible evidence is required to meet the criteria set forth by *Daubert* or to meet rigorous standards judged appropriate to the field, such as nursing or medicine. The standard for admissibility of evidence in criminal cases is equally applicable to civil litigation and should not be thought of as a separate or distinct standard.

The Court replaced *Frye* with a new standard that requires the trial court to act in a gatekeeping function to "ensure that any and all scientific testimony or evidence admitted is not only relevant, but reliable" (*Daubert v. Merrell Dow Pharmaceuticals, Inc.*, 1993). This requirement stems from a belief that the rules on expert testimony serve to relax "the usual requirement of firsthand knowledge" to ensure reliability on the part of a witness. This relaxation is justified so long as "the expert's opinion has a reliable basis in the knowledge and experience of his discipline" (*Daubert v. Merrell Dow Pharmaceuticals, Inc.*, 1993).

The reliability of expert testimony is to be ensured by a requirement that there be "a valid scientific connection to the pertinent inquiry as a precondition to admissibility." This connection is to be examined in light of "a preliminary assessment" by the trial court "of whether the reasoning or methodology underlying the testimony is scientifically valid and of whether the reasoning or methodology properly can be applied to the facts in issue." The Court went on to make some suggestions as to how a court could fulfill its gate-keeping role. These involve whether or not the technique had been subjected to peer review and/or publication, the "known or potential rate of error," the existence of "standards controlling the technique's operation," the technique's "refutability," or, more simply put, testability, and finally an incorporation of the *Frye* general acceptance in the scientific community as only a factor in the analysis (*Daubert v. Merrell Dow Pharmaceuticals, Inc.*, 1993).

The Court also stated that other rules of evidence govern this testimony, mainly Federal Rule of Evidence 403's balancing test that will exclude probative evidence if outweighed by its potential for unfair prejudice. The Court noted the possibility that the expert's testimony can be quite misleading and prejudicial if this gate-keeping role is not properly satisfied, requiring a flexible approach and a careful evaluation of the methodology surrounding the testimony and its conclusions. Conjectures that are probably wrong are of little use. However, in the process of reaching a quick, final, and binding legal judgment, they are often of great consequence regarding a particular set of past events. In practice, a gate-keeping role for the judge, no matter how flexible, inevitably on occasion will prevent the jury from learning of authentic insights and innovations. That, nevertheless, is the balance struck by rules of evidence designed not for the exhaustive search for cosmic understanding but for the particularized resolution of legal disputes.

This raises the question of the admissibility of the latest scientific evidence, such as DNA testing, to be commonly used in criminal law and civil law. Both federal and state courts have found that, in general, DNA profiling is a reliable technique and is admissible, for example, in *United States v. Jackboots* (1992), *Hayes v. State* (1995), *Commonwealth v. Rodgers* (1992), *Trimboli v. State* (1991), and *Caldwell v. State* (1990). Courts have agreed that the principles of DNA profiling and restriction fragment length polymorphism analysis are both relevant and reliable and thus are admissible.

In DNA analysis, as with any type of scientific evidence, it is of utmost importance that the party wishing to introduce such evidence be able to show a chain of custody. The "chain of custody" relates to the handling of evidence from the time of retrieval up to testing and until presentation before the trier of fact. The chain of custody is a requirement for admissibility, because it substantiates the reliability of the evidence by seeking to prevent altering of or tampering with evidence. Although different methods are used from jurisdiction to jurisdiction to protect the chain of custody for different types of evidence, the most common method used for medical evidence is to place the evidence in sealed containers. The containers are sealed with tape upon which identification information is written. As the evidence travels from one individual or agency to another, records are kept of the date, time, and person who handled the evidence. At trial, these persons are called to testify as to when and how they received the evidence, and what they did with it while it was in their possession. This procedure is necessary to illustrate to the court that the evidence is reliable and has not been tampered with or altered in any way. This is a key concept for any medical examiner. The proper procedure must be followed for all evidence or potential evidence.

Last, when attempting to present scientific evidence, the presenter is required to prove that the witness is qualified to render an expert opinion in the field for which the witness has been called. This requires the party calling the witness to show that the witness has knowledge, experience, and training that is sufficient to support his statements and conclusions. Generally, courts will look to the educational background, work experience, and training of a potential witness when considering allowing him to testify as an expert. Additionally, the court will consider whether or not the potential expert has published any materials on the topic and whether or not the witness has been qualified or refused qualification in any other court. Only after a witness has been qualified as an expert will the court allow a witness to render opinion evidence; otherwise, witnesses are limited to factual testimony only.

The effect of scientific evidence on a criminal case can best be illustrated by the following example. In a rape case, there are generally only two defenses available to defense counsel. The first is consent of the victim. This is tantamount to the defendant's admitting to engaging in sexual intercourse with the victim, but denying that it was against the victim's will. The second defense is one of faulty identification. In a trial where the first defense was employed, the prosecution would seek to introduce evidence to show that the sex act was not consensual. This evidence would include the victim's testimony, photographs of the victim's physical appearance shortly after the incident, and medical evidence of bruising or tearing. Scientific evidence may not be especially useful in this situation because of the defendant's admission of engaging in sexual intercourse with the victim. However, it is very useful in corroborating the history such as "he licked my ear and then bent me over the sink and put his penis in me. I was facing the wall." This case may come down to the DNA evidence on her ear and the fact that she might have finger tip bruises on the outside of her thighs that show she was bent over the sink and facing the wall versus facing him. Scientific evidence, in particular DNA testing, becomes especially relevant under the second defense. When an accused claims incorrect identification, the case hinges upon the prosecution's ability to establish that the victim's identification is not incorrect. If the health care professional who examines the patient shortly after the rape is able to swab body areas for fluids or stains, then the crime lab can locate DNA that can be used to link the accused to the crime. The accessibility of DNA testing has resulted in convictions of sex offenders who in the past would have escaped conviction. DNA testing, which is available today, has also freed men who were charged with rape and have been imprisoned for many years. Current research supports that best practice is to swab the cervical os as well as the vaginal vault in cases of alleged sexual assault. This may provide DNA information for many days after the event in an alleged sexual assault (Morgan, 2008).

DNA and its analysis and testing keep changing, so it is important to understand that evidence collected yesterday or today may be analyzed differently tomorrow due to changing technology (Fredland, 2008).

Investigation

Criminal investigation is a complex profession. With the advances in forensic science, criminal investigations require the cooperative efforts of professionals from many different disciplines within the criminal justice system. Law enforcement, forensic scientists, forensic nurses, pathologists, and attorneys must work together in the investigation and solution of criminal acts. In reviewing criminal cases, the LNC becomes a medical investigator whose main responsibility is to provide the defense or prosecution with nursing expertise as to the medico-legal aspects of the case.

Law enforcement officers take the leading role in criminal investigations. In order to be successful, investigators must have the education and experience to recognize, collect, and use evidence in criminal investigations. An important aspect of any criminal case is the crime scene. The primary goal in crime scene assessment is to detect all traces that indicate that a crime has been committed and establish any association between the crime and victim, or victim and perpetrator. The crime scene is the place from which much physical evidence is obtained and, in the majority of cases, is the key to the solution of a crime. The crime scene provides the investigator with a starting point, a beginning of the investigation to determine the identities of the suspect and victim and to piece together the circumstances of what happened during the crime.

All physical evidence collected at the crime scene will be carefully processed, documented, and placed in the proper custody until such time as it is utilized in the legal process. Any physical evidence that may be introduced in court must be identified, described, and maintained in proper custody. In handling evidentiary material, care must be taken not to disturb the viability of the material for later examination (Reece, 1994). Any variance in the above can result in physical evidence being inadmissible in court. This is an especially important consideration when reviewing a criminal case.

Forensic science is that which is applied to answering legal questions by examining, evaluating, and explaining evidence. It encompasses pathology, toxicology, biology, serology, chemistry, anthropology, odontology, and psychiatry, among other fields. One branch of forensic science is criminalistics, which deals with the study of physical evidence related to a crime. It encompasses firearms, questioned documents, tool mark comparison, fingerprints, photography, evidence collection kits, and trace elements, among other fields (Swanson et al., 1999). The written and oral testimony generated by experts in the various forensic fields may play important roles in the presentation of evidence during a trial. LNCs interact with many of these experts in understanding and applying the specific field of science. This represents another aspect of their involvement in a criminal case.

Preliminary Hearing, Arraignment, Indictment

Once a suspect has been arrested and accused of a crime, the accused is entitled to a timely hearing to determine whether probable cause exists that a crime was committed and whether the accused committed it. The accused cannot be detained prior to trial unless this has occurred. The exact process will be determined by the seriousness of the crime and the jurisdiction in which the matter is pending. The accused is brought before a judge for an initial appearance, at which time he is told what charges are pending, advised of his rights, and given the date for a preliminary hearing. The information gathered during the initial investigation is presented to a judge in the form of a preliminary hearing or to a grand jury for review. In some jurisdictions and in some instances, preliminary hearings are not held.

If a grand jury determines that enough evidence exists to hold a defendant for trial, an indictment is returned charging the defendant with a crime or crimes. At the time of arraignment, the accused is given a copy of formal charges, is once again informed of his or her rights, and is asked to enter a plea. Criminal trials are usually held within a year of the indictment as opposed to civil cases in which several years may pass before a case reaches a trial calendar. This is because the defendant may be incarcerated during this period of time, depending on the seriousness of the crime, and has the constitutional right of an accused to a speedy trial.

Prosecution

The job of prosecuting the accused is within the purview of the prosecuting attorney's office. The prosecutor attempts to determine that the right person (the accused) has been identified, located, and apprehended, and that there is sufficient evidence to indict. If an indictment is not possible, neither is a conviction. The burden of proof in a criminal case rests solely on the prosecution and proof should be beyond a reasonable doubt. The verdict must be unanimous and is returned as guilty or not guilty. Since a crime by definition is against the state, the prosecution has the state's resources at its disposal in investigating and developing cases. This includes law enforcement agencies, the office of the medical examiner, the coroner, the state crime laboratory, and other state agencies (such as family and children's services, mental health, etc).

Defense

The job of the criminal defense attorney is to be an advocate for the client. This gives the attorney the responsibility of ensuring that the client's civil rights are respected. The Constitution guarantees everyone the right to a fair and speedy trial regardless of the evidence concerning guilt or innocence. The criminal defense attorney does not enjoy the same readily available access to the state's resources as the prosecution does, and at times must utilize private laboratories and forensic scientists in private practice for testing and consulting. The conclusions or test results provided by these private entities might challenge or refute the conclusions or tests provided by the state. The conclusions or test results may also provide a sufficient basis on which to create a reasonable doubt for a jury concerning the state's case.

Civil proceedings have rules governing the disclosure of information (discovery) prior to trial, which are broad and entitle every party to relevant information. The same rules do not apply in criminal proceedings. The type and amount of information that is discoverable in a criminal case will vary from state to state. Therefore, the criminal defense attorney may or may not be privy to the state's case theory, depending on the working relationship between the criminal defense attorney and the district attorney's office or the usual practices of the municipality. The criminal defense attorney will need to become an expert on any anticipated theory that the state may utilize. The LNC can assist the defense attorney in developing case theories and strategies. For example, if the state is pursuing DNA evidence, it would behoove defense counsel to know as much as possible about DNA in order to present testimony or additional evidence that could create reasonable doubt about the evidence. The LNC can produce medical literature on the topic. The LNC can also locate, identify, retain, and work with experts in the field as part of case development.

The LNC's Role

The LNC's analysis of the facts of the case will be the same regardless of the side of a criminal case for which one might be working. The scope of the LNC's duties may include one or more of the following. (Note: The following list is not intended to be all-inclusive, as the actions of the LNC will be determined by the type of case and the LNC's work environment.) The LNC may be involved in the analysis of the following:

1. Medical or forensic reports to assess the extent of injuries and determine whether injuries could be consistent with the time frame and history given. Other factors to consider would be old injuries (in the case of domestic violence or child abuse) or whether an underlying medical condition or disease could be present.

2. Autopsy reports to
   a. Assess the extent of injuries
   b. Determine whether injuries match history (victim strangled, then house set on fire to make the death appear accidental)
   c. Determine whether previous untreated injuries exist (especially in domestic violence cases)
   d. Determine whether gunshot wounds are entrance or exit wounds (to substantiate claims of self-defense when the victim is shot at a distance from behind)
   e. Identify the type of weapon used (blunt instrument, tire iron, rock, knife, electrical cord) from wounds in, on, and through the body; cause and manner of death; whether the body had been moved, mutilated, or further injured postmortem; and the approximate time of death
   f. Determine whether the death was an accident, suicide, or homicide
   g. Identify how much time elapsed between the fatal injury and the time of death
3. Police reports to assess the initial crime scene (from measurements, photographs, drawings, and descriptions contained in the report), to identify witnesses, to determine persons and objects removed from the scene and their destination (by the police, hospital, morgue), and to determine the investigating officer and who made the initial call to the police.
4. Supplemental investigative reports, including reports of police detectives, fire, emergency medical services, or investigations from the prosecuting attorney's office or private investigators working for the criminal defense attorney. These reports may provide additional information concerning witnesses and witness statements and the additional gathering of evidence by the investigators involved in the case.
5. Sexual assault reports to assess the presence or absence of injuries. The presence or lack of injuries in sexual assault cases is related to the history and time frame. One cannot determine from injuries whether the sexual contact was consensual or nonconsensual (Anderson, McClain, & Riviello, 2006). The findings or lack of findings will be based on the history and time frame as stated in the report. Sometimes there is no history. The sexual assault report is only one piece of the evidence in a large investigation that must be evaluated. An example of a standardized form used in the documenting of sexual assault comes from the Cal E-M-A hyperlink http://rimsin land.oes.ca.gov/WebPage/oeswebsite.nsf/content/BD564E51EE1121F1882575DD00692A1. Psychological testing/reports to evaluate the competency of the accused to stand trial, to assess the state of mind of both the perpetrator and the victim at the time of the crime, to evaluate the effect of the crime on the victim, to determine whether the accused had a history of mental illness (diagnosis, treatment, medications, compliance), to assess recommendations made by health care professionals, and to assess psychological profiles in the case of serial offenders.
6. Forensic science reports to determine whether the accused can be linked to the scene by trace evidence, fingerprints, blood, semen, DNA; to determine whether illicit or prescription drugs or alcohol were involved; to determine whether bite marks on the victim match the accuser's bite; to determine the sex and race of skeletal remains; to assess the evidence gathered during a sexual assault exam (semen in body orifices or on the body, pubic hair not belonging to the victim); and to determine whether the weapon (if located) is consistent with the type of weapon used in the commission of the crime.

In addition to analyzing reports, the LNC may be involved in the following:

1. Interviewing clients, witnesses, and potential experts to gather information about the crime from clients and witnesses and to determine whether the information supports or refutes

physical evidence. If differences do exist, the task is to determine how to reconcile the differences and to provide information to experts regarding the case.

2. Assisting in obtaining experts and acting as liaison between expert and attorney, which may involve researching the literature, to determine experts in a given science and then contacting the experts to determine whether they are willing to review the case. LNCs may also be involved in providing information to experts regarding the case, determining whether their conclusions or findings support or refute issues of the case, and learning as much as possible about a particular issue from the experts.

3. Performing medical research as indicated. This could involve searches through medical literature, forensic science literature, and law enforcement literature. Research could also include interviews, telephone calls, and correspondence.

4. Providing information regarding case development based on the above and to assess and evaluate the ongoing development of issues of the case.

5. Preparing transcription of medical records and chronologies of events.

Examples of Types of Criminal Case Analyses Performed by the LNC

Child Abuse

In the case of alleged child sexual abuse, it is important to consider the concept of the differential diagnosis to ensure that premature decisions about what might have happened are avoided (Adams, 2008). The best approach to child abuse is utilizing a multidisciplinary center that provides services in the local community. These centers are called Child Abuse Centers (CAC) (Monteleone, 1998). The evaluation of the child is multifaceted when components include past and current medical history, physical examination with diagnostic and forensic testing, forensic interview, and all the referrals that might be needed for this child and family. Most children who are being abused do not report the incident in a timely fashion (72–120 h or less). This is important to understand as many times there is little visible evidence present due to the delay in reporting. Children heal quickly and often do not report the abuse for many reasons (McCann, Miyamto, Boyle, & Rogers, 2007). The perpetrators of this crime usually know and have access to the child.

Example 23.1

Patty, a five-year-old, disclosed to her mother that "Uncle John" had touched her bottom. Her mother notified the sheriff, and the child was interviewed. Patty was a poor historian and could only state that this had happened 10–15 times when Uncle John was her babysitter. The medical examination revealed no findings.

The LNC can help the attorney by knowing how to locate child sexual abuse experts in this arena. The medical expert in child sexual abuse will be able to speak to the genital findings or lack of findings in children (Merritt, 2008). The LNC will also be able to pull together all forensic and medical multidisciplinary reports and help in the analysis for the prosecution or defense. Other variables that the LNC would need to consider include the following. The medical history of the child, both past and present, must be assessed. Also, are there medical problems that mimic sexual abuse? Does the child have acute injuries, such as bruises or bite marks? Are any of accidental nature? Did the child have a forensic interview? Was this interview videotaped with a written report? Who interviewed the child? Is this evidence or report kept separate from a medical record? Is there a written protocol that is followed for the interview? Is there a family history with child protective services (CPS)? Has the child been removed from the family before?

Who are the childcare providers? Are the school records and school history available?

Are there changes in the child's behavior? What are the changes and how were they reported?

It is frightening for a child to testify and confront the adult in court. Many children do not make good witnesses. There are court programs that will assist the child in learning about the courts and advocates who help during the testimony process for children (Burkhart, 1998).

In many incidents of child abuse, the LNC will also be utilized to help in civil suits that may be filed after the criminal case has closed. The LNC would not only be able to help with record summaries but would also be used to locate expert witnesses related to the child abuse field for case review and possible expert testimony that might be needed.

Elder Abuse

Elder abuse and/or neglect is the act of/or failure of appropriate actions that a reasonably prudent person would use under similar circumstances, where there is an expectation of trust, which results in harm to an *at-risk adult*. An at-risk adult as defined by the majority of states is an individual 18 years old and older. This individual is unable to perform activities of living necessary for his or her health, safety, or welfare. This individual may also lack the understanding or capacity to make and/or communicate appropriate and responsible decisions concerning health, safety, and welfare. The LNC needs to be knowledgeable of the state definitions pertaining to the case.

Prevalence studies estimate that between one and two million Americans aged 65 and older have been injured, exploited, or otherwise mistreated by someone whom they depended on for care and protection. Based on statistical figures, the total number of reports of elder abuse was approximately 472,813 in 2003. Where does elder abuse happen: own homes—67%, nursing homes—12%, residential care—10%, hospitals—5%, and other locations—6%. Litigation against health care facilities alleging elder abuse and neglect is on the rise in this country. There are thousands of claims annually. Of all of the claims reviewed, less than 10% of these cases go to trial (National Center on Elder Abuse, 2005).

Adult protective services (APS) serve adults aged 18 or older who are mentally or physically incapacitated to the extent that they cannot provide self-care or manage their own affairs. The APS is utilized for those residing in the community setting. In long-term care facilities, the Ombudsman advocates for residents. Complaints of abuse are also reportable to the state regulatory agency for health and safety.

Medical personnel, law enforcement, government agencies, and care custodians are mandated reporters of elder abuse, neglect by others, financial abuse, and self-neglect. If the LNC is involved in interviewing the person who was allegedly abused, the LNC should investigate the following concerns:

- What is the state of the person's nutrition?
- Is there evidence of lack of food or inappropriate food in the house (e.g., candy, fast food)?
- Is the person malnourished?
- Are the utilities working?
- Is the person receiving in-home assistance, housecleaning, and personal care?
- The LNC should make these observations or look for this type of documentation.
- Is the person unkempt or malodorous?
- Is the person inappropriately dressed?
- Is the person agitated?
- Are there bruises, cuts, scrapes, or evidence of poor health?

- Are there pressure ulcers?
- Is the person confused or afraid?
- Was there a delay in seeking care?

Elder and dependent victims may be embarrassed, fearful, reluctant to be a nuisance, and unwilling or unable to go to court. A multidisciplinary team approach from the district attorney's office to APS provides the best approach for care, complete services with comprehensive follow-up, secondary assessments, and documentation (Grey, 2001). APS has an 800 hotline in each state. The majority of cases from health care facilities will be complaints filed by family members after their loved one has passed away. Nursing homes are prime targets for litigation for elder abuse. An area of concern often overlooked or not reported in nursing home patients is sexual abuse perpetrated not only by staff members responsible for the care of the elder, but also by sex offenders placed in long-term care because this care cannot be provided by the prison system or they have a record as a sex offender. Most states do not require notification of the long-term care facility that the new resident is a known sex offender.

The LNC can help attorneys in the record review for these elder abuse cases. The LNC must look beyond the documentation while performing these chart reviews. Ask yourself: What is the precipitating event? What is the medical history? While performing the record reviews, factors related to patient outcomes are identified. The LNC identifies the strengths, weaknesses, and breaches in standard of care. The LNC also identifies key players: family members, caregivers, nurses, doctors, certified nursing assistants, rehabilitation therapists, dieticians, supervisors, administrators, chief nursing officers, director of nurses, and any other person responsible for the patient's care. An interview of the key players may be necessary. It is also imperative to review all facility policies and procedures.

Requests for production and interrogatories are a very important responsibility of the LNC. Requests for production include the following:

1. All medical records and reports from all health care providers/facilities in the past 10 years
2. All policies and procedures of the health care facilities involved in the case
3. Diagnostic procedures and results
4. Relevant photos
5. Complaints and allegations of the plaintiff
6. Expert witness declarations
7. The curriculum vitae for each expert witness
8. All depositions taken
9. Any article or other source of reference utilized by experts in forming their opinion
10. Regulatory State Survey Results

Interrogatories include the following:

1. Names of all licensed and unlicensed personnel involved in the care of the patient
2. Names of all nursing supervisors
3. Names of all involved physicians
4. Names of administrators, chief nursing officers, and directors of nursing

It is important for the LNC to know when to involve a subcontractor for specific elements of the case. The LNC will also be key in identifying expert witnesses for the case. An example of why it is so important to review all relevant medical records and to contract with the appropriate sub-contractor or expert witness is demonstrated in the following case study.

The patient underwent surgery for an excision of an abscess. The procedure left a deep narrow open wound. The treatment order was to pack the wound with nu-gauze strips. The patient was sent home with home health to provide this wound care treatment. The wound did not heal and became infected. Subsequently, the patient was rehospitalized and underwent surgical debridement of this wound. During the debridement procedure, a 4 × 4 inch gauze packing was found in the wound cavity. Allegations of elder abuse by the patient (plaintiff) were that the home health nurses had not removed all of the packing material during dressing changes, resulting in the wound infection requiring surgery, longer rehabilitation, and emotional and physical pain and suffering.

The LNC reviewing this case identified that she needed to request for all medical records from both hospitalizations as well as the home health records. Once the LNC reviewed these records, an expert certified in wounds was contracted to review the records. The expert was able to establish that the 4 × 4 inch gauze found by the surgical team while debriding the infected wound was left there during the first surgery. The home health nurses had comprehensively documented the wound treatment and the use of Nu-gauze strips. The use of 4 × 4 gauze had been documented in the initial surgical report. Nu-gauze strips are 0.5 inch packing strips.

Issues of elder abuse are very complex. The aging of baby boomers comprises the fastest growing group over the next 15 years. This aging cohort creates huge implications for areas of care and abuse. The LNC utilizes the nursing process of assessment, diagnosis, intervention, and evaluation in the performance of the scope of the LNC role when working with elder abuse cases.

Domestic Violence

Some large urban areas may have domestic violence emergency response teams (DVERT), or rapid response to domestic violence that have formed to deal with variables of this issue in a timely manner. This team consists of law enforcement, advocates, social workers, and medical personnel. All of these team members generate documentation and reports. Many areas or communities may not have teams that respond to domestic violence. Typically, the patient will seek out a health care provider or go to the local emergency department (ED) for health care.

In a case of domestic violence, the LNC should ask whether this is the first such incident. If not, are there previous police reports, arrests, or convictions? What steps had the victim taken (if any) to separate or move away from the perpetrator or have the perpetrator removed? Had any previous protective orders or warrants been served on the perpetrator? If so, what was the response of the perpetrator? Had the victim dropped previous charges against the perpetrator? If so, why? Had the victim ever sought refuge in a shelter? If so, what happened? Had the couple undergone any type of counseling or therapy? If so, what were the conclusions? What was the victim's account of the incidents?

There are also other questions the LNC should ask:

■ What is the medical history of the victim?
■ Is there a history of pet abuse?
■ What is the medical history of the perpetrator?
■ Are there children involved? If so, what is the medical history of the children?
■ Have the children been removed from the home? If so, how many times?
■ Was CPS involved?
■ Were the children interviewed?

- Are the children in foster care or in the care of other family members?
- Who is the caseworker?
- Was there any evidence or indication of emotional, physical, or sexual abuse of the children?

Over 50% of children in DV homes will have been maltreated. If the victim was examined by a medical professional, what were the findings? Many states are filing child endangerment charges against the parent or parents if a child witnesses the domestic violence. Considerations with the DV patient are the following:

- Were physical injuries photographed?
- Was evidence obtained? If so, where is the evidence?
- What diagnostic tests were performed, and what were the results?
- Were statements made to medical professionals documented?
- What was the psychological/emotional state of the victim at the time of exam?
- How much time elapsed from the time of the physical abuse to the time treatment was sought?
- If rape occurred, was it reported?
- Was a sexual assault examination performed? If so, what were the findings?

Variables for the LNC to consider in the record review of the perpetrator of this crime include the following:

- Is there a previous criminal history?
- What does the police report say?
- Are the officers who took the report available to discuss the report?
- What is the medical history of the perpetrator? Does he use drugs and alcohol? Does he have a history of psychological or mental problems?
- Has there been an evaluation by a mental health provider?

The LNC's role in this area would be to assist with the record review and analysis.

Sexual Assault

Sexual assault or rape is defined as the act of forced penetration, meaning vulvar, anal, or oral penetration by a penis, object, or body part without consent (Satin et al., 1991). This crime is a violent act that may be motivated by a desire for power and control. Sex is the mechanism. A female is sexually assaulted every 6 minutes in the USA, but 80–90% of the cases are never reported (11,995) (Tjaden & Thoennes, 2006). SANEs are forensic nurses or sexual assault forensic examiners (SAFEs) who have received special training (International Association of Forensic Nurses, 2008a,b), and demonstrate competency in performing sexual assault examinations. The role of the SANE/SAFE is to collect evidence, document the evidence collected, and testify in court (International Association of Forensic Nurses, 2008b).

Example 23.2

Crystal and Rick were drinking at a party. Crystal passed out on a bed in the back of the house. When she woke up, Rick was on top of her. She told him to get off, but he had intercourse with her. She got up and grabbed her clothes and went into the bathroom and dressed. She was very upset and left shortly thereafter. She went home and showered. She told a friend and then called the sheriff and consented to an evidentiary examination. She was transported to a Sexual Assault Response Team (SART) center by law enforcement for her examination. Crystal was concerned that she might have been slipped a drug in her drink as well. Blood and urine were obtained for toxicology per protocol (LeBeau, 2008). This examination took several hours. She was treated, given referrals, and then taken home. There was an investigation and arrest, and now the LNC is helping prepare for the defense or prosecution of the case. This case defense would not be about who did this but rather the defense will be consenting sex versus nonconsenting sex. Current literature and research do support similar findings of genital injuries in consenting and nonconsenting sex in both adults and adolescents (Jones, Rossman, Hartman, & Alexander, 2003). Variables and issues for the LNC to consider in assisting with this case include the following.

Review of all documentation should occur from the 911 calls, interviews, examination, and investigation (Girardin et al., 1997). Alcohol was involved, so the crime lab reports would provide the results of this information. The LNC might need to find an expert in ETOH levels to present this information in a trial.

- Did the crime lab analyze the evidence collection kit?
- Can the chain of evidence be followed and documented?
- Were the evidentiary examination findings positive or negative? Was a suspect examination completed? By whom?
- Were there positive findings on the suspect examination?

A health history should be present (International Association of Forensic Nurses, 2008b). There are only three defenses in sexual assault:

1. I did not do this.
2. Some other dude did it.
3. There was consent.

Driving Under the Influence

The presence or absence of drugs or alcohol in a person's body and whether the subject was under the influence of a drug are important issues in traffic investigations, in cases of driving under the influence (DUI), in the legal defense of diminished capacity, and in public intoxication cases.

The majority of states in the United States set 0.08% as the alcohol level at which a person is presumed to be under the influence of alcohol such that the driver is unable to operate a motor vehicle in a safe and prudent manner. The amount of alcohol necessary to reach a level of 0.08% varies from one individual to another. Law enforcement agencies across the country have routine procedures for analyzing blood, breath, and urine for blood alcohol levels. Blood and urine samples should be collected in a medically approved manner. Breath tests are conducted by technicians/officers who have been certified in the use of breath intoxilyzers.

The LNC's analysis of this type of case should include searching for answers to questions. In the case of someone DUI and causing a motor vehicle accident, does the driver have a previous history of DUI?

Has the driver's license ever been revoked or suspended? If so, why? What is the driving history of the driver? What facts are documented on the police report concerning driving conditions, road conditions, speed at the time of impact, skid marks, time of day, appearance and behavior of driver, etc.? If injuries occurred, how serious were the injuries? Was emergency assistance required? Was anyone removed from the scene by ambulance? If so, to which facility was the person taken? What was the driver's condition at the scene and at the time of arrival at the emergency room? If a field sobriety test was performed, what was the tester's training and the process followed? What was the training and process followed by the person who administered the breath test? Is there a record or log of the intoxylzer calibrations? What treatment was required? What were the findings? If drug or alcohol tests were performed, were they blood or urine or both? What were the results? How much time had elapsed since the time of ingestion of drug and alcohol and the time of the accident and also the time that the drug or alcohol tests were performed? Were any narcotics administered in the ED before the urine or blood was tested for substances?

The LNC should consider the following factors when evaluating a DUI case:

Physical makeup of the individual
Existing and pre-existing medical conditions
Use of central nervous system depressants
Proper evidence collection and preservation of physical evidence
Use of nonprescription drugs that may elevate blood alcohol levels

Forensic Nursing within the ED

The ED is naturally a chaotic environment due to the inability to predict acute injury events. According to the Center for Disease Control, violence causes approximately 50,000 deaths and 2.5 billion injuries yearly in the United States (NCIPC, 2007). This is not to say that all of the injuries were treated in an ED but often they do need emergent care.

With injuries numbering in the billions, the following information is important to consider when dealing with any case that involves someone receiving treatment within an ED. Sometimes the ED has warning that a patient will be arriving; first responders call ahead to the department, which gives the department time to prepare. Other times there is no warning such as when a patient is driven in by friends or family. EDs also have the potential to receive patients from other area EDs if the victim needs a higher level of care than the first ED can provide. These would be potential areas of lost evidence during treatment prior to arrival. The ED environment is driven by the goal to preserve life and limb. Crime victims are treated in emergency rooms across America everyday with the goal of preserving life; evidence is routinely lost during resuscitation efforts. This is not to say that this is wrong—preservation of life should always be the primary concern; however, there are some hospitals that do attempt to preserve evidence during treatment. The hospital's capability of evidence collection at the time the victim receives treatment can have a significant impact when the victim's case goes to trial.

Forensic nursing within the ED has and remains an ever-changing opportunity for nurses to be on the front lines of forensic nursing. With daily changes in the forensic sciences, what may have not been considered useful as evidence in the past may now help solve cases. Forensic nurses are often SANEs who have expanded their training and services beyond the sexual assault victim to include other victims of crimes. This may include but is not limited to suspected elder abuse and/or neglect, suspected child abuse and/or neglect, domestic violence victims, and victims of violent crimes who have injuries that result in the need for acute medical treatment. A few examples of violent crimes victims would be those sustaining gunshot wounds, stabbing victims, and assault resulting in blunt force trauma, such as a bat to the head. A few other forensic patients who may be seen by the forensic nurse are pedestrians struck by motor vehicles, attempted suicides and motor vehicle collision with multiple injuries and a question as to who was the driver. Some forensic teams also participate in suspect examinations.

Many SANE programs would like to expand, but do not have the administrative and financial backing of the hospitals during these difficult times. Programs work differently from hospital to hospital. Many are able to offer forensic nursing services to victims of domestic violence and sexual assault only. Many ED-based SANE/Forensic programs function on an on-call basis. Only a few have a forensic nurse in-house 24 hours a day. Some have a forensic nurse on call for sexual assaults but have 24-hour coverage for victims with traumatic injuries. A problem with having a forensic nurse on call for traumatic injuries is the risk of loss of evidence until the forensic nurse arrives.

Education and Training

Educational levels of forensic nurses range from the completion of certificate programs to advanced degree programs. Forensic nurses may be certified in a practice area, such as sexual assault examination of adult or pediatric patients. Certifications involve the nurse taking an examination that verifies a knowledge base in a certain specialty. Finally, graduate degree programs in forensic nursing at both the master's and doctoral levels in nursing are available in several areas of the United States (Hammer, Moynihan, & Pagliaro, 2006). Bedside nurses in the emergency room will usually have a degree in nursing and either a certification or a certificate in the forensic issues that their program addresses.

Scope and Standards of Practice

Standards of practice related to forensic nursing have been published by the International Association of Forensic Nurses (IAFN). They include *The Sexual Assault Nurse Examiner Standards of Practice, Intimate Partner Violence Standards of Practice,* and *Scope and Standards of Forensic Nursing Practice* (IAFN, 2009). Best practices can be found in Lynch's *Forensic Nursing* (2006).

Hospitals have not only hospital-wide policy and procedures but also unit-based policies and procedures. Nursing also has clinical practice guidelines (CPGs), in which the purpose is to provide evidence-based standards of care. The LNC should be aware that sometimes the forensic team may have their own policies and/or CPGs. The LNC may need to ask if the forensic program has policies or CPGs specific to their program. All forensic programs should have standard definitions used for documentation such as one using descriptions for all wounds from a standard Medical Encyclopedia.

The forensic nurse may testify for the defense or prosecution. "The forensic nurses' objective is to relay the information about evidentiary findings and to educate the court as to what those findings mean" (Lynch & Duval, 2006). The forensic nurse should have an up-to-date curriculum vitae at all times and may testify as a fact or an expert witness, depending on experience. As a fact witness, the forensic nurse may provide what is in the chart, verify chain of custody as to collection and preservation of evidence, and authenticate photographs taken by the forensic nurse. Depending on the forensic nurse's experience, the forensic nurse may testify as to the severity of injuries and whether injuries are or are not consistent with the history given.

Reviewing Forensic Records

When it comes to reviewing forensic documentation of injuries in an ED record, the LNC may see what appears to be conflicting documentation, or different types of documentation. With the average ED visit, a triage sheet is generated, which will have the least amount of information on it. This is meant to be a very quick assessment to make decisions as to the level of care needed. Few, if any, details will be found on the triage sheet, and sometimes the whole complaint changes when the victim is in an actual room. For example, someone might make a complaint at triage that they fell down the steps, but once in the privacy of a treatment room, they may disclose that their boy-friend hit them. Depending on whether the hospital is a teaching institution, the LNC may see one to two physician documentation sheets with a history and injury documentation: resident and attending physician documentation.

If a forensic nurse was involved, they may have their own documentation tool. When a victim is a trauma patient the trauma flow sheet will also contain injury documentation. The trauma flow sheet has injuries written that are found during resuscitation efforts depending on the condition of the victim. Minor injuries that are not life threatening may be missed by the trauma team, but may be very important in the forensic nurse's assessment. Although the trauma team makes every effort to do a full assessment, the presence of life-threatening injuries takes immediate priority, and a forensic evaluation may be deferred, which can explain any gaps in the patient's time of arrival and the beginning of a forensic assessment. For example, if a victim presents as a trauma victim with a knife wound in the chest, causing massive amounts of blood loss, and also has multiple abrasions on the knees, addressing the cause of blood loss will stop the assessment until the bleeding is under control, which normally means immediate transfer to the operating room. The abrasions may not show up on the ED documentation at all. If there was a forensic nurse in the room in addition to the bedside nurse who is delivering immediate care, missed injury documentation decreases.

When reviewing documentation of gunshot wounds, be aware of the fact that the documentation can lead the reader down the wrong path. Some staff, including nursing, emergency physicians, and surgeons, think they can identify an entrance versus an exit wound. This documentation, however, should be left to the experts in ballistics and forensic pathology. For instance, consider a victim who states that he was running away when shot in the back and the bullet exited through the chest, yet the shooter claims self-defense and that the victim was attacking him. The documentation in the ED can play a very important role and can also be very wrong. Forensic nurses should document only what they see, for example "an opening in the skin with irregular edges with black material noted around edges." Conflicts in documentation between the regular emergency chart and the forensic chart can happen. The forensic nurse has received specialized training in injury recognition and documentation. A common error seen in nonforensic nurse documentation is confusion when documenting a laceration versus an incised wound. A laceration occurs from blunt force trauma and an incised wound occurs from a sharp edge such as a knife. The forensic team should always use proper injury terminology.

Consent

Consent for all forensic patients should be obtained in writing or verbally whenever possible. For victims who are unable to give consent, refer to the individual hospital's policy for handling those situations.

The LNC should consider the following factors when evaluating any forensic case in which the victim or accused received emergent care in an ED.

Physical Evidence Collection

Clothing

Clothing has potential for evidence to relate the person to a scene or the crime itself. See the following examples: (1) a pedestrian struck by a vehicle may have identifiable tire marks on the clothing, (2) a belt buckle on the pedestrian may have left a mark on the vehicle, and (3) the clothing of a gunshot victim may have soot and powder that can assist with range determination.

Care and treatment of the victim can directly affect the clothing. When a person has life-threatening injuries, articles of clothing are removed as fast as possible with little movement of the victim to prevent further injury. The best way to do this is to cut the clothing off the victim. Many first responders have been educated on not to cut through existing holes or tears, but this does not mean it does not happen in the rush to save a life. Not all clothing arrives at the ED with the victim. Sometimes it may be left at the scene or in the ambulance that was used to transport the victim, or if the victim was transported from another medical facility the clothing may have been left at the first facility.

There are several questions the LNC may consider with regard to collection techniques, as techniques can affect the clothing as evidence. For instance, was the clothing placed in paper or plastic? Plastic can facilitate the growth of mold if clothing is not completely dry. Was each article of clothing placed altogether in one bag or in individual bags? Who collected the clothing—was it a police officer or a forensic nurse who has been trained to collect clothing, or was it placed in a bag by the treating nurse. When the clothing was collected, was it photographed prior to being placed in the bag? A forensic nurse may or may not photograph the clothing, and if so it would be for the purpose of basic identification of the clothing. Photographing the clothing would depend on individual policies of the program. A normal expectation would be that upon the clothing's arrival at the police department's evidence detection unit, the clothing would be removed from the bags or packaging, dried if needed, and photographed with focus on any marks, cuts, or holes (Citation). If there is a forensic nurse involved with the victim within the ED, there would be an expectation that the clothing was collected with evidence preservation in mind.

Sources of DNA

Potential DNA can be obtained from a victim if it is recognized by someone trained to collect it. For example, if a victim of assault arrived in the ED and was unable to speak but there was an injury that appeared to be a bite mark, it can be swabbed for potential DNA. Broken or chipped fingernails can indicate a struggle and that the victim may have scratched the attacker. Swabbing the fingernails can potentially yield the DNA of the attacker.

Bullets

Bullets have potential identifiable marks on them that may match them to the individual firearm used. Due to the marks left on a bullet, how a bullet has been removed from a victim is important. Soft tipped hemostats would decrease the chances of adding a mark onto the bullet during removal. Most hemostats are of stainless steel and it would take preparation on the hospital's part to have soft-tipped hemostats available for a surgeon. The LNC would want to know if chain of custody was documented upon removal of the bullet. Another consideration would be whether the bullet was even removed. Within our society we have people walking around with bullets in their bodies. If the LNC knows someone was treated for a gunshot wound in a hospital, that does not guarantee that the bullet was removed. Sometimes surgeons make the decision of leaving the bullet in place.

Trace Evidence

Trace evidence, that is, small bits of evidence such as skin, hair, blood flecks, fibers, grass, soil, or glass, can easily be lost in an ED. When rolling a victim during injury assessment, things such as leaves or grass may come off the victim and fall to the floor. The sheet from the stretcher of the transporting ambulance has potential evidence since the victim would have been removed from the scene and placed on that stretcher. On occasion, if the victim has been removed from a bed, the ambulance attendants sometimes use the sheet from that bed to move the victim to the stretcher. If the victim's clothing is dropped on the floor of the ED, that has potential to pick up trace evidence not related to the crime.

Unidentified Substances

Potential drugs or unidentified substances such as pills, powder, leafy material, and/or liquids found on victims should be described as best as possible and collected and transferred to the police using chain of custody.

Weapons

Weapons found on victims pose a safety risk to the victim and staff. When dealing with any weapon in the ED, safety always comes first. Knives should be handled with care in order to preserve potential fingerprints that may be on them, and packaged to avoid risk of injury to others handling them. Firearms should never be handled by someone unfamiliar with firearms. Most hospitals have policies for handling weapons, especially firearms. As far as evidence is concerned, it is rare to find an identifiable fingerprint on a firearm. This is partially due to the firearm design of irregular surfaces and recoil when firing, which tends to cause smudging of fingerprints (DiMaio, 1999). Handling firearms may necessitate the involvement of a third party in the chain of custody such as hospital security. The forensic nurse may document where the firearm was found and who removed it prior to transferring to the police.

Photographic Evidence

Photographic documentation of injuries can be a very powerful tool in explaining injuries to a jury. It is one thing to describe an 18 cm incised wound of the neck but another for the jury to see that the neck had been cut with a knife from ear to ear. When a jury views a photo of a gunshot wound of the thigh, it may not show the extent of the injury, but when a photo of the x-ray showing the bullet fragments and a shattered femur is viewed, it tends to promote an understanding of the significance of the injury that was received at that time. Taking photos in focus, before and after treatment, is the optimal goal. However, if the victim is critical, the forensic nurse may only have seconds to take photos while the physical assessment is taking place. This means that the photos may not all be perfect and they may be taken while the victim is being rolled or moved. The appearance of injuries can change with medical resuscitation efforts. They can change quickly if invasive interventions need to be done in an attempt to save the victim's life. If the victim came in as critical with life-threatening injuries, he or she may only have been in the ED for 5 min or less before going to the operating room. In a case like this, the forensic nurse may have had time to take one or two photos or nothing at all. For this reason, when it comes to critical victims, photos may not be perfect. When using cameras in the ED, all photos taken must be documented and with a procedure for proper storage. When reviewing a chart, if the LNC does not find detailed forensic photo documentation, there should still be some indication that photos were taken or that a forensic nurse was present during resuscitation efforts.

When requesting records from a hospital that may include a SANE or forensic chart and/or photographs, the LNC must therefore be very specific with record requests. Some hospital SANE or forensic programs are their own keepers of the photographs and/or forensic records (or have onsite provisions to store forensic records and photographs that adhere to principles of the chain of custody). In other words, they may not be kept at the normal medical records department, and that department may miss your request for photographs if not clearly written. The medical records department may not know that the forensic/SANE chart or photographs exist. Some hospitals may print out photos or copy photos while others who use digital cameras may just make a duplicate photo compact disc for law enforcement.

Most EDs do not have a SANE nurse or forensic nurse in-house 24 h a day. This diminishes the chances of evidence being collected; however, some nurses have received education on the principles of evidence collection and preservation. These nurses must maintain the care of the patient as their first priority, and may not have opportunities for activities such as putting clothing in separate paper bags and documenting and photographing injury and evidence. Items may be collected, but not according to the standards of an established forensic team. Emergency room nurses can testify to their observations and their procedures of care, injury assessment, and evidence collection, but the LNC should keep in mind that they will not be as comfortable and may even be fearful to testify.

Death Investigations

Of all criminal cases, death investigation is the most difficult and requires the greatest effort on the part of law enforcement. In sudden and violent death investigations, it is important to determine as quickly as possible whether the deceased died from an accident, suicide, or the act of another person. The finding of a body is the starting point and initial focus of any death investigation. The first officer on the scene is responsible for determining whether the victim is dead or alive and maintaining the integrity of the crime scene. Determination of suspicious death at this point is critical. In many cases, the first officer to arrive at the scene has erred and pronounced the death as due to natural causes, only to learn at a later time that the actual cause of death was the result of an unnoticed bullet wound. Care and attention to detail are critical in this type of case. In order to conduct an efficient and effective investigation, the investigator must concentrate on the mechanical aspects of the death (i.e., motives and methods; wound structures; autopsy; crime scene reconstruction; the cause, manner, and time of death; and the other factors that provide clues to the dynamics of the event).

From an investigative point of view, it is imperative that an LNC have a practical understanding of the manner, means, and mode of several kinds of death:

■ Gunshot and firearm wounds
■ Cutting wounds
■ Stabbing wounds
■ Blunt force injuries

- Poisoning
- Asphyxia deaths
- Autoerotic deaths
- Arson and fire deaths
- Drowning
- Suicides

Example 23.3

A female body was reported in a shallow riverbed. The story given to police investigators was that the victim fell off an overpass and into the river. Attempts to rescue the victim by a male friend were in vain. There were noticeable cuts and bruises on the body, which would corroborate the story. After the autopsy, it was determined that many of the injuries did not match the description of the incident. Upon further investigation, it was determined that the person who attempted the rescue had recently taken out an insurance policy on the victim.

Was there a history of domestic violence with this couple? What interpersonal characteristics did this couple display prior to this event? What were the toxicology findings of the autopsy? Was anything found at the scene that would be consistent with the types of blunt injury wounds to the victim's head? Were there any findings at the time of autopsy to indicate that the head trauma was the fatal injury? Were there any findings consistent with drowning? What was the affect and response of the rescuer at the time police arrived on the scene? Who reported the incident? What was the financial situation of the couple? What was the work history of the rescuer? Was anyone else with the couple? If so, what was their relationship to the victim?

Death investigation requires a team effort. The actions and responsibilities of each person involved in this type of case are highly scrutinized during litigation. The successful solution to any death case relies on a professional, thorough, and intelligent investigation.

Summary

As is true in any case analysis, the processes of assessment, planning, implementation, and evaluation are ongoing as new information becomes available. The LNC who pursues this area of practice will benefit from objectivity, thoroughness, and inductive and deductive reasoning.

References

Adams, J. (2008). *Genital complaints in prepubertal girls*. E Medicine on Medscape. Retrieved February, 15, 2009, from http://www.medscape.com

Aiken, T. D. (2004). *Legal, ethical, and political issues in nursing* (2nd ed.). Philadelphia: F. A. Davis.

Anderson, S., McClain, N., & Riviello, R. (2006). Genital findings of women after consensual and non-consensual intercourse. *Journal of Emergency Nursing, 2*(2), 59–65.

Brayton Purcell. (2005) App. in No. 92-9049, p. 49 (emphasis added) (Sandoval App).

Burkhart. (1998). *Preparing children for court* (Vol. 11, No. 8). Alexandria, VA: National District Attorney Association (APRIA). Retrieved from /www.ndaa.org/publications/newsletters/apri_ 2/15/09

Caldwell v. State, 260 Ga. 278, 393 S.E.2d 436 (1990).

Cal E-M-A hyperlink http://rimsinland.oes.ca.gov/WebPage/oeswebsite.nsf/content/BD564E51EE1121 F1882575DD00692A1

Center for Disease Control and Prevention Center National Center for Injury Prevention and Control (NCIPC). (2007). The *cost of violence in the United States* [fact sheet]. Retrieved August 27, 2008, from http:www.cdc.gov./ncipc/factsheets/costof violence.htm

Commonwealth v. Rodgers, 413 Pa.Super.Ct. 498, 605 A.2d 1228 (1992).

Daubert v. Merrell Dow Pharmaceuticals, Inc., 509 U.S. 579 (1993).

DiMaio, V. (1999). *Gunshot wounds practical aspects of firearms, ballistics and forensic techniques* (2nd ed.). Washington, DC: CRC Press.

Grey, H., Elder abuse, handout outline, San Diego, CA, January 12, 2001.

Fredland, N. M. (2008 April/June). Sexual bullying: Addressing the gap between bullying and dating violence. [Article.]Advances in Nursing Science. *Violence, Injury, and Human Safety 31*(2), 95–105.

Frye v. United States, 54 App. DC 46, 293 F. 1013 (1923).

Girardin, B., Faugno, D., Seneski, P., Slaughter, L., & Whelan, M. (1997). *The color atlas of sexual assault*. St. Louis: C.V. Mosby.

Hammer, R., Moynihan, B., & Pagliaro, E. (2006). *Forensic nursing a handbook for practice*. Sudbury, MA: Jones and Bartlett.

Hayes v. State, 660 So. 2d 257 (Fla. 1995).

International Association of Forensic Nurses. (2008a). *Sexual assault nurse examiner educational guidelines*. Arnold, MD: International Association of Forensic Nurses.

International Association of Forensic Nurses. (2008b). *Sexual assault nurse examiner standards of practice*. Arnold, MD: International Association of Forensic Nurses.

International Association of Forensic Nurses (2009). *Forensic Nursing: Scope and Standards of Practice*. Arnold, MD: American Nurses Association and International Association of Forensic Nurses.

Jones, J., Rossman, L., Hartman, M, & Alexander, C. (2003). Anogential injuries in adolescents after consensual sexual intercourse. *Academic Emergency Medicine*, *10*, 1378–1383.

Kumho Tire Co. v. Carmichael, 526 U.S. 137 (1999).

LeBeau, M. A. (2008). Guidance for improved detection of drugs used to facilitate crimes. *Therapeutic Drug Monitoring*, *30*(2), 229–233.

Lynch, V., & Duval, J. (2006). *Forensic nursing*. St Louis, MO: Mosby. Retrieved December 1, 2007, from: http://www.medscape.com/viewarticle/565600

McCann, J., Miyamto, S., Boyle, C., & Rogers, K. (2007). Healing of nonhymenal injuries in prepubertal and adolescent girls: A descriptive study. *Pediatrics*, *120*(5), 100–1011.

Merritt, D. F. (2008, June). Genital trauma in children and adolescents. *Clinical Obstetrics & Gynecology*, *51*(2), 237–248.

Miranda v. Arizona, 384 U.S. 436 (1966).

Monteleone, J. (1998). *Physical examination in sexual abuse, child maltreatment* (2nd ed.). St. Louis: GW Medical.

Morgan, J. (2008, April). A comparison of cervical os versus vaginal evidentiary findings during sexual assault exam. *Journal of Emergency Nursing*, *34*(2), 102–105.

National Center on Elder Abuse. (2005). www.elderabusecenter.org

Reece, R. M. (1994). *Child abuse: Medical diagnosis and management*. Philadelphia: Lea & Febiger.

Satin, A., Hemsell, D. L., Stone, I. C. Jr., Theriot, S., Wendel Jr., G. (1991). Sexual assault during pregnancy. *Obstetrics and Gynecology*, *77*(5), 710–714.

State v. Cressey, 137 NH 402, 628 A.2d 696, 698 (1993).

Strickland v. Washington, 466 U.S. 668 (1984).

Swanson, C. R., Chamelin, N.C., & Territo, L. (1999). *Criminal investigation* (7th ed.) New York: McGraw-Hill,

Tjaden, P., & Thoennes, N. (2006). *Extent, nature, and consequences of rape victimization: Findings from the National Violence Against Women Survey* (NCJ 210346). Washington, DC: National Institute of Justice, Office of Justice Programs, U.S. Department of Justice and the Centers for Disease Control and Prevention. Retrieved February 15, 2009, from www.ncjrs.gov

Trimboli v. State, 817 S.W.2d 785 (Tex. App. Waco 1991), aff'd, 826 S.W.2d 953 (Tex. Crim.App. 1992).

United States v. Jackboots, 955 F.2d 786 (2d Cir. 1992).

U.S. v. Cronic, 466 U.S. 648 (1983).

Test Questions

1. In order to be found guilty of a crime, the defendant must be
   A. Proven guilty by a preponderance of the evidence
   B. Proven guilty by 51% of the evidence
   C. Required to testify
   D. Proven guilty beyond a reasonable doubt

2. All of the following are types of evidence that can be relied upon EXCEPT:
   A. Scientific
   B. Physical
   C. Testimonial
   D. Circumstantial

3. The chain of custody refers to
   A. Ankle chains
   B. The reporting hierarchy in health care
   C. Handling of evidence
   D. Disputes between separated parents regarding custody of the child

4. Which of the following is the LNC least likely to analyze in a criminal case?
   A. Emergency room record
   B. Psychological testing results
   C. Autopsy report
   D. Auto body shop reports

5. Which of the following statements is NOT true?
   A. A felony is a crime punishable by imprisonment up to a year
   B. An incident may give rise to both a criminal and civil suit
   C. Criminal laws may vary from state to state
   D. Violations of criminal law generally require some level of intent

Answers: 1. D, 2. D, 3. C, 4. D, 5. A

Appendix 1

Glossary

Noreen M. Sisko, PhD, RN

Second Edition
Sherri Reed, BSN, RN, LNCC and Bruce Kehoe, JD

Access: Approach to electronic information through any storage medium. When used in relation to the term online, it implies the availability of suitable telecommunications, plus user IDs and passwords for the online host system.

Access to medical and exposure records standard: One of the standards developed by the Occupational Safety and Health Administration in order to provide the employee who has a possible exposure to, or uses toxic substances or harmful physical agents in the workplace, with the right to access employee exposure records, and any analyses of employee medical and exposure records provided all employee identifiers have been removed.

Account balance: Difference between debit and credit sides of an account.

Account debtor: A person who is obligated on an account, chattel, paper, or general intangible.

Account payable: A debt owed by an enterprise that arises in the normal course of business dealings and has not been replaced by a note payable of a debtor. A liability representing an amount owed to a creditor usually arising from purchase of merchandise or materials and supplies; not necessarily due or past due.

Account receivable: A debt owed to an enterprise that arises in the normal course of business dealings and is not supported by negotiable paper. A claim against a debtor usually arising from sales or services rendered that is not necessarily due or past due.

Account rendered: An account made out by the creditor, and presented to the debtor for his examination and acceptance. When accepted, it becomes an account stated.

Account settled: An agreed balance between parties to a settlement.

Account stated: An account that accumulates additions to another account.

Accountability: An obligation of providing or being prepared to provide an account of one's actions.

Accountant: A person who works in the field of accounting and is skilled in keeping books or accounts. This person is also skilled in designing and controlling systems of account and in giving tax advice and preparing tax returns.

Accreditation: The act of granting credit or recognition, especially with respect to an education institution that maintains applicable standards.

Action level: If the 8-hour time-weighted average (TWA) for noise levels equals or exceeds 85 decibels (dB) in a department, the employees must be included in a hearing conversation program according to OSHA's Occupational Noise Exposure Standard (29 CFR 1910.95).

Acute coronary syndrome: A continuum of disease processes that include life-threatening cardiac conditions including unstable angina, non-ST segment elevation myocardial infarction (MI), and ST segment elevation MI.

Address: (1) A label or number, which identifies a database disk location where information is stored in the computer. (2) May also refer to the location of a host computer on an online network.

ADL: Activities of daily living, includes bathing, dressing, toileting, feeding, and grooming.

Administrative controls/work practice controls: A method of controlling hazards that involves management practices, such as training and education or job rotation to limit exposure.

Advanced cardiac life support provider: A health care professional who is certified as a BLS provider and passes certification to enhance their resuscitation skills in an adult cardiopulmonary emergency. These skills include CPR, airway management, cardiac rhythm recognition, emergency medication administration, and the use of treatment algorithms.

Adverse drug reaction reports: Summaries of adverse experiences with a specific product reported to the Food and Drug Administration.

Adverse event (AE): Any untoward change in health or medical status, such as a new medical occurrence, or a change (such as an exacerbation) in a pre-existing medical condition. This occurs during the course of a study from the signing of the informed consent by the study participant to the final study visit (study completion). The medical condition does not have to be considered as related to the study drug or device to be termed an AE. The AE must be evaluated by the investigator (not the study coordinator) to examine the relationship of the study drug and designate the results as possibly related, probably related, definitely related, or definitely not related.

Advice protocols: Written guidelines that establish protocols for evaluating the urgency of patient problems and differentiating cases requiring emergency intervention from those better addressed through office visits or home care.

Affidavit: Sworn, voluntary statement of fact or declaration.

Affirmative defense: A defense to a cause of action (claim) for which the defendant has the burden of proof. Comparative negligence is an example of an affirmative defense.

AHCPR: Agency for Health Care Policy and Research. Established standards of practice for a variety of patient care issues.

AHRQ: Agency for Healthcare Research and Quality (formerly AHCPR).

Allegations: The claims, statements, or assertions made by a party to a legal action or a potential legal action. These assertions may be incorporated in the complaint or the answer.

American Board of Nursing Specialties (ABNS): The certifier of certifiers for nursing specialties. The ABNS mission is to provide assurance to the public that the nurse holding the credential from an accredited certification program possesses the knowledge, skills, and competency for quality practice in his or her particular specialty (Bernreuter, 2001; www.Nursingcertification.org).

American Legal Nurse Consultant Certification Board (ALNCCB): The certification board associated with AALNC that develops its budget, determines the eligibility criteria for the examination, audits applications for compliance with the criteria, sets fees, and sets maintenance criteria for renewal of certification. ALNCCB is charged with the responsibility of maintaining the examination so that it is valid, reliable, and legally defensible.

ANA: American Nurses Association, which is the national association of nurses.

Analysis and issue identification: As an LNC standard, analysis of data to identify the health care issues related to a case or claim.

Annotation: The process of highlighting, drawing circles, underlining, and so on, on an exhibit.

Answer: The formal written statement made by a defendant in response to the complaint, setting forth the grounds of his defense.

Aortic dissection: A condition in which a violation to the aorta, such as a tear, allows blood to leak, resulting in a life-threatening vascular emergency. For example, a thoracic aortic dissection occurs when there is a violation to the internal layer of the aorta allowing blood to leak between the medial and adventitial layers. Dissection can occur above or below the original site of the tear.

APA 5 format: The Publication Manual of the American Psychological Association (5th Ed.). Used as a reference for manuscript citations.

Apportionment of liability: Assigning a percentage of the total negligence to each culpable party (e.g., a jury could find that the plaintiff was 20% liable, one defendant was 30% liable, and another defendant was 50% liable).

Arbitration: Informal hearing held before a neutral third party who renders a decision and issues an award.

Arbitrator: Disinterested third party chosen by the parties or appointed by the court to render a decision.

Arraignment: The stage of the criminal process in which the defendant is formally informed of the charges and is allowed to enter a plea.

ASCII: Acronym for the American Standard Code for Information Interchange. Pronounced "askee" (e.g., ASCII is a code for representing English characters as numbers, with each letter assigned a number from 0 to 127. For example, the ASCII code for uppercase M is 77). Most computers use ASCII codes to represent text, which makes it possible to transfer data computer to another.

Assault: Unlawful, intentional inflicting, or attempted inflicting of injury upon another.

Assessment: As an LNC standard, a collection of data to support the systematic assessment of health care issues related to a case or a claim.

Assessment: The first step of the nursing process during which data are gathered and examined in preparation for the second step, diagnosis.

Assigned risk: A risk underwriters do not wish to insure but, because of state law or otherwise, must be insured. The coverage is assigned through a pool of handlers each taking turns.

Attorney work product: Materials that are protected from discovery. It includes materials prepared by an attorney in anticipation of litigation, including private memoranda, written statements of witnesses, and mental impressions of personal recollections prepared or formed by an attorney in anticipation of litigation or for trial.

Attorney–client privilege: The protection of communication between the attorney and the client, which is made for furnishing or obtaining professional legal advice; the privilege that allows the client to refuse to disclose and to prevent any other person from disclosing confidential communications between the client and attorney (Black's Law Dictionary, 2009).

Audit trails: The capability to identify who entered or altered data in a computer system and in which field the information was located, as well as the date and time.

Authorization: The process by which permission is granted by the plan for a member to receive a treatment or service by a health care provider.

Autonomy: The right to self-determination and independence. Autonomy pertains to decisions individuals make to serve their interests.

AVI: Acronym for Audio Video Interleave, the file format for Microsoft's Video for Windows.

Award: A decision rendered by an arbitrator or a panel of arbitrators. If the parties are satisfied with the arbitrator's award, a judgment is entered.

B&B: Bowel and Bladder, as in bowel and bladder incontinence or training.

Back file: A portion of a database or directory that is separate from the original file. Used as a backup for information that may somehow become lost or deleted.

Backup and recovery: Sometimes referred to as DBAR (disaster backup and recovery)—the necessary computer programs written to ensure that data are not lost during nightly processing or any disaster that would prevent normal computer access and function.

Banana peel effect: Refers to the possibility that progression of the pre-existing condition(s) could be primarily responsible for the plaintiff's postaccident health status, not the alleged injury.

Basic life support (BLS) provider: One who is certified to recognize and respond to life-threatening conditions such as MI, choking, and respiratory arrest, and can provide CPR and operate an automatic external defibrillator (AED). A BLS provider can be a health care provider or a layperson.

Bates stamping: Organizational labeling system that places a number on medical and legal documents.

Battery: The unlawful use of violence against another.

Benchmarking: Serving as a standard of reference or comparison.

Beneficence: The ethical view that the right action is to protect the patients and to provide treatment that promotes the good of the individual.

Beyond a reasonable doubt: The degree of certainty required for a juror to legally find a criminal defendant guilty. It means that the proof must be so conclusive and complete that all reasonable doubts of the fact are removed from the mind of the ordinary person.

Bias: Inclination; prejudice.

Bill of particulars: A legal document in which the plaintiff sets forth the specific negligence and damage claims.

Billable hours: Hours worked that have a direct relationship to the project at hand.

Biomechanics: Mechanics as applied to the body and encompasses the responses of the human body to various forces.

Bit: A binary digit, that is, either 0 or 1; the smallest storage unit for data in a computer.

Blocked account: Placement of a conservatee's money in a bank or other financial institution that cannot be withdrawn without court approval.

Bloodborne Pathogens Standard: One of the standards developed by the Occupational Safety and Health Administration in order to limit workers' occupational exposure to blood, bodily fluids, and other potentially infectious materials.

BMP: The standard bit-mapped graphics format used in the Windows environment.

Bond: A judge will require that a conservator of the estate obtain a bond to guarantee that there will be no loss to the conservatorship estate if the money is mismanaged or taken by the conservator. The bonding agency will reimburse the estate for any loss, dishonesty, or negligence. The bonding company may then sue the conservator to repay the loss.

Book of business: The specific type(s) of insurance products an insurance company might provide; for example a company may have a book that is comprised of 50% automobile, 40% workers' compensation, and 10% group life and health.

Boolean logic: Consists of logical operators also referred to as Boolean operators (AND, OR, and NOT), which allow a searcher to create logical search statements or sets that show relationships (e.g., Meperidine or Demerol®).

B-Reader: A licensed radiologist who has received special training and experience in reading x-rays for the purpose of identifying lung disease, such as asbestosis and silicosis. The National Institute for Occupational Safety and Health (NIOSH) certifies physicians through their B-Reader Examination for proficiency in the classification of chest radiographs for the pneumoconiosis. Each B-Reader is required to recertify at 4-year intervals.

Brief: A formal written presentation of an argument that sets forth the main points with supporting precedents and evidence.

Burden of proof: The amount of proof required to prove an element of a cause of action or an affirmative defense. In civil cases, the amount of proof required is "a preponderance of the evidence."

Business plan: A business plan should include a description of the business and its purpose, marketing, a financial plan, and a plan for its implementation and management. See also http://www.sba.gov/smallbusinessplanner/plan/writeabusinessplan/SERV_WRRITINGBUSPLAN.html

Byte: A group of bits sufficient to define a character. Usually represents eight bits but ten bits are used per character for online transmission.

Capitation: A specific dollar amount for the coverage of cost of health care delivered per person. It is usually a negotiated per capita rate paid periodically, usually monthly, to a health care provider for the delivery of services to a covered member. In most situations, the provider receives a specific amount of money each month for every member who has selected that provider as their primary care giver. The provider is paid the capitation rate for each assigned member, regardless of whether or not the member receives any services from the provider during the time period.

Cardiopulmonary resuscitation: A restoration of cardiac output and pulmonary ventilation following cardiac arrest and apnea, using artificial respiration and closed chest massage.

Carrier: A company that provides the insurance.

Catastrophic injury: Injury or illness that permanently alters an individual's functional status.

Catastrophic loss: Loss of an extraordinary large value.

Cause of action: A claim in a lawsuit with specific elements that must be proven. For example, to state a cause of action for negligence, there must be sufficient proof of the four elements of negligence. The plaintiff has the burden of proof regarding these elements.

Certificate: Typically are offered at the completion of an educational process, demonstrating knowledge of course content at the completion of the course. Certificates are accessible to newcomers as well as experienced professionals, and are often awarded by for-profit institutions and programs. Certificates indicate completion of a course or series of courses with a specific focus, not a degree granting program. Course content is determined by the specific provider or institution and is not standardized, so quality may vary with different providers.

Certification: The formal recognition of the specialized knowledge, skills, and experience demonstrated by the achievement of standards identified by a nursing specialty to promote optimal health outcomes (ABNS, 2005).

Certified emergency nurse (CEN): A nurse who is proficient in the specialty of emergency nursing and has passed a national certification examination produced by the Board of Certification of the Emergency Nurses' Association. Certification as an emergency nurse measures the attainment of a defined body of knowledge pertinent to the specialty of emergency nursing.

CFR: Code of Federal Regulations which contains regulations that govern nursing homes.

Chronological chart summary: A written document, which consists of a summary of pertinent information from medical records. The summary includes the date and the page number of the referenced information.

Citation: The bibliographic information (author, title, publication, volume, date, pages) in a complete reference; often used synonymously with the term "reference."

Claim: Used in reference to insurance, this is a demand by an individual or corporation to recover, under a policy of insurance, for losses that may come within that policy.

Claimant: The individual petitioning for, or receiving benefits.

Claim processor: Carrier's employee responsible for handling claims as they are received from patients and providers.

Claims analysis data: Data compiled through the analysis of legal claims including type of legal claim filed, prevailing party, and financial payout, in an effort to identify trends in litigation.

Claims consultant: Person designated to represent the insurance company in investigations and negotiations in order to reach an agreement on the amount of a loss or the insurer's liability.

Claims management: A mechanism that can substantially reduce the overall cost of claims.

Claims specialist/adjuster: The independent agent or insurance company employee who investigates claims, sets insurance reserves, and settles claims against the insured.

Client: The purchaser of services.

Clinical pathways: A precalculated plan of routine services usually required by a patient for a given disease, based on average medical recovery outcomes.

Clinical trials: Premarketing evaluations of a drug or medical device performed by the manufacturer to determine the safety and effectiveness of the drug or device.

CMS: Center for Medicare and Medicaid Services (formerly HCFA).

CMS 1500 (HCFA 1500): A standard claim form for submission of charges.

CNA: Certified Nursing Assistant. An assistant who has completed standardized training and is employed in a nursing home.

Code of Ethics: An explicit statement of the primary goals and values of a profession.

Co-efficient of friction (COF): A measurement of friction (or the degree of slipperiness) of the floor or other surface. On ice, and on wet and oily surfaces, the COF is low (.10). Excellent traction is at a COF of .40 to .50 or more. "Slip resistant" is defined a COF of .50.

Collaboration: As it applies to the LNC, the LNC collaborates with legal professionals and health care professionals when necessary.

Collegiality: As it applies to the LNC, the LNC shares knowledge and contributes to the development of peers, colleagues, and others.

Command language: Instructions entered by a searcher that direct the computer retrieval program to perform specific tasks or operations. The command languages vary by vendor system, and symbols may be utilized.

Common law: In general, a body of law that develops and derives through judicial decisions, and is as distinguished from legislative enhancements.

Communication: The transmission and reception of information.

Comparative negligence: A proportional division of the damages between the plaintiff and the defendant in a tort action according to their respective share of fault contributing to the injury.

Competent: Duly qualified; answering all requirements; having sufficient capacity, ability, or authority; possessing the requisite physical, mental, natural, or legal qualifications; able; adequate; sufficient; capable; legally fit.

Complaint: The original or initial pleading by which an action is commenced under codes or Rules of Civil Procedure. It is the pleading that sets forth a claim for relief.

Complex litigation: Usually involves many parties in numerous related cases, and often in different jurisdictions. This involves large numbers of documents, witnesses, and extensive discovery that will require judicial management generally assigned to the same judge.

Conceptual framework: A categorization or classification of a mental image.

Concept analysis: The method for examining attributes and characteristics of a concept as a foundation for theory development.

Concept derivation: A process in which a previously defined concept from a parent field is transposed to a new field and then redefined as a new concept in the new field.

Concept: A term used to describe a phenomenon or group of phenomena.

Conciliation: Adjustment and settlement of a dispute in a friendly, nonantagonistic manner.

Concordance: An index showing the context in which words occur.

Confidentiality: The duty to keep private all information provided by a client or acquired from other sources before, during, and after the course of the professional relationship. This includes information from the client's medical records.

Conflict of interest: A situation where one person has information that may potentially be used to influence a case and cause harm, injury, or prejudice to the client.

Connect time: The time between log-on to a database and/or termination. It is one of the primary components of online searching costs.

Conservatee: A person who a judge has deemed unable to care for himself or herself or to manage financial affairs and for whom a conservator is appointed.

Conservator: Either an organization or a person whom the court appoints to handle either the financial or personal affairs of an individual or both, as a result of the individual being deemed incompetent.

Conservator of the estate: A person or organization who the court appoints to handle the financial affairs of an individual (conservatee), as a result of having been deemed unable to do so for themselves.

Conservator of the person: A person or organization who the court appoints to handle the personal care and protection of a person (conservatee) whom a judge has decided is unable to do so.

Consulting or reviewing expert: An expert offering an opinion on a particular subject, but not expected to testify at trial.

Consumer expectation test: Consumers of a product may have reasonable, widely accepted minimum expectations about the circumstances under which it should perform safely.

Contingency fee: A fee arrangement in which the attorney receives a percentage of the plaintiff's settlement or verdict.

Contract: Voluntary agreement that creates legally binding responsibilities for the parties named in it to facilitate predetermined amount or type of service or work to be performed for a specific reason or period of time.

Contractor: One who contracts to perform a work for another party; the person who retains the control of the means, method, and manner of the project result.

Contributory negligence: Negligent conduct by the plaintiff that contributed to his or her injury.

Controlled vocabulary: An authorized listing of subject heading or descriptor strings used by indexers to assign subject terminology to items described in records in a database or in files.

Co-payment: A sharing in the cost of certain covered expenses on the part of the insured on a percentage basis.

Coverage: The assurance against losses provided under the terms of a policy of insurance. It is used synonymously with the term insurance or protection.

CPT (Current Procedural Terminology): A systematic listing of descriptive terms and corresponding five-digit codes for reporting services and procedures performed by medical providers.

Credentialing: A review process to approve a provider applying for a contract with a health plan.

Credentials: Degree credentials (for example BS, MS, PhD, JD) awarded based on the completion of a particular educational program. Licensure credentials (RN, LPN) awarded based on completion of a specified educational program and the successful passing of a national licensure exam. Credentials required or designated by specific states are similar to licensure credentials, but are usually beyond basic licensure and designate authority and recognition to practice at a more advanced level in that state (APN, APRN, ARNP, CNS), and are based on meeting certain criteria that may include advanced education or work experience (ANCC, 2008). National certifications are credentials awarded by a nationally recognized, usually accredited, certifying body, such as the LNCC, accredited by the American Board of Nursing Specialties. See also: http://www.nursecredentialing. org/Certification/HowtoListYourCredentials.aspx

Credibility: Worthy of belief; must be preceded by establishment of competency (legally fit to testify).

Crime: Performance of an act that is forbidden by law or the omission of an act required by law.

Criteria: Variables known to be relevant; measurable indicators of the standards of clinical nursing practice.

Cross-jurisdictional advocacy: An LNC who manages care interventions for clients in differing jurisdictions by bridging the paradigms of law and health care for the purpose of reducing conflict and producing change.

Culture brokering: The act of bridging, linking, or mediating between groups or persons of differing cultural backgrounds for the purpose of reducing conflict or producing change.

Curriculum vitae: A more formal, academically oriented resume that includes presentations, publications, professional associations, and continuing education, as well work experience.

Damage mitigation: Actions or steps that reduce or limit the damage resulting from an event.

Damages: A pecuniary compensation or indemnity, which may be recovered in the courts by any person who has suffered loss, detriment, or injury, whether to his person, property, or rights, through the unlawful act or omission or negligence of another. A sum of money awarded to a person injured by the tort of another.

Database: An organized collection of data in electronic form, generally related by subject, concept, or idea (e.g., MEDLINE, TOXLINE, and CHEMLINE).

Declarant: A person who makes a declaration; one who makes a sworn statement.

Declaration of Helsinki: International guidelines for investigators conducting biomedical research involving human subjects. Recommendations, adopted by the 18th World Medical Assembly in Helsinki in 1964, include procedures to ensure subject safety in clinical trials.

Deductible: A preset amount which each insured must pay toward the cost of treatment before benefits go into effect.

Defective design: A drug or device that is not reasonably safe for its intended use or a use that can be reasonably anticipated.

Defective manufacture: A product that is not reasonably safe as a result of the manner in which it is manufactured and the defect existed when the product left the manufacturer's control.

Defendant: The person or entity against whom a lawsuit is brought.

Defense client: Any entity referred to as the defense client of the LNC. The LNC may work with one or more entities in assisting the defense in a professional liability case. These entities may include the HCPD, the defense attorney, an insurance company, a third-party administrator, or a self-insured company.

Defense team member: The individuals working on behalf of the defense. The team may include the trial attorney, associate attorneys, LNCs, expert witnesses, and other consultants.

Delta V: Change in velocity; the delta V is the difference between the speed just prior to the impact, and the speed immediately after the impact. A low-velocity motor vehicle crash is one with a delta V approximately 10 mph or less. The greater the delta V, the greater the forces, and the greater the likelihood of severe injury. An accident reconstructionist will calculate the delta V(s) in a collision.

Demand letter: A letter to the insurance company by the plaintiff's attorney demanding settlement of the case.

Demonstrative evidence: Evidence in the form of objects (as maps, diagrams, or models) that has in itself no probative value but is used to illustrate and clarify the factual matter at issue broadly.

Deposition: Pretrial sworn testimony of parties or others, such as witnesses to elicit information about the claims and defenses. Deposition testimony may be used for various purposes at trial (e.g., to impeach a witness). Depositions are conducted outside of the courtroom, usually at a law firm.

Derivative claim: The claim of an injured party's spouse, child, or parent for damages resulting to them, which may include one or more of the following: loss of companionship; loss of services; and expenses incurred.

Descriptor: A word or phrase used to describe a subject, concept, or idea.

Designated nonparty: A party deemed responsible for all or part of damages that was not named in the suit.

Diagnosis: The second step of the nursing process, during which data are analyzed and pulled together for the purpose of identifying and describing health status (strengths, or actual and potential health problems).

Digitalization: The process of making a 2D or 3D exhibit into a computer file format that can then be stored and retrieved from a disc on a computer. This allows easy access, quick retrieval, and simplified method of transporting exhibits.

Disbursements: Attorney's out-of-pocket expenses incurred on behalf of a specific case (e.g., expert witness fees or copying charges for medical records).

Disclosure: Communication of information regarding the results of a diagnostic test, medical treatment, or surgical intervention.

Disclosure of adverse events: The forthright and empathetic discussion of clinically significant facts between providers of care, patients, and/or their representatives about the occurrence of an adverse event that has resulted in patient harm, or could result in harm in the foreseeable future.

Discoverable: That which can be brought into discovery, pretrial, or acquisition of knowledge from opposing side.

Discovery: Pretrial devices that can be used by one party to obtain facts and information about the case from the other party in order to assist the party's preparation for trial.

Disk: A circular, hard or floppy, plate coated with magnetic material used to store digital or machine-readable data.

Docket: A formal record, entered in brief, of the proceedings in a court of justice.

Docket control order: Order from a judge outlining deadlines for discovery, and so on.

Domains: Territories that shape practice.

Do-not-resuscitate order (DNR): An order by a physician following the discussion with and informed consent by a legally competent patient or the patient's legal representative, which orders health care providers NOT to perform resuscitation procedures on this patient when these procedures are necessary for sustaining the patient's life. A DNR order is frequently initiated by the patient's living will or the legal representative's medical power of attorney.

Dose–response: The process of quantifying the relationship between the level of exposure and increased risk of adverse effects such as cancer.

Downloading: The practice of copying data in electronic form on a computer, which may then be manipulated or stored permanently on a personal computer.

DRG (Diagnosis Related Group): A classification scheme whose patient types are defined by the patient's diagnoses or procedures, and in some cases by the patient's age or discharge status.

DRI: A company specializing in retrieving defense testimony.

Drug formulary: A listing of medications preferred for use by the health plan. An "open" or "voluntary" formulary will cover both formulary and nonformulary drugs, and a "closed" formulary covers only those drugs in the formulary. The patient must pay for any drugs purchased by the patient not listed on a closed formulary, even if the ordering physician specifies the drug and even when no generic or alternative form exists.

Duty: An action or observation that is expected to occur once a relationship has been established between two people, such as health care provider and patient.

DVERT: Domestic Violence Emergency Response Team.

E/M (Evaluation and Management): CPT codes that represent services (e.g., office, emergency department, inpatient visits) that are the most frequently performed by medical providers.

eCommunity: An online or virtual listserve.

Ectopic pregnancy: Occurs when a fertilized egg implants outside the endometrial cavity, most often in a fallopian tube (95% of the time). If the fetus continues to grow, the fallopian tube will eventually rupture causing potential life-threatening hemorrhage.

ED overcrowding: Any situation involving an influx of patients to the emergency department that will tax the department's resources and services beyond its capacity. Examples include disaster situations, mass casualty incidents, and multiple victims from a motor vehicle crash.

Eggshell plaintiff: A fragile plaintiff with significant pre-existing conditions that affects the risk as well as the recovery from injury.

Employee: One who is engaged in paid services of another.

Engineering controls: The preferred method of controlling hazards that stops the hazard at its source or in the pathway of transmission before it reaches the worker and does not depend on the worker to control the hazard, such as elimination of a hazardous substance.

Entrepreneur: One who organizes, manages, and assumes the risks of a business or enterprise, usually self-employed.

Enterprise risk management (ERM): Is a structured and analytical process that focuses on identifying and estimating the financial impact and volatility of a defined portfolio of risks.

EPO: Managed Care Organization known as the Exclusive Provider Organization. In this plan, the providers are exclusive to the plan and its membership.

ERISA: Employee Retirement Income Security Act of 1974, a law designed to protect the rights of employees who receive employer-provided benefits such as pensions, deferred retirement income, and health care benefits such as HMOs, long-term and short-term disability coverage.

Errata sheet: A document that shows corrections to the text of the deposition.

Ethics: The systematic investigation of questions about right and wrong. Ethics involves critical analysis of different views of right and wrong, with particular attention paid to the underlying values of each view, its coherence and consistency, and its implications in actual situations.

Euthanasia: The act, by commission or omission, of painlessly ending the life of persons suffering from incurable and distressing disease as an act of mercy.

Evaluation: The fifth step of the nursing process, during which the extent of goal achievement is determined; each of the previous four steps is analyzed to identify factors that enhanced or hindered progress, and the plan of care is modified or terminated as indicated.

Excess (Insurance) coverage: Insurance that provides coverage when damages reach a certain level. This is also the function of umbrella coverage. Excess coverage may involve an additional insurance carrier.

Exclusions: Noted services or conditions, which the policy will not cover.

Exemplary damages: Also known as punitive damages; an award made to the plaintiff for the purpose of punishing the defendant when oppressive, malicious, or fraudulent conduct is involved.

Exhibit: A document or object produced and identified in court as evidence; a document labeled with an identifying mark (as a number or letter) and appended to a writing (as a brief) to which it is relevant; something exhibited; an act or instance of exhibiting.

Experience: The history of injuries or accidents, which is used for substantiating the setting of a current premium amount.

Expert: A person possessing the knowledge, skills, and expertise concerning a particular subject who is capable of rendering an opinion.

Expert fact witness: One who by virtue of special knowledge, skill, training, or experience is qualified to provide testimony to aid the fact finder in matters that exceed the common knowledge of ordinary people, but does not offer opinions on the standard of care.

Expert witness: A witness (as a medical specialist) who by virtue of special knowledge, skill, training, or experience is qualified to provide testimony to aid the fact finder in matters that exceed the common knowledge of ordinary people.

Exposure records: Documentation of environmental workplace monitoring or measuring of a toxic substance or a harmful agent or biological monitoring, which directly assesses the absorption of a toxic substance or a harmful physical agent.

Exposure: The maximum amount of money that an insurer could spend on one claim (often coincided with the policy limit).

External standards: Standards that stem from sources such as state nurse practice acts, state boards of nursing, federal organizations, independent, not-for-profit organizations, such as the Joint Commission, professional nursing organizations, nursing literature, and continuing education programs.

Fabricate: To invent; to devise falsely.

Fact witness: One not named as a defendant in a lawsuit, who has knowledge of events that have occurred.

Failure mode effects analysis (FMEA): A proactive analysis to look at a particular process and look for ways that it might fail as opposed to a postevent evaluation. The first step is to define the process to be analyzed and find evidence-based data to support your analysis. Next, a multidisciplinary team will break the process into subprocesses and identify failure modes for each followed by the assignment of risk priorities. An analysis of each failure mode will lead to recommendations for improvement and corrective action.

Federal Rules of Civil Procedure: Body of procedural rules that govern all civil actions in U.S. District Courts and after which most of the states have modeled their own rules of procedure.

Federal question jurisdiction: A term used in the U.S. law of civil procedure to refer to the situation in which a U.S. federal court has subject matter jurisdiction to hear a civil case because the plaintiff has alleged a violation of the Constitution, laws, or treaties of the United States (http://en.wikipedia.org/wiki/Federal_question_jurisdiction).

Field: An area of a unit record used to store a defined category of data.

Field case management: Case management services provided face to face through visits with the client at home, in an inpatient setting, and at treatment provider's offices.

File: A collection of related records. The term is often used as a synonym for database, sometimes used to refer to part of a database structure.

Five C's of communication: Five elements that represent effective communication skills: clear, concise, complete, cohesive, and courteous.

Floppy disk: A thin, flexible disk with magnetic surfaces that is used to store computer programs and data.

Food and Drug Administration (FDA): U.S. government agency established for the provision of regulations and guidelines for compliance with the Food, Drug and Cosmetic Act.

Forensic science: Science applied to answering legal questions by the examination, evaluation, and exploration of evidence.

Foreseeability: The implication that the damages must be the foreseeable, or reasonably anticipated, result of substandard practice of the defendant health care provider.

Free text: A method by which a searcher may select the terms on which searching will be performed without the requirement of matching them to a controlled vocabulary list or thesaurus; also referred to as text words.

G: This is the unit of measurement of a load caused by acceleration or deceleration. One G is the force that holds us onto the Earth (the force of gravity, hence the "G"). A person on a roller coaster experiences more than one G. A jet pilot might experience as much as 6 Gs in a turn. Acceleration/deceleration in an accident subjects the occupants to increased Gs. The Gs in a motor vehicle collision are calculated by an accident reconstructionist.

Gatekeeper: The secretary, paralegal, or other personnel who take and screen calls for the professional.

General acceptance test: A standard for the admissibility of expert testimony. Expert testimony based on a scientific technique is inadmissible unless the technique has been accepted as reliable by the relevant scientific community.

General damages: Also referred to as noneconomic damages. General damages are nonpecuniary damages recognized as compensable, but on which the law is unable to place a dollar amount. Examples of general damages are *pain and suffering and loss of consortium.*

Gigabyte: The largest unit of mass storage used in common parlance. One gigabyte is equal to 1000 megabytes, 1 billion bytes, or 500,000 pages of information. Used in huge computer storage depots by major vendors of online databases.

Goal-oriented planning: The identification of a goal and the steps it will take to reach that goal, including objectives, leadership, target date, resources, training, support, budget, communication, and evaluation.

Gopher: A service that provides a menu-like interface to voluminous amounts of information available on the Internet. The data in *Gopherspace* may be efficiently browsed using a Gopher client.

Grand jury: A group of people randomly selected in a manner similar to trial jurors whose purpose is to investigate and inform on crimes committed within its jurisdiction and to accuse (indict) persons of crimes when it has discovered sufficient evidence to warrant holding a person for trial.

Guardian: A person lawfully invested with the power, and charged with the duty, of taking care of and managing the property and rights of another person, who, for defect of age, understanding, or self-control, is considered incapable of administering his or her own affairs.

Guardianship: A court proceeding in which a judge appoints an individual to care for a person under the age of 18 and/or manage the estate.

Guideline: A resource tool to assist employers in recognizing and controlling hazards. It is voluntary and not enforceable, as are standards. Also a process of client care management that has the potential of improving the quality of clinical and consumer decision-making; includes assessment and diagnosis, planning, intervention, evaluation, and outcome.

Hard disk: A rigid storage device coated with a magnetic surface on which computer programs and data may be stored. Typical capacities for personal computers range from 5 megabytes to 120 megabytes.

Hardware: The equipment and computers used in data storage and processing systems.

Hazard Communication Standard: One of the standards developed by the Occupational Safety and Health Administration in order to prevent workplace illness and injury to workers who are exposed to hazardous chemicals by providing information to employees about chemical hazards.

HCFA: Health Care Finance Administration, involved in regulating nursing homes (now Centers for Medicare & Medicaid Services).

HCPCS: (HCFA Common Procedural Coding System)—A uniform method for health care providers and medical suppliers to report professional services, procedures, and supplies.

Health care provider defendants: Any of the individuals involved in providing care for the plaintiff who are alleged to have fallen below the standard of care resulting in the claimed damages.

Health Maintenance Organization (HMO): Groups of participating health care providers (physicians, hospitals, clinics) that provide medical services to enrolled members of group health insurance plan (Black's Law Dictionary, 2009).

HIPPA: The Health Insurance Portability and Accountability Act of 1996. Establishes privacy and security standards to protect a patient's health care information. In December 2000, the Department of Health and Human Services issued final regulations governing privacy of this information under HIPPA.

Hired Gun: A person hired to handle a difficult problem. In the legal arena, a person who may be perceived as someone who will provide any desired testimony for a price.

HMO: Health Maintenance Organization. This type of plan is based on the premise of preventative medicine and management of dollars spent for the health care benefits of its members.

Home health care conditions of participation: Minimum health and safety conditions that must be met by providers in order to begin and continue to participate in the Medicare Home Health Care program.

Homebound: Medicare criteria for home health care services. Leaving the home must take a substantial effort, and patients normally leave for medical care or for short and infrequent nonmedical reasons.

HTML: Short for HyperText Markup Language. The authoring language used to create documents on the World Wide Web. HTML defines the structure and layout of a Web document by using a variety of tags and attributes.

Hypermedia: Similar in concept to hypertext except that it also includes multimedia capabilities such as sounds and graphics related to the subject.

Hypertext: A hypertext document contains live links, which when pressed send the reader to another document related by terms or concepts.

ICD-9CM (International Classification of Diseases and Clinical Modification): These are three-digit codes, required by Medicare Part B, referring to a disease with additional number of up to two decimal places for specificity.

ID Code: A code issued by a vendor to individual users for identification.

IDEX: A company specializing in retrieving defense testimony.

IDT: Interdisciplinary team consisting of the nurse, physician, and therapists.

Impeachment: To call into question the veracity of the witness by means of evidence offered.

Implementation: As an LNC standard, implementation of the plan of action.

Implied consent: When a consent form is not signed, but patient's actions or circumstances surrounding the procedure or treatment at issue indicate consent; that is, filling a prescription, getting blood drawn, and so on.

Improper joinder: Joining of unrelated defendants in single lawsuit.

In camera: To the judge only.

Incident: A broad term used to describe any occurrence that is not consistent with routine hospital activities.

Incompetency: A relative term that may be employed as meaning disqualification, inability, or incapacity, and it can refer to lack of legal qualifications or fitness to discharge the required duty and to show want of physical or intellectual or moral fitness.

Independent LNC: A legal nurse consultant whose LNC practice is independent of a law insurance company, hospital, and so on. Frequently works solo, either as an expert witness or as a behind the scenes consultant for multiple attorneys, in her (his) own small business venture, charging hourly fees for service.

Independent medical examination: An examination requested by the carrier to determine appropriateness of medical care to date, causality of work/accident-related injury, length of disability, and work status.

Indictment: A formal accusation from a grand jury of a criminal offense made against a person.

Individuals with disabilities: A person with a physical or mental impairment, which substantially limits one or more major life activities.

Informed consent: The process of disclosure of information, usually regarding proposed medical or surgical treatment, by health care professionals to a competent patient who is presumed to have the capacity to understand the information, and a decision by that patient based on the information received. An agreement to do something or to allow something to happen only after all the relevant facts are known (Law.com Dictionary, 2009).

Informed consent form: A document that outlines and fully explains a research study that includes required elements. The form is to be approved by the IRB designated for the particular jurisdiction of study location and investigator, prior to presentation to the potential study participant. The study subject is to read, sign, and date this form prior to performance of designated study procedures, to indicate acceptance to voluntarily participate in the study. The subject is considered as enrolled into a study at the time the consent form is signed and dated by the participant.

Informed consent in research: An aspect of research in which consent of the subject is obtained after the subject is informed about the possible risks and benefits of participating in the research study. The process is similar to that of informed consent for medical decisions, but includes additional information that must be understood by the subject, such as what is known or not known about aspects of the research study and their effects (American Cancer Society, n.d.).

Informed refusal: The right of a patient to refuse treatment or diagnostic tests after the physician/health care provider has informed the patient of all the risks and likely outcomes of the choice to refuse treatment or testing (American Cancer Society, n.d.).

Inherent risk: A risk of a complication or condition that is existent in and inseparable from the medical procedure or treatment.

In-house LNC: Usually references LNCs working within a law firm, insurance company, and so on, and typically salaried, full time employment.

Institutional Review Board (IRB): A committee that reviews clinical study protocols, informed consent documents, and other relevant study materials to evaluate that the protection of the rights and welfare of human study subjects is maintained.

Insurance: A contract for the provision of coverage for services, injuries, or damages as set forth in the conditions, types, and terms of the contract.

Insurer: The party agreeing to reimburse another party for loss by designated contingencies.

Integrity: The distinctive element of being honest; the soundness or moral principle and character, as shown by one person dealing with others in the making and performance of contracts and fidelity and honesty in the discharge of trusts (Black's Law Dictionary, 2009). Firm adherence to a code, especially moral or artistic (Webster's New College Dictionary, 2008).

Intellectual property: Refers to copyrights, trademarks, and patents.

Intensity of service/severity of illness: Also referred to as IS/SI, this is a description of how sick a patient is and the level of health care services the patient requires.

Interfacing: The ability to send and/or receive information from one computer system to another.

Internal standards: Institutional standards that stem from internal sources such as policies and procedures, professional job descriptions, or internal educational materials.

(the) Internet: The name given to the worldwide collection of data networks (an Internet or internet work) which all speak the TCP/IP network protocol, or language.

Internet work: A collection of two or more distinct networks joined together typically using a router to form a larger "network of networks."

Interrogatories: A set or series of written questions about the case submitted by one party to the other party or witness. The answers to the interrogatories are usually given under oath, that is, the person answering the questions signs a sworn statement that the answers are true.

Intrapreneur: A nurse who creates innovation within the health care organization through the introduction of a new product, a different service, or simply a new way of doing something.

***In vitro* study:** A biologic or biochemical process occurring outside a living organism.

***In vivo* study:** A biologic or biochemical process occurring within a living organism.

IPA: Individual Practice Association. Physicians contract with one or more specific plans and provide services to patients for an agreed-upon rate, and bill the plan on a fee-for-service basis.

Item bank: References certification test items (questions) that have been developed by the Item Writing Committee and are ready for use, but that have not yet been used on the certification exam.

Job analysis: Process of looking at a job to determine physical requirements needed to perform the essential functions of the job.

Joinder: Union; a joining of elements or causes of action or defense in a law suit.

JPG: Short for Joint Photographic Experts Group and pronounced "jay-peg." JPEG is a glossy data compression technique for color images. Although it can reduce files sizes to about 5% of their normal size, some detail is lost in the compression.

Justice: The principle of ethics that involves the obligation to be fair to all persons. Distributive justice is the allocation of a good as fairly as possible. The good of health care is distributed on the basis of need, which means that some people will get more than others because their need is greater.

Kantianism: This view holds that consequences do not make an action right or wrong. The moral rightness of a person's actions is dependent upon whether or not those actions uphold a principle, regardless of outcome.

Keogh plan: A designation for tax deductible retirement plans available to self-employed taxpayers. Such plans extend to the self-employed tax benefits similar to those available to employees under qualified pension and profit sharing plans.

Key words: Single words or terms of importance in an article drawn from titles, abstracts, subject headings, or any part of a record that is used for indexing.

Kilobyte: The most common memory storage unit quoted. It is 1000 bytes, or approximately one-half page of single-spaced, printed material.

Leadership: The office, position, or capacity of a leader who gives guidance and has the ability to lead or exert authority.

Learned intermediary: The person with knowledge who prescribes the drug to the patient.

Learned treatises: Facts, standards, methods, and principles of care.

Legal assistant: A person qualified by education, training, or work experience, employed by an attorney, who performs specifically delegated substantive legal work for which a lawyer is responsible (ABA).

Legal causation: Causation in fact and foreseeability or the *but for* test. (See proximate cause.)

Legal Nurse Consultant Certified (LNCC): The Gold Standard of Legal Nurse Consulting Certification, accredited by ABNS. Not an entry-level exam, the qualifications to sit for the American Association of Legal Nurse Consultants' exam include active licensure as an RN, at least five years experience as a practicing RN, and 2000 hours of qualified LNC practice within the previous three years.

Legal writing: Writing pertaining to, or intended to be used in, the legal process; in style and execution it need not differ from other writing.

Level I trauma center: A health care facility or center with dedicated resources to the care of trauma patients 24 hours a day, seven days a week. Level I is the highest level, and has the most available resources, as designated by the American College of Surgeons. Level I trauma centers should have resources that include but are not limited to, a dedicated trauma service, a trauma director, in-house surgeon availability, emergency resuscitation equipment for patients of all ages, a performance improvement program, coordination and/or participation in community prevention programs.

Liability: Any legally enforceable obligation. In insurance, this usually is associated with a monetary value.

Liberty interest: An interest recognized as protected by the due process clauses of state and federal constitutions.

Lien: A right or claim against an asset (e.g., Medicare may have a right to reimbursement of health care benefits it paid for treatment of the injury giving rise to the lawsuit from the damages recovered in that lawsuit).

Life-sustaining medical treatment: Medical treatment that sustains a person's life functions, including respiratory and cardiopulmonary functions, preventing the person's body from reaching that state where it is declared legally dead.

Limits: The amount the payer covers.

Litigation: A lawsuit, legal action, including all proceedings therein. Contest in a court of law for the purpose of enforcing a right or seeking a remedy.

Living will: A document executed by a competent person which governs the withholding or withdrawal of life-sustaining treatment from an individual in the event of an incurable or irreversible condition that will cause death within a relatively short time, and when such person is no longer able to make decisions regarding his or her medical treatment.

Logical operators: Also called Boolean operators (see Boolean logic).

Loss control: An application of techniques that is designed to minimize loss in a cost-effective manner.

Loss of chance: A theory of recovery in medical malpractice cases for a patient's loss of chance of survival or loss of chance of a better recovery. This theory applies where the patient is suffering from a pre-existing injury or illness that is aggravated by the alleged negligence of the health care provider to the extent that (1) the patient dies, when without negligence there might have been a substantial chance of survival; or (2) the patient survives, but the actual recovery is substantially less than it might have been absent the alleged malpractice.

Loss of consortium: A claim brought by the spouse of an injured party for loss of the benefits of companionship caused by the injuries suffered in the accident.

Loss prevention: A program that seeks to reduce or eliminate the chance of loss or the potential severity of a loss.

Mainframe: A very large computer, which has many megabytes in the central processing unit, or CPU. Because it can store many gigabytes of disk memory, it may act as a host computer, which controls searches from instructions or commands from many remote terminals.

Malpractice: Misconduct, negligence, or failure to properly perform duties according to professional standards of care.

Marginalization: Peripheralization, to be situated on the border or edge so that there is memberships in dual domains.

Markup: See "annotation."

Mass tort: A civil wrong that injures many people. Examples include toxic emissions from a factory, the crash of a commercial airliner, and contamination from an industrial waste-disposal site.

Material risk: A risk that, if the patient was informed about it, could influence his or her decision to consent to the proposed treatment or procedure.

Material Safety Data Sheet (MSDS): Documentation provided by the manufacturer that provides valuable information about the chemical, including a brief summary about the hazards and personal protective equipment that must be used when working with the chemical.

MCO: Managed Care Organization such as an HMO, EPO, IPA, or PPO. All types of MCOs utilize health care cost containment methods such as providing care within a specific network of providers and facilities, utilization management, and case management.

MDS: Minimum data set, a national tool used to assess the resident's needs and used to determine reimbursement.

Mechanism of injury: The way in which an injury was sustained.

Mediation: A problem-solving process involving a neutral third party who facilitates the parties in reaching a resolution but lacks authority to render a decision.

Mediator: A neutral third party who assists the parties in negotiating a compromise.

Medical review panel process: Requires the submission of a medical malpractice claim to a medical review panel for its opinion prior to the institution of the judicial action.

Medical surveillance: A program that requires monitoring specific exposures that is conducted to protect workers from adverse health effects of exposures to hazards in the workplace and to ensure ability to perform job activities.

Megabyte: One million bytes, 1000 kilobytes, or 500 pages of data.

Memo of understanding: A document of agreement between parties with a shared commitment. Depending on the wording, may have the binding power of a contract. May be synonymous with a letter of intent.

Meningeal signs: Refers to signs and symptoms that may signify possible meningeal irritation and raise the index of suspicion for a diagnosis of meningitis. Signs include nuccal rigidity spinal rigidity, Kernig's sign, and Brudzinski's sign. Besides meningitis, other possible causes are subarachnoid hemorrhage, fossa tumor, and increased intracranial pressure.

Mentor: A wise legal advisor, trusted teacher, or guide.

Middle range theory: Theories that are more limited in scope, with less abstraction, and that reflect practice.

Mitigation of damages: Claim that plaintiff has responsibility to minimize the adverse impact of his injury and, therefore, his failure to do so should reduce the amount awarded to him by the damages that would have been avoided had he done so. This claim is typically used in the context of a defendant's assertion that plaintiff's award should be reduced by a prior act/omission of plaintiff (e.g., failure to wear a seat belt) because it would have lessened the injury, or because a treatment (e.g., a medicine, physical therapy, or a surgical procedure) is available to cure plaintiff's condition or diminish the effects of it.

Model: A mental image; a conceptualization of a phenomenon.

Model cases: The process of defining and identifying exemplars to illustrate a concept.

Modem: Acronym for Modulator-Demodulator. It is a device that allows a terminal to interface with the telecommunications network and converts the electrical or digital signals of a terminal.

Morality: Refers to the common societal conceptions of what is right and what is wrong. Our morality and morals are reflected in how we live, the decisions we make, and what we hold as valuable.

Motion: An application to a court or judge for the purpose of obtaining a rule or order direct some act to be done in favor of the applicant.

Motion in limine: A pretrial motion that requests the court to issue an interlocutory order which prevents an opposing party from introducing or referring to potentially irrelevant, prejudicial, or otherwise inadmissible evidence until the court has finally ruled on its admissibility.

Motivation: A conscious or unconscious need, drive, and so on that incites a person to some action, behavior, or goal.

MPEG1: Short for Moving Picture Experts Group, and pronounced "m-peg." The term also refers to the family of digital video compression standards and file formats developed by the group. MPEG generally produces better-quality video than competing formats, such as Video for Windows, Indeo, and QuickTime. MPEG files can be decoded by special hardware or by software.

NANDA: North American Nursing Diagnosis Association, an organization involved in developing and promoting the use of nursing diagnoses.

National Committee for Quality Assurance: It is an independent, nonprofit organization that evaluates health care coverage provided by insurers and managed care organizations by reviewing the clinical outcomes of its members, contracting practices, and member satisfaction surveys. Successful accreditation by the NCQA is considered a standard by which MCOs can be compared. Accreditation also implies a higher standard of service.

National Institute for Occupational Safety and Health (NIOSH): One of three separate bodies created by the OSH Act to administer the major requirement of the Act. The role of this agency is to conduct research, education, and training.

Native Resolution: In referring to a projector's resolution, it is common to refer to true or native resolution. If a projector's native resolution is 800×600, that means that the actual number of physical pixels on the display device is 800×600. The projector needs to match the resolution of the computer. Resolution is usually quoted in two numbers, where the first number refers to the number of pixels from side to side across the screen and the second number refers to the number of pixels vertically from top to bottom.

Natural language: A language that uses natural speech (words) rather than symbols.

NCQA: The National Committee for Quality Assurance. It is an independent, nonprofit organization that evaluates health care coverage provided by insurers and managed care organizations by reviewing the clinical outcomes of its members, contracting practices, and member satisfaction surveys. Successful accreditation by the NCQA is considered a standard by which MCOs can be compared. Accreditation also implies a higher standard of service.

NEC: (Not elsewhere classifiable). Indicates that the condition specified does not have a separate more specific listing; used only in Volume 2 of the ICD-9.

Negligence: Negligence is a failure to act as an ordinary prudent person or "reasonable man" would do under similar circumstances. There are four elements of negligence that must be proved in order for there to be a viable medical malpractice claim.

Nettiquette: Etiquette (manners) on the "net."

Network: A collection of computers linked together by a physical medium (wires, microwaves, etc.) for transmission of data between computers or "nodes" on the network.

Networking: Meeting and establishing a network of other like professionals to enhance information exchange and business relationships.

Network protocol: The set of rules or language used by computers on a network to communicate (e.g., Novell IPX, Appletalk, and TCP/IP).

Newton's Laws of Motion: Three basic laws of physics utilized to determine whether the mechanism of the claimed injury existed in the subject incident.

NIC: Nursing Interventions Classification, a method of placing interventions in a taxonomy.

No fault system: Under a no-fault system, each party's own insurance covers the damages (up to policy limits regardless of which party is at fault).

NOC: Nursing Outcomes Classification, a method of placing outcomes in taxonomy.

Nonbillable hours: Hours worked that does not directly relate to the client/customer's project; hours spent in administrative or other support areas of a business project.

Nonparty witness: A witness who is not a plaintiff or defendant or employee or agent of a plaintiff or defendant.

NOS: (Not otherwise specified). Used, only in Volume 1 of the ICD-9, when the available information does not permit assignment to a more specific code.

Notice of intent: A document sent to a health care facility, which puts that facility on notice that a party has initiated legal action against the facility.

NPA: Nursing Practice Act.

Nursing process: An organized, systematic method of giving individualized nursing care that focuses on identifying and treating unique responses of individuals or groups to actual or potential alterations in health.

Objection: (form, hearsay, privilege). Legal format for not allowing testimony into evidence based on various legal reasons such as form of question, hearsay, or privilege.

OBRA: Omnibus Budget Reconciliation Act of 1987, changed the standard of care in nursing homes by defining minimum standards

Occupant kinematics: The movement of the occupants of a vehicle due to the motor vehicle collision.

Occupational and Environmental Health Nurse (OEHN): A professional licensed nurse whose specialty area of practice is the worker and the work environment.

Occupational Noise Exposure Standard: One of the standards developed by the Occupational Safety and Health Administration in order to protect workers from hearing impairment when there is significant noise exposure.

Occupational Safety and Health Administration (OSHA): One of three separate bodies created by the OSH Act to administer the major requirements of the Act. The role of this agency is to set and enforce safety and health standards; provide training outreach and education; establish partnerships; and encourage continual process improvement in workplace safety and health.

Off-line printing: Printed records generated at the mainframe after the user has logged off the computer system. They are usually mailed or faxed to the user.

Off-line searching: Computer processing of a search after the user has entered the appropriate strategy and has logged off the system.

Ombudsman: An official or semiofficial office or person to which people may come with grievances connected with the government. The ombudsman stands between, and represents, the citizen before the government.

Online: The term describes the status of a searcher conversing with the host computer in the interactive mode.

Open account: An account that has not been finally settled or closed, but is still running or open to future adjustment or liquidation. Open account, in legal as well as in ordinary language, means indebtedness subject to future adjustment, and which may be reduced or modified by proof.

Open book pelvic fracture: An unstable pelvic fracture caused by a high energy injury resulting in the posterior aspects or the integrity of the ring are disrupted. This can be an open or closed fracture and is a potentially life-threatening injury due to the possibility of severe hemorrhage.

Opt-out: After a class action is certified, a deadline is set, typically by the court, as to when one may voluntarily decide to not participate in a class action; after the date passes, plaintiffs who have not opted-out will be bound by the decisions of the court.

Ostensible authority: Ostensible authority is a doctrine of law whereby a hospital is liable for the negligence of an independent contractor if the patient has a rational basis to believe that the independent contractor is a hospital employee, for example, a physician in the emergency department.

Outcome identification: As an LNC standard, the identification of desired activities as related to the health care issues of a case or claim.

Outcomes: Result of medical treatment and medical case management services. These should be measurable.

Outcomes and Assessment Information Set (OASIS): Quality information collected from Medicare home health care patients and submitted regularly to fiscal intermediaries who analyze the data in order to implement quality initiatives and calculate Medicare payments for services.

Paradigm: The body of values, commitment, beliefs, and knowledge shared by members of a profession.

Paralegal: A person qualified by education, training, or work experience employed by an attorney who performs specifically delegated substantive legal work for which a lawyer is responsible.

Partnership: A business owned by two or more persons that is not organized as a corporation. For income tax purposes, a partnership includes a syndicate, group, pool, or joint venture, as well as ordinary partnerships. Partnerships are treated as a conduit and are, therefore, not subject to taxation. The various items of partnership income, gains, and losses, and so on flow through to the individual partners and are reported on their personal income tax returns.

Password: A unique set of characters assigned to a user for security purposes to grant access to specific databases.

Paternalism: An extension of beneficence. Paternalism is the view that professionals understand patients' best interests better than patients do and are entitled to act on behalf of the patient's well being even when the patient does not agree.

Pathognomic: Characteristic or indicative of a disease (Stedman's Medical Dictionary, 28th Edition 2005).

Payroll tax: A type of tax that is collected by deduction from an employee's wages. Federal, state, and half of the social security tax is paid by employees, with the social security tax matched by the employer.

PDF: Short for Portable Document Format, a file format developed by Adobe Systems.

Pediatric advanced life support provider: A health care professional who is certified as a BLS provider and passes certification to enhance their resuscitation skills in a pediatric cardio-pulmonary emergency. These skills include CPR, airway management, cardiac rhythm recognition, emergency medication administration, and the use of treatment algorithms.

Peer-reviewed: A process used by professions for monitoring and regulating member practice.

Percentile: Percentile fees arranged in sequence from highest to lowest, which results in a range, which contains 100% of the fees, received, the 80th and 90th percentile fees would be the actual fees which are higher than (or equal to) 80% or 90% of all fees in the range, respectively.

Performance appraisal: Evaluation of the practice of the LNC in relation to professional standards and relevant statutes and regulations. PDF captures formatting information from a variety of desktop publishing applications, making it possible to send formatted documents and have them appear on the recipient's monitor or printer as they were intended.

Persistent vegetative state: Denoting especially an enduring state of grossly impaired consciousness, as after severe head trauma or brain disease, in which an individual is incapable of voluntary or purposeful acts and only responds reflexively to painful stimuli.

Personal protective equipment (PPE): Devices worn by workers to protect against hazards in the workplace, such as the use of earplugs or earmuffs in high noise areas or gloves for protection against blood or other body fluid exposures.

Personal Protective Equipment Standard: One of the standards developed by the Occupational Safety and Health Administration in order to provide information on the types of protection available for employees where engineering and administrative controls were not available or effective in reducing occupational hazards.

Perspective: The way members of a group characterize, define, and view a situation.

Phenomena: An aspect of reality that is sensed or experienced.

PIP: (Personal Injury Protection). Coverage by the client's own auto insurance carrier for medical expenses. Dictated by state auto law and amount of coverage purchased.

Plaintiff: A person who brings an action; the person who complains or sues in a civil action and is so named on the record. A person who seeks remedial relief for an injury to rights; it designates a complainant.

Planning: As an LNC standard; formulation of a plan of action. The formal allegations by the parties of their respective claims and defenses. Under rules of civil procedure, the pleadings consist of a complaint, an answer, a reply to counterclaim, a third-party complaint, and a third-party answer.

Planning: The third step of the nursing process. In this step, specific measures are identified to put into action based upon the initial assessment.

PMPM: Per member per month. The formula by which utilization management calculates average utilization and cost for each member of the plan.

Position statement: Consensus statements providing the generally accepted opinions of a group.

Postings: The number of citations or references retrieved as a result of a search. Synonymous with hits.

Power of attorney: An instrument in writing whereby one person, as principal, appoints another as his agent and confers authority to perform certain specified acts or kinds of acts on behalf of principal.

PowerPoint: A Microsoft software product commonly used for computer-based "slide" presentations, may contain text and graphics.

PPO: Preferred Provider Organization. Members of this type of plan receive benefits at a discounted rate as long as they utilize only the providers who have a contract with the plan.

PPS (Prospective Payment System): A payment system, such as DRGs, that pays on historical data of case mix and regional differences.

Practice analysis: A study and analysis of critical skills and concepts needed to be proficient in the specialty, as identified by nurses practicing in the specialty. A practice analysis is a critical early step in creating a certification exam that accurately reflects specialty practice, the exam blueprint. This periodic analysis is required to meet ABNS standards and maintain accreditation.

Premium: The amount of money paid to an insurer in return for insurance coverage.

Preponderance of the evidence: A standard of proof that is more probable than not; just over 50% of the evidence favors the party.

Principal investigator (PI): An individual, usually a physician, with appropriate qualifications (eligibility usually evaluated and determined by an IRB and/or pharmaceutical sponsor) who is responsible for the research study trial conduct.

Proactive: Planned action towards a goal.

Probable cause: Standard used to determine if a crime has been committed and if there is sufficient evidence to believe a specific individual committed it.

Probate court: The department of each county's superior court that deals with probate conservatorships, guardianships, and the estates of people who have died.

Procedure creep: Billing for a higher level of service than provided; see upcoding.

Procedures: A series of recommended actions for the completion of a specific task or function. Procedures may be either specific to an institution or applicable across settings.

Process server: One who serves papers on parties.

Product liability: Concept in the law holding a manufacturer responsible for the article placed on the market.

Products liability: A tort arising out of defective products, including medical devices and medications.

Profession: An occupation that requires considerable training and specialized study. Professionals experience a high level of dedication and an acceptance of responsibility for the quality of their work. Society holds professionals in a position of high regard, with a high level of accountability in their practices.

Professional: A person with a specialized training in a field of learning, art or science.

Professional Code of Ethics: Rules that govern the conduct of an organization and its members.

Profit and loss: The gain or loss arising from goods bought or sold, or from carrying on any other business, the former of which, in bookkeeping, is placed on the creditor's side; the latter on the debtor's side.

Properties of the nursing process: Purposeful, systematic, dynamic, interactive, and flexible.

Provider: The party providing services and supplies to the beneficiary.

Proximate cause: An act or omission that was a substantial factor in bringing about or failing to prevent an injury. An action that produces a result legally sufficient to result in liability

Psychometric Testing Standards: Postadministration testing analysis to ensure that the certification exam questions are directly related to the roles of experienced LNCs who meet eligibility criteria and perform successfully on the examination. Statistical analysis indicates high consistency of performance of individual candidates throughout the examination.

Punitive damages: Also known as exemplary damages. Punitive damages exceed the amount intended to make the plaintiff whole. Punitive damages are awarded with the intent to punish the defendant, to set an example, and to deter future behavior considered outrageous. Most jurisdictions determine if punitive damages can be awarded and often set a cap on the amount of punitive damages that can be awarded.

Qualification: Quality or circumstance that is legally or inherently necessary to perform a function (West's Legal Thesaurus/Dictionary, 2001).

Qualified individual with a disability: A person who with reasonable accommodation can perform the essential functions of the job.

Qualities and traits: Characteristics that personify the behaviors of an individual

Quality assurance: Ongoing program that objectively and systematically monitors and evaluates quality and resolves identified problems.

Quality improvement: Focuses on processes or systems that contribute to or distract from outcomes.

Quality of practice: Evaluation of the quality and effectiveness of practice.

RAI: Resident Assessment Instrument that consists of the MDS, RAPS, and the care plan.

RAP: Resident Assessment Protocol. Defines the problems that were identified through the use of the MDS.

Rating: The quantifying of an insured or group's activity or experience.

Reader-friendly writing: Writing that is tailored to the audience and the purpose, that attempts to minimize the effort required by the reader; typically characterized by brevity, clarity, simplicity, and structure.

Reasonable accommodation: The Rehabilitation Act of 1973 requires the employer to take reasonable steps to accommodate the individual with a disability unless it causes the employer undue hardship.

Recording and Reporting of Occupational Injuries and Illness Standard: One of the standards developed by the Occupational Safety and Health Administration in order to identify high hazard industries and permit employees to be aware of their employer's safety record.

Records: Groups of related elements that, when handled as units, make up files.

Redaction: The act of deleting identifying information.

Refereed journal: A professional journal that publishes material only after comprehensive review by the author's peers.

Reference: See citation.

Referral: The process of sending a member to a second care provider for a consultation, second opinion, or further diagnosis and treatment of an existing condition.

Reflective reaction: Incorporates thought and action with reflection to analyze actions.

Request for admissions: Written statements of fact concerning the case, which are submitted to an adverse party and which that party is required to admit or deny; those statements that are admitted will be treated by the court as having been established and need not be proven at trial.

Request for production: A formal written request compelling a party to produce materials subject to discovery rules.

Res ipsa loquitur: Latin for the thing speaks for itself; the mere facts provide information supporting negligence.

Reserves: Monies set aside by the insurance company for the future expenditures on a claim based on an educated projection.

Resource management: As it applies to the LNC, the LNC selects expert assistance on the needs of the case or the claim.

Respondeat superior: Latin for "let the superior make answer;" employer liability for employee's wrongful actions within the scope of employment.

Restatement (Third) Tort Products Liability Section 6: A statement which reflects that prescription drug or medical device is not reasonably safe due to defective design. If the foreseeable risks of harm posed by the drug or medical device are sufficiently great in relation to its foreseeable therapeutic benefits, the reasonable health care providers, knowing of such foreseeable risks and therapeutic benefits, would not prescribe the drug or medical device for any class of patients.

Retainer: The act of withholding what one has in one's own hands by virtue of some right. In the practice of law, when a client hires an attorney to represent him, the client is said to have retained the attorney. This act of employment is called the retainer.

Risk: A chance of loss. Risk is a variation in possible outcomes that exist in any given situation or event. Risk may include two categories: (1) objective, variations that exist in nature and that are the same for all individuals facing the same situation; and (2) subjective, an individual's estimation of the objective risk.

Risk management: A process that identifies, evaluates, and takes corrective action against potential or actual risks to patients, visitors, employees, or property.

Root cause analysis (RCA): A process designed to uncover how and why something happened and to identify ways to prevent it from happening again. The four-step process includes data collection, organization of contributing factors, identification of the root causes, and recommendations for corrective action.

RUG (Resource Utilization Group): A federally mandated standardized clinical assessment, to classify residents into one of 44 payment categories.

Rule 702: A federal rule of evidence governing the admissibility of expert testimony.

RVS (Relative Value System): A procedure/service is assigned a value multiplied by cost factor.

SART: Sexual Assault Response Team.

Search Statement: A user-entered instruction that combines key terms and Boolean operators (which see) to retrieve a set of citations or records.

Search Strategy: The selection of an essential set of planned search statements.

Securing: The protection portion of a computer system that prevents access to sensitive material.

Self-insured companies: Companies or businesses that set aside a fund to cover potential business liability losses instead of insuring against such a loss through a separate insurance company.

Sentinel event: An unexpected occurrence of variation involving death, serious physical or psychological injury, or risk thereof. Serious injury specifically includes loss of limb or function. The phrase *"or risk thereof"* includes any process variations for which a recurrence would carry a significant chance of a serious adverse outcome.

Sepsis: The most common kind of distributive shock caused by an overwhelming systemic infection resulting in cellular destruction, microvascular occlusion, and systemic vasodilatation.

Shadow jury: Acts as a surrogate for the real jury by sitting in a courtroom whenever the real jury is present and agrees to be interviewed at regular intervals during a trial.

Sick building syndrome: The term used to describe the cluster of symptoms found to occur in office environments, particularly in sealed buildings with centrally controlled mechanical ventilation.

Software: Computer program or sets of computer-readable messages/language that instructs a computer to perform specified tasks.

Sole proprietorship: A form of business in which one person owns all the assets of the business in contrast to a partnership, trust, or corporation. The sole proprietor is solely liable for all the debts of the business.

Special damages: Out-of-pocket expenses incurred by the plaintiff as a result of the negligence.

Standard: A model accepted as correct by custom.

Standard of care: The degree of care that a reasonably prudent person should exercise under the same or similar circumstances. In the case of a professional (e.g., nurse, doctor, lawyer), it is the degree of care that a reasonably prudent person in that profession should exercise under the same or similar circumstances.

Statute: A formal written enactment of a legislative body, whether federal, state, county, or city. A particular law enacted or established by the will of the legislative department of the government.

Statute: Law enacted by the legislature.

Statute of limitations: Specific period of time between an occurrence and the filing of the lawsuit. In malpractice claims, this is usually when the party claiming injury first discovers or should have discovered the injury.

Statutory: Relating to a statute.

Stop word List: A list of terms that are ignored for online searching, such as articles and prepositions.

Strict liability: Doctrine by which the one who sells any product in a defective condition deemed unsafe to the user or consumer or to their property is subject to liability for physical harm or property damage; the plaintiff must prove the product was in a condition not contemplated by the ultimate consumer, which would make the product unreasonably dangerous.

Sub Rosa: A technique of investigation that uses videotape surveillance of a plaintiff or claimant; carried out by a private investigator for the defense.

Subcontract: An agreement between a party of the original contract and a third party.

Subcontractor: One who has entered into a contract, express or implied, for the performance of an act with the person who has already contracted for its performance.

Subpoena: A command to appear at a certain time and place to give testimony upon a certain matter.

Subpoena duces tecum: A process by which the court commands a witness who has in his possession or control some document or paper that is pertinent to the issues of a pending controversy, to produce it at the trial.

Sullivan v. Edward Hospital: The 2004 court decision which affirmed that the profession of nursing involves a unique body of knowledge and expertise, and nurses are the most appropriate experts to testify to nursing standards of care.

Summary judgment: The process by which a court decides, based on evidence presented by the defendant doctor, that there is no genuine issue of material fact for a jury to consider.

Therefore, the court dismisses the case against the defendant as a matter of law and the case does not go to trial.

Summary plan description: An overview of the benefits elected by a plan member, detailing the expectations a member can expect covered by the plan. It is an overview of the benefits elected by a plan member, detailing what the member can expect to be covered by the plan, and possibly, what is not covered. The structure and wording of SPDs is stipulated in ERISA.

Summons and complaint: A document also known as petition, that sets forth allegations against the defendant(s) that the plaintiff intends to prove. The document is formal notification and initiates the legal action against the facility. The method of instituting a legal proceeding and notification of such action to all concerned parities is regulated by the individual.

Tax: A charge by the government on the income of an individual, corporation, or trust, as well as the value of an estate or gift.

Taxonomy: A common language in event reporting for use in and across health care organizations to promote reliable and accurate information.

Technical nurse consultant: A nurse who has advanced skills and expertise in the use of computerized presentations for legal proceedings.

Telecommunications: Transmission of voice or data by means of telephone networks or carriers.

Telephonic case management: Coordination of services provided through telephone contact only.

Terminal: An electronic device for transmitting to and receiving signals from a computer.

Terminal illness: A medical practitioner's term for a disease that is incurable or irreversible and which will, with a high degree of probability, cause the death of a patient, within a relatively short period of time.

Testifying expert: An expert who is capable of rendering an opinion as a potential trial witness.

Testimony: Spoken or written evidence by a competent witness under oath.

Text word: A single word that appears in the title or abstract of a citation, which may be used as a search tool rather than, or in addition to, the subject terms (such as MeSH terms) assigned by an indexer. Also see free text.

The Joint Commission: An independent, not-for-profit organization, formerly known as Joint Commission on Accreditation of Healthcare Organizations or the acronym, JCAHO, whose mission is to continuously improve the safety and quality of care provided to the public through the provision of health care accreditation and related services that support performance improvement in health care organizations. The Joint Commission accredits and certifies more than 15,000 health care organizations and programs in the United States. Joint Commission accreditation and certification is recognized nationwide as a symbol of quality that reflects an organization's commitment to meeting certain performance standards.

Theory: A conceptualization of an aspect of reality for the purpose of describing phenomena, concepts that are interrelated in a coherent whole for some purpose.

Theory development: The process or integrated approach by which theory is developed including the evolution of an idea, the concept analysis, the proposal of a framework and theoretical definition, substantiation through research, and critique of the theory.

Third-party administrator: A person or company hired to oversee and resolve claims and actions. Third-party administrators, known as TPAs, are often utilized by large self-insured companies such as health maintenance organization or large health care conglomerates to handle claims against the company.

Third-party counterclaim: A separate cause of action, which a defendant asserts against a third person or party.

TIF: Acronym for tagged image file format, one of the most widely supported file formats for storing bit-mapped images on personal computers. TIFF graphics can be any resolution, and they can be black and white, gray-scaled, or color.

Time management: A method of efficient use of energy, space, and time to enhance task completion.

Time-weighted average (TWA): Averages the levels and duration of noise exposure over the work shift to give an equivalent 8-hour exposure.

Tort: A civil wrong or injury other than breach of contract.

Total quality management: Process used to improve the ability to satisfy customer expectations; based on belief that quality is a positive strategy for growth and integrated into the business plan.

Toxic tort: A civil wrong arising from exposure to a toxic substance, such as asbestos, radiation, or hazardous waste. A toxic tort can be remedied by a civil lawsuit (usually a class action) or by administrative action.

Tracking: Following and monitoring the awareness of a direction or idea.

Trauma bays: Treatment rooms in an emergency department that are equipped and dedicated to the care of trauma patients who arrive in the ED.

Trauma Nurse Core Course (TNCC): TNCC is a course produced by the Emergency Nurses Association that serves as a standard of practice for nurses who provide care for patients who have sustained traumatic injuries.

Trending: Maintaining a consistent way or direction.

Trial consultant: A consultant employed or hired to assist with trial preparation, typically through the preparation of witnesses and parties for testifying at trial. Trial consultants may also assist in jury selection, through the creation of a profile of desirable jurors. Trial consultants often have background education in psychology and/or communication.

Trier of fact: Judge, arbitrator, or juror.

Truncation: A means of retrieving words that share a common root or stem.

Trustee: A person or an institution that manages the assets for the benefit of someone else, perhaps the consevatee.

U&C (Usual and Customary): A fee defined as the charge for health care that is consistent with the average rate or charge for identical or similar services in a certain geographical area.

UB-92 (Universal Bill 1992): The form used by hospital-based providers to bill for services.

Unbundling: Breaking a single service into its multiple components to increase total billing charges.

Underwriting: The analysis done for accepting insurance risk and determining the amount of insurance the company will write on each risk.

Upcoding: The process of assigning a code that represents a more complex or involved service than actually provided and thus receives a higher reimbursement.

Update service: A periodic online search of a previously selected topic. The search strategy is stored and activated periodically (i.e., monthly or quarterly) to provide new citations. Also known as "Selective Dissemination of Information" or "SDI."

UCR: Usual, customary, and reasonable. A method for determining benefits by comparing the charges of one provider to like charges of others in the same area and specialty.

Utilitarianism: The ethical view that the right action is that which promotes a greater balance of good over harm for everyone concerned in a situation.

Utilization management: A method employed by the insurance and managed care industry to track and manage the use of medical benefits by covered beneficiaries. It is a formal assessment of medical necessity, efficiency, appropriateness of health care services, and treatment plans. This assessment can occur prior to, during, and after delivery of services.

Utilization review: A process of evaluation of health care based on medical necessity and appropriateness. Utilization review can include preadmission review, concurrent review, discharge planning, and retrospective review.

Vendor: A service company that stores databases electronically and makes them available, via telecommunications, to clients for a fee.

Venture capital: Funding for new companies or others embarking on new or turnaround ventures that entails some investment risk but offers the potential for above average profits. Venture capital is often provided by firms that specialize in financing new ventures with capital supplied by investors interested in speculative or high-risk investments (Black's Law Dictionary, 2009).

Veracity: The principle of telling the truth without deception.

Vicarious liability: Vicarious liability occurs when the law, in certain limited instances, imposes liability on a principal of the acts or omissions of an agent.

Vision statement: Articulation of a view of a realistic, credible, attractive future for the organization.

Voir dire: The questioning of prospective jurors by a judge and attorneys in court.

Warranty: An assurance by the manufacturer that the product is merchantable or fit for the purpose for which it was sold.

WAV: The format for storing sound in files developed jointly by Microsoft and IBM. Support or WAV files were built into Windows 95 making it the de facto standard for sound on PCs.

Whistleblower: An employee who reports an employer wrongdoing to a government or law enforcement agency.

Witness: One who is called on to be present at a transaction so as to be able to testify to its occurrence (Merriam-Webster's Dictionary of Law, 1996).

Word: When capitalized, short for Microsoft Word, a word processing software.

Worker's compensation: A Federal and State mandated insurance program that provides medical care and wage loss replacement for workers injured on the job.

World Wide Web (WWW): A collection of hypermedia documents that reside on computers (Web servers) located all over the Internet that is linked together in a "worldwide web" of information. A Web browser (such as Mosaic or Lynx) is needed to gain access to the World Wide Web.

Wrongful death: Type of legal theory argued on behalf of a deceased person's beneficiaries that allege that death was attributable to the willful or negligent act of another.

Wrongful life: Refers to a type of medical malpractice claim brought on behalf of a child, alleging that the child would not have been born but for negligent advice to, or treatment of, the parents.

Appendix 2

Acronyms

Joyce M. Collins, RN, BSBA, CLNC, LNCC

Acronym	Definition
AALNC	American Association of Legal Nurse Consultants
AARP	American Association of Retired Persons
ABA	American Bar Association
ABNS	American Board of Nursing Specialties
ADL	Activities of daily living
ALNCCB	American Legal Nurse Consultant Certification Board
ANA	American Nurses Association
ANCC	American Nurses Credentialing Center
ATD	Anthropomorphic test devices (crash dummies)
CNA	Certified nursing assistants
CARF	Commission on Accreditation of Rehabilitation Facilities
CBT	Computer-based testing
CCI	Competency and Credentialing Institute
CCRN	Critical Care RN
CDC	Centers for Disease Control
CDHP	Consumer-Directed Health Plan
CEN	Certified Emergency Nurse
CEO	Chief Executive Officer
CFR	Code of Federal Regulations
CGA	Contact guard assist, required to physically have a hand on the resident
CMS	Centers for Medicare and Medicaid Services
C-NET	Center for Nursing Education and Testing
COBRA	Consolidated Omnibus Budget Reconciliation Act
CPR	Cardiopulmonary resuscitation
CPT	Current procedural codes

CRPS	Complex regional pain syndrome
CV	Curriculum vitae
DME	Durable medical equipment
DME	Defense Medical Exam
DRG	Diagnostic-related groups
ED	Emergency department
EMTALA	Emergency Medical Treatment and Labor Act
ER	Emergency room
ERISA	Employee Retirement Income Security Act
FAM	Functional Assessment Measure
FDA	Food and Drug Administration
FIM	Functional Independence Measure
FWB	Full weight bearing
HCFA	Health Care Financing Administration
HCP	Health care provider
HEDIS	Health Plan Employer Data and Information Set
HHS	Department of Health and Human Services
HIPAA	Health Insurance Portability and Accountability Act
HMO	Health Maintenance Organization
ICD–9–CM	International Classification of Diseases, Clinical Modification
IDLH	Immediately dangerous to life and health
IME	Independent Medical Exam
INR	International Normalized Ratio
IND	Independent
IPA	Independent Practice Association
JCAHO	Joint Commission on Accreditation of Healthcare Organizations
LNC	Legal nurse consultant
LNCC	Legal Nurse Consultant Certified
LOC	Loss of consciousness
LOS	Length of stay
MAX A	Maximal assistance from 50% to 75%
MCO	Managed Care Organization
MDS	Minimum Data Sets
MIN A	Minimal assistance from 1% to 24%
MOD A	Moderate assistance from 25% to 49%
MSDS	Material safety data sheet
MTBI	Mild traumatic brain injury
MVA	Motor vehicle accident
NCQA	National Committee for Quality Assurance
NFSNO	National Federation of Specialty Nursing Organizations
NHBR	Nursing Home Bill of Rights
NIH	National Institutes of Health
NOA	Nursing Organizations Alliance, or The Alliance
NOLF	Nursing Organization Liaison Forum
NWB	Nonweight bearing
OBRA	Omnibus Budget Reconciliation Act of 1987
OR	Operating room

PEL	Permissible exposure limit
PI	Personal injury
POS	Point of service
PPE	Personal protective equipment
PPO	Preferred Provider Organization
PTSD	Post-traumatic stress disorder
PVCT	Perceived Value of Certification Tool
PWB	Partial weight bearing
RAI	Resident Assessment Instrument
RAP	Resident Assessment Protocol
RM	Risk Manager
RN, BC	Board certified RN (ANCC)
RSD	Reflex sympathetic dystrophy
RUG	Resource Utilization Group
SBA	Stand by assist, be ready to help if needed
SBA	Small Business Administration
SCI	Spinal cord injury
SCORE	Service Corps of Retired Executives
SMT	Schroeder Measurement Technologies
SOAP	Subjective data, objective data, assessment, plan
SOL	Statute of limitations
SPD	Summary Plan Description
SSA	Social Security Administration
STEL	Short-term exposure limit
TLV	Threshold limit value
TA	Total assist
TBI	Traumatic brain injury
URL	Uniform Resource Locator
VBAC	Vaginal birth after caesarean section
WFL	Within functional limits
WNL	Within normal limits

Index